Jeremy M. Hutton
The Transjordanian Palimpsest

Beihefte zur Zeitschrift für die alttestamentliche Wissenschaft

Band 396

Walter de Gruyter · Berlin · New York

Jeremy M. Hutton

The Transjordanian Palimpsest

The Overwritten Texts of Personal Exile and Transformation in the Deuteronomistic History

Walter de Gruyter · Berlin · New York

∞ Printed on acid-free paper which falls within the guidelines of the ANSI to ensure permanence and durability.

ISBN 978-3-11-020410-0

ISSN 0934-2575

Library of Congress Cataloging-in-Publication Data

A CIP catalogue record for this book is available from the Library of Congress.

Bibliographic information published by the Deutsche Nationalbibliothek

The Deutsche Nationalbibliothek lists this publication in the Deutsche Nationalbibliografie; detailed bibliographic data are available in the Internet at http://dnb.d-nb.de.

Printed in Germany

Cover design: Christopher Schneider, Laufen

For my wife, Anne,
and our sons,
Daniel and James

Foreword

This book is a significantly revised version of my doctoral dissertation, directed by Professor Jo Ann Hackett of Harvard University. At a late stage in the development of the dissertation, I lamented to Prof. Hackett that I could not decide whether this study was a 300-page prospectus for a four-volume opus or a complete overworking of a 100-page monograph. The reader will discover that I have decided the piece worked best as it stood (approximately) at the end of the 2004–2005 academic year, at which point I set it aside to complete several smaller projects. I returned to the manuscript during the late months of 2007 after having eliminated the need to list several of my own planned articles as "forthcoming." Since then, the study has undergone much elaboration and revision. Although the basic thesis has not changed markedly, I believe my revisions have strengthened the argument and added nuance on several occasions. While I hope the redactional strata are not so apparent as I fear in my worst moments, their presence here is indisputable; the opportunity for revision has been much appreciated, and I have attempted to strike a balance between a much needed comprehensive study of the composition of the book of Samuel and a much terser exploration of the Jordan River's symbolic geography.

Many individuals and institutions have assisted me in this endeavor and have made it possible for me to complete this book. As with the structure of the book itself, I begin at the end and work in reverse (with one exception). First, I must extend my thanks to Princeton Theological Seminary, whose generous sabbatical policy for Assistant Professors, as well as childcare facilities, provided me with an extended period of time in which to complete the research for this book. The members of the support staff at Speer Library have gone out of their way at times to procure rare research materials. Ms. Kate Skrebutenas deserves particular mention here. The seminary also provided me with a number of research assistants, two of whom in particular aided my work on this project: Raymond Bonwell and Paul Kurtz. The latter did a good deal of proofreading, compiling of bibliography, and several other small and onerous tasks associated with publication. Especially important in my formation here have been my colleagues in the Biblical Studies department. Professors Katharine Sakenfeld, Dennis Olson, Choon-Leong Seow, Beverley Gaventa,

Clifton Black, Jim Charlesworth, Brian Blount, Jacqueline Lapsley, Chip Dobbs-Allsopp, Ross Wagner, Eunny Lee, George Parsenios, and Shane Berg have all proffered ample mentoring and sound advice, sometimes unwittingly. Foremost among these individuals is Professor Seow, at whose invitation I submitted the manuscript for consideration in the BZAW series. I owe thanks also to the editors of that series for accepting the manuscript for publication, and especially to Professor Reinhard Kratz, whose comments challenged me to engage more thoroughly with recent European scholarship than I had previously attempted. While I have not always agreed with him, it is with heartfelt gratitude that I have engaged his scholarship. The staff at de Gruyter Press has been patient and diligent. Particularly gracious in this regard were Albrecht Döhnert and Sabina Dabrowski. I thank also Koninklijke Brill N.V. for allowing me to republish material in §1.2.1 previously published in *Vetus Testamentum*.

A grant from the Mrs. Giles Whiting Foundation supported me in my final year at Harvard University; it was the last in a bevy of financial supports that the University extended to me. The faculty of the NELC Department at Harvard University contributed much of their own time to conversations with me, and I will be forever thankful for the opportunities presented to me there. Because this dissertation has its genesis in the Hebrew 200 seminar, each one of the faculty members should be named: Professors Jon Levenson, Paul Hanson, and Richard Saley sat in on the seminar and offered critique. Professors Peter Machinist and Larry Stager served as astute and demanding readers on my dissertation committee, and each contributed immeasurably to various aspects of my professional development; Prof. Stager also managed to keep me employed in his offices through most of my tenure as a graduate student at Harvard. Professor John Huehnergard remained a source of inspiration, and the bibliography of this piece cannot begin to indicate the influence he has had on my thought processes. I owe my deep gratitude to Professor Jo Ann Hackett, who spent many long hours reading and rereading, editing and writing, and who sometimes just let me sit and talk a problem out. Mention should also be made of Professor Hugh Page of the University of Notre Dame, who was the catalyst of my interest in Biblical Studies and an early and patient mentor.

Several colleagues at Harvard University deserve mention for their collegiality in the throes of dissertating; Aaron Rubin, Adam Aja, and Joel Baden were particularly reliable conversation partners. But it is to Eugene McGarry that I owe the topic of this study. During my years in Cambridge, Mr. McGarry was a frequent companion on long-distance hiking trips, and much of the material in this thesis was formulated—although not always vocalized—within earshot of him, often as we experienced together the power of the landscape. Gene, thank you.

My parents, Rodney Hutton and Kathleen Zwanziger, deserve my gratitude for their patience and intellectual generosity during my childhood years. Our many road trips, taken along with my brother Eric, may account for the *Wanderlust* that fueled the present project.

Finally, I owe my deepest gratitude to my wife Anne. Our engagement at the headwaters of the Cutler River in New Hampshire in July of 2001 provided more inspiration for a project on the emotional and cognitive engagement of humans with *place* than any other single event in my life. She has suffered nobly through my writing binges and exuded calm when I was frantic. She has provided safety and security for both of us throughout the years of hard work. She has helped to focus my attention when it was necessary and allowed me to drift off when relaxation was the order of the day. Most recently, she has shared with me in the joys and trials of raising two children in this magnificent world. Our sons Daniel and James are the joy of my life and serve as a constant inspiration to work hard, play hard, and impart a love of *places* to them, one journey at a time.

Princeton, N.J. March, 2009

Abbreviations

Note: this piece follows conventions of abbreviations published in *The SBL Handbook of Style* (ed. Patrick H. Alexander et al.; Peabody, Mass.: Hendrickson, 1989). The following abbreviations are not included there:

ABG	Arbeiten zur Bibel und ihrer Geschichte
AmAnthropol	*American Anthropologist*
ArchDial	*Archaeological Dialogues*
ATD	Das Alte Testament Deutsch
BAT	Die Botschaft des Alten Testaments
BritJSociol	*The British Journal of Sociology*
BVB	Beiträge zum Verstehen der Bibel
CanGeogr	*The Canadian Geographer*
ConBib	Connaissance de la bible
CornArch	*Cornish Archaeology*
ETB	Evangelisch-theologische Bibliothek
GeogrRev	*The Geographical Review*
GTW	Grundriss der theologischen Wissenschaften
HTIBS	Historical Texts and Interpreters in Biblical Scholarship
IB	*Interpreter's Bible* (12 vols.; Nashville: Abingdon, 1953).
JEconHist	*Journal of Economic History*
IntBT	Interpreting Biblical Texts
LibAncIsr	Library of Ancient Israel
NEBAT	Die Neue Echter Bibel, Altes Testament
NTG	Neue theologische Grundrisse
PPS	*Proceedings of the Prehistoric Society*
SBLBibEnc	SBL Biblical Encyclopedia
SHC	Studies in the History and Culture of the Ancient Near East.
SHVL	Skrifter utgivna av Kungl. Humanistiska Vetenskapssamfundet i Lund
SWBA	The Social World of Biblical Antiquity
UCNES	University of California Publications: Near Eastern Studies
WorldArch	*World Archaeology*

Contents

1. Echoes of the Past and Topos as Text: The Transjordanian Motif and Landscape Criticism

1.1. The Transjordanian Motif: A Literary Feature in the Deuteronomistic History

The landscape east of the Jordan River holds a special significance in the Deuteronomistic History (i.e., the narrative of Israel's history in the land of Canaan found in Deuteronomy–Kings; hereafter DtrH).[1] The book of Deuteronomy begins with the Israelites stationed on the eastern side of the river, poised to cross over into the Promised Land, an event narrated in Joshua 3–4. Beginning with the biblical narration concerned with the period of the Judges, and persisting through the Babylonian exile of the Judahite kingdom, the journey to Transjordan and back to Cisjordan serves as a frequent motif that aids in the characterization of several important biblical figures. Throughout the DtrH, these figures cross eastward over the Jordan River for various reasons.

In some cases, the characters are waging battles against invaders from the East. Ehud crosses the Jordan in order to kill Israel's oppressor, Eglon the Moabite (Judg 3:15–30). He does so, escapes, rallies the Ephraimites, and kills ten thousand Moabites at the fords of the Jordan. The Ephraimites, at the behest of the Manassite Gideon, wage a similar battle at the fords of the Jordan against the Midianites (Judg 7:24–25). Gideon and his Manassite companions pursue the routed Midianites across the Jordan and up the Jabbok River. On the return journey, they stop to deal with the hostile residents of Sukkoth and then with the belligerent inhabitants of

1 I follow here the classic definition of the DtrH first articulated by Martin Noth (*The Deuteronomistic History* [trans. J. A. Clines et al.; JSOTSup 15; Sheffield: JSOT Press, 1981; repr., Sheffield: Sheffield Academic Press, 2001]; trans. of *Überlieferungsgeschichtliche Studien* [2d ed.; Tübingen: Niemeyer, 1957], 1–110), while at the same time recognizing the recent contribution by those interested in an Enneateuch (see, e.g., the various essays in Markus Witte et al., eds., *Die deuteronomistischen Geschichtswerke: Redaktions- und religionsgeschichtliche Perspektiven zur "Deuteronomismus"-Diskussion in Tora und Vorderen Propheten* [BZAW 365; Berlin: de Gruyter, 2006]). I will not be treating here the Wilderness Wanderings. Although the Pentateuch's vision of Transjordan is clearly related to the perception of DtrH (and especially to that of Joshua 3–4), a full comparison of the two exceeds the scope of the present study.

Penuel.[2] Gideon defeats the Midianite army, destroys the (presumably Israelite) towns of Penuel and Sukkoth, and then returns home. In response to these acts, the Israelites offer to him the dynastic kingship, which he declines (Judg 8:1–23). Both Ehud and Gideon perform their military duties while east of the Jordan, returning westward to reap the benefits.

In other cases, the figures are fleeing political circumstances that would otherwise result in their death or subjugation to another's rule. In most of these cases, political events have transpired that necessitate the flight of the character, and many of the figures who make their way eastward as fugitives do not survive long enough to return to Cisjordan with aspirations for success. For example, after Saul's defeat at Gilboa (1 Samuel 31–2 Samuel 1), Abner transfers Ishbosheth[3] to Mahanaim in order to crown him king over "Gilead, Asher, Jezreel, Ephraim, Benjamin and all Israel" (2 Sam 2:8–9). Joab brutally murders Abner in a time of peace (2 Sam 3:27), and Ishbosheth—dejected at the loss of his commander—is similarly slain in his own house by Rekab and Baanah (2 Sam 4:5–8). Sheba ben-Bikri, a secessionist Benjaminite, flees to Abel Beth-Maakah after rallying the northern tribes after himself and to the detriment of David's Judah.[4] David's general Joab pursues Sheba, invests the city, and collects another notch in the hilt of his sword, thanks to some heads-up (-and-over) thinking by the wise woman of Abel (2 Samuel 20). Neither Ishbosheth nor Abner is able to convert the dream of return from exile in Transjordan to power in Cisjordan into reality; both are killed ignobly and fade from biblical and literary memory. Sheba's fate is similar; he is trapped in a hostile city, surrounded by an enemy army, and finally surrendered over by the city's beleaguered inhabitants.

---

2 For a discussion of the location of those cities, see Jeremy M. Hutton, "Mahanaim, Penuel and Transhumance Routes: Observations on Genesis 32–33 and Judges 8," *JNES* 65 (2006): 161–78.

3 I use here the name "Ishbosheth" rather than the commonly accepted "Ishbaal" (1 Chr 8:33; 9:39; see similarly below "Mephibosheth" rather than "Mephibaal" or "Meribaal") primarily for reasons of consistency within the Deuteronomistic portion of MT. For the form of the name in antiquity, cf. Matitiahu Tsevat, "Ishbosheth and Congeners: The Names and Their Study," *HUCA* 46 (1975): 71–87; P. Kyle McCarter, *II Samuel: A New Translation with Introduction and Commentary* (AB 9; New York: Doubleday, 1984), 85–87; and Gordon J. Hamilton, "New Evidence for the Authenticity of *bšt* in Hebrew Personal Names and for Its Use as a Divine Epithet in Biblical Texts," *CBQ* 60 (1998): 228–50, esp. 241.

4 Although at the head of the Hula River (the major source of the Jordan north of the Sea of Galilee), Abel Beth-Maakah nonetheless would have had resonances relevant to the discussion: the main heartland of the tiny kingdom of Maakah, as well as the kingdom of Geshur with which Maakah was conceptually paired (Josh 13:13), lay on the eastern side of the Sea of Galilee. See, e.g., William G. Dever, "ʾAbel-Beth-Maʿacah: 'Northern Gateway of Ancient Israel," in *The Archaeology of Jordan and Other Studies: Presented to Siegfried H. Horn* (ed. Lawrence T. Geraty and Larry G. Herr; Berrien Springs, Mich.: Andrews University Press, 1986), 207–22.

On the other hand, some of the characters who retreat eastward as exiles return westward with their intentions to procure prosperity and autonomy realized. David brings Mephibosheth ben-Jonathan back to the Cisjordan from his refuge in Lo-debar in order to instate him as a regular fixture at the king's table in Jerusalem and to return his ancestral lands to him (2 Sam 9:5–10). Although David gives the lands to Mephibosheth's servant Ziba in retribution for perceived treason during David's flight from Jerusalem (2 Sam 16:3–4), a portion of the inheritance is eventually allotted to Mephibosheth when he insists that Ziba had deceived him for personal gain (2 Sam 19:30). Since little else is said about the son of Jonathan after this episode, the reader is left with at least the impression that Saul's grandson maintained some semblance of prestige in David's court.[5]

Absalom flees to Geshur, on the eastern bank of the Sea of Galilee, after murdering his half-brother and the heir to the throne, Amnon (2 Samuel 13). After Absalom resides in Geshur for three years, Joab develops an ultimately convincing scheme that motivates David to bring Absalom back to Jerusalem (2 Samuel 14). Although Absalom's position in the court is rather limited—he finds himself unable to gain access to the king (2 Sam 14:24)—he nonetheless remains in a position to have himself crowned king a little while later. Absalom's grip on the kingship is tenuous at best and short lived, but the apparent literary role of his exile in Transjordan with respect to his rise to power should be noted.

When David and his army are forced to flee Jerusalem in the face of Absalom's rebellion, they make their way to the stronghold city Mahanaim (2 Sam 15:14–16:13; 17:27–29)—the same location of exile to which Abner and Ishbosheth had retreated earlier in the narrative. Absalom is killed in a battle in the Forest of Ephraim (2 Sam 18:6,15), paving the way for David's pyrrhic return to his capital city and kingship over both Judah and Israel (2 Samuel 19).[6]

Only three cases occur in which the character enters (or stays) in Transjordan *without* the explicit intention of improving his political situation. Elijah is a native Transjordanian called by Yahweh to serve as a prophet in Israel. The deity's first instruction to Elijah—a Gileadite by birth—is to seek refuge in the *Naḥal Cherith*, specifically identified twice

5 2 Sam 21:7–8 notes that "David had compassion on Mephibosheth," preserving him from the fate of several relatives, including the uncle for which he was named (but cf. §5.3.4.1)

6 Here I follow to some extent the recent work of Baruch Halpern, who argues that David's hegemony over Ephraim and Manasseh, as well as over the Israelite tribes even further north, was not complete until *after* Absalom's revolt and subsequent demise (*David's Secret Demons: Messiah, Murderer, Traitor, King* [Grand Rapids, Mich.: Eerdmans, 2001], 357–81).

as being על־פני הירדן "in front of (= east of) the Jordan" (1 Kgs 17:3,5).[7] While there, Elijah relies upon the ravens for his food—the first such occurrence of the supernatural in Transjordan that we have seen so far in the DtrH. The extent of this incubational period lasts until the water in the torrent-valley dries up because of drought. God then sends Elijah to Zarepthah, a dependency of Sidon (and west of the Jordan Valley), to begin his ministry. Elijah's connection with the numinous is furthered in the scene of his translation. This event happens as well to be the moment of Elisha's professional maturation in which he inherits—among other things—Elijah's mantle, despite the fact that Elisha has obstinately followed his master, against the master's wishes. The two characters cross dry-shod over the Jordan (thanks to Elijah's cloak) to their respective moments of destiny (2 Kgs 2:6–14).

The motif of the triumphant and empowered return from the eastern side of the Jordan River culminates in the DtrH's portrayal of Jehu, one of Israel's generals stationed in Ramoth-gilead, when he is anointed king of Israel by an unnamed follower of Elisha (2 Kgs 9:4–13). Jehu's rule is prophetically ordained and favored by Israel's God. Jehu responds to this devotion on Yahweh's part by cleansing the Israelite monarchy of Baal worship. However, despite the empowering moment of anointing in Transjordan, a blotch remains on the king's record. The Deuteronomistic text impugns Jehu's Yahwistic legacy, pointing out that Jehu perpetuated the "pagan" cult of the golden calves in Bethel and Dan (2 Kgs 10:29).[8]

Now, the scope of what has so far been called "Transjordan" or the "Israelite Transjordan" must be narrowed and defined with reference to Elisha. Elisha accompanies the armies of Israel and Judah on a punitive raid against Mesha of Moab (2 Kgs 3:4–27). Although Moab sat on the eastern scarp of the Great Rift Valley, the route taken went around the

7 For the historical and traditional locations of the *N. Cherith*, see Jeremy M. Hutton, "Topography, Biblical Traditions, and Reflections on John's Baptism of Jesus," in *Proceedings of the Princeton-Prague Symposium on the Historical Jesus* (ed. J. H. Charlesworth; Grand Rapids, Mich.: Eerdmans, forthcoming).

8 Two qualifications should be made here that mitigate this Deuteronomistic impeachment of Jehu: (a) The cult of the golden calves has long been recognized as a contemporarily appropriate expression of Yahwism (e.g., Frank Moore Cross, *Canaanite Myth and Hebrew Epic: Essays in the History of the Religion of Israel* [*CMHE*] [Cambridge, Mass.: Harvard University Press, 1973], 74); Halpern has gone so far as to argue that the bull figurines were a *more* appropriate local expression of Yahwism than was David's ark, a Gibeonite cultic implement (*David's Secret Demons*, 420); and (b) It is possible that Jehu originally received a land-grant-style oracle (such as that in 2 Samuel 7) mandating an eternal Jehuide rule over the northern kingdom, which was only secondarily emended by the Deuteronomistic Historian—*after* Shallum's coup that killed Zechariah, Jehu's great-great-grandson—to extend only four generations past Jehu (Jon D. Levenson, *Sinai and Zion: An Entry into the Jewish Bible* [San Francisco: HarperCollins, 1985], 203–5).

southern end of the Dead Sea and therefore did not pass through the Jordan. Similarly, David moves his family to Moab (1 Sam 22:3–5), but the lack of detail with which this story is narrated renders difficult any attempt to provide a full analysis of its significance in the present study. Two observations result from these journeys east of the Jordan Rift that do not seem to fit into the Transjordanian Motif as outlined here. First, Transjordan's meaningfulness in the present study is situated primarily in that area populated and controlled by recognized "Israelites" and deemed to be part of the "Promised Land" in the Deuteronomistic sense (i.e., in the land north of the Arnon River, the traditional boundary between Israel and Moab; see, e.g., Josh 12:1–5).[9] This includes, in some time periods and to some extent, Geshur and Maakah and, accordingly, the cases of Absalom and Sheba. It does not include, though, the land of Moab, which remained outside the scope of Israelite settlement. Second, it may be the case that Elisha's trip to Moab is concerned more with the *execution* of prophetic authority than with the *justification* of it and therefore does not necessarily recognize any specific topographic importance of the journey. Cognate episodes may be 1 Kgs 20:26–34, in which the "king of Israel" campaigns in Transjordan with no specific reference to leadership or to the legitimization of authority, and 22:29–38, in which the "king of Israel" is killed in battle east of the Jordan.

The nuanced literary links between these characters and their situations are palpable: in the literary logic of the DtrH, Transjordan serves as a place of exile, refuge, and incubative transformation for prospective personages of power.[10] Throughout the History, the motif of the return from Transjordan serves as a powerful metaphor for the return (or entry) of a character into a high degree of personal authority, previously lost or non-existent. I intend to demonstrate in this study that this literary *Transjordanian Motif* is directly linked to the topography and the human geography of the area. In this motif, the area of Transjordan purportedly occupied by ethnic Israelites, and under Israelite political influence, serves to symbolize

9 See Moshe Weinfeld, "The Extent of the Promised Land—The Status of Transjordan," in *Das Land Israel in biblischer Zeit* (ed. Georg Strecker; Göttingen: Vandenhoeck & Ruprecht, 1983), 59–75; and David Jobling, "'The Jordan a Boundary:' Transjordan in Israel's Ideological Geography," in idem, *The Sense of Biblical Narrative II: Structural Analyses in the Hebrew Bible* (JSOTSup 39; Sheffield: JSOT Press, 1986), 88–133, 142–47.

10 Rachel S. Havrelock reached a similar conclusion in her dissertation ("The Jordan River: Crossing a Biblical Boundary" [Ph.D. diss.; University of California, Berkeley, 2004]). That piece appeared only a year before the submission of my own, which forms the basis of the present book. Unfortunately, I was unaware of Havrelock's dissertation at the time and have subsequently been delighted to discover that our conclusions as to the literary significance of journeys through the Jordan River overlap and are, as I see it, mutually supportive. See also Harold Brodsky, "The Jordan—Symbol of Spiritual Transition," *BRev* 8.3 (1992): 34–43, 52.

and encode biblical characters' transformation and legitimization within the Cisjordanian Israelite and Judahite communities.

That Transjordan functions as a liminal space in which Cisjordanian figures undergo a sort of incubation should come as no surprise. The entire Transjordanian landscape stands at a liminal position at the edge of Israelite territory: only a few steps farther and one enters the foreign territories of Aram and Ammon; beyond those polities sprawls the eastern wilderness of the Syrian Desert. They are physically and metaphorically at the edge of Israelite existence. With this understanding of the region's situation—both its geographical position and its literary significance—the narratives of the Bible (Jewish and Christian) may be read in a new light. The ad hoc military leader whose campaigns take him east of the Jordan should expect some form of institutionalized authority upon his return; the aspiring or deposed monarch's retreat to Mahanaim-Penuel (and to Transjordan in general by extension) becomes a literary retreat to the murkiness of political liminality. In each case, the figure is not quite king and not quite commoner. In the former cases, the leader may unwittingly cross the boundary comprised of the Jordan River, but in the latter, the character flees with the intention of seeking refuge beyond the river and must wait until conditions in the Cisjordan are ripe for his triumphant return. We may discern a third vision of Transjordan's transforming effects on individuals in the prophet's incubation east of the Jordan River and its corresponding shift in status. As opposed to the previous visions of Transjordan's significance, here the reasons for the eastward movement are no longer purely mundane. Instead, they are the result of a divine calling, whether received directly from Yahweh (1 Kgs 17:2–3), or through the word of a prophet (1 Kgs 19:19–21; 2 Kgs 2:1–14[11]).

1.2. Deep River: The Jordan as *Limen* and Its Position in Israelite Society

A synchronic reading of three texts, one from each of the groups delineated in §1.1, demonstrates the singularity of meaning obtaining in the final form of the biblical text. Indeed, the continued significance and stability of this motif in subsequently composed episodes of the Hebrew Bible, the New

11 Although Elisha's dialogue with Elijah seems to indicate the intention of the former to enter into Transjordan, the corresponding trope of the אדרת should be noted (1 Kgs 19:19; 2 Kgs 2:8,13,14). Elisha is simply following his master, as he was called to do.

Testament, and in Judaean thought of the first centuries CE[12] is a witness to the motif's vibrant metaphorical and literary depth for the Israelites and their genealogical and spiritual descendants. However, that the journey of the prospective authority figure was ever explicitly conceived in Israelite society as an institutionalized, proscriptive, and self-supporting ritual is unlikely. Despite the change in status—actual or assumed—accorded to the individual after a journey or sojourn in Transjordan, none of the narratives that has been mentioned so far displays an explicit recognition that the character has partaken in a ritual, per se. While it has been previously suggested that the Jordan River was crossed in the rituals of the early Israelite cultus,[13] that suggestion is based on inference and the assumption that the biblical text preserves liturgical texts beside its narratives. Skepticism leveled at this claim is justified but should not dissuade an examination of the *ritualistic aspects* that accompany some of the narratives of crossings of the Jordan River. I will not argue that the narratives explored here serve as evidence of liturgical rituals, performed at regular intervals or at particular points in the characters' lives. None of them bears any indication of such institutional regularity or of the assumption of prescribed efficacy appropriate to such ritualistic actions. However, an examination of the *ritualistic aspects* of each narrative takes into account the structure of the *textus receptus*, analyzing it as a properly organized narrative recollection of an event.

I discuss here three *ritualized* narratives of the crossing of the Jordan River in light of the anthropological theories of A. van Gennep and V. Turner: the return of David across the Jordan from Mahanaim in 2 Samuel 19 (and, by extension, the king's journey *to* Mahanaim in 2 Samuel 15–17); the ascension of Elijah and the concurrent beginning of Elisha's ministry (2 Kings 2); and the Transjordanian campaign of Gideon to defeat the fleeing Midianites. These three texts have been selected intentionally—one from each of the categories delineated roughly above—with the goal of demonstrating the overall coherence of the Transjordanian Motif and its transformational effects. To the extent that all three texts show corresponding narrative logic, despite various histories of composition and development, this assertion is born out at the synchronic level.

12 See, e.g., Jeremy M. Hutton, "'Bethany Beyond the Jordan' in Text, Tradition, and Historical Geography," *Bib* 89 (2008): 305–28; and idem, "Topography."

13 E.g., Cross, *CMHE*, 123–44, esp. 138–41.

1.2.1. The Left Bank of the River and the Rites of Passage: 2 Sam 19:12–44[14]

2 Sam 19:12–44 (Eng. vv. 11–43) describes David's return to Jerusalem from the eastern side of the Jordan River. Having fled to Mahanaim to escape his son Absalom's coup in chs. 15 and 16, and having subsequently won the battle with Absalom and his army of "all Israel" in ch. 18, David has once again secured the kingdom and is prepared to return to his capital Jerusalem. Before he can return, however, he must make arrangements for the journey with the members of his court who have remained behind in Jerusalem. These arrangements consist not only in reestablishing political connections with his former subjects, who have been the very ones forming the basis of Absalom's rebellion, but also in placating the surviving political structure of the rebellion, particularly Absalom's general Amasa (vv. 12–15). Only after David has reclaimed his position atop the hierarchical structure of the kingdom does he make his way toward the river (vv. 16–19a).

Three episodes characterize the larger pericope of David's crossing of the Jordan. From the historical critic's point of view, in which the proper narrative structure should follow a natural progression from east to west, the order of these conversations seems to be jumbled. One expects the following order of David's meetings: First, David converses with Barzillai on the eastern bank. Barzillai turns down the king's invitation to reside in Jerusalem, but escorts the king into the river, and after exchanging pleasantries turns back. When the king has crossed the river, the reformed Shimei meets him on the western bank. Later, upon his return to Jerusalem, David's exchange with Mephibosheth solidifies the king's confidence in his subject's loyalty sufficiently so that the monarch returns to Mephibosheth half of his family's ancestral land. Yet, the text has not

14 This section is an expansion of an article originally published as "The Left Bank of the Jordan and the Rites of Passage: An Anthropological Interpretation of 2 Samuel xix," *VT* 56 (2006): 470–84. It is republished here with the kind permission of Koninklijke Brill N.V. That study was itself a revision and expansion of a paper given at the "Bible and Social Sciences" section of the 2004 SBL Annual Meeting in San Antonio, Tex. I would like to thank Professors Jo Ann Hackett, Peter Machinist, Carol Newsom, David P. Wright, and an anonymous reviewer at *VT* for their comments on earlier drafts of the paper, and Professor Steve Caton of Harvard University's anthropology department for allowing me to engage him in discussion on the anthropological responses to the theories of van Gennep and Turner. Yet as always, the views expressed here—as well as any mistakes—are solely my own. While many detailed literary and historical discussions of 2 Samuel 19 exist, I have kept my references to those works to a minimum in an attempt to conserve space. The recent discussion by Jeremy Schipper provides a thorough bibliography of literary studies, and the reader is referred there ("'Why Do You Still Speak of Your Affairs?' Polyphony in Mephibosheth's Exchanges with David in 2 Samuel," *VT* 54 [2004]: 344–51).

been presented in this order. Rather, once David has been met by a contingent of Benjaminites and Judahites at the river,[15] an odd ordering of episodes occurs. In the first position is the conversation with Shimei (2 Sam 19:19b–24).[16] Next, the structure of the narrative places the chronologically later conversation between David and Mephibosheth (vv. 25–31)[17] *before* David's conversation with Barzillai (vv. 32–40).[18]

---

15 Ziba, the servant of the house of Saul, leads the contingent of Benjaminites to the Jordan. This figure's presence at the fords of the Jordan is, not insignificantly, overlooked for the most part in the remainder of the biblical text because his master Mephibosheth has also come down to the river to accompany David to the Cisjordanian side of the river (see discussion below). In opposition to Shimei ben-Gera, with whom Ziba arrives at this time, Ziba has acted loyally toward David in the past. Upon the king's departure from Jerusalem, Ziba had met David with supplies for the journey. When asked where his master Mephibosheth was, Ziba claimed that the Saulide heir had not accompanied David and his entourage on their flight from Jerusalem because Mephibosheth had aspired to the throne of Israel immediately upon learning of David's departure. In reward for this apparent display of loyalty, David granted by decree that Ziba should inherit the familial lands that had been left to Mephibosheth as Saul's descendent (2 Sam 16:1–4). Upon David's departure from Jerusalem, then, the text presents two Benjaminites who are noted for their manifestations of loyalty toward David: Shimei for his extreme *disloyalty* toward the crown (and complementarily, loyalty toward his family, that of Saul), and conversely, Ziba for his apparently extreme loyalty toward David. The two appear again together here in 2 Samuel 19, both now demonstrating apparent fealty to the Judahite king.

16 Upon David's hasty departure from Jerusalem, Shimei had cursed the king, throwing rocks and dust at the royal entourage (2 Sam 16:5–8,13). Now, upon David's triumphant return from Transjordan, Shimei has thought better of his past behavior. At the news of David's imminent return, Shimei hurries down with the people of Judah who are going to Gilgal to "meet the king to bring the king across the Jordan" (2 Sam 19:16–17). Shimei's possible entry into the river itself is suggested by the phrase בעברו "while he [David] was crossing" in v. 19b (see, e. g., Jan P. Fokkelman, *King David (II Sam. 9–20 & 1 Kings 1–2)*, vol. 1 of *Narrative Art and Poetry in the Books of Samuel* [Assen: Van Gorcum, 1981], 299). Two possible interpretations of this phrase exist, the first a definitive statement of immediacy ("while [David] was in the act of crossing the Jordan"), the second a more circumstantial and therefore ambiguous statement of time ("at the time that [David] crossed the Jordan"). In either case, Shimei falls at the king's feet in order to ask David's mercy and forgiveness, which he receives for the time being, despite Abishai's protestations (vv. 20–24).

17 Mephibosheth had come to meet David at the Jordan, with the appearance of a man in mourning. While Mephibosheth has come to the river to escort David across (v. 25), the bulk of this episode consists of a conversation between the two that seems to take place later in Jerusalem, according to the time signature in v. 26. In that conversation, David asks why Mephibosheth had not accompanied him on his way out of Jerusalem, to which Mephibosheth responds that he had made an attempt to accompany the king, but that Ziba had failed to follow his orders, deciding instead to slander Mephibosheth to David (vv. 26–28). David responds to Mephibosheth's apparent loyalty by dividing in half the property he had formerly granted to Ziba (v. 30), but Mephibosheth delivers the ultimate rhetorical coup by turning down his share in v. 31: "Let him take it all, since my lord the king has come home safely." With this testimony from Mephibosheth it then seems as though Ziba's presence at the river in 2 Samuel 19 is designed more as damage-control to maintain his newfound property than as a sincere outpouring of loyalty to David (e.g., Hans Wilhelm Hertzberg, *I & II Samuel: A Commentary* [trans. John S. Bowden; OTL; London: SCM, 1964; repr., Philadelphia: Westminster, n.d.], 365), but see Schipper, who concludes that "[r]ather than clarifying his position, [Mephibosheth's] exchanges with David only add to the ambiguity of the situation

Therefore, David's encounters with Shimei and Barzillai now form an *inclusio* surrounding the Mephibosheth episode. From this perspective, the two characters who have appeared the most disloyal to David during the course of Absalom's revolt—other than Absalom himself, of course—*seem* to meet David in the middle of the river, *before* he sets foot back in Cisjordan.[19] The conversation with Mephibosheth concludes in a compromise designed to stem any further hopes of revolt by the House of Saul. Likewise, the conversation with Shimei makes it clear that David can expect no more trouble from the Benjaminite. The text thereby leaves nothing in doubt concerning the security of the kingdom, into which the king is now free to enter.

The entire scene is designed around David's crossing of the Jordan as the centerpiece.[20] All the transactions and interactions—both human and

---

and the complexity of his character" ("Polyphony," 351). For a discussion of the chronology of the exchanges, particularly the exchange between David and Mephibosheth, see McCarter, who notes that David's conversation with Mephibosheth need not have taken place until David had returned to Jerusalem (*II Samuel*, 424). The situation of the word ירושלם in v. 26 seems to assume that Mephibosheth came *to* Jerusalem rather than *from* that city. McCarter therefore reads vv. 26–31 as a parenthetical description of future events, but still placing the lame and unkempt Mephibosheth at the Jordan during David's crossing. The conversation, he asserts, is included because it forms the logical conclusion to Mephibosheth's presence at the river. At the time of the conversation, David decides what appears to be a "contest of obsequiousness" (ibid., 424) by dividing the land evenly between Mephibosheth who seems to be telling the truth—since surely one could not forge the unchecked growth of toenails and mustache (but cf. Schipper, "Polyphony," 344–45, esp. sources cited in nn. 1–4)—and Ziba whose household has so diligently assisted David's westward crossing of the Jordan (vv. 18b–19). For a very thorough discussion of this pericope as an example of the Israelite land-grant system, see Zafrira Ben-Barak, "Meribaal and the System of Land Grants in Ancient Israel," *Bib* 62 (1981): 73–91.

18 Barzillai the Gileadite, one of David's supporters in Mahanaim, has also come to the Jordan to send David across (vv. 32–33). For his loyalty, David invites the aged Barzillai to live out the remainder of his years in Jerusalem, presumably as a member of David's court (v. 34). Barzillai refuses politely (vv. 35–36), instead expressing a desire to die in his own town, near the graves of his ancestors (v. 38a), but he offers to accompany the king a little way across the river (v. 37a). In his stead, he sends his servant Kimham along with David to Jerusalem (v. 38b), a proposal that David accepts (v. 39). David then takes leave of Barzillai in v. 40 by kissing and blessing his subject.

19 The passage of the river crossing concludes in vv. 41–44. When the entirety of David's army has crossed the Jordan, the king finally crosses over in v. 41a. Verses 41–44 detail the confrontation between Israel and Judah on the west bank that leads directly into the revolt of Sheba ben-Bikri in 2 Samuel 20.

20 See the observation of Robert Alter that there is a symmetry between David's exit from Jerusalem and his return to Cisjordan: "Then he met a hostile Shimei, now he meets a contrite Shimei. Then he met Ziba, who denounces his master Mephibosheth; now he meets Mephibosheth himself, who defends his own loyalty. Then he spoke with Ittai, the loyalist who insisted on accompanying him; now he speaks with Barzillai, the proven loyalist who refuses to accompany him back to the capital" (*The David Story: A Translation with Commentary of 1 and 2 Samuel* [New York: Norton, 1999], 315). Unfortunately, these interludes do not follow the same order that Alter must put them in to line up with the current

economic—take place in the narrative between David's arrival at the Jordan River and his entry into Cisjordan. Furthermore, according to the logic of the narrative structure, David *never stands alone while crossing the river*. He is accompanied into the river by Barzillai (and implicitly by Kimham) and met by Shimei in the river "while he was crossing" (בעברו).[21] Only after David has taken his leave of Barzillai (and after the entire army has crossed over) does he complete the westward crossing. He is escorted at all times by those subservient to him.

The apparently intentional organization of this pericope, with its discontinuous order of events, suggests that something more than the relatively simple chronological implications of the crossing and the various conversations is at stake.[22] In the following discussion, I appeal to two well-known anthropological models of human behavior: the rites of passage, as described by A. van Gennep, and the notion of *communitas*, as posed by V. Turner. While both theories have been utilized in biblical studies for quite some time,[23] I suggest that they have not been outmoded

---

set of conversations. In 2 Samuel 15–17, Ittai appears first, followed by the priests Zadok and Abiathar along with their sons, then Hushai the Archite (whom Alter recognizes as having no cognate in 2 Samuel 19), and finally Ziba and Shimei. K. K. Sacon has made a similar observation, arguing that the two "sincere characters" of 2 Sam 15:19–37a (Ittai and Hushai) parallel the two similarly sincere characters Meribbaal (Mephibosheth) and Barzillai in 19:25–39 ("A Study of the Literary Structure of the 'Succession Narrative'," in *Studies in the Period of David and Solomon and Other Essays* [ed. Tomoo Ishida; Winona Lake, Ind.: Eisenbrauns, 1982], 27–54). Together these episodes form an *inclusio* around the insincere characters found in 15:37b–17:23 and 19:16a–24 (Shimei and Ziba). See also Gillian Keys, *The Wages of Sin: A Reappraisal of the "Succession Narrative"* (JSOTSup 221; Sheffield: Sheffield Academic Press, 1996), 75–76; Fokkelman, *King David*, 282–314. François Langlamet attributed 2 Sam 16:1–13 and 2 Sam 19:17–41a to a "theological redactor" of the earlier Succession Narrative ("Ahitofel et Houshaï: Rédaction prosalomonienne en 2 S 15–17?" in *Studies in Bible and the Ancient Near East: Presented to Samuel E. Loewenstamm on His Seventieth Birthday* [ed. Yitschak Avishur and Joshua Blau; Jerusalem: Rubinstein, 1978], 29–32); see also recently Alexander A. Fischer, "Flucht und Heimkehr Davids als integraler Rahmen der Abschalomerzählung," in *Ideales Königtum: Studien zu David und Salomo* (ed. Rüdiger Lux; ABG 16; Leipzig: Evangelische Verlagsanstalt, 2005), 43–69. I doubt that these episodes can be so easily divorced from the rest of the story, but Langlamet's structural arrangement points to the centrality of Absalom's death and David's mourning in the present text.

21 Whether Barzillai has accompanied the king part of the way or all the way across is nowhere explicitly stated. Verse 32 suggests that he has accompanied the king all the way across; however, Barzillai's speech in v. 37a (כמעט יעבר עבדך) and text-critical issues in v. 40a (see McCarter, *II Samuel*, 418) mitigate the strength of this impression, suggesting only a partial crossing by Barzillai, or none at all.

22 For a study that analyzes the literary logic of "passages" as more meaningful components of narratives than those texts' historical implications, see Don Seeman, "The Watcher at the Window: Cultural Poetics of a Biblical Motif," *Proof* 24 (2004): 1–50, esp. 26–33.

23 Jack R. Lundbom has already analyzed Psalm 23 in conjunction with 2 Samuel 15–19 according to van Gennep's model of the *rites of passage* ("Psalm 23: Song of Passage," *Int* 40 [1986]: 5–16). I do not discount the conjunction of the Psalm with the narrative pericope

and may be particularly instructive in elucidating the reasons for the organization of 2 Samuel 19.

An analysis of 2 Samuel 19 with reference to the rites of passage does not require that we reconstruct a yearly Conquest Ritual at Gilgal[24] as the model for David's confirmation as king. 2 Samuel 19 does not describe a ritual per se, because the event portrayed is a one-time occurrence.[25] Clearly, though, the pericope does display aspects of a singular crossing of the Jordan River that show a modification of the subject's relationship to the mundane. The actions performed during David's crossing of the Jordan River are thereby *ritualistic*, insofar as they give the appearance of participating in a ritual where there is evidently none assumed. Moreover, one is not dealing here with David's historical crossing of the Jordan River but instead with a narratively emplotted account of such a crossing. This account of David's crossing has been constructed precisely in order to display the ritualistic augmentation of the mundane action of river crossings, a feature characteristic of certain other pericopes of crossing the Jordan River (e.g., Joshua 3–4; 2 Kgs 2:1–18). David's crossing of the Jordan in 2 Samuel 19 should be recognized as a crossing in which the normal aspects—mediation by fellows, difficulty in crossing, etc.—have been exaggerated and which has implications for David's subsequent position within the Judahite and Israelite communities. Therefore, I use the term "narratively ritualized" to describe those literarily emplotted actions or sequences of actions which partake of certain conventions of ritual action—in appearance or in actuality—without necessarily portraying a ritual per se.[26]

---

at hand, since Lundbom makes a nice case for much congruence; however, that is not my interest here. Rather, I intend to show how van Gennep's model may be specifically correlated to the actions observable in 2 Samuel 19. In this regard Lundbom did not provide a detailed description of the precision with which van Gennep's model fits the biblical passage. See also L. G. Perdue, "Liminality as a Social Setting for Wisdom Instructions," *ZAW* 93 (1981): 114–26.

24 E.g., Cross, *CMHE*, 103–6.

25 "Rituals" are generally viewed as regular occurrences; on the difficulty of defining "ritual" and the term's attendant connotations of empty regularity, see Jack Goody, "Against 'Ritual': Loosely Structured Thoughts on a Loosely Defined Topic," in *Secular Ritual* (ed. Sally F. Moore and Barbara G. Meyerhoff; Assen: Van Gorcum, 1977), 25–35. Cf., though, two other essays in the same volume: Sally F. Moore and Barbara G. Meyerhoff, "Secular Ritual: Forms and Meanings," 8–9; Barbara G. Meyerhoff, "We Don't Wrap Herring in a Printed Page: Fusion, Fictions and Continuity in Secular Ritual," 199–224. Catherine Bell contests viewing formality, fixity, and repetition as primary features of ritual behavior (*Ritual Theory, Ritual Practice* [New York: Oxford University Press, 1992]).

26 For early discussions of "ritualization," see, e.g., Max Gluckman, "*Les Rites de Passage*," in *Essays on the Ritual of Social Relations* (ed. Max Gluckman; Manchester: Manchester University Press, 1962), 20–25; Mary Catherine Bateson, "Ritualization: A Study in Texture and Texture Change," in *Religious Movements in Contemporary America* (ed. Irving I. Zaretsky and Mark P. Leone (Princeton, N.J.: Princeton University Press, 1974), 150–65. Bell has more recently argued for "ritualization" as a mode of practice that sets itself off from

Therefore, insofar as this study concentrates on the text of 2 Samuel 19—as opposed to its historical referent—it analyzes the narratively ritualized emplotment of David's crossing in two important and complementary ways. First, the theories of rites of passage and of liminal communitas are used here to articulate the logic behind the narrative in 2 Samuel 19 with no reference to whether an actual crossing by David employed similar strategies or commanded similar symbolic recognition by those involved.[27] Second, this study examines how 2 Samuel 19 functions within the context of the rest of 2 Samuel as a literary—not necessarily historical—entity.[28]

The particular innovation of Arnold van Gennep's groundbreaking work, *The Rites of Passage*,[29] lies in its departure from the position of previous discussions of rites performed at times of life crises. Van Gennep delineated the rites of passage as rites denoting a transition in state through a physical transition of place and utilizing a particular structure. The rites themselves are performed in order to mitigate the harmful effects thrust upon society by such transitions of state.[30] Each rite of passage can be broken down to its constituent elements, and frequently a connection may

---

the mundane not in terms of elements specific only to "ritual," but as an elaboration of the mundane—differentiated from the commonplace only by varying degrees of augmentation (*Ritual Theory*, 88–93). For instance, the "ritual" of Christian communion should not be viewed as separate from everyday meals by virtue of its formality, regularized practice, and the regularity with which it occurs. Instead, its significance differs from that of normal consumption precisely because of the degree to which it is not *normal* consumption (ibid., 90–91). For a recent discussion of Bell's "ritualization," see David P. Wright, *Ritual in Narrative: The Dynamics of Feasting, Mourning, and Retaliation Rites in the Ugaritic Tale of Aqhat* (Winona Lake, Ind.: Eisenbrauns, 2001), 11–13.

27 Historically, however, it is possible that the participants could have understood David's crossing of the Jordan on multiple levels of significance; see Stefan Bekaert, "Multiple Levels of Meaning and the Tension of Consciousness: How to Interpret Iron Technology in Bantua Africa," *ArchDial* 5 (1998): 6–29.

28 The stated goal of Wright's *Ritual in Narrative* is "the examination of how ritual functions within the narrative context of stories" (ibid., 6). This differs from the goal of the present paper only insofar as 2 Samuel 19 provides a narrative account of a singular "narratively ritualized" crossing of the Jordan instead of a regularly repeated "ritual" crossing.

29 Arnold van Gennep, *The Rites of Passage* (trans. Monika B. Vizedom and Gabrielle L. Caffee; 1909; repr., Chicago: University of Chicago Press, 1960).

30 E.g., Terence S. Turner, "Transformation, Hierarchy and Transcendence: A Reformulation of van Gennep's Model of the Structure of Rites of Passage," in *Secular Ritual* (ed. Sally F. Moore and Barbara G. Meyerhoff; Assen: Van Gorcum, 1977), 60–64. On the continuing need in modern society for rituals at times of major life transitions, see W. S. F. Pickering, "The Persistence of Rites of Passage: Towards an Explanation," *BritJSociol* 25 (1974): 63–78; Louise Carus Mahdi, Nancy G. Christopher, and Michael Meade, eds., *Crossroads: The Quest for Contemporary Rites of Passage* (Chicago: Carus, 1996); Ronald L. Grimes, *Deeply into the Bone: Re-Inventing the Rites of Passage* (Berkeley and Los Angeles: University of California Press, 2000). For a summary of V. Turner's view of rites not just as actions expected to preserve the community's integrity but as communicative practices that establish order in society, see Robert A. Segal, "Victor Turner's Theory of Ritual," *Zygon* 18 (1983): 327–35; and Moore and Meyerhoff, "Secular Ritual," 4–5.

be drawn between stages of the process and the physical locus of the individual undergoing the transition.[31] The preliminal rites (rites of separation) consist of rituals centered on the subject's movement away from the group, at a *threshold of some sort*, usually taken to be the threshold between the common and the incubational worlds. The liminal rites (rites of transition) are those performed while in this incubational world. Finally, the community performs postliminal rites (rites of incorporation) to welcome the subject back into the mundane world, albeit a newly reworked world in which the subject bears a different status and therefore plays a modified role.[32] Often, the bracketing sets of rites (i.e., the preliminal and postliminal sets) can be read as complementary sets within themselves; that is to say, every rite of separation from the community is at the same time a rite of incorporation into the transitional (liminal) stage, and every rite of incorporation back into the community is a rite of separation from the liminal.

Throughout this study, I do not mean to argue that David underwent any project of ritual engagement construed by the text as a "rite of passage." Rather, I intend to indicate the emplotment of David's Transjordanian exile as structurally parallel to van Gennep's model of the "rites of passage." That said, the time David spends in Transjordan serves as an incubational period in the narrative logic of the text.[33] During this exile,

31 The subject who undergoes such matrices of ritual acts is believed to be "in a special situation for a certain length of time: he wavers between two worlds" (van Gennep, *Rites of Passage*, 18).

32 Ibid., 10–11. For a discussion of the reasons for the structure of these rites, see T. Turner, "Transformation," 53–70. Bruce Lincoln has argued that women undergo a different series of elements in their initiations—namely, enclosure, metamorphosis, and emergence—since the locus of their transitional period (i.e., the home) shows continuity with their predominant locus in the mundane world (*Emerging from the Chrysalis: Rituals of Women's Initiation* [New York: Oxford University Press, 1981], 99–101; see also Carol Walker Bynum, "Women's Stories, Women's Symbols: A Critique of Victor Turner's Theory of Liminality," in *Anthropology and the Study of Religion* [ed. Robert L. Moore and Frank E. Reynolds; Chicago: Center for the Scientific Study of Religion, 1984], 105–25). However, this should probably be considered a refinement of van Gennep's schema rather than an outright challenge, because it preserves the tripartite schema of separation, transformation, and reintegration vis-à-vis the *community*. The location of seclusion from the community is not in and of itself critical in van Gennep's schema, as I read it. Instead, it is the movements into and out of seclusion that are paradigmatic for the rites of passage. See, e.g., the distinction made between "sequestered" and "public" liminality in Victor Turner, "Variations on a Theme of Liminality," in *Secular Ritual* (ed. Sally F. Moore and Barbara G. Meyerhoff; Assen: Van Gorcum, 1977), 38–39. Furthermore, while we should take note of Grimes's caveat that male initiation rites held a privileged position in van Gennep's organization (*Deeply into the Bone*, 105), it is precisely an initiation—or better, confirmation—of a male that is described in 2 Samuel 19.

33 For a similar view, see the assertion of Sacon that 18:1–19:9 "is located at the turning point from David's retreat and resignation to his return and restoration" ("Literary Structure," 34). J. W. Wesselius argued that 2 Samuel 18 serves as "the central scene in the entire Succession

David's state—his political *status*—changes dramatically. He leaves Jerusalem in 2 Samuel 15–16 a broken monarch whose own son has revolted and taken the throne, supported by a groundswell of popular outrage. Only the most loyal of David's subjects accompany him to the city of Mahanaim or remain in Cisjordan to plot against the newly ascendant king Absalom. David garners little broad-based support other than that of his personally loyal army. Upon his return, however, David has the support of the entire tribe of Judah (2 Sam 19:15–16; 20:2).[34] The transition of David's state has therefore occurred while he dwelled in Mahanaim. David's geographic double-movement from Cisjordan to Transjordan and back to Cisjordan parallels narratively his interstitial double-movement from king to exile back to king. To quote van Gennep, "A rite of spatial passage has become a rite of spiritual passage."[35]

The complementary structure of rites of separation and incorporation proposed by van Gennep allows for a further refinement of scope. While in the larger presentation Transjordan is the site of David's "rite" of transition, we may also note the two locations of the threshold between the mundane world and the liminal world, when viewed at a smaller scale. The Mount of Olives and the Jordan River are each represented as the locales of further transformation.[36] David's experiences centered on the summit of the Mount of Olives in chapters 15 and 16 prepare him for the ordeal to come; his experiences at the Jordan River in chapter 19 prepare him for reentry into the hierarchical society of Cisjordan. On either side of these two thresholds, David undergoes ritualized elements both of separation from and incorporation into the community (fig. 1).

Narrative" ("Joab's Death and the Central Theme of the Succession Narrative [2 Samuel ix–1 Kings ii]," *VT* 40 [1990]: 340–43). Also see Charles Conroy, *Absalom Absalom! Narrative and Language in 2 Sam 13–20* (AnBib 81; Rome: Biblical Institute Press, 1978), 89.

34 It is debatable whether Israel (i.e., the northern tribes), ever really considered themselves rightful subjects of David's Judahite hegemony. In both 2 Sam 20:1 and 1 Kgs 12:16, the cry "every man to his tent, Israel," and "to your tents, Israel, " respectively, quickly galvanizes the resolve of the (northern) Israelites—in stern juxtaposition to the Judahites—to break free of any exertion of power by the (southern) Judahite Davidic dynasty.

35 Van Gennep, *Rites of Passage*, 22. Gluckman has argued that shifts in status are more likely to be accompanied by spatial separation in "modern societies" than in "tribal societies" because modern societies exhibit a more radical break between the loci of a single subject's variant social positions ("*Les Rites de Passage*," 35–36; but cf. 35 n. 1). However, that rites of passage as a whole are integrally embedded in spatial relationships has been argued and elaborated by Edward S. Casey ("How to Get from Space to Place in a Fairly Short Stretch of Time: Phenomenological Prolegomena," in *Senses of Place* [ed. Steven Feld and Keith H. Basso; Santa Fe, N.M.: School of American Research, 1996], 39–40).

36 For the Jordan River as a boundary, see Jobling, "'Jordan a Boundary'," 88–133, 142–47; Weinfeld, "Extent," 59–75; Brodsky, "The Jordan," 34–43, 52; Lori Rowlett, "Inclusion, Exclusion, and Marginality in the Book of Joshua," *JSOT* 55 (1992): 15–23; and Havrelock, "Jordan River," esp. 1–4.

Fig. 1. The Nested Rites of David's Passage (2 Sam 15:13–19:43):

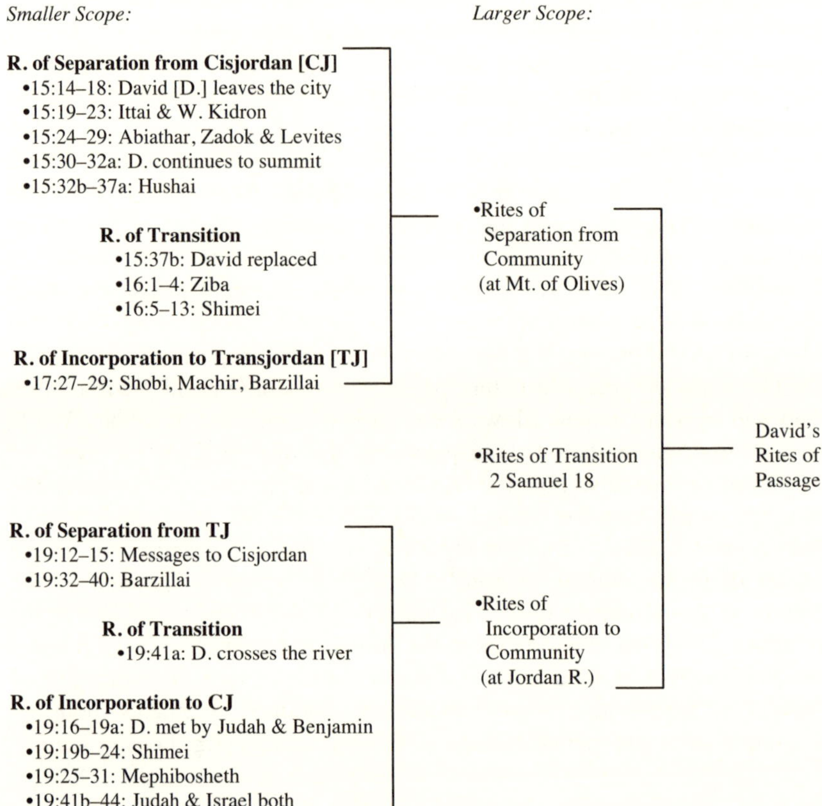

2 Samuel 15–16 details the "preliminal rites" performed during the royal entourage's flight from the city of Jerusalem. At each step, David becomes further removed from the quotidian world of Cisjordan. After making and implementing the decision to flee Jerusalem in 2 Sam 15:14–18, David's various sequential interludes serve to divorce him slowly from his kingdom. In vv. 19–22, David meets Ittai the Gittite before crossing the Kidron Valley in v. 23. David next takes his leave from the priests Abiathar and Zadok and their respective sons, along with the rest of the Levites carrying the Ark of the Covenant in vv. 24–29. After continuing to the summit of the Mount of Olives in vv. 30–32a, David sends back Hushai the Archite to serve as a spy in Absalom's court (vv. 32–37a). David has thus begun his physical and geographical separation from the land by slowly engaging in a narratively ritualized separation from his

community until he reaches the topographical high point of his journey.[37] Having crested the Mount, David's separation from his own community of loyal subjects is finished, and the period of his transition has begun, signaled by Absalom's move into the city in v. 37b. Yet the circles of loyal Judahite subjects are themselves nested in larger concentric demographic circles.

Just after the high point of the Mount of Olives, David encounters the family steward of his longtime rival Saul. Ziba has brought food and drink as a parting gift and a sign of fealty to the crown (16:1–4). While not a member of David's immediate agnatic group, Ziba shows loyalty akin to that of the members of David's tribe. In return for his loyalty, David gives the ancestral land of Saul's house to the steward. But with his departure from Ziba, David has left the mundane world of loyal Israelites and Judahites and has stepped into the liminal abyss. After continuing some distance, David is castigated and humiliated by Shimei, another Benjaminite of the House of Saul, who hurls insults—both verbal and geological—at the king (vv. 5–13).

We recognize here a narrative logic that articulates with van Gennep's model of the rites of separation from the community[38] and the concomitant sundering of the subject's bond to the quotidian world. In his encounter with Shimei, David has reached the threshold between the everyday world pervaded by hierarchical structure and the larger liminal world. The world on the other side of this boundary will serve as the site of David's ultimate transformation into a monarch with renewed legitimacy.[39]

David and his entourage quickly pass the threshold marked by Shimei's insults and finally reach Mahanaim (17:27), where they are met by three Transjordanian personages: Shobi ben-Nahash the Ammonite, Machir ben-Ammiel from Lo-debar, and Barzillai the Gileadite. During these rites of incorporation, these men greet David with all sorts of supplies and provisions in vv. 28–29.[40]

37 Notice here the phrase "When David was coming to the summit where one bows/would bow down to God..." (ויהי דוד בא עד־הראש אשר־ישתחוה שם לאלהים; v. 32a). We can distinguish here another textual rite of separation. The traveler headed east out of Jerusalem, upon reaching the summit of the Mount of Olives, partook of yet another frequent ceremony of territorial passage—that occurring at the mountain pass. See van Gennep, *Rites of Passage*, 22.

38 Ibid., 36. Fischer makes passing reference to the structure of *rites de passage* ("Flucht und Heimkehr," 47).

39 For the significance of Shimei's insults in van Gennep's model of the rite of passage, see the discussion of V. Turner's *communitas* below. For *communitas* in this passage, see, briefly, Fischer ("Flucht und Heimkehr," 54).

40 Lundbom also recognized this feast as an important element of David's rite of passage but again did not correlate it specifically to elements of the model proposed by van Gennep ("Psalm 23," 13–14).

After David's transformation of state during his stay in Mahanaim,[41] David initiates "postliminal rites" that will ultimately serve to reincorporate the king into the Cisjordanian hierarchy. Like the "preliminal rites" centered on the threshold at the Mount of Olives, these "rites" (performed at the threshold of the Jordan River) also consist of more finely grained narratively ritualized elements of separation and incorporation.[42] David sends word to Zadok and Abiathar saying, "Speak to the elders of Judah and say, 'why would you be the last to bring the king back to his house?'" The priests do so, and the Judahites consent to further Davidic rule, sending word back to the king: "Return, you and all your servants" (2 Sam 19:12,15). Yet, David's efforts at separation from Transjordan consist not only of his message to Zadok and Abiathar and the Judahite response in 2 Sam 19:12–15, but also in his final interaction with Barzillai, the good-byes they exchange, their kissing and blessing (vv. 32–40). These nested narratively ritualized actions serve to sunder David's ties to the eastern shore at which point he is then free to make his westward crossing.

David's crossing of the river in v. 40a forms the transitional stage of this smaller, nested rite of passage,[43] after which his various interactions with his subjects—Mephibosheth, Shimei, the Judahites and Israelites—

41 It is naturally somewhat foreign to us as moderns that the liminal, transformative nature of Transjordan does not seem to affect those who dwell there. Why should Barzillai be able to take his leave of the king and then return to that sacred land—juxtaposed to the profane Cisjordan—in which David has recently undergone his incubation? The answer again might be found in the tripartite structure of the rites of passage, in which the liminal area (here, *neutral zone*) is clearly set off from the world of the everyday by the threshold, or *limen*: "Because of the pivoting of sacredness, the territories on either side of the neutral zone are sacred in relation to whoever is in the zone, but the zone, in turn, is sacred for the inhabitants of the adjacent territories" (van Gennep, *Rites of Passage*, 18). The places of transitional importance are therefore relative and can be described only from one subject's point of view. In the schema presented so far, Transjordan forms the neutral zone, the place of transition, with respect to the Cisjordanian Israelites. The Transjordanians, however, implicitly live quite comfortably and without any self-aware contradictions to the western Israelite outlook. They are the Other, then, in the mindset of the Cisjordanian narrative (e.g., Denis Baly, "The Pitfalls of Biblical Geography in Relation to Jordan," in *Studies in the History and Archaeology of Jordan* 3 [ed. Adnan Hadidi; Amman: Jordanian Department of Antiquities, 1987], 124).

42 Fokkelman noticed the narrative connection of the "crossings" of the Kidron Valley and the Mount of Olives in 2 Samuel 15–16 and of the Jordan River in ch. 19 (*King David*, 313–14, 322–23). However, Fokkelman's outlook on the narrative of David's transformation in 2 Samuel 15–19 differs from my own in that Fokkelman views the transformation negatively: "David the refugee is composed, strong and adequate versus David the conqueror who is broken, not composed, and inadequate" (ibid., 322).

43 In addition, a group of intermediaries aids David's transition from the conceptually liminal world of Transjordan. Intermediaries comprise a frequent element in the rites of passage (van Gennep, *Rites of Passage*, 48). The text has been deliberately constructed such that David is implicitly escorted part of the way by Barzillai, then met and escorted the rest of the way across by Shimei, who "rushed into the Jordan before the king," (v. 18) and Kimham.

serve to reincorporate the king into the community. A circumstantial summary of action at the time of the crossing (19:41) states that David, along with Kimham, crosses towards Gilgal (הגלגלה). The Judahites, as well as half the people Israel[44] have brought the king over (or crossed over, depending on the proper reading of the word ויעברו) and are confronted by a hostile group of Israelites claiming their "ten shares" of the king (19:42–20:1). This confrontation, presumably in the area of Gilgal, bears several commonalities with other stories of the fulfillment of personal destiny that take place at Gilgal (e.g., Josh 4:19–24; 1 Sam 13:8–15), as well as episodes of convening to crown a new king (e.g., 2 Sam 5:1;[45] 1 Kgs 12:1).[46] The literarily emplotted preliminal rite—coming to an agreement concerning the proper hierarchicalization of society—and the postliminal rite—crowning the new monarch—bracket David's ritualized movement through the Jordan River. The smaller set of episodes in ch. 19 itself serves as a nested rite of passage within the larger double-movement of disenfranchisement and re-empowerment (fig. 1).[47]

The centrality of the hierarchicalization of society fundamental to the structure of this double-movement suggests that a closer investigation of the liminal transitional period is warranted. Just as the liminal period of the crossing of the Jordan is bracketed off from ordinary society by interactions revolving around prospective power dynamics in the reconstituted Davidic monarchy, so too does the issue of power and hierarchicalization permeate the larger-scale double-movement of the journey to Transjordan and back. In his book *The Ritual Process*, Victor Turner identified the power-dynamics of the rites of passage and proposed a vocabulary with which to discuss them.[48] His term "structure" designates the static hierarchical assemblage of rules in society.[49] The structural mode of society for Turner is hierarchically differentiated, often fraught with conflict, and predicated on the continuity between the past and the future, rooted in the politics and economics of power relations, including

44 Notice the clear juxtaposition between the Judahites and Israelites. One wonders from the context of the following verse whether "half the people Israel" was not an addition designed to emphasize David's appeal to both groups.

45 Significant as well here is the Israelites' assertion of familial relation, הננו עצמך ובשרך אנחנו, parallel to that in 19:13.

46 Cf., however, 2 Sam 20:1 and 1 Kgs 12:16 in both of which the denial of any stake in the Davidic dynasty appears.

47 See van Gennep, *Rites of Passage*, 185.

48 Victor Turner, *The Ritual Process: Structure and Anti-Structure* (Ithaca, N.Y.: Cornell University Press, 1969).

49 In terms of its semantic field, Turner's *structure* seems to me completely different from the (deep) structures of the Structuralist school of linguistics and anthropology, but cf. Theodore Schwartz, who explicitly compares Turner to Lévi-Strauss (review of V. Turner, *The Ritual Process*, *AmAnthropol* n.s. 74 [1972]: 904–8).

and deriving from laws and customs. David's Judahite monarchy before and after Absalom's revolt qualifies as such. Over against this structure stands liminality, a "movement in and out of time,"[50] posed in opposition to the temporal rootedness of social structure. One of the elements commonly found during periods of liminality is a mode of being that Turner calls *communitas*.

As the ideological but complementary opposite of structure, communitas entails a leveling of social class during the liminal period.[51] The community's hierarchy temporarily breaks down, and social position goes unrecognized or is intentionally ignored. On the night before an Ndembu chief-elect becomes chief, the rites of transition consist of the rest of his tribe insulting him directly to his face with no fear of reprisal:

> ...any person who considers that he has been wronged by the chief-elect in the past is entitled to revile him and most fully express his resentment, going into as much detail as he desires. The chief-elect, during all this, has to sit silently with downcast head, "the pattern of all patience" and humility.... The chief may not resent any of this or hold it against the perpetrators in times to come.[52]

The transitional period outlined by van Gennep is the temporal locus of communitas (and complementarily, the physical location at and beyond the *limen* is its site). Because communitas "emerges where social structure is not,"[53] it engages in a mutually enriching dialectic with structure. One cannot be fully grasped without recourse to an understanding of the other. Communitas at the same time embraces social structure as its mutually

---

50 Ibid., *Ritual Process*, 96.

51 However, we should perhaps be wary of locating communitas solely within the liminal, thereby assuming its coextensive relationship with the practice of ritual. See, e.g., Michael Heyd, who suggests that structure may appropriate "certain themes which were traditionally elements of anti-structure" ("The Reaction to Enthusiasm in the 17th Century: From Structure to Anti-Structure," *Religion* 15 [1985]: 287). Brian Morris has noted that Turner's rigid division of structure and communitas is misleading, arguing instead that there can be egalitarian and spontaneous action within the confines of structure and that a few of Turner's examples (especially Turner's use of Goffman's *Asylums*) are more appropriately understood as the stripping off of the individuals' personalities—Goffman's "mortification"—rather than merely the elements of social status (*Anthropological Studies of Religion: An Introductory Text* [Cambridge: Cambridge University Press, 1987], 258–63, esp. 260). Mathieu Deflem has suggested that "at least some marginal phenomena of the liminal...are not at all challenging to the wider social structures and involve no feeling of humankindness or communitas, but on the contrary offer an outlet for the social order and involve mechanisms of depersonalization...by which the whole personality of the marginal individual is stripped off" ("Ritual, Anti-Structure, and Religion: A Discussion of Victor Turner's Processual Symbolic Analysis," *JSSR* 30 [1991]: 19). This may be true, but does not seem to me to be an argument that discounts entirely Turner's assertion of those features of communitas that do offer a challenge to the hierarchicalization of structure.

52 V. Turner, *Ritual Process*, 101.

53 Ibid., 96, 126.

affirming and defining partner and pushes it away, as its ideological opposite.[54]

The transitional period, the time in which communitas comes to the fore, yields a disconcerting homogeneity or even reversal of political power.[55] The radical destabilization of Israelite social structure during Absalom's revolt appears to contain elements of the social dehierarchicalization of communitas. During the flight from Jerusalem, Shimei castigates David as the king makes his way slowly down to the Jordan River: "Out! Out! Murderer! Scoundrel!" (2 Sam 16:7).[56] Shimei peppers the king's entourage with rocks and dust, and David does nothing in retaliation, even though Abishai ben-Zeruiah, the brother of David's general Joab, offers to kill Shimei on the spot (v. 9). Perhaps, David argues, Shimei curses because God has told him to (v. 11). In this episode, David recognizes the situation into which both he and Shimei have been thrust. David's kingship has come to an end at the hands of his own son, and in order to regain the kingship, he must undergo an ordeal of transition that consists of humiliation and retribution for past grievances—in particular, his behavior towards the Saulide family.[57] Shimei, as a newly

54 This point has been emphasized by Mary Gluckman and Max Gluckman ("On Drama, and Games and Athletic Contests," in *Secular Ritual* [ed. Sally F. Moore and Barbara G. Meyerhoff; Assen: Van Gorcum, 1977], 242). Bynum suggests that "liminality itself...may be less a universal moment of meaning needed by human beings as they move through social dramas than an escape for those who bear the burdens and reap the benefits of a high place in the social structure" ("Women's Stories," 109).

55 While this reversal serves as a potent juxtaposition to the normal structure of society, it is necessarily limited in duration. Attempts to prolong the presence of communitas ultimately fail. The community based on widespread egalitarianism, in order to be viable, must gradually instill strata of social relations. The dialectic between structure and communitas is one of constant flux, a dynamic complementary relation in which both partners are mutually interdependent, yet the pragmatic partner (structure), with its temporal connections to past and future, asserts its own agenda as strongly as does the egalitarian partner (communitas) of the immediate moment. Neither wins out in the end, since the existence of each is contingent upon the existence of the other, but the pragmatic partner structure finds itself in the temporal duration as the more practical and therefore more common (see V. Turner, *Ritual Process*, 131–203).

56 I use here the translation of NRSV, which, while not a literal translation, properly conveys the sentiment expressed. Unless otherwise noted, all translations are my own.

57 See McCarter for a discussion of Shimei's wording (*II Samuel*, 373–77, 436–46). Is he calling David a murderer because of his evident collaboration with the Philistines and the ensuing death of Saul (1 Samuel 29), his apparent complicity in the deaths of Abner and Ishbosheth (2 Samuel 3–4), his outright murder of the Saulide household (2 Samuel 21—which McCarter places temporally at the beginning of David's reign), or his brutal elimination of Uriah (2 Samuel 11)? With so many unsavory narratives of David's callous brutality and shady dealings, it is difficult to pick a clear winner. One is inclined to believe that the reason lay in David's rough treatment of the Saulides (three of the four cases listed above), since the author of the text takes special care to mention that Shimei himself is a Benjaminite, but the answer is not important for the time being: Shimei has enough of the narrative's testimony on his side to be unimpeachable.

empowered former subject, sees only the imminence of David's downfall and places himself in a position to condemn the king's actions. Even though Shimei cannot predict the impending reversal of fortunes brought about by David's stay in Transjordan, he nonetheless partakes of the imminent presence of communitas coursing up through the fissures in the Judahite-controlled Israelite social structure. The Benjaminite's curses articulate a shift in the dynamics of power as well as the presence of a former king caught in a period of liminality.

The positioning of Shimei's diatribe is significant as well. In the smaller, nested, more focused scope of David's "rite of passage," Shimei's insults themselves take the character of rites of incorporation into Transjordan (even though David has, topologically speaking, not made it there yet). But at the level of the larger scope, these insults only serve as the beginning of David's ordeal during his period of liminality. Shimei, standing clearly within the threshold, is free to insult David, since the former king's separation from his community is well underway.

In the textual event of his return trip, David's liminality takes a different form. Here he is implicitly one of the first to wade into the river (since Shimei and Ziba rush into the river to meet him)[58] and the last to finish the crossing. David is stuck precisely at the *limen* until his entire army has passed over; in this regard he is both the one mediated—since Barzillai and Shimei escort him across in the implicit logic of the narrative—and the mediator of his army's passage. This is perhaps a further indication of David's renewed power and authority, resonating from and an implicit allusion to the people Israel's assumption of power in Canaan at this same ford over the Jordan in Josh 3:14–4:18. In that passage, the priests carrying the Ark of the Covenant step into the river. The river's flow comes to a halt until the entire people of Israel has crossed the dry river bed, at which point the priests carrying the ark step foot on dry ground and the river resumes its flow.[59]

58 However, cf. McCarter's discussion, cited above (n. 17), which places historically David's encounter with Barzillai on the east bank and his encounter with Shimei on the west.

59 This short description of Joshua 3–4 disregards the complex transmission history of the pericope. Brian Peckham provides a review of literature on the traditio-historical work up until that time ("The Composition of Joshua 3–4," *CBQ* 46 [1984]: 413–31, esp. 413–18), but Peckham flattens the literary history to two basic sources, dtr_1 and dtr_2, thereby dating the episode to the late seventh century. This may be contrasted with the recent work of Antony F. Campbell and Mark A. O'Brien, who attribute the bulk of Joshua 3–4 to an undated pre-Deuteronomistic "Conquest Narrative" and its expansions (*Unfolding the Deuteronomistic History: Origins, Upgrades, Present Text* [Minneapolis: Fortress, 2000], 23–24, 112–17). For them, the pericope is clearly liturgical and has been supplemented with several "liturgical annotations" (3:5,9,11,12,13; 4:4,6–7,9,15) that would have aided in the ritual celebration of one of God's foundational acts on behalf of Israel (e.g., Cross, *CMHE*, 79, 103–5). However we interpret the community's use of the text, it is clear from the final parallelism between

One further theme of liminal communitas—or even status reversal—might also be picked up in David's final encounter with Barzillai, whom he seems to treat as an equal. The interaction between the two figures may not be surprising from a historical point of view, given that Barzillai is one of a trio of hosts who have supported David during his exile (2 Sam 17:27). Having provided for David during his sojourn in Transjordan, Barzillai (along with Shobi ben-Nahash the Ammonite and Machir ben-Ammiel from Lo-debar) has implicitly established a patrimonial-style relationship of benefactor and beneficiary with David.[60] David's invitation to Barzillai to become part of the royal court in Jerusalem serves the purpose of role-reversal precisely at this moment of (post)liminal transformation. David's offer is at the same time an explicit recognition of the role that Barzillai has played in his succor and an implicit request to reverse the benefactor-beneficiary relationship, reinstating David as the more powerful partner in that relationship. Barzillai tactfully declines the invitation but sends Kimham—possibly his own son[61]—in his stead. This concession displays Barzillai's implicit recognition of the newly reinstated political status. Even though Barzillai is an important man (2 Sam 19:33) in the social structure of Transjordan, Kimham, a member of his household, resides in the royal court. No longer does Barzillai have a claim to power over the king in the king's disenfranchised state.[62] The

---

Joshua 3–4 and Exodus 14, in both of which the Israelites cross a waterbed on dry ground (Joshua 4:23), that the two pericopes were conceived of as bracketing a period of transformation in which Israel became ready to assume its stature as rightful possessor of the Canaanite hill-country (Hutton, "Topography"). This is demonstrated by the function of the forty years' wandering in the Pentateuch's final form (e.g., Num 14:20–35) to weed out the entire Exodus generation aside from Caleb and Joshua (but including Moses: Deut 3:25–27; 4:21–22).

60 For patrimonialism and its embeddedness in Israelite cultural thought, consult Max Weber, *Economy and Society: An Outline of Interpretive Sociology* (ed. Guenther Roth and Claus Wittich; 2 vols.; Berkeley and Los Angeles: University of California Press, 1968), 2:1006–69; Stager, "Archaeology of the Family," 24–28; and Philip J. King and Lawrence E. Stager, *Life in Biblical Israel* (LibAncIsr; Louisville, Ky.: WJKP, 2001), 36–40.

61 See McCarter, *II Samuel*, 418.

62 Historically, the invitation would not be untenable. Having enjoyed such a relation of power over the king, Barzillai's descendants might have seen this as a certain degree of legitimization for their own possible rule over Judah and Israel. Cf. the case of David's care of Mephibosheth in his court, probably as an attempt to keep close tabs on the surviving Saulide's dynastic hopes (see e.g., McCarter, *II Samuel*, 265). It is possible that here, too, the invitation carries some reminiscence of historical facticity since David should have wanted to stem any such dynastic hopes emanating from Transjordan as well. Barzillai's deliverance of Kimham, then, might have been a concession made to David in order to ensure good relations between the two regions, an assurance that Gilead was Judah's ally and held no interest in acceding to the Judahite/Israelite throne. Assuming that the Barzillai "the Gileadite" of 2 Samuel 19 was the same as the Barzillai "the Meholatite" the father of Adriel (2 Sam 21:8; see also 1 Sam 18:19), this solution becomes even more credible, since the marriage of Saul's daughter Merob (reading with a few Hebrew manuscripts, *Tg. Jon.*, and LXX^{L} at 2 Sam 21:8;

social world of the Judahite monarchy, through David's sojourn in Mahanaim, has regained its proper structure. The period of David's liminality has ended; he may safely and unqualifiedly reassert his control.

1.2.2. Double-Crossing Prophets: Elijah and Elisha in 2 Kgs 2:1–18

The Elijah/Elisha scene of 2 Kings 2 shows a similar reliance upon the binary oppositions west : east :: mundane : liminal. It has often been recognized that the pericope in 2 Kings 2 inaugurates Elisha's ministry while at the same time drawing Elijah's to a close.[63] Moreover, R. Havrelock has recently discussed the passage in the terms of the rites of passage.[64] The centerpiece of the passage details a short journey to the eastern bank of the Jordan. This journey functions differently for each character, but the function in both cases is that of a rite of passage. For Elijah, the pericope centers on his disappearance from the mundane world, his vacating of the prophetic office in this world.[65] For Elisha, the scene describes his investiture with the prophetic powers of his predecessor. In both cases elements of van Gennep's model apply, because both figures experience changes in status encoded narratively through changes in geographical location. In some ways, the recognition of this pericope as a rite of passage has already been formulated in the passage's chiastic structure:

> Elijah crosses the Jordan to go up alive, when Elisha crosses back he has Elijah's powers and *twice* his spirit. He may not go up in his lifetime but he can make the

---

see also Robert B. Lawton, "David, Merob, and Michal," *CBQ* 51 [1989]: 423–25) to Adriel, Barzillai's son, would have solidified relational bonds between the Benjaminite Saulides and the Gileadite Meholatites. In this case, one wonders how sincere Barzillai's loyalty to David actually was if McCarter is correct in his assertion that David's execution of Barzillai's grandchildren ("the five sons that Merob daughter of Saul had borne to Adri[el]"; 2 Sam 21:8) took place *before* David's instatement of Mephibosheth (McCarter, *II Samuel*, 262–65).

63 E.g., Richard D. Nelson, *First and Second Kings* (Interpretation; Atlanta: John Knox, 1987), 157–63; Mordechai Cogan and Hayim Tadmor, *II Kings: A New Translation with Introduction and Commentary* (AB 11; New York: Doubleday, 1988), 33; Burke O. Long, *2 Kings* (FOTL 10: Grand Rapids, Mich.: Eerdmans, 1991), 19–22; Philip E. Satterthwaite, "The Elisha Narratives and Coherence of 2 Kings 2–8," *TynBul* 49 (1998): 8; Mark A. O'Brien, "The Protrayal of Prophets in 2 Kings 2," *ABR* 46 (1998): 1–16; Marvin A. Sweeney, *I & II Kings: A Commentary* (OTL; Louisville, Ky.: WJKP, 2007), 271–74; Havrelock, "Jordan River," 136–43.

64 Havrelock, "Jordan River," 138–42; see previously Long, *2 Kings*, 22. Although our readings differ, our simultaneous and independent interpretations of this passage as modeled on the structure of the rites of passage mitigate the need for a detailed analysis.

65 The question of Elijah's ascension to heaven and its attendant conceptions of Elijah's end status is avoided here. For a short discussion, see Cogan and Tadmor, *II Kings*, 33–34.

dead live even after he dies (ch. 13). Elijah *splits* the Jordan with his coat and the *two* of them walk through. The chariots and horses *separate* between the *two* of them. When Elijah goes up Elisha *tears* his clothes to *two* pieces but now lifts up Elijah's coat that is now his, *splits* the Jordan with it and crosses back alone now with *twice* Elijah's spirit.[66]

Even without an explicit decision regarding the *portion* of Elijah's spirit received by Elisha,[67] Levine has correctly pointed to the symmetry of the structure. If we take his italicized key words as the points to be mapped in sequence, it is possible to establish the chiastic structure of the pericope:

A Elijah splits the Jordan and both cross (ויחצו [המים]; v. 8a)
B Both cross through (ויעברו שניהם; v. 8b)
C Elisha asks for a double portion of Elijah's spirit (פי־שנים ברוחך; v. 9)
D If Elisha sees, he will be rewarded (אם־תראה; v. 10)
E The chariot of fire separates the two (ויפרדו בין שניהם; v. 11)
D' Elisha is watching (ואלישע ראה; v. 12)
C' Elisha tears his own garments in two (ויקרעם לשנים קרעים; v. 12)
B' Elisha crosses the Jordan… (ויעבר; v. 14)
A' …after it has been split with Elijah's cloak (ויחצו; v. 14)

As Levine's model makes clear, the centerpiece of this scene is Elijah's ascension to heaven when the whirlwind separates him from his disciple. This point is exactly the culmination of Elijah's prophetic office and the inauguration of Elisha's. Verses 9–13 describe the liminal period in which the status of each shifts while on the eastern bank of the river, and v. 11 clearly acts as the focal point of that transformative experience. Elisha's double movement through the Jordan River brackets his shift in status. The rites of separation that sever his mundane ties to the world and prepare him for the liminal should be recognized in his conversations with the sons of the prophets in vv. 3 and 5: they ask Elisha "Do you know that today the Lord is taking your master from you?" (הידעת כי היום יהוה לקח את־אדניך מעל ראשך), to which he responds, "Yes, I know; be quiet" (גם־אני ידעתי החשו). At this point, the sons of the prophets know what Elisha knows. A similar conversation with the prophetic novices comprises the

66 Nachman Levine, "Twice as Much of Your Spirit: Pattern, Parallel and Paranomasia in the Miracles of Elijah and Elisha," *JSOT* 85 (1999): 41–42, his italics.

67 Levine, following much rabbinic interpretation, analyzes Elisha's reception of Elijah's spirit as *twice that* of Elijah, since his miracles repeat and *double* those performed by Elijah, according to Midrash (ibid., 44; see also Havrelock, "Jordan River," 140–41). However, the original understanding of the phrase פי־שנים ברוחך probably would have been "two shares," a reference to the traditional share of the first-born in the father's patrimony when there is more than one son (Deut 21:17; Nelson, *Kings*, 159; John Gray, *I & II Kings* [2d ed.; OTL; Philadelphia: Westminster, 1970], 475; Cogan and Tadmor, *II Kings*, 32; Iain Provan, *1 and 2 Kings* [NIBCom; Peabody, Mass.: Hendrikson, 1995], 173; Sweeney, *I & II Kings*, 273); cf. "two thirds" in Zech 13:8. In either case, argues O'Brien, the request for less than the full amount of Elijah's spirit signals Elisha's humility ("Portrayal," 10).

narrative analogue to "rites of incorporation" for Elisha, performed upon his reentry into the community. Now he knows what they *do not*, namely, that Elijah will not be found (vv. 15–18[68]), proving his elevation in status. Elijah's experience in Transjordan follows a similar trajectory but differs in a single important way. As in the case of Elisha, Elijah's "rites of separation" from the community consist of his admonitions to Elisha to stay behind and the latter's refusal to comply (vv. 2,4,6).[69] Again, these rites of separation culminate in the crossing of the Jordan River. But because Elijah undergoes translation on the eastern bank of the Jordan River, he never experiences any sort of reincorporation into the Cisjordanian community. This significant departure from van Gennep's model is at the same time a recognition of its efficacy: because Elijah is never reincorporated into the community, his existence as a liminal figure is fixed in Israelite and later Jewish and Christian belief (see, e.g., Mal 3:23–24; Matt 17:1–8; Mark 9:2–8; Luke 9:28–36).[70]

Unlike the passage concerning David's crossing examined above, the Jordan River serves in this episode only as a line of demarcation. Because the double crossing is narrated much more concisely, the nested structure of rites of passage that was demonstrated for 2 Samuel 15–19 does not seem to obtain in the present scene, and the action occurs at a single scope of significance. Nonetheless, in 2 Kings 2 the Jordan River is portrayed as separating the mundane world from the liminal world. The journey across the river and the subsequent return again exhibit a narrative structure that bears commonalities to the rites of passage.[71]

---

68 For this scene as part of Elisha's confirmation, see also Judith A. Todd, "The Pre-Deuteronomistic Elijah Cycle," in *Elijah and Elisha in Socioliterary Perspective* (ed. Robert B. Coote; Atlanta: Scholars Press, 1992), 29–30; cf. Havrelock, who argues that the prophetic novices' mistrust indicates that the succession has not been entirely successful ("Jordan River," 140–41).

69 In this regard, it is appropriate to point out that already Elisha serves as the mediator between Elijah and the community, since the prophet himself never comes in contact with the "sons of the prophets," who seem to know of his immanent departure. It is Elisha who must act as the conduit between the two.

70 The New Testament passages concerning Jesus's transfiguration point to an added facet of the Transjordanian motif in Jewish and early Christian thought. The three figures present at that event were all somehow associated with the Jordan River: Moses could not cross it westward; Elijah crossed it eastward at the culmination of his career and did not return; Jesus was baptized in it at the beginning of his own ministry. The symbolic significance of the Jordan River as a boundary between the mundane and the liminal does not end with the closure of the Hebrew Scriptures.

71 I have not dealt with issues surrounding the concept of communitas in this passage, since the leveling of social status does not seem to have been as explicitly demarcated as it was in 2 Samuel 19. However, one might point to the fact that Elijah asks Elisha what the master might do for the disciple (v. 9) and that Elisha seems to be incorporated into the realm of authority when he is able to see Elijah's ascension (v. 12). These notices suggest some degree of parity between the two prophetic figures.

1.2.3. Derision in the East: Judges 8

The recognition that both 2 Samuel 19 and 2 Kings 2 comprise narratives—not necessarily historical—whose respective meanings follow the same logic accorded to actual rites of passage by van Gennep and Turner suggests that we might make similar conclusions with regard to the symbolic matrix employed by some of the deliverer-narratives in the book of Judges. I examine here briefly the ritualized logic of the Judges 8 pericope, in which Gideon crosses the Jordan River, defeats the Midianite invaders, and is offered the kingship. As with the previous cases, it should not be taken from this short investigation that I assume any sort of actual *ritual* to have been performed upon the defeat of the Midianites and the attempt to crown Gideon king. Rather, the narrative has been constructed to follow the same foundational logic that underlies the rites of passage, namely, that geographical movement through—both entrance into and return from—a *liminal space* (in this case as in the former examples, Transjordan) immediately occasions a change in the *state* (political or religious status) of the character. Regardless of whether vv. 22–23 comprises a secondary insertion,[72] Gideon must have experienced some form of literarily emplotted elevation in the original form of the story.[73]

The eastward crossing of the Jordan River is only cursorily mentioned in this passage (v. 4), and no return crossing appears explicitly in the Gideon story. The river itself clearly plays no obviously necessary role in the story, and although the action of the battles—both against the retreating Midianites and against the (presumably Israelite) people of Sukkoth and Penuel[74]—takes place on the eastern side of the Jordan River, that

72 That the offer of the kingship (vv. 22–23) has been secondarily inserted is frequently accepted (e.g., George Foot Moore, *Judges* [ICC; New York: Scribner, 1895], 217, 229–30; J. Alberto Soggin, *Das Königtum in Israel: Ursprünge, Spannungen, Entwicklung* [BZAW 104; Berlin: Töpelmann, 1967], 15–20; Uwe Becker, *Richterzeit und Königtum: Redaktionsgeschichtliche Studien zum Richterbuch* [BZAW 192; Berlin: de Gruyter, 1990], 174–83, esp. 176–83; Reinhard Müller, *Königtum und Gottesherrschaft: Untersuchungen zur alttestamentlichen Monarchiekritik* [FAT II/3; Tübingen: Mohr Siebeck, 2004], 35–92). It is difficult to know, however, when that interpolation was performed; suggested dates for the intrusion range from the 10th cent. (Frank Crüsemann, *Der Widerstand gegen das Königtum: Die antiköniglichen Texte des Alten Testaments und der Kampf um den frühen israelitischen Staat* [WMANT 49; Neukirchen-Vluyn: Neukirchener Verlag, 1978], 42–54, esp. 52), to the 9th cent. during Jehu's reign (Wolfgang Richter, *Traditionsgeschichtliche Untersuchungen zum Richterbuch* [BBB 18; Bonn: Heinstein, 1963], 236), to the 8th cent. before the fall of the northern kingdom (Moore, *Judges*, 230), to the exile (Becker, *Richterzeit*, 177), to the Persian Period (Müller, *Königtum*, esp. 237–49; but cf. Soggin, *Königtum*, 18–20).

73 Soggin, *Königtum*, 20.

74 A. Malamat allows that the two cities had previously entered into a vassalage treaty with Gideon but shies away from claiming Israelite or non-Israelite ethnicity for either city ("The Punishment of Succoth and Penuel by Gideon in Light of Ancient Near Eastern Treaties," in

positioning seems in the story's logic to be accidental: Gideon was chasing the Midianites back to the hinterland from which they had come. That hinterland simply *happened* to be in Transjordan. But if no particular symbolic importance was initially attributed to the battle's location in Transjordan, why has the Gideon story been included in the present discussion? Nothing about the narrative seems explicitly ritualistic, as did the narratives in 2 Samuel 19 and 2 Kings 2. The positioning of the story in Transjordan probably *was* originally incidental, insofar as the battles fought there would have originally been conceived of as commonplace practicalities.

Assuming that Judges 8 preserves the memory of a historical event, or of a politico-historical milieu in which such cultural conflicts occurred, Gideon's intention in following the Midianites across the Jordan River was under no circumstances intended as a symbolic action. Instead, it was aimed at eliminating further threats to the agricultural resources upon which he and his tribe relied for survival (e.g., Judg 6:3–4).[75] Until the battle with the Midianites, Gideon's authority has been recognized but provisional and ad hoc.[76] Yet, in 8:22 the Israelites attempt to crown him king. Clearly, something has taken place in the interval that provides the Israelites with a reason to elevate Gideon's status. But how might we go about deciphering the clues that point to how this story functions within the context of the DtrH as a whole? A few of the lessons learned from the study of 2 Samuel 19 and 2 Kings 2 help us to understand the present problem. Without recourse to comparison to several of the narratives concerning the transformative nature of Transjordan, it would be difficult to draw out any explicit connections that the movement through the *landscape* might have with the fortunes of the hero. More specifically, it is quite difficult to argue cogently that van Gennep's model of the rites of passage may be used to describe the narrative logic of Judges 8; there is little particularly ritualistic about the narrative, and the narrative logic encoded in Gideon's geographic movement was not mapped across the

---

Sefer Moshe: Studies in the Bible and the Ancient Near East, Qumran, and Post-Biblical Judaism [ed. Chaim Cohen, Avi Hurvitz, and Shalom M. Paul; Winona Lake, Ind.: Eisenbrauns, 2004], 69–71).

75 Jo Ann Hackett, "'There Was No King in Israel': The Era of the Judges," in *The Oxford History of the Biblical World* (ed. Michael D. Coogan; New York: Oxford University Press, 1998), 199–200.

76 There is no need here to discuss in depth the Weberian categories of "Charismatic" vs. "Institutional" authority. Gideon's leadership is that of a fully capable deliverer, appointed through the agency of a messenger of God (מלאך יהוה; v. 6:11), and whether or not his position as the son of a freeman who owned his agricultural land suggests raised socioeconomic status (cf. the stereotypical response in 6:15), the received text *presents* the authority as provisional.

Jordan River in any easily intelligible way (as was 2 Kings 2). Nonetheless, the story recognizes implicitly that the geographic movement was the occasion of the inauguration of Gideon's kingship (if we may interpret the Israelites' offer as such).[77]

More immediately effective in explaining the implicit structure of Judges 8 as a narrativized "rite of passage" is Turner's notion of communitas. Just as Shimei hurls dust and insults at the retreating David in 2 Sam 16:5–7, so too do the Transjordanian Israelites in Sukkoth and Penuel challenge Gideon's request for sustenance: "Have you already gotten the hands of Zeba and Zalmunna that we should give you food for your army?" (8:6). The hierarchical structure of Cisjordan, to the extent that it existed there, has been turned on its head. The provisional leader of the (Cisjordanian) Manassite contingent is disregarded and scorned by the people of two cities that should—it is assumed—be allied with Gideon's forces.[78] The disrespect leveled at Gideon by the inhabitants of these two cities is reversed in Judg 8:22, after he has taken the Midianite camp by surprise and captured the offending kings. Only the battle at Qarqor and the ensuing destructions of Penuel and Sukkoth intervene. If there is any historicity that may be attributed to Gideon's Transjordanian campaign and subsequent crowning, I find it unlikely that the geographical movements of Gideon's band were motivating factors in the accession. However, the narrative has undergone a complex tradition history, the final result of which recognizes a component of social dehierarchicalization during the establishment of Gideon's authority, which corresponds with his military foray into Transjordan.

1.2.4. Transjordan in the Cisjordanian Worldview

In concluding this juxtaposition of biblical narratives with the structural markers of the rites of passage, a few remarks are necessary. I have not attempted a historical reconstruction of the order of events in David's return from his Transjordanian exile, of Elisha's inauguration as a prophet, or of the existence of Gideon's kingship; I am, for the purposes of this study, uninterested in *what any of these characters actually did*. While the historical-critical method takes account of the difficulties encountered in a study of the textual transmission, it fails in the case of David to explain the chronological order of the narrative text itself. Similarly, it simply glosses

77 See G. Henton Davies, "Judges viii 22–23," *VT* 13 (1963): 151–57.

78 If this passage is read historically (and if Sukkoth and Penuel were even Israelite), it points to the intertribal struggles that prevented any large-scale unifications of Israelite identity during the Iron Age I.

over the tight narrative structuring of 2 Kings 2 and misses the narrative function of Gideon's humiliation by the people of Sukkoth and Penuel. By approaching the unexpected or overly schematic canonical order of episodes in these texts with recourse to interpretational models provided by anthropological theory, I have attempted to show that the present order and form of each text is not only intentional, but meaningfully structured as well. As a literary representation of David's "rite of passage" from transformed and prospective king to fully empowered monarch, 2 Samuel 19 serves as the culmination of the narratively ritualized emplotment of an event through which David regains his authority in Israelite society. Van Gennep's analysis of the rites of passage provides a model by which we might better understand the position held by Elijah in subsequent Israelite, Jewish, and Christian tradition, as well as Elisha's corresponding elevation in status in 2 Kings 2. Finally, the importance of Gideon's humiliation at Sukkoth and Penuel is brought to light through comparison to David's humiliation at the hands of Shimei in 2 Samuel 16. These narratives, I have argued, all exhibit a roughly uniform narrative logic that envisions a journey to Transjordan as a transformative experience. Yet, underlying that uniformity, fissures emerge between the variant assumptions as to the actors' reasons for crossing over to Transjordan and their resultant expectations upon their return westward. The first narrative examined most clearly presents Transjordan as a politically autonomous region to which exiled political figures could escape in exile (2 Samuel 15:16–16:13; 17:27–29; 19:12–44). This escape is narrated such that it inevitably occurs with a very pragmatic purpose: survival. The narrator never seems to indicate any explicit attempt on the David's part to achieve any other end. This outlook is shared with several other texts from 2 Samuel (e.g., 2:8–10a,29–32; 9:3–5; 13:37–38). Sometimes the exile presented is self-imposed, and sometimes it comes as the result of external pressure, but in all cases, the exiled figure is a monarch or an aspirant monarch. Therefore, this sub-motif will be designated the *monarch-type* vision of Transjordan.

The second narrative (2 Kgs 2:1–14) schematizes and systematizes the journey to Transjordan as significant in the individual's transformation of state. Along with, for example, Joshua 3–4, it conceptualizes the passage through the Jordan in terms of a codic opposition: the eastern bank remains outside the pale of mundane Israelite experience and therefore as Other. Conversely, the western bank embodies the quotidian, everyday experience of being "at home." Because prophets and their followers play the dominant roles in these passages, they are designated here members of the *prophet-type* subset of the Transjordanian Motif.

Although similar to the monarch-type view in its recognition of a primarily pragmatic purpose to the hero's double-movement across the Jordan, Judges 8 is differentiated from the former by its recognition of Transjordan as a hinterland from which enemies come and back to which they must be pursued. This assessment is shared with Judges 3; 8; 12; and 1 Samuel 11. In each one of these deliverer-narratives, the battles fought east of the Jordan—or even more fully developed by some of the tales, *at* the fords of the Jordan—occasion increased authority for the head figure but are not otherwise seen as metaphysically transformative. It is not improper, then, to delineate a *deliverer-type* subset of the Transjordanian Motif.

These fissures between three distinct perceptions of the landscape east of the Jordan River in the Cisjordanian collective consciousness invite examination of their interrelationships and development. The three schematic designations of these subsets as deliverer-, monarch-, or prophet-type proceed merely from a cursory analysis of the dominant actors in each group. However, the very nature of these designations warrants a more detailed analysis of the relationships between the members of each set. Each set seems to cluster. The deliverer-type vision is found primarily in Judges, with one exemplar in 1 Samuel. The monarch-type is found nearly exclusively in 2 Samuel. The prophet-type is found mainly in the other books of the DtrH: it is implied in Deuteronomy, but it undergirds the Israelites' entry into the land in Joshua and the formation of the prophets in 1–2 Kings. This circumstance can hardly be accidental. Yet, before an analysis of the Transjordanian Motif's diachronic development may proceed, it is necessary to examine the emotive and affective capabilities that landscapes have, so that we may achieve a clearer understanding of how different visions of landscape may be compounded and compiled to effect an augmented and novel understanding of a landscape's narrative significance.

1.3. Landscape Criticism as a Means of Interpretation

The core focus of this study is the Transjordanian *landscape*: the actual physical topography, the human geography, and the historical and cognitive interactions between the inhabitants of the area and the physical topography itself. This interaction, I argue throughout this study, has led to the solidification of a literary feature that was used frequently in the historiographic emplotment of Israel's political and religious history to indicate or suggest the divinely sanctioned authority—or the *presumption* of such authority—attributed to the characters who make the journey to Transjordan and return westward. But what, exactly, is meant by the term *landscape*? Of what is landscape comprised? And might a nuanced view of landscape help us understand how the narrative portrayal of certain landscapes holds meaning for societies? Section 1.3 offers an overview of landscape criticism as it has come to be practiced in recent years along with a discussion of its various axioms and recognitions that will aid in the present discussion.

Human geography was the first field to adopt studies of humanity's embeddedness in its landscape.[79] Archaeology followed soon afterwards and has since added much fruitful study to the field of discussion.[80] Recently, the need for a specifically landscape-oriented synthetic study in ancient Near Eastern archaeology has been recognized and fulfilled by T. J. Wilkinson in his spectacular survey of *Archaeological Landscapes of the Near East*.[81] The classification of all these studies as "landscape"-based scholarship, however, should not be taken as an indication that their methodologies, findings, and even definitions of the term "landscape" are all the same.[82]

---

79 Yi-Fu Tuan, "Geography, Phenomenology and the Study of Human Nature," *CanGeogr* 15 (1971): 181–92; idem, *Topophilia: A Study of Environmental Perception, Attitudes, and Values* (New York: Columbia University Press, 1974); D. Cosgrove, "Place, Landscape, and the Dialectics of Cultural Geography," *CanGeogr* 22 (1978): 66–72; idem, *Social Formation and Symbolic Landscape* (Madison, Wis.: The University of Wisconsin Press, 1984).

80 Ian Hodder, "Converging Traditions: The Search for Symbolic Meanings in Archaeology and Geography," in *Landscape and Culture: Geographical and Archaeological Perspectives* (ed. J. M. Wagstaff; Oxford: Basil Blackwell, 1987), 134–45; Tim Ingold, "The Temporality of the Landscape," *WorldArch* 25 (1993): 152–74; Barbara Bender, "Theorising Landscapes, and the Prehistoric Landscapes of Stonehenge," *Man* 27 (1992): 735–55; idem, "Introduction: Landscape—Meaning and Action," in *Landscape: Politics and Perspectives* (ed. Barbara Bender; Oxford: Berg, 1993), 1–17; Christopher Tilley, *A Phenomenology of Landscape: Places, Paths and Monuments* (Oxford: Berg, 1994); idem, "Rocks as Resources: Landscapes and Power," *CornArch* 34 (1995): 5–57; idem, "The Powers of Rocks: Topography and Monument Construction on Bodmin Moor," *WorldArch* 28 (1996): 161–76; Barbara Bender, Sue Hamilton, and Christopher Tilley, "Leskernick: The Biography of an Excavation," *CornArch* 34 (1995): 58–73; idem, "Leskernick: Stone Worlds; Alternative Narratives; Nested Landscapes," *PPS* 63 (1997): 147–78. For the interaction between human geography and archaeology, see particularly Hodder, "Converging Traditions," 134–45; and A. Bernard Knapp and Wendy Ashmore, "Archaeological Landscapes: Constructed, Conceptualized, Ideational," in *Archaeologies of Landscape: Contemporary Perspectives* (ed. Wendy Ashmore and A. Bernard Knapp; Malden, Mass.: Blackwell, 1999), 1–30.

81 T. J. Wilkinson, *Archaeological Landscapes of the Near East* (Tucson, Ariz.: The University of Arizona Press, 2003). See also the call for further sensitivity toward the effects of environment on culture made by Denis Baly ("The Nature of Environment, with Special Relation to the Country of Jordan," in *Studies in the History and Archaeology of Jordan* 2 [ed. Adnan Hadidi; Amman: Jordanian Department of Antiquities, 1985], 19–24).

82 See, e.g., the methodological criticisms of Hodder and Tilley in J. David Schloen, *The House of the Father as Fact and Symbol: Patrimonialism in Ugarit and the Ancient Near East* (SAHL 2; Winona Lake, Ind.: Eisenbrauns, 2001), 29–36.

T. Lemaire, for example, understands the term "landscape" to be "already an arrangement and structuring of the environment by the human gaze," which presupposes a loss of mythical conceptions of space. He thus treats the term as a descriptor of a completed artistic portrayal of topography, rather than a dynamic process.[83] D. Cosgrove's notion of landscape is much more a notion of an interactive *process*: "Human ideas mould the landscape, human intentions create and maintain spaces, but our experience of space and place itself moulds human ideas."[84] According to Cosgrove, our interaction with landscape, even though it begins with seeing and experiencing, soon becomes an ideological mode—rooted in the struggle between classes—of manipulating the visible forms of the environment in order to impose or encode rational order and design into or onto the topographic features of the land.[85]

Two problems arise in the application of Cosgrove's definition of landscape to the Israelite systems of thought about the land. First, it relies too much on the physical manipulation of the land as a site of rational encoding of meaning. While this facet of human-worked landscape would be appropriate to landscape studies dealing with Israelite *building practices*,[86] it is less appropriate for the study of the Jordan's fords. So far as can be determined, the actual physical manipulation of the topography at the fords seems to have been quite minimal (despite the literary commemoration of Israel's crossing through the erection of stones in Joshua 3–4). Instead, the meaning latent at those fords was encoded primarily *textually*. Cosgrove's notion of the manipulation of the physical topography distinguishes too greatly between the inner (cognitive) and outer (physical) worlds.[87] Second, Cosgrove's definition seems too predicatively Marxist to describe accurately the situation with respect to the Israelites' attribution of meaning to geographical and topological features of their environment. Although the application and maintenance of power clearly played a role in

83 Ton Lemaire, "Archaeology between the Invention and the Destruction of the Landscape," *ArchDial* 4 (1997): 5–21, esp. 5; see also idem, "Ambiguous Landscape(s)," *ArchDial* 4 (1997): 32–38; cf. Augustin Berque, "There is Only Mount Jingting," *ArchDial* 4 (1997): 22–23; Dennis E. Cosgrove, "Inhabiting Modern Landscape," *ArchDial* 4 (1997): 23–28; and Tim Ingold, "The Picture Is Not the Terrain: Maps, Paintings and the Dwellt-In World," *ArchDial* 4 (1997): 29–31.

84 Cosgrove, "Place," 66.

85 Cosgrove, *Social Formation*, 13–38; idem, "Geography is Everywhere: Culture and Symbolism in Human Landscapes," in *Horizons in Human Geography* (ed. Derek Gregory and Rex Walford; Totowa, N.J.: Barnes & Noble, 1989), 118–35.

86 E.g., Lawrence E. Stager, "Jerusalem and the Garden of Eden," in *ErIsr* 26 (ed. Baruch A. Levine et al.; Jerusalem: Israel Exploration Society, 1999), 183*–94*.

87 Ingold, "Temporality," 152–72.

the Israelite cultural milieu,[88] it is quite difficult to justify the application of a specifically Marxist interpretation of well-defined self-identifying strata of "classes," as N. K. Gottwald has done.[89] Furthermore, it is overly simplistic in this situation to adopt Marxism's inherent interest in the control of production.[90] A less materialist definition of landscape is appropriate to discuss the Israelite attribution of meaning to places.

For B. Bender, the term landscape designates the full range of human perceptions of and interactions with their physical environment: the perception of landscape is "the way in which people—all people—understand and engage with the material world around them."[91] For C. Tilley, landscape is "a set of relationships between named locales."[92] B. A. Knapp and W. Ashmore suggest a useful division of landscapes into three basic types: constructed, conceptualized, and ideational.[93] "Constructed landscapes" are those physical landscapes that have been intentionally designed or created or that display an evolution from their natural state.[94] "Conceptualized landscapes," in their schema, "offer a variety of images which are interpreted and given meaning through localized social practice and experience" and are thus increasingly cognitive but remain physically perceptible.[95] "Ideational landscapes" are both imaginative and emotional. Not to be equated wholesale with "sacred" or "symbolic" landscapes (and even less limitable to "ideological landscapes"), they comprise a more

88 Any number of historical-critical studies may be cited here, including Halpern's study of David and Solomon's succession history (*David's Secret Demons*), Paul D. Hanson's study of the internecine struggles between the restoration-era Zadokite priests and their Levitical underlings (*The Dawn of Apocalyptic: The Historical and Sociological Roots of Jewish Apocalyptic Eschatology* [rev. ed.; Philadelphia: Fortress, 1979]), and Cross's study of the conflicting priestly houses (*CMHE*, 195–215).

89 Norman K. Gottwald, *The Tribes of Yahweh: A Sociology of the Religion of Liberated Israel, 1250–1050 BCE* (Maryknoll, N.Y.: Orbis, 1979; repr., Biblical Seminar 66; Sheffield: Sheffield Academic Press, 1999); cf. George Mendenhall, "The Hebrew Conquest of Palestine," *BA* 25 (1962): 66–87. I wish to thank here Professor Lawrence E. Stager for his willingness to engage me in conversations concerning political and economic theory. Those conversations have greatly influenced—but not entirely overridden—my thought on this matter.

90 See Robert Layton, *An Introduction to Theory in Anthropology* (Cambridge: Cambridge University Press, 1997), 127–56.

91 Barbara Bender, "Introduction," in *Contested Landscapes: Movement, Exile and Place* (ed. Barbara Bender and Margot Winer; Oxford: Berg, 2001), 3; see also idem, "Theorising Landscapes," 735–55; and idem, "Introduction: Landscape," 1–17.

92 Tilley, "Rocks as Resources," 5; see also idem, "Powers of Rocks," 161–75; for "locales" see §1.4 below.

93 Knapp and Ashmore, "Archaeological Landscapes," 10–13. Notice that the *topography* itself plays only a basic role in all of these definitions. Topography may be considered as the raw material from which human notions of *landscape* are worked.

94 This is the type most closely related to Cosgrove's landscapes. See also Baly's *cultural environment* ("Nature," 19–20).

95 Knapp and Ashmore, "Archaeological Landscapes," 11.

wide-ranging group of emotionally important and evocative landscapes. Ideational landscapes encompass both the interpretation of the landscape and the previously mentioned analytic categories, "constructed" and "conceptualized" landscapes. In short, ideational landscapes are the combination of the physical interconnections of places and the cognitive appropriations of those sets of locales. Although several writers have studied the Jordan River as a conceptualized landscape,[96] it is at the level of the ideational that the following analysis will seek to proceed.

These three sets of definitions—Bender's and Tilley's of "landscape" as well as Knapp and Ashmore's "ideational landscape"—are sufficiently broad so as to permit a reworking of their contents into a viable way of talking about the Israelite landscape, while not being so vague as to limit meaningful discourse about the landscape. A combination of the three yields this formulation that shall serve as a benchmark for the following discussion: *landscape* is the total perceived and conceptualized set of relationships existing between humans and named locales. To talk about the Israelite landscape, therefore, is not to talk merely about Cisjordanian or Transjordanian topography. Rather, it is to point to the set of emotional and cognitive relationships bound up with the physical topography that is both constituted by and at the same time constitutive of the Israelite worldview.

Proceeding from this definition of landscape, four basic themes will serve to clarify the salient issues encountered while discussing the Israelite (and particularly the Transjordanian) landscape: (a) landscape is potentially polyvalent; (b) landscape can function as social currency; (c) smaller landscapes are nested within larger ones; and (d) landscape is a cognitive entity.

1.3.1. Landscape Is Potentially Polyvalent

In §1.1 of this study, Transjordan was presented as exhibiting or expressing a single, monolithic meaning in the DtrH under the rubric "a place of exile, refuge, and incubative transformation for prospective personages of power." Indeed, the landscapes of Transjordan and the Jordan River often display only one property at a time. This property usually manifests itself as magico-religious (e.g., 2 Kgs 6:1–7) or mundane and pragmatic (e.g., Judges 8 and 2 Samuel 19). Sometimes, however, these landscapes may appear to embody both magico-religious and pragmatic properties at the

96 See, e.g., Weinfeld, "Extent," 59–75; Jobling, "Jordan a Boundary," 88–133; Brodsky, "The Jordan," 34–43, 52.

same time (Joshua 3–4; 2 Kings 2; see §1.2.4). This dichotomy suggests that landscape as a *meaningful* entity is subject to the application or bestowal of more than one meaning by more than one source (individual or corporate). For T. Ingold, "landscape is constituted as an enduring record of—and testimony to—the lives and works of past generations who have dwelt within it, and in so doing, have left there something of themselves."[97] Because human interaction with the landscape changes over time, it is possible that the specific cognitive and emotional resonations of that place motivated by that interaction would change as well. It stands to reason that if there is continuity in the human culture interacting with the landscape, there will be continuity in the meaning attributed to the landscape, even if that continuity exhibits some degree of diachronic development. By this reasoning, the continued reattribution of meaning, slightly varied, builds up a cognitive patina of significance in the landscape. Places may "contain sedimented meanings,"[98] or they may serve as "palimpsests of past activity."[99] Without further qualifications, one would expect a disjoint between cultural conceptions of the meaning of Transjordan between the Canaanite and Israelite cultures and a relative degree of continuity between conceptions attributed to the Transjordanian landscape by various factions within Israelite culture.

But social meaning is by no means synchronically monolithic, even within a single culture. Any model that purports to be useful must take into account the dramatic differences in the respective experiences of the world on the part of the various groups of individuals in society. One may still show through social-scientific study of the Hebrew Bible that several groups, some empowered, some disenfranchised—most identified roughly along familial lineages—inhabited the Cisjordanian and Transjordanian highlands, without arguing for any crosscutting sodalities such as Neo-Marxism might assume.[100] To assume that these various groups all held a monolithic conception of a plot of land is surely fallacious.[101] We must allow for variations—some slight, some significant—in their respective symbolic systems. "As with landscapes that encode belief, so too can social, political, ethnic, and other distinctions be embedded in the landscape."[102] Places, along with their attendant meanings, form landscapes

97 Ingold, "Temporality," 152.

98 Tilley, *Phenomenology*, 15.

99 Bender, "Introduction: Landscape," 9.

100 E.g., Lawrence E. Stager, "The Archaeology of the Family in Ancient Israel," *BASOR* 260 (1985): 1–35.

101 Bender, "Theorising Landscapes," 740.

102 Carole L. Crumley, "Sacred Landscapes: Constructed and Conceptualized," in *Archaeologies of Landscape: Contemporary Perspectives* (ed. Wendy Ashmore and A. Bernard Knapp; Malden, Mass.: Blackwell, 1999), 273.

that are "*polyvalent*, because the mixing together of so many micro-stories gives them functions that change according to the groups in which they circulate."[103] Given this qualification, if the DtrH were as monolithic (and perhaps "monovalent") as it evidently seeks to portray itself, we should expect that the picture of Transjordan that it presents should be monolithic as well. However, the thesis that springs from this theme, and which will be analyzed in the present study, is this: the process of the formation of the DtrH brought together shorter sources in a larger attempt to unify Israel, to present it as a single political unit under the control of the Davidic dynast Josiah.[104] These sources can be shown to have had divergent conceptions of the *meanings* latent in the Transjordan landscape and the fords of Gilgal. The DtrH's Transjordanian landscape is therefore a palimpsest of past intellectual activity, to use Bender's formulation.

1.3.2. Landscape Can Function as Social Currency

It was recognized above that the very mention of a certain topological feature is meaningful. Within any given unified social unit, such mention refers to a commonly accepted perception of that topological feature. When I mention the geographical name "Timbuktu," a competent interlocutor skilled in conversing in late twentieth/early twenty-first century America will know that my speech refers to one of two things: it is either directly referential and refers specifically to the city of Timbuktu in western sub-Saharan Africa, or it is metaphorical, in which case I really mean the "middle of nowhere."[105] A skilled interlocutor will be able to interpret from my demeanor, my delivery, and the context of the situation, which of the two I intend to indicate.

A second example, with somewhat different connotations, comes from the movie *Casablanca*. At the time of their final parting, Rick tells Ilsa, "We'll always have Paris." The name of the city evokes strong emotions and memories for many people; often those memories are romantically inclined. Even people who have never been to Paris often associate the city with lovers and romantic moments. Rick's words bear this connotation even without knowledge of the back-story of the couple's love affair

---

103 Michel de Certeau, *The Practice of Everyday Life* (trans. Steven Rendall; Berkeley and Los Angeles: University of California Press, 1984), 125.

104 See, e.g., Cross, *CMHE*, 284.

105 See, e.g., the metaphorical usage of the phrase in the travel memoire of Tony Hawks (*Playing the Moldovans at Tennis* [New York: Thomas Dunne, 2000], 174).

that had taken place in Paris a few years before.[106] But the *precise* meaning of Paris in the *Casablanca* narrative's constructed world lies in the back-story; those movie goers who fully understand the line, "We'll always have Paris," are that subset who have not stepped out for popcorn during the flashback to the couple's time together in Paris. In turn, the enduring popularity of *Casablanca* and the corresponding dissemination of Rick's lovelorn line have augmented and cemented in the American psyche the romantic nature of the Parisian cityscape, now commemorated in countless movies, television shows, and so on.

Landscape can serve as common currency while at the same time retaining mystery for the outsider uninitiated in the proper associated cultural traditions. Knowledge of these traditions can become commodified, and this knowledge is an empowering commodity.[107] As such, it is also appropriable, but this fact is only useful to those who have access to the knowledge.[108] Concomitant with the possibility of appropriation comes the possibility of contestation. The polysemy of place described above can lead to outright conflict over culturally embedded *meanings* of a place. See, for instance, the altar in Joshua 22—probably built in Transjordan (אל־מול ארץ כנען; v. 11). The Cisjordanian Israelites mustered under Phinehas consider the building of the altar treachery (v. 16: המעל הזה), while the Transjordanian Israelites claim that the altar is meant merely to signify and preserve their religious unity with the Cisjordanians (vv. 21–29). When traditions conflict, any power differential involved in that conflict will necessarily polarize the variant conceptions of the contested landscape.[109]

Landscapes of power and landscapes of exclusion are two corollary and derivative *types* of landscape that can develop from this contestation.[110] As is apparent from Joshua 22, Transjordan was a contested landscape, the struggle over which occurred historically not only between the Cisjordanian and Transjordanian Israelites (see also the stories of internecine strife in Judges 12), but also between various textual sources of the

106 The reason for this possibility lies in places' currency as containers (or more properly, *embodiments*) of socially imposed and recognized meanings. The identification of Paris as a city of romance is at the same time an implicit identification of ourselves as members of a social group that recognizes the (apparently) inherent romantic nature of that city (Knapp and Ashmore, "Archaeological Landscapes," 15).

107 Tilley, "Rocks as Resources," 5–57; idem, "Powers of Rocks," 161–75; see also Michel Foucault, *Discipline and Punish* (New York: Vintage, 1977).

108 Bender, "Introduction: Landscape," 752.

109 For a more thorough discussion of the polar oppositions encoded into this story, see Jobling, "Jordan a Boundary," 88–133, esp. 98–103; and Havrelock, "Jordan River," 63–70.

110 For the former, see Bender, "Introduction," in *Contested Landscapes*, 4–5; for the latter, Cosgrove, "Geography is Everywhere," 118–35.

DtrH.[111] Through the efforts of the Deuteronomistic Historian (hereafter Dtr) and of later editors, the literary and ideological credibility of earlier Cisjordanian authors increased with respect to their perspectives of the contested history of the Transjordanian landscape. Part of Dtr's project was apparently to *relocalize* the *center* of "Israelite" corporate identity (away, specifically, from Shiloh, Shechem, Bethel, and Dan as religious centers of the Joseph tribes—themselves all contested landscapes). But in doing so, the Deuteronomistic Historian was disenfranchising Transjordanian Israelites as well.[112]

1.3.3. Smaller Landscapes Are Nested within Larger Landscapes

Lived space is an ordered collection of *places*, with landscapes nested inside one another. For example, the inhabited space of a settlement is situated within the margins of the domestic landscape. That larger domestic landscape includes boundary markers, the surrounding fields and pastures, the city's "daughters" (i.e., satellite towns), and so on. Outside of that lie the other towns and boundaries of the tribal territory, and beyond that still, the tribe.[113] Stager's model of the social structure of Israel provides for nested patrimonial groups, with the kingship as the *bēt ʾāb* ("father's house") writ large.[114] This nesting is not only conceptual and genealogical, but physical and geographical as well, as Stager shows. In the same way, nested places can embody identical meanings. Frequently,

111 In teasing out the tensions latent in the text, one should keep in mind the applicability of one method adopted by Steven Feld and Keith H. Basso: "A more radical way to create sharp textual juxtapositions…was to emphasize places and populations whose geographical closeness and presumed familiarity made them, ironically, *more*, not less, 'other' and remote…" ("Introduction," in *Senses of Place* [ed. Steven Feld and Keith H. Basso; Santa Fe, N.M.: School of American Research, 1996], 7).

112 Historically speaking, there were likely very few Transjordanian "Israelites" left at the time of the Deuteronomistic Historian's work (assuming a Josianic compilation of the DtrH), since Tiglath-Pileser III had conquered most of northern Transjordan in 743, and before that the territory had been ruled for several decades by Aram (see §2.3). However, as will be argued in chs. 3–7, many of the sources in which the Transjordanian Motif is embedded had been compiled into a single source already sometime during the Jehuite dynasty (late 9th–mid-8th cent.). For most of that period, neither Assyria nor Aram had as yet subsumed the Israelite community in northern Transjordan.

113 See also Bender, Hamilton, and Tilley, "Leskernick: Biography," 59; idem, "Leskernick: Stone Worlds," 147–78.

114 Stager, "Archaeology of the Family," 18–24; idem, "The Patrimonial Kingdom of Solomon," in *Symbiosis, Symbolism, and the Power of the Past: Canaan, Ancient Israel, and Their Neighbors, from the Late Bronze Age through Roman Palaestina* (ed. W. G. Dever and S. Gitin; Winona Lake, Ind.: Eisenbrauns, 2003), 63–74. Cf., however, the important qualifications of the model in Carol Meyers's review of P. King and L. Stager, *Life in Biblical Israel* (*BASOR* 331 [2003]: 84–86).

the heads of households are called out to serve as representatives of their houses or as representatives of their tribes (e.g., Josh 22:14). Similarly, refined locales often serve to embody the meaning of the larger landscape. For example, in the accounts of Jesus' baptism at the Jordan (Matt 3:13–17; Mark 1:9–11; cf. Luke 3:21–22 and John 1:29–34), the authors did not merely *forget* to narrate Jesus' crossing to Transjordan for a period of transformative incubation before returning to his baptism, and then to Cisjordan.[115] Rather, the Jordan itself serves *pars pro toto* as a metonym for Transjordan. Likewise, Elijah and Elisha do not seem to make it very far into Transjordan before Elijah is assumed and Elisha turns back around (2 Kings 2). The two cases suggest that in later applications of the Transjordanian motif, the effect of the Transjordanian landscape is delivered through even minimal contact with it. This is not to say, however, that the symbolism contained in the individual *locale* is always the same as that contained in the larger landscape. Mahanaim, a city of quotidian exile in the context of the monarch-type vision of Transjordan (2 Sam 2:8; 17:24–27), never exhibits the magico-religious property of a locus of incubative transformation. It is only in these texts' juxtaposition to other narratives in the DtrH that the city's transformative properties emerge.

1.3.4. Landscape Is a Cognitive Entity

As the set of symbolic relationships between humans and named locales, landscape is subject not only to human *action* but to human *thought* as well. Just as physical topography is subject to spatial movement, so too is the ideational landscape subject to "cognitive movement."[116] This cognitive movement, often taking the form of the imagining of migration or exile (or of the imagining of physical rootedness), serves as a means of manipulating identity, both social and individual. Such movement can be *just as meaningful* as physical movement. A. Dawson and M. Johnson cite the case of a mayoral election in a coal-town in northeast England. One candidate was a coal-miner with extensive historical familial embeddedness in the area who had for a time been forced to leave the region in order

115 Matt 3:13–17 and Mark 1:9–11 state only that Jesus went to the Jordan directly from Galilee, with no mention of crossing the river. Luke 3:21–22 gives no geographical indications at all, only stating that Jesus was baptized with other people. John 1:31–34 relates no baptism of Jesus in narrated time but implies its past occurrence. Like the passage from Luke, it gives no geographical indication of Jesus' movements (although see Hutton, "'Bethany Beyond the Jordan'," 305–28).

116 Andrew Dawson and Mark Johnson, "Migration, Exile and Landscapes of the Imagination," in *Contested Landscapes: Movement, Exile and Place* (ed. Barbara Bender and Margot Winer; Oxford: Berg, 2001), 319.

to find work. Socioeconomically, he was paradigmatic of the town's experience. The other candidate was a teacher who had been a long-term resident but who did not have extensive familial history in the area. This candidate knew the history of the town, its economic peculiarities, its habits, its "particular lifeways," and relied upon that cognitive familiarity with a somewhat *imagined* and perhaps romanticized landscape rather than genealogical or economic familiarity with the region in order to build his campaign strategy. This dichotomy of self-identification with respect to both the landscape and its inhabitants juxtaposes the historical rootedness but temporary "routedness" of the coal-miner and the historical "routedness" but cognitive rootedness of the teacher in the town.[117] The disparity between these two mayoral candidates draws into sharper relief the fact that embeddedness in—and complementarily, disembeddedness from—the landscape are fundamental elements in the formation of identity as a function of landscape. Even though the teacher had what Dawson and Johnson implicitly deem to be an *inferior* personal link to the community,[118] he was able to manipulate symbols through his knowledge of the historical—but romanticized—self-identity of the town to have "condensed historical meaning." This winning strategy ultimately deprived the coal-miner of the primary conceptual buttress of his credibility: his historical rootedness in the community.

Dawson and Johnson relate a second story of the interface between self-identity and landscape. In the coal-miner's case, an economically imposed physical exile diminished the miner's perceived connection to the town; an imagined exile takes place in this other case. The town of Hue in Vietnam is romanticized in the memories of (exiled) American Vietnamese as a paradigmatically Vietnamese town. Some ethnically Vietnamese-American men imagine Hue as a town where a "properly" Vietnamese woman may be found and married. Quite often, these men return with

117 The clever linguistic play of exile as "routes over roots" is that of Dawson and Johnson.

118 Dawson and Johnson, "Migration," 322. I do not agree with what I take to be the implication of Dawson and Johnson's assertion that "community is being refined as a discourse by a middle class that manipulate images and symbols that have only a condensed historical meaning for them, rather than a more personal link" (ibid., 322), namely, that this manipulation is a less authentic mode of existence. I *do* believe that relations of power manipulate historical data and symbols, forming a condensed historical meaning—the vision of the Transjordan presented by the Dtr is exactly such a manipulation and synchronization (i.e., detemporalization) of the historically developed traditions about Transjordan (e.g., Weinfeld, "Extent," 59–75). But to oppose this flattening over against "a more personal link" seems to me arbitrarily to privilege one mode of being in the world (i.e., working a blue collar job) over another (investing one's academic interest in one's newly-chosen home). In their apparent rush to protect the coal-miner from some sort of neocolonialist appropriation by the middle-class, it appears to me that Dawson and Johnson have themselves appropriated his case for their own purposes.

their new wives to the United States to maintain the economic and political connections that they had fostered before the marriage. Such a marriage with an "authentic" Vietnamese woman fulfills a "longing" latent in these men for a return to their roots, so to speak. But as Dawson and Johnson articulate elegantly, a paradox develops in which "the imagined longing of the exiled ... in part creates the burden of an authentic self which they see themselves as carrying."[119] This case study underscores a salient theme in the cognition of landscape. The story reinvigorates our need to recognize the phenomenological subjectivity of perception. Whether the Vietnamese-Americans' experience is indeed an "exile"—"a discontinuous state of being"[120]—is arguable; they benefit economically and politically in the United States. But their self-constituted *experience* is one of living an "inauthentic," incomplete life. Their longing for "authentic" self-identity manifests itself as a longing for a return to an embeddedness in their cultural identity. This sought-after embeddedness consists of marrying an "authentic" Vietnamese woman. In short, "the *imagining* of migration and exile become constitutive parts of the construction and experience of place and landscape."[121]

From a synchronic standpoint, it would appear that the individual whose work eventually came to form the DtrH, like the Vietnamese-American men who seek an authentic self-identity in women appropriated from the perceived *source* of Vietnamese authenticity, sought to alleviate the burden of a perceived need for an "authentic" Israelite self by manipulating historically-constituted symbols (including the Transjordanian landscape). This manipulation included the portrayal of the Davidic political exile in the Transjordan as an exile with the politically allied "friendly stranger."[122] This portrayal of Barzillai the Gileadite ostensibly incorporated him as a "real" or "authentic" Israelite. But this attempt at identification suggests more about the perception of the Cisjordanian historian(s) than it does about Barzillai's self-identification as Israelite.[123] As a budding nationalist, Dtr felt the burden of the imagined need for an "authentic" self as a member of the greater Israelite totality composed of

119 Dawson and Johnson, "Migration," 327.

120 Edward W. Said, "Reflections on Exile," *Granta* 13 (1984): 159, cited in Beverley Butler, "Egypt: Constructed Exiles of the Imagination," in *Contested Landscapes: Movement, Exile and Place* (ed. Barbara Bender and Margot Winer; Oxford: Berg, 2001), 315.

121 Dawson and Johnson, "Migration," 319.

122 Yi-Fu Tuan, "Strangers and Strangeness," *GeogrRev* 76 (1986): 10–19.

123 See Jobling ("Jordan a Boundary," esp. 106) and Weinfeld ("Extent," 59–75), both of whom argue that the Cisjordanians saw the inhabitants of Transjordan as ambiguous Israelites. Uriah Y. Kim has recently published a study of identity in the DtrH (*Decolonizing Josiah: Toward a Postcolonial Reading of the Deuteronomistic History* [The Bible in the Modern World 5; Sheffield: Sheffield Phoenix, 2005]).

Judahites, northern Israelites, and Transjordanian Israelites. But these three ethnically related groups were probably never politically unified to the degree that the historian presents in the Israelite metanarrative (and were certainly not unified at the time of the full History's compilation). Instead, Dtr has gone to Transjordan—one of the landscapes at stake in this construction of history—cognitively and textually rather than physically. This self-imposed "incubation" consists of constructing a Transjordanian landscape that can be recognized as monovalent and totalized (and therefore detemporalized) in order to justify the assertion that David's Israelite empire had in fact existed to the extent that Josiah's was forecasted to encompass, despite never having actually achieved such a span. At the same time, this constructed symbolic matrix of the Transjordanian landscape presents it as just "Other" enough to justify Yahweh's dwelling in the Cisjordan's Jerusalem, rather than elsewhere (e.g., Transjordan's Mahanaim).[124] Therefore, although Dtr's efforts at historiography may give access to real historical events, one must recognize that they also construct a historicizing discourse that displays the ideological tendency to imply a unified polity "Israel" where in fact none existed and to legitimize Jerusalem as the seat of Yahweh's authority. In short, the conceptualization of the Transjordanian landscape in the final form of the text has a two-pronged ideology: (a) Transjordan is an Israelite territory, not only ethnically, but politically and economically; and (b) Transjordan is *not* the site of God's dwelling on earth, a distinction that belongs only to Jerusalem.[125]

Drawing on these four thematic observations concerning the meaningfulness of landscape—polyvalence, social relevance, nested structure, and cognitive existence—the present study investigates the interface between landscape, history, and the literary presentation of history. The basic question of the project is this: Why did the matrix of polarities formed by crossing and recrossing, liminality and homogeneity, incubation and fulfillment become part of the *Weltanschauung* of the ancient Cisjordanian Israelite, and how was that worldview appropriated and perpetuated by the various authors and compilers whose work came to form the DtrH as we know it? The answer to this question lies in the tangible and textual histories of Israel, histories that I hope to uncover in this study.

---

124 See, e.g., Jobling, "Jordan a Boundary," 98–103.

125 Similarly, Havrelock, "Jordan River," 43–50; also see idem, "The Two Maps of Israel's Land," *JBL* 126 (2007): 649–67.

1.4. The Fords of the Jordan: The Development of Meaning and Metaphor

The importance of the fords of the Jordan in narratives as well as the potency of the Transjordanian Motif has already been noted. The natural environment of the Jordan River was such that easy crossings of the river could not be made at points other than at well-known fords. For the most part, the narratives of crossings of the Jordan River take place at the fords east of Gilgal (the *Maḫāḍat Ḥağla* and *al-Maġtas*, and the *M. al-Ġoranīya*, ca. 8 km to the north),[126] but there were several other fords over the river in antiquity.[127] Had the Jordan been fordable at any spot along its course, one suspects the forty-two thousand dead Ephraimites of Judges 12 might have survived a bit longer. So many salient events of personal transformation occur specifically at the Jordan River—Ehud's victory over the Moabites in Judges 3; Jephthah's over the Ephraimites in Judges 12; David's crossing over in victory after the death of Absalom in 2 Samuel 19, to name a few—that it is impossible to ignore their position of symbolic prominence in the narratives. Consequently, the fords of the Jordan contain and exude a significance more than merely that of the pragmatic. Individuals and armies did not *simply* cross at the fords in any sense of the quotidian. Rather, many of the biblical stories have been presented so that their central episodes revolve around the fords of the Jordan. Meaning is latent in the fords. It dwells there, waiting to be alluded to by the writer, and this allusion evokes a matrix of imagery whose tangents spread out through the entirety of the Bible. The Jordan and its fords appear as the site of Elijah's ascension to heaven in a fiery chariot and Elisha's concomi-

126 For the location of the two former, see Michele Piccirillo, "The Jerusalem-Esbus Road and Its Sanctuaries in Transjordan," in *Studies in the History and Archaeology of Jordan* 3 (ed. Adnan Hadidi; Amman: Jordanian Department of Antiquities, 1987), 167 n. 31; see also Hutton, "Topography."

127 Two fords close to the *W. Zarqa* were potentially used by the major road from Samaria into the Transjordanian highlands: the ford at Adam (modern *T. Dāmīya*; André Lemaire, "Les benê Jacob: Essai d'interprétation histoirique d'une tradition patriarcale," *RB* 85 [1978]: 333, 335) and *M. Umm Sidre* (Gustav Dalman, "Jahresbericht des Deutschen Evangelischen Instituts für Altertumswissenschaft des Heiligen Landes für das Arbeitsjahr 1912/13," *PJ* 9 [1913]: 70; Carl Steuernagel, "Der ᶜAdschlūn," *ZDPV* 48 [1925]: 92, 97; republished as idem, *Der ᶜAdschlūn* [Leipzig: Hinrichs, 1927], 140, 145; idem, "Wo lag Pnuel?" *JPOS* 8 [1928]: 206; see also David A. Dorsey, *The Roads and Highways of Ancient Israel* [Baltimore: The Johns Hopkins University Press, 1991], 37, 174–75 [S 16]). Edward Robinson tells of the presence of a ford south of Beth-shean, as well as a tripartite ford closer to that city (cited by Dorsey, *Roads and Highways*, 325). Often, the accessibility of these fords was subject to factors such as time of year or weather. Josh 3:15 notes that "the Jordan overflows its banks throughout the harvest" (והירדן מלא על־כל־גדתיו כל ימי קציר; see also 1 Chr 12:16), and Josephus (*J.W.* 4.7.5 [=4.433–35]) states that some Jewish fugitives from the Romans were caught at the river because it had been swollen by rain.

tant accession to prophetic power (2 Kings 2). During the Babylonian exile, Deutero-Isaiah used the related imagery of the Exodus and the crossing of the Jordan River to reassure the exiled Judahites in Babylon:

> Thus says the LORD,
> your Redeemer, the Holy One of Israel:
> For your sake I will send to Babylon,
> and break down all the bars,
> and the shouting of the Chaldeans will be turned to lamentation.
> I am the LORD, your Holy One,
> the Creator of Israel, your King.
> Thus says the LORD,
> who makes a way in the sea,
> a path in the mighty waters... (Isa 43:14–16; NRSV)

That the people of Judah were transformed—forged into a new Israel—by their sojourn in the East and reentry into Canaan was a typological association made by the prophet.

The productivity of the Transjordanian Motif did not end with the closure of the corpus of Hebrew Scriptures, however. The motif continued to be fruitful in the Jewish community, as is proved by the movement of John the Baptist to the Jordan River (Matt 3:1–3; Mark 1:2–5; Luke 3:3–6; John 1:24) and of the ensuing baptism of Jesus in the Gospels (Matt 3:13–17; Mark 1:9–11; Luke 3:21–22; cf. John 1:29–33).[128] This baptism inaugurates Jesus' ministry, thus presuming the lasting potency of the motif of transformative power inherent to the River Jordan. The historical and literary motif of the passage through the Jordan as an Israelite, Jewish, and early Christian rite designating increased authority was subsumed by imagery of purification and cleansing, and thereby rendered moot for the Christian community in the Gospel of John. Baptism, as a sacrament of the early church, began to signify the cleansing of the individual, his or her entry into the Christian community:

> While the Gospels do not tell that Christ parted the river's waters or Himself crossed the Jordan, it was His Baptism that enabled all Christians to 'cross over' to salvation just as their Israelite forebears had crossed the Red Sea and the Jordan into the promised land; and in a long tradition of patristic and medieval exegesis, these narratives of deliverance through parted waters came to be construed as foretokens of the Baptism and of the sacrament it established.[129]

Even in modern times, the Jordan holds symbolic significance and retains a certain degree of cultural and political importance. The African-American

128 Thomas N. Hall provides a collection of Medieval Christian literature in which Jesus' Baptism was accompanied by the parting and reversal or halt of the Jordan's waters, on analogy with Ps 114:3,5 ("The Reversal of the Jordan in Vercelli Homily 16 and in Old English Literature," *Traditio* 45 [1990]: 53–86).

129 Ibid., 56.

spiritual whose words are "Deep river/ My home is over Jordan" implicitly conceptualizes the freedom of crossing the Ohio River northwards as a means of coming "home," that is, to the promised land. The song "Swing Low, Sweet Chariot" explicitly identifies the crossing of the river with the assumption of Elijah:

I looked over Jordan and what did I see,
Coming for to carry me home?
A band of angels coming after me,
Coming for to carry me home.[130]

The potency of the allusion in American culture has, fortunately, been mitigated in some respects by the abolishment of slavery. The song is in the process of becoming a relic, a frozen form, so to speak, of a cultural milieu in which crossing a river—this time the Ohio River—held the cognitive association of newfound freedom parallel to the freedom gained by Israel during their Exodus. Thanks to the geographical rootedness prevalent in today's American society, the words of "Deep River" cannot possibly evoke the same feelings of longing for "home" in the hearer that they once did.

The emplacement of Jesus's baptism at the Jordan River has been almost entirely worked out of the conscious references in mainline Christian liturgical practice, yet the motif of crossing the Jordan River remains an easily accessible and frequently appropriated metaphor for *coming home, newly empowered.* As Harold Brodsky has recognized, "The Jordan of the Bible was not so much a physical river as a symbol of spiritual yearning. To cross over the Jordan was to attain freedom in this life, or in the life to come."[131] It is with this final typological association of crossing the Jordan River with death and the corresponding spiritual fulfillment that many modern Christian hymns are imbued. One need only survey the final stanzas of a hymnal to recognize the import of this association, found as the culminating theme in "Thine Is the Glory":

No more we doubt thee,
Glorious Prince of life;
Life is nought without thee;
Aid us in our strife;
Make us more than conqu'rors,
Through thy deathless love;
Bring us safe through Jordan
To thy home above.[132]

130 African-American spiritual quoted in Robert St. John, *Roll Jordan Roll: The Life Story of a River and Its People* (Garden City, N.Y.: Doubleday, 1965), 16.

131 Brodsky, "The Jordan," 41, sidebar; Jeremy M. Hutton, "Jordan River," *NIDB* 3:385–92.

132 Edmond Budry, "Thine Is the Glory," in *Lutheran Book of Worship* (trans. R. Birch Hoyle; Minneapolis: Augsburg, 1978), hymn #145, verse 3.

The same theme is made even more explicit in the final verse of "Guide Me Ever, Great Redeemer":

> When I tread the verge of Jordan,
> Bid my anxious fears subside;
> Death of death and hell's destruction,
> Land me safe on Canaan's side...[133]

Just how the literary importance of the fords of the Jordan came historically to transcend a merely pragmatic meaning and to become a common coin of almost worldwide currency, is the subject of this section (§1.4) and, indeed, of this study. But the dramatic shift from the particularization of the biblical passages examined in §1.2 to the abstraction of the Transjordanian Motif's efficacy as a whole requires first a consideration of people's engagement with the landscape that they exhibit in their everyday lives. An accurate understanding of the attribution of specific *meanings* to places begins with attentiveness to the perception of places' characteristics. The endowment of places with meaning is a specifically *human* endeavor that is conducted historically. That is to say, the rootedness in *place* that people experience and which causes them to bestow, donate, or impose meaning on topologically distinct features is embedded not only in place, but in *time* as well.

The discussion throughout the remainder of this section will focus on several themes centered on one problem. The problem is of the meaning apparently inherent (but quite obviously human-imposed) in the fords of the Jordan River. Textually speaking, the narrative *passages* concerning characters' *passages* across the river are caught up in a web of interrelated meanings. Moreover, the fords of the Jordan River play an integral part in the literary traditions of both the Jewish and Christian Bibles. Every instance of events explicitly narrated as occurring at the fords of the Jordan (and more specifically at the ford east of Gilgal) involves one of two themes: the crossing through (or happening at) the river is somehow magico-religious (e.g., the floating axe-head in 2 Kgs 6:1–7) or instrumental in the formation of the pragmatic character's subsequent life (Judges 8; 2 Samuel 19). Frequently, the episodes contain elements of both (e.g., Joshua 3–4; 2 Kgs 2:1–14). While analysis at the narrative level recognizes the importance of the stories for the delimitation of territory,[134] a historically-oriented interest in these narratives demands a demythologized exploration of these events of magico-religious qualities.

---

133 William Williams, "Guide Me Ever, Great Redeemer," in *Lutheran Book of Worship* (trans. composite; Minneapolis: Augsburg, 1978), hymn #343, verse 3.

134 De Certeau, *Practice*, 123.

By virtue of their inherent qualities, river fords—and specifically, those across the Jordan—*always already* have a certain cultural significance: the very criterion that defines their existence as specific *locales*—namely, the shallowness that allows them to be crossed relatively easily when other areas along the river could not be crossed as simply—becomes an ineluctable element of their essence and an indispensable characteristic of the place. Because humans are already fundamentally embedded in the world, we encounter such *places* and their functions as given. In other words, these places already contain uses or significances that we perceive, appropriate, articulate, and sometimes even invent: "there must be, as an ingredient in perception from the start, a conveyance of what being in places is all about."[135] Moreover, because each of the fords of the Jordan is one of a limited number of practical crossings over that river, human travel is necessarily funneled through those areas. This concentration of usage provides an impetus for, and the possibility of, the consideration of the ford as significant.

The fact that the *al-Maġtas/Ḥağla* fords east of Gilgal served as a funnel for such meaningful and symbolic human narrative action throughout the DtrH displays the very tension latent in fords (and, for that matter, border crossings in general).[136] The fords of the Jordan mark out and exemplify what de M. Certeau calls the "paradox of the frontier: created by contacts, the points of differentiation between two bodies are also their common points."[137] The characters perceive themselves as crossing borders,[138] yet it is precisely the site of the border crossing that is a *locale* at which the borders break down. This paradox draws attention to the *locale* and demands an explanation in terms that can no longer be considered merely pragmatic.

---

135 Casey, "Space to Place," 13–46, quote from 17; Maurice Merleau-Ponty, *Phenomenology of Perception* (1945; trans. Colin Smith, 1962; repr., London: Routledge, 2002), 112–70, 283–347.

136 For a discussion of borders in biblical literature, see Steven Weitzman, "The Samson Story as Border Fiction," *BibInt* 10 (2002): 158–74, and bibliography therein.

137 De Certeau, *Practice*, 127.

138 But "it is important to note that no feature of the landscape is, of itself, a boundary. It can only become a boundary, or the indicator of a boundary, in relation to the activities of the people (or animals) for whom it is recognized or experienced as such" (Ingold, "Temporality,"156; see also van Gennep, *Rites of Passage*, 15–16). Therefore, the narratives of the Bible either invent or perpetuate the identification of the two banks as separate entities. Based on the Bible's recollection of historical events, the latter appears the more likely (see e.g., Baly, "Pitfalls," 124; Weinfeld, "Extent," 59–75). This perpetuation of a demographic identity based upon *difference* is itself a perpetuation of older geographical distinctions between the eastern and western landmasses (Yohanan Aharoni, *The Land of the Bible: A Historical Geography* [rev. ed.; trans. A. F. Rainey; Philadelphia: Westminster, 1979], 73–77, esp. 75).

These two features, that is, fords' immediate identity as obvious *locales* (i.e., places that were topographically distinctive enough to be able to bear discrete identities) and their necessary concentration of human activity (literary or otherwise) through a point of paradoxical value are the conditioning factors—necessary but *not sufficient* causes[139]—of the attribution of meaning. In the diachronic progression of humans' movement through places, there develops a continuity of the significance of any given *locale*. Socially imposed interpretations of places in turn impose themselves on other humans. Although locales normally acquire and sustain continuous significances within societies, decisive breaks in this continuity may occur as the result of historical events that effect disjunctures in meaning. Place, as a function of use, is thus set in a dialectic relationship with both social context and historical event—locales become particularized through their history of human usage, and associated with and infused by historical events and humans' memories and interpretations thereof.

Two conclusions are self-evident from this vantage point. First, we may conclude that the "environment"—a descriptor of the world including factors such as climate, topography, and geology—is an inexorable factor in the formation of human societies.[140] Second, the continuity of a cultural group's experience of any given place is subject to the same conditions of continuity outlined by Bourdieu in his study of the *habitus*—human practice—which is at the same time an arbitrary expression of human nature and a culturally motivated mode of acting.[141] These conclusions provide a touchstone for the remainder of this study. Chapter 2 investigates the social and historical contexts of the Transjordanian Motif's development. Humans' variegated relationships with the topography lying behind the narratives of the DtrH, it will be assumed, can only be understood in connection with the socially- and economically-expressed history of those relationships. In chs. 3–7, I work towards a model describing the *diachronic* development of the Transjordanian Motif in its specifically Deuteronomistic instantiation. The questions asked there will focus on the processes of textual compilation, redaction, and engineering. Although the focus of chs. 3–7 very rarely touches on the Jordan River or Transjordan in any explicit way, the analysis of these interrelated processes makes it possible to discern several divergent individual conceptions of Transjordan that were held by apparently different authors, editors, and tradents. This

---

139 Crumley, "Sacred Landscapes," 273.

140 Casey, "Space to Place," 13–46; Fernand Braudel, *The Mediterranean and the Mediterranean World in the Age of Philip II* (1949; rev. ed.; trans. Siân Reynolds; New York: Harper & Row, 1972).

141 Pierre Bourdieu, *Outline of a Theory of Practice* (trans. Richard Nice; rev. and expanded ed.; Cambridge: Cambridge University Press, 1977), esp. 96–158.

analysis will further enable us to ask questions such as: What is the earliest traceable conception of Transjordan in the Cisjordanian worldview? What kinds of development did that conception undergo, and why? Are there demonstrable and dateable stages in the development of the motif? How does landscape become part of a symbolic system to begin with? Is the Transjordanian Motif, as it appears in the DtrH, a consciously constructed symbolic system, or was the final outcome of the motif unintentional from the standpoint of the Deuteronomistic compilers? Finally, did the motif cease to bear meaning in Israelite culture with the closure of the Deuteronomistic corpus, or did it remain a productive hermeneutic system for interpreting historical events and inherited religious traditions and for formulating and disclosing theological assessments thereof? These questions will be addressed in the remainder of this study.

2. Exiles and Textiles: Transjordan in History

Thus far I have spoken of "the Israelite Transjordan" as a single entity, a topographic unit. But was this the experience of the biblical writers? Did *they* experience the land as such? Despite the fact that the Hebrew Bible uses the term עֵבֶר הירדן 36 times to mark the eastern bank of the Jordan,[1] other appellations are given as well: the Mishor (i.e., the Plain), (the) Gilead, and Bashan. Each one of these names designates a particular topographic unit in the area "across the Jordan" from present-day Israel (excluding the Golan). The task of the present section will be to define more precisely the world in which the biblical narratives were set and in which the fords of the Jordan accumulated their meaning. This investigation will occur under three general headings. The first two, socioeconomic dynamics (§2.1) and ethnicity (§2.2), operate at the level of *conjuncture*,[2] in which we can trace trends in social change. The third, history (§2.3), takes into consideration the political and theological *events* (*histoire événementielle*) that can be traced through texts and, in some cases, archaeology (most often, destructions).[3]

---

1 This is opposed to the nine times in which the term is applied to the Western (Cisjordanian) bank (see BDB, 719a, עֵבֶר I). Those instances generally occur when the speaker is perceived to be standing on its eastern flank, and thus their designation of the western bank is consistent with the narrative story line.

2 Fernand Braudel, *The Mediterranean and the Mediterranean World in the Age of Philip II* (1949; rev. ed.; trans. Siân Reynolds; New York: Harper & Row, 1972).

3 An overview of the Transjordanian topological *longue durée* will not be given here. A bevy of studies can provide access to the topography, geology, and climate of Transjordan: e.g., Yohanan Aharoni, *The Land of the Bible: A Historical Geography* (rev. ed.; trans. A. F. Rainey; Philadelphia: Westminster, 1979), 36–42; Denis Baly, "The Nature of Environment, with Special Relation to the Country of Jordan," in *Studies in the History and Archaeology of Jordan* 2 (ed. Adnan Hadidi; Amman: Jordanian Department of Antiquities, 1985), 19–24; idem, "The Pitfalls of Biblical Geography in Relation to Jordan," in *Studies in the History and Archaeology of Jordan* 3 (ed. Adnan Hadidi; Amman: Jordanian Department of Antiquities, 1987), 123–24; Karl-Heinz Bernhardt, "Natural Conditions and Resources in East Jordan According to Biblical Literature," in *Studies in the History and Archaeology of Jordan* 2 (ed. Adnan Hadidi; Amman: Jordanian Department of Antiquities, 1985), 179–82; Harold Brodsky, "The Jordan—Symbol of Spiritual Transition," *BRev* 8.3 (1992): 34–43, 52; Dawud M. Al-Eisawi, "Vegetation in Jordan," in *Studies in the History and Archaeology of Jordan* 2 (ed. Adnan Hadidi; Amman: Jordanian Department of Antiquities, 1985), 45–57; Jonathan Mabry and Gaetano Palumbo, "Environmental, Economic and Political Constraints on Ancient Settlement Patterns in the Wadi al-Yabis Region," in *Studies in the History and Archaeology of Jordan* 4 (ed. Muna Zaghloul et al.; Amman: Jordanian Department of Antiquities, 1992), 67–72; Robert North, "Quirks of Jordan River Cartography," in *Studies in the History and Archaeology of Jordan* 2 (ed. Adnan Hadidi; Amman: Jordanian Department

The current recognition that the Late Bronze Age constituted a period of relatively low population density demands a short discussion of those sociological and ecological factors that conditioned the proportion of settled peoples to nomadic peoples during the Iron Age—and which continue to do so in our own time. I assume the applicability of two operative models to the Israelite settlement. One, ruralization, explains much of the early Iron Age population increase in the Cisjordanian and Transjordanian highlands, especially over against those models espousing a large conquest, a settlement from outside, or an urban revolt. The other—sedentarization, in itself a sub-category of the former model—provides a model that accounts for the various agricultural systems of production in Israelite society and for those systems' interactions with the physical environment. It will become apparent in the discussion below that the factors controlling the fluctuation between settlement and nomadization, and which finally brought about a large-scale highland settlement at the end of the Late Bronze Age and beginning of the Iron Age, did not disappear completely from the sociological milieu of the Iron Age Transjordan but rather continued to condition the interaction of the population with the environment throughout the Iron Age.[4]

The position of this "Israelite" Transjordan geographically at the point of junction among several ethnic groups in antiquity warrants a short discussion concerning the ethnic composition of the population of the area. The Israelites, the Geshurites and Maakites, the Ammonites, the Moabites, and to a lesser extent the Edomites, the Aramaeans, and the Phoenicians all played a role culturally or militarily in the area. In all likelihood, therefore, the population of Transjordan by the time of the divided Israelite monarchies was one of mixed ethnicity, which recognized itself as only nominally Israelite at most, and which, throughout its long association with the Cisjordanian kingdoms (ca. 1250–742 BCE), attempted to maintain some degree of autonomy. This autonomy, however, was never more than short-lived on account of the superior economic position of the Cisjordani-

---

of Antiquities, 1985), 205–15; Numan Shehadeh, "The Climate of Jordan in the Past and Present," in *Studies in the History and Archaeology of Jordan* 2 (ed. Adnan Hadidi; Amman: Jordanian Department of Antiquities, 1985), 25–37; W. Van Zeist, "Past and Present Environments of the Jordan Valley," in *Studies in the History and Archaeology of Jordan* 2 (ed. Adnan Hadidi; Amman: Jordanian Department of Antiquities, 1985), 199–204; Gerd Wiesemann, "Remarks on the Geomorphogeny of the Yarmuk Valley, Jordan," in *Studies in the History and Archaeology of Jordan* 2 (ed. Adnan Hadidi; Amman: Jordanian Department of Antiquities, 1985), 79; Michael Zohary, *Vegetation of Israel and Adjacent Areas* (BTAVO A/7; Wiesbaden: Reichert, 1982).

4 See, e.g., Michael B. Rowton (e.g., "Urban Autonomy in a Nomadic Environment," *JNES* 32 [1973]: 201–15; idem, "Dimorphic Structure and Topology," *OrAnt* 15 [1976]: 17–31; idem, "Dimorphic Structure and the Problem of the ᶜApirû-ᶜIbrîm," *JNES* 35 [1976]: 13–20; idem, "Dimorphic Structure and the Parasocial Element," *JNES* 36 [1977]: 181–98).

an kingdoms, as well as the relatively unfavorable juxtaposition of the Israelite Transjordan up against several less-closely related corporate groups.

2.1. Nomads in ANE Society

2.1.1. Nomadization and Sedentarization

According to classical scholarly analyses, one of the fundamental hallmarks of social structure throughout the ancient Near Eastern world was the bifurcation of the systems of production into pastoralism and sedentarism. M. B. Rowton has described and analyzed this *dimorphic society* extensively.[5] As part and parcel of this system, enclosed nomadism—that is, nomadism or semi-nomadism that is closely associated with urban and village sites,[6] over against fully peripheral nomadism, which takes place outside of settled society—seems to have functioned on a transhumance basis. In practical terms, Rowton developed a picture of a society whose systems of production operated in two interrelated and mutually supportive manners. The sedentary component of society dwelled year-round in one place and concentrated its productive efforts primarily on farming. The crops planted by these sedentarists demanded continual presence for the most part[7] and—so long as there was enough rainfall to sustain the year's crop—allowed the group to be reasonably self-sufficient. Yet the climatic variation of certain areas in the Levant was

---

5 Rowton's studies of dimorphic society were published in a series of sixteen articles throughout the 1970's. The full list of articles can be found in Rowton, "Typology," 17 n. 4. Leon Marfoe has challenged the strict dichotomy between transhumant nomadism and sedentary agriculture on the grounds that such a distinction does not allow for social evolution or for movement between the two poles ("The Integrative Transformation: Patterns of Sociopolitical Organization in Southern Syria," *BASOR* 234 [1979]: 1–42). As will be seen below, my own conception of early highland culture allows for families to participate in both systems simultaneously.

6 Rowton makes the identification between his "enclosed" nomadism and the common usage of the term "semi-nomadism" ("Urban Autonomy," 207–8). Lawrence E. Stager cautions against the concept of "seminomadism" because of its overly simplistic participation in a "(pseudo-) evolutionary" model that envisions a predetermined movement "from tent-to-hut-to-house" ("Response," in *Biblical Archaeology Today: Proceedings of the International Congress on Biblical Archaeology, Jerusalem, April 1984* [Jerusalem: Israel Exploration Society, 1985], 85). When applicable, I have used the terms "enclosed nomadism" and "transhumant pastoralism" to indicate this model in which pastoralists circulated within and in conjunction with settled society.

7 Fredrik Barth, "A General Perspective on Nomad-Sedentary Relations in the Middle East," in *The Desert and the Sown: Nomads in the Wider Society* (ed. Cynthia Nelson; Berkeley: Institute of International Studies, University of California at Berkeley, 1973), 13 n.; but cf. Carol Palmer, "Traditional Agriculture," in *The Archaeology of Jordan* (ed. Burton MacDonald, Russell Adams, and Piotr Bienkowski; Sheffield: Sheffield Academic Press, 2001), 622.

such that in some seasons those areas would suffer from drought severe enough to prohibit the adequate growth of the year's produce. In these cases, it was necessary for the sedentarists to be associated—directly or indirectly—with the pastoralist sector of society, whose herds were moveable and could therefore be transferred to a climate more favorable to survival. This association could be at any number of agnatic levels but was possible even at that of the household. Some members of the household would manage the family's plots of farming land, while some would take charge of the herds and flocks. The movement of the herds—typically small cattle such as sheep and goats—could range several days' journey in order to find cool, well-watered land during the summer, and warmer weather during the winter.[8] This process of seasonal transhumance was practiced primarily as a means of ensuring the survival of the corporate group, since even the mitigated success of the flocks could supplement the unmitigated failure of a poor season's crop. Because of this fundamental reliance upon pastoralism as the supplement to sedentarist dry-farming, and despite the fact that pastoralism actually forms a relatively small component of society's economic production, the constituents of sociological systems in which pastoralism plays a significant role often conceive of their herds as "the principal economic branch and as the mainstay of their culture."[9]

This composite system, agropastoralism (i.e., the mixed economy founded on both systems of production discussed here), was most likely the dominant model of production in the Iron Age Levant. Although studies tend to pose the relationship in terms of a dichotomy, it may be more accurate to analyze the composite system in terms of a spectrum (with families concentrating in one system or the other to varying degrees but participating in both for the most part).[10] While this twofold system of production is usually the most practical system over the long run, economic factors can either motivate families to leave the nomadic or pastoralist lifestyle behind when they have acquired a great deal of wealth or, conversely, force them to abandon their flocks and other moveable wealth, constraining them to a life of servitude.[11] The former—which E. J. van der Steen calls "falling out of nomadization at the top"—occurs when a nomadic or semi-nomadic family gains enough wealth and political stature

8 Palmer, "Traditional Agriculture," 622.

9 Emanuel Marx, "The Tribe as a Unit of Subsistence: Nomadic Pastoralism in the Middle East," *AmAnthropol* n.s. 79 (1977): 344; see also Barth, "General Perspective," 17.

10 E. J. van der Steen, *Tribes and Territories in Transition: The Central East Jordan Valley in the Late Bronze Age and Early Iron Ages. A Study of the Sources* (OLA 130; Leuven: Peeters, 2004), 102–31, esp. 105–6.

11 Eveline J. van der Steen, "Aspects of Nomadism and Settlement in the Central Jordan Valley," *PEQ* 127 (1995): 155–56.

to enable the group to settle down permanently, divesting themselves of their flocks and herds without the fear of starvation generated by the cycles of rainfall proliferation and abatement. In contrast, the latter she calls "falling out of nomadization at the bottom," i.e., becoming poor enough through loss or mismanagement of the herds that survival predicated on nomadism or pastoralism is impossible.[12] The family would then be forced to subsist on its agricultural possessions, where any year with below-normal rainfall could potentially spell disaster for the group. Therefore, in outlining the systems of production used in Iron Age Transjordan, we cannot fail to take into account the spectrum of systems employed simultaneously by families over the years. Still, sedentarization from nomadism can account for only a small fraction of the population surge that covered the Cisjordanian and Transjordanian highlands in the Early Iron Age.

2.1.2. Ruralization

Following a model proposed by O. Lattimore for early China and adapted by R. McC. Adams for Mesopotamia, L. Marfoe and I. Finkelstein have attributed the sharp diminution of settled population in the Levant during the EB–MB transition, as well as the LB–Iron I transition, to cycles of ruralization and sedentarization.[13] But L. E. Stager has challenged the oscillatory nature of the model for two reasons.[14] First, the group entering the Levantine highlands in MB IIB is a *new* group whose architecture displays commonalities with that of Syrian cities to the north (e.g., rabbetted facades and free-standing city walls). Second, the population that coalesced in the Levantine highlands during the Iron I period was too

---

12 If I have understood her correctly, van der Steen's model applies equally to full nomadism and to the enclosed, transhumant pastoralism that has been described here, insofar as vastly increased wealth may occasion the selling-off of the herds that might be considered extraneous, whereas any great decrease in wealth could demand the overuse of the herd for survival. Both eventualities produce the ultimate result of no longer possessing a self-sustaining herd.

13 Marfoe, "Integrative Transformation," 1–42; Israel Finkelstein, *The Archaeology of the Israelite Settlement* (Jerusalem: Israel Exploration Society, 1988), 339–48; see earlier Owen Lattimore, *Inner Asian Frontiers of China* (1940; Irvington-on-Hudson, N.Y.: Capitol, 1951); Robert McC. Adams, "The Mesopotamian Social Landscape: A View from the Frontier," in *Reconstructing Complex Societies: An Archaeological Colloquium* (BASORSup 20; ed. Charlotte B. Moore; Cambridge, Mass.: ASOR, 1974), 1–20.

14 Cf. Lawrence E. Stager, "Forging an Identity: The Emergence of Ancient Israel," in *The Oxford History of the Biblical World* (ed. Michael D. Coogan; New York: Oxford University Press, 1998), 141–42; idem, "The Archaeology of the Family in Ancient Israel," *BASOR* 260 (1985): 1–35; idem, "Response," 83–87. This metaphor of the oscillation of nomadic and settled population as a sine wave is not mine; I thank Professor Lawrence E. Stager for the analogy and for references to the history of the idea.

large to have come solely from settled nomads.[15] Stager therefore proposes a model of "ruralization" in which he envisions the establishment of agropastoralist villages in the Israelite highlands by people of multiple origins. Perhaps foremost among these origins were the lowland city-states. As the peasants and pastoralists linked to those Bronze Age city-states recognized opportunities for free land in the highlands,[16] the resultant shift of population into the sparsely populated highlands, coupled with the simultaneous sedentarization of some nomadic groups, created a boom in the highland agropastoralist village lifestyle, which participated in a range of agricultural subsistence strategies.[17] Insofar as Stager's model describes the increase in settled population of the Levant during the early Iron I, it provides a more archaeologically and sociologically viable alternative to the classical models of Israel's origins: conquest,[18] external settlement,[19]

15 Stager, "Response," 83.

16 Stager, "Forging an Identity," 141; Evsey D. Domar, "The Causes of Slavery or Serfdom: A Hypothesis," *JEconHist* 30 (1970): 18–32, cited by Stager, "Response," 85.

17 We should not overestimate the population of this new society, however. Ilse Köhler-Rollefson points to the seasonal transhumance rates of modern Jordanian pastoralists, arguing that in the village where she performed an ethnographic investigation "40% of the buildings in the village belonged to pastoral specialists who were tent-dwellers during the entire year" ("A Model for the Development of Nomadic Pastoralism on the Transjordanian Plateau," in *Pastoralism in the Levant: Archaeological Materials in Anthropological Perspectives* [ed. Ofer Bar-Yosef and Anatoly Khazanov; Madison, Wis.: Prehistory Press, 1992], 15). These houses are virtually identical to those belonging to sedentary occupants and are used only for storage. Neither should we confuse sedentarism with cultivation or pastoralism with a nomadic or semi-nomadic lifestyle. Stager's model of "agropastoralism" would consist of two opposed axes, one describing the form of settlement, i.e., nomadic vs. sedentary, and the second describing the system of production, i.e., agricultural cultivation vs. pastoralism (see also Barth, "General Perspective," 11–21). The boundaries between these two systems become blurred by the fact that some sedentarists also keep a minimal number of animals while some pastoralists raise crops when they have the opportunity. It should be kept in mind that no theoretical description in a heuristic model can pigeonhole a group of people into a single mode of production and that individual strategies for survival can fluctuate with the political exigencies of society. Some modern Bedouin practice farming (van der Steen, "Aspects," 146–47), which suggests that the model of ruralization/sedentarization does not simply present a system of polar opposites, but rather a continuum of possible systems of economic production in which even the nomadic element of society can engage in limited seasonal agriculture when their flocks have sufficient water to remain in one place for an entire season or when their survival strategy entails a shift to a predominantly agriculturally-based system (Barth, "General Perspective," 16–18; Emanuel Marx, "Are There Pastoral Nomads in the Middle East?" in *Pastoralism in the Levant: Archaeological Materials in Anthropological Perspectives* [ed. Ofer Bar-Yosef and Anatoly Khazanov; Madison, Wis.: Prehistory Press, 1992], 255–60; see also Köhler-Rollefson, "Model," 14; Palmer "Traditional Agriculture," 622).

18 William F. Albright, "The Israelite Conquest in the Light of Archaeology," *BASOR* 74 (1939): 11–22.

19 Albrecht Alt, "The Settlement of the Israelites in Palestine," in *Essays in Old Testament History and Religion* (trans. R. A. Wilson; Garden City, N.Y.: Doubleday, 1968), 172–221; translation of "Die Landnahme der Israeliten in Palästina," in *Kleine Schriften zur Geschich-*

and urban revolt.[20] Although the ruralization model had Cisjordan primarily in mind, it applies equally well to Transjordan, although the archaeological evidence from the Transjordanian plateau shows fewer tendencies toward the wide-scale destruction of urban centers than does that from Cisjordan.[21]

We find, then, two ways of entering the highland agro-pastoralist village society. Not only could families "fall out" of nomadism at the top or the bottom, so too could a family "fall into" village settlement from the top (i.e., from the lowland urban city-states) or from the bottom (i.e., from nomadism). Again, socioeconomic reasons must have governed much of the demographic movement between the two extremes of urbanization and fully nomadic life.[22] In this regard, Stager's model is much like that of urban revolt proposed by G. E. Mendenhall and given its most complete explanation by N. K. Gottwald,[23] but the urban-revolt theory in which a

---

te des Volkes Israel (Munich: Beck, 1953), 1:89–125; idem, "Erwägungen über die Landnahme der Israeliten in Palästina," *PJ* 35 (1939): 8–63; Martin Noth, *The History of Israel* (2d ed.; trans. P. R. Ackroyd; London: Adam & Charles Black, 1960), 68–84.

20 George E. Mendenhall, "The Hebrew Conquest of Palestine," *BA* 25 (1962): 66–87; Norman K. Gottwald, *The Tribes of Yahweh: A Sociology of the Religion of Liberated Israel, 1250–1050 BCE* (Maryknoll, N.Y.: Orbis, 1979; repr., Biblical Seminar 66; Sheffield: Sheffield Academic Press, 1999).

21 For the settlement of northern Transjordan (i.e., much of the area under investigation) during the Iron I period, see, e.g., Siegfried Mittmann, *Beiträge zur Siedlungs- und Territorialgeschichte des nördlichen Ostjordanlandes* (ADPV 2; Wiesbaden: Harrassowitz, 1970); Patrick E. McGovern, "Central Transjordan in the Late Bronze and Early Iron Ages: An Alternative Hypothesis of Socio-Economic Transformation and Collapse," in *Studies in the History and Archaeology of Jordan* 3 (ed. Adnan Hadidi; Amman: Jordanian Department of Antiquities, 1987), 268–70; idem, "Settlement Patterns of the Late Bronze and Iron Ages in the Greater Amman Area," in *Studies in the History and Archaeology of Jordan* 4 (ed. Muna Zaghloul et al.; Amman: Jordanian Department of Antiquities, 1992), 181; Robert G. Boling, *The Early Biblical Community in Transjordan* (SWBA 6; Sheffield: Almond, 1988), 13–18; and Chang-Ho C. Ji, "Iron Age I in Central and Northern Transjordan: An Interim Summary of Archaeological Data," *PEQ* 127 (1995): 129. Cf. Köhler-Rollefson's reconstruction of the establishment of transhumant pastoralism in Transjordan during the Neolithic Age centered around the hypothesized clash over space in urban areas between the sedentarist population, whose primary mode of production was crop cultivation, and the pastoralist population, who was not nomadic—or, at least, not *fully* nomadic—and whose flocks "interfered with, and probably prevented, the regeneration of arboreal resources and endangered the crop harvest" ("Model," 13). Köhler-Rollefson views not only ruralization as an upshot of this contention, but the development of transhumance as well.

22 The movement from urbanization to small-scale settlement, like that from nomadization to sedentarization, is reversible. The Iron IC period marked a period of reurbanization, according to McGovern ("Central Transjordan," 268). For the threefold organization of settlement (nomads/sedentarized peasants/urban populations), see Ernest Gellner, "Introduction: Approaches to Nomadism," in *The Desert and the Sown: Nomads in the Wider Society* (ed. Cynthia Nelson; Berkeley: Institute of International Studies, University of California at Berkeley, 1973), 2.

23 Mendenhall, "Hebrew Conquest," 66–87; Gottwald, *Tribes of Yahweh*, esp. 210–19. The models proposed by Mendenhall and Gottwald are, of course, hardly identical. Whereas

peasant population leaves the major cities behind in some kind of socialist uprising both imposes a quasi-Marxist and anachronistic framework on what must have been a much more complex and "long-term socioeconomic transformation"[24] and fails to account fully for the highland's increased population in Iron I.[25] Because of its recognized and more fully nuanced complexity, the ruralization-sedentarization model is preferable.

Despite the symbiotic relationship between nomadic and sedentary components,[26] one cannot argue that the coexistence of the two elements was always peaceful. Some modern Bedouin maintain an antagonistic relationship with the settled population, robbing them or, it may be assumed, charging "protection money" for the towns' defense.[27] This antagonistic aspect of the relationship must have obtained during the Iron Age as well, and it may be related to the raids of the Midianites and the peoples of the East in Judg 6:1–6 in particular, if that text may be taken at face value. The depredations of nomadic raids could have caused ruralization during the Iron Age as well, since economic and political stability seems to be one of the factors both conditioning and conditioned by the increase of settled society:

> It would seem that in times of peace, stability and effective government people are inclined to settle permanently and to utilize and develop landscape resources.... On the contrary, in times of political uncertainty, excessive tax claims and social disorder, people seem to revert to other forms of existence, either in fortified enclosures or in caves and dolmens in the inaccessible marginalized zones such as indicated by a few sites on the slopes of the escarpment or as pastoral nomads.[28]

Mendenhall's model assumes a cognitive revolt with Moses as the leader, Gottwald's presumes a "grass-roots" materialist movement in which Moses' Yahwism functions interactively as an expression of the frustration of the peasants and as a motivation and justification of their separation from the cities.

24 McGovern, "Central Transjordan," 270.

25 Stager, "Response," 84.

26 Alison Betts, "Pastoralism," in *The Archaeology of Jordan* (ed. Burton MacDonald, Russell Adams, and Piotr Bienkowski; Sheffield: Sheffield Academic Press, 2001), 616.

27 Van der Steen, "Aspects," 147; Palmer, "Traditional Agriculture," 622. The extent of this negative interaction can be mitigated by the presence of a shrine to a saint (van der Steen, "Aspects," 147), or—as in the Atlas Mountains of Morocco—the problem is worked out through the agency of a corporate group that functions as a means of arbitration (Ernest Gellner, *The Saints of the Atlas* [London: Weidenfeld & Nicholson, 1969]; Jeremy M. Hutton, "The Levitical Diaspora (I): A Sociological Comparison with Morocco's Ahansal," in *Exploring the* Longue Durée*: Essays in Honor of Lawrence E. Stager* [ed. David Schloen; Winona Lake, Ind.: Eisenbrauns, 2009], 223–34). Obviously, this model of mobile thugs should not be applied to the vast majority of modern nomadic Bedouin, who remain outside of settled society or inside a favorable trade relationship with it (McGovern, "Central Transjordan," 268).

28 Hannes Olivier, "Remarks on Landscape Resources and Human Occupation in Jordan According to Some Nineteenth Century Travelogues," in *Studies in the History and Archaeology of Jordan* 6 (ed. Ghazi Bisheh, Muna Zaghloul, and Ina Kehrberg; Amman: Jordanian Department of Antiquities, 1997), 396.

The ruralization/sedentarization model of the Israelite settlement in the Levant not only provides an explanation for the apparent population explosion in the hill-country during the early Iron Age but also demonstrates an awareness of the continuity of the languages and isoglosses in the area. The various ethnic populations of the Cisjordanian and Transjordanian tribal kingdoms of the early Iron Age must have been in place for quite some time prior to early Iron Age settlement of those populations,[29] since the isoglosses between various linguistic aspects—both phonological and morphological—can be traced with little difficulty from as early as the Amarna Letters.[30] The continuity of the linguistic traditions of the tribal kingdoms in the Levant suggests that the Israelite settlement was primarily an indigenous one, not an external one.[31]

Furthermore, a strict application of the ruralization model precludes the necessity of the eastward settlement of the tribes of Reuben, Gad, and eastern Manasseh as proposed by M. Noth.[32] Far more likely, the population of Transjordan that developed during the Iron Age was indigenous to the area, having settled like a precipitant out of the demographic solution onto the geographic features of the land.[33] While some of the nomadic element remained in solution, much of the settled-out precipitant coagulated in pockets across the land, aggregating with agriculturalists moving away from the urban centers. As the need for mutual defense—as well as other

---

29 E.g., Lawrence E. Stager, "The Patrimonial Kingdom of Solomon," in *Symbiosis, Symbolism, and the Power of the Past: Canaan, Ancient Israel, and Their Neighbors, from the Late Bronze Age through Roman Palaestina* (ed. W. G. Dever and S. Gitin; Winona Lake, Ind.: Eisenbrauns, 2003), 63–74; Øystein S. LaBianca and Randall W. Younker, "The Kingdoms of Ammon, Moab and Edom: The Archaeology of Society in Late Bronze/Iron Age Transjordan (ca. 1400–500 B.C.E.)," in *The Archaeology of Society in the Holy Land* (ed. Thomas E. Levy; London: Leicester University Press, 1998), 399–411.

30 E.g., W. Randall Garr, *Dialect-Geography of Syria-Palestine, 1000–586 B.C.E.* (Philadelphia: University of Pennsylvania Press, 1985).

31 Cf., though, Anson F. Rainey's recent challenges to the consensus opinion ("Whence Came the Israelites and Their Language?" *IEJ* 57 [2007]: 41–64; idem, "Redefining Hebrew—A Transjordanian Language," *Maarav* 14 [2007]: 67–81). I leave open here the question of an Exodus community that entered Cisjordan. If the traditions of Israel's entry into Canaan are historical in some respects, then the Israelite highland settlement was not *entirely* indigenous (e.g., Peter Machinist, "Outsiders or Insiders: The Biblical View of Emergent Israel and Its Context," in *The Other in Jewish Thought and History: Constructions of Jewish Culture and Identity* [ed. Laurence J. Silberstein and Robert L. Cohn; New York: NYU Press, 1994], 35–60). I thank Jo Ann Hackett and Peter Machinist for their insights into this problem in private conversations.

32 Martin Noth, "Das Land Gilead als Siedlungsgebiet israelitischer Sippen," *PJ* 37 (1941): 50–101, esp. 37, 75–77; idem, "Gilead und Gad," *ZDPV* 75 (1959): 14–73, esp. 60–61.

33 This may provide a bit of an explanation for traditions of the Israelites' kinship with the non-Israelite groups, which can be found in the Bible (e.g., Genesis 19–32; see also Larry G. Herr, "Social Systems in Central Jordan: Moving toward the First Millennium BC and the Earliest Iron Age Politics," in *Studies in the History and Archaeology of Jordan* 7 [ed. Ghazi Bisheh; Amman: Jordanian Department of Antiquities, 2001], 282).

factors in the formation of corporate identity—increased, these pockets became more and more consolidated into larger corporate identities. L. G. Herr argues that these corporate groups should not be confused with the nation states into which they gradually developed:

> ...during the 13th and 12th centuries, we should speak of "tribal entities" rather than "national" ones. Tribal relationships consist of fluid coalitions or alliances that rise, fall, swap loyalties, and come and go.... Thus, there would be no "national" groups called Ammon, Moāb, or Israel in early Iron I. Instead, there were tribes and tribal alliances. The biblical remembrances of these tribes as "nations" in premonarchic times are anachronisms, placing the Iron II concepts of monarchy and nationhood onto the earlier tribal entities.[34]

However, the movement from tribe to tribal kingdom should perhaps not be isolated so stringently. Stager argues that the movement from tribal society to tribal kingdom is cognitively only a short jump since both are founded upon the sociological ideal of the בית אב ("House of the Father") institution.[35]

Finally, while the "Israelite" tribes of Transjordan may have had several important ethnic, political, and religious ties to those of Cisjordan, we should not discount the possibility that they shared more immediate economic ties with corporate groups other than the Cisjordanian Israelite tribes, i.e., the Ammonites and the Moabites. A major transitional LB–Early Iron Age caravan route passed through the Jabbok River Valley (i.e., the modern *W. Zarqa*), connecting Shechem with the Beqᶜah Valley and Amman.[36] This route would have served as a primary route for transhumant pastoralists between their summer and winter herding grounds, while allowing for trade between the two areas of highland culture as well. Thus, there are indications not only of a long history of human movement through the area of the Jordan River—a *necessary* cause of the attribution of meaning to locals in the model proposed above—but also of connections between the Transjordanian Israelites and the polities to the east. Because of the relative ease of travel, the Transjordanian Israelites would have

34 Ibid.

35 Stager, "Patrimonial Kingdom," 63–74.

36 Roland de Vaux, "Notes d'histoire et de topographie transjordaniennes," in *Vivre et Penser I: Recherches d'exégèse et d'histoire I* (=*RB* 50 [1941]): 34; Noth, "Gilead und Gad," 32–33; Siegfried Mittmann, "Die Steige des Sonnengottes (Ri. 8,13)," *ZDPV* 81 (1965): 80 n. 1; Patrick E. McGovern, *The Late Bronze and Early Iron Ages of Central Transjordan: The Baqᶜah Valley Project, 1977–1981* (University Museum Monograph 65; Philadelphia: University of Pennsylvania Museum of Archaeology, 1986); V. C. Pigott, P. E. McGovern, and M. R. Notis, "The Earliest Steel from Transjordan," *MASCA Journal* 2 (1982): 35–39; Hutton, "Mahanaim," 173–78; Eveline J. van der Steen, "A Walk through the Wadi Zerqa," in *Sacred and Sweet: Studies on the Material Culture of Tell Deir ᶜAlla and Tell Abu Sarbut* (ed. Margreet L. Steiner and Eveline J. van der Steen; ANESSup 24; Leuven: Peeters, 2008), 109–33.

looked more immediately to the Ammonites and Moabites as trading partners than to their ethnic congeners in Cisjordan.

2.2. Ethnic Diversity in Iron Age Transjordan

Concomitant with the application of the ruralization theory to the territory east of the Jordan River comes the question as to the identity of the settled and nomadic populations. Unfortunately, it is impossible to determine with any certainty the original ethnic identities of the groups. Furthermore, the corporate groups must be thought of as small, tribally based units, rather than as the nations into which they developed most fully during the late Iron I or early Iron II.[37] In the end, the reconstruction of ethnicity in the Transjordan is a fully speculative project, based entirely on what may or may not be circumstantial data, such as the presence of certain types of pottery in excavated sites, or on later classifications of ethnicity that are retrojected secondarily onto the original population.

For example, over against the usual assumption that the presence of collared-rim store jars indicates specifically Israelite sites, C.-H. C. Ji has pointed to the proliferation of Iron I collared-rim store jars throughout the Transjordanian highlands, arguing that "a variety of ethnic groups should be included when trying to determine the ethnicity of the users" of those jars.[38] Indeed, collared-rim store jars appear at a variety of sites in Transjordan, many of which are recognized to have been non-Israelite, or only so temporarily: Sahab, Jalul, Safut, Dhiban, and Amman.[39] The jar-style's common usage across a wide area of the Levant thus suggests some degree of interaction between regions, so it cannot be used as a diagnostic criterion of ethnicity.[40] Only during the Iron II period do the pottery assemblages from Edom, Moab, Ammon, and the "Israelite" Transjordan diverge from one another, with the regional variations appearing roughly along east-west boundary lines.[41] This discrepancy would seem to suggest that

---

37 Herr, "Social Systems," 282.

38 Ji, "Iron Age I," 137–38; see earlier Stager, "Response," 83–84.

39 Rudolph H. Dornemann, "The Beginning of the Iron Age in Transjordan," in *Studies in the History and Archeology of Jordan* 1 (ed. Adnan Hadidi; Amman: Jordanian Department of Antiquities, 1982), 138.

40 E.g., Kathryn A. Kamp and Norman Yoffee, "Ethnicity in Western Asia During the Early Second Millennium B.C.: Archaeological Assessments and Ethnoarchaeological Perspectives," *BASOR* 237 (1980): 85–104.

41 Piotr Bienkowski, "The North-South Divide in Ancient Jordan: Ceramics, Regionalism and Routes," in *Culture Through Objects: Ancient Near Eastern Studies in Honour of P. R. S. Moorey* (ed. Timothy F. Potts, M. Roaf, and Diana Stein; Oxford: Griffith Institute, 2003), 97–98.

the common cultural heritage of the highland collared-rim store jars that was shared by at least those groups that later became Reuben, Gad, and Ammon (as well as the Cisjordanian Israelite tribes) began to break down along the lines of ethnicity, which became more openly recognized at the beginning of the Iron II period. The heterogeneous population of the Iron II Transjordan (and of the biblical texts) may offer a skewed view into the actual demographic realities of the early Iron I period, in which the population of Transjordan was more homogeneous, or at the very least did not differentiate itself to the extent that the biblical narratives imply. This does not mean, however, that there were no cultural differences between certain segments of the Transjordanian population during the Iron I, only that the large-scale cultural differences were probably not delineated with the rigor found in the biblical texts. Ethnicity, as a function of self-recognition,[42] was ambiguous in Transjordan from the very beginning of the Iron Age. The close proximity of so many ethnic groups in the Iron II can only serve as a testament to the processes of differentiation and alliance within a difficult matrix of tribal affinities and alliances; after all, "'national' groups may change over time."[43] In short, the purported *national* heterogenization of the Iron I population may only have begun during the Iron II.

This ambiguity with respect to tribal and national ethnicity during the Iron Age poses the problem of the commonalities shared by those tribes that became the nation of Israel during the transitional Iron I–II (ca. 1000–900). To what extent did the populations of the Transjordan and the Cisjordan consider themselves homogenous? Certainly, the biblical genealogical accounts of the twelve-tribe system were designed to unite the tribal entities into a mutually defensive nation. As Kallai points out, "the inclusion of Jair within the general framework of Machir or Manasseh, and the styling of Machir as the father of Gilead, is a generalization that expresses the assimilation and absorption of the clans in northern Trans-Jordan into the strongest tribal framework that had the necessary standing in the tribal league of Israel in that area."[44] The same ambiguity of genealogical relationship may have applied to Reuben and Gad with respect to each tribe's inclusion in the larger nation of Israel, yet the coherence and unity portrayed by the twelve-tribe system belie the constant bickering and "infighting" narrated in other sections of the Bible (e.g., the rebuke of

42 Fredrik Barth, "Introduction," in *Ethnic Groups and Boundaries: The Social Organization of Cultural Difference* (ed. Fredrik Barth; Boston: Little, Brown, 1969), 9–38.

43 Piotr Bienkowski, "The Iron Age and Persian Periods in Jordan," in *Studies in the History and Archaeology of Jordan* 7 (ed. Ghazi Bisheh; Amman: Jordanian Department of Antiquities, 2001), 268.

44 Zecharia Kallai, "Conquest and Settlement of Trans-Jordan: A Historiographical Study," *ZDPV* 99 (1983): 114.

certain tribes in Judg 5:17–23;[45] the rebuke of the Transjordanian tribes in Joshua 22; intertribal quarrels and battles at the fords of the Jordan in Judg 8:1–3 and Judg 12:1–5; the civil war narrated in Judges 20; not to mention the internecine strife between the Judahite Davidic dynasty and the northern Israelite tribes in 2 Sam 2:8–3:1; 16:5–8; 19:40–20:22; 1 Kgs 12:1–19).

In many respects, the Transjordanian tribes that became "Israelite" seem to have been originally autonomous ethnic units that considered themselves, to some extent, separate from the Cisjordanian groups.[46] I contend that the various Transjordanian tribes considered themselves only nominally Israelite and that although they often remained allied with the Cisjordanian kingdoms, there is evidence in the Bible that a separatist movement operated in Transjordanian society as well (see §2.3). I view Saul's rescue of Jabesh-gilead (1 Samuel 11) and David's overtures to the same city (2 Sam 2:4b–7) not as actions performed out of any feelings of solidarity, but rather as movements towards sovereignty over the northern Israelite Transjordan.[47] In §1.2.1, I presented the offer of hospitality made by David to Barzillai as a political ploy to defuse any subsequent pretension to the throne—or separation from it—before a Gileadite revolt. Linguistically speaking, it is possible that Barzillai the Gileadite bore an Aramaean patronymic, bar-Zillai ("son of Zillai"), rather than a Hebrew name implying mastery of iron-working skills.[48] This interpretation is bolstered by the fact that Barzillai's son bears a distinctively Aramaic or Aramaizing name, in which the Proto-Semitic *ḏ was realized as /d/ (עדריאל: 1 Sam 18:19; 2 Sam 21:8). If the name were Hebrew, one would

---

45 For an excellent socio-ecological study of this rebuke, see Lawrence E. Stager, "Archaeology, Ecology, and Social History: Background Themes to the Song of Deborah," in *Congress Volume: Jerusalem, 1986* (ed. J. A. Emerton; Leiden: Brill, 1988), 221–34.

46 Manfred Weippert, "Israélites, Araméens et Assyriens dans la Transjordanie septentrionale," *ZDPV* 113 (1997): 27.

47 Insofar as this attempt at kingship building is endemic to the Saul story, I agree with Diana Edelman in her assessment of 1 Samuel 11 ("Saul's Rescue of Jabesh-Gilead [I Sam 11 1–11]: Sorting Story from History," *ZAW* 96 [1984]: 195–209).

48 *Pace* Robert A. Coughenour, "A Search for Maḥanaim," *BASOR* 273 (1989): 63. The Aramaic name זילאי (Zilay?) is known from the Talmud, as a rabbinical authority (*Ber.* 53b). An original name בַּר־זִלַּי thus seems to have been misanalyzed at least by Coughenour and other modern commentators, if not by the biblical authors themselves, as deriving from Hebrew ברזל ("iron": thus, בַּרְזִלַּי) consequent to the knowledge of Iron mines in Transjordan (e.g., Robert A. Coughenour, "Preliminary Report on the Exploration and Excavation of Mugharat el Wardeh and Abu Thawab," *ADAJ* 21 [1976]: 71–78, 186–89; Xander Veldhuijzen and Eveline van der Steen, "Iron Production Center Found in the Jordan Valley," *NEA* 62.3 [1999]: 195–99). My thanks are due to Gene McGarry, who suggested this onomastic interpretation to me.

expect the form to have been the cognate form עזריאל.[49] The traditions linking Jacob to the Aramaean Laban (Gen 28:1–32:1) have suggested to Humbert that the "Israelite" Transjordan was of "mixed ethnicity" (i.e., Aramaeo-Israelite) already by the 10th cent. BCE, and he adduces, moreover, the "Aramaean influence" of some pottery at *T. Deir ᶜAllā* as archaeological proof of economic or demographic ties with Aram.[50]

Linguistic and paleographic ties between Aram and the various ethnic groups of Transjordan attest to similarly complex connections. The Ammonite language's position within the Canaanite family[51] attests to an ethnic affiliation to the Israelites whose Hebrew language also fell within the rubric of the family of Canaanite, yet the Ammonite script developed more directly from the lapidary Aramaic script.[52] Moabite, with its Gt-stem, at first seems to resemble Aramaic more closely than it does Hebrew. Yet Moabite clearly belongs to the Canaanite family of languages, and the presence of the stem can be attributed to the retention of the Proto-Northwest Semitic construction.[53] Even within "Israelite" society, linguistic differences obtain. For example, one may point to the narrative of Jephthah's battle against the Ephraimites at the fords of the Jordan (Judg 12:1–5). The inability of the Ephraimites to reproduce the Gileadite sibilant in *šibbōlet* leads to their demise. While the narrative clearly holds the Ephraimites in contempt,[54] the account could plausibly be based on an actual

49 See, e.g., Hans Joachim Stoebe, "David und Mikal: Überlegungen zur Jugendgeschichte Davids," in *Von Ugarit nach Qumran: Beiträge zur alttestamentlichen und altorientalischen Forschung* (ed. J. Hempel et al.; BZAW 77; Berlin: Töpelmann, 1958), 230–33.

50 Jean-Baptiste Humbert, "L'occupation de l'espace à l'âge du Fer en Jordanie," in *Studies in the History and Archaeology of Jordan* 4 (ed. Muna Zaghloul et al.; Amman: Jordanian Department of Antiquities, 1992), 200, citing H. J. Franken, "Deir ᶜAllâ," in *EAEHL*, 1:322; see also van der Steen, *Tribes*, 288–94; H. J. Franken, "Deir ᶜAllā and Its Religion," in *Sacred and Sweet: Studies on the Material Culture of Tell Deir ᶜAlla and Tell Abu Sarbut* (ed. Margreet L. Steiner and Eveline J. van der Steen; ANESSup 24; Leuven: Peeters, 2008), 25–52. Franken's inscriptions, found on a rock and a potsherd (respectively, אבן שרעא and זי שרעא), *are* distinctively Aramaic, but, as Jo Ann Hackett points out, the necessity of adducing evidence for Aramean presence suggests that the majority of the population was of other ethnicity ("Response to Baruch Levine and André Lemaire," in *The Balaam Text from Deir ᶜAlla Re-Evaluated: Proceedings of the International Symposium Held at Leiden 21–24 August 1989* [ed. J. Hoftijzer and G. van der Kooij; Leiden: Brill, 1991], 82–83; see also Baruch A. Levine, "The Balaam Inscription from Deir ᶜAlla: Historical Aspects," in *Biblical Archaeology Today: Proceedings of the International Congress on Biblical Archaeology, Jerusalem, April 1984* [Jerusalem: Israel Exploration Society, 1985], 328, 332).

51 Kent P. Jackson, *The Ammonite Language of the Iron Age* (HSM 27; Chico, Calif.: Scholars Press, 1983), 107–9.

52 Frank M. Cross, "Epigraphic Notes on the ᶜAmmān Citadel Inscription," *BASOR* 193 (1969): 13.

53 Kent P. Jackson, "The Language of the Mesha Inscription," in *Studies in the Mesha Inscription and Moab* (ed. Andrew Dearman; Atlanta: Scholars Press, 1991), 130.

54 David Marcus, "Ridiculing the Ephraimites: The Shibboleth Incident (Judg 12:6)," *Maarav* 8 (1992): 95–105.

phonological phenomenon.[55] The most anomalous linguistic conundrum is that discovered at *T. Deir ᶜAllā*, a site located well within the boundaries of the early "Israelite" Transjordan. While written in a script clearly derived from the Aramaic script (like Ammonite), the language seems to be separate from both Hebrew and Aramaic.[56] Furthermore, the religious tradition that seems to be preserved in the text was certainly not normative Yahwism, and—if Yahwistic at all—presumably comprised a rival cult to the one centered in Jerusalem.[57] The presence at *T. Deir ᶜAllā* of such a cult may attest to further disparities in culture between the two groups.[58]

In the end, it is proper to heed Ji's warning that "we should be careful before attributing ethnic labels to the LB/Iron I sedentary peoples,"[59] but this does not preclude a recognition that the ethnicity of the Transjordanian plateau was of mixed or heterogeneous origin. Not only was this admixture socioeconomic and ecologically based (§2.1), but the linguistic differences that persisted long enough to leave textual and archaeological records also testify to diverse ethnic origins. While it is certainly appropriate to be careful about such ethnic observations, Barth's suggestion that self-identification holds the key to ethnic identification may be applied in this instance.[60] In all probability, the Israelite Transjordan of the Iron Age

---

55 E.g., Alice Faber, "Second Harvest: *šibbōlεθ* Revisted (Yet Again)," *JSS* 37 (1992): 1–10.

56 See three essays in *The Balaam Text from Deir ᶜAlla Re-Evaluated: Proceedings of the International Symposium Held at Leiden 21–24 August 1989* (ed. J. Hoftijzer and G. van der Kooij; Leiden: Brill, 1991): John Huehnergard, "Remarks on the Classification of the Northwest Semitic Languages," 282–93; P. Kyle McCarter, "The Dialect of the Deir ᶜAlla Texts," 87–99, esp. 97; Dennis Pardee, "The Linguistic Classification of the Deir ᶜAlla Text Written on Plaster," 104–5; see also Jo Ann Hackett, who argues that "if a choice must be made between South Canaanite and Aramaic, South Canaanite dialects are considerably closer to the dialect of our text than is any known Aramaic" (*The Balaam Text from Deir ᶜAllā* [HSM 31; Chico, Calif.: Scholars Press, 1984], 124). This comparison was, of course, written before the discovery of the Tel Dan inscription. Cf. those who argue for the language as an early offshoot of Aramaic (J. Hoftijzer and G. van der Kooij, eds. *Aramaic Texts from Deir ᶜAlla* [Leiden: Brill, 1976], 300; P. Kyle McCarter, "The Balaam Texts from Deir ᶜAllā: The First Combination," *BASOR* 222 [1980]: 49–60, esp. 50–51; Al Wolters, "The Balaamites of Deir ᶜAllā as Aramean Deportees," *HUCA* 59 [1988]: 101–113, esp. 108–11; André Lemaire, "Les inscriptions sur plâtre de Deir ᶜAlla et leur signification histoirique et culturelle," in *The Balaam Text from Deir ᶜAlla Re-Evaluated: Proceedings of the International Symposium Held at Leiden 21–24 August 1989* [ed. J. Hoftijzer and G. van der Kooij; Leiden: Brill, 1991], 33–57; Weippert, "Israélites," 30).

57 Hackett, *Balaam Text*, 125; idem, "Some Observations on the Balaam Tradition at Deir ᶜAllā," *BA* 49 (1986): 216–22; idem, "Religious Traditions in Israelite Transjordan," in *Ancient Israelite Religion: Essays in Honor of Frank Moore Cross* (ed. Patrick D. Miller, Paul D. Hanson, and S. Dean McBride; Philadelphia: Fortress, 1987), 134.

58 For a more thorough discussion, see Jeremy M. Hutton, "Southern, Northern, and Transjordanian Perspectives," in *Religious Diversity* (ed. John Barton and Francesca Stavrakopoulou; London: T&T Clark, forthcoming).

59 Ji, "Iron Age I," 138.

60 Barth, "Introduction," 9–38.

was the home of an ethnically diverse population comprised of several tribal entities all derived from multiform economic and sociological backgrounds, some of which left archaeological, textual, and linguistic records of their perceived heterogeneity. Since ethnicity is a nebulous subject, defined variably to suit the context, we must then seek to understand the ethnicity of the Transjordanian Israelites in a complex manner—one that takes into account the shifting alliances of the tribes involved, as well as the constantly shifting genealogical schemas adduced in order to outline the various corporate groups' positions within the later nation-bound system. Ethnicity is subject to the contingencies of diachrony, and our notions of ethnicity must reflect this fact.

2.3. Transjordan in History

It is quite difficult to trace the political history of Transjordan without recourse to the biblical account. There is no written extra-biblical evidence for the formative Iron I period, and only a few extra-biblical documents attest to the history of relations between the Transjordanian Israelites and the surrounding polities during the Iron II period. Aside from a few Assyrian chronicles, which seem to be the most systematically organized documents available, only the Aramaic Tel Dan Inscription[61] and the Moabite (Mesha) Stela[62] give any specific indication of politico-historical events. Roughly contemporaneous, these two natively authored inscriptions provide only the barest outline of the situation in the mid-9th

61 The *editio princeps* of the bulk of the inscription can be found in Avraham Biran and Joseph Naveh, "An Aramaic Stele Fragment from Tel Dan," *IEJ* 43 (1993): 81–98; another portion of the same inscription was found subsequently and published in idem, "The Tel Dan Inscription: A New Fragment," *IEJ* 45 (1995): 1–18. The authenticity of the stela has been impugned (unfairly), and the more compelling discussions of the stele's meaning have focused on the authorship of the stele and the significance of the phrase "House of David" (*bytdwd*), rather than on any hypothetical "House of Dôd." Scores of studies treating the stele have appeared in the intervening years (see, e.g., Bob Becking, "Did Jehu Write the Tel Dan Inscription?" *SJOT* 13 [1999]: 187–201, which, by my count, cites 23 sources—excluding the two by Biran and Naveh!). Despite the assessment of Jan Wim Wesselius that the author was Jehu ("The First Royal Inscription from Ancient Israel: The Tel Dan Inscription Reconsidered," *SJOT* 13 [1999]: 163–86; cf. Becking, ibid., for the response), the general trend in interpretation among epigraphers at the time of this writing remains that of the initial assessment of the excavators—after finding the second major portion—was correct in assigning the stele to Hazael, ca. 842–841 (Biran and Naveh, "Tel Dan Inscription," 17; cf. idem, "Aramaic Stele Fragment," 96–98, where the question is left somewhat open).

62 In the ca. 135 years since the discovery of the Mesha Inscription, countless articles have been written about its discovery, its translation and language, and its historical significance. A good introduction to the range of topics that touch on the stele is Andrew Dearman, *Studies in the Mesha Inscription and Moab* (Atlanta: Scholars Press, 1989).

century, but insofar as they both deal with the continuing struggle between Israel and its neighbors, they corroborate the rough contours of biblical historiography in two important ways. First, if we assume that the consensus holding Hazael's authorship of the Tel Dan Inscription is correct,[63] the inscription attests to what the Bible describes as an almost continual state of warfare between the Aramaean kingdom of Damascus and the Israelite kingdom under the Omrides.[64] Second, the Mesha Inscription confirms the continued presence of ethnic Israelites in Transjordan between the Jabbok and Arnon Valleys,[65] as well as the lingering antagonism between the Israelite kingdom and the Moabite kingdom under Mesha (2 Kings 3).

The other primary extra-biblical sources for the event history of Transjordan are the Assyrian records of the 9th and 8th centuries BCE. The northern Israelite kingdom is first mentioned in Assyrian records in an inscription of Shalmaneser III, commemorating the Battle of Qarqar in 853 (the "Monolith Inscription," found at Kurkh).[66] In that text, Ahab is listed with several other kings of small Levantine kingdoms, all of whom banded together to oppose the invading Assyrian forces. Of the other kings on the list, only the territory of Hadadezer of Damascus was sufficiently close enough to Transjordan to have been an effective contender for control over the area,[67] but it seems unlikely that Ahab and Hadadezer would have been locked in struggle with one another over such a small matter as territory at that time. Thanks to the overthrow of both dynasties shortly thereafter, however, the Assyrian Empire conquered Damascus (now ruled by Hazael) and extracted tribute from Israel. Jehu is pictured doing obeisance to Shalmaneser III on that king's black obelisk (ca. 840), found at Kalhu/Calah.[68] This appearance of the Israelite king in a humble state may provide some corroboration for the biblical notice that "Hazael struck every border of Israel: from Jordan eastward, all the land of Gilead, the Gadites,

---

63 See n. 61.

64 Judah, whose king also appears to be mentioned in the text ([אחזי]הו . בר [. יהורם . מל]ך . ביתדוד; lines 8–9), was also tied up in the relations between these two kingdoms, but not to the same extent.

65 While the Mesha Inscription never explicitly identifies the Gadites as an Israelite tribe, we should probably disregard the suggestion of Weippert that Mesha was himself a Gadite and was using the fact that "Gadites had lived in the area of Atarot for ages" (ואש גד ישב בארץ עטרת מעלם; line 10) as justification for the attack on the city that the "king of Israel had built for himself (ויבן לה מלך ישראל את עטרת; lines 10–11; "Israélites," 26 n. 32).

66 *ANET*, 278–79.

67 The name commonly transcribed as Baesa (or Baasha) of Beth-Rehob the Ammonite (*Baʾsa mār Ruḥūbi* KUR *Amanaya*) probably does not refer to the Ammonite kingdom of Transjordan, but rather to the Aramaean kingdom of Beth-Rehob in the Amanus, the northern portion of the Anti-Lebanon mountain range. The area was also known as Zobah (see Nadav Na'aman, "Hazael of ʿAmqi and Hadadezer of Beth-rehob," *UF* 27 [1995]: 385–86, for transcription and discussion).

68 See *ANET*, 281 for accompanying text.

the Reubenites, and the Manassites..." (2 Kgs 10:32–33).[69] It thus seems that already during the reign of Jehu, Israel had lost the bulk of its Transjordanian possessions.[70] This loss may have been temporary, since Jehoash and Jeroboam II may have reclaimed the eastern territories (2 Kgs 13:25; 14:25[71]), but by the time Tiglath-Pileser III overran the Transjordanian area in 734–732, the territory had apparently reverted to Aramaean control.[72] Thus, by the time of Dtr, Transjordan had already been separated politically from both Judah and Israel for at least a century, and probably for much closer to two centuries, if the Israelite resurgence under Jehoash and Jeroboam is as optimistic and idealized as is commonly assumed.

If we are to flesh out this skeletal structure any further, we must rely on the reconstructive efforts of biblical historians.[73] A few more salient

69 The coincidence of Jehu's subjection to the Assyrian Empire and the loss of Transjordan to the Aramaeans is somewhat surprising, given that Hazael had similarly been subjugated by the invading Assyrians. One wonders how the Aramaean coalition had made such a quick turnaround, when Israel's subjugation prevented an adequate military response.

70 Iain W. Provan, V. Philips Long, and Tremper Longman III, *A Biblical History of Israel* (Louisville, Ky.: WJKP, 2003), 267.

71 This latter verse describes the reinstated boundaries as "from Lebo-Hamath to the Dead Sea," the traditional expanse of Israelite possession in the east.

72 Two inscriptions of Tiglath-Pileser III describe the taking of the lands of Aram Damascus (*Bīt Ḫazaili*; see Na'aman, "Hazael," 381–94). Na'aman identifies the city *Galʕaza* with Mizpah-gilead (modern *Jelʕād*) rather than with the more northerly Ramoth-gilead (so H. Tadmor, "The Southern Border of Aram," *IEJ* 12 [1962]: 118–19; B. Oded, "Observations on Methods of Assyrian Rule in Transjordania after the Palestinian Campaign of Tiglath-Pileser III," *JNES* 29 [1970]: 179–80), regardless of whether that city is to be identified with *T. er-Rumeith* (e.g., Nancy L. Lapp, "Rumeith, Tell er-," *NEAEHL* 4:1291–93), *T. er-Ramṯa* (Ernst Axel Knauf, "The Mists of Ramthalon, or: How Ramoth-Gilead Disappeared from the Archaeological Record," *BN* 110 [2001]: 33–36), or *T. el-Ḥuṣn* (Noth, "Land Gilead," 92; Gustaf Dalman, "Jahresbericht des Deutschen Evangelischen Instituts für Altertumswissenschaft des Heiligen Landes für das Arbeitsjahr 1912/13," *PJ* 9 [1913]: 63–66). Accordingly, the other cities listed in the inscription confirm that the annexation extended much further south than previously thought: in Na'aman's reconstruction, the territory extended south from the Jabbok River as far as the northern border of Moab (which, beginning with Mesha's conquest, had controlled all of the formerly Israelite possessions on the Mishor). 1 Chr 5:26 states that it was at this time that the tribes of Reuben and Gad and the half-tribe of Manasseh were displaced. Undoubtedly, the ethnic affiliation of the peoples east of the Jordan was more complex than this. Moreover, because the the Aramaeans could have ruled over the Israelite tribes of Transjordan, the two sets of data are not *necessarily* diametrically opposed. In all likelihood, however, Reuben had disappeared several centuries earlier (Frank M. Cross, *From Epic to Canaan: History and Literature in Ancient Israel* [Baltimore: The Johns Hopkins University Press, 1998], 53–70).

73 The problems with biblical historiography are prolix and will not be rehearsed here; see, e.g., Provan, Long, and Longman (*Biblical History*, 3–35; cf., e.g., John Bright, *A History of Israel* [4th ed.; Louisville, Ky.: WJKP, 2000]; John H. Hayes and J. Maxwell Miller, eds., *Israelite and Judaean History* [OTL; Philadelphia: Westminster, 1977]). A short overview of Israelite history in the context of ancient Near Eastern geo-politics is provided in Amélie Kuhrt (*The Ancient Near East: c. 3000–330 BC* [London: Routledge, 1995], 466–72).

political events may be indicated here on the basis of the historical notices contained in the DtrH and the Chronicles, but the interpretation of each event requires a proper understanding of the historical sources. The first account of Cisjordanian dealings with Transjordanian Israelites in the DtrH that does not have the appearance of pure folklore is the notice in 2 Sam 2:8–9, which reports that Saul's son Ishbosheth[74] ruled the northern kingdom ("Gilead,[75] Asher,[76] Jezreel,[77] Ephraim, Benjamin, and all

---

74 Ishbosheth was presumably the oldest living son of Saul. According to the text, he was forty years old when he began to reign (2 Sam 2:10), but it is unclear whether he was also at Gilboa when Saul died. If he was, it strikes the historian as odd that he survived (although one wonders as well how Abner survived while Saul and three of his sons perished; cf. 1 Sam 31:2). However, it would also be odd to conclude that Ishbosheth had not been at the battle, given that he is said to have been of sufficient age for battle. J. Alberto Soggin points out that even a liberal reading of the figure of forty years still suggests that Ishbosheth was past the time of his youth, making it even more disconcerting that he was so weak-willed and powerless ("The Reign of ᵓEšbaᶜal, Son of Saul," in *Old Testament and Oriental Studies* [BibOr 29; Rome: Biblical Institute Press, 1975], 41).

75 The name Gilead refers to the hill country in Transjordan split in the middle by the Jabbok River (Baly, "Pitfalls," 61–63; idem, *The Geography of the Bible: A Study in Historical Geography* [New York: Harper & Brothers, 1957], 226–31). Cf. J. R. Bartlett, who argues that "Gilead" was typically used to refer only to the territory north of the Jabbok ("Sihon and Og, Kings of the Amorites," *VT* 20 [1970]: 262, cf. 263; also André Lemaire, "Galaad et Makîr," *VT* 31 [1981]: 39–61).

76 It is at least highly unlikely that Abner crowned Ishbosheth king over Assyria (Soggin, "Reign," 41), and while the name might suggest "the Asherites" (this reading is supported by *Tg. Jon.* and perhaps LXX^{L}), most commentators follow LXX in reading "Geshurites" (see, e.g., P. Kyle McCarter, *II Samuel: A New Translation with Introduction and Commentary* [AB 9; New York: Doubleday, 1984], 83, 87). Reading with LXX produces a nice sequence in which Geshur is read between Gilead and Jezreel, an approximation of its geographic location (see also Bartlett, "Sihon and Og," 264). Contrast, though, the work of Soggin, who finds it difficult to believe that Ishbosheth was crowned king over Geshur, given that around this same time David married Maakah, the daughter of the king of Geshur ("Reign," 41). Benjamin Mazar reminds us that Geshur and Maakah were classically considered by the Israelites to be lands *yet to be possessed* ("Geshur and Maacah," *JBL* 80 [1961]: 16–28). This would suggest that an Israelite claim to Geshur is only a pipedream, especially in such a tumultuous time as Ishbosheth's. Diana Edelman has argued for the reading "Asher," with the stipulation that a portion of that tribe had some smallholdings on Mt. Ephraim ("The 'Ashurites' of Eshbaal's State [2 Sam 2:9]," *PEQ* 117 [1985]: 85–91; idem, "The Asherite Genealogy in 1 Chr 7:30–40," *BR* 33 [1988]: 13–23).

77 Jezreel here might refer to the area immediately surrounding *T. Jezreel* rather than the entire Jezreel Valley, since that had presumably been captured recently by the Philistines (McCarter, *II Samuel*, 87). Although Ishbosheth may have only been able to exert control over the area immediately surrounding *T. Jezreel*, the assertion that Ishbosheth was king over Jezreel may betray a fundamental obstinacy on the part of the Israelite monarchy to admit that the Jezreel Valley—through which the important *Via Maris* ran—had been lost. Additionally, I would argue that the strategic position of *T. Jezreel* almost necessitates its capture by any force that claims to have dominance over the valley. If the Philistines *did* control the Jezreel Valley, along with its trade route, then they probably controlled the major sites overlooking the valley as well. Ishbosheth's government probably saw itself as a government in exile, a government that rightfully possessed the Jezreel but was simply unable to exert control over it.

Israel";[78] 2 Sam 2:9) from Mahanaim.[79] Initially, this relocalization seems odd since the distance required to travel from there to the Benjaminite *Kerngebiet* centered on Gibeah was substantial. However, the city was favorably located in a highly defensible position,[80] and distance from

---

78 Ephraim and Benjamin classically refer to two of the major tribal inheritances in the central hill country, and as James W. Flanagan has shown, "all Israel"—a technical term with a specific meaning during the time of the United Monarchy later reinterpreted by redactors of the source material—probably refers to the northern confederation of Ephraim and Manasseh ("Judah in All Israel," in *No Famine in the Land: Studies in Honor of John L. McKenzie* [ed. James W. Flanagan and Anita Weisbrod Robinson; Missoula, Mont.: Scholars, 1975], 101–16).

79 Scholars have traditionally considered the establishment of Ishbosheth's government at Mahanaim to have been a defensive move to counteract the Philistine pressure exerted on the Israelite highlands: Gibeah, along with the rest of the Benjaminite hill-country, was too close to the border with Philistia to ensure the safety of the ruling family (McCarter, *II Samuel*, 87; Soggin, "Reign," 37). Even if the list of Ishbosheth's holdings is accurate, it makes relatively little sense that the Saulide general would move his king and capital to Gilead, unless under extreme external pressure. One usually expects the capital of a region to be roughly in the center of that region, in order to facilitate control throughout the area. See J. Alberto Soggin ("The Davidic-Solomonic Kingdom," in *Israelite and Judaean History* [ed. John H. Hayes and J. Maxwell Miller; London: SCM, 1977], 346). My assumption follows on the case of Jerusalem, a city that David apparently selected on account of its neutral position between the nations of Israel and Judah. Its proximity to the newly ruled Israel was no doubt a favorable attribute when compared to Hebron. Klaus-Dietrich Schunk raises the possibility that Mahanaim was one of a series of Transjordanian Benjaminite enclaves ("Erwägungen zur Geschichte und Bedeutung von Maḥanaim," *ZDMG* 113 [1963]: 36–38). For Schunk, this possibility solves many problems; for instance, it explains why the Benjaminites appear to be fleeing across the Jordan in Judg 20:45,47; it provides justification for the refusal by the people of Sukkoth and Penuel to aid Gideon; finally, it explains Abner's selection of Mahanaim over Jabesh or Penuel for the center of Ishbosheth's kingdom. But each of these explanations raises further questions. The assumption that Judg 20:45,47 portrays the Benjaminites as fleeing with a Transjordanian destination in mind, while possible, simply seems unnecessary. Furthermore, it could have been that they were merely trying to remove themselves from the theater of destruction, rather than making their way to any specific place. Schunk's proposition does not, in my opinion, explain the refusal of the inhabitants of Sukkoth and Penuel to aid Gideon any more than a Gadite lineage would. Clearly, Abner's decision to move the center of the kingdom east to Mahanaim removes Ishbosheth from the Philistine threat, as well as from the threat of the newly-established rival dynasty in Judah, but the argument that this transfer of the seat of power indicates the specifically Benjaminite background of the city is neither necessary nor especially convincing. Far more likely reasons for the selection are the positioning of Mahanaim as a secure but convenient staging area for military operations into the west as well as its preexistent political and religious significance (both of which Schunk recognizes as well). Finally, Schunk's intimation that David's move to Mahanaim was predicated on that monarch's desire to appropriate the symbolic capital "left over" from the Saulide family's stay there in order to bolster his own legitimacy to the Israelite throne can hardly stand against the evidence we have from the Biblical text that David was a *persona non grata* to the Benjaminites (e.g., 2 Sam 16:5–13). In general, Mittmann's assessment that both moves were made for reasons of geographical rather than tribal nature is most likely true (*Beiträge*, 216 n. 22).

80 If the identification of the city with *T. aḏ-Ḏahab al-Ǵarbīya* is correct (Hutton, "Mahanaim," 161–78; see previously Coughenour, "Search," 57–66; Gustaf Dalman, *Sacred Sites and Ways: Studies in the Topography of the Gospels* [trans. Paul Philip Levertoff; New York:

David's upstart government may have been a key component in the decision.[81] Ultimately, the rump government of Ishbosheth failed in the

---

Macmillan, 1935], 238; Benjamin Mazar, "The Campaign of Pharaoh Shishak to Palestine," in *Volume du Congrès: Strasbourg, 1956* [ed. G. W. Anderson et al.; VTSup 4; Leiden: Brill, 1957], 61; Diana Edelman, "Mahanaim," *ABD* 4:472–73; F. M. T. Böhl, *Palestina in het licht der jongste opgravingen en onderzoekingen* [Amsterdam: Paris, 1931], 81–82), the city probably was equipped to withstand a siege of significant proportions (Robert L. Gordon and Linda E. Villiers, "Tulul edh Dhahab and Its Environs Surveys of 1980 and 1982: A Preliminary Report," *ADAJ* 27 [1983]: 284; Siegfried Mittmann, "Amathous, Essa, Ragaba: Drei hellenistische Festungen im östlichen Randbereich des mittleren Jordangrabens," *ZDPV* 103 [1987]: 59–60; Robert L. Gordon, "Notes on Some Sites in the Lower Wādī ez-Zerqa and Wādī Rāġib," *ZDPV* 103 [1987]: 67).

81 Interpreters have so far generally neglected (or at least not adequately stressed) another important development that probably forced the retreat of the Israelite government across the Jordan. The problem is rooted in the chronology of David's reign in Hebron. Since the biblical text does not report that David was crowned in Hebron until after Saul's death, it has been commonly assumed that David's reign over Judah began after Saul had died. This scheme, however, creates two major problems. First, it neglects to give a reason for the fact that Israel does not immediately make a covenant with David, but rather delays until after Saul's successor Ishbosheth has been killed ignominiously in his home (2 Sam 4:1–3,5–8; 5:1–3; cf. the majority manuscripts of LXX at 2 Kgdms 4:1–3,5–8, which read Mephibosheth). If the elders of Israel had perceived that David held a more legitimate claim to the throne than Ishbosheth (as the anointed one of Yahweh), we should expect them to reject the insurrection of Abner and Ishbosheth and turn to David to be their leader. Instead, the picture presented is that Israel willingly followed Ishbosheth's government. This being the case, we would expect the biblical writers to reprove Israel for its initial rejection of the anointed David. But the Bible's silence on this matter suggests that the writers did not find this dichotomy between Israel (under Ishbosheth) and Judah (under David) problematic. The notion of a prophetically anointed king appears to be a separate—and later—accretion retrojected or overlaid onto the template of David's rise to power (Antony F. Campbell, *Of Prophets and Kings: A Late Ninth-Century Document [1 Samuel 1–2 Kings 10]* [CBQMS 17; Washington DC: Catholic Biblical Association of America, 1986]; cf. Nils P. Lemche, "David's Rise," *JSOT* 10 [1978]: 4 and n. 10).

Second, the problem of chronology arises. David is said to have reigned seven and a half years in Hebron over Judah before moving to Jerusalem (2 Sam 2:11; 5:5). Ishbosheth reigned a mere two years over Israel (2 Sam 2:10). There is no reason to assume that the biblical text does not represent an actual discrepancy in the two reigns. That the actual discrepancy amounted to exactly five and a half years is irrelevant; even when taken as a rough figure, this difference arouses suspicion. Notice also that the biblical text presents Ishbosheth's rule over Israel as legitimate and that no polemic is made stating anything to the effect that the Saulide had conspired or rebelled against David. Benjamin Mazar suggests that Ishbosheth's reign was contemporaneous with the first two years of David's reign in Hebron ("David's Reign in Hebron and the Conquest of Jerusalem," in *In the Time of Harvest: Essays in Honor of Abba Hillel Silver on the Occasion of His 70th Birthday* [ed. Daniel Jeremy Silver; New York: Macmillan, 1963], 235–44). When David was crowned king of Israel as well, he continued to reign in Hebron for five and a half years before eventually moving his capital to Jerusalem. While initially compelling, this argument ignores the notice that David reigned *over Judah* from Hebron, whereas he reigned over all Israel and Judah during his time in Jerusalem (2 Sam 5:5). However, Mazar's point that David probably did not move his capital to Jerusalem immediately after his accession to the throne of Israel is well taken. On the other hand, if Ishbosheth's two-year reign was roughly contemporaneous with the last two years of David's reign in Hebron, there was then an approximately five and a half year difference in the length of the two monarchs' reigns at the

face of pressures from the Davidic kingdom and dissatisfaction among his own subjects. Whatever the final judgment on David's role in the murder of Ishbosheth,[82] the biblical text gives little reason to believe that Ishbo-

---

beginning of David's reign. Typically, scholars have elected to posit an interregnum of five and a half years between Saul's death and the beginning of Ishbosheth's reign. During this time, Abner was attempting to solidify his own control over Israel and finally had to give up—presumably because of some concerns over legitimacy—eventually crowning his puppet Ishbosheth as king (Soggin, "Reign," 37–39). However, some scholars have attributed the difference in the length of Ishbosheth's and David's respective reigns to another cause: the contemporaneous reigns of David over Judah and Saul over Israel. That Judah and Israel were separate political entities even during this formative period of the Israelite state(s) is clear from the technical usage of the term "all Israel" (Flanagan, "Judah," 105–9; see also P. Kyle McCarter, "The Historical David," *Int* 40 [1986]: 125). David's rise to ascendancy in Judah is perhaps a little surprising. After all, he was the youngest son in a family that probably did not belong to the Calebite clan (1 Chr 2:9–17), the major power center of the tribe of Judah. But it is precisely the same category of factors that legitimates both David's claim to the Judahite throne and his claim to the Israelite throne: his marriages. Reading 1 Samuel 25 carefully, Levenson has pointed out that David's marriage to Abigail can be understood as the fulfillment of a precondition for David's rise to power and his subsequent inclusion in the Calebite clan (Jon D. Levenson, "1 Samuel 25 as Literature and as History," *CBQ* 40 [1978]: 11–28). According to the text of Samuel, before she became David's wife, Abigail was married to a man named Nabal, whose position David probably took as his own. Most likely the head of the Calebite clan, this figure should be associated with Ithra/Jether the Jezreelite (2 Sam 17:25; 1 Chr 2:17), the father of Amasa (who figures later as Absalom's legitimizing link to the Calebite clan; Jon D. Levenson and Baruch Halpern, "The Political Import of David's Marriages," *JBL* 99 [1980]: 511–12). When David married Abigail, the wife of the former Calebite leader, the stage was set for the Bethlehemite's rise in Judah. The name of David's other wife, Ahinoam, appears in only one other place in the Bible: as Saul's wife (1 Sam 14:50)! This identification of the two is bolstered by the prophet Nathan's reproof of David in 2 Sam 12:8, in which Nathan alludes to Saul's wives as having been given to David. Because of this, Levenson concludes that Ahinoam had previously been Saul's wife but that David had claimed her—and therefore Saul's throne—as his own while Saul was still alive (Levenson, "1 Samuel 25," 27). If this reconstruction is correct, it may suggest the contemporaneous reigns of Saul in Israel and David in Judah.

82 The text of Samuel-Kings displays a marked tendency to argue for David's legitimacy as king by downplaying or negating David's role in counter-Saulide activities (see esp. §5.4, below). The text contains two stories of David's respect for the anointed monarch Saul (1 Samuel 24, 26), provides its hero with an alibi for the Battle of Gilboa (1 Samuel 29–30; Baruch Halpern, *David's Secret Demons: Messiah, Murder, Traitor, King* [Grand Rapids, Mich.: Eerdmans, 2001], 23–24), distances David from the deaths of Ishbosheth and Abner (2 Samuel 3–4; James C. Vanderkam, "Davidic Complicity in the Deaths of Abner and Eshbaal: A Historical and Redactional Study," *JBL* 99 [1980]: 521–39; cf. Tomoo Ishida, "The Story of Abner's Murder: A Problem Posed by the Solomonic Apologist," in *ErIsr* 24 [ed. S. Aḥituv and B. A. Levine; Jerusalem: Israel Exploration Society, 1993], 109*–13*; Mazar, "David's Reign," 235–44, esp. 239–42; Jean-Claude Haelewyck, "L'assassinat d'Ishbaal [2 Samuel iv 1–12]," *VT* 47 [1997]: 145–53), and maintains David's relative innocence in the slaughter of Saul's few remaining heirs by the Gibeonites (2 Samuel 21; Arvid S. Kapelrud, "König David und die Söhne des Saul," *ZAW* 67 [1956]: 198–205). The picture of David the text presents is one of respect for the institution of the monarch, but this reverence would seem to be in direct contradiction to the underlying suggestion that David was less true to Saul than has been presented elsewhere in the text. Vanderkam has pointed to several events narrated in Samuel–Kings that betray a less admirable historical David than the text seems to indicate ("Davidic Complicity," 521–39): (a) David was the leader of a

sheth's move to Mahanaim is unhistorical, and judgments to the contrary proceed from the *a priori* assumption that later or ideologically founded documents cannot accurately convey historical data.

Similarly, David's flight to Mahanaim upon Absalom's ill-fated coup attempt seems to be a reasonable strategy, especially when considered as an analogue to Ishbosheth's flight across the Jordan. According to the text, David's exile in Mahanaim was supported by three individuals, all of whom were probably tribal or clan leaders: Shobi son of Nahash from Rabbah of the Ammonites; Machir son of Ammiel from Lo-debar; and Barzillai the Gileadite from Rogelim (2 Sam 17:27–29).[83] The three dignitaries are portrayed as being personally loyal to him in a patrimonial sense.[84]

---

band of outlaws, possibly in a vassal relationship with Israel's archenemy, the Philistines (see also Halpern, *David's Secret Demons*, 22–26); (b) David's political moves in the south suggest more than a lap-dog loyalty to Saul and his household (also Levenson and Halpern, "Political Import," 507–18); (c) there is the possibility that David became king over Judah in Hebron before Saul's death, setting himself directly against Saul (see n. 81); and (d) David continually denounces those who have killed Saul and those related to him in an attempt to divert the listener's suspicion. In general, Vanderkam argues, the historian has attempted to whitewash these points, but his silence speaks volumes, and his protestations fall on unsympathetic ears. Given these rifts in the DtrH's presentation of David, it seems much more consistent to picture David as a rival king in Hebron whose biography has been somewhat refined by later interpreters than as the committed vassal of the king to the north (see also David N. Freedman, "Early Israelite History in the Light of Early Israelite Poetry," in *Unity and Diversity: Essays in the History, Literature, and Religion of the Ancient Near East* [ed. Hans Goedicke and J. J. M. Roberts; Baltimore: The Johns Hopkins University Press, 1975], 16).

83 Scholars differ on how to interpret the goodwill towards David on the part of these noteworthy individuals. Especially surprising is the notice that Machir, who had formerly been the guardian of Mephibosheth, has now become aligned with David. As McCarter notes, it would be easy for the modern historian to surmise that these leaders were acting more out of fear of an army in their backyard than out of any sense of personal loyalty to David (McCarter, *II Samuel*, 395).

84 The fact that the notables of Gilead (Barzillai) and Manasseh (Machir) remain loyal to the ousted David, rather than to the bureaucratic kingship Absalom assumed, suggests exactly the opposite of what Martin A. Cohen has argued—namely, that Absalom's core value facilitating the rebellion was a stated traditionalism based on the premonarchical elements of family ties and that David's non-traditional bureaucracy was the target of the rebellion ("The Rebellions During the Reign of David: An Inquiry into Social Dynamics in Ancient Israel," in *Studies in Jewish Bibliography, History and Literature in Honor of I. Edward Kiev* [ed. Charles Berlin; New York: KTAV, 1971], 91–112). Instead, we see here that David, who depended upon the loyalty of his soldiers and supporters, was probably a throwback to an earlier day when the patrimonial household was the primary social arrangement (e.g., Stager "Archaeology of the Family," 18–23; Max Weber, *Economy and Society: An Outline of Interpretive Sociology* [ed. Guenther Roth and Claus Wittich; 2 vols.; Berkeley and Los Angeles: University of California Press, 1978], 2:1006–69).

If we can, in fact, read these two episodes as authentic portrayals of history—at least in their broad strokes[85]—the events centered on Ishbosheth's and David's respective journeys to Transjordan serve to elucidate the political status of the Israelite tribes inhabiting that territory: clearly not Judahite, neither do they seem to belong to a northern Israelite confederation. When Israel and Judah retracted their support from David, the Transjordanian tribes seem to have supported him, not out of a bureaucratically monolithic devotion to the institution of Israel's kingship, but out of fealty to the person of the king. It is no wonder, then, that Transjordan may have served as a political haven for exiles from the Cisjordan: the inhabitants of the ethnically Israelite Transjordan were able to support whomever they pleased, precisely because they were not inherently politically aligned with either Judah or Israel. It seems likely that Transjordan existed as a separate political entity.

To summarize, it is reasonable to believe that Mahanaim was largely already gaining recognition as a favorable location for exiled Israelite and Judahite monarchs during the period of the early monarchy,[86] even if David's exile in Transjordan occurred only in the literary emplotment of historical memory and not historically per se. For Abner and Ishbosheth, the decision to move to Mahanaim was most likely based on the city's strong fortifications (over against a lowland valley site like Sukkoth) and its relative proximity to the Cisjordanian arena (as opposed to a city further north in Cisjordan), although presumably, the fact that the area had a material culture and ethnic affiliations similar to those of the Cisjordanian monarchies figured into the decision as well. Over time—and with the collectively remembered exiles of two Cisjordanian kings at the city—Mahanaim's reputation would have become more and more favorable towards those seeking asylum. The biblical historiographic narratives, along with the theory of locales' particularization through history proposed in §1.4, provide some indication of *why* and *how* the Israelite portion of northern Transjordan came to symbolize safe refuge in the Cisjordanian worldview. Although this worldview was preserved in the writings detailing the early monarchy, it seems to have faded very quickly. What events

85 Cf., though, the recent redactionally-based challenges to the historicity of David's exile in Transjordan put forth by Reinhard G. Kratz, *The Composition of the Narrative Books of the Old Testament* (Trans. John Bowden; London: T&T Clark, 2005), 175–76; Erik Aurelius, "David's Unschuld: Die Hofgeschichte und Psalm 7," in *Gott und Mensch im Dialog: Festschrift für Otto Kaiser zum 80. Geburtstag* (ed. Markus Witte; BZAW 345; 2 vols.; Berlin: de Gruyter, 2004), 1:391–412; and Alexander A. Fischer, "Flucht und Heimkehr Davids als integraler Rahmen der Abschalomerzählung," in *Ideales Königtum: Studien zu David und Salomo* (ed. Rüdiger Lux; ABG 16; Leipzig: Evangelische Verlagsanstalt, 2005), 43–69. For further discussion, see below, §3.4.4 and §5.3.3.

86 E.g., Noth, "Land Gilead," 82–83.

can be traced out that might have brought about the loss of the connotation of refuge in Transjordan?

The city of Mahanaim garnered increased centrality in the Solomonic kingdom's power structure, becoming a major center of authority (1 Kgs 4:14). Moreover, after Solomon's death and the resultant schism of the kingdom, Jeroboam "went out" from his newly fortified city of Shechem, and "built Penuel" (ויצא משם ויבן את־פנואל; 1 Kgs 12:25).[87] While the significance of this notice is debated,[88] at the very least it suggests that the area surrounding Penuel and Mahanaim persisted as a recognized place of Cisjordanian influence until the destruction of Mahanaim and Penuel at the hands of Shishak in the late 10th cent.[89] This depredation of the Israelite

87 The latter phrase is commonly taken to mean that Jeroboam *rebuilt* or *fortified* Penuel.

88 Several scholars have argued that Jeroboam moved his capital to the east once it had become clear that Shishak would invade his kingdom (e.g., Aharoni, *Land of the Bible*, 327; Mazar, "Campaign," 62–63), but the phrase "and he went out from there" hardly indicates that Jeroboam made Penuel his new capital. As Mordechai Cogan reminds the reader, "[t]ranslating *wayyēṣēʾ* as 'he left' (NAB) or 'moved out' (NJPSV) implies that Jeroboam transferred his residence to Transjordan, but there is nothing to suggest that Penuel, far removed from the Israelite heartland, became his capital" (*I Kings: A New Translation with Introduction and Commentary* [AB 10; New York: Doubleday, 2000], 357–58). Rather, the fortification of Penuel may have been an attempt to maintain a strong presence in the Transjordan, whose inhabitants may have remained sympathetic to the Davidic dynasty (ibid., 364). Since it is clear from a reconstruction of Shishak's itinerary during his campaign that the major cities of the northern kingdom were targeted, Mazar suggests that "the rich areas of the Kingdom of Israel were the main object of the expedition...perhaps because after seizing power Jeroboam refused to admit the suzerainty of the Pharaoh, contrary to what he had consented during his revolt and the days he had spent in Egypt" ("Campaign," 62–63). While it may indeed be the case that Jeroboam had taken refuge in Penuel—assuming with Mazar that the main goal of Shishak's expedition was punitive—it need not be the case that Jeroboam had rebuilt Penuel to house the central Israelite government. Although he accepts the theory that Jeroboam fled to Penuel during Shishak's campaign, Noth has argued that Jeroboam rebuilt the city in the face of an earlier resurgent Philistine threat ("Land Gilead," 88–89). There would not have been enough time to refortify the city once it was realized that fortification was needed for the oncoming Egyptian expedition, and the availability of labor for building projects would have been scarce during times of battle. Accordingly, the fortification may have already been well underway, or even complete, by the time that Shishak entered Palestine.

89 Noth argued: "Daß Jeroboam nun nicht wie Esbaal und David Mahanaim als Zufluchtsort wählte, sondern Pnuel, mag damit zusammenhängen, daß Mahanaim den Soldaten Schoschenks in die Hände gefallen war, Pnuel dagegen anscheinend nicht" ("Land Gilead," 89). A significant argument can be marshaled against this statement. Noth's suggestion does not take into account the order of the Shishak list, as Aharoni and Mazar have reconstructed it (Aharoni, *Land of the Bible*, 325; Mazar, "Campaign," 57–66). The order of the list remained difficult until Mazar's proposal that the first four lines should be read in *boustrophedon* order, with the second and fourth lines being read backwards (that is, *into the backs* of the hieroglyphs, contrary to normal Egyptian practice; Aharoni, *Land of the Bible*, 325). The cities listed in the fifth line of the inscription had been omitted from the second line. According to the order given by Mazar, this omission apparently occurred in two groups, although Mazar does not explicitly acknowledge this. Mazar inserts numbers 56–53 (Adamah–Penuel) before number 22 (Mahanaim), and 59–65 (Tirzah–*Paʿ Emeq* [= the Valley?]) *after* 18 (Hapharaim), the last city of the Transjordanian section of the list ("Campaign," 60).

Transjordan could potentially have affected the Cisjordanian perception of that area, forcing a reevaluation of the inherited perception and symbolism of Transjordan as a *safe haven*. The realization that Transjordan was not as safe as the dominant Cisjordanian worldview (represented by the Davidic Court History) would have been further compounded by the flight of Jeroboam to Egypt (1 Kgs 11:40). As more "evidence" mounted in opposition to the formerly dominant view that Transjordan was an effective place of refuge, the habitual tendency of Cisjordanian Israelites to perceive the area as such would have diminished, forcing the Israelite and Judahite authors to come to grips with the "true" theological importance of the Transjordanian sojourn: spiritual transformation.

This proposed order seems difficult, however, if only because the omission occurred in two separate places in the text. Aharoni's proposed order (*Land of the Bible*, 325) seems superior to me, because it assumes an omission *en masse* of 64–60 (only one of which, 64, is legible), along with 59–53 (Tirzah–Penuel). This order places the conquest of Tirzah *before* the Transjordanian component of the campaign, a more logical position, both geographically and historically. We can thereby reconstruct the route from the highlands into the valley that Shishak's force took as being through the *W. Farᶜah* (see, e.g., Aharoni, *Land of the Bible*, 324 map 24; contra Mazar, "Campaign," 58, map). Topologically, it makes little sense for Shishak's army to descend from the central highlands in the area of Gibeon into the Valley—commencing the Transjordanian thrust of the campaign—only to march back into the hill country to attack Tirzah (59) and then to return again to the Valley in order to press the cities Rehob (17) and Beth-shean (16). Not only would the severe relief have been detrimental to the strength of an army, but also the road system, as David A. Dorsey has reconstructed it for the area between the central highlands and the Jordan Valley around Adam, would not have been conducive to such a strategy (*The Roads and Highways of Ancient Israel* [Baltimore: The Johns Hopkins University Press, 1991], esp. 163–80). The route proposed by Mazar crosses an area of the eastern escarpment of the Central Hill country where the lateral valleys would have cut perpendicularly to the direction of Shishak's travel, exaggerating the already tiresome relief and frustrating any cross-country travel. Far more probable geographically is Aharoni's reconstruction of events: having taken the major cities of the highlands, Shishak then descended the *W. Farᶜah* (the location of the main road between Tirzah and Adam—the site of a major ford; Dorsey, *Roads and Highways*, 174; see also Aharoni, *Land of the Bible*, 327 for the site of the ford), pressed the Transjordan, then continued his attack in the Jordan Valley. This route proves more reasonable both geographically and historically. If it were indeed the case that Jeroboam had taken refuge in Penuel (e.g., Aharoni, *Land of the Bible*, 327; Noth, "Land Gilead," 88–89), then it would make more sense for Shishak to have first besieged Tirzah, the capital of Israel at the time, and having found Jeroboam not there, then to have proceeded to the eastern side of the river. Aharoni's proposed order, however, still leaves out number 65 (*PaᶜEmeq* = the Valley?), which he takes as the Valley of Beth-shean, and inserts between numbers 18 (Hapharaim, an otherwise unknown city) and 17 (Rehob). One wonders if this is entirely reasonable because, like the suggestion of Mazar, it seems to demand a twofold omission from line 2. Unfortunately, I have no better suggestion for its position in the list.

2.4. Surveying the Terrain Ahead

In the remaining chapters of this study, I attempt to establish an outline of the process whereby both Israelite history and its emplotted presentation in Israelite historiographic literature affect the meaning ascribed to the Transjordanian landscape. The main question on which I will focus is this: when was it that the development of the Transjordanian Motif occurred? A bevy of subsidiary questions follows: What were the steps involved in the formation of the Cisjordanian conception of Transjordan? What latent meanings of that landscape were assumed at each traceable node of this development, and can these nodes be linked to each of the distinct types of Transjordanian vision laid out here? Were the texts in which the Transjordanian Motif operates juxtaposed to one another by Dtr, or had the significant theological work already been done by the time of Dtr? (In short, what was the role of the DtrH's primary compiler in the formulation of the Cisjordanian conception of Israelite Transjordan that pervades the DtrH?) Alternatively, did the authors and editors of the DtrH intentionally establish the journey to Transjordan as a meaningful literary motif in order to account for the diversity of sources that had been inherited and for the contingencies of history (as suggested above in §1.4), or is the motif merely an accident of tradition and redaction history?

The division of the biblical text into its fundamental sources is not a new endeavor. Chapter 3 attempts to provide a schematic overview of the various models of the formation of the DtrH and to carve out theoretical space for the existence of a pre-Deuteronomistic redaction produced by a member or members of the prophetic guild in northern Israel during the late-9th or early- to mid-8th centuries BCE. While I accept that redactional strata have, in fact, changed the shape of the DtrH, particularly in its later editions, this study is primarily concerned with the constituent source texts from which the DtrH—and particularly, the book of Samuel—was compiled. Therefore, ch. 4 continues the methodological and theoretical investigation of the DtrH's production, taking into account newer research on ancient Near Eastern scribal culture and the possible context(s) in which the component documents of the DtrH were produced, as well as what those documents can tell us both about Israel's and Judah's respective histories and their own formative contexts. In chs. 5–7, I examine the large constituent documentary sources of Samuel. Since the time of L. Rost, the "Succession Narrative" (2 Samuel [2–9*]; 10–20*; 1 Kgs 1–2) has been regarded, until only recently, as a single document that—although its *Tendenz* and limits can be debated—nonetheless remained fairly consistent in its essentials.[90] Chapter 5 explores many of the issues associated with that document in an attempt to show that not only was it a composite document, but also it was never a document entirely independent of its literary predecessor, the History of David's Rise.[91] In recent years, the History of David's Rise has also generally been discussed as a literary unit, as has the Ark Narrative. In chapter 6, I argue that the History of David's Rise is a composite document, comprising two long traditional collections detailing David's ascent to the Judahite throne, each with its own narrative logic and apologetic purpose. Although a few scholars have discussed the "Narrative of Saul's Rise" as such, scores of scholars have worked on the traditions of the early Israelite monarchy, and only the siglum used to designate that body of work (NSR) is new here (ch. 7). I present in this part of the larger study my own schematic synthesis of the original documents and redactional process(es) whereby they were combined to form the basic pre-Deuteronomistic text underlying the DtrH.

The widely synthetic project encompassed by this part of the study attempts to bridge the gaps between several sub-fields of research in the DtrH. Because of this breadth, none of the sections on the constituent documents and traditions can provide as much detailed discussion as a monograph fully dedicated to the subject. The present division's purpose is solely to delineate the basic contours of the original sources used in the composition of the DtrH and to show that the contingencies of the History's redaction influenced the way in which the Transjordanian Motif developed throughout the nascent biblical text's history. As a secondary component of this argument, it will become necessary not only to reevaluate those schemas that have been proposed to explain the composition history of Samuel, but to propose a new model of the evolution of that complex of material as well. This study thus proposes a developmental history of the process whereby the sedimented meanings of exile and incubation in Transjordan entered the Israelite—and later, the Jewish and Christian communities—as a productive motif that maintained its force in subsequent theological thought and literature.

90 Leonhard Rost, *The Succession to the Throne of David* (trans. Michael D. Rutter and David M. Gunn, with an introduction by Edward Ball; HTIBS 1; Sheffield: Almond, 1982); trans. of *Die Überlieferungen von der Thronnachfolge Davids* (BWANT 42; Stuttgart: Kohlhammer, 1926).

91 It is only recently that the Succession Narrative's independent existence has been called into question; see, e.g., Serge Frolov, "Succession Narrative: A 'Document' or a 'Phantom'?" *JBL* 121 (2002): 81–104; and Steven L. McKenzie, "The So-Called Succession Narrative in the Deuteronomistic History," in *Die sogenannte Thronfolgegeschichte Davids: Neue Einsichten und Anfragen* (ed. Albert de Pury and Thomas Römer; OBO 176; Fribourg: University Press; Göttingen: Vandenhoeck & Ruprecht, 2000), 123–35.

3. Vexed Texts: Sources of the Deuteronomistic History

3.1. The Question

In the preceding chapters, I have used the basic terminology of "the Deuteronomistic History" (DtrH) and "the Deuteronomistic Historian" (Dtr) without clarification or relation to the history of scholarship on that corpus, which pervades the background of this study. Dtr, as I have suggested, may be responsible for the ultimate juxtaposition of the tales of various journeys across the Jordan River, for a multiplicity of purposes, and I asked at the end of ch. 1 whether the juxtaposition of these various sources and the subsequent formulation of the Transjordanian Motif as I have described it were an intentional theological movement made by Dtr, or an accidental product of the very process by which the literary corpus was formed. If the Historian was in fact the primary compiler of the corpus Deuteronomy–Kings, then it is highly likely that the Transjordanian Motif was the intentional literary production of that theologically motivated individual. However, a reinvestigation of the composition and redaction history of the Deuteronomistic corpus calls into question the supposedly overarching nature of Dtr's involvement in the formation of that narrative body. In chs. 3–8, I argue that the Historian used a large body of early monarchic traditions that had already been assembled to a great extent before its incorporation into the DtrH. This narrative body included examples of both the deliverer-type vision of Transjordan (1 Sam 11:1–11,15) and the monarch-type thereof (e.g., 2 Sam 19:12–44). The prophet-type (e.g., Joshua 3–4; 2 Kings 2:1–18), however, was not represented in this pre-Deuteronomistic stratum of redaction.

If this model is correct, then the exact role that Dtr played in the reception, formulation, and augmentation of the Transjordanian Motif must be clarified and refined. For example, the inclusion of the deliverer-type vision in the postulated pre-Deuteronomistic text is not an assertion that any part of the book of Judges was connected to Samuel at any point before the formation of the larger DtrH. In juxtaposing these two narrative complexes, Dtr utilized an already extant structural system, augmenting it and adjusting it to fit within the larger narrative corpus. On the other hand, the Historian's inclusion of the Elijah-Elisha Cycle and the Joshua traditions displays that author's continued innovation underlying the Transjordanian Motif. Therefore, I argue in the remainder of this study that the

Transjordanian Motif can be attributed in part, but not solely, to the work of a Deuteronomistic compiler-author who had a singular theological aim, since that compiler had received the primary corpus of the Transjordanian Motif already in a rudimentary form.

This being the case, to whom—or at least, to what time—may we attribute the composition of the textual stratum in which the Transjordanian Motif came to its earliest expression? Can it be shown that the earlier compiler had intentionally formulated the Transjordanian Motif, or is the motif even at its earliest stage the product of a system and process of compilation that admitted little authorial ingenuity, at least in regard to the literary trope under discussion, and instead left the compiler with a limited set of possible textual strategies, forcing the accidental formation of the motif? The answers to these questions are not only dependent upon the reconstruction of the redactional work performed by the Deuteronomistic Historian(s), of which I provide a rough outline in this section, but far more importantly, they are affected by the early transmission history of the source(s) used by Dtr in that author's own reconstruction and formulation of the history of Israel. No matter the process by which the Transjordanian motif came to be—intentionally or not, compiled at one time from scraps of history and legend or the product of a slow accumulative aggregation of stories—we can presume that the post-exilic Israelite community received the DtrH as a relatively complete unity, a textbook of the triumphs and foibles of the Israelite people in their attainment and loss of the land promised by Yahweh to their ancestors.[1] As such, the communal theological reception of the document provided the returning Israelite community of the Persian period (along with all subsequent periods of the early Jewish and Christian communities) with an already formed understanding of its position in the land and the symbolism involved in the period of testing beyond the Jordan.[2]

---

1 That this document was "relatively complete" is an assertion that does not exclude the possibility of a layer of post-exilic redactional work; see recently, e.g., Thomas Römer; *The So-Called Deuteronomistic History: A Sociological, Historical, and Literary Introduction* (London: T&T Clark, 2005), 165–83; idem, "Entstehungsphasen des 'deuteronomistischen Geschichtswerkes," in *Die deuteronomistischen Geschichtswerke: Redaktions- und religionsgeschichtliche Perspektiven zur "Deuteronomismus"-Diskussion in Tora und Vorderen Propheten* (ed. Markus Witte et al.; BZAW 365; Berlin: de Gruyter, 2006), 45–70; and Raymond F. Person, *The Deuteronomic School: History, Social Setting, and Literature* (SBLStBL 2; Atlanta: SBL, 2002). Römer's post-exilic reworking is perhaps a bit broader than I would have suggested, but the schema is conceivable; cf. Serge Frolov, "Evil-Merodach and the Deuteronomist: The Sociohistorical Setting of Dtr in the Light of 2 Kgs 25,27–30," *Bib* 88 (2007): 174–90.

2 I suggest that two cases in particular attest to the continued productivity (and therefore normativity) of the Transjordanian Motif within the exilic community. First, the eastward escape of Zedekiah and his men toward the Arabah (2 Kgs 25:4–7 [=Jer 52:7–11])—while

3.2. Early Models of the Redaction of the Deuteronomistic History as a Whole

3.2.1. Noth, Jepsen, and Their Immediate Respondents

3.2.1.1. Noth's Überlieferungsgeschichtliche Studien

Any contemporary discussion of the formation of the Deuteronomistic History cannot but begin with the work of M. Noth, which appeared originally in 1943.[3] Although he was not the first to recognize the literary

perhaps historically performed merely as a purely pragmatic attempt at escape, much like David's flight to Mahanaim in 2 Samuel 15–16—can only be fully understood symbolically within the unified literary context of the Transjordanian Motif as a stymied attempt at transformative exile, occasioned by a movement to Transjordan and resulting in renewed power and legitimacy within Israelite Realpolitik. More obviously, the continued unified productivity of the motif is played upon in Deutero-Isaiah's comparison of exiled Israel's return to the land to its own exodus from Egypt and, concomitantly, its entry into Canaan several centuries before (e.g., Isa 43:2,16–19; 48:20–21; 50:2; 51:9–11; 52:3–4; etc.; cf. Joshua 3–4). For the continued symbolic significance of passage through the Jordan in the New Testament, see Rachel S. Havrelock, "The Jordan River: Crossing a Biblical Boundary" (Ph.D. diss.; University of California, Berkeley, 2004); and Jeremy M. Hutton, "Topography, Biblical Traditions, and Reflections on John's Baptism of Jesus," in *Proceedings of the Princeton-Prague Symposium on the Historical Jesus* (ed. J. H. Charlesworth; Grand Rapids, Mich.: Eerdmans, forthcoming).

3 Martin Noth, *The Deuteronomistic History* (trans. J. A. Clines et al.; JSOTSup 15; Sheffield: JSOT Press, 1981; repr., Sheffield: Sheffield Academic Press, 2001); trans. of *Überlieferungsgeschichtliche Studien* (2d ed.; Tübingen: Niemeyer, 1957), 1–110. Page numbers given refer to the 2001 English edition, hereafter abbreviated *DH*. Comprehensive discussions of Noth's initial scholarship on the DtrH and of the subsequent development of that scholarship can be found in Iain Provan, *Hezekiah and the Books of Kings: A Contribution to the Debate about the Composition of the Deuteronomistic History* (BZAW 172; Berlin: de Gruyter, 1988), 1–31; Mark A. O'Brien, *The Deuteronomistic History Hypothesis: A Reassessment* (OBO 92; Fribourg: University Press; Göttingen: Vandenhoeck & Ruprecht, 1989), 3–23; Antony F. Campbell, "Martin Noth and the Deuteronomistic History," in *The History of Israel's Traditions: The Heritage of Martin Noth* (ed. S. L. McKenzie and M. P. Graham; JSOTSup 182; Sheffield: Sheffield Academic Press, 1994), 31–62; Erik Eynikel, *The Reform of King Josiah and the Composition of the Deuteronomistic History* (OTS 33; Leiden: Brill, 1996), 7–31; Thomas Römer and Albert de Pury, "Deuteronomistic Historiography (DH): History of Research and Debated Issues," in *Israel Constructs Its Identity: Deuteronomistic Historiography in Recent Research* (ed. A. de Pury, T. Römer, and J.-D. Macchi; JSOTSup 306; Sheffield: Sheffield Academic Press, 2000), 24–141; trans. of "L'histriographie deutéronomiste (HD): Histoire de la recherche et enjeux du débat," in *Israël construit son histoire: L'historiographie deutéronomiste à la lumière des recherches récentes* (ed. A. de Pury, T. Römer, and J.-D. Macchi; *MdB* 34; Geneva: Labor et Fides, 1996), 9–120; Gary N. Knoppers, "Introduction," in *Reconsidering Israel and Judah: Recent Studies on the Deuteronomistic History* (ed. G. N. Knoppers and J. G. McConville; SBTS 8; Winona Lake, Ind.: Eisenbrauns, 2000), 1–18; and Römer, *So-Called Deuteronomistic History*, 13–43. My very basic summary of research on the DtrH is heavily indebted to these studies. For a much more comprehensive overview of almost six decades' worth of material than can be given here, the reader is referred to these studies, as well as to other reviews of the literature: e.g.,

coherence of the books of the former prophets, Noth was the first to make a systematic study of the corpus Deuteronomy–2 Kings and to propose an overarching picture of the process of its compilation and subsequent transmission.[4] Earlier endeavors had sought to trace the extension of the Pentateuchal sources (JEDP) past Deuteronomy into Joshua (and therefore were receptive to the notion of a Hexateuch)[5] and, in some models, even as far as 1–2 Kings.[6] Noth, however, postulated a single creative and produc-

---

Norman H. Snaith, "The Historical Books," in *The Old Testament and Modern Study: A Generation of Discovery and Research* (ed. H. H. Rowley; Oxford: Clarendon, 1951), 84–114; Ernst Jenni, "Zwei Jahrzehnte Forschung an den Büchern Josua bis Könige," *TRu* 27 (1961): 1–32, 97–146; Arnold Nicolaas Radjawane, "Das deuteronomistische Geschichtswerk: Ein Forschungsbericht," *TRu* 38 (1974): 177–216; J. R. Porter, "Old Testament Historiography," in *Tradition and Interpretation: Essays by Members of the Society for Old Testament Study* (ed. G. W. Anderson; Oxford: Clarendon, 1979), 125–62; Norbert Lohfink, "Zur neueren Diskussion über 2 Kön 22–23," in *Das Deuteronomium: Entstehung, Gestalt und Botschaft* (ed. Norbert Lohfink; BETL 68; Leuven: University Press and Peeters, 1985), 24–48, esp. 34 n. 53; Helga Weippert, "Das deuteronomistische Geschichtswerk: Sein Ziel und Ende in der neueren Forschung," *TRu* 50 (1985): 213–49; Horst Dietrich Preuß, "Zum deuteronomistischen Geschichtswerk," *TRu* 58 (1993): 229–64, 341–95; Léo Laberge, "Le deutéronomiste," in *"De bien des maniéres": La recherche biblique aux abords du XXIe siècle* (ed. Michel Gourgues and Léo Laberge; LD 163; Paris: Cerf; Montreal: Fides, 1995), 47–77; Douglas A. Knight, "Deuteronomy and the Deuteronomists," in *Old Testament Interpretation: Past, Present, and Future: Essays in Honor of Gene M. Tucker* (ed. James Luther Mays, David L. Petersen, and Kent Harold Richards; Nashville: Abingdon, 1995), 61–79; Timo Veijola, "Deuteronomismusforschung zwischen Tradition und Innovation," parts 1–3, *TRu* 67 (2002): 273–327, 391–424; 68 (2003): 1–44; Michael Avioz, "The Book of Kings in Recent Research," parts 1–2, *CurBR* 4 (2005): 11–55; 5 (2006): 11–57; Reinhard G. Kratz, *The Composition of the Narrative Books of the Old Testament* (trans. John Bowden; London: T&T Clark, 2005), 153–221; trans. of *Die Komposition der erzählenden Bücher des Alten Testaments* (Göttingen: Vandenhoeck & Ruprecht, 2000), 155–225.

4 See Noth (*DH*, 17–26) and literature cited therein for his acknowledged predecessors in the endeavor.

5 J. Wellhausen, *Die Composition des Hexateuchs und der historischen Bücher des Alten Testaments* (4th ed.; Berlin: de Gruyter, 1963; = repr. of 3d ed.; 1895); originally published as vol. 2 of idem, *Skizzen und Vorarbeiten* (6 vols.; Berlin: Reimer, 1885); idem, *Prolegomena to the History of Israel* (trans. J. S. Black and Allan Menzies, with a preface by W. Robertson Smith; 1885; repr., with a foreword by Douglas A. Knight, Atlanta: Scholars, 1994); trans. of *Prolegomena zur Geschichte Israels* (Berlin: Reimer, 1883); S. R. Driver, *An Introduction to the Literature of the Old Testament* (1897; repr., Cleveland: Meridian, 1967); Gerhard von Rad, *Das formgeschichtliche Problem des Hexateuchs* (BWANT 78; Stuttgart: Kohlhammer, 1938); Theodore H. Robinson, *The Old Testament: A Conspectus* (London: Duckworth, 1953), 36; Georg Fohrer, *Introduction to the Old Testament* (trans. David E. Green; Nashville: Abingdon, 1968); trans. of *Einleitung in das Alte Testament* (10th ed.; Heidelberg: Quelle & Meyer, 1965); Otto Eissfeldt, "Deuteronomium und Hexateuch," *Mitteilungen des Instituts für Orientforschung* 12 (1966): 17–39.

6 Karl Budde, *Die Bücher Richter und Samuel, ihre Quellen und ihr Aufbau* (Giessen: Ricker, 1890); Carl Heinrich Cornill, *Einleitung in das Alte Testament* (GTW 2/1; Freiburg: Mohr Siebeck, 1891); Immanuel Benzinger, *Jahvist und Elohist in den Königsbüchern* (BWANT 27; Berlin: Kohlhammer, 1921); Ernst Sellin, *Introduction to the Old Testament* (trans. W. Montgomery; London: Hodder & Stoughton, 1923); trans. of *Einleitung in das Alte Testament* (ETB 2; Leipzig: Quelle & Meyer, 1910); R. Smend (Sr.), "J E in den

tive author (rather than simply a redactor and compiler) whom he called Dtr, living in Palestine during the Babylonian Exile and writing with a distinctive and easily recognized style. This author gathered records, legends, and various other sources for Israelite history and compiled them into a single, coherent, and theologized history of Israel's occupation and loss of the land.[7] Moreover, the historian intentionally structured this document, adding a few major speeches or summarizations during climactic moments of communal transition (Joshua 1; 12; 23; Judg 2:11–23; 1 Samuel 12; 1 Kings 8:14–53; 2 Kgs 17:7–23)[8] in order to depict the history of Israel's failure and the causes of the community's ultimate loss of the land. Taking the core of the book of Deuteronomy (4:44–30:20*) as its model of the godly life[9]—a document that Noth identified with that found by Hilkiah in the temple (2 Kgs 22:8–10)[10]—Dtr evaluated the meaning of the history of corporate Israel (i.e., including Judah), particularly its suffering at the hands of Assyria and Babylon. According to Noth, the goal of this theologized history was to provide an accounting of the transgressions that had led to the exile, an exposition of the meaning of a historical calamity that served as proof of the failure of the monarchy. Noth's model now serves as the benchmark from which scholarship on the DtrH proceeds.[11]

---

geschichtlichen Büchern des AT," *ZAW* 39 (1921): 181–217; Gustav Hölscher, "Das Buch der Könige, seine Quellen und seine Redaktion," in *ΕΥΧΑΡΙΣΤΗΡΙΟΝ: Studien zur Religion und Literatur des Alten und Neuen Testaments* (ed. Hans Schmidt; FRLANT 36; Göttingen: Vandenhoeck & Ruprecht, 1923), 1:158–213; idem, *Geschichtsschreibung in Israel: Untersuchungen zum Jahvisten und Elohisten* (SHVL 50; Lund: Gleerup, 1952); cf. Otto Eissfeldt, *The Old Testament: An Introduction* (trans. Peter R. Ackroyd; New York: Harper & Row, 1965), 242–301, esp. 244–48, 271–80; trans. of *Einleitung in das Alte Testament* (3d ed.; NTG; Tübingen: Mohr Siebeck, 1934); idem, *Geschichtsschreibung im Alten Testament: Ein kritischer Bericht über die neueste Literatur dazu* (Berlin: Evangelische Verlagsanstalt, 1948); Hannelis Schulte, *Die Entstehung der Geschichtsschreibung im Alten Israel* (BZAW 128; Berlin: de Gruyter, 1972), 216–18; for a summary of the work of Hölscher, Eissfeldt, and von Rad, see Radajawane, "Deuteronomistische Geschichtswerk," 192–206.

7 Noth, *DH*, 17–27.

8 For the discussion, see ibid., 18–20; and Campbell, "Martin Noth," 32.

9 Noth, *DH*, 31–33.

10 Ibid., 116 n. 1; see Norbert Lohfink, "Kerygmata des Deuteronomistischen Geschichtswerks," in *Die Botschaft und die Boten: Festschrift für Hans Walter Wolff* (ed. Jörg Jeremias and Lothar Perlitt; Neukirchen-Vluyn: Neukirchener Verlag, 1981), 87–100.

11 Although the hypothesis initially garnered criticism from some quarters (e.g., Otto Eissfeldt, *Geschichtsschreibung*; idem, "Die Geschichtswerke im Alten Testament," *TLZ* 72 [1947]: 71–76), it was quickly picked up by many commentators and is now generally assumed to be the dominant model from which all other models are derived. See, e.g., Hans Joachim Krause, "Gesetz und Geschichte: Zum Geschichtsbild des Deuteronomisten," *EvT* 11 (1951–52): 415–28; Enno Janssen, *Juda in der Exilszeit: Ein Beitrag zur Frage nach der Entstehung des Judentums* (FRLANT 69; Göttingen: Vandenhoeck & Ruprecht, 1956); Johannes Fichtner, *Das erste Buch von den Königen* (BAT 12/1; Stuttgart: Calwer Verlag, 1964), 15–31, esp. 25–26; Peter R. Ackroyd, *Exile and Restoration: A Study of Hebrew Thought of the*

3.2.1.2. Jepsen's Quellen des Königsbuches

Working independently from Noth in the late 1930's, A. Jepsen arrived at a schema of Deuteronomistic redaction that most contemporary scholars recognize to have been fundamentally supportive of Noth's hypothesis.[12] One can only imagine the frustration of Jepsen, whose work—although finished nearly contemporaneously with that of Noth—was delayed in publication by the Second World War, necessitating at least slight revision to take what now appears as only minimal account of Noth's thesis.[13] While Noth's piece garnered serious and thoughtful responses already by the late 1940's (see below) and has come to be seen therefore as the first, primary, or paradigmatic statement of the theory of the DtrH,[14] Jepsen's

---

Sixth Century B.C. (Philadelphia: Westminster, 1968), 62–83; Hans Jochen Boecker, *Die Beurteilung der Anfänge des Königtums in den deuteronomistischen Abschnitten des I. Samuelbuches: Ein Beitrag zum Problem des 'deuteronomistischen Geschichtswerks'* (WMANT 31; Neukirchen-Vluyn; Neukirchener Verlag, 1969); Terence E. Fretheim, *Deuteronomic History* (IntBT; Nashville: Abingdon, 1983); Thomas Römer, ed., *The Future of the Deuteronomistic History* (BETL 147; Leuven: University Press; Leuven: Peeters, 2000). Several studies have attempted to support the fundamental accuracy of Noth's singular Dtr: Moshe Weinfeld analyzed broadly the themes and phraseology employed by the Deuteronomistic circles, but although he allowed for the "distinct character" of each "major branch" of "deuteronomistic composition… i.e., Deuteronomy, Dtr, and the Jeremian prose sermons," did not attempt to distinguish their particularities, preferring instead to allow that "they exhibit signs of linguistic and ideological independence" (*Deuteronomy and the Deuteronomic School* [Oxford: Clarendon Press, 1972], esp. 8–9); see also idem, "The Emergence of the Deuteronomic Movement: The Historical Antecedents," in *Das Deuteronomium: Entstehung, Gestalt und Botschaft* (ed. Norbert Lohfink; BETL 68; Leuven: University Press and Peeters, 1985), 76–98. Hans-Detlef Hoffmann argued that the minor stylistic and thematic tensions in Deuteronomistic passages that others had previously recognized as signs of redactional work (see below) can only be read as stylistic variation on the part of one author (*Reform und Reformen: Untersuchungen zu einem Grundthema der deuteronomistischen Geschichtsschreibung* [ATANT 66; Zurich: Theologischer Verlag, 1980], esp. 316–18). For similar movements toward an undifferentiated Deuteronomistic layer, see also John Van Seters, "Histories and Historians of the Ancient Near East: The Israelites," *Or* 50 (1981): 137–85; idem, *In Search of History: Historiography in the Ancient World and the Origins of Biblical History* (New Haven: Yale University Press, 1983; repr. Winona Lake, Ind.: Eisenbrauns, 1997); Burke O. Long, *1 Kings: With an Introduction to Historical Literature* (FOTL 9; Grand Rapids, Mich.: Eerdmans, 1984), 14–21; Rainer Albertz, "Die Intentionen und Träger des deuteronomistischen Geschichtswerks," in *Schöpfung und Befreiung: Für Claus Westermann zum 80. Geburtstag* (ed. Rainer Albertz, Friedemann W. Golka, and Jürgen Kegler; Stuttgart: Calwer Verlag, 1989), 37–53.

12 Alfred Jepsen, *Die Quellen des Königsbuches* (Halle: Niemeyer, 1953).

13 Jepsen, *Quellen*, 100–101.

14 See, e.g., the assessment of O'Brien that Noth's work "received *initial support* in the independent work of Ivan Engnell in Scandanavia, and Alfred Jepsen in Germany" (O'Brien, *DHH*, 3; my emphasis). Engnell's work on the Deuteronomistic History is not, in my experience, widely discussed in the literature (Ivan Engnell, *Gamla testamentet: En traditionshistorisk inledning* [Stockholm: Svenska Kyrkans Diakonistyrelses Bokförlag, 1945]; idem, "The Pentateuch," in idem, *A Rigid Scrutiny: Critical Essays on the Old Testament* [trans. John T. Willis with Helmer Ringgren; Nashville: Vanderbilt University

thesis, published only in 1953, stands on its own when properly contextualized as a nuanced and appropriately complicated statement of the problem, even if its fundamental methodology remains problematic.

Through a detailed form-critical study of the entire book of Kings, Jepsen isolated several source documents and three significant layers of redaction that united them. The first of these redactional strata (R^{I}) was composed early in the exilic period (ca. 580), comprised two different sources (a Synchronic Chronicle [S], which synchronized the reigns of the Israelite and Judean kings until the reign of Hezekiah, and an annalistic source [A]), which the author-redactor wove together artfully with his own composition, and was focused on the Jerusalem temple. Hence, Jepsen assigned a Priestly context to this redaction and suggested that those passages composed by the redactor sprang both from historical traditions preserved among the members of the Temple Priesthood and from personal experience.[15] On the other hand, the second major layer of redaction (R^{II}) was composed ca. 550 in a Palestinian context associated with both prophetic *nabi*'s and wisdom practitioners.[16] The author-redactor of this stratum utilized several various prophetic traditions (his siglum N, not to be recognized as a single source per se) that were preserved among prophetic circles, adding his own notations and framing elements.[17] The third stratum (R^{III}) was a fairly unobtrusive touch-up and argued for the maintenance of Levitical authority within post-exilic (end of the 6th cent.) Judean society.[18]

Before note can be made of the important contributions Jepsen made to early study of the DtrH, it must be admitted that at least three significant

---

Press, 1969], 50–67 esp. 62; published in Great Britain as *Critical Essays on the Old Testament* [London: SPCK, 1970]). Cf., though, Römer and de Pury, who provide a short synopsis of Engnell's contribution ("Deuteronomistic Historiography," 55). Richard Nelson further minimizes Jepsen's contribution with his (specious) claim that Jepsen's thesis "has not found much of a following" other than in a few articles by Gustavo Baena (Richard D. Nelson, *The Double Redaction of the Deuteronomistic History* [JSOTSup 18; Sheffield: JSOT Press, 1981], 20 and 134 n. 39, citing Gustavo Baena, "El vocabulario de II Reyes 17, 7–23. 35–39," *EstBib* 32 [1973]: 357–84; idem, "Carácter literario de 2 Reyes 17, 7–23," *EstBib* 33 [1974]: 5–29; and idem, "Carácter literario de II Reyes 17, 13. 35–39," *EstBib* 33 [1974]: 157–79; see also Christoph Levin, *Der Sturz der Königin Atalja: Ein Kapitel zur Geschichte Judas im 9. Jahrhundert v. Chr.* [SBS 105; Stuttgart: Verlag Katholisches Bibelwerk, 1982]).

15 Jepsen, *Quellen*, 41–76.

16 Jepsen's claim (ibid., 94–100) that R^{II} was working in a Palestinian (and specifically Benjaminite) context dovetailed with Noth's placement of Dtr as well; cf., however, the assessment that the author/editor was working in Babylon: e.g., J. A. Soggin, "Der Entstehungsort des Deuteronomistischen Geschichtswerkes: Ein Beitrag zur Geschichte desselben," *TLZ* 100 (1975): 3–8; but cf. Ackroyd, *Exile and Restoration*, 65–68.

17 Jepsen, *Quellen*, 76–101.

18 Ibid., 102–5.

problems dog the thesis. First, Nelson correctly offered the criticism that Jepsen's schema seems to be predicated on the "common and erroneous opinion that the prophetic and cultic sides of Israel's life were in constant, irreconcilable conflict."[19] Jepsen provides no argument why the "prophetic" and "priestly" concerns require separation from one another or why they necessarily stand as complete blocks. Second, Jepsen's methodology assumes that all verses displaying traits of a given *Gattung* may be uniformly assigned to the same redactor without further examination. This is a particularly weak basis on which to undertake a study of this magnitude. In my view, there is nothing that requires all notices concerning the Temple, for example, to have been composed by the same author or preserved in a single environment. Finally, one cannot help but notice that R^{II}, decidedly the most important stratum in Jepsen's schema, is the most theologically variegated and, in fact, seems most likely to be a catchall category for those verses that did not fit easily with any of the other *Gattungen* assigned to different redactors or sources. Although the conclusion that R^{II} was composed in a context influenced by both prophets and sages is hardly impossible, the question may nonetheless be asked what exactly demands that this juxtaposition be the work of a single redactor aligning 1 Kgs 3:16–27 or 12:3b–14 (both assigned to N) with 11:29–31,33–38abα (an admixture of N and R^{II}).[20] (A constituent problem, but wholly beside the point here, is the impropriety of assigning 1 Kgs 3:16–27 or 12:3b–14 to "wisdom" influence, presumably—and merely—on the basis of the presence of counselors or clarity of thought in the narrative[21]). The unity of R^{II} is far from proven.

Regardless of the methodological shortcomings of Jepsen's work, he did make several important insights concerning the DtrH, two of which are especially salient in the current discussion. Both observations complement and serve to elaborate those of Noth. First, Jepsen recognized the continuous filament of prophetic activity threaded through and holding together much of the history. Second, he perceived the vital importance of reconstructing the history of the development of the constituent documents used by later redactors (for example, the assertion of the existence of a Syn-

19 Nelson, *Double Redaction*, 20.

20 Jepsen, *Quellen*, table; vv. 29–31a are attributed to N, whereas vv. 31b,33–38abα are credited to R^{II}. One wonders whether Jepsen's schema does not underlie that of Kratz, who treats "prophetic narratives and other legends which tell of the wisdom and wealth of Solomon (1 Kgs 3f.; 10.1ff.) or of Naboth's vineyard (1 Kgs 21.1–16), of the miracles and the political oracles of Elijah and Elisha and others (1 Kgs 17; 18.41–46; 20; 22; 2 Kgs 2–8; 13.14ff.), or of Isaiah's miracles and signs (1 Kgs 19–20)" in the same paragraph (*Composition*, 170).

21 E.g., Jepsen, *Quellen*, 78 and table; both passages are assigned wholly to N. For the problem of assigning such passages specifically to wisdom circles, see J. L. Crenshaw, "Method in Determining Wisdom Influence upon 'Historical' Literature," *JBL* 88 (1969): 129–42.

chronic History that had been compiled from extant Judahite and Israelite records of the reigns of kings).[22] Moreover, Jepsen concluded much in the same vein as Noth that Israel's history is one of abject apostasy and that the author wanted chiefly to record his understanding of Israel's disgraced history.[23] Yet this picture of a cynical redactor theologizing what modern historians would consider the historical contingency of Judah's exile in Babylon was soon contested.

3.2.1.3. Von Rad and Wolff

Although G. von Rad did not challenge Noth's presumption of an exilic author, he did seek to clarify the extent of the author's negativity for which Noth argued.[24] While it was certainly the case that the kings of Israel had failed in those criteria by which the Historian judged them (i.e., the practice of centralized worship and abolition of cultic sin), von Rad argued, the Historian included several notices articulating God's enduring support for the Davidic monarchy and for the city Jerusalem (1 Kgs 2:4; 8:20,25; 11:13,32,36; 15:4; 2 Kgs 8:19; i.e., those oracles and speeches referring to the promise of a Davidic dynasty in 2 Samuel 7).[25] The Historian expressed hope in this divine grace through the final verses of the compilation, which narrate Jehoiachin's release from prison (2 Kgs 25:27–30): "the passage must be interpreted...as an indication that the line of David has not yet come to an irrevocable end."[26] In short, the author of the DtrH was not so decisively negative as Noth had argued.

H. W. Wolff took up von Rad's argument and pointed out its fundamental opposition to the Deuteronomistic judgment in 2 Kgs 24:2 that the destruction of Jerusalem had come "according to the word which YHWH had spoken through his servants the prophets."[27] Wolff argued that the

---

22 Jepsen, *Quellen*, 40.

23 Ibid., 112–14.

24 Gerhard von Rad, *Studies in Deuteronomy* (trans. D. Stalker; SBT 9; London: SCM, 1953; repr., 1961), 74–91; trans. of *Deuteronomium-Studien* (2d ed.; Göttingen: Vandenhoeck & Ruprecht, 1948). See also idem, *Old Testament Theology* (trans. D. M. G. Stalker, with an introduction by W. Brueggemann; 2 vols.; OTL; Edinburgh: Oliver & Boyd, 1962; repr., Louisville, Ky.: WJKP, 2001), 1:334–47; trans. of *Theologie des alten Testaments* (2 vols.; 2d ed.; Munich: Kaiser, 1957). For the exilic authorship of the history see idem, *Studies*, 76–77; *OTT*, 1:342.

25 Von Rad, *Studies*, 84–85, 89.

26 Ibid., 90–91. See also Soggin, "Deuteronomistische Geschichtsauslegung während des babylonischen Exils," in *Oikonomia: Heilsgeschichte als Thema der Theologie* (ed. Felix Christ; Hamburg-Bergstedt: Herbert Reich Evangelische Verlag, 1967), 11–17.

27 Hans Walter Wolff, "The Kerygma of the Deuteronomic Historical Work," in *The Vitality of Old Testament Traditions* (ed. W. Brueggemann and H. W. Wolff; trans. F. C. Prussner; 2d

"windfall hope" represented by Jehoiachin's release was "flatly inconsistent with the Nathan oracle, whose fulfillment...is contingent on obedience to the word of Moses in Deuteronomy."[28] Pointing to the cyclical nature of the sin-and-salvation schema of Judges, Wolff located a significant theological intent in the final four verses of the DtrH, the same verses to which von Rad had referred in his earlier study (2 Kgs 25:27–30): the passage was not so much the historian's holding out a small hope for a restoration of divine grace as it was rather an adjuration to the people of Judah to "return" (שׁוּב) to YHWH.[29] The catchword appears repeatedly throughout the history, argued Wolff, both in the passages that were to serve as models of the people's behavior (e.g., 1 Sam 7:3; 1 Kgs 8:33,35,46–53; 2 Kgs 23:25) and in those that encapsulated the law, or the prophets' exhortations to abide by it (Deut 28:45–68[69]; 30:1–10; 2 Kgs 17:13). The possibility for Israel's salvation, then, could only be actualized through the people's "unqualified turning to Yahweh in prayer"[30] and did not necessarily include the Davidic (or "messianic") component that von Rad had recognized in the historian's specification of Jehoiachin's release.[31]

Although von Rad eventually accepted the basic thrust of Wolff's argument for the centrality of the historian's adjuration to "return," he remained somewhat unconvinced by the larger hypothesis on account of the apparent incongruity of the cyclical nature of sin and salvation portrayed by the historian in the book of Judges, over against the more linear portrayal of the monarchy in 1–2 Kings.[32] Yet, Wolff had—apparently unwittingly—discerned a possible cause for the disparity with his recognition that the hand of a second Deuteronomistic author was at work in Deuteronomy (specifically, Deut 4:29–31; 28:45–68[69]; and 30:1–10), an

---

ed.; Atlanta: John Knox, 1982), 86; trans. of "Das Kerygma des deuteronomistischen Geschichtswerks," *ZAW* 73 (1961): 171–86.

28 Wolff, "The Kerygma," 86.

29 Ibid., 90–97. Following Wolff's model, Walter Brueggemann finds another important *leitmotif* in the word "good" (טוֹב) ("The Kerygma of the Deuteronomistic Historian: Gospel for Exiles," *Int* 22 [1968]: 387–402).

30 Wolff, "The Kerygma," 98.

31 Ibid., 99.

32 Von Rad, *OTT*, 1:346–47. A further complicating factor is the apparent paucity of Deuteronomistic editorial material in Samuel; Artur Weiser, *The Old Testament: Its Formation and Development* (trans. Dorothea M. Barton; New York: Association, 1961), 157–70, esp. 166–69; published in Great Britain as *Introduction to the Old Testament: The Canon, the Apocrypha and Pseudopigrapha* (London: Darton, Longman & Todd, 1961); trans. of *Einleitung in das Alte Testament* (1939; 4th ed.; repr. Göttingen: Vandenhoeck & Ruprecht, 1957), 131–66; Fohrer, *Introduction*, 193–94; but cf. R. A. Carlson, *David, the Chosen King: A Traditio-Historical Approach to the Second Book of Samuel* (trans. Eric J. Sharpe and Stanley Rudman; Uppsala: Almqvist & Wiksell, 1964), esp. 20–37.

author "trying to graft not only DtrH kerygma but also Jeremiah traditions onto the older material of Deuteronomy."[33]

Noth's assessment that Dtr used only one large-scale compilation (i.e., the Saul-David matrix that he had received as "extended writings on Saul and David [that] were linked with one another"[34]) both structured and limited his perceived goal of the DtrH, such that its entirety could only have been written from the standpoint of the exile. However, as von Rad and Wolff pointed out, this solution cannot account for much of the optimism latent in the promises to the Davidic dynasty, centered primarily on David and on his descendant Josiah (e.g., 2 Samuel 7; 2 Kgs 22:1–23:25). Wolff's suggestion that Deuteronomy displayed evidence for editorial insertions by a second (and slightly later) member of a Deuteronomistic "circle" pointed the way toward an increasingly important development in studies of the DtrH.[35]

3.2.2. The Cross (Harvard) School

3.2.2.1. Cross's "The Themes of the Book of Kings"

The supposition that a significant portion of the DtrH had been composed already before the exile, well before the period of composition that Noth hypothesized, was not a new theory. Since the time of A. Kuenen, a model of double redaction—with the first edition appearing *before* the Exile—had been the norm, and this model persisted despite the gravitation of many scholars towards Noth's proposal.[36] In 1968 F. M. Cross rearticulated the

33 Wolff, "The Kerygma," 96. Wolff pointed out that Deut 4:29–31; 28:45–68[69]; and 30:1–10 contained manifold resonations of Jeremiah's language; cf. נדח *hiphil* "to disperse" in Deut 30:1; Jer 16:15; 32:37; 46:28; שׁוב שְׁבוּת in Deut 30:3; Jer 29:14; 30:3,18; "YHWH's delighting (שׂושׂ) in Israel" in Deut 30:9b; Jer 32:41; etc. (ibid., 94–97). His argument presumes, of course, that the "editorial additions" in Deuteronomy were Deuteronomistic uses of Jeremiah's language and not vice versa. For a similar view, see Jepsen, who considered his own Deuteronomistic compiler (R^{II}) to have been a student of Jeremiah (*Quellen*, 100). It is not entirely clear to me, however, that the reverse is impossible, or even improbable: Jeremiah clearly displays much dependence on the basic tenets of Deuteronomistic thought, and it does not seem at all unlikely that he (or the book named after him) could not have picked up a few elements of vocabulary from an earlier (and complete) text of Deuteronomy. Nonetheless, the literary- and redactional-critical models separating these layers are not a significant concern here and require no thoroughgoing analysis.

34 Noth *DH*, 25; see also the discussion provided by Campbell, "Martin Noth," 33.

35 For Wolff's use of the term "circle," see idem, "The Kerygma," 96.

36 Abraham Kuenen, *Het onstaan van de Historische Boeken des Ouden Verbonds* (vol. 1 of *Historisch-kritisch onderzoek naar het ontstaan en de verzameling van de boeken des Ouden Verbonds*; 3 vols.; Leiden: Engels, 1861), 249–82; for an outline of the idea's history, see Nelson, *Double Redaction*, 14–19; and Provan, *Hezekiah*, 8–11. Formulations of the thesis

model of a double redaction of the DtrH, thereby challenging the purported intent of the historiographic work proposed by Noth. Cross argued that two significant thematic limitations negated Noth's model.[37] The first theme—the wickedness of the sin of Jeroboam (1 Kgs 12:26–33)—culminated in the destruction of Israel at the hands of Assyria (2 Kgs 17:1–23).[38] In and of itself, this theme is not mutually exclusive with a dating in the exile, since it parallels the Judahite theme that occasions the downfall of Jerusalem: the sin of Manasseh (e.g., 2 Kgs 23:26–27).[39] But the second theme of the DtrH recognized by Cross—God's faithful attention to the Davidic dynasty and its capital city Jerusalem[40]—is directly contradicted by an exilic dating, since the Babylonian desecration and destruction of Jerusalem would negate the divine promise of an eternal house made in 2 Sam 7:4–17, especially v. 16.[41] Cross found the culmination of this positively structured theme in the reign and religious reforms of Josiah (2 Kgs 22:1–23:25).[42] The culmination of this theme in the reign of Josiah suggested to Cross that Noth had neglected one of the major projects of the bulk of the DtrH (i.e., the text up to 2 Kgs 23:25): the ideological foundation and legitimization of Josiah's reform and its correspondent retrospective call to the northern kingdom to join in the proper worship of Yahweh in Jerusalem.[43] This bulk of the history could only have been formulated and productive during the reign of Josiah and before his death at the hands of the army of Necho II in 609. It was only *after* the early death of Josiah

---

dating after 1943 include: William Foxwell Albright, "The Biblical Period," in *The Jews: Their History, Culture, and Religion* (ed. Louis Finkelstein; 2 vols.; New York: Harper, 1949), 1:3–69, esp. 45–46 and 62 n. 108; G. Ernest Wright, "Deuteronomy: Introduction," *IB* 2:311–30, esp. 316–17; John Bright, "The Book of Joshua: Introduction," *IB* 2:541–50, esp. 542–46; John Gray, *I & II Kings* (2d ed.; OTL; Philadelphia: Westminster, 1970), 6–9; and idem, *Joshua, Judges and Ruth* (NCB; London: Nelson, 1967), 7–8.

37 Frank M. Cross, "The Themes of the Book of Kings and the Structure of the Deuteronomistic History," in idem, *Canaanite Myth and Hebrew Epic: Essays in the History of the Religion of Israel* (Cambridge: Harvard University Press, 1973), 274–89.

38 Cross, "Themes," 279–81.

39 Ibid., 285–87.

40 Although Cross deemed 2 Kgs 25:27–30 "a thin thread upon which to hang the expectation of the fulfilment of the promises to David," he recognized the value of von Rad's observations concerning the divine promise to the Davidic dynasty (ibid., 277).

41 Ibid., 278. Indeed, although Cross did not argue this explicitly, the trope seems to be closely related to the prophetic adjuration calling for the people's repentance *before* a violent destruction, in the hopes that the destruction would be averted (e.g., Amos 5:14–15). However, it could also be argued that even in the prophetic conceptualization the salvation was to have taken place *after* the destruction, since already in the 8th cent. Amos talks of a "remnant of Joseph" (v. 15).

42 Ibid., 281–84. Insofar as Wolff's postulated Deuteronomistic call to "return" was predicated upon the assumption that the book of Judges had been collated during the exile, Cross found better reason to understand the trope as an "exhortation to reform with the hope of national salvation," contextualized in the pre-exilic situation of Judah.

43 Ibid., 284–85.

(2 Kgs 23:28–30) and the ensuing downward spiral of the Judahite kingdom, resulting eventually in its destruction by Babylon (2 Kings 25), that the DtrH was updated with the theme of Manasseh's sin to provide an account of the kingdom's end. Oddly, given Dtr's frequent use of prophecies to anticipate political events, the DtrH contains no prophecies concerning the gravity of Manasseh's offenses.[44] For Cross, it was especially confusing that,

> given the Deuteronomist's penchant for composing final addresses, edifying prayers, and theological exhortations on significant events... [t]he omission of a final, edifying discourse on the fall of chosen Zion and the Davidic crown is better explained by attributing these final terse paragraphs of the history to a less articulate Exilic editor.[45]

The two editions could therefore be separated primarily on the basis of thematic coherence or disjunction into a primary Josianic edition (Dtr[1]) and an exilic reworking thereof (Dtr[2]).[46] These two editions could be dated to ca. 620 and 550, respectively.[47] Negative judgments of the exilic redactor's style aside, Cross's rearticulation of the theory of double redaction presented a consistent and valuable set of concerns with Noth's proposal. However, because Cross's evidence was primarily thematic, the hypothesis required additional support.

3.2.2.2. Cross's Supporters: Nelson, Friedman, and Others

That support came during the 1970's and 1980's in the form of the work of several of Cross's students, who provided linguistic arguments to bolster the thesis of the Deuteronomistic double redaction. R. D. Nelson, the student of P. D. Miller, who was himself one of Cross's early students at Harvard, and R. E. Friedman and B. Halpern, two of Cross's own students, all contributed significant monographs in 1981.[48] To these may be added

---

44 Ibid., 286; for the historian's propensity to use prophecy as a means of schematizing and theologizing historical events, see, e.g., von Rad, *Studies*, 78–81.

45 Cross, "Themes," 288.

46 This exilic reworking was apparently, for Cross (ibid., 287), rather light, comprising Deut 4:27–31; 28:36–37,63–68; 29:27; 30:1–10 (cf. discussion of Wolff, above); Josh 23:11–13, 15–16; 1 Sam 12:25; 1 Kgs 2:4; 6:11–13; 8:25b,46–53; 9:4–9; 2 Kgs 17:19; 20:17–18; 23:26–25:30; and possibly Deut 30:11–20; and 1 Kgs 3:14.

47 Ibid., 287–89.

48 Nelson, *Double Redaction*; Richard E. Friedman, *The Exile and Biblical Narrative: The Formation of the Deuteronomic and Priestly Works* (HSM 22; Chico, Calif.: Scholars Press, 1981); Baruch Halpern, *The Constitution of the Monarchy in Israel* (HSM 25; Chico, Calif.: Scholars Press, 1981). All three monographs were reworked dissertations, the first from 1973, and the latter two from 1978. See also Steven L. McKenzie, *The Chronicler's Use of the Deuteronomistic History* (HSM 33; Atlanta: Scholars Press, 1984), although contrast his

several shorter articles in support of the thesis by Nelson, Friedman, Halpern, and J. D. Levenson, as well as the contributions—either bolstering or assuming the model—of several others, many of whom had no official association to Cross.[49] In his monograph, Nelson expanded and re-

---

revised schema that leans back towards Noth's original model (i.e., a single pre-exilic edition with secondary, but not systematic, revisions) in idem, *The Trouble with Kings: The Composition of the Book of Kings in the Deuteronomistic History* (VTSup 42; Leiden: Brill, 1991), esp. 135–45, 148–49.

49 Richard D. Nelson, "Josiah in the Book of Joshua," *JBL* 100 (1981): 531–40; see also the recent restatement of the hypothesis in idem, "The Double Redaction of the Deuteronomistic History: The Case is Still Compelling," *JSOT* 29 (2005): 319–37; and Richard Elliot Friedman's slightly abbreviated republication of *Exile*, 1–43, as "From Egypt to Egypt: Dtr^1 and Dtr^2," in *Traditions in Transformation: Turning Points in Biblical Faith* (ed. J. D. Levenson and B. Halpern; Winona Lake, Ind.: Eisenbrauns, 1981), 167–92; Baruch Halpern, "Sacred History and Ideology: Chronicles' Thematic Structure—Indications of an Earlier Source," in *The Creation of Sacred Literature: Composition and Redaction of the Biblical Text* (ed. Richard Elliott Friedman; UCNES 22; Berkeley and Los Angeles: University of California Press, 1981), 35–54; Jon D. Levenson, "From Temple to Synagogue: 1 Kings 8," in *Traditions in Transformation: Turning Points in Biblical Faith* (ed. J. D. Levenson and B. Halpern; Winona Lake, Ind.: Eisenbrauns, 1981), 143–66; idem, "Who Inserted the Book of the Torah?" *HTR* 68 (1975): 203–33; see also Robert G. Boling, *Judges: Introduction, Translation, and Commentary* (AB 6b; Garden City, N.Y.: Doubleday, 1975), 29–38; idem, "Levitical History and the Role of Joshua," in *The Word of the Lord Shall Go Forth: Essays in Honor of David Noel Freedman in Celebration of His Sixtieth Birthday* (ed. Carol L. Meyers and M. O'Connor; ASORSVS 1; Winona Lake, Ind.: Eisenbrauns, 1983), 241–61; G. Ernest Wright, "Introduction," in Robert G. Boling, *Joshua: A New Translation with Notes and Commentary* (AB 6a; Garden City, N.Y.: Doubleday, 1982), 41–51; Mordechai Cogan, "Israel in Exile—The View of a Josianic Historian," *JBL* 97 (1978): 40–44; Jonathan Rosenbaum, "Hezekiah's Reform and the Deuteronomistic Tradition," *HTR* 72 (1979): 23–43; P. Kyle McCarter, *I Samuel: A New Translation with Introduction and Commentary* (AB 8; Garden City, N.Y.: Doubleday, 1980), 14–17; idem, *II Samuel: A New Translation with Introduction and Commentary* (AB 9; New York: Doubleday, 1984), 6–7; A. D. H. Mayes, *The Story of Israel between Settlement and Exile: A Redactional Study of the Deuteronomistic History* (London: SCM, 1983); Brian J. Peckham, "The Composition of Deuteronomy 5–11," in *The Word of the Lord Shall Go Forth: Essays in Honor of David Noel Freedman in Celebration of His Sixtieth Birthday* (ed. Carol L. Meyers and M. O'Connor; ASORSVS 1; Winona Lake, Ind.: Eisenbrauns, 1983), 241–61; idem, *The Compostion of the Deuteronomistic History* (HSM 35; Atlanta: Scholars Press, 1985), although in both of Peckham's works a schema is introduced that bears several tensions with Cross's hypothesis; Rolf Rendtorff, *The Old Testament: An Introduction* (trans. John Bowden; Philadelphia: Fortress, 1986), 183–88; esp. 186–87; trans. of *Das Alte Testament: Eine Einführung* (Neukirchen-Vluyn: Neukirchener Verlag, 1983); Robert L. Cohn, "Convention and Creativity in the Book of Kings: The Case of the Dying Monarch," *CBQ* 47 (1985): 603–16, esp. 603; Simon J. De Vries, *1 Kings* (WBC 12; Waco: Word Books, 1985), xlii–xliii; Gottfried Vanoni, "Beobachtungen zur deuteronomistischen Terminologie in 2 Kön 23,25–25,30," in *Das Deuteronomium: Entstehung, Gestalt und Botschaft* (ed. Norbert Lohfink; BETL 68; Leuven: University Press and Peeters, 1985), 357–62; Ziony Zevit, "Deuteronomistic Historiography in 1 Kings 12–2 Kings 17 and the Reinvestiture of the Israelian Cult," *JSOT* 32 (1985): 57–73, esp. 66–67 n. 1; idem, *The Religions of Ancient Israel: A Synthesis of Parallactic Approaches* (London: Continuum, 2001), 439–79; Gerald Eddie Gerbrandt, *Kingship According to the Deuteronomistic History* (SBLDS 87; Atlanta: Scholars Press, 1986), 13–18.

fined Cross's essay, adding several theological sub-themes, adducing twenty-seven idiomatic expressions that could be traced in those demonstrably exilic passages,[50] and distinguishing these passages from those that were pre-exilic. Perhaps most importantly, Nelson attempted to mitigate the presumed importance of reading 2 Kgs 25:27–30 as the historian's extension of hope that the unconditional promise in 2 Samuel 7 remained in effect and would someday come to fruition, as von Rad had argued earlier. Nelson suggested that the conditionality of the Davidic covenant assumed in 1 Kgs 2:2–4; 8:25; 9:4–5 applied only to Solomon (and was therefore to be fulfilled or rejected within the confines of 1 Kings 2–11) and was meant to threaten only the loss of Davidic control over the throne of the northern kingdom, *not* over corporate Israel (including Judah).[51] Not only did this recognition free Nelson from having to reconcile the two different categories of promises, but it also removed the specter of a necessarily exilic date for Dtr^1. Nonetheless, although this specific argument stands in conflict with the argument of Cross that the unconditional promise to the Davidic dynasty (2 Sam 7:1–17) and the conditioning reassessments thereof (1 Kgs 2:2–4; 8:25; 9:4–9) should be traced to two different editors,[52] Nelson's work supports and expands that of Cross for the most part.

Friedman, on the other hand, was more summary in his treatment of the double redaction hypothesis,[53] but he adduced valuable confirmation for the hypothesis in non-Deuteronomistic literature by arguing for a double redaction of the Priestly material, where the first knew only of Dtr^1, while the second was exilic and knew both Dtr^1 and Dtr^2.[54]

The work of the Cross school has alleviated much of the tension noted by von Rad between the prophetic proclamations of divine support for the Davidic monarchy (2 Sam 7:8–17; 1 Kgs 2:4; 8:20,25; 11:13,32,36; 15:4; 2 Kgs 8:19) and the apparently cynical fatalism of the Deuteronomistic Historian, as profiled by Noth. It proposes a realistic and genuinely thoughtful analysis of the variegated theological traditions found in the

50 Nelson began with the five passages that accused the Israelites of "not having listened" (לא שמע): Judg 2:1–5; 6:7–10; 2 Kgs 17:7–20,23b; 17:24–28,34b–40; 21:3bβ–15. He then extrapolated the grammatical and lexical observations he had made in order to isolate other exilic passages: Deut 4:19–20; 2 Kings 23:4b–5,19–20,24(?),26–30; 23:31–25:30.

51 Nelson, *Double Redaction*, 99–118, esp. 102–4; for further discussion of this point, see Friedman, *Exile*, 12–13; cf. Provan, *Hezekiah*, 106–11; Jon D. Levenson, "The Last Four Verses in Kings," *JBL* 103 (1984): 353–61; and Baruch Halpern and David S. Vanderhooft, "The Editions of Kings in the 7th–6th Centuries B.C.E.," *HUCA* 62 (1991): 242–43.

52 Cross, "Themes," 287.

53 Friedman, *Exile*, 1–43. Friedman's list of exilic passages includes: Deut 4:25–31; 8:19–20; 28:36–37,63–68; 29:21–27; 30:1–10,15–20; 31:16–22,28–30; 1 Kgs 9:6–9; 2 Kgs 21:8–15; and, less certainly, Josh 23:15–16; 1 Kgs 6:11–13; 2 Kgs 17:19,35–40a; 22:16–20.

54 Ibid., 44–119.

Former Prophets. However, the work of the scholars discussed here is dissatisfying when the issue turns to the precise nature and extent of Dtr[1]. As M. A. O'Brien points out, "[w]hat is missing in the work of this school…is a thoroughgoing analysis of the Josianic history from beginning to end, and a convincing formulation of its unity and conceptual plan. The school has shown the importance of prophecy in DtrH but has not explored the full significance of its prophecy-fulfillment schema."[55] It is precisely this failure to reckon adequately with the prophecy-fulfillment schema recognized by von Rad (therefore, with the nature of the DtrH as an ostensibly *prophetic* document in its earliest form) that has obfuscated the nature of the History's earliest sources for which Noth argued so stringently and effectively. In omitting significant discussion of the prophetic background and structure of the DtrH, Cross and his conjoiners inadvertently removed from discussion an essential and salient aspect of the text's identity.

3.2.3. The Smend (Göttingen) School

3.2.3.1. Smend's "Das Gesetz und die Völker"

In 1971, shortly after the initial publication of Cross's article, but not in response to that essay, R. Smend published his own criticism of Noth's hypothesis.[56] Like Cross, Smend argued that Noth's hypothesis of a single layer of the DtrH was lacking. But Smend's methodology and conclusions were completely different from those of Cross. Instead of examining the broad themes of the Deuteronomistic corpus, Smend studied several smaller pericopes in Joshua and Judges that exhibited smaller-scale repetitions of words and phrases (as well as what could reasonably be understood as

---

55 O'Brien, *DHH*, 12.

56 Rudolf Smend, "The Law and the Nations: A Contribution to Deuteronomistic Tradition History," in *Reconsidering Israel and Judah: Recent Studies on the Deuteronomistic History* (ed. G. N. Knoppers and J. G. McConville; trans. P. T. Daniels; SBTS 8; Winona Lake, Ind.: Eisenbrauns, 2000), 95–111; trans. of "Das Gesetz und die Völker: Ein Beitrag zur deuteronomistischen Redaktionsgeschichte," in *Probleme biblischer Theologie: Gerhard von Rad zum 70. Geburtstag* (ed. H. W. Wolff; Munich: Kaiser, 1971), 494–509; see also his later and more comprehensive statement: idem, *Die Entstehung des alten Testaments* (1978; 4th ed.; Stuttgart: Kohlhammer, 1989), 110–66. As with Cross's model, earlier studies had moved in the same direction but were not taken up as rallying points to the same degree: e.g., Odil Hannes Steck, *Israel und das gewaltsame Geschick der Propheten: Untersuchungen zur Überlieferung des deuteronomistischen Geschichtsbildes im Alten Testament, Spätjudentum und Urchristentum* (WMANT 23; Neukirchen-Vluyn: Neukirchener Verlag, 1967), esp. 66 n. 3 and 137–43; Georg Braulik, "Spuren einer Neubearbeitung des deuteronomistischen Geschichtswerkes in 1 Kön 8,52–53.59–60," *Bib* 52 (1971): 20–33.

interpretive additions and glosses) within the Deuteronomistic speeches, literary features that he felt Noth's thesis did not adequately explain. These indications of redactional disjunction suggested to Smend several nuanced differences in theology discernable within the speeches themselves. Smend perceived and attempted to isolate a law-oriented "nomistic" layer of redaction within these texts (Josh 1:7–9; 13:1bβ–6; 23:1–16; Judg 1:1–2:9; 2:17,20–21,23). Smend noted that in those framing elements of Judges (2:17,20–21), the judges figured not as military leaders (as they did in the bulk of the stories themselves) but as teachers of the law.[57] Accordingly, this redaction held as paramount the people's—rather than the king's—obedience to the laws delivered by Moses in the book of Deuteronomy and suggested to Smend that "alongside the author of the Deuteronomistic History...there was thus another author (or several)."[58] This redaction, produced by a single redactor or a school of redaction, Smend dubbed DtrN ("Nomistic" redaction), a siglum that indicates the dependence of the redactor's thought on that of the original Historian (DtrG)[59] and seems to have presumed the exile. A second major motif in this redaction was the problem occasioned by the continued presence of a non-Israelite element in the land,[60] comparable to the binary themes of Ezra: adherence to the law and the preservation of Israelite identity despite the mixed or different ethnicity of the surrounding enclaves. The solution for Smend, then, was not one of "block-redaction," as it was for Cross, but of "stratum-redaction."[61] DtrN's craft is first discernable in Deut 1:5 and persists in small interpretive additions and glosses throughout the DtrH until the final chapter of 2 Kings.[62]

57 Smend, "Law," 106. Smend correctly discerned that the perennial cycle of the people's sin and the salvation of the judges sent by God was established in the framework of the book rather than in the stories themselves.

58 Ibid., 98.

59 Ibid., 106. Smend originally used the siglum DtrG for the foundational edition (with G presumably standing for Noth's "Geschichtswerk," although it is possible that in the original Smend intended the antecendent of the siglum to be "Grundbestand"). This convention was initially followed in the works of his students mentioned below but was soon adapted to the "more international" DtrH (H = history/histoire/Historie); see Tryggve N. D. Mettinger, *King and Messiah: The Civil and Sacral Legitimation of the Israelite Kings* (ConBOT 8; Lund: Gleerup, 1976), 20; Walter Dietrich, "David in Überlieferung und Geschichte," *VF* 22 (1977): 48 n. 11; and Smend, *Entstehung*, 115. Because DtrH designates the totality of the Deuteronomistic History in the present study, DtrG is used in the following pages to indicate Smend's original Historian. Much confusion can arise through the use of such sigla; I have therefore tried to keep their use to a minimum throughout this study.

60 Smend, "Law," 109.

61 For this terminology, see Weippert, "Geschichtswerk," 235. Smend regarded his methodology and insights, as well as those of his students, as in line with the basic thrust of Jepsen's initial observations and conclusions concerning multiple reworkings of the material (*Entstehung*, 123).

62 Smend, "Law," 110.

3.2.3.2. Smend's Students: Dietrich and Veijola

W. Dietrich and T. Veijola quickly picked up on Smend's suggested reconstruction, but both added a second major redactional stratum, DtrP, the "Prophetic" redaction.[63] This redactional layer, which Dietrich dated between ca. 580–560—and which thus preceded the work of DtrN, ca. 560[64]—comprised various small glosses and interpretive additions of a prophetic nature. Some of the additions were comprised of pre-existent prophetic traditions that DtrP incorporated into the body of the history, sometimes adding only short redactional statements to provide a more fluid feel to the text. Veijola's minute source-division of Samuel proposes a similar exilic layer of redaction in that sub-corpus.[65]

Like the Cross school, the Smend school has gained a number of proponents and more casual adherents.[66] This is doubtless due to the fact

63 Walter Dietrich, *Prophetie und Geschichte: Eine redaktionsgeschichtliche Untersuchung zum deuteronomistischen Geschichtswerk* (FRLANT 108; Göttingen: Vandenhoeck & Ruprecht, 1972); Timo Veijola, *Die Ewige Dynastie: David und die Entstehung seiner Dynastie nach der deuteronomistischen Darstellung* (AASF B 193; Helsinki: Suomalainen Tiedeakatemia, 1975); idem, *Das Königtum in der Beurteilung der deuteronomistischen Historiographie: Eine redaktionsgeschichtliche Untersuchung* (AASF B 198; Helsinki: Suomalainen Tiedeakatemia, 1977). To say that Dietrich "picked up" on Smend's hypothesis is not altogether accurate, since his 1970 dissertation must have been assumed by Smend as a given (Smend references the dissertation in "Law," n. 57 [n. 58 in original]). Perhaps more accurate would be to say that their respective components of the theory were developed in tandem.

64 Dietrich, *Prophetie und Geschichte*, 144.

65 Lists of Dietrich and Veijola's respective attributions to DtrG, DtrP, and DtrN have been compiled by Campbell ("Martin Noth," 48–50) and will not be reproduced here.

66 Wolfgang Roth, "The Deuteronomic Rest Theology: A Redaction-Critical Study," *BR* 21 (1976): 5–14; idem, "Deuteronomistisches Geschichtswerk/Deuteronomistische Schule," *TRE* 8 (1981): 543–52; Ernst Würthwein, *Die Bücher der Könige: 1. Könige 1–16* (ATD 11/1; Göttingen: Vandenhoeck & Ruprecht, 1985); idem, *Die Bücher der Könige: 1. Kön. 17–2. Kön. 25* (ATD 11/2; Göttingen: Vandenhoeck & Ruprecht, 1984), esp. 489–501; Rainer Bickert, "Die Geschichte und das Handeln Jahwes: Zur Eigenart einer deuteronomistischen Offenbarungsauffassung in den Samuelbüchern," in *Textgemäß: Aufsätze und Beiträge zur Hermeneutik des Alten Testaments* (ed. A. H. J. Gunneweg and Otto Kaiser; Göttingen: Vandenhoeck & Ruprecht, 1979), 9–27; idem, "Die List Joabs und der Sinneswandel Davids: Eine dtr bearbeitete Einschaltung in die Thronfolgeerzählung: 2 Sam. xiv 2–22," in *Studies in the Historical Books of the Old Testament* (VTSup 30; Leiden: Brill, 1979), 30–51; A. Graeme Auld, *Joshua, Moses and the Land: Tetrateuch-Pentateuch-Hexateuch in a Generation since 1938* (Edinburgh: T&T Clark, 1980); Leslie J. Hoppe, "The Meaning of Deuteronomy," *BTB* 10 (1980): 111–17; J. Alberto Soggin, *Judges: A Commentary* (trans. J. S. Bowden; OTL; Philadelphia: Westminster, 1981), 5; idem, "Problemi di storia e di storiografia nell'antico Israele," *Hen* 4 (1982): 1–16, French summary, 15–16; although cf. the unity of Dtr in idem, *Joshua: A Commentary* (OTL; London: SCM, 1972), published before wide acceptance of Smend's hypothesis; Hermann Spieckermann, *Judah unter Assur in der Sargonidenzeit* (FRLANT 129; Göttingen: Vandenhoeck & Ruprecht, 1982); Rainer Stahl, "Aspekte der Geschichte deuteronomistischer Theologie: Zur Traditionsgeschichte der Terminologie und zur Redaktionsgeschichte der Redekompositionen" (Ph.D. diss.; Jena, 1982), reviewed in *TLZ* 108 (1983): 74–76; Ralph W. Klein, *1 Samuel* (WBC 10; Waco:

that the work of the Smend school has much to recommend it; I would single out two areas of methodological and theoretical precision in particular: first, we must commend the exegetical importance of Smend's recognition of the intricacies with which redactors could deal with extant texts.[67] Second, and more importantly for the present discussion, the members of this school were much more deliberate than those of the Cross school in their acknowledgment of the underlying prophetic nature of the DtrH, which had been recognized within Continental scholarship for some time (see above).

3.2.4. Objections to the Smend School

Despite the aptitude of many of the Smend school's observations, the project remains quite tentative and hypothetical, often assuming the results of its own manufacture before those results have been adequately grounded.[68] Fundamental to the problem is Smend's isolation of DtrN as a stratum so myopically concerned with the law that any possible redactional passages are necessarily assigned to that layer.[69] This assumption is then carried through the studies of Dietrich and Veijola in such a manner that it obfuscates the true import of each scholar's observations. A perfect example of the school's misplaced confidence in the existence and nature

Word Books, 1983), xxviii–xxxii; Fabrizio Foresti, *The Rejection of Saul in the Perspective of the Deuteronomistic School: A Study of 1 Sm 15 and Related Texts* (Studia Theologica [Teresianum] 5; Rome: Edizioni del Teresianum, 1984); Georg Hentschel, *1 Könige* (NEchtB 10; Würzburg: Echter Verlag, 1984); idem, *2 Könige* (NEchtB 11; Würzburg: Echter Verlag, 1984); Jacques Vermeylen, "L'affaire du veau d'or (Ex 32–34): Une clé pour la 'question deutéronomiste'?" *ZAW* 97 (1985): 1–23; idem, *La loi du plus fort: Histoire de la rédaction des récits davidiques de 1 Samuel à 1 Rois 2* (BETL 154; Leuven: University Press, 2000); Uwe Becker, *Richterzeit und Königtum: Redaktionsgeschichtliche Studien zum Richterbuch* (BZAW 192; Berlin: de Gruyter, 1990); Ehud Ben Zvi, "The Account of the Reign of Manasseh in II Reg 21,1–18 and the Redactional History of the Book of Kings," *ZAW* 103 (1991): 355–74; Otto Kaiser, *Grundriß der Einleitung in die kanonischen und deuterokanonischen Schriften des Alten Testaments* (3 vols.; Gütersloh: Gerd Mohn, 1992), 1:85–131; Jochen Nentel, *Trägerschaft und Intentionen des deuteronomistischen Geschichtswerks: Untersuchungen zu den Reflexionsreden Jos 1; 23; 24; 1 Sam 12 und 1 Kön 8* (BZAW 297; Berlin: de Gruyter, 2000).

67 E.g., Smend, "Law," 101. There, he argues that DtrN's insertion of Josh 13:2 immediately after the already extant [DtrG] text v. 1bβ so thoroughly reinterprets the earlier text that the latter textual unit (v. 1bβ) can now only be rightfully attributed to the later redactor.

68 For a thorough and incisive critique of the school's most common methods of argumentation, see Antony F. Campbell, *Of Prophets and Kings: A Late Ninth-Century Document (1 Samuel 1–2 Kings 10)* (CBQMS 17; Washington DC: Catholic Biblical Association of America, 1986), 4–14; see also O'Brien, *DHH*, 7–10.

69 For further critique of DtrN, see Provan, *Hezekiah*, 25–26.

of DtrP and DtrN is Dietrich's discussion of 1 Kgs 11:29–38.[70] Dietrich isolates an original, pre-Deuteronomistic narrative (vv. 29–31,33a,34a, 35abα,37aβγb) in which the prophet Ahijah meets Jeroboam, tears a cloak (the owner of the cloak, while a thorny issue, remains unimportant in the context of this discussion) and delivers a divinely-granted oracle of Jeroboam:

> (31) Take for yourself ten pieces; for thus says the LORD, the God of Israel, "See, I am about to tear (הנני קרע) the kingdom from the hand of Solomon, and will give you ten tribes... (33a) this is because (יען אשׁר) he[71] has forsaken me, worshiped Astarte the goddess of the Sidonians, Chemosh the god of Moab, and Milcom the god of the Ammonites... (34a) Nevertheless I will not take the whole kingdom away from him; ... (35abα) but I will take the kingdom away from his son and give it to you,... (37aβγb) and you shall reign over all that your soul desires; you shall be king over Israel."[72]

All in all, Dietrich's redactional division of the passage into an early, coherent narrative and a later layer comprising editorial emendations (vv. 32,33b,34b,35bβ,36,37aα,38abα) is plausible, although I would disagree with a few specifics. Dietrich establishes as a criterion for the secondary nature of the text "interest in Judah, David, and Jerusalem..., the chosen city."[73] Although it is not at all self-evident that this concern to limit the Davidides' loss of control over the northern kingdom was not also a concern of the original story, a certain amount of leeway may be granted for the sake of argumentation. Allowing for the operation of this criterion, we may omit, with Dietrich, vv. 32,34b,36.[74] Furthermore, v. 33b is terminologically similar to v. 38abα, which may be omitted as a concealed threat ("versteckte Drohung").[75] Finally, v. 35bβ can be tied to the secondarily derived "fuzzy math" produced by the insertion of v. 32, whereas v. 37aα can be explained as an editorial resumption to introduce v. 37aβb after the insertion of v. 36.[76] Because vv. 29–39 have the appearance of being secondarily inserted into the DtrG story of Jeroboam's revolt (1 Kgs 11:26–28,40), this added complex (vv. 29–39) is to be attributed to a

70 Dietrich, *Prophetie und Geschichte*, 15–20.

71 Although LXX, Syr., and Vulg. all have the singular here, it seems likely that these versions are deliberately bringing the difficult 3.m.pl. עֲזָבוּנִי וַיִּשְׁתַּחֲווּ of MT into conformity with the context of the passage.

72 Translation NRSV, adjusted to reflect Dietrich's omissions.

73 Dietrich, *Prophetie und Geschichte*, 17, my translation.

74 Ibid., 16–19. The difficulty of the math in vv. 31–32 will not be discussed here.

75 Ibid., 19. As will become clear below, v. 38a may fall in the column of Dietrich's "later insertions" easily, but v. 38bα does not permit such easy dismissal; it speaks only of an "enduring house," a concept known from 2 Sam 7:16, which could easily be pre-Deuteronomistic.

76 Ibid., 17–18.

secondary editor.[77] Moreover, several elements of the editorial work may be correlated with an interest in nomism (e.g., הלך בדרכי יהוה vv. 33b,38a; חקות vv. 33b,34b; משפטים vv. 33b,34b; etc.)[78] and thus displays indications of subsequent reworking by the already assumed DtrN. Therefore, the composition of 1 Kgs 11:29–39 seems to be interposed between the formulation of the original DtrG (vv. 26–28,40) and the redactional emendations DtrN. In combination with similar evidence adduced from several other such passages, this reading of 1 Kgs 11:29–39 leads Dietrich to argue for the editorial reworking and insertion of earlier prophetic traditions by a post-DtrG but pre-DtrN editor. It thus appears that a relatively unified redactional stratum, which foregrounds prophetic concerns (hence, DtrP), may be traced throughout the DtrH. But as I. Provan has pointed out—a point by then already recognized by Würthwein as well—not all the material in the DtrH with prophetic affinities derives necessarily from the same hand (hence, E. Würthwein's DtrP1 and DtrP2), nor does it preclude DtrG's incorporation of extant, organized prophetic material.[79] As A. F. Campbell has cogently argued, the flaw in Dietrich's methodology consists of the fact that it does not permit Dtr (= DtrG) to have been building upon earlier texts.[80] Moreover, operating from the assumption that law-oriented passages must spring from a third level of redaction (DtrN) is a form of circular argumentation that can only bear out its own assumptions. Without having provided a thorough critical and literary study of the differences between the "nomistic" redactor DtrN and the earlier DtrG, any study attempting to isolate an intermediate layer is founded on shaky ground. A final flaw in Dietrich's proposal here is an all-too-rigid reliance on the formal model of the prophetic oracles of doom that he outlined earlier in his study (1 Kgs 14:7–11; 16:1–4; 21:20bβ–24; 2 Kgs 9:7–10a), in which the foundational cause of the punishment is introduced by (אשר) יען—cf. תחת אשר in 2 Kgs 22:16–17—and the pronouncement by הנני + *participle*.[81] Reliance on such a fixed form ignores the astute methodological observation by Smend that a redactor could reshape the text at hand, appropriating a passage

77 Ibid., 54–55.

78 Ibid., 20, 28–29.

79 Provan, *Hezekiah*, 24–25; Würthwein, *Könige*, 496–98; see also already Mayes, *Story*, 117–20.

80 Campbell, *Of Prophets and Kings*, 6–7.

81 True enough, Claus Westermann's schema of prophetic oracles of judgment includes both an accusation and an announcement, but there are a few examples in which no reason for the announcement is present (*Basic Forms of Prophetic Speech* [trans. H. C. White, with a forward by G. M. Tucker; Louisville, Ky.: Westminster, 1967; repr., 1991], 161–63; trans. of *Grundformen prophetischer Rede* [Munich: Kaiser, 1960]).

verbatim and adding his own insertion that alters the extant text grammatically or thematically.

A better reading of 1 Kgs 11:31–38 would have been to omit v. 33a (the יען אשׁר clause), which members of the Cross school would argue bears numerous similarities to the language of Dtr^2.[82] Moreover, much of what Dietrich omitted as belonging to DtrN in fact displays no particularly "nomistic" view, other than adherence to the Deuteronomic law (which, one may assume with Noth, was the core of Deuteronomy found in the temple); this is the case with vv. 32b,33b,34b,36,38a. Verse 38bα, on the other hand, displays no evidence of quintessential Deuteronomistic vocabulary or concern, but only knows of the Davidic land-grant of 2 Sam 7:16 (בית נאמן). Finally, vv. 34a,35abα act as delaying agents, both in conflict with the initial announcement that the kingdom would be ripped from Solomon's hand, and they therefore appear as secondary insertions already in their context. It seems far more natural to reconstruct the development of the text in the following manner: assuming that the earliest possible form of the tradition could have been nearly contemporaneous with the events described in vv. 26–28,40, it is logical to think that the oracle would have predicted the ripping of the kingdom from Solomon's hand—hence, the king's attempt to kill Jeroboam in v. 40. When the expected upheaval did not materialize, but instead came about after Jeroboam's return from Egypt, later tradents could easily add to the tradition the delaying elements in vv. 34a,35abα to account for the historical realities (see also v. 11*, with the prolongation added in v. 12), along with other glosses, clarifications, etc.[83] In this understanding, vv. 26a,40 form an independent and early traditum that Dtr (or probably an earlier compiler) worked together with a variety of other extant traditions, including the description of Solomon's

82 Compare, e.g., עזב + חוה *hishtaphel* in v. 33a with 1 Kgs 9:9, which Nelson attributes to Dtr^2 on the basis of the sequence וַיִּשְׁתַּחֲוֻּ...וַיַּעַבְדֻם (*Double Redaction*, 65; see also O'Brien, *DHH*, 169). Although the verb עבד does not occur in 11:33, חוה *hishtaphel* + עזב are coupled in verses that are often relegated to Dtr^2 status (e.g., 1 Kgs 9:9; 17:16; see also Jer 1:16; 22:19; although, cf. Judg 2:12 [Nelson, *Double Redaction*, 122]; Jer 16:11 [וַיַּעַבְדוּם...וַיִּשְׁתַּחֲווּ, which is a Dtr^1 sequence, according to ibid., 65]).

83 Cf. Helga Weippert, "Die Ätiologie des Nordreiches und seines Königshauses (1 Reg 11:29–40)," *ZAW* 95 (1983): 355–360. Weippert argues that Ahijah's oracle, which Weippert dates to the second half of Solomon's reign (ca. 945–925) (ibid., 359), claimed that Jeroboam would wrestle the kingdom from Solomon. The additions in vv. 34a,35a,36a,40bβ were inserted by two later editors in literary attempts to bring the oracle into conformity with the actual passage of events. The corrections made in the "delaying elements," as I have called them here, could easily have been inserted into the tradition after the division of the kingdom (during Jeroboam's reign) and before Baasha's rebellion (ca. 905) in order to clarify the oracle and bring it into alignment with historical fact. Outside of the biblical text, which has undergone much redaction, there is little or no evidence for the date (and historicity) of Jeroboam's coup. Any reconstruction is, therefore, speculative.

building activities (vv. 27–28) and the prophetic episode of vv. 29–39*, which the editor reworked. A later, possibly "nomistic," redactor then added a few glosses to the episode.[84] A plausible early form of the oracle would then comprise only vv. 31,(37aα),37aβγb, 38bα:

> (31) Take for yourself ten pieces; for thus says the LORD, the God of Israel, "See, I am about to tear the kingdom from the hand of Solomon, and will give you ten tribes.... (37aα) I will take you, (37aβγb) and you shall reign over all that your soul desires; you shall be king over Israel... (38bα*), and I will be with you, and I will build you an enduring house."

There is nothing particularly Deuteronomistic about this passage, and especially not in what I have reconstructed here as the original content of the oracle (vv. 31,[37aα],37aβγb), a brief report of a prophetic utterance.[85] Although Dietrich has correctly isolated a prophetic element in 1 Kgs 11:29–40, no intermediate DtrP stratum is required to take account of the remaining material, regardless of whether it should all be assigned to a single redactor or to two individuals working consecutively. In large agreement with this criticism, Campbell observes that "once the three great minatory pillars have been removed and clearly identified with later redactional levels, the likelihood of a Josianic Deuteronomistic History suddenly gains weight and momentum."[86] However, this observation of Campbell's seems to gloss over too readily a more recent model of the development of the DtrH that is more in keeping with his own interests in pre-Deuteronomistic strata.

84 Jepsen proposed a similar order of redaction (*Quellen*, 10, 15, table). Notice that the first indication that "[Jeroboam] raised a hand against the king (וירם יד במלך; v. 26b) is missing in the OG and may be an indication that the phrase was added to anticipate vv. 27–28 after those verses' insertion.

85 For a much more detailed discussion of the passage, including a more thorough critique of Dietrich's position, see Campbell, *Of Prophets and Kings*, 25–32; O'Brien, *DHH*, 163–71; Weippert, "Ätiologie," 344–75; and Mayes, *Story*, 118–19. I am in large agreement with Campbell and Weippert, less so with Mayes. Both Campbell and Weippert limited the text, including introductory and concluding notes, to vv. 29–31,37,38bαβ(=38bα*),40abα. I follow them in including v. 37aα in this original oracle, because, as Weippert pointed out, a literary parallel is thereby formed in which Jeroboam is instructed to "take for [him]self" (קח לך) ten pieces of the garment because "[YHWH] will take [him]" (ואתך אקח) ("Ätiologie," 354). Mayes included vv. 34,35bβ, and omitted v. 38 as Deuteronomistic. Cf., however, the discussion of McKenzie, who attributes the entire passage to Dtr (*Trouble*, 41–47).

86 Campbell, "Martin Noth," 50.

3.3. Models Incorporating a Pre-Deuteronomistic Edition: Focus on Formulae in 1–2 Kings

The last four decades have seen the propagation of theories of multiple pre-exilic redactions of the DtrH. This third major model of the development of the History builds to a large degree on the work of Jepsen, whether admittedly so or not, despite the obvious fact that Jepsen reconstructed only exilic layers of redaction. Many of his insights, though (e.g., the recognition that the Synchronic Chronicle's form ended with the reign of Hezekiah[87]), provided fertile ground for scholars of the 1980's to till. The theories that have developed in this trend have often come into some degree of conflict with the earlier models of multiple redaction, particularly with that generated by the Smend school. This conflict can be traced in large part to their respective working methodologies: the rationale behind the multiple-redaction model finds its basis both in thematic structures and in close analysis of formulary structures (as with the Cross school), but not in the minute redactional study performed by Smend and his followers. Moreover, it holds that the present form of the DtrH is the product of a much longer process than even Cross's model necessitates.[88] Working from the principle that the DtrH served as an operative textual commentary on Israelite historiography through much of the history of the divided kingdom, the various exemplars of this model argue: (a) that several stages of textual redaction existed and (b) that "[a]t each of these literary stages these books [of the DtrH] were revised and updated: not only was recent history appended to the text, but previously recorded history was revised and systematically corrected when necessary."[89] In this second regard, the principles of the multiple-redaction model still have much in common with Cross's double-redaction model, since both assume the updating of the text over time to reflect the contingencies of historical events and to provide those events with a (reasonably) consistent interpretive framework. But the multiple-redaction model differs from its predecessors in that it disregards to some extent the overarching importance of the themes of the Josianic-era History as proposed by Cross and instead finds its coherence in themes of a slightly smaller scale. The two models are, in fact, hardly mutually exclusive, but they do have two very different foci: the Cross

87 Jepsen, *Quellen*, 10.

88 This is not to say that Cross's model is incompatible with this third model; see below.

89 André Lemaire, "Toward a Redactional History of the Book of Kings," in *Reconsidering Israel and Judah: Recent Studies on the Deuteronomistic History* (ed. G. N. Knoppers and J. G. McConville; trans. Samuel W. Heldenbrand; SBTS 8; Winona Lake, Ind.: Eisenbrauns, 2000), 446–61, here 459; trans. from "Vers l'Histoire de la Rédaction des Livres des Rois," *ZAW* 98 (1986): 221–36.

model technically allows for earlier complexes of material (see, e.g., Nelson's allowance for a "prophetic source" of 1 Kgs 11:29–40[90]) but concentrates on the later stages of the history. In comparison, the multiple-redaction model concentrates on the redactional stages and smaller-scale textual complexes that were added to the base layer of the DtrH, and displays an even greater regard for the subsequent redaction thereof. Two basic components of the model may be discerned here on the basis of the themes on which they concentrate. In principle, although not necessarily in their various presentations, they are not mutually exclusive, but are instead two relatively independent concerns within the same larger synthetic model. The first component, a focus on formulae in 1–2 Kings, will be treated in this section. The second component, the establishment of a pre-Deuteronomistic prophetic edition, will be treated below in §3.4.

3.3.1. Arguments in Favor of a Pre- or Proto-Deuteronomistic Edition

3.3.1.1. H. Weippert

The first component of the model, exemplified by the work of H. Weippert, finds its motivation and primary focus in the variant forms and concerns of the evaluations of the kings of Israel and Judah.[91] Weippert noticed that several of the short evaluative statements of kings which Noth had attributed to the structuring author Dtr—those from Jehoshaphat to Ahaz for Judah—utilized a single criterion: the non-removal of the high places (במות) during the reign of the king under scrutiny as a mitigating factor to the favorable reports of certain southern kings' having done "what was right in Yahweh's eyes" (עשה הישר בעיני יהוה; pattern IS1; 1 Kgs 22:43–44; 2 Kgs 12:3–4; 14:3–4; 15:3–4,34–35; 16:2b,4),[92] whereas the two southern kings evaluated negatively had "walked in the way of the kings of Israel/House of Ahab" (מלכי ישראל or בית אחאב + הלך בדרך; pattern IS2; 2 Kgs 8:18,27). On the other hand, the northern kings had done "what was evil in Yahweh's eyes" (עשה הרע בעיני יהוה) by "persisting in" (מן + סור *qal* + לא) the "sin of Jeroboam ben-Nebat which he had caused Israel to sin" (חטאות ירבעם בן נבט אשר החטיא את ישראל; pattern IN; 2 Kgs 3:2–3; 10:29,31; 13:2–3,11; 14:24; 15:9,18,24,28). The

90 Nelson, *Double Redaction*, 110–11.

91 Helga Weippert, "Die 'deuteronomistischen' Beurteilungen der Könige von Israel und Juda und das Problem der Redaktion der Königsbücher," *Bib* 53 (1972): 301–39; idem, "Der Ort, den Jahwe erwählen wird, um dort seinen Namen wohnen zu lassen: Die Geschichte einer alttestamentlichen Formel," *BZ* 24 (1980): 76–94.

92 Cf. 1 Kgs 3:2–3, which provides the justification for this neglect.

redactional unity produced in these remarks, argued Weippert, suggests that a pre- (or perhaps better *proto-*) Deuteronomistic edition of the History (R^{I}) had been compiled under Hezekiah. The evaluations of the Judahite kings from Rehoboam to Asa and from Hezekiah to Josiah, as well as of the Israelite kings from Jeroboam I to Ahaziah, exhibit a different form. The Judahite kings Asa, Hezekiah, and Josiah were credited with doing "what was right in Yahweh's eyes" (עשׂה הישר בעיני יהוה), and following in the footsteps of "his ancestor David" (דוד אביו; pattern IIS; 1 Kgs 15:11; 2 Kgs 18:3; 22:2; cf. 1 Kgs 11:33,38; 14:8; 15:5). All northern kings—and some southern kings—were evaluated, as in the earlier pattern IN, as having done "evil in Yahweh's eyes (עשׂה הרע בעיני יהוה) and having sinned or caused Israel to sin (Pattern IIN; 1 Kgs 15:26,34; 16:19,25–26,30–31; 22:53,54b; cf. the southern kings' evaluations in 1 Kgs 15:3; 2 Kgs 21:2; 21:20–21). Weippert did admit that Pattern IIN is the most troublesome to represent, but he nonetheless maintained that minor variations did separate it from IN. She asserted that these two patterns, IIS and IIN, could also be attributed to a single layer of redaction (R^{II}), one more focused than R^{I} on the guilt or sin of the individual kings and attributable to the time of Josiah. Weippert then discerned a third (exilic) redaction (R^{III}), roughly equated with Cross's Dtr^2, which naturally evaluated the final four kings of Judah homogenously and negatively (2 Kgs 23:32,37; 24:9,19).[93] In addition to the support of Weippert's separation of R^{III} provided by Nelson,[94] several subsequent studies offered emendations or modifications to Weippert's hypothesis.[95]

---

93 Weippert, "'Deuteronomistischen' Beurteilungen," 307–34. I disregard here the issue of whether the different forms of northern and southern formularies necessitates different authors. Others who critique this theory are: Nelson, *Double Redaction*, 29–42; Campbell, *Prophets and Kings*, 139–202; Provan, *Hezekiah*, 35–55; and Enzo Cortese, "Lo schema deuteronomistico per i re di Giuda e d'Israele," *Bib* 56 (1975): 37–52, conveniently summarized by Provan (*Hezekiah*, 40–41).

94 Nelson, *Double Redaction*, 36–41.

95 Those not discussed here include Francolino J. Gonçalves, *L'expédition de Sennachérib en Palestine dans la littérature hébraïque ancienne* (Ebib n.s. 7; Paris: Gabalda, 1986), 73–76; George C. Heider, *The Cult of Molek: A Reassessment* (JSOTSup 43; Sheffield: JSOT Press, 1985), 286–89; and Konrad Schmid, "Hatte Wellhausen Recht? Das Problem der literarhistorischen Anfänge des Deuteronomismus in den Königebüchern," in *Die deuteronomistischen Geschichtswerke: Redaktions- und religionsgeschichtliche Perspektiven zur "Deuteronomismus"-Diskussion in Tora und Vorderen Propheten* (ed. Markus Witte et al.; BZAW 365; Berlin: de Gruyter, 2006), 19–43. Mayes (*Story*, 120–24) also followed Weippert's lead in pointing to the importance of the evaluations; his work is discussed more fully in a different context below (§3.4.2.3).

3.3.1.2. Slight Modifications: Barrick, Campbell, Lemaire, and Others

W. B. Barrick slightly modified Weippert's position by suggesting that 1 Kgs 15:14a and 2 Kgs 18:4a—the evaluations of Asa and Hezekiah, respectively—may arguably be placed within the scope of R^{I}, based on an examination of vocabulary and structure, as well as a common concern with the fate of the *bāmôt*-sanctuaries.[96] While the hand of the author of R^{II} may indeed be seen in those accounts, he argued, it comes as no surprise that the redactor may have added redactional elements at the join. This solution is somewhat more satisfying than Weippert's, particularly in the case of Hezekiah, who now becomes the climactic figure of the R^{I}.[97]

Campbell, too, accepted Weippert's emphasis on the judgment formulae as correctly placed, but he divided the authorship primarily geographically, rather than both geographically and temporally, as Weippert had done.[98] He argued that an extant "Prophetic Record," produced in a northern context, was subsequently expanded with the northern kings' judgment formulae after the fall of Samaria in 722 (Campbell's pattern A, dubbed the "Northern Expansion"), which recorded the evaluations of the Israelite kings from Jehu to Hoshea (2 Kgs 10:29; 13:2,11; 14:24; 15:9,18, 24,28; 17:2).[99] This expansion was designed to "bring [the Prophetic Record, which ended in 2 Kgs 10:28] down to the fall of the northern kingdom."[100] That complex was then expanded by a parallel document of southern origin (pattern B, the "Southern Document"), which culminated in the reign of Hezekiah (1 Kgs 14:22a,23a; 15:3a,11–12a,14a; 22:43a,44; 2 Kgs 8:18,27; 12:3–4; 14:3–4; 15:3–4,34–35a; 16:2b–3a; 18:3–5).[101] It is this Southern Document that formed the basis of Dtr's work. Dtr overlaid the extant evaluations of southern kings from Rehoboam to Asa with additional material (1 Kgs 14:22–24; 15:3–5,11–14) and composed evaluations for those northern kings who had not already received such evaluation (1 Kgs 14:15–16; 15:26,30,34; 16:13,19,25–26,30–33; 22:53–54; 2 Kgs 3:2–3)

96 W. Boyd Barrick, "On the Removal of the 'High Places' in 1–2 Kings," *Bib* 55 (1974): 257–59; see also Campbell, *Of Prophets and Kings*, 169–87.

97 Barrick, "Removal," 258–59; this position was also adopted by Manfred Weippert, "Fragen des israelitischen Geschichtsbewusstseins," *VT* 23 (1973): 437–38; Gonçalves, *L'expédition de Sennachérib*, 73–76; and Ansgar Moenikes, "Zur Redaktionsgeschichte des sogenannten Deuteronomistischen Geschichtswerks," *ZAW* 104 (1992): 333–48, esp. 340–45.

98 Campbell, *Of Prophets and Kings*, 139–202.

99 Ibid., 144. According to Campbell, the minimal text of the Northern Expansion comprised 2 Kgs 10:29,32–33,35; 13:2–3,7,9,11; 14:16,24,29; 15:9–10,14,18–20,22,24–25,28–29,30*; 17:2–6,20–21,23b (ibid., 158–61).

100 Ibid., 142.

101 The minimal text of the Southern Document was extensive, comprising 1 Kgs 12:1–15bα,16, 18–19,20b,26–29,30b–32; 14:21–23*,25–26a,31*; etc. For full text, see ibid., 187–97.

and for those southern kings from Hezekiah to Josiah (2 Kgs 21:2–6,20–22; 22:2).[102]

A. Lemaire also followed Weippert's reconstruction of the later layers of the DtrH in his own presentation but proposed four *earlier* redactional levels of the material:[103]

1) The Abiatharite account of David, written around 970, probably at the end of David's reign and ending with the crowning of Solomon.[104]
2) The Zadokite (or Nathanite?) edition of the same account, probably written during the first years of Solomon's reign, perhaps around 960.
3) The redaction of the history of Solomon's reign, ending with the divided kingdom, probably written around 920 during the reign of Rehoboam.
4) The redaction/edition comprising the history of the two kingdoms of Judah and Israel until their reconciliation, written around 850, during the reign of Jehoshaphat.[105]

The first three redactional levels are more likely to be explained somewhat differently (see below, chs. 5–7), but ultimately, Lemaire's reorganization of Weippert's system provides an explanation as to why her Stratum I oddly began only with those kings who ruled ca. 850, since the earlier kings would already have been covered in an earlier document. The next redactional level would then have been Weippert's Hezekian Redaction I, with the fall of the northern kingdom viewed in retrospect (written ca. 710–705), followed by the Josianic Redaction II (= Cross's Dtr[1]; ca. 620–609) and the exilic Redaction III (= Cross's Dtr[2]; ca. 560).

---

102 Ibid., 148–49, 179–85. See also O'Brien for a defense of Campbell's theory (*DHH* 174–226).

103 The following quotation can be found in Lemaire, "Redactional History," 458. A full account of Lemaire's sources will not be given here, but the reader is referred in particular to ibid., 457–58, esp. nn. 34–43. The footnotes in the quoted block of text are my own.

104 Lemaire bases this view on the work of François Langlamet, "Pour ou contre Salomon? La rédaction prosalomonienne de 1 Rois i–ii," parts 1 and 2, *RB* 83 (1976): 321–79, 481–528; see also idem, "Ahitofel et Houshaï: Rédaction prosalomonienne en 2 S 15–17?" in *Studies in Bible and the Ancient Near East: Presented to Samuel E. Loewenstamm on His Seventieth Birthday* (ed. Yitschak Avishur and Joshua Blau; Jerusalem: Rubinstein, 1978), 57–90. This redactional level, ending with 1 Kings 2, corresponds roughly to the combined History of David's Rise and Solomonic Succession Narrative. For the breakdown of those two texts, see below, chs. 5 and 6.

105 For discussion of this stratum, see Lemaire, "Redactional History," 454–56.

3.3.2. Arguments and Counter-arguments Concerning a Pre-Deuteronomistic Edition of 1–2 Kings

3.3.2.1. Provan, Halpern and Vanderhooft, Eynikel

I. Provan in turn offered a criticism of Weippert's model and of the various responses thereto. He argued that the rigidity of the last four evaluations adduced by Nelson (2 Kgs 23:32,37; 24:9,19)[106] was not so diagnostic of authorial discontinuity at Josiah's reign as had been previously assumed, that Weippert's analysis unfairly privileges some data while ignoring or suppressing other indications of authorship, and that Campbell's schema inappropriately divides the northern evaluations, forcing a difficult reconstruction of the post-722 development of the DtrH.[107] These criticisms and others led Provan to the conclusion that an early DtrH concluding with the reign of Hezekiah (2 Kgs 18:17–19:8 + 19:35–37), not Josiah, was produced before the exile early in the reign of Josiah.[108]

Although they agreed that a document ending with the reign of Hezekiah could be isolated, B. Halpern and D. S. Vanderhooft challenged Provan's thesis (and anticipated that of Aurelius; see below) that no document ending with Josiah's reign existed and instead returned to the earlier model that maintains essential breaks in authorship both at Hezekiah's reign and at Josiah's reign.[109] They based their argument both on thematic concerns (viz-à-viz the evaluations of northern kings) and on the formal dissimilarities between Hezekiah's evaluation (2 Kgs 18:3–5) and that of Josiah (2 Kgs 22:2).[110] With Barrick, they argued that formal changes between the evaluations of Rehoboam (1 Kgs 14:21–24) and Abijam (1 Kgs 15:3), on one hand, and Asa (1 Kgs 15:9–14), on the other, can actually be explained as features of stylistic consistency on the part of a single author, rather than as markers of two separate hands.[111] This recognition ultimately negates R^{II}'s authorship of the evaluations preceding that of Asa, as Weippert had supposed, and instead supports a block of Deuteronomistic text that comprises much of the text of 1–2 Kings, ending

106 Nelson, *Double Redaction*, 36–41; see also O'Brien, *DHH*, 268–71.

107 Provan, *Hezekiah*, 48–55. For discussion of the debate through Provan's work, see McKenzie, *Trouble*, 117–22.

108 Ibid., 120–30, esp. 128, and 153–55. For similar conclusions, see H. R. Macy, "The Sources of the Book of Chronicles" (Ph.D. diss., Harvard University, 1975).

109 Halpern was, to some extent, building on his own "Sacred History," 35–54.

110 Ibid., 206–7. Weippert's R^{III} remains uncontested by Halpern and Vanderhooft (ibid., 208–12).

111 Ibid., 199–208.

only with Hezekiah's reign.[112] This conclusion receives further substantiation from a study of the death and burial formulae, which normally begin with the notice of death (וישכב PN עם אבתיו) and continue with a statement to the effect that the king "was buried with his fathers" in a specific place (ויקבר עם אבתיו); until and including the notice for Ahaz's burial in 1 Kgs 16:20, this location is the City of David (בעיר דוד). As with the evaluations beginning with Hezekiah, the regularity of these formulae breaks down, and only the first element remains consistent.[113] The similarity of Hezekiah's evaluation (2 Kgs 18:4a) to those preceding, combined with the dissimilarity of his death formulary (20:21) to its antecedents, may thus indicate the date and extent of one pre- or proto-Deuteronomistic text complex fairly precisely.[114]

E. Eynikel had independently reached a substantially similar conclusion in his 1989 dissertation and was able to take note of Halpern and Vanderhooft's thesis in his dissertation's final published form.[115] Eynikel differed from Halpern and Vanderhooft primarily in two areas. First, he limited the work of the proto-Deuteronomist (his RI) to the book of Kings, beginning only with the evaluation of Solomon in 1 Kgs 3:3a. Second, and less importantly, he asserted that the first and second editions should be dated *after* the completion of the reigns of Hezekiah and Josiah, respectively, since each contains a notice of the duration of the king's reign (2 Kgs 18:2; 22:2) that need not be separated from the accompanying evaluations.[116]

3.3.2.2. Aurelius

Recently, a reactionary position has been espoused by E. Aurelius, who argues only for a redactional boundary between 2 Kings 17 and 18, which

112 The interaction of Halpern and Vanderhooft's model with that of Campbell requires much fuller analysis than can be devoted in this modest review.

113 Halpern and Vanderhooft, "Editions of Kings," 189–90, 194. Moreover, a study of the preservation of the names of Queen Mothers in Chronicles suggests "that the edition of Kings that served as the *Vorlage* of Chronicles (Chr^1?) named no QM's [Queen Mothers] after Hezekiah" (ibid., 198); see also Provan, *Hezekiah*, 139–41.

114 Halpern and Vanderhooft, "Editions of Kings," 194–97, 221; see also Provan, *Hezekiah*, 134–38. Compare already the observations of Jepsen that the Synchronic History ended with Hezekiah (*Quellen*, 10).

115 Eynikel, *Reform*, 33–135, esp. 52–60, 107–11, 120–21, 132–35.

116 Ibid., 134–35. A further point of minor divergence is reached in Eynikel's reassertion of the primary importance of the evaluations over and above the remaining data adduced by Halpern and Vanderhooft (ibid., 135).

can be traced to post-Dtr redactional activity.[117] His methodology includes a thorough reanalysis of the argumentation concerning the evaluations of the kings. Aurelius's argument proceeds in several steps. First of all, he disputes the claim that there existed a redactional boundary somewhere after the reign of Abijam (1 Kgs 15:9–14), that is, the first boundary between Weippert's R^{II} (1 Kings) and R^{I} (2 Kings). This is not simply a refutation of parts of Weippert's model, which finds this boundary between the evaluations of Asa (1 Kgs 15:14) and Jehoshaphat (22:41–44), but also of Barrick's, which found the boundary before the reign of Asa (1 Kgs 15:14), and of Campbell's, which, Aurelius implied, had argued that the evaluations of the northern kings before 2 Kgs 10:28 had been composed by the pre-Deuteronomistic author of Campbell's "Prophetic Record":

> Sowohl Campbell als auch Lemaire bauen die Annahme einer alten, bis einschließlich 1 R 22 oder 2 R 10:28 reichenden Geschichte im wesentlichen auf H. Weipperts Untersuchung der Königsbeurteilungen. H. Weippert betont indessen nicht nur die Unterschiede zwischen den Beurteilungen in 1 R (RII) und 2 R 3–17 (RI), sondern ebensosehr die Verwandtschaft zwischen denjenigen in 1 R und 2 R 18–22 (beidemal RII). Wenn die ersten nicht RII, sondern vielmehr einem Vorgänger von RI entstammen sollen, dann wird ihre Verwandtschaft mit den Beurteilungen in 2 R 18–22 zum Problem. Diese Kapitel müßte mann dann eigentlich auch um 850 datieren, obwohl sie die Geschichte bis 622 darstellen.[118]

Aurelius's second task was to examine Provan's (and others') claim that there exists a literary boundary at the reign of Hezekiah. This, too, Aureli-

117 Erik Aurelius, *Zukunft jenseits des Gerichts: Eine redaktionsgeschichtliche Studie zum Enneateuch* (BZAW 319; Berlin: de Gruyter, 2003), esp. 1–110.

118 Aurelius, *Zukunft*, 24–25; cf. Barrick, "Removal"; Campbell, *Of Prophets and Kings*. Careful scrutiny suggests that this is a too facile dismissal of Campbell's proposed redactional schema. Had Aurelius not been so flippant in his criticism of Campbell's discussion of the problem, he might have noticed that Campbell *did not* attribute the evaluations of the northern kings (1 Kgs 14:15–16; 15:26,30,34; 16:13,19,25–26,30–33; 22:53–54; 2 Kgs 3:2–3) to his pre-Deuteronomistic "Prophetic Record" source (i.e., the "Vorgänger von RI"); that condemnatory function had already been fulfilled by the prophetic oracles of the Prophetic Record (see discussion below), so the evaluations would therefore have been superfluous in that document. Instead, Campbell attributed these evaluations in 1 Kings to Dtr (Weippert's R^{II}), who had already received the Prophetic Record along with the Northern Expansion, roughly analogous to the northern notices of Weippert's R^{I} (=IN). The Deuteronomist then composed the evaluations of the earlier northern kings in conformity with the evaluations of the southern kings beginning with Hezekiah and ending with Josiah (2 Kgs 21:2–6,20–22; 22:2). Moreover, Campbell *did* include the evaluations of Rehoboam (1 Kgs 14:21–23a*) and Abijam (15:3a) in the pre-Deuteronomistic Southern Document, but he allowed for Deuteronomistic editing of both those evaluations (14:22b,23b,24b; 15:3b–5; *Of Prophets and Kings*, 148–49, 179–85, 198; see discussion above). Whether or not Campbell's schema is the best model through which to understand the evaluations, Aurelius has apparently misread the former's work, and his objections to Campbell's hypothesis miss the mark entirely; the literary boundary between the evaluations of 1 Kings and 2 Kings is not at stake and is a position that is not held by the majority of interpreters.

us denied.[119] Furthermore, Aurelius distinguished his position from that of any that claims a redactional boundary at the reign of Josiah. Here, Aurelius joined Provan in his criticism that other interpreters had too easily claimed an epigonic status for the author of the last four royal evaluations (2 Kgs 23:32,37; 24:9,19).[120] He then asserted that the passages reiterating the Davidic covenant were best understood as exilic, implicitly a retroversion to von Rad's position, which, it should be remembered, found the presence of a graceful divine promise in Jehoiachin's establishment in the Babylonian court.

Although Aurelius has provided a valuable critique of the Weippert-Lemaire schema and a meaningful theological reading of the DtrH as a component of the Enneateuch, the thesis is not without its own methodological problems. By denying that Hezekiah had indeed carried through a cultic centralization of his own volition in history, Aurelius is able to claim that the Deuteronomistic condemnation of Manasseh, which was founded on Manasseh's renewal of "pagan" cultic practices and reestablishment of the high places, was predicated on a literary (but not historically accurate) claim that Hezekiah had first removed those installations and ended those practices.[121] While it may be the case that Hezekiah's "centralization" was a literary construct crafted to justify the very real historical shrinking of Judah during the Assyrian period,[122] this logic is particularly weak, since it assumes a priori that the DtrH was composed all at one time and that Manasseh was condemned for Judah's downfall from the inception of that document. As should be clear by now, this is not necessarily the case, and any such assumption rests on the same type of circular methodology as does the Cross school's supposition that the DtrH could be the product of an ongoing process. Moreover, any argument that Manasseh was blamed for Judah's downfall from the beginning, rather than retrospectively in a set of secondary Deuteronomistic additions (e.g., the Cross school's Dtr^2), requires much more stringent argumentation than Aurelius provides. In short, because it tacitly assumes the exilic provenance of the DtrH, his argument here can only arrive at that same conclusion.

The same criticism applies to Aurelius's dismissal of Josiah's reform as well.[123] Aurelius argues that although it would have been impossible for the temple reform to be carried out during the exile, since the temple lay in

119 Aurelius, *Zukunft*, 29–38.

120 Ibid., 45; see also Thomas Römer, *Israels Väter: Untersuchungen zur Väterthematik im Deuteronomium und in der deuteronomistischen Tradition* (OBO 99; Fribourg: University Press; Göttingen: Vandenhoeck & Ruprecht, 1990), 271–85, esp. 284.

121 Ibid., 30–33, esp. 33.

122 See recently Diana Edelman, "Hezekiah's Alleged Cultic Centralization," *JSOT* 32 (2008): 395–434, and bibliography there.

123 Ibid., 39–44, esp. 39–40. Cf. Schmid, "Hatte Wellhausen Recht?" 35–36.

ruins, the exile constitutes the most likely scenario in which the *idea* of a cultic centralization would have been imagined. The continued presence of any peripheral cultic installations after the Temple's destruction would have posed severe problems for the cult's claim to centrality, calling into question the effectiveness of the Yahwistic cult itself. "Das Anliegen wäre in beiden Fällen, die nun zum ersten Mal gefährdete Stellung Jerusalems als Zentrum der Jhwh-Verehrung für die Zukunft zu verteidigen."[124] This claim is specious and too flatly assumes that the Cross school's interpretation of the Deuteronomistic account of Josiah's reform lays claim to the text's unshakeable historical accuracy. Ironically, Aurelius's reading also suffers from the assumption that the Yahwistic cult of the period was already irrevocably unified and centralized in Jerusalem and that the DtrH itself could only have been trying to portray history, albeit in a heavily theologized manner. Yet a more responsible reading from the general perspective of the Cross school would assert that the DtrH account of Josiah's reform was not historically accurate but rather was meant to be *programmatic*, an attempt by the Josianic-era temple priesthood to capitalize on the young age and corresponding inexperience of an ascendant king in order to centralize their own station within Judah, whether theologically or economically.[125] This viewpoint would furthermore allow that Josiah's (or, more properly, "Josiah's") reform was never carried through thoroughly and that peripheral cultic installations naturally continued to exist. After the downfall of the kingdom—and with it, the centralized temple cultus—Deuteronomistic editors had to come to grips with the ultimate failure of the reform. The claim that a "reform movement" finds its most fitting locus in the exile is patently false; this was hardly the first time that the centrality of the Yahwistic cultus had been threatened: it had been under the threat of centrifugal forces from the beginning and likely remained so until the temple's destruction in 587.

3.3.3. Concluding Remarks

Although a full critique of Aurelius's study remains outside the scope of the present investigation, due respect must be paid to the present status of that book within the current discussion. *Zukunft jenseits des Gerichts* is without doubt one of the two or three most important works by a theoretical adherent of the Smend school—and certainly one of the most often-

124 Ibid., 40.

125 Aurelius flatly denies both of these possibilities (ibid., 40–42). It is not immediately apparent to me that his argument holds up under a different set of assumptions.

cited. Overall, the study is a thorough and well-articulated statement of that school's basic position, since it remains grounded in the same logic and on the same set of basic assumptions concerning the process whereby the DtrH was formed as well as the theological intention of that document—just as the present study remains fundamentally centered within the model established by the Cross school. However, Aurelius has begun to move away from the Smend school in a few important ways, which unfortunately cannot be discussed in great detail here.[126] Nonetheless, while some degree of consensus has been reached concerning the "nomistic" nature of much of the post-Dtr material in the DtrH (see discussions of Mayes and O'Brien below), it seems to me unlikely that a consensus or even a medial position between the two dominant schools will ever be reached concerning the date and intention of the original edition of the Deuteronomistic corpus, and Aurelius's study remains symptomatic (and perhaps emblematic) of the theoretical gulf between the two.

It might—with some difficulty—be argued that the majority of scholars who have analyzed the evaluations and other formulae in 1–2 Kings have reached the conclusion that Hezekiah's reign exhibits signs of editorial disjunction, after which the hand of a different author may be discerned.[127] This difficulty is fortunately mitigated by the fact that the thesis of the present study is not fundamentally reliant on the accuracy of one or another particular view of the precise date of the formation of the DtrH, since the pre-Deuteronomistic edition(s) of 1–2 Samuel remain(s) the focal point of this source- and redaction-critical investigation and since the existence of a Hezekian- or Josianic- or exilic-era Deuteronomistic edition is only of subsidiary importance in that discussion. We therefore need not delve much further into these disagreements between the proponents of the various models of the development of the larger DtrH, except as they apply specifically to the relationships between 1–2 Samuel and the surrounding materials. Because of this primary concern to isolate the pre-Deuteronomistic edition of 1–2 Samuel, this study finds welcome conver-

126 First and foremost, this movement is effected by Aurelius's limitation of the extent of the original edition of DtrH to 1 Samuel–2 Kings (see discussion below, §3.4). It may be the case that we are witnessing the birth of a new Göttinger school, a Kratz-Aurelius school, which has as its primary object of study the composition of the Enneateuch. Although I remain somewhat skeptical that such study can be effectively carried through without first coming to a settlement on the fundamental problems faced by scholars of both the DtrH and the Pentateuch—since all such investigation continues to ground itself in the foundational theoretical and methodological assumptions inherited from the Smend school—its goal is admittedly a noble one. A larger contextualization of the problems faced by students of both corpora may eventually lead to increased understanding of each.

127 Cf. McKenzie, who is disinclined to see more than one organizer for the larger history. He therefore must revert to the Cross school's model of a single Josianic author (*Trouble*, 117–34).

sation partners among the respective memberships of both the Cross and Smend schools.

3.4. Models Incorporating a Pre-Deuteronomistic Edition: Focus on Prophetic Redaction in Samuel-Kings

The second component of this model of the development of pre-Deuteronomistic sources, under discussion in §§3.3–3.4, provides a supplement to the focus on formulae in the Weippert-Lemaire component. Because Weippert was most concerned to explain the development of the Deuteronomistic structure of 1–2 Kings, neither her study nor those seeking to supplement and refine it took into sufficient account the development of 1–2 Samuel. In my view, Weippert's component of the model provides a reasonable basis for an understanding of the evaluations, but it does not adequately explain the development of much of the rest of the pre-Deuteronomistic material in Samuel-Kings. A second component of the model is required. The hypothesis of a pre-Deuteronomistic "Prophetic Record" (hereafter PR) treats 1–2 Samuel and much of 1–2 Kings as an accumulation of traditions that only solidified around the time of Jehu (ca. 840).[128]

The influence of prophetically oriented schools of redaction in the prehistory of the Deuteronomistic writings was hardly an innovation of the 1970's or 1980's, and it is therefore somewhat anachronistic to delay discussion of this model until this point; already in the late 1940's, the "prophetic" nature of the DtrH was accepted as obvious. As described above, Jepsen, von Rad, and Wolff (among many others) had all noted the centrality of prophetic tropes in the history: Jepsen's postulation of a "nebiistische Redaktion" as the primary edition of the DtrH, von Rad's clarification of the prophecy-fulfillment schema undergirding the history's structure, and Wolff's foregrounding of the prophetic call to "return!" all point the way towards the recognition of the DtrH as prophetically oriented, at least in its origins and initial expression (DtrG or Dtr^1), although that structure has been somewhat masked by a later redactor concerned specifically with the people's adherence to a *written* law (DtrN

128 E.g., Antony F. Campbell, *1 Samuel* (FOTL 7; Grand Rapids, Mich.: Eerdmans, 2003), 319–20. Note that this document therefore effectively post-dates Lemaire's supposed compilation of the royal evaluations during the time of Jehoshaphat (ca. 850; Lemaire, "Redactional History," 458). As discussed briefly above, Cambell's particular permutation of the theory was commensurate with the basic outline of Weippert's model.

or Dtr^2).[129] The Smend School's recognition of a strongly prophetic component of Deuteronomistic redaction (DtrP) solidified the case for the existence of prophetic tropes in the DtrH, even if that school's practitioners were perhaps too quick to lump together prophetic pronouncements, narratives, and other literature into a single layer of redaction. Undoubtedly, several passages dealing with prophetic concerns may be traced to the Deuteronomistic layers of editing (especially those passages in which the prophetic intermediary remains unnamed; e.g., 1 Kgs 12:31–13:34; 2 Kgs 21:10–15; cf. the naming of Huldah in 2 Kgs 22:14);[130] the same cannot necessarily be said for the earliest isolatable incidents of prophetic pronouncement against the northern dynasties (all of which are uttered by a named prophet; 1 Kgs 11:30–39*; 14:7–11*; 21:17–24*; and 2 Kgs 9:6–10*).[131] The widespread extent of these passages indicates that the PR reaches potentially as far forward as 2 Kings 10, and as far backward as 1 Samuel 1, claims Campbell. Moreover, the bulk of identifiable pre-Deuteronomistic prophetic collection and edition of materials can be found throughout the book of Samuel. It is to that more narrowly confined textual unit that we must turn our attention in the remainder of this study, because it is in the book of Samuel that the fractures and seams of the DtrH—and with it, the Transjordanian Motif—are both most visible and most complexly interwoven. In this section I intend to demonstrate two points through a survey of critical approaches to Samuel: first, I find that there is ample reason to posit the existence of a pre-Deuteronomistic prophetic document that was subsequently incorporated in the DtrH and overlaid with at least one, but probably two, layer(s) of Deuteronomistic redaction. Second, a concurrent examination of the composition history of that document and the processes whereby it was incorporated into the DtrH suggests that the earlier document's boundaries may be found at 1 Sam 1:1 and somewhere in 2 Kings 9–10. This means that of the three different views of Transjordan outlined in §1.2.4—the deliverer-type, the monarch-type, and the prophet-type—examples of the first two occur already in the

129 Jepsen, *Quellen*, 76–101; von Rad, *Studies*, 78–81; Wolff, "The Kerygma," 93–99, esp. 98; compare also O'Brien's claim that Dtr intentionally structured several episodes with a "four-part pattern" centered on the person and function of the prophet. The four constituent elements were: (1) the "critical element in the king's reign," (2) the "prophetic consultation," (3) delivery of the prophecy, and (4) the "fulfillment of the prophecy." The combination of these elements may be found, for example, in the episodes of the Assyrian crisis (2 Kgs 18:17–37; 19:1–2,5–7,8–9a,36–37) and Josiah's reform (2 Kgs 22:3–10,11–14,15–20; 23:1–23).

130 See also the discussion below of McKenzie, *Trouble*; and O'Brien, *DHH*, 272–87, esp. 273–80.

131 See Mayes, *Story*, 117–20, esp. 119; Campbell, *Of Prophets and Kings*, 23–41; see also Nelson, *Double Redaction*, 110–11; cf. McKenzie, *Trouble*, 61–80.

pre-Deuteronomistic compilation (1 Sam 11:1–15* as deliverer-type; 2 Sam 19:12–44 as monarch-type). Only the third type, the prophet-type, remained outside the boundaries of this document (Joshua 3–4) or was later interpolated (e.g., 2 Kgs 2:1–18).

3.4.1. The Formation of the Theory of Prophetic Redaction: Origins in Continental Scholarship

3.4.1.1. Noth

Noth's hypothesis allowed for the Historian's use of extant prophetic and narrative *legenda* as building blocks for the DtrH. The largest documents that Dtr used in the composition of what is now 1–2 Samuel, according to Noth, were the "old Samuel story" (1 Sam 1:1–4:12), itself a "self-contained prophetic tradition";[132] the "old tradition on Saul" (1 Sam 9:1–10:16 + 10:27b–11:15 + 13–14), ostensibly the "pro-monarchic" source adduced by Wellhausen; the "story of the rise of David" (1 Sam 16:14–2 Sam 5:25*); and the "story of the Davidic succession" ([1 Sam 4:1b–7:1], 2 Samuel 6–7; 9–20; and 1 Kings 1–2), ostensibly Rost's "Succession Narrative."[133] Although the precise delineation of each and the description of the process whereby the text reached its final form did not especially concern Noth, he did admit much pre-Deuteronomistic combination of these textual complexes, each of which had already potentially undergone a formation by the juxtaposition and editorial compilation of earlier texts (e.g., the combination of the Ark Narrative of 1 Sam 4:1b–7:1 + 2 Samuel 6 in Rost's formulation). Noth suggests, for example, that the old Saul tradition (originally 1 Sam 13:2–14:52* with the subsequent addition of 1 Samuel 15; 16:1–13) had already been fused with the story of the rise of David (beginning with 1 Sam 16:14) by the time Dtr received the traditions.[134] Therefore, despite the fact that his acceptance of a large pre-Deuteronomistic complex remained of secondary importance, one of the complexes of tradition that Noth allotted to a pre-Deuteronomistic tradition spanned at least 1 Sam 1:1–2 Sam 2:7. This admission opened the door to the study of those smaller complexes of tradition within the context of study of the DtrH.

132 Noth, *DH*, 84.
133 Ibid., 86; see also Rost, *Succession*.
134 Ibid., 86 n. 1, and 87.

3.4.1.2. Nübel, Mildenberger, Macholz, and Schüpphaus

Several scholars quickly picked up on the space left open for pre-Deuteronomistic redaction in Noth's formulation, many of whose studies appeared as inaugural dissertations now not widely available. The first, H.-U. Nübel, examined 1 Samuel 16–2 Samuel 12, in which he saw a relatively unified History of David's Rise (*Geschichte von Davids Aufstieg*).[135] This corpus had been compiled and composed by someone operating in a northern context and with knowledge of—if not influence from—the prophetic guild with which Elijah and Elisha were associated.[136] F. Mildenberger completed his dissertation three years later under K. Elliger and A. Weiser (see below).[137] Because he was primarily concerned with the book of Samuel, Mildenberger limited the prophetic editing to 1 Sam 9:1–10:16; 11; 13:4b–5,7b–15a; 15; 16:1–14a; 18:10–16*; 25(?); 28:3–25; 2 Sam 3:18(?); 5:1–2; 5:12(?); 6:16,20–23; 7:8–17*, but he did recognize signs of Deuteronomistic appropriation of earlier prophetic traditions in 1 Kgs 11:26–13:18.[138] In Heidelberg, G. C. Macholz completed a dissertation in 1966 also arguing for a pre-Deuteronomistic, prophetic redactional stratum.[139] The next year, J. Schüpphaus, working in Bonn under O. Plöger, found a pre-Deuteronomistic edition reaching from Joshua 24 to the reign of Hezekiah.[140] But these new scholars were not the only ones to find evidence of pre-Deuteronomistic editions in the Judges–Kings complex.

---

135 Hans-Ulrich Nübel, "Davids Aufstieg in der frühe israelitischer Geschichtsschreibung" (Ph.D. diss., Bonn, 1959). Nübel was a former student of Noth who completed his dissertation under O. Plöger.

136 Ibid., 145–47.

137 Friedrich Mildenberger, "Die vordeuteronomistische Saul-Davidüberlieferung" (Ph.D. diss., Tübingen, 1962).

138 Ibid., 29, 60–70; the review of Mildenberger (*TLZ* 87 [1962]: 778–79) incorrectly omits 1 Samuel 11 from the list of prophetically reworked passages in Samuel.

139 Georg Christian Macholz, "Untersuchungen zur Geschichte der Samuel Überlieferungen" (Th.D. diss., Heidelberg, 1966). Unfortunately, I have been unable to gain access to this dissertation.

140 Joachim Schüpphaus, "Richter- und Prophetengeschichten als Glieder der Geschichtsdarstellung der Richter- und Königzeit" (Th.D. diss., Bonn, 1967). For pre-Deuteronomistic redaction in the book of Judges, see especially Wolfgang Richter, *Traditionsgeschichtliche Untersuchungen zum Richterbuch* (BBB 18; Bonn: Heinstein, 1963); idem, *Die Bearbeitungen des "Retterbuches" in der deuteronomistischen Epoche* (BBB 21; Bonn: Hanstein, 1964); idem, "Die Überlieferungen um Jephtah: Ri 10,17–12,6," *Bib* 47 (1966): 485–556. A narrative spanning a similarly broad range of the DtrH was proposed by Giovanni Garbini, who found a coherent—albeit truncated—story in Judg 9:1–25,50–55*; 1 Sam 9:1–10:16*; 16:14–23; 18:6b–9,12–13,20–29; 19:8–17; 21:11–22:5; 24*; 31:1–10; 2 Sam 2:17–32; 3:6–32; 4; 1 Kgs 21; 22:29–38; 2 Kgs 9:1–10:14 ("'Narrativa della Successione' o 'Storia dei Rei'?" *Hen* 1 [1979]: 19–41, French summary on 40–41).

3.4.1.3. Weiser

Weiser himself had been working on the problem of the composition of Samuel concurrently with his student Mildenberger, and he published two studies in the years immediately before and after the completion of his student's thesis theorizing the existence of multiple *legenda*, originally independent of one another, that had been gathered and organized in a pre-Deuteronomistic prophetic edition.[141] That edition included the earlier legends and the prophetic additions in 1 Sam 1–3; 7–8; 10:8,17–27; 13:7–15; 15; 16:1–13; 28 and possibly the "late narrative" of David and Goliath in 1 Sam 17–18.[142] Weiser understood that these disparate episodes did not "represent a literary unity" but suggested, rather, that they were "associated together in the same intellectual and religious context of a theological presentation of history."[143] He therefore answered von Rad's complaint that 1–2 Samuel does not display significant evidence of Deuteronomistic reworking: because this pre-Deuteronomistic prophetic edition had already done much of the shaping of 1–2 Samuel, it was unnecessary for Dtr to add more than a few unifying theological notes and revisions (1 Sam 2:35–36; 2 Sam 7:13) or chronological statements (1 Sam 4:18b; 7:2b; 2 Sam 5:4–5).[144]

3.4.1.4. Fohrer

G. Fohrer, too, found a "supplementary stratum" running through Samuel. This stratum of redaction appropriated an already somewhat loosely assembled collection of "independent narratives and more comprehensive presentations, partially popular, partially deriving from the royal court," consisting of the full span of the original Ark Narrative (1 Sam 4:1–7,17; 2 Sam 6:1–12,14,20–23; 7:1–7,17); the "narrative of Saul's rise and end" (1 Sam 9:1–10:16; 11; 13–14; 31); the History of David's Rise (1 Sam 16:14–2 Sam 5*); a revised version of Nathan's oracle (2 Samuel 7), which thematically divorced that episode from its original position with the Ark

---

141 Weiser, *Old Testament*, 166–69; see also idem, *Samuel: Seine geschichtliche Aufgabe und religiöse Bedeutung* (FRLANT 81; Göttingen: Vandenhoeck & Ruprecht, 1962).

142 Weiser, *Old Testament*, 166. By "late narrative" Weiser intended to indicate those passages missing from the LXX of 1 Samuel 17–18 (17:12–14,16–18,20–23a,24–30,41,48b,50,55–58; 18:1–5,10–11,12b,17–19,29b–30). However, it seems as though Weiser felt himself unable to solve the riddle of the manuscript evidence, and therefore also allowed the attribution of this narrative to a post-Deuteronomistic editor. This solution is unnecessary; see discussion below, §6.5.2).

143 Ibid.

144 Ibid., 168–70.

Narrative; and the "Court History of David" (2 Sam 9–20*; 1 Kgs 1–2*).[145] This "basic stratum" had been supplemented with a few scattered episodes (1 Sam 14:49–51; 2 Sam 8:16–18; 21:1–14,15–22; 23:8–39; 24) before its inclusion in the supplementary stratum, in which "prophetical thought comes to grips with the early history of the monarchy and its traditions." This supplementary stratum did not simply comprise an organization of the various constituent traditions; in addition, the editor added material articulating the prophetic viewpoint (1 Sam 1–3*; 7:2–17; 8; 10:17–27; 12; 13:7b–15bα; 15; 16:1–13; expansions of 1 Samuel 17, esp. vv. 45–47; and 28).[146] Fohrer found reason as well to attribute several of the prophetic narratives in 1–2 Kings (1 Kings 17–19; 21; 2 Kgs 1:1–17; 2; 3:4–27; 4:1–8,15; 9:1–10; 13:14–21) to a long process of transmission culminating in the work of a (presumably northern?) redactor working in the late-9th century.[147]

3.4.2. Adding Fuel to the Prophetic Fire: Anglophone Scholarship in Favor of pre-Deuteronomistic Redaction

3.4.2.1. Birch

The explosion of studies finding pre-Deuteronomistic prophetic editorial work quickly crossed the Atlantic and became a widely propagated theory in the Anglophone world during the 1970's and 1980's. In his 1970 Yale dissertation, B. C. Birch attempted a thorough exegetical analysis of the prophetic elements in 1 Samuel 7–15. The resulting publications of the piece appeared in the early and mid-1970's and continue to lay a foundational cornerstone for models of prophetic redaction in Samuel.[148] In each of the chapters narrating the institution of the monarchy in Israel, Birch detected both traditional prophetically reworked antecedents and the work of Dtr (generally construed as an undifferentiated stratum). The prophetic reworking of the section was extensive, comprising several older preserved traditions and etiologies (7:5–6abα,7–12,16–17; 8:1–7*,[19–22, edited];

145 Fohrer, *Introduction*, 218–22, quote from 218.

146 Ibid., 222–25, quote from 223.

147 Ibid., 232–34. See also Rolf P. Knierem, "The Messianic Concept in The First Book of Samuel," in *Jesus and the Historian: Written in Honor of Ernest Cadman Colwell* (ed. F. Thomas Trotter; Philadelphia: Westminster, 1968), 20–51.

148 Bruce C. Birch, *The Rise of the Israelite Monarchy: The Growth and Development of 1 Samuel 7–15* (SBLDS 27; Missoula, Mont.: Scholars Press, 1976); see also idem, "The Development of the Tradition on the Anointing of Saul in 1 Sam. 9:1–10:16," *JBL* 90 (1971): 55–68; and idem, "The Choosing of Saul at Mizpah," *CBQ* 37 (1975): 447–57. The two latter pieces were slightly reworked versions of chapters from the dissertation.

9:1–14,18–19,22–24; 10:2–4,9,14–16a,20–21bα,21bβ–24; 11:1–11*,15; 13:2–7a,15b–18,23; 14:1–46,47–51[149]) and the prophetic redactional material that linked them together (7:6bβ,15; 9:15–17,20–21,[25–26],27–10:1[LXX]; 10:5–8,10–13,[150]16b,17–19,25–27a; 11:7*[ואחר שמואל],8bβ, 12–14; [12:1–5]; 13:7b–15a; 15:1–35). Birch detected the work of a Deuteronomistic editor, but in comparison to the assertions of earlier figures such as Wellhausen and Noth, the work of Dtr appears quite minimal in Birch's reconstruction (especially in 1 Samuel 10), comprising only 7:(2),3–4,13–14; 8:5b* (ככל־הגוים),8,(9–10),11–18; 12:6–25; 13:1.[151]

3.4.2.2. McCarter

In his commentaries on 1–2 Samuel, P. K. McCarter laid out his own theory of the Deuteronomistic and prophetic (which he considered proto-Deuteronomistic) editing of the books of Samuel.[152] McCarter distinguished signs of Deuteronomistic editing only in 1 Sam 2:27–36; 3:11–14; 4:18b; 7:2aβ–4,6b,13–14,15–17; 8:8; 12:6–15,19b(?),20b–22,24–25; 13:1–2; 14:47–51; 17*; 20:11–17, 23, 40–42; 23:14–24:23; 25:28–31; 2 Sam 2:10a(?), 11(?); 3:9–10, 17–18a(?), 18b, 28–29; 5:1–2, 4–5(?), 12; 6:21; 7:1b, 9b–11a, 13a, 16, 22b–24(Dtr^{2}?), 25–26, 29bα; 8:14b–15(?); 14:9; 15:24aβ*(Dtr^{2}?); 21:7(?). Most of these verses serve to anticipate or recall episodes in the book that belonged to other original source texts or to express the Deuteronomistic perspective in the context of the narrative.[153] But McCarter considered the bulk of the book of Samuel to have attained its present order before the Deuteronomistic edition in the form of a "Prophetic History," which was "prophetic in perspective and suspicious of the monarchy" (with Weiser). This history comprised a redactional, "supplementary *stratum*" (following Fohrer), over against Birch's claim of a prophetic, "pre-Deuteronomistic *edition*." [154] While the precise nature of the document at hand remains up for debate—and I remain unconvinced

149 Birch views much of chs. 13 and 14 (including 14:47–51) as an undifferentiated collection of stories about Saul's kingship which had already been formed by the time of its inclusion by the prophetic redactor, but he is unable to determine how to classify the note in 14:52 (*Rise*, 94).

150 Although Birch considers the insertion of 10:10–13 as having been effected by the prophetic redactor, he argues (correctly, in my estimation) that its origins lay independent from that source (ibid., 41).

151 Ibid., 20, 28–29, 42, 53–54, 62–63, 74, 84–85, 93–94. Cf. the slightly condensed list of Prophetic passages at ibid., 141.

152 McCarter, *I Samuel*, 14–30; idem, *II Samuel*, 7–8.

153 Idem, *I Samuel*, 16–17; idem, *II Samuel*, 8.

154 Idem, *I Samuel*, 18; his emphasis. See also Weiser, *Old Testament*, 166–69; and Fohrer, *Introduction*, 223–25.

that McCarter's juxtaposition of Birch and Fohrer is a helpful dichotomy—McCarter envisioned a process of development in 1 Samuel whereby an editor picked up several large narrative units and

> amplified them and reworked parts of them, sometimes with considerable license, to reflect his particular *Tendenz*. Everywhere he introduced the dominant figure of the prophet Samuel, whose activity became the organizing feature of his work. The result was a systematic narrative in three sections, each structurally complete within itself, but pointedly interconnected with the others.[155]

The "three sections" of 1 Samuel—the story of Samuel (1 Samuel 1–7*), the story of Saul (1 Samuel 8–15*), and the story of David's Rise (1 Samuel 16–2 Samuel 5*)—were themselves not originally discrete units. Instead, each of these smaller thematic sections was a compilation of even earlier traditions and narratives, which can be briefly enumerated as follows:

1. The Ark Narrative (1 Sam 2:12–17,22–25 + 4:1b–7:1)
2. The Saul Cycle, "a loose collection of materials about Saul's early career" (1 Samuel 1; 9:1–10:16*; 10:27b–11:15*; 13:2–7a,15b–23; 14:1–46)
3. The History of David's Rise (1 Sam 16:14–2 Sam 5:10)
4. The Account of the Transfer of the Ark to Jerusalem (2 Sam 6:1–13,17–19)
5. The Account of David's Ammonite War (2 Sam 10:1–19 + 8:3–8 + 11:1 + 12:25–31)
6. The Story of Abishalom's Revolt (2 Samuel 13–20)
7. The Story of the Gibeonites' Revenge and David's Patronage of Meribbaal (2 Sam 21:1–14 + 9:1–13)[156]

Eventually, toward the end of the 8th century, a prophetic editor assembled these written documents into a single large account of the institution of Israel's early monarchy, inserting a few unifying narratives and verses containing older traditional material (e.g., 1 Sam 1:20,27,28; 10:17–27a; 28:3–25) or of his own manufacture (e.g., 1 Sam 2:11–26; 3; 7:2–17; 12; 13:7b–15; 15:1–34; 19:18–24[?]; 25:1; 2 Sam 7:4–9a,15b,20–21; 11:2–12:24; 24:10–14,16a,17–19).[157] The prophetic shaping of 1 Samuel was, according to McCarter, effected in order "to present the advent of the kingship in Israel as a concession to a wanton demand of the people. Beyond this purely negative purpose, however, the history was written to set forth according to a prophetic perspective the essential elements of the new system by which Israel would be governed."[158] This perspective

155 McCarter, *I Samuel*, 18.

156 The titles and passages listed here are those of McCarter, with some slight clarifying adjustments (*I Samuel*, 23–30; *II Samuel*, 9–16).

157 List compiled from McCarter, *I Samuel*, 19–21; idem, *II Samuel*, 8. Steven L. McKenzie intially supported McCarter's proposal of an eighth-century prophetic history ("The Prophetic History and the Redaction of Kings," *HAR* 9 [1985]: 203–20) but later implicitly retracted that support (see below).

158 McCarter, *I Samuel*, 21.

"cautiously accepts the monarchy as an unwelcome but inevitable reality."[159] However, the negativity of this outlook with respect to the monarchy is only tenable if one assumes that chs. 8 and 12—or at least, substantial portions of them—were in fact already part of the prophetic arrangement of the text and not simply a Deuteronomistic elaboration thereof (with, e.g., Noth and Wellhausen), a challenge that was reintroduced by A. D. H. Mayes, among others.

3.4.2.3. Mayes

For the most part, Mayes followed these early attempts to find prophetic elaboration in the Samuel-Kings corpus, although he did not consider the question as minutely as Birch had but was instead interested in providing a more overarching study of the strata of Deuteronomistic redaction in the DtrH.[160] He allowed that a prophetic redactor had been at work in 1–2 Samuel but limited that editor's work to the early material on Samuel (1 Samuel 1–3; 7:15–8:3), the first and third parts of Wellhausen's and Noth's "old tradition" of Saul (1 Sam 9:1–10:16[161] + 13–14) in addition to the History of David's Rise and the Succession Narrative (1 Samuel 16–2 Kgs 2*).[162] However, Mayes contested Birch's attribution of 1 Samuel 11 to the prophetic redactor because he found the addition of that tradition (originally comprising vv. 1–11*,15) only in the work of the Historian (vv. 7*[ואחר שמואל],12–14).[163] Mayes also countered McCarter's claim that much of 1 Samuel 8; 10:17–27a; and 12 belonged to the Prophetic History: those passages all display "strong deuteronomistic influence" and can be linked decisively to a Deuteronomistic context in which the importance of covenant (as articulated in 10:17–27a; 12:1–25, two of those chapters considered by Wellhausen and Noth to have been quintessentially Deuteronomistic) "achieves definitive expression."[164] Mayes recognized the work there of two different Deuteronomistic hands; the work of the (Josianic) Dtr he detected in 1 Sam 7:2,5–8:6a,11–22*; 9:15–19(?[165]),21; 10:1,5–7,17–18aα,19b–21bα,25–27; 11:7*,12–14. The work of this author "gives expression to both views [i.e., favorable and unfavorable] of the monarchy

159 Idem, *II Samuel*, 8.

160 Mayes, *Story*, 81–132.

161 Specifically, Mayes points to "9.15ff., 21; 10.1,5–7" as points of Deuteronomistic editing.

162 Mayes, *Story*, esp. 83–84, 88–89, 105.

163 Ibid., 81–105, esp. 88–89, and 117–20.

164 Ibid., 93.

165 Mayes is rather unspecific with the precise delineation in 1 Samuel 9, citing only "9.15ff" (*Story*, 88).

while itself remaining not unfavourable."[166] The historian's inclusion of the pro-monarchic material in 1 Sam 9:1–10:16 admits the deficiencies of the political structure of the pre-monarchic period, justifying the need for the kingship on the failure of the preceding institution to guarantee safety (1 Sam 4:1–7:1*; cf. 7:10–11) and just leadership (8:1–3), thematically echoing Judg 21:25. However, it also acknowledges the fallible nature of the monarchy and provides a stern warning against it (1 Sam 8:11–17). This first edition was nuanced in outlook and presented an ambivalent portrait of the monarchy. The second Deuteronomistic hand left its traces in 1 Sam 7:3–4; 8:6b–10; 10:18aβb–19a; 12:1–25, in additions that manifest an unambiguous anti-monarchical tendency.[167] Here, the institution of kingship comprises a religious offence, in that the rebellious people Israel has rejected the divine kingship of Yahweh (8:7) and ignored its covenantal obligation to avoid worshipping other deities (8:8).[168]

Further in conflict with McCarter, Mayes argued that the Ark Narrative (1 Sam 4:1–7:1) had been introduced only by a Deuteronomistic editor through the addition in 7:2 and that the entire complex of so-called "anti-monarchic" tradition (although Mayes would not use that term) in 1 Samuel 7–8; 10:17–21bα,25–27; 12:1–25, along with its connective tissue, was similarly an insertion of the Deuteronomists (see below for a discussion of his more precise delineation), although 7:15–8:3,11–17* were,

166 Ibid., 101.

167 Ibid., 87–89, 96–102. Incidentally, Mayes described the second, exilic redactor's work in the following manner: "Legal forms and ideas predominate" (ibid., 101). This assessment has led many to see Mayes's work as attempting to bridge the gap between the Cross and Smend schools, since it seems to allow for a rough identification of Dtr^2 with DtrN (e.g., Römer and de Pury, "Deuteronomistic Historiography," 95). Römer and de Pury also point to O'Brien's work in this context, since he too delineated several exilic redactions aside from assorted independent additions (ibid.; see also O'Brien, *DHH*, 272–87). Indeed, the third of these four strata O'Brien described as "nomistic"; for example, O'Brien discerned the work of Dtr in 1 Sam 8:1–3,4–6a,11–17,19–22; 10:17,20–27; 11:7*,12–13 but argued that secondary post-Dtr additions are found in 1 Sam 8:6b–8,9–10,18; 10:18–19; 12:1–25, of which 8:7aβb(8); 10:18–19; and the entirety of ch. 12 are considered definitively nomistic (ibid., 109–28). Although O'Brien expressly denied identification of this nomistic redactional stratum with the Smend school's DtrN (*DHH*, 47–48), his model moves much closer towards that of the Smend school than does that of Mayes. The designation of a "nomistic" redactor seems to me not an unlikely scenario—especially in light of its possible identification with Dtr^2 (although O'Brien attributes the text most typically attributed to Dtr^2, 2 Kgs 23:28–25:21, to his *first* "subsequent dtr redaction"). A fuller discussion of the possibility cannot be enjoined here.

168 The work of a third, post-Deuteronomistic editor, which Mayes detected in Deuteronomy, Joshua, and Judges, does not appear to have infiltrated 1–2 Samuel. Mayes qualified the third editor's work as "very enigmatic, but its constant ritualistic and levitical concerns perhaps suggest a time and place of origin in priestly circles from which the combination of deuteronomistic history and Tetrateuch ultimately derives" (ibid., 134–36, quote from 135). Although outside the bounds of this study, is it possible that one might fruitfully compare Mayes's post-Deuteronomistic redactor with Jepsen's R^{III} (*Quellen*, 102–5)?

tradition-historically speaking, not the original work of those individuals.[169]

As will be argued below (ch. 7), it is clear that 1 Samuel 11* originally comprised a narrative independent of the truncated tradition in 9:1–10:16, but it is not at all clear, as Mayes would have us believe, that the two traditions were combined only by Dtr at such a relatively late date. Similarly, it is quite obvious that vv. 12–13 presuppose the derogatory remarks of the בני בליעל in 10:27a and that 11:14 serves both (a) as a transition between Samuel's command for Saul to wait at Gilgal (10:8, itself an editorial insertion) and the episode of Saul's first rejection at Gilgal (13:7b–15) and (b) as a confirmation of the public institution of the monarchy in 10:17–27a. However, none of those verses (vv. 12–14) bears particularly Deuteronomistic traits. Although Mayes's reconstruction of the prophetic layer of editing in much of 1–2 Samuel agreed in principle with the work of many of his precursors, the ordering of the inclusion of one of its primary episodes (i.e., 1 Samuel 11*), I believe, can be shown to be inaccurate (see §7.3).

Like the proponents of the Double Redaction model in whose wake he was working, Mayes found traces of two Deuteronomists throughout the DtrH. Because Mayes's primary consideration was simply to trace the contours of the Deuteronomistic redaction throughout that corpus, his discussion of the extent of pre-Deuteronomistic narrative structures was relatively minimal (although he did accept a pre-Deuteronomistic prophetic stratum of redaction in Samuel, as well as Richter's theory of a pre-Deuteronomistic *Retterbuch* in Judges[170]), making it difficult to discern his position on the original independence or interdependence of Samuel and Judges. The lack of any specific discussion on the subject suggests that Mayes considered it to have been Dtr, the earlier of the two major editors—as opposed to any pre-Deuteronomistic redactor—who initially combined the larger traditional structures of Samuel with those of Judges. A similar lack of concern with the Elijah-Elisha Cycle precludes comment on how Mayes would have reconstructed the process of development whereby Dtr joined Samuel and Kings.

169 Ibid., 96–102, esp. 98. However, Mayes does account 8:11b,15,16b as secondary additions (by the Historian?) (ibid., 99).

170 Ibid., 62–66, 162 n. 12.

3.4.2.4. Campbell

Building on the work of these previous studies,[171] A. F. Campbell's model of the PR is perhaps the most clearly enunciated vision of a proto-Deuteronomistic kernel within the DtrH. While Noth himself allowed for Dtr's reception of the traditions that later formed the large compositions that came to be known as the "[Solomonic] Succession Narrative" and the "History of David's Rise,"[172] Noth himself was much more concerned to enunciate the work done by Dtr in collecting and editing the material. Campbell did not discount the majority of Noth's observations with respect to the glossating work performed by Dtr, but argued that widespread literary clues point to a single corpus of historiographic work that had been redacted together during the late-9th century.[173] A series of literary inter-relationships permeates the DtrH between the narratives beginning in 1 Samuel 1 and those ending around 2 Kings 9. Campbell's proof-texts may be grouped into three sets:

(a) Those texts in which prophets figure as the legitimating figures of a newly ascendant royal lineage, specifically, in the three cases of prophetic anointment: Saul (1 Sam 9:1–10:16*); David (1 Sam 16:1–13); and Jehu (2 Kgs 9:1–13*).[174]

(b) Those texts in which prophets figure as the mediators of divine punishment, specifically, within the cases of the rejection of Judahite and Israelite kings:

171 For a bibliography of earlier attempts to account for the prophetically associated elements of the DtrH, see Campbell, *Of Prophets and Kings*, 2 n. 3; and, less fully, above. Omitted from the present survey for space considerations is the work of W. Lee Humphreys, "The Tragedy of King Saul: A Study of the Structure of 1 Samuel 9–31," *JSOT* 6 (1978): 18–27; idem, "The Rise and Fall of King Saul: A Study of an Ancient Narrative Stratum in 1 Samuel," *JSOT* 18 (1980): 74–90; idem, "From Tragic Hero to Villain: A Study of the Figure of Saul and the Development of 1 Samuel," *JSOT* 22 (1982): 95–117. A. F. Campbell and M. A. O'Brien have provided a comprehensive redactional overview of the DtrH and the position of the PR within that corpus with their book *Unfolding the Deuteronomistic History: Origins, Upgrades, Present Text* (Minneapolis: Fortress, 2000). The most recent statement of the PR may be found in Campbell's commentary (*1 Samuel*).

172 Campbell, "Martin Noth," 38. See below (§5.1) for a summary of Leonhard Rost's establishment of this model (*The Succession to the Throne of David* [trans. Michael D. Rutter and David M. Gunn, with an introduction by Edward Ball; HTIBS 1; Sheffield: Almond, 1982]). The chapters forming these disparate traditions were: 1 Sam 4:1b–7:1; 9:1–10:16; 10:27b–11:15; 13–15; 16:1–13; 16:14–2 Sam 5:25; 6–7; 9–20; 1 Kgs 1–2; see also Noth, *DH*, 86 nn. 1–3.

173 Campbell, *Of Prophets and Kings*, 111–23.

174 Five basic elements may be found in each of these stories: (a) prophetic anointing, (b) in private, (c) the call from Yahweh, (d) the use of the language of kingship (מלך or נגיד), and (e) the empowerment of the individual that results from the anointing (ibid., 17–23, esp. Table I).

Jeroboam's designation (and Solomon's concurrent rejection;[175] 1 Kgs 11:31–39*); the rejection of Jeroboam (1 Kgs 14:7–11*); the rejection of Ahab (1 Kgs 21:17–24*); and the designation of Jehu (2 Kgs 9:6–10*).[176]

(c) Those texts that point to the manifold relationships of the pericopes contained in the preceding sets.[177]

It will be noticed that many of Campbell's texts overlap with those that Dietrich adduced as DtrP (1 Kgs 14:7–11; 21:20bβ–24; 2 Kgs 9:7–10a),[178] yet Campbell's reading of them was much different from that of Dietrich. Instead of demonstrating the presence of a prophetically-oriented Deuteronomistic redactional stratum, argued Campbell, these three sets of prophetically-influenced pericopes point roughly to a unified literary text established during the latter part of the 9th cent. in circles associated with the prophetic school of Elisha and comprising much of the text of the DtrH between 1 Samuel 1 and 2 Kings 9 (and perhaps the prophetically-legitimized purges of the Omrides in chs. 10–11).[179] Although the PR utilized earlier extant traditions such as Saul's search for his father's donkeys and the History of David's Rise in order to provide a theological narrative

175 Cf. Weippert for a discussion of the process whereby *Solomon's* rejection in 1 Kgs 9:31–39 was subsequently amended to be *Rehoboam's* rejection in light of historical events ("Ätiologie," 344–75).

176 Campbell's discussion of the four designation/rejection pericopes provides a list of seven elements that are found in these four narratives, although never are all seven found together: (a) a notice that the kingdom will be torn away, (b) the concomitant prophetic designation of another as king, (c) the "bringing of evil" upon the rejected dynasty, (d) the dynasty's complete annihilation, which entails (e) the extermination of all males in the dynasty, (f) comparison to the house of Jeroboam (not found, of course, in the case of the rejection of Jeroboam's house), and (g) a notice as to the fate of those who will die in the city or in the country (*Of Prophets and Kings*, 23–41, esp. Table II).

177 See Campbell, *Of Prophets and Kings*, 41–63, esp. Table III. Included here are: the fact that Jehu is to be found in both of the preceding sets; the recognition of the literary motif of the "ripping away" of the kingdom in the prophetic rejection of Saul (1 Sam 15:27–28); the function of the prophet as "one empowered for acts of such consequence in Israel as the designation and rejection of kings, so guiding the destiny of Israel" (ibid., 45). The last theme leads one to look for evidence of prophetic redaction in 1 Samuel 28 and to measure the degree to which 2 Samuel 7 represents a particularly "prophetic" approach to the maintenance of the Davidic kingship (ibid., 46, 72–81).

178 The omission of 1 Kgs 16:1–4 from this list is not accidental. Campbell, *contra* Weinfeld, argues cogently that those verses comprise an epigonic Deuteronomistic attempt to imitate these earlier PR texts (Campbell, *Of Prophets and Kings*, 24–25, 33 n. 28, 36, and esp. 39–41; Weinfeld, *Deuteronomy and the Deuteronomic School*). Cf., however, McKenzie's poignant critique: "[Campbell] never explains why his Prophetic Record had a gap in its treatment of the house of Baasha. It is hard to imagine a running prophetic account of the Israelite monarchy that would not include an oracle against one of its dynasties" (*Trouble*, 64–66, quote from 66).

179 See also H. N. Wallace, who argues that the present form of each of these oracles is Deuteronomistic but who allows for a pre-Deuteronomistic antecedent ("The Oracles Against the Israelite Dynasties in 1 and 2 Kings," *Bib* 67 [1986]: 21–40, esp. 34–35).

account of the history of Israelite monarchy,[180] the PR in its final form argued specifically for the legitimacy of Jehu's overthrow of the Omride dynasty while at the same time making larger claims to the divinely-granted authority of Yahweh's prophets within the Israelite and Judahite political spheres. In short, the text argued that "this role—the designation and rejection of kings—has been the prerogative and duty of the prophets through Israel's history."[181]

3.4.2.5. Campbell and McCarter in Dialogue

In his commentary on 1 Samuel, Campbell argued that neither Mildenberger nor Birch considered extensively enough the prophetic reworking of several traditions extending into the book of Kings, since each had studied only slight reworkings of earlier material in the Saul-David complex. Yet McCarter went too far, Campbell argued, in concluding that the central theme of the history was "the advent of kingship in Israel as a concession to a wanton demand of the people."[182] This somewhat unnuanced reading of 1 Samuel had arisen because McCarter counted within the Prophetic History all texts containing prophetic motifs and *Gattungen*.[183] But none of these texts was adequately defended as a central passage in a specific, prophetically edited document. This criticism is very much in line with Campbell's earlier criticism of Dietrich's failure to distinguish those "prophetic" passages predating the Deuteronomistic edition from those that are part and parcel of the Deuteronomistic revisions of the exilic period. Campbell himself had provided the following list of passages that he considered integral to the PR: 1 Samuel 1–3*; 4:1a,1b–2,4,10–11,12–18a; 7:2b,5–6a,7–12; 9:1–10:16*; 11:1–11,14–15*; 14:52; 15:1–35; 16:1–13; 16:14–2 Sam 5:25*; 2 Sam 7:1a,2–5,7*–10,11b–12,14–17; 8:1–15 (or only 8:15); 2 Samuel 11–20; 1 Kgs 1:1a,5–15a,16–48; 2:1a,10,12; 3:1; 9:15–24*; 11:7,26–31,37,38b,40; 12:1,3b–15a,16–18,20,25,28a,29; 13:33b–34; 14:1–8a,9bβ–13,17–18,20b; 15:27–29*; 16:6,9–11*,15–24*,28,31b–32;

180 Campbell, *Of Prophets and Kings*, 64–101.

181 Ibid., 103–10, quote from 109. In his 1994 essay ("Martin Noth"), Campbell considered himself a "restorer" of "the house that Noth built"—over against "rebuilders" and "remodelers"—but his argument for the PR seems to me to be a significant departure from Noth's limitation of the pre-Deuteronomistic compilation to 1 Sam 1:1–2 Sam 2:7*. Not only does Campbell argue that the PR was basically intact as early as the late-9th cent., but he also makes the case for the inclusion of much of 1–2 Kings in the pre-Deuteronomistic expansions of the PR, a scenario with which Noth's initial understanding of the textual work done by Dtr conflicts.

182 McCarter, *I Samuel*, 18–23, esp. 21.

183 Campbell, *1 Samuel*, 320.

17:1; 18:2b–3a,5–12a,15–18a,19*,20–36a*,37–40,42b,45–46; 21:1–7a,8, 11a,14–19a,21–22a*,24; 22:40; 2 Kgs 1:2–8,17a; 9:1–7a,8–9a,10b,11–13, 14–27,30–35; 10:1–9,12–17,18–28.[184] The omission here of any parts of 1 Samuel 8; 10:17–27; and 12 is particularly important when comparing Campbell with Birch and McCarter.

That Campbell's criticism of McCarter relied on an altogether fair characterization of McCarter's thesis and methodology is debatable. For example, Campbell criticized McCarter's inclusion of the Ark Narrative in the Prophetic History because "Samuel plays no part in it; it makes a claim for the working out of Yahweh's will in history which bypasses the prophets completely."[185] Yet this critical remark betrays a certain myopia that can see only confrontational prophetic tropes and a priori excludes a realistic and methodical consideration of the probable—or even necessary—conditions of editorial collection and arrangement. Campbell focused more on the finalized form of the textual tradition than on its development; such a methodology allowed him to include with great specificity the *minimum text* belonging to the PR. Yet while Campbell did not discount the possibility of the diachronic development of the PR,[186] his discussion of its unity in the final form shies away from presenting a detailed overview of the processes by which the PR came into existence. The methodology whereby Campbell lays out the analysis of the Record's structure is therefore somewhat specious. Without definitive evidence that this is, in fact, the true structure—or even the most logical possible structure—the discussion remains founded quite problematically on the assumption that a structural analysis proceeding from a hypothesized minimal text can account for the entirety of editorial additions and insertions required by the pre-existence of the utilized traditions. In short, Campbell's structural analysis can do nothing more than confirm the *minimal* skeletal structural of the text; it cannot a priori exclude passages by claiming perfunctorily that they display a different concern. Therefore, I tend to side with McCarter's more expansive view of the PR's contents, tempered with a thorough consideration of the diachronic development of that early text. For example, I argue below that the original Ark Narrative (1 Sam 4:1–7:1*, without 2 Samuel 6*), although perhaps completely ancillary to any prophetic editorial *Tendenz*, must have already been integrated into the larger Saul-David complex (through the addition of 2 Samuel 6) at latest by the time of the formation of the PR (§6.5).[187]

184 Idem, *Of Prophets and Kings*, 101–3.

185 Ibid., 67.

186 Ibid., 108.

187 The fact that McCarter included in his Prophetic History the heavily Deuteronomistic passages 1 Samuel 8; 10:17–27a; 12 may lend some additional weight to Campbell's criti-

Nonetheless, McCarter's formulation of the milieu in which the PR developed is not altogether satisfactory. He traced the development of the various original sources used in the Prophetic History—the Ark Narrative, the Saul Cycle, and the History of David's Rise—until that document was compiled in the northern kingdom around the end of the 8th cent. by an author whose "background was northern" but whose "orientation was to the south, to which he looked for hope and in which he knew the future of Israel to be."[188] Indeed, on the basis of this principle, McCarter has identified a possible solution to an important conundrum in 1–2 Samuel—namely, that there appears to be little reason for the presence of primarily *southern* concerns (e.g., the promised duration of the Davidic dynasty) in a document whose prophetic outlook seems as though it can only have been derived from *northern* prophetic circles.[189] But McCarter finds the reason for this southern theme in Saul's replacement by David, which came to serve as "a paradigm for the prophetic rejection and election of kings."[190] Moreover, writing around the time of the northern kingdom's destruction at the hands of the Assyrian empire, the prophetic editor would have been able to contrast the failed, fragmented, and discontinuous monarchy of the north to the successful, purportedly monolithic, and continuous Davidic dynasty of the south.

These two themes, the latter of which is left fairly implicit in McCarter's presentation, seem to be at cross-purposes. The prophetic designation of the king is always and everywhere in 1 Samuel–2 Kings presented by the PR as a divinely ordained action, designed to punish those kings or dynasties that have departed from Yahweh's desired course of action (e.g., 1 Sam 13:7b–15; 15:10–29*; 1 Kgs 14:7–11*; 21:17–24*; 2 Kgs 9:6–10*), and as such, it serves in part to justify the north's secession from the Davidic kingdom (1 Kgs 11:29–40*). It thus seems somewhat counterintuitive to me that the same author would both express this north-

---

cism (cf. also Mayes, *Study*, 89–102). I take no explicit stance on those chapters in this study (see below) but hope to comment more extensively on their relationship to the pre-Deuteronomistic prophetic edition of Samuel in the future. My criticism of Campbell here is nearly the polar opposite of that of McKenzie, who faults Campbell for (uncritically) basing much of his source-critical delineation on the theme of prophecy: "are all stories about prophets written by prophets?" (*Trouble*, 14). This criticism strikes me not as unfounded but more appropriately leveled against McCarter.

188 McCarter, *I Samuel*, 21–22, quote from 22; see also Birch, *Rise*, 152–54; Mildenberger, "Saul-Davidüberlieferung," 12; and Humphreys, who similarly places the early development of 1–2 Samuel in a northern context ("Rise and Fall," 75, 85; "Tragic Hero," 103, 107).

189 McKenzie poses the flip side of this problem: "The problem is that the stories about Northern prophets do not always accord well with the Southern royalist interests of redactors in the times of Hezekiah, Josiah, and the exile whom scholars have credited with composing the D[euteronomistic] H[istory]" (*Trouble*, 10).

190 McCarter, *I Samuel*, 22.

ern withdrawal positively (i.e., as divinely mandated) and yet continue to hold out hope in the stability and success of the Davidic dynasty. Moreover, Campbell challenged the strictly northern provenience of the document (a tenet that was based implicitly on the hypothesized text's perceived anti-monarchical views) and argued that Alt's differentiation between northern charismatic and southern dynastic kingship was not as diagnostic a distinction as Alt had suggested.[191]

A final consideration that calls into question the details of McCarter's hypothesis is the apparent cessation of prophetic intervention in the transfer of the kingship at 2 Kgs 9:10 with the flight of the unnamed prophet. McCarter's dating thus seems too late, since it must assume—but nowhere explains—that a central principle in the author's theological interpretation of historical events became inoperative during the final decades of the northern kingdom's existence, despite the fact that the regime changed frequently during that time, beginning with the assassination of Zechariah in ca. 745 (2 Kgs 15:8–10),[192] and that the downfall of the kingdom could later be claimed by a Deuteronomistic author to have been similarly due to the divine wrath (2 Kgs 17:7–18). In opposition to McCarter's relatively late dating of the Prophetic History, Campbell dated the PR much earlier (late-9th cent.), connecting its final form with the overarching political thrust in support of Jehu (as described above). In this regard, Campbell's early dating is a bit more tenable, since the final form of the PR—which ended more plausibly with Jehu's accession to the Israelite throne (2 Kgs 9:1–13*), extermination of his Omride rivals (10:1–17*), and annihilation of the Baal cult (10:18–28*)—would have been coherent beginning in the mid- to late-9th cent., when Jehu faced opposition from the remnants of the shattered Omride political system and was forced to provide an account of his divinely granted legitimacy. The anti-Baal thrust of the PR, however, would have remained current throughout the early- and mid-8th cent., as a cursory reading of Hosea indicates; moreover, the PR would work equally

191 Campbell, *Of Prophets and Kings*, 113; see also T. C. G. Thornton, "Charismatic Kingship in Israel and Judah," *JTS* 14 (1963): 1–11; Giorgio Buccellati, *Cities and Nations of Ancient Syria: An Essay on Political Institutions with Special Reference to the Israelite Kingdoms* (Studi Semitici 26; Rome: Instituto di Studi del Vicino Oriente, Università di Roma, 1967), 195–212; Tomoo Ishida, *The Royal Dynasties in Ancient Israel: A Study on the Formation and Development of Royal-Dynastic Ideology* (BZAW 142; Berlin: de Gruyter, 1977), 151–82; cf. Albrecht Alt, "The Monarchy in the Kingdoms of Israel and Judah," *Essays on Old Testament History and Religion* (trans. R. A. Wilson; Oxford: Blackwell, 1966), 239–60; trans. of "Das Königtum in den Reichen Israel und Juda," *VT* 1 (1951): 2–22.

192 The mention in 2 Kgs 14:25 of the prophet Jonah ben Amittai of Gath-Hepher can hardly serve as evidence that a Prophetic History extended this far into 2 Kings, since the oracle attributed to Jonah was of a positive character and bears no formal resemblance to the other oracles attributable to Campbell's PR (1 Kgs 11:29–40; 14:7–11; 21:17–24; 2 Kgs 9:6–10). For a similar criticism, see McKenzie, *Trouble*, 14.

well as a narrative written to explain the downfall of the Jehuide dynasty and thus may plausibly be dated between the late-9th and mid-8th cent.

3.4.2.6. O'Brien

Campbell's student M. A. O'Brien followed his teacher closely in maintaining the existence of a Prophetic Record and adducing support for that document.[193] But while Campbell's primary concern was to plot out the contours and boundaries of the PR, that project receives less attention in O'Brien's work. The latter was much more concerned with providing an account of how Dtr appropriated the disparate traditions from which the DtrH was formed and edited them together. Most pertinent for the present discussion is the admixture of Campbell's work on the PR and Mayes's concern with the entire Deuteronomistic corpus that O'Brien's scholarship represents. Picking up Richter's earlier work on the pre-Deuteronomistic (or better, proto-Deuteronomistic) and Deuteronomistic editorial work on Judges, O'Brien argued that Dtr not only periodized Israel's history but also structured the period of the judges (Judg 2:11–1 Sam 11:15) in a two-stage system. The first stage ostensibly comprised Richter's proto-Deuteronomistic southern edition of the *Retterbuch* (Judges 3:7–9:57*), in which Israel's deliverers were finally (and disastrously) replaced by the abortive monarchy of Abimelech. With the failure of Abimelech's kingship, order was restored in the second stage of the structure in the form of the judges (Judges 10:6aα,7–8*,9b,17–13:1*; 1 Sam 1:1–7:17*). These judges, who were Dtr's own addition to the *Retterbuch* and eventually gave their name to the whole corpus, continued to provide Israel with leadership and order—to the degree made possible by such an ad hoc form of leadership—until the eventual failure of the system (1 Sam 1:1–2:34), again led to the establishment of a new form of leadership (i.e., that of the prophet; 1 Sam 3:1–7:17*) and culminated in the people's request for a king.[194]

3.4.2.7. Summary of the Consensus on the Prophetic Record

Although the multitude of commentators I have discussed here have argued for different schemas by which to understand the phenomenon, they agree that 1 Samuel–2 Kings displays evidence for a pre-Deuteronomistic, prophetically edited collection of texts. This collection began most likely

193 O'Brien, *DHH*, esp. 98–109, 289.
194 Ibid., 88–94, esp. 93.

with 1 Samuel 1 (Noth, Weiser, Fohrer, McCarter, Mayes, Campbell, O'Brien), although it has been suggested that the collection extended forward into Judges (Schüpphaus). The collection ended somewhere as late as Jehu's accession in Kings (McCarter, Campbell), although the ending is now intertwined with the (pre- or proto-) Deuteronomistic evaluations of the kings (see §3.3) and is no longer easily discernable. In between these two textual limits, those who argue for the existence of a pre-Deuteronomistic, prophetically edited collection of texts are nearly unanimous in their inclusion in that body of three major complexes of traditional material: (a) the so-called "early narrative" of Saul's Rise (1 Sam 9:1–10:16*; 11:1–15*; 13–14); (b) the History of David's Rise (1 Sam 16:14–2 Samuel 5*); (c) the Solomonic Succession Narrative (2 Samuel [2–9]10–1 Kings 2*). Over these three complexes was spread the editorial and redactional material that unified these disparate but related traditions into a single body of work (e.g., 1 Samuel 15; 16:1–13; etc.).

3.4.3. Anglophone Arguments to the Contrary

3.4.3.1. Provan

That 1–2 Samuel was early on connected literarily, and not just thematically and linguistically, to 1–2 Kings was accepted almost as a given by Provan in his short discussion of the subject. But Provan quite intentionally rejected the possibility of pre-Deuteronomistic prophetic editing: "the case for differentiating prophetic and Dtr *editors*, however, and thus for denying the two strand theory, does not seem very strong."[195] Moreover, in contradistinction to the established model, he adduced a much shorter original edition of the DtrH, claiming that "the first DH, although influenced by Dtn laws, probably did not contain the books of Deuteronomy and Joshua. It was simply a history of the monarchy from Saul to Hezekiah, with its necessary prologue in 1 Samuel 1–8, and perhaps in Judges 17–21. Deuteronomy and Joshua were added, along with Judges, at a later time."[196] Within this shorter history of the monarchy, Provan included both the Succession Narrative and, partially because it was not easily separated from that document, and especially because its presence was "essential to the credibility of the David theme" (which he took to be

195 Provan, *Hezekiah*, 160 n. 10, his italics, citing also R. E. Clements, review of B. C. Birch, *The Rise of the Israelite Monarchy*, *JTS* 29 (1978): 507–8. Clements's review is short, however, and provides little firm argumentation.

196 Provan, *Hezekiah*, 169. Cf. O'Brien, who excludes Judges 17–21 from the DtrH (*DHH*, 97–98).

foundational to his argument), the History of David's Rise.[197] Provan also included the few early traditions about Saul in 1 Sam 1:1–28; 9:1–10:16 in the early history but attributed the tensions and apparent shifts in assessment of the monarchy (especially 7:2–8:22; 10:17–27; 12:1–25) to his second (exilic) Deuteronomist.[198]

Yet Provan's schema exhibits several shortcomings. Because his postulated DtrH was already effectively so early and encompassed such a minimal text,[199] he was unable to permit a full compilation of the DtrH before the completion of the exilic edition. This meant, in turn, that Provan could not account for what might otherwise be called pre-Deuteronomistic composition. Provan's proposal accordingly has the adverse effect of telescoping an evidently long process of transmission and composition into a mere two editions. Thus, the schema cannot reasonably sustain the methodological rigor attained in Mayes's more nuanced reading, in which (at least) two Deuteronomistic editors contributed material foregrounding their own particular concerns to an already substantially formed tradition. Provan's attribution of 1 Sam 9:1–10:16; 1 Sam 11:1–11,15 to his first Deuteronomistic edition and 1 Sam 7:3–8:22; 10:17–27; 12:25 in its entirety to his second, exilic edition simply does not adequately address the tensions distinguishable within the latter sequence.[200]

3.4.3.2. McKenzie

Although he had initially supported McCarter's proposal of an 8th century prophetic redaction stretching from 1 Samuel 1 as far as 2 Kings 13, S. L. McKenzie again in 1991 picked up the theory of prophetic literature predating the DtrH, this time implicitly repudiating his earlier assessment.[201] He began the study with an analysis of 3 Reigns 12:24a–z, which united textual and redactional criticism with a literary sensitivity.[202]

---

197 Ibid., 158–59, quote from 159; for the importance of the "David theme," see 91–131.

198 Ibid., 159–60.

199 Compare, for example, McCarter's Prophetic History of ca. 721 to Provan's Josianic author, whose work ended with the events of 701.

200 A similar inability—or at least lack of concern—to distinguish not only between the first and second strata of Deuteronomistic edition but between the first Deuteronomistic stratum and any pre-Deuteronomistic traditional material as well is evidenced in Provan's discussion of 1 Kgs 11:29–39 (*Hezekiah*, 100–105), in which he attributes vv. 29–31,33(singular),34a,36–38 to Dtr. Although this is not an unreasonable attribution when distinguishing Dtr[1] from Dtr[2] (or something like those categories), it displays little concern to attempt to trace earlier traditions.

201 McKenzie, "Prophetic History"; cf. idem, *Trouble*.

202 McKenzie, *Trouble*, 21–40. McKenzie acknowledges several predecessors in the text-critical study of 3 Reigns 12:24a–z (i.e., the LXX[B] supplement to MT 1 Kings 12), foremost among

McKenzie argued convincingly that Trebolle had overstepped the evidence in suggesting that the LXX^B supplement in 3 Reigns 12:24a–z was a pre-Deuteronomistic prophetic narrative inherited by Dtr and preserved in the *Vorlage* of LXX^B. Although McKenzie admitted that the refutation of Trabolle's argument here did not constitute adequate evidence to disprove the existence of a pre-Deuteronomistic, prophetic stratum of redaction,[203] he systematically challenged the "prophetic" nature of several key passages in Campbell's PR (1 Kgs 11:29–39; 1 Kgs 14:7–18; 16:1–4,11–13; 21:21–24; 2 Kgs 9:6–10), insisting instead that they are to be attributed most readily to the single Nothian Dtr, who crafted the history from an assortment of traditions without relying on an already compiled document.[204]

Despite the fact that McKenzie's arguments provide a valuable caveat to schemas that too readily splinter the Deuteronomistic text into a fractious mélange of redactional tidbits, I find specious his claim to have shown that "[t]here is *no evidence* for any kind of earlier running history, prophetic or otherwise, beneath Dtr's composition in the book of Kings."[205] While many of his observations detailing the Deuteronomistic nature of purported pieces of evidence for Campbell's PR are well-founded and

whom is Julio C. Trebolle Barrera (*Salomón y Jeroboán: Historia de la recensión y redacción de I Reyes 2–12, 14* [Bibliotheca Salmanticensis, Dissertationes 3; Salamanca: Universidad Pontificia, Inst. Español Bibl. y Arqueologico, 1980]).

203 McKenzie, *Trouble*, 40.

204 Ibid., 41–47, 61–80; McKenzie has added argumentation in favor of dating the DtrH in the Babylonian Exile ("Mizpah of Benjamin and the Date of the Deuteronomistic History," in *"Lasset uns Brücken bauen...": Collected Communications to the XVth Congress of the International Organization for the Study of the Old Testament, Cambridge 1995* [ed. Klaus-Dietrich Schunk and Matthias Augustin; BEATAJ 42; Frankfurt a.M.: Lang, 1998], 149–55). However, McKenzie's analysis assumes a unified "late source" in 1 Samuel 7–8 + 10:17–27a + 12—a premise of which I am entirely unconvinced—in order to argue that the ultimate failure of the kingship at Mizpah in 2 Kgs 25:23–26 provides a fitting literary ending to the institution established at Mizpah in 10:17–27a. McKenzie has undoubtedly recognized an important literary trope constructed by an exilic editor of the DtrH, but the literary-critical assignment of the entire series 1 Samuel 7–8; 10:17–27a; 12 neglects several important aspects of those passages that speak in favor of the Deuteronomists' combination of several traditions. Primarily, it overlooks the fact that 10:17–27a seems to follow most naturally on 1 Samuel 8, where the location of the people's petition occurs in Ramah rather than Mizpah (v. 4). The notice of 10:17 that the people were called together in Mizpah is most likely an editorial insertion made at the time of the combination of the sequence 9:1–10:16 + 11:1–15*. However, this does not mean that the insertion originally located the episode at Mizpah; it is just as possible, I believe, that a pre-exilic Dtr inserted the notice here that the people were gathered in Ramah to follow up on the request made in ch. 8. A later Deuteronomistic editor working in the exile then added parts of ch. 7 (especially the notice in v. 5 locating the episode at Mizpah), not to mention the bulk of ch. 12, while at the same time readjusting the notice of locale in 10:17 to conform to the newly inserted material. While a complete analysis of the problem is not within the scope of this study, I hope to be able to provide fuller argumentation of this point in the near future.

205 McKenzie, *Trouble*, 147–48, my emphasis.

deserve closer scrutiny than can be presented in this survey, much of McKenzie's argument attacks pericopes that remain outside of the PR. For example, the demonstration that 1 Kings 13 is relatively late, perhaps even post-Deuteronomistic,[206] is readily admissible and hardly a controversion of Campbell's thesis, since he included only the surrounding verses (1 Kgs 12:29; 13:33b–34) in the PR. Moreover, the late insertion of the story does not negate the possibility of its early origination in and traditional preservation by prophetic circles that came to be associated with the Deuteronomistic movement; McKenzie himself allows that "1 Kgs 13:11–32a likely derives from Northern prophetic legends like those of Elijah and Elisha and 1 Kings 20."[207] Only slightly more problematic for Campbell's thesis are the cases of 1 Kings 17–19; 20; 22:1–38; 2 Kings 1; 2; 3:4–27; 4:1–8:15; 13:14–21, which McKenzie argues are all secondary insertions into the DtrH,[208] since those chapters all hint at the historical presence of a prophetic school in the Northern Kingdom during the 9th cent. But even

---

206 Ibid., 51–56; McKenzie cites Van Seters, "Histories and Historians," esp. 171; Alexander Rofé, "Classes in the Prophetical Stories: Didactic Legenda and Parable," in *Studies on Prophecy: A Collection of Twelve Papers* (ed. G. W. Anderson et al.; VTSup 26; Leiden: Brill, 1974), 143–64, esp. 163 (see also idem, *The Prophetical Stories: The Stories about the Prophets in the Hebrew Bible—Their Literary Types and History* [Jerusalem: Magnes Press, 1988], 140–82); Werner E. Lemke, "The Way of Obedience: I Kings 13 and the Structure of the Deuteronomistic History," in *Magnalia Dei: The Mighty Acts of God* (ed. Frank Moore Cross, Werner E. Lemke, and Patrick D. Miller; Garden City, N.Y.: Doubleday, 1976), 301–26; and Thomas B. Dozeman, "The Way of the Man of God from Judah: True and False Prophecy in the Pre-Deuteronomic Legend of 1 Kings 13," *CBQ* 44 (1982): 379–93. This position remains compatible with the theory of pre-Deuteronomistic prophetic redaction espoused by O'Brien (*DHH*, 263–64).

207 McKenzie, *Trouble*, 55. The apparent—but clearly secondary—association of the unnamed prophet with the writing prophet Amos, along with the close interaction between Deuteronomistic and prophetic schools in the Latter Prophets, may help to explain the overlap in Deuteronomistic and prophetic concerns, even after the initial formation of the DtrH (e.g., Wellhausen, *Composition*, 277–78; Julian Morgenstern, *Amos Studies* [2 vols.; Cincinnati: Hebrew Union College Press, 1941], 1:161–79; Otto Eissfeldt, "Amos und Jona in volkstümlicher Überlieferung," in *Kleine Schriften* [ed. Rudolf Sellheim and Fritz Maass; 6 vols.; Tübingen: Mohr Siebeck, 1962–1979], 4:137–42, esp. 138–39; James L. Crenshaw, *Prophetic Conflict: Its Effect upon Israelite Religion* [BZAW 124; Berlin: de Gruyter, 1971], 41–42).

208 McKenzie, *Trouble*, 81–100. Much of his argumentation here is founded on the authority of such scholars as J. Maxwell Miller ("The Elisha Cycle and the Accounts of the Omride Wars," *JBL* 85 [1966]: 441–54); Celso Alcaina Canosa ("Panorama crítico del circlo de Eliseo," *EstBib* 23 [1964]: 217–34; idem, "Vocación de Eliseo [1 Re 19,19–21]," *EstBib* 29 [1970]: 137–51; idem, "Eliseo secede a Elias [2 Re 2, 1–18]," *EstBib* 31 [1972]: 321–36); Stefan Timm, *Die Dynastie Omri: Quellen und Untersuchungen zur Geschichte Israels im 9. Jahrhundert vor Christus* (FRLANT 124; Göttingen: Vandenhoeck & Ruprecht, 1982); and Hermann-Josef Stipp (*Elischa—Propheten—Gottesmänner* [Arbeiten zu Text und Sprache im Alten Testament 24; St. Ottilien: EOS Verlag, 1987]); Lloyd M. Barré, *The Rhetoric of Political Persuasion: The Narrative Artistry and Political Intentions of 2 Kings 9–11* (CBQMS 20; Washington DC: Catholic Biblical Association of America, 1988); and Rofé, *Prophetical Stories*.

here, the overlap with Campbell's proposed text of the PR is minimal, the coinciding material encompassing only 1 Kgs 17:1; 18*; 22:40; 2 Kgs 1:2–8,17a. McKenzie considers the rest of Campbell's text in 1–2 Kings,[209] with some exceptions, as Deuteronomistic.[210] McKenzie seems to assume that his refutation of the traditional and textual priority of much of the Elijah-Elisha "cycle" (if the assorted *legenda* can properly be called by that term) negates Campbell's theory, but it is, in fact, only the claim that the basic anti-dynastic oracles (1 Kgs 11:29–39; 14:7–18; 16:1–4,11–13; 21:21–24; 2 Kgs 9:6–10) are in fact Deuteronomistic, rather than proto-Deuteronomistic, that bears any weight in the dispute.[211] In the dispute concerning the Deuteronomistic or pre-Deuteronomistic nature of these passages, McKenzie's objections by necessity run up against Campbell's initial thesis that the Deuteronomistic language overlaid on the original curses is only a secondary Deuteronomistic adaptation of the earlier prophetic text to the new context in which the Historian wished to set it. Without a full investigation of these constituent texts, which would be too expansive for the present argument, it is difficult to arbitrate this variance in opinion. Although I appreciate the precision and clarity with which McKenzie has argued his case, I remain unpersuaded that significant Deuteronomistic *shaping* necessarily negates the plausibility of an underlying prophetically-edited document of some sort. In combination with what Campbell has shown to be the distinctively prophetic reworking of 1–2 Samuel, the enduring suspicion that some sort of traditional material underlies at least portions of 1–2 Kings suggests that McKenzie's argument was not entirely successful in closing the door on a pre-Deuteronomistic edition hypothesis. Stated differently, the admission that an exilic or post-exilic editor of the DtrH who utilized concepts, themes, and *Gattungen* normally correlated with Israelite prophetic literature—and thus

209 Recapitulated here for convenience's sake: 1 Kgs 1:1a,5–15a,16–48; 2:1a,10,12; 3:1; 9:15–24*; 11:7,26–31,37,38b,40; 12:1,3b–15a,16–18,20,25,28a,29; 13:33b–34; 14:1–8a,9bβ–13, 17–18,20b; 15:27–29*; 16:6,9–11*,15–24*,28,31b–32; 21:1–7a,8,11a,14–19a,21–22a*,24; 2 Kgs 9:1–7a,8–9a,10b,11–13,14–27,30–35; 10:1–9,12–17,18–28.

210 McKenzie, *Trouble*, 151–52, tables. The only additional exceptions (i.e., further elements that McKenzie considers post-Deuteronomistic) are 1 Kgs 11:38bβ; 12:12 (ירבעם); 13:33b; 21:18a,19b (אשר בשמרון); 2 Kgs 9:14–15a,27bβ; 10:18–28.

211 Problematic, but not insurmountable, for Campbell's theory is McKenzie's claim that 2 Kgs 10:18–28 is post-Deuteronomistic (*Trouble*, 78, 151–52; see also Yoshikazu Minokami, *Die Revolution des Jehu* [Göttinger Theologische Arbeiten 38; Göttingen: Vandenhoeck & Ruprecht, 1989], 96–97; and Würthwein, *Könige*, 340–42). The presence of this passage in the PR—a point on which I am hardly convinced—is not necessary for the maintenance of Campbell's thesis and may, in fact, detract from its elegance. That Jehu slaughtered the priests of Baal seems to me to be more properly considered a secondary (Dtr^2?) concern, rather than one primary to a Jehuite apologetic work; at the very least, the PR nowhere else exhibits in my mind such anti-Baalistic fervor.

typologically analogous to the Smend school's DtrP—in no way requires the complete abrogation of the proposal that an earlier prophetically-oriented stratum of redaction already underlay the DtrH.[212]

3.4.4. Pushing New Directions in the DtrH: Recent Continental Scholarship Favoring a Pre-Deuteronomistic Edition of Samuel

It is virtually impossible in such narrow confines to depict the broad history of scholarship accurately, much less to make generalizations about dominant trends in scholarship without danger. At first glance, it might appear that the prevailing trend towards the study of pre-Deuteronomistic traditions in Samuel during the 1980's seems to have been a concern primarily of the Anglophone world (e.g., Campbell and O'Brien in Australia; Mayes and Provan—who later began teaching in Canada—in Ireland and Great Britain, respectively; Birch and McCarter in the United States), and this impression is borne out when considering the hypothesis of specifically *prophetic* editorial work on the pre-Deuteronomistic traditions. But the considerable mass of Anglophone scholarship dealing with pre-Deuteronomistic prophetic redaction is dwarfed by the sheer magnitude of Continental scholarship on the pre-Deuteronomistic stages of redaction. Generally speaking, the continental scholarship does not derive—or, more appropriately, no longer derives—its impetus from the attempt to isolate specifically "prophetic" redaction as did Mildenberger and Weiser,[213] in part because of the near ubiquity with which the Smend school's model has permeated the continental academy: once the "prophetic" concern has been isolated as a sub-set of the Deuteronomistic concern (DtrP), there remains little need to attribute pre-Deuteronomistic redaction to an editor whose *Sitz im Leben* is so consciously identified on the basis purely of thematic and lexical unity.

The Continental method may provide some guidance in circumventing the problems that arise in the Anglophone model of a pre-Deuteronomistic prophetic edition. The Anglophone model—although it has much to recommend it—has the propensity to become so myopically focused on generic and thematic considerations that it loses sight of the complete

212 For a similar separation of a pre-Deuteronomistic prophetic edition from secondary post-Dtr editing, see O'Brien's second stage of "subsequent dtr redaction" (*DHH*, 273–80).

213 Although cf. the work of Peter Mommer, who, in the tradition of Weiser and Mildenberger, continued to find strongly prophetic influence in the pre-Deuteronomistic redaction of Samuel (*Samuel: Geschichte und Überlieferung* [WMANT 65; Neukirchen-Vluyn: Neukirchener Verlag, 1991], 192–202, esp. 194).

redactional process(es) necessitated by the style and status of the texts themselves (e.g., the omission of the Ark Narrative from Campbell's PR) or, at the opposite extreme, to cast its thematic net so broadly—e.g., searching for passages about "prophets"—that it draws in many texts that are not necessarily to be enumerated with the others (e.g., McCarter's inclusion in his pre-Deuteronomistic Prophetic History of what may very well be Deuteronomistically composed texts: e.g., 1 Sam 7–8; 10:17–27a; 12). Instead, in Continental scholarship it has remained the norm to isolate redactional strata on the basis of form and genre; linguistic data, both syntactic and lexical; and apparent political and theological concerns. Only after careful analysis of these categories are the thematic concerns of each identifiable stratum laid out. This means that while one cannot talk of a specifically "prophetic"-oriented pre-Deuteronomistic edition, there nonetheless remains the possibility of pre-Deuteronomistic compilation by various parties.

Some recent proposals have held open the possibility that 1–2 Samuel was not fully structured before the composition of the DtrH itself, or they deny such structuring outright. In 1999, H. Rösel stated his lack of concern with a pre-Deuteronomistic edition of Samuel quite clearly:

> So bleibt die Frage zu beantworten, ob das Buch Samuel als sebstständiges Buch bestanden hat, bevor es vor das Buch der Könige gestellt wurde, oder ob einzelne Quellenschriften, die *jetzt* im Buch Samuel vereint sind, als Blöcke vor Könige gestellt wurden. M.E. ist diese Frage weniger entscheidend, da jede Antwort in gleicher Weise die Besonderheit der in Samuel vereinten Überlieferungen und damit die Besonderheit des Buches Samuel erklären kann. Schließlich sind auch mittlere Lösungen denkbar, wonach einige „Blöcke" schon zusammengestellt wurden, bevor man sie mit dem Buch der Könige verband.[214]

But this indeterminacy is not the norm for Continental scholars, who usually provide quite thorough analyses of their schemas. A few recent interpretive representations of the developmental history of Samuel may be discussed briefly here.

3.4.4.1. Vermeylen

Jacques Vermeylen traced several much older traditions in the early history of the Deuteronomistic writings. As is the case with my own reconstruction presented below, Vermeylen's study discerned several successive

214 Hartmut N. Rösel, *Von Josua bis Jojachin: Untersuchungen zu den deuteronomistischen Geschichtsbüchern des Alten Testaments* (VTSup 75; Leiden: Brill, 1999), 70–76, quote from 75–76. See also the recent entropic analysis of K. L. Noll ("Deuteronomistic History or Deuteronomistic Debate? [A Thought Experiment]," *JSOT* 31 [2007]: 311–45).

layers of composition in 1–2 Samuel. The earliest of the constituent texts were written during or shortly after David's lifetime. These were the short report in 2 Sam 21:15–21*; the list in 2 Sam 23:8–39*; the Saul-David narrative in 1 Samuel 11–2 Samuel 7; the Absalom-David narrative in 2 Samuel 13–20*; and the anti-Solomonic narrative in 1 Kgs 1–2*. These individual narratives were collected and assembled already during the time of Solomon to craft a composite Solomonic edition, spanning 1 Samuel 1–1 Kings 2. This edition was created to defend Solomon's legitimacy over against that of Adonijah and elaborated shortly afterwards with the account of Solomon's temple-building activities. There was thus already by the end of the 10th century, Vermeylen proposed, a text that reached from 1 Samuel 1 as far as 1 Kings 11.[215]

Although I am in basic agreement with the relative antiquity of several components of the document proposed by Vermeylen, as well as with the supposition that much of the early redactional history of the texts displays a tendency toward propaganda and apology, a few of his suppositions seem quite spurious to me. First, Vermeylen's schema apparently suggests a redactional disregard for a nearly complete text between the end of Solomon's reign and the (exilic) Deuteronomistic incorporation of that text in the first complete edition of the DtrH. This amounts almost to a textual neglect and must be considered quite specious, simply from the standpoint of probability. I find it immensely difficult to believe that a composite text such as the early history of the Israelite monarchy would have gone relatively untouched for over 300 years. Moreover, such a reconstruction flagrantly disregards the clear editorial continuities between the scenes of prophetic anointing in 1 Sam 9:1–10:16; 16:1–13; and 1 Kgs 9:1–10, the last of which in Vermeylen's schema could only be derivative from the other two.

3.4.4.2. Dietrich

Although it will become clear throughout the following chapters that I am in large agreement with Vermeylen's early dating of these texts, the proposal that the basic structure of 1–2 Samuel can be assigned a date already in the 10th century represents a very early estimate of that text's composition and a minority position within Continental scholarship. Walter Dietrich has recently taken a more moderate position in his encyclopedic *The Early Monarchy in Israel*. This book, originally published in 1997, contains a sizeable discussion of the literature dealing with

215 Vermeylen, *Loi du plus fort*, 471–624, English summary on 731–33.

the earliest period of the Israelite monarchy.[216] While his earlier work, *Prophetie und Geschichte*, dealt almost exclusively with the various Deuteronomistic additions to the historical documents, this book, based to a large extent on his earlier monograph *David, Saul und die Propheten*, surveyed the older traditional literature that was gathered together into the books of Samuel.[217] Some parts of the narratives were nearly contemporaneous with the events they purport to describe. For example, claims Dietrich, the Solomonic Succession Narrative "was written soon after the events themselves" although it has undergone subsequent thematic and textual emendation "by later redactors who placed these narratives in the service of quite different intentions."[218] The History (or Narrative) of David's Rise, too, seems to Dietrich to have existed before its inclusion in the DtrH, although not nearly as early as the Succession Narrative. Instead, Dietrich dates "the history of David's rise (or better, the textual layer in the books of Samuel connected to this history) to the time of Hezekiah. This would imply dating the text to the time assumed for the supplementary redactional layer by historical-critical exegesis."[219] This "supplementary redactional layer," which should be recognizable as loosely akin to Fohrer's "supplementary stratum" or to the prophetically edited document postulated by Anglophone scholarship, could not be propagandistic in the strictest sense of the term, since it no longer argued for the Davidic dynasty over against the Saulides or even those northern kings whose kingdom had recently fallen to the Assyrians at the time of the document's composition. But its framing was such that it acquired a distinctly pro-Davidic tone of election by God, a tone that resonated with Judahites in light of the recent destruction of the northern kingdom.[220]

Despite the validity of many of Dietrich's observations, and his work's general complementarity with the project of this study, there does exist a fundamental problem with Dietrich's "composition-critical" methodology, namely, his odd reconstruction of the texts' redactional development. My criticism of McCarter's methodology above applies equally to Dietrich here. It is readily apparent that the Succession Narrative and the History of David's Rise were at some point in time joined together and forced by a redactor to operate in tandem, and Dietrich's very clear discussion of the problems involved in peeling away the clear redactional suture in 2 Samuel

216 Walter Dietrich, *The Early Monarchy in Israel: The Tenth Century B.C.E.* (trans. Joachim Vette; SBLBibEnc 3; Atlanta: SBL, 2007), 227–316; trans. of *Die frühe Königszeit in Israel: 10. Jahrhundert v. Chr.* (Biblische Enzyklopädie 3; Stuttgart: Kohlhammer, 1997).

217 Walter Dietrich, *David, Saul und die Propheten* (BWANT 122; Stuttgart: Kohlhammer, 1987).

218 Dietrich, *The Early Monarchy*, 236.

219 Ibid., 247.

220 Ibid., 249.

2–5 (or even 6–7?) demonstrates the difficulty in treating the two separately. However, the apparent assumption that the *primary* and *original* themes of the History of David's Rise should be limited to those that are continued in the Succession Narrative—

> the dialectic between election and rejection; the relation between human and divine wills; the interrelatedness of faith and sin; the need for and the limits of state power; the tension between politically advantageous and ethically responsible action; the relation between politics and religion; the double existence of Israel as an independent polity and as the people of God; and the contrast and comparison of different political interest groups in Israel[221]

—cannot comprise adequate reason for maintaining the basic unity of the two in a diachronic schema. Form- and redaction-critical considerations must be brought to bear as well in order to move beyond the pre-Deuteronomistic compilation of these texts. Those considerations suggest that the set of documents loosely designated as the "History of David's Rise" originated in a context in which it *did* function as state-endorsed propaganda, separate from and prior to the Succession Narrative (see ch. 6).

An additional complication arises from Dietrich's synthetic discussion of the "literary precursors" to the Deuteronomistic "history of the early monarchy."[222] Citing D. W. Jamieson-Drake and H. M. Niemann, Dietrich concludes that

> the events were recorded only considerably after the events themselves occurred. The tenth and the ninth centuries were not yet time periods in which we can assume large-scale literary production and intellectual activity. Then as now, there certainly were individuals capable of such activity, but the external circumstances and the educational possibilities simply did not yet exist for most. There was also no audience for such literature; there were but a few people capable of reading and writing. A market for literature did not exist even in rudimentary form.[223]

Dietrich therefore assumes the priority of shorter, individual traditions that only later "crystallized" into "larger, thematically unified narratives."[224] These shorter traditions included songs and proverbs (e.g., 1 Sam 18:7; 21:12; 29:5; 2 Sam 1:19–27; 20:1), lists (e.g., 1 Sam 7:16; 14:47; 14:49–51, etc.), short narratives (e.g., 2 Samuel 8; 21:15–22; 23:8–17,18–23), and notes (1 Sam 8:2),[225] but none of the longer documents that constitute political narratives. The origination of 1–2 Samuel in a variety of "extend-

---

221 Ibid., 249–50.

222 Ibid., 262–316.

223 Ibid., 263. Dietrich cites here David W. Jamieson-Drake, *Scribes and Schools in Monarchic Judah: A Socio-Archeological Approach* (JSOTSup 109; SWBA 9; Sheffield: Almond, 1991); and Hermann Michael Niemann, *Herrschaft, Königtum und Staat: Skizzen zur soziokulturellen Entwicklung im monarchischen Israel* (FAT I/6; Tübingen: Mohr Siebeck, 1993).

224 Ibid., 264.

225 Ibid., 264–67.

ed narratives" is also apparent (e.g., 1 Samuel 17 [itself a composite]; 1 Sam 9:1–10:16 + 13–14; 1 Sam 10:10–12 [~19:18–24]), and these short stories were combined into the longer "narrative collections and novellas," which themselves, Dietrich allows, were "gathered into a narrative opus prior to the creation of the Deuteronomistic History," which stretched from "1 Sam 9 (or 1 Sam 1) to 1 Kgs 1 (or 1 Kgs 12)."[226]

In principle, I agree with Dietrich's basic model in which older, shorter traditions were gathered into larger thematic structures; this process he has termed "crystallization" best accounts for the multitude of various episodes in the History of David's Rise. But Dietrich and I hold disparate views as to the speed with which this process occurred. Because he pushes the date of the compilation of the History of David's Rise so late, relatively speaking, Dietrich allows little lag-time between that document's formation and the inception of the pre-Deuteronomistic structure comprising most of 1–2 Samuel and possibly much of 1 Kings. As will become clear below (chs. 5–6), my proposal allows for a much longer period between the initial composition of the primary History of David's Rise and its eventual inclusion in the pre-Deuteronomistic narrative stratum.

3.4.4.3. Recent Reactions to the Early Dating of the Constituent Traditions of 1–2 Samuel

Despite the admirable moderation with which Dietrich lays out his proposal, younger voices have found difficulty in locating any of the text of 1–2 Samuel in the 10th or 9th centuries. Thomas Römer has recently opined, "[t]he opinion that most of these traditions were written down very shortly after the event during the tenth or ninth century BCE is still very popular. *But this view should definitely be given up*."[227] In the most recent (and most widely accepted) presentations of Continental scholarship, the establishment of the basic text of 1–2 Samuel is located much closer to the composition of the DtrH as a whole. This general trend among Continental scholars has been to push the dates of composition of the various constituent episodes in 1–2 Samuel as late as possible and to attribute the combination of Samuel and Kings only to Dtr's first edition of the DtrH (and thus

226 For the "extended narratives," see ibid., 268–71; for "narrative collections and novellas," see 271–98; for the "narrative history of the early monarchy," see 298–316; for the extent of the pre-Deuteronomistic text, see 298. Dietrich provided a similar treatment of the documents underlying 1–2 Samuel in "Prophetie im deuteronomistischen Geschichtswerk," in *The Future of the Deuteronomistic History* (ed. T. Römer; BETL 147; Leuven: University Press, 2000), 47–65.

227 Römer, *So-Called Deuteronomistic History*, 93, my emphasis.

usually to the exile) at the earliest. We have already seen this position taken by Aurelius.[228] The detailed analyses of R. G. Kratz and—with a slightly earlier date—T. C. Römer may be examined more closely in this regard as well.

3.4.4.4. Kratz

In the same year Vermeylen's work appeared (2000) and in general conformity with Dietrich's work both methodologically and theoretically, Kratz published his own schema of the development of the DtrH. He, too, claimed that portions of Samuel existed before the formation of the DtrH, as we find that "in 1–2 Samuel the narrative material is original and the Deuteronomistic framework is secondary."[229] This is in contradistinction to most of 1–2 Kings, where the framework comprises the earliest portion of the text (except for 1 Kings 1–2, which naturally comprised the epilogue of the material concerned with the succession to David's throne in 2 Samuel 9–20).[230] This schema continues to hold the consensus opinion that the narrative complex of 1–2 Samuel was literarily distinct from Judges even at the formation of the DtrG: "1 Samuel 1.1 ('There was once a man…') is the beginning of an independent narrative, and indeed the beginning of a wide narrative arch which leads through the birth of Samuel (1 Sam. 1) to the elevation of Saul to be king over Israel (1 Sam. 9–11) and from here beyond 1 Sam. 16–2 Sam. 10 to David and Solomon in 2 Sam. 11–1 Kgs 2."[231]

For Kratz, as for Vermeylen, the early form of Samuel has been overlaid with several layers of the Deuteronomistic "annalistic framework" (1 Sam 13:1; 2 Sam 2:10–11; 5:4–5 [~1 Kgs 2:10–12; 3:1–3]), as well as the now-familiar Deuteronomistic editing throughout 1 Samuel 7–12. Yet Kratz accounts much more of the book of Samuel to later interpreters. Therefore, as is perhaps by now to be expected, Kratz's model is missing much of what I consider to have been necessary to the pre-Deuteronomistic structure of Samuel.[232] For the most part, he espouses what is essentially a multiple-redaction version of the Wellhausian model, assigning the various constituent episodes of those chapters to an apparently pro-monarchic

---

228 Aurelius, *Zukunft*, 71–95, 207.

229 Kratz, *Composition*, 170–71.

230 Ibid., 171.

231 Ibid., 170–71. Aurelius adduced a similarly restricted first edition of the Deuteronomistic History (*Zukunft*, 71–95, 207); compare also Provan, who found the beginning of the first (albeit pre-exilic) edition of the DtrH at 1 Samuel 1 (*Trouble*).

232 Kratz, *Composition*, 171.

narrative (1:1–20 + 9:1–10:16* + 11:1–5 + 13–14* with anti-Saulide redactional insertions in 10:8; 13:1,4b,7b–12,15a) and an ostensibly anti-monarchic sequence "in the spirit of the book of Judges" (1 Samuel 7:5–17; 8:1–22; 10:17,20–27a*; 11:5–8,12–14; 12:1–25*) that was overlaid with a third stratum of later nomistic editing (7:3–4; 8:7b–9a; 10:18–19; 12:1–25; 13:13–14).[233] The most conspicuous anomaly in Kratz's schema is the assignment of 1 Sam 11:5–8,12–14 to the intermediate stage of redaction (which, despite Kratz's attempt to remain fairly vague, sounds much like the DtrP of the Smend school). Verses 12–14 are quite regularly assigned to Deuteronomistic redaction, but the assignment of vv. 5–8 to an implicitly "prophet-judge" stratum of redaction—on the basis of the "spirit of the judges" that comes upon Saul—arbitrarily interrupts the story and imposes an anachronistic criterion on the composition of the passage. Merely because the older version of the institution of the monarchy (9:1–10:16*, etc.) was combined with the Judges narratives at a relatively late date does not preclude the possibility that its traditio-historical composers were aware of the traditions of the deliverers.[234]

Moreover, although he considers the narrative of Samuel's birth (which was already pre-Deuteronomistic; 1:1–20) and the Ark Narrative (4:1–7:2, originally perhaps "an earlier episode with the ark in which the ark is irretrievably lost," 4:1b–2 [=v.10]; vv. 11–22) within the body of the DtrH, Kratz removes much of 1 Samuel 1–7 and 13–14 from that corpus because of its apparently priestly concern (1:3b,21–2:11,18–21,26 + 2:12–17,22–25,27–36; 3:1–21; 14:15–16,18–19,23,24–51*).[235] There are undoubtedly elements of priestly concern in these chapters (especially, e.g., 14:31–35), but a thoroughgoing relegation of that concern to a single late textual stratum too flatly combines all things priestly and is subject to the same criticism, already mentioned above, that Nelson applied to Jepsen's R^{I}-R^{II} dichotomy: it evinces a vestige of the "common and erroneous opinion that the prophetic and cultic sides of Israel's life were in constant,

233 Ibid., 171–73.

234 Kratz claims that "[q]uite clearly we can trace the influence of Joshua and above all of course Judges here, so that here too we have a revision which presupposes the combination of Samuel–Kings with the Hexateuch" (ibid., 173). It is quite unnecessary, however, to assume that Deuteronomistic editors required the presence of Judges to be able to construct the episode in a deliverer-style manner; what is required is simply knowledge of—or the appropriation of—deliverer-narratives at the time of the composition. The necessary *terminus post quem* of this episode (1 Sam 11:1–11,15*) cannot reasonably be pushed any further forward than the formation of the *Retterbuch* in the period of the divided monarchy, at least on the basis of vv. 5–8. See also my argument below in §§7.3–4. The presupposition that Samuel's combination with the Hexateuch was a pre-requisite for the introduction of this motif does not follow by necessity either.

235 Kratz, *Composition*, 173–74.

irreconcilable conflict."[236] Despite these points of divergence between my own redactional hypothesis and that of Kratz, there are many points of tangency as well.

As was the case with his reconstruction of the minimal pre-Deuteronomistic text of the independent Saul-narrative (1 Sam 1:1–20* + 9:1–10:16* + 11:1–15* + 13–14*), the remainder of 1–2 Samuel must be divided in Kratz's model between those passages that can be claimed for a pre-Deuteronomistic layer and those that cannot. In the former group can be found much of the so-called Succession Narrative, originally comprised of a series of individual narrative units. Kratz distinguishes the Amnon-Absalom material in 2 Samuel 13–14 from the story of Absalom's insurrection (2 Samuel 15–19), as well as from the story of Sheba's rebellion (2 Samuel 20). Further distinction can be drawn between the combination of these originally independent sources (thus, 2 Samuel 13–14 + 15–19 + 20) and the Solomon narratives in 2 Samuel 11–12; 1 Kings 1–2, which were "put round the Absalom cycle in 2 Sam. 13–20 as a framework. 2 Samuel 21–24, which are inserted between the Absalom episodes and the end of the succession narrative, are generally held to be appendices which presuppose the linking of the traditions about Saul and David…."[237] As will be demonstrated in ch. 5, I concur with Kratz's supposition that the bulk of the chapters relating to Solomon (2 Sam 11–12* + 1 Kgs 1–2) must be assigned to a secondary stratum of redaction in which the "Succession Narrative," which originally anticipated the ascendency of Adonijah, was brought up to date. But I do not fully agree with his assertions concerning the secondary nature of the literary links between this complex and the History of David's Rise in 1 Samuel 16–2 Samuel 10. These literary links are intimately intertwined with the Transjordanian Motif and so will be discussed in some detail in ch. 5. Nonetheless, despite my quite different methodological assumptions and my continued divergence of opinion from that of Kratz concerning the degree to which the Succession Narrative knew of the ending of the so-called "History of David's Rise" in 2 Samuel 2–9 (see below, ch. 5), there is much here with which I can fundamentally agree. Kratz's redactional hypothesis may be seen as generally complementary with that held throughout the present study, since he points out that

> [t]he prehistory, namely the kingship of the sons of Saul in Mahanaim (2 Sam. 2.8f.; 4.4) and the kingship of David over Israel (5.3; 8.15), is completely presupposed, but only in the account of the flight in chs 15–17 and 19 and in the Benjaminite episodes 2 Sam. 9; 16:1–14 (with a resumption of 15.37 in 16.15–19); 17.27–29 and 19.17–41, which are taken up by the additions in 1 Kgs 2.5–9, 36ff.

236 Nelson, *Double Redaction*, 20.

237 Kratz, *Composition*, 175.

(v. 44), and also when a basic stratum and a supplementary stratum are distinguished in 2 Sam. 9.[238]

In the following chapters it will become clear, I hope, that I have no particular stake in the original unity of the Succession Narrative. After all, the passages in which I am the most interested for purposes of studying the Transjordanian Motif are the purported "pre-history" to the Succession Narrative in 2 Sam 2:1–5:5* (especially 2:8–9,12,29); David's self-imposed Transjordanian exile in 2 Sam 15:14–20:1; and Sheba ben-Bichri's flight to Abel Beth-maacah in 2 Samuel 20, since those are the passages pertinent to the Transjordanian Motif as I have sketched it out. Contrary to Kratz's argumentation, I stress only that the "Succession Narrative" reached something closely resembling its present form at a pre-Deuteronomistic point of redaction history.

In fact, Kratz's reconstruction of the original status of the Succession Narrative as a narrative complex in which "David need not be Saul's successor, and 'the Israelites' appear merely as an indefinable and uncontrollable potential danger of which Absalom skilfully makes use"[239] bolsters my own hypothesis that the History of David's Rise, to which the Succession Narrative was eventually connected, was itself in fact originally bifurcated. Although full discussion of this hypothesis must wait until chapters 5 and 6, its fundamental points may be anticipated here briefly: I hypothesize that there existed *two* Histories of David's Rise, only one of which knew the Narrative(s) of Saul's Rise. It was to the *other* History of David' Rise, which intentionally—but problematically, from a historical point of view—presented David as Jonathan's replacement, that the Succession Narrative was originally fastened. Moreover, in the following chapters, I make no explicit claim that David's journey to Transjordan was historical—only that it was presented as such. The author of the Court History was evidently working with an already established body of tradition in which the Transjordanian excursion (or flight) of the prospective ruler was a conventional motif, and it very well may be the case that this motif was utilized in the formation of the narrative.

This discussion leads to the most salient differences between our respective redactional reconstructions, which are to be found in the span of literature between the narratives concerning Saul's Rise (1 Samuel 1–14) and the Succession Narrative (for Kratz, 2 Samuel 10–1 Kings 2). This bridge is commonly known as the History of David's Rise (1 Samuel [15] 16–2 Sam 2 [3–9?]). The narrative complex was formed from a congeries of traditions, and discussions of this middle part of Samuel inevitably

238 Kratz, *Composition*, 176.
239 Ibid., 176.

involve various complicated attempts to distinguish those traditions original to the most basic form of the narrative from those that accrued in later editions. Although I withhold analysis here of the specifics of Kratz's own understanding of the History of David's Rise until ch. 6, the basic thrust of his argument may be anticipated. Beginning with the three introductions to David (1 Sam 16:1–13; 16:14–23; 17:1–15, esp. vv. 12–14), of which he deems 1 Sam 16:14–23 to have priority, Kratz assembles a reasonable minimal text for the History of David's Rise. This assemblage is performed through a supplementary stratum model, so that the original text is deemed to have comprised 1 Sam 14:52; 16:14–23 + 18:17–27 + 19:9–10,11–12 + 21–31 + 2 Samuel 2–5 (8–10).[240] As will be discussed below, I do not consider Kratz's schema to be the most logical representation of the textual and literary data in 1 Samuel 15–2 Sam 9; it certainly does not take full consideration of the witness provided by the Old Greek (as represented by LXX^{B}) of 1 Samuel 17–18 (see §6.2.2). Moreover, our respective datings of the formation of this large textual complex differ substantially, since Kratz's model finds that this earliest form of 1–2 Samuel was compiled only at the turn of the 7th century and that the corpus was combined with a preliminary edition of 1–2 Kings during the exile (as the original DtrG).[241] Despite these differences, I agree with Kratz's basic view that there existed a pre-Deuteronomistic edition of 1–2 Samuel, encompassing three narrative complexes: a Narrative of Saul's Rise, the History of David's Rise, and the Succession Narrative.

3.4.4.5. Römer

T. Römer seems to have adopted a position similar to that of Kratz in his own monograph-length treatment of *The So-called Deuteronomistic History*. In some ways, though, Römer's model leans back toward the more classical position espoused by Dietrich: Römer carves out theoretical space for a first edition of the DtrH during the monarchic period (specifically, in the reign of Josiah), which included the loosely bound 1 Samuel–2 Kings complex.[242] In allowing for this loose connection between 1–2 Samuel and

240 Ibid., 174–86, esp. 184, Table B.II.1, and 186; the complete text of Kratz's pre-Deuteronomistic source is: 1 Sam 1:1–20 + 9:1–10:16* + 11:1–5 + 13–14* (at least 14:52); 16:14–23 + 18:17–27 + 19:9–10,11–12 + 21–31 + 2 Samuel 2–5 (8–10) + 11:1–27; 12:24b + 13–14 + 15:1–6,13; 18:1–19:9a; 20:1–22 + 1 Kings 1–2 (ibid., 183, 186).

241 Ibid., 181–82, 186.

242 Römer, *So-Called Deuteronomistic History*, 67–106, esp. 68–69, 104; idem, "Entstehungsphasen," 56–59. It is important to stress that Römer does not seem to allow a tight connection at this point in time between the present books of 1–2 Samuel and 1–2 Kings, because

1–2 Kings already in the pre-exilic period, Römer moves away from the position espoused by Aurelius and Kratz. But Römer's schema is slightly more minimalist in how it views the development of Samuel: he considers that early collection of documents to have contained, minimally, fewer narratives than even in Kratz's model. Römer's reconstructed text of 1–2 Samuel includes 1 Sam 1; 9:1–10:16; 11:1–15*; 13–14*; 16–27; 29; 31; and 2 Samuel 2–5 (i.e., the early Samuel-Saul narratives and the basic structure of the History of David's Rise), but he expresses doubt that the Succession Narrative was originally included in this pre-exilic edition of Samuel, while holding open exactly that possibility: "David's presentation in the SN, where he appears as a rather weak, if not faulty, character (2 Sam. 11–12) makes it rather unlikely that the SN would have been part of the Josianic library. It is nevertheless possible that a shorter account of the court history, without the 'scandalous chapters' 2 Sam. 11–12; 15–17* and 19*."[243]

A brief survey of the reasons for expunging this material from 1–2 Samuel provides some insight into the assumptions with which Römer is working and an entrée into the problem posed for biblical studies by recent examinations of scribal culture in the ancient Near East. Römer's reservation in adducing the Succession Narrative as part of what is an effectively proto-Deuteronomistic edition seems to be based on the odd juxtaposition of the divergent characterizations of David between the bulk of the narrative (e.g., 2 Samuel 13–20*) and chs. 11–12. That this is an altogether accurate portrayal of David's character in chs. 11–12 viz-à-viz his character in 2 Samuel 13 is imminently debatable: is David *not* portrayed as effete and ineffective in his dealings with Amnon and Absalom in chs. 13–14? But more problematic is the assumption that David's weak character in 2 Samuel 11–12 should—or even can—serve as an indicator that the *rest* of the narrative does not belong in the pre-exilic edition of Samuel. As we saw in the recapitulation of Kratz's argument above, these tensions may be explained by a reasonable and responsible apportioning of the narrative into its constituent traditions or redactional layers, in which David's character may in fact have been rendered quite differently (see below, ch. 5). Römer's "possible...shorter account" is far more preferable than complete omission.

The hesitation to include the Succession Narrative is not the only interpretive decision that requires comment here. Römer also excises the Ark Narrative from the Josianic library, because although it

---

those texts may have been maintained on separate scrolls (e.g., *So-Called Deuteronomistic History*, 91, 105). For this reason, Römer speaks of a "Josianic library" (ibid., 72).

243 Ibid., 93–97, quote from 94.

> probably preserves an older tradition…, the present arrangement of 1 Sam. 1–6 already seems to reflect the destruction of the temple of Jerusalem in 587/586 BCE. The redactional comment upon the loss of the ark in 4.21 ('The Glory is banished from Israel') is very close to the description of the departure of the Glory from the temple in Ezek. 8–10, suggesting that the story of the loss of the ark foreshadows the later destruction of the Jerusalem temple. Also, the fact that Samuel is raised as a priest in the sanctuary at Shiloh, but ultimately becomes a prophet (3.19–4.1a) and survives the destruction of the sanctuary *in his office as prophet* and intercessor for 'all Israel' (cf. 1 Sam. 7.2–14) also recalls the replacement of the temple by the prophetic word as a medium of access to the divine will, a central theme of the Deuteronomistic theology in the exilic and postexilic periods.[244]

Two salient objections must be raised to Römer's line of argumentation here. First of all, that 1 Sam 4:21 "is very close to the description of the departure of the Glory from the temple in Ezek. 8–10" is at best a misleading claim that does not carefully enough consider the distinction between similarity of imagery and similarity of language. In 1 Sam 4:19–20, the wife of Phinehas gives birth to a boy upon hearing the news of her husband's and father-in-law's deaths; then, "she named the boy Ichabod, saying 'The Glory has departed from Israel (גלה כבוד מישׂראל)', because of the removal of the ark of God (אֶל־הִלָּקַח ארון האלהים), and because of her father-in-law and her husband (וְאֶל־חמיה ואישׁה)"[245] (v. 21). True enough, the term "glory" (כבוד) occurs in Ezekiel 8–10 five times with the connotation of God's presence (8:4; 9:3; 10:4,18,19); however, in each of those occurrences the term is always clarified as the "Glory of the God of Israel" (כבוד אלהי ישׂראל; 8:4; 9:3; 10:19) or the "Glory of the LORD" (כבוד־יהוה; 10:4,18),[246] and it never occurs alone. Moreover, the verb "depart" (גלה) never occurs in Ezekiel 8–10 and appears in the MT in conjunction with כבוד on only five occasions (1 Sam 4:21,22; Isa 5:13; 40:5; and Hos 10:5). Aside from the closely related recapitulation of 1 Sam 4:21 in the following verse ("She said 'The Glory has departed from Israel [גלה כבוד מישׂראל]' because the ark of God had been removed [כי נלקח ארון האלהים]"; v. 22), none of the other passages bears any resemblance to the text at hand. The alternate, middle/passive semantic value of גלה as "to be exposed," specific to the *niphal*, is used in Isa 40:5: "The Glory of the LORD will be *revealed* (ונגלה כבוד יהוה)"[247] and can hardly merit further consideration here. In Isa 5:13, the "Glory" neither

244 Ibid., 93–94; his emphasis.

245 The use of אל here where על ("over, concerning") is expected is anomalous, but not unheard of (see *HALOT*, 50, and bibliography therein; and Gary A. Rendsburg, *Israelian Hebrew in the Book of Kings* [Bethesda, Mary.: CDL, 2002], 32–36).

246 Cf. the *BHS* note at Ezek 8:4a, which points to two manuscripts of LXX that add a rendering of יהוה here as well.

247 *HALOT*, 191–92.

refers to God (it refers instead to a sub-set of the population), nor does it serve as the subject of the verb גלה:

> Therefore my people go into exile (גָּלָה) without knowledge;
> their nobles (וּכְבוֹדוֹ) are dying of hunger,
> and their multitude is parched with thirst. (NRSV)

Finally, and most tellingly, Hos 10:5–6a announces that

> The inhabitants of Samaria tremble
> for the calf of Beth-aven.
> Its people shall mourn for it,
> and its idolatrous priests shall wail over it,[248]
> over its glory that has departed from it (על־כבודו כי־גלה ממנו).
> The thing itself shall be carried to Assyria
> as tribute to the great king. (NRSV)

Here, the "glory" refers the object of the idolatrous priests' (כמרים) veneration, the golden calf at Bethel. Despite this divergence in reference, the syntactic structure מן + כבוד + גלה *qal* found in Hos 10:5 is identical to that found elsewhere only in 1 Sam 4:21,22. The following verse, Hos 10:6, provides further information as to the exact context of this sequence's usage, namely, cases in which a divine image was carried off passively after a military defeat—and *not* in which the deity initiates a visitation of an exiled people.[249] Hosea is well known for citing Israel's early traditions, although not necessarily in the reworked forms most familiar from other biblical texts. For example, one might point to the reference to the exodus in 11:1–3 or to Jacob's life in 12:3–6. Given the identical syntax and socio-political situation, it is not irresponsible to suggest that Hosea alluded here to a traditional trope from Israel's past—the loss of the ark preserved in 1 Samuel—in order to present the illegiti-

---

248 Karl Elliger reads here ייליל, parallel to אבל in the preceding stich, rather than MT's יגילו (*BHS* n. 10:5e). James L. Mays, who suggests that "*gīl* in the sense of 'howl, shriek' is used as a word-play on *gālā*" (*Hosea: A Commentary* [OTL; Philadelphia: Westminster, 1969], 138 n. c). David N. Freedman and Francis I. Anderson suggest translating "will be in agony" based on Ps 2:11 (*Hosea: A New Translation with Introduction and Commentary* [AB 24; New York: Doubleday, 1980], 556–57; see also Mitchell J. Dahood, *Psalms I: 1–50* [AB 17; Garden City, N.Y.: Doubleday, 1966], 13; idem, "New Readings in Lamentations," *Bib* 59 [1978], 178 n. 11; Ehud Ben Zvi, *Hosea* [FOTL 21A/1; Grand Rapids, Mich.: Eerdmans, 2005], 211–12).

249 See, e.g., Patrick D. Miller and J. J. M. Roberts, *The Hand of the Lord: A Reassessment of the "Ark Narrative" of 1 Samuel* (JHNES; Baltimore: The Johns Hopkins University Press, 1977; repr., Atlanta: SBL, 2008), 10–17, and esp. 42; see also Mays, *Hosea*, 141; Freedman and Anderson, *Hosea*, 556–57. While it may be the case that Ezekiel is framing a Babylonian plundering of the Jerusalem temple as Yahweh's intentional initiation of a visitation of the Judahite exiles in Babylon, the prophetic oracle itself constitutes a deliberate transformation and thorough reinterpretation of a trope well established in ancient Near Eastern society and hardly represents a reasonable *terminus post quem* of the Ark Narrative in its present form and context, as Römer's argument suggests.

mate Bethel priests' mourning over their lost divine image in an ironic, condemnatory light. Hosea reframed the traditional trope, in which the loss of the divine image is truly a tragedy, and here cast the Bethel calf's removal to Assyria in the same language, implicitly stressing the priests' misplaced anguish.[250] Therefore, it is both possible and reasonable to establish the *terminus ante quem* of 1 Sam 4:21 or 22 (if one verse has priority over the over), set by Hos 10:5, sometime in the 8th cent. The original tradition, now represented by 1 Samuel 4–7*, presumably predated the Assyrian invasion, since it must have been known commonly enough to have been meaningful for at least a portion of Hosea's audience. And while the text of Hosea made allusion to the ark tradition to bolster its own theology, the Ark Narrative itself—or, the book of Samuel, if compiled already by this time—would have accumulated additional layers of meaning aside from simply the triumph of Yahweh over the Philistines in the narrative's historical referent. In the aftermath of the Assyrian invasion and subjugation of the northern kingdom, the Ark Narrative, which had all along been theologically fertile, now provided eschatological hope for the Israelite people that their cultic images—and fellow Israelites whom the Assyrians had deported along with those images—would someday return to the land. Contrast to this diachronically-expressed re-interpretive theological framework the cynicism latent in Römer's argument concerning the connection between 1 Sam 4:21 and Ezekiel 8–10, which arbitrarily assigns the passage to the latest available date at which its reference is theologically, politically, or historically meaningful. Not only is Römer's assertion linguistically unfounded, but it also appears to be predicated only on the superficial similarity of the image of divine movement, which breaks down upon closer thematic inspection.

The second significant objection to Römer's mode of argumentation here derives from the purportedly problematic oscillation that is to be found between Samuel as priest (e.g., 1 Sam 1:24–28; 2:11,18; 3:1; cf. Jer 15:1) and Samuel as prophet (1 Sam 3:19–4:1a). To recapitulate the text quoted above, the cognitive movement from the temple as the locus of the divine encounter to prophecy as the legitimate "medium of access to the divine will," argues Römer, serves as "a central theme of the Deuteronomistic theology in the exilic and postexilic periods." Scrutiny of the assumptions underlying this assertion, however, lays bare the fundamental difficulties with Römer's claims. We have already encountered the problematic underlying principle whereby the somewhat oversimplified, if not

250 For a similar example of deliberate prophetic allusion to a traditional motif with the intention of reframing a position inimical to the prophet's own in an ironic manner, see Jeremy M. Hutton, "Isaiah 51:9–11 and the Rhetorical Appropriation and Subversion of Hostile Theologies," *JBL* 126 (2007): 271–303.

artificial, distinction between priest and prophet is held up as a valid and unbiased criterion for redactional division, so the recrudescence of that principle need only be noted here.[251] But acknowledging that principle's continued operation leads to a second recognition, namely that most interpreters would readily admit the variant origins of the two texts on which Römer founds this distinction (1 Sam 3:19–4:1a; 7:2–14). The latter passage is a miscellany of traditional material and Deuteronomistic editorial material that serves to unite two major sub-corpora of the DtrH, Judges and Samuel.[252] The former is somewhat indeterminate in origin, as it could be an authentically traditional, prophetic (pre-Deuteronomistic) claim or a Deuteronomistic (or DtrP?) reframing of the text.[253] The primary point is that Römer's attribution of these homogenized textual blocks to the exilic or post-exilic period makes certain preliminary assumptions—for example, the lateness of the prophetic influence on the Deuteronomistic corpus and the reification of the conceptual or cultural tensions between divergent forms of Israelite religious practice—without adequate explanation or defense. To say that Samuel "survives the destruction of the sanctuary *in his office as prophet* and intercessor for 'all Israel' (cf. 1 Sam. 7.2–14)" implies the operation of more deliberate compositional techniques than may have been available to Dtr or a pre-Deuteronomistic redactor in the compilation of the originally independent traditions.

Much of this interpretive matrix—which is often expressed in an unconditional syntax—derives from Römer's acceptance of much recent work on scribal culture, as it was described in several studies during the 1990's and early 2000's. In the following chapter on history and historiographic methodology, I examine the problems with those redactional schemas that rely too strictly on the work of Jamieson-Drake. Several recent scholars have refined the work on scribal culture, making possible a reevaluation of the necessary dates of composition of the component documents of the books of Samuel (see below, §4.3).

251 See, e.g., Hans Joachim Stoebe, *Das erste Buch Samuelis* (KAT 8/1; Gütersloh: Mohn, 1973), 126.

252 Compare, for example, the works of Hans Wilhelm Hertzberg, *I & II Samuel: A Commentary* (trans. John S. Bowden; OTL; London: SCM, 1964; repr. Philadelphia: Westminster, n.d.), 66–70; trans. of *Die Samuelbücher* (2d ed.; DATD 10; Göttingen: Vandenhoeck & Ruprecht, 1960); Stoebe, *Erste Buch Samuelis*, 170–72; Birch, *Rise*, 11–21; McCarter, *I Samuel*, 148–51; Campbell, *Of Prophets and Kings*, 68 n. 7; idem, *1 Samuel*, 95 and bibliography there.

253 E.g., Hertzberg, *I & II Samuel*, 42–43; McCarter attributes 1 Sam 3:19–4:1a to his "prophetic writer" (*I Samuel*, 100); Campbell, *Of Prophets and Kings*, 66; idem, *1 Samuel*, 57.

3.5. Summary Comments on the Prophetic Record Hypothesis

Despite the many and significant divergences of opinion between proponents of an early, pre- or proto-Deuteronomistic prophetic edition, the basic model provides a viable and plausible alternative to the Smend school's relegation of nearly all prophetically oriented passages to an exilic redactor DtrP. The proposed text of this Prophetic Record encompasses much of 1–2 Samuel, most likely beginning with 1 Sam 1:1. The prophetic author organized several earlier narratives into a fluid and cogent presentation that described the work(s) of prophets in the early years of the Israelite and Judahite monarchies and articulated a theological justification for the continuation of prophetic authority—Israelite and Judahite kings would surely have substituted here "prophetic interference"—in the political realm. This consensus opinion that the pre-Deuteronomistic form of Samuel—or in more ambitious presentations the PR—most logically began at 1 Sam 1:1 comes with the concomitant recognition that the *Ritterbuch*, which contained the predominant examples of the deliverer-type vision of Transjordan (except for 1 Samuel 11), most likely remained separated from the PR until the conjoining of those two bodies of literature in the DtrH. This is not to claim however that the book of Samuel was without its own deliverer-narrative and accompanying deliverer-type view of Transjordan. As will be demonstrated below (§7.3.1), 1 Sam 11:1–11,15 bears much in common with the deliverer-type narratives in Judges, not least of which is their common use of the deliverer-type view of Transjordan. In this regard, the Transjordanian *theologumenon* of 1 Sam 11:1–15 finds its closest parallel in the deliverer-type vision found in the narratives of Judges, rather than the monarch-type found in the remainder of Samuel (e.g., 2 Sam 19:12–44), or the prophet type found in Josh 3–4 and 2 Kgs 2:1–18.

The sole remaining task of this chapter is to analyze the position of the Elijah-Elisha Cycle (1 Kgs 17:1–2 Kgs 13:21*) and with it the third typological component of the Transjordanian Motif (i.e., the prophet-type) viz-à-viz its inclusion in or exclusion from the PR. Here, too, it will become clear that no matter the precise dating of the prophetic narrative in 2 Kgs 2:1–18, that passage originally stood independent of the PR. Only through the process whereby the passage was interpolated by a later editor (either a pre-Deuteronomistic editor of prophetic persuasion or one of the Deuteronomists) did 2 Kgs 2:1–18 come into close literary contact with the view of Transjordan taking shape in the books of Samuel, and augment that already composite vision.

In 1997, M. C. White argued independently of Campbell for the existence of a mid-9th cent. document supporting the bloody coup of Jehu.[254] She did not cite Campbell at all and avoided significant discussion of the books of Samuel, yet her conclusions were remarkably in line with those of Campbell. White's literary study suggested that the several chapters of 1–2 Kings centered on Elijah, Elisha, and Jehu (1 Kgs 17–19; 21; 2 Kgs 2; 8:7–15; 9–10) were "literary creations produced to serve Jehuite apologetic purposes."[255]

White's study argues in principle that (presumably secular) supporters of Jehu compiled the legendary prophetic texts in order to provide an apology exculpating Jehu's great massacre of the preceding Omride dynasty. This compilation proceeded in at least five steps. First, we can point to the historical existence of a "legendary rainmaker (Elijah)," which was preserved in a narrative centered on the wonder-worker's contest with Baalite prophets (1 Kings 18*), and in a short tradition of Ahab's misuse of royal prerogative (2 Kgs 9:25b–26a). Second, early in Jehu's reign, the story of Naboth's vineyard (1 Kings 21) was composed in tandem with the recitation of Jehu's rebellion against the Omride dynasty (2 Kings 9–10). Third, later in Jehu's reign, the drought legend was appended at the beginning of the burgeoning cycle in order to provide a framework for the various *legenda*. Fourth, an editor working at the earliest during the reign of Joahaz effected the "composition and insertion of I Kgs 19:1–21, II Kgs 2:1–18, and 8:7–15 to enhance Elijah as Moses and to reinforce the prediction of the coup." Finally, after the Jehuite Dynasty had met its end, the legend in 2 Kgs 1 was composed by one of the Deuteronomists as an expression of the southern disdain for northern religious practices.[256]

Clearly, in White's schema, it is the second stage of traditional development that most closely resembles the text of Campell's PR in 1 Kings 17–2 Kgs 10* (Campbell's reconstructed PR encompasses 1 Kgs 17:1; 18:2b–3a,5–12a,15–18a,19*,20–36a*,37–40,42b,45–46; 21:1–7a,8, 11a,14–19a,21–22a*,24; 22:40; 2 Kgs 1:2–8,17a*; 9:1–7a,8–9a,10b,11–

---

254 Marsha C. White, *The Elijah Legends and Jehu's Coup* (BJS; Atlanta: Scholars, 1997). This is a revised publication of White's 1994 Harvard dissertation written under P. Machinist.

255 Ibid., 78. Cf. Rofé, who argues that careful study of the date of Elisha's activity suggests the prophet was not active before 841 (*Prophetical Stories*, 70–74). Although the various *legenda* surrounding him suggest he was closely allied with the Jehuite dynasty, it appears as though the relationship between Elijah and Elisha was forged redactionally and that it was not, in fact, Elisha who commanded that Jehu be anointed as king (ibid., 79–88, esp. 82; cf. also Mayes, *Story*, 109, 170 n. 6). Yet this observation of redactional disjunction does not necessarily negate the possibility of a propagandistic purpose to 2 Kings 9–11 but would, in fact, support Campbell's thesis that a prophetic redactor had combined and edited several earlier narratives.

256 White, *Elijah Legends*, 42–43.

13, 14–27,30–35; 10:1–9,12–17,18–28). There is so much overlap here that the two arrangements may be considered virtually identical treatments of the cycle's literary development, at least as regards the first two steps of White's reconstruction.[257] But no matter the theoretical and methodological differences between the two schemas, both allow for a post-PR introduction of the prophet-type view of Transjordan.

---

257 Insofar as White's concentration is on the *political* ramifications of the narratives, her presentation conflicts with that of Campbell, whose emphasis lies on the *theological* purposes of the text. White's solution, in my mind, has as its assumption the separation of the religious and political spheres and may thus be somewhat divorced from the actual worldview of the ancient Israelites in its formulation. She argues, for example, that Hosea considered the coup against the Omrides "as lacking YHWH's sanction and therefore illegitimate," suggesting instead that the prophetic elements of the text of 2 Kings 9–11 were designed to cast what had been a purely political overthrow in a more friendly, legitimizing religious light (ibid., 76). We should note, however, that Hosea's diatribe against the Jehuite dynasty (e.g., Hos 1:4) is purportedly dated to the reign of Jeroboam II in the early-8th cent. Jeroboam was the fourth in the Jehuite line, and it is entirely possible—if not probable—that the prophetic community that had initially supported Jehu in his coup later turned on the members of his house because of transgressions of the later monarchs in that lineage, or because of a feeling of political disenfranchisement and anger at Jehu's broken "campaign promises." Jon D. Levenson has argued that Jehu was most likely "rewarded...an eternal covenant" for his extermination of the Omrides (*Sinai and Zion: An Entry into the Jewish Bible* [San Francisco: HarperCollins, 1985], 205). Cf. Amos 7:10–11; the anger of the people at Amos's negative evaluation of Jeroboam II suggests just such an arrangement. The prophetically mediated land grant was probably subsequently modified to cover only four generations when Amos's prophecy against the Jehuite dynasty came true. Thus, White's objection to the *historical* prophetic involvement in the overthrow of the Omride dynasty is founded on the assumption of the continuity of prophetic evaluation of the Jehuite dynasty, an assumption that cannot reasonably serve as a solid foundation for the argument. I find far more probable Campbell's assertion that the prophetic school that was centered on Elijah and Elisha supported Jehu's coup, at least textually and theologically, if not historically (See also Judith A. Todd, "The Pre-Deuteronomistic Elijah Cycle," in *Elijah and Elisha in Socioliterary Perspective* [ed. Robert B. Coote; Atlanta: Scholars Press, 1992], 1–35). Yet when Jehu and his followers failed to live up to the expectations placed upon the dynasty by the heavily Yahwistic prophetic guild, the prophets' evaluation of the house of Jehu darkened, and the prophets succumbed to a feeling of regret for their initial support. But this explanation assumes a unity of prophetic outlook in Israel, an assumption which itself may not be grounded on much more than the suppositions of earlier scholars. While Hosea is generally recognized as a thoroughly Deuteronomistic and anti-Baalist prophet, it does not *necessarily* mean that his mediation of divine judgment against the Jehuite lineage would have been shared by *all* of his contemporaries. The same goes for Amos's condemnation of Jeroboam II. If Deut 18:22 was ever actually applied in the process of canonization, it theoretically would have weeded out or called for the amendment of the writings of those anti-Baalist, (proto-) Deuteronomistic prophets who uttered oracles in favor of the Jehuite dynasty. Moreover, Peter B. Machinist argues that Hosea's negative attitude towards the Jehuite dynasty may be indicative of a general perception that the northern monarchy as a whole had proved to be a failure ("Hosea and the Ambiguity of Kingship in Ancient Israel," in *Constituting the Community: Studies on the Polity of Ancient Israel in Honor of S. Dean McBride Jr.* [ed. J. T. Strong and S. S. Tuell; Winona Lake, Ind.: Eisenbrauns, 2005], 153–81; cf. Michael S. Moore, "Jehu's Coronation and Purge of Israel," *VT* 53 [2003]: 97–114).

Therefore, it is in the development of the earlier, prophetically organized document that two of the three foundational visions of Transjordan—the deliverer-type (1 Sam 11:1–15) and the monarch-type (e.g., 2 Sam 19:12–44)—came to be juxtaposed to one another, each thereby augmenting the other. Unless the PR were composed with the destruction of the Jehuite dynasty in mind rather than its legitimate inception, the third vision of Transjordan—the prophet-type—was most likely added subsequent to the formation of the PR and should thus be traced at the earliest to a pre-exilic Deuteronomistic redaction (Dtr^1). Because the primary concern both of the prophetic author and of Dtr was to present the history of the early Israelite and Judahite monarchies as essentially under Yahweh's purview, albeit in different ways, the selection of texts was limited to those that the author could appropriate and reshape to suit the intended purpose. This means that the juxtaposition of the views of the Transjordan was most likely an accidental by-product of the authors' own methodologies, constrained by the relatively static nature of the extant source texts, the socially-located circumscriptions concerning the permissibility of certain editorial methods, and the theological *Tendenz* of the authors and their respective assumed audiences. It is therefore appropriate to give some indication of the various developmental schemata by which the PR may have come into its final form. It is my argument in the remainder of this book that the sources of the PR[258] can be traced back to the situation and motivation of their inception, based on the comparison of the reconstructed documents' concerns as they may be related to the life-world of the Israelite community. Furthermore, I argue, a reconstruction of the historical development of the PR is possible, based on the same sociological concerns. In short, the relation of the various documents contained in and elaborated by the PR to the genre of extra-biblical apologetic texts discussed below (§4.2) leads to a reasonable hypothesis detailing the concerns, motivations, and sources of the various stages of the PR at each step of the way. The Prophetic Record, I will argue, is a medial node in the network of traditions and texts that eventually coalesced to form the DtrH. It is only by tracing a few of the respective functions of the hypothesized core documents outlined above—specifically, the Narrative of Saul's Rise (NSR = ca. 1 Samuel 7–14*),[259] the History of David's Rise (HDR = ca. 1 Samuel 15–2 Samuel 5*),[260] and the so-called Succession Narrative (SSN

258 In the remainder of this study, references to "the PR" should no longer be taken to refer exclusively to the Prophetic Record as outlined by Campbell, *Of Prophets and Kings*. Instead, I have appropriated the term for reference to a slightly larger body of work than Campbell would allow.

259 See below, ch. 6.

260 See below, ch. 5.

= ca. 2 Samuel 2–1 Kings 2*)—as living, *coherent* texts both politically meaningful and theologically cogent at the time of their composition that we may arrive at a more complete understanding of the temporal and conceptual interrelationships of the varied layers of the text. In the following chapters, I lay out my understanding of the source-critical separation of 1 Samuel 9–1 Kings 2.

4. Royal Apology and Scribalism in Iron Age Israel

4.1. Method

As the composition-critical component of this study proceeds, it is mandatory that the delineation of the sources and redactional layers of 1–2 Samuel be performed with absolutely no regard for each discerned source's understanding of the Transjordanian landscape in order to eliminate—or to reduce—the possibility of circularity in the argument. Instead, the distinctions between the hypothesized documents must be drawn on the basis of factors *other* than their respective phenomenological interpretations of the area. In the following analyses, I attempt to pay attention to the markers of literary disjuncture long considered integral to the composition-critical method: "doublets, abrupt changes, differences of vocabulary and style, references to earlier accounts...."[1] I supplement these standard criteria governing source- and redaction-critical studies with one additional literarily- and historically-informed criterion, namely, similarity to (and, conversely, divergence from) the *form* and *function* of Judahite and Israelite royal apology as these features may be reconstructed through study of cognate texts from Mesopotamia and Anatolia.

Part and parcel of this method is the reading of these types of texts. Such readings are never performed without assumptions and are therefore always subjective.[2] I admit, therefore, to holding the fundamental assumption that the biblical texts were written, at least in part, with the intention of addressing a real situation or potentiality. It is imperative in this model that each text be analyzed with its initial and subsequent meanings in mind. Whom or what was the passage intended to support? How has that intention been augmented by secondary accretions or by the passage's juxtaposition with another text?

---

1 Adolphe Lods, *Israel from Its Beginnings to the Middle of the Eighth Century* (trans. S. H. Hooke; London: Routledge, 1932), 11; cited by Edward L. Greenstein, "The Formation of the Biblical Narrative Corpus," *AJSR* 15 (1990): 154.

2 Ina Willi-Plein, "ISam 18–19 und die Davidshausgeschichte," in *David und Saul im Widerstreit—Diachronie und Synchronie im Wettstreit: Beiträge zur Auslegung des ersten Samuelbuches* (ed. Walter Dietrich; OBO 206; Fribourg: University Press; Göttingen: Vandenhoeck & Ruprecht, 2005), 138–41.

In many respects, this method is one of skepticism, yet several attempts at absolute skepticism towards the Bible's mimetic properties have drawn criticism in recent years, and rightfully so. Those readings that disavow all possibility of a historical project on the Bible's part before the reading of any biblical text too readily equate the apologetic with the fanciful and the polemic with the fantastic. Despite claims to the contrary, extra-biblical sources describing historical events during the period of the Israelite divided monarchy corroborate several biblical historiographic notices.[3] Moreover, however idealized the Deuteronomistic sources are, however much the narrative presentation has been shaped to provide Israelite history with a coherent direction and the manifestation of God's sovereign hand guiding that history, the general contours of divided Israelite history resonate in extra-biblical documents from the mid-9th cent. onwards. One may not, therefore, automatically consider intentionally apologetic statements as unhistorical fabrications concocted in contexts to which they do not—and cannot—speak.

A medial position between the two extremes of naive belief and absolute doubt is possible;[4] the project thus becomes one of determining the most salient criteria by which the biblical historian may determine the *plausibility* of various narratives and scenarios, as well as of the force of apologetic documents within Israelite society. Historical plausibility does not consist of a one-to-one system of representation of a historical event. That is to say, the exact narrative features of each source—reported speech, character motivation, the action of God in history—may be attributed to the narrational style of the historian, the *emplotment* of history,[5] without any negative judgment applied to the representative quality of the author's attempt to engage the world. I assume that ultimately the historiographic works composed by the Israelites—whether theologized, polemicized, or politicized—were intended to serve as reminders of past ramifications of humans' actions, and thus as models for effective and efficient present action.

Therefore, the literary judgment of correspondence to or divergence from genre-based models of apologetic texts is coterminous with the

---

3 See, e.g., Baruch Halpern, "The State of Israelite History," in *Reconsidering Israel and Judah: Recent Studies on the Deuteronomistic History* (ed. G. N. Knoppers and J. G. McConville; SBTS 8; Winona Lake, Ind.: Eisenbrauns, 2000), 540–65; see also Walter Dietrich, *The Early Monarchy in Israel: The Tenth Century B.C.E.* (trans. Joachim Vette; SBL Biblical Encyclopedia 3; Atlanta: SBL, 2007), 145–54.

4 See, e.g., Baruch Halpern, "Biblical or Israelite History?" in *The Future of Biblical Studies: The Hebrew Scriptures* (ed. Richard Elliot Friedman and H. G. M. Williamson; Atlanta: Scholars Press, 1987), 103–39.

5 For the emplotment of history, see, e.g., Hayden White, *Tropics of Discourse: Essays in Cultural Criticism* (Baltimore: The Johns Hopkins University Press, 1978).

historical judgment that such an application of the genre is plausible, possible, and warranted within the parameters established for the claimed text's inception and augmentation. These judgments, then, are necessarily mutually-supporting and mutually-affirming; the potential for circularity is present but may be accounted for and mitigated. Subjectivity in the comparative method is ever present but may be overcome through detailed textual study. The likelihood of an accurate comparison increases as lexical, syntactical, thematic, and other indicators accumulate. With these caveats stated, it is now possible to articulate the model whereby several early sources of 1–2 Samuel become both recognizable and dateable. The next section (§4.2) focuses on the nature of Assyrian and Hittite documents as *royal apology* and their formal convergence with—and, in some cases, divergence from—the various source texts of 1–2 Samuel. As apologetic texts, these documents responded to the particular social and historical contexts within which they were composed. Insofar as they were written for apologetic purposes, they give an emplotted account of history. Moreover, their very existence bespeaks a historical situation in which they were necessary (or at least desired) sociologically, politically, and theologically. While these apologetic documents do not give an objective view of history, they betray the workings of history, allowing a view into the mechanics of historical politics, such that the gears and machinations of *real historical agents* (i.e., what we might call the "historical substrate" underlying the literary emplottment of history) may be discerned in them, albeit from our subjective position as modern readers.

4.2. Royal Apology in Hittite and Assyrian Literature

4.2.1. Formal and Conventional Considerations

Ancient Near Eastern exemplars of royal apology abound. A few important articles dating from the mid-1970's to the mid-1980's attempted to schematize the conventions of such texts. In a 1974 article, H. A. Hoffner offered a specialized definition of the term "apology" when discussing literature produced in the Hittite court: "a document composed for a king who had usurped the throne, composed in order to defend or justify his assumption of the kingship by force."[6] The documents that fall under this

6 Harry A. Hoffner, "Propaganda and Political Justification in Hittite Historiography," in *Unity and Diversity: Essays in the History, Literature, and Religion of the Ancient Near East* (ed. Hans Goedicke and J. J. M. Roberts; JNHES; Baltimore: The Johns Hopkins University Press, 1975), 49.

rubric were written as elements in a tactic designed to countermand the power of rumors which would, if left uncontested, undermine the legitimacy of the ruler. In Hoffner's proposal, each royal apologetic document exhibits a conventional, six-part structure offering specific reasons as to why the usurper was, in fact, legitimate (see further below). K. W. Whitelam later extended this category in his discussion of "The Defence of David" to include "the successful use and manipulation of all available media."[7] Instituted at a time of inherent and profound political instability, any such campaign of royal apology is designed to affect the recipient of the message through the use of heavily freighted symbolism that, once actualized, causes the message to appear matter-of-fact, while at the same time dissuading the recipient's further investigation into the *reasons* for the message's production in the first place. As Whitelam noted, this type of message "is an extremely subtle form of communication which cannot be divorced from the audience involved."[8] In short, the specificity of the audience constrains and, to some extent, determines the form of the message so that it might successfully persuade its recipients of the usurper's legitimacy and naturalize the message by drawing the rhetorical methodology into the background where it will remain unquestioned or tacitly assumed.

Soon after Hoffner's study was published, H. Tadmor followed with a description of the causes and mechanisms by which autobiographical apology served to endorse and sustain the legitimacy of unexpected claimants to the throne in Assyrian custom.[9] Around the same time, T. Ishida recognized that the same features of apology Hoffner had proposed could be recognized in the Samʾalian apologetic literature of the Kilamuwa stele (*KAI* 24 = *COS* 2.30), as well as in Judahite royal literature (specifically, the portions of the Succession Narrative in 1 Kings 1–2).[10] Tadmor did not use Hoffner's structuring system of the apology, but Ishida applied Hoffner's six-step structure to Esarhaddon's apology in a seven-step variation, thus bringing the Assyrian literature into the discourse estab-

7 Keith W. Whitelam, "The Defence of David," *JSOT* 29 (1984): 61.

8 Whitelam, "Defence," 66.

9 Hayim Tadmor, "Autobiographical Apology in the Royal Assyrian Literature," in *History, Historiography and Interpretation* (ed. H. Tadmor and M. Weinfeld; Jerusalem: Magnes, 1983), 36–57. Tadmor was apparently familiar with Hoffner's article and made reference to it (ibid., 36–37) but cited several viewpoints opposed to the article as well (ibid., 37 n. 3).

10 Tomoo Ishida, "'Solomon Who is Greater than David': Solomon's Succession in 1 Kings i–ii in the Light of the Inscription of Kilamuwa, King of YʾDY-Śamʾal," in *Congress Volume: Salamanca, 1983* (ed. J. A. Emerton; VTSup 36; Leiden: Brill, 1985), 145–53.

lished by Hoffner (see further below, §4.2).[11] Furthermore, although Hoffner and, to some extent, Tadmor recognized the applicability of the model to the Judahite kingship,[12] it was Ishida who first formalized the exact nature of the various correspondences between the biblical and extra-biblical sets of literature.[13] More recent analyses have added to this constellation of ANE apologetic texts both the History of David's Rise (ca. 1 Samuel 16–2 Samuel 5*) and the Tel Dan Inscription (*KAI* 310 = *COS* 2.39).[14] The general commonality and correspondence of typical elements of apology in wide usage across the cultural and temporal boundaries of the ancient Near East suggests that despite the cultural rootedness and particularity of the motifs, features, and elements hypothesized by Whitelam, there obtains some continuity in the basic forms of Near Eastern apologetic. The six traits identified as common to this literary category are as follows:[15]

1. *Introduction.* The first element of each royal apology provides what might be considered the genealogical justifications notifying the reader how the usurper is qualified through familial relations of some type or another to take the throne. In some cases (e.g., those of the Hittite king Ḫattušili III[16] and Esarhaddon[17]), recourse to a genealogy derived from

---

11 Tomoo Ishida, "The Succession Narrative and Esarhaddon's Apology: A Comparison," in *Ah, Assyria...: Studies in Assyrian History and Ancient Near Eastern Historiography Presented to Hayim Tadmor* (ed. M. Cogan and I. Ephᶜal; Jersalem: Magnes, 1991), 167.

12 Hoffner, "Propaganda," 50; Tadmor, "Autobiographical Apology," 56.

13 Ishida, "Solomon," 145–53; idem, "Succession Narrative," 175–87.

14 Respectively, Michael B. Dick, "The 'History of David's Rise to Power' and the Neo-Babylonian Succession Apologies," in *David and Zion: Biblical Studies in Honor of J. J. M. Roberts* (ed. Bernard F. Batto and Kathryn L. Roberts; Winona Lake, Ind.: Eisenbrauns, 2004), 3–19, citing already Herbert M. Wolf, "The Apology of Ḫattušiliš Compared with Other Political Self-Justifications of the Ancient Near East" (Ph.D. diss, Brandeis, 1967); and Matthew J. Soriano, "The Apology of Hazael: A Literary and Historical Analysis of the Tel Dan Inscription," *JNES* 66 (2007): 163–76, esp. 172–73.

15 The names of the elements presented here are those originally adduced by Hoffner ("Propaganda," 51). Ishida applied a seven-element framework to the Apology of Esarhaddon instead of the more familiar six-element framework ("Succession Narrative," 167), but it should be noted that the fourth and fifth elements identified by Ishida in Esarhaddon's apology—respectively, "Rebellion [by the rival princes]" and "The legitimate successor's counter-attack and victory"—may be collapsed, corresponding to the fourth element of Hoffner's model, the "coup d'état." Since Esarhaddon at least *claims* to have been the legitimate successor, designated before his brothers' revolt, he must portray the coup negatively, rather than offer the positive portrayal recognized in the Hittite variations. In both cases, though, it is clear that a battle was fought in which the legitimacy of one or more of the participants was at stake.

16 For English translation and references to previous editions, see *COS* 1.77. The text is abbreviated here as *ApḪattu*.

17 For the text of Esarhaddon's prism inscription from Nineveh, see Riekele Borger, *Die Inschriften Asarhaddons Königs von Assyrien* (AfOB 9; Osnabrück: Biblio-Verlag, 1956; repr., 1967), 39–64. For English translation, see *ANET*, 289–90. The text is abbreviated here as NinA.

the extant dynasty can be made, claiming direct and therefore legitimate descent from an earlier king. For example, Ḫattušili III is able to point not only to his genealogy (as the younger brother of his competitor Muwattalli) but also to the superiority of his name as a recollection of the name of the dynasty's founder and to his divine care and designation by Ištar (*ApḪattu*. §§1,3, 10a,11).[18] Similarly, Esarhaddon is the son of the king and the dominant queen. However, as a younger son of Sennacherib, he remains an unexpected heir to the throne and hence bases his claim on the throne to a designation by the deities "Ashur, Shamash, Bel and Nabu, the Ishtar of Nineveh (and) the Ishtar of Arbela," which has been confirmed by a liver omen (NinA i.5–7,13–14).[19] Other cases require more ingenuity in the construction of the argument for legitimate succession; the apology of another Hittite king, Telepinu,[20] for instance, points to that king's marriage to a member of the royal family, namely, the previous king's sister Ištapariya, sister of Ḫuzziya (*ApTele*. §22)[21].

2–3. *Historical Survey: noble antecedents and unworthy predecessor*. The second and third elements common to apologetic literature provide both a model of the desirable kingship (*ApTele*. §§1–6,8, but cf. §7; *ApḪattu*. §§1–9) implicitly found to be lacking (according to the usurper) in the reign of the immediately preceding ruler and a direct reference to the immediately preceding ruler(s) who, it is claimed, had failed to attain the standards of divinely ordained leadership (*ApTele*. §§18–21; *ApḪattu*. §10c).[22] For Esarhaddon, these two elements are comprised of Sennacherib's specific designation of Esarhaddon as the royal successor and his older brothers' slander, spoken in an apparent attempt to drive a wedge between the ruling father Sennacherib and the crown prince Esarhaddon (NinA i.8–12,26–34).[23] In a variation on the schema presented by Hoffner, the Kilamuwa inscription also speaks of the subject's predecessors (הלפנים; *KAI* 24.5) but assesses each one negatively with the caveat, "but he did nothing (ובל.פעל; lines 2–4).

---

18 Hoffner, "Propaganda," 51.

19 Tadmor, "Autobiographical Apology," 38–39; Ishida, "Succession Narrative," 167. See also the discussion of the genealogical notices of *KAI* 24.1–5 (Ishida, "Solomon," 147–48) and of *KAI* 310.3–5 (Suriano, "Apology," 64–67).

20 For English translation and references to previous editions, see *COS* 1.76. The text is abbreviated here as *ApTele*.

21 Hoffner, "Propaganda," 51; cf. particularly the argument for David's legitimacy made in the HDR_I (§6.5).

22 Hoffner remarks, "[t]he common theme [of the discussion of the 'noble antecedents'] is unity and strength" (ibid., 52). Remembrance of the antecedents' military victories as well as their coherent and unifying domestic policies seems to have been paramount in the usurper's recognition of their worthy stature.

23 Ibid., 169.

Only Kilamuwa's own actions have been worthy of mention: "[w]hat I have done my predecessors did not do" (מאש.פעלת / בל.פעל.הלפנים; lines 4–5).[24]

4. *Coup d'état*. The fourth element of Hittite apology describes the coup by which the protagonist came to power. For Telepinu, his act of usurpation is a just culmination of the period of unjust and disgraceful leadership that itself had begun in some sort of palace coup (*ApTele*. §19–21).[25] Yet not only was the ruler whom Telepinu has overthrown an unjust and inept one, but he has also made an attempt on Telepinu's life, further justifying Telepinu's response (*ApTele*. §22).[26] Similarly, Ḫattušili III responds with a revolt against the ruling king only after the king makes an attempt on his life (*ApḪattu*. §10c).[27] The description of the coup need not be extensive; Telepinu's is contained in a matter of only a few lines.[28] Ishida has recognized in the Apology of Esarhaddon a slight variation from the original model in which it is the *rightful successor* who is under attack in an inappropriate and unjust coup. As opposed to the Hittite models in which the usurper was the rightful ruler, the role is reversed in the Assyrian model. Since Esarhaddon has based his legitimacy *a priori* on his designation by his father and by the gods, this negative evaluation of the coup is ultimately unsurprising. In any case, Esarhaddon's struggle for power with his brothers results in his ultimate victory, after which he wins the people's support (NinA I.41–52), although one wonders, of course, how unmotivated by an instinct of self-preservation this support was.
5. *Merciful victor*. Following the reprehensible behavior of the preceding kings, the protagonist (i.e., the usurper) is portrayed as a paragon of virtue. This upstanding moral character is first displayed in his actions after the coup's success when the usurper treats his defeated opponents with compassion and forgiveness. Hoffner attributes the magnanimity of the victors to social necessity: "the situation was still delicate and the stakes for survival too high. Thus both documents [i.e., the apologies of Telepinu and Ḫattušili] are at pains to portray the new kings as men of mercy."[29] Whatever the reasons for this merciful behavior—

24 Both translations here are Ishida's ("Solomon," 149). There are no noble antecedents in the Kilamuwa inscription.

25 Muršili, the last of the just kings, was killed by Ḫanteli, the husband of his sister. In the same way, Telepinu—the husband of the ruling king's sister—brought an end to the dynasty of Ḫanteli, perhaps implying poetic justice. For further details of the coup, see Hoffner, "Propaganda," 52–53.

26 Ibid., 53.

27 Ibid., 52–53.

28 Ibid., 53.

29 Ibid., 54.

and furthermore, whatever the actuality behind such statements—it is clear that this element became a meaningful motif in royal apology because it established unqualifiedly the mercy and benefaction of the protagonist, particularly in the face of the predecessor's depredations and criminal behavior. Both Telepinu and Ḫattušili act with comparable graciousness toward their enemies, building houses for the vanquished foe and putting them to work as farmers[30] (in the case of Telepinu; *ApTele.* §23), or publicly humiliating them while refraining from executing them (as was the case of Ḫattušili; *ApḪattu.* §12b).[31] In contrast to the Hittite model, Esarhaddon was apparently not so beneficently inclined toward his opponents; although many of them flee "to an unknown country" (*ana māt lā idû*), those left within Esarhaddon's reach are exterminated, along with their male descendants (NinA i.80–110).[32]

6. *Edict.* Both of the Hittite texts conclude with what Hoffner has termed "quasi-legal sections": "[i]n Telepinu the regulations concern the conduct of justice as it affects the royal family [*ApTele.* §28–50]. In Ḫattušili the regulations concern only the disposition of royal property to the cult of the goddess Ištar of Šamuḫa [*ApḪattu.* §12b]."[33] The legitimacy of the legal codes is in effect *founded* on the narrative portions of the texts but also seems to provide proof of the usurper's ultimate legitimacy. A similar situation is found in the apology of Esarhaddon, where his extermination of the rival princes signifies "the establishment of a just kingship."[34] No law code is present in the Esarhaddon text, but the just punishment of the rebellious older brothers moves the kingdom back into a position in which the appropriate administrator of justice holds power.

As noted already, Ishida has discussed the applicability of the Assyrian variation of this model to the Solomonic Succession Narrative (SSN). This applicability will be explained in greater detail below (§5.3.2.3). However, before that discussion may proceed, a final observation on the ramifications of Tadmor's discussion of the Esarhaddon inscription is warranted.

30 Whether this latter action is indeed a form of graciousness is debatable. Hoffner notes in his translation that the henchmen were made into "real" farmers, designating those who actually performed the work of agriculture, rather than "absentee landlords, whose serfs tilled the soil" (Ibid., 54, 61 n. 41).

31 Ibid., 54–55.

32 The gracious display of beneficence is similarly failing in the Samʾalian text.

33 Hoffner, "Propaganda," 55.

34 Ishida, "Succession Narrative," 173.

4.2.2. Contextual Considerations

Most politically-minded commentators have recognized the function of the SSN as a piece of literature that takes part in a genre Ishida calls "Royal Historical Writings of an Apologetic Nature."[35] As such, its use for the reconstruction of the details of actual historical events has been rightfully impugned.[36] There is some credibility to the recognition that as political documents—and particularly as instances of royal apology—these texts may hedge the truth, conceal the truth, avoid the truth, or dismiss the truth altogether. But it is possible to reconstruct with some detail the sociological situation in which royal apology was written, and which it apparently intends to subvert. In short, the very existence of apologetic writing allows historians to reconstruct a historical set of events that necessitated, occasioned, and conditioned the apologetic writing to begin with. This recognition does not necessarily provide us with an accurate chronology of events in the Davidic monarchy—a register with which the present study is relatively unconcerned—but rather with the sociological situation(s) harboring the taproots of the two apologies, the History of David's Rise (ch. 6) and the Solomonic Succession Narrative (ch. 5).

Esarhaddon's apology gives neither explicit *proof* of his designation—neither by his father nor by the gods—nor strictly representative access to the historical events behind the document; its existence and the argumentative style of its composition are representative of a historical social situation in which such a document could be written meaningfully. That is to

35 Ibid.

36 For various voices in the debate over the historical accuracy of the biblical record, see, e.g., Nils Peter Lemche, "David's Rise," *JSOT* 10 (1978): 2–25; P. Kyle McCarter, "The Apology of David," *JBL* 99 (1980): 489–504; James C. Vanderkam, "Davidic Complicity in the Deaths of Abner and Eshbaal: A Historical and Redactional Study," *JBL* 99 (1980): 521–39; Whitelam, "Defence," 61–87; Tomoo Ishida, "The Story of Abner's Murder: A Problem Posed by the Solomonic Apologist," in *ErIsr* 24 (ed. S. Aḥituv and B. A. Levine; Jerusalem: Israel Exploration Society, 1993), 109*–13*; Steven L. McKenzie, *King David: A Biography* (New York: Oxford University Press, 2000); Baruch Halpern, *David's Secret Demons: Messiah, Murderer, Traitor, King* (Grand Rapids, Mich.: Eerdmans, 2001), esp. 37, 292–94, 332; Timo Veijola, "Solomon: Bathsheba's Firstborn," in *Reconsidering Israel and Judah: Recent Studies on the Deuteronomistic History* (ed. G. N. Knoppers and J. G. McConville; trans. Peter T. Daniels; SBTS 8; Winona Lake, Ind.: Eisenbrauns, 2000), 340–57; trans. of "Salomo: Der Erstgeborene Bathsebas," in *Studies in the Historical Books of the Old Testament* (VTSup 30; Leiden: Brill, 1979), 230–50. Despite their critical stance towards the *accuracy* of the biblical historiography, these authors all recognize that the text was composed in order to address issues in the lives of the subjects. This assumption must be contrasted to that of those who argue the text took shape as a response to significantly later (and completely unrelated) events and circumstances; see, e.g., Philip R. Davies, *In Search of "Ancient Israel"* (JSOTSup 148; Sheffield: Sheffield Academic Press, 1992; repr., 1999); Thomas L. Thompson, *The Mythic Past: Biblical Archaeology and the Myth of Israel* (New York: Basic Books, 1994).

say, strictly speaking, we cannot *know* with certainty that Sennacherib had designated the younger son Esarhaddon as crown prince, since the designation could have been coerced or fabricated;[37] we cannot presume to have full historical access to the oracle given by the deities in Esarhaddon's favor, since any records of alternative extispicy may have been lost or destroyed subsequent to Esarhaddon's assumption of power;[38] we cannot even trust without reservation Esarhaddon's claim to have established a *just* kingship. These claims are, in the end, interpretations or polemical representations of the actual events to which, it must be admitted, we do not have direct access. However, our own faculties allow for the reconstruction of the events and contingencies surrounding the publication of this text: Esarhaddon's distribution and preservation of this polemical, subjective, and purportedly representative text is indicative of a situation in which some (or all) of these claims—and concomitantly, his claim to the Assyrian throne—were contested.

For the historian of traditions, the demonstrable political bias of royal propagandistic and apologetic literature can provide a key to the function and dating of the tradition. In order for the argument to have been effective, we assume, it must have made sense to its audience, addressing the issues at hand in a way that was both rational and steeped in symbolism most likely to convince the audience of its truthfulness and certainty. For example, historians place the initial composition and promulgation of the Apology of Esarhaddon within the timeframe of Esarhaddon's rule precisely because the text's existence only makes sense during the reign of Esarhaddon (i.e., before it was able to become outdated and therefore irrelevent). Similarly, Ishida has argued that "[t]he date of composition [of the Succession Narrative] could not be as late as the second half of Solomon's reign. For the regime of Solomon must have felt it necessary to make this sort of legitimation only in its early years."[39] However, no matter how rational these respective datings, they overlook a single salient feature of apology that has direct bearing on the text's provenance: the anticipation of a conflict over the designated heir's legitimacy. Although, as Tadmor remarked, "it has usually been assumed that these compositions [i.e., royal apologies] stem from that psychological and political situation

---

37 See, of course, the arguments mustered against the accuracy of Solomon's designation by David (recently, Mordechai Cogan, *I Kings: A New Translation with Introduction and Commentary* [AB 10; New York: Doubleday, 2000], 164–68).

38 Cf. the various prophetic designations of Israelite and Judahite rulers and the ways in which they have come to be understood as *ex eventu* justifications rather than authentic representations of Yahweh's will.

39 Tomoo Ishida, "Solomon's Succession to the Throne of David—A Political Analysis," in *Studies in the Period of David and Solomon and Other Essays* (ed. Tomoo Ishida; Winona Lake, Ind.: Eisenbrauns, 1982), 187.

which confronted the usurper at the beginning of his reign,"—an assumption borne out in some instances, particularly the apologetic texts of the Chaldean kings of Babylonia and the Achaemenid kings of the early Persian Empire—the assumption does not hold true for the Apology of Esarhaddon. Not only was the document intended to justify the Assyrian king's ascendance, but it was also "written…in conjunction with the appointment of the successor—a crucial moment in the life of every king and especially of those whose own coming to the throne was not entirely in order."[40] In short, the anomalous nature of Esarhaddon's accession to the throne of Assyria fostered a political situation in which the succession of his own chosen crown prince Ashurbanipal to the throne of Assyria was at stake and for which the Apology had to make provision, even though it nowhere mentions this contingency explicitly.[41]

This recognition of a second significant function of Esarhaddon's apology suggests that an augmentation in the common assumptions concerning biblical royal apologies (especially those of Solomon and David) may be in order. Both of the apologetic documents purporting to describe the Davidic Kingdom show signs of a concern for the legitimacy of the ruling monarch (who, in both cases, has come to power in a situation of ambiguous legitimacy).[42] In addition, each provides at least an ideological foundation for the legitimization of the ruler's successor. In neither case, I allow, is the successor explicitly named in the document itself; rather, the specific selection of the successor is left open, and the primary concern seems to be a defense of the continued legitimacy of the Davidic dynasty over against the Saulides in the Davidic apology (referred to below as the HDR_1) and, more broadly, the generalized threat from splinter factions in

40 Tadmor, "Autobiographical Apology," 37–38.

41 As is well known, the succession of Ashurbanipal was not without difficulties, since Esarhaddon's relegation of his older son Shamash-shum-ukin to the (less prestigious) kingship of Babylonia brought about a schism in the empire, a civil war between the two factions, and—because of the severe punishment of Babylonia at the culmination of the civil war—increased hostility between the two political entities that ultimately resulted in the utter destruction of the Assyrian empire in the years 612–605 (Tadmor, "Autobiographical Apology," 43–45; Amélie Kuhrt, *The Ancient Near East: c. 3000–330 BC* [2 vols.; London: Routledge, 1995], 2:540–41).

42 Recently, Klaus-Peter Adam has examined the Succession Narrative as concerned with "the securing of monarchic power" (*die Sicherung der königlichen Macht*) ("Motivik, Figuren und Konzeption der Erzählung vom Absalomaufstand," in *Die deuteronomistischen Geschichtswerke: Redaktions- und religionsgeschichtliche Perspektiven zur "Deuteronomismus"-Diskussion in Tora und Vorderen Propheten* [ed. Markus Witte et al.; BZAW 365; Berlin: de Gruyter, 2006], 183–211). It may be noted here, in anticipation of the discussion below concerning David's marriage to Saul's daughter (§6.3.2.2), that the Apology of Telepinu provides a hierarchy of legitimacy: naturally, the highest ranking claimant to the throne is a first-born prince. The next is a subsequently born prince, and if none of these exists, then the husband of the highest-ranked daughter (*ApTele.* §28).

the north—which continue to be led most prominently by Benjaminites—in the Solomonic apology (see below, the HDR_2 + SSN).

A tentative proposal as to the social and historical contexts of the Succession Narrative emerges: if the document can be shown to have significant formal similarities to other instances of royal apologetic from the ancient Near East, then we must at least ask the question whether the text is most firmly rooted in the late-10th cent., towards the end of Solomon's reign. This comparison will proceed in the following chapter. Before it begins, however, it is necessary to consider briefly an ancillary issue that arises from this investigation into the *form* and *function* of royal apologetic. Given our increasing—but still quite limited—knowledge of scribal practices and culture in Israel and Judah of the 10th cent., is it even *possible* that a written document legitimizing the reign of Solomon (or more properly, of Rehoboam), was in circulation already by the late-10th cent.? If so, then we must ask who the intended audience was and how widely the document was circulated. The next section examines these questions.

4.3. Scribalism and Audience in Iron Age Israel

In 1991, D. W. Jamieson-Drake published a seminal study calling into question the common assumption that scribal "schools" were prevalent in Iron Age Judah.[43] Because Jamieson-Drake was able to demonstrate conclusively that the archaeological evidence supported neither the assumption of widespread literacy in the Judahite highlands during the Iron Age, nor the presence of scribal "schools" in the peripheral areas outside of Jerusalem, nor the systematization of learning representative of large-scale educational institutions, the study is frequently cited as a compelling argument against the possibility of literary production in highland Israel before the 8th cent. Although several of Jamieson-Drake's conclusions

43 David W. Jamieson-Drake, *Scribes and Schools in Monarchic Judah: A Socio-Archaeological Approach* (JSOTSup 109; SWBA 9; Sheffield: Almond, 1991); for subsequent works on scribes, scribalism, and scribal schools in monarchic Israel, see, e.g., Susan Niditch, *Oral World and Written Word: Ancient Israelite Literature* (LibAncIsr; Louisville, Ky.: WJKP, 1996); Philip R. Davies, *Scribes and Schools: The Canonization of the Hebrew Scriptures* (LibAncIsr; Louisville, Ky.: WJKP, 1998); Raymond F. Person, *The Deuteronomic School: History, Social Setting, and Literature* (SBLStBL 2; Atlanta: SBL, 2002); William M. Schniedewind, *How the Bible Became a Book: The Textualization of Ancient Israel* (Cambridge: Cambridge University Press, 2004); David M. Carr, *Writing on the Tablet of the Heart: Origins of Scripture and Literature* (Oxford: Oxford University Press, 2005); Karel van der Toorn, *Scribal Culture and the Making of the Hebrew Bible* (Cambridge, Mass.: Harvard University Press, 2007).

may go unchallenged—e.g., literacy in the Israelite and Judahite highlands of the 10th and 9th centuries was simply not widespread—the assumptions on which Jamieson-Drake based his arguments must be reexamined. Recent reevaluation of Jamieson-Drake's work, along with attentiveness to the precise conclusions he reached, calls into question the too-hasty eschewal of a relatively early dating of a few biblical texts.[44]

As part of his "socio-archaeological" survey, Jamieson-Drake adopted the theoretical position developed by Mendenhall and Gottwald of a highland Israelite "rejection of...the urban Canaanite city-state regime and its socioeconomic control (or attempts at control) of the rural hinterland."[45] This Israelite rejection was not only a political rejection, but a rejection of culture—including scribal culture—as well: "little, if any, centralized administrative control, social stratification..., or full-time non-agricultural professionalism characterized Israelite society during the first two-century period of this study."[46] W. M. Schniedewind has challenged Jamieson-Drake's assessment, however: Israel's cultural "rejection" of Canaanite systems cannot have been nearly so thorough as represented in the biblical text, since "[i]t was the later Josianic reform narrative...that emphasized the need for cultural distinction.... In contrast, continuity is evident in the archaeological record that demonstrates continued Egyptian presence in Canaan from the Late Bronze Age (1550–1200 B.C.E.) through the early Iron Age I period (1200–1000 B.C.E.)."[47] Accordingly, Jamieson-Drake's claim of utter rejection is predicated upon a "simplistic reading" of the biblical text.[48] Moreover, a more sophisticated reading of the biblical witness suggests exactly the opposite:

> Although some later biblical narratives advocate a cultural break, the stories of Judges and the accounts of the early monarchy from Samuel and Kings suggest that the early Israelite kings drew heavily upon a Canaanite administrative infrastructure. It was only the Deuteronomistic ideology stemming from the late seventh century Josianic religious reforms that advanced the notion of a complete cultural break with Canaanite social institutions.[49]

Although the explosion of writing in non-institutional settings was, admittedly, only made possible by increased urbanization during the 8th and 7th centuries, recourse to Stager's ruralization model presented above (§2.1.2) suggests, in agreement with Schniedewind, that a basic cultural continuity obtained between the lowland city-states and the highland settlement of the Early Iron Age. The Amarna corpus confirms the presence of at least a

44 For the acrimony that developed during the 1990's, see, e.g., Baruch Halpern, "Erasing History—The Minimalist Assault on Ancient Israel," *BRev* 11.6 (1995): 26–35, 47.

45 Jamieson-Drake, *Scribes and Scribal Culture*, 45.

46 Ibid.

47 Schniedewind, *How the Bible Became a Book*, 57.

48 Ibid.

49 Ibid.

few scribes (and therefore of the traditions of scribal training) in the Levant during the Late Bronze Age, and these most likely persisted, if in isolated pockets, into the Iron Age.[50] The presence of these scribes in the central highlands during the 10th cent. is confirmed by the existence of the Gezer Calendar (*KAI* 182 = *COS* 2.85) and the recently discovered T. Zayit and Kh. Qeiyafeh inscriptions, among others.[51] During the 9th cent., two neighboring cultures evince the work of professional scribes in the form of monumental inscriptions: the Aramaic dialectal Tel Dan Inscription (*KAI* 310 = *COS* 2.39) and the Mesha (or Moabite) Inscription (*KAI* 181 = *COS* 2.23) demonstrate the work of a still relatively uniform scribal culture in the southern Levant.[52]

Undoubtedly, scribal training in the highlands was minimal during this period, and where present, it was surely performed in small-scale domestic settings, in which a parent (usually a father) would educate his son and perhaps a few other students under his tutelage.[53] Commentators generally seem to agree that this education was conducted with the intention of providing marketable services to the royal house or the temple apparatus—the major emergent institutions of the day. While we have little sure evidence to make a decision favoring one or the other, a few sociologically-conditioned observations may suggest a provisional solution to the problem. Those who argue most stringently against the presence of a large scribal economy in the southern Levantine highlands during the 10th and 9th

---

50 See, e.g., Ryan Byrne, "The Refuge of Scribalism in Iron I Palestine," *BASOR* 345 (2007): 1–31; and Seth L. Sanders, "Writing and Early Iron Age Israel: Before National Scripts, Beyond Nations and States," in *Literate Culture and Tenth-Century Canaan: The Tel Zayit Abecedry in Context* (ed. Ron E. Tappy and P. Kyle McCarter Jr.; Winona Lake, Ind.: Eisenbrauns, 2008), 97–112.

51 For the inscription from T. Zayit, see Ron E. Tappy et al., "An Abecedary of the Mid-Tenth Century B.C.E. from the Judaean Shephelah," *BASOR* 344 (2006): 5–46; and the various essays in Ron E. Tappy and P. Kyle McCarter Jr., eds., *Literate Culture and Tenth-Century Canaan: The Tel Zayit Abecedry in Context* (Winona Lake, Ind.: Eisenbrauns, 2008). The inscription found at Kh. Qeiyafeh has, at the time of this writing, not yet been made available in a scholarly venue; see the preliminary notification of its find in Ethan Bronner, "Find of Ancient City Could Alter Notions of Biblical David," *New York Times* (Oct. 30, 2008), accessed online at: http://www.nytimes.com/2008/10/30/world/middleeast/30david.html?_r=2&ref=world&oref=slogin. The article's implication that the inscription's find may prove that "literacy may have been more widespread than is generally assumed" is certainly an overstatement, as is the article's title. See also the various other 10th and 9th cent. inscriptions that have come to light over the last ten years, listed in Aren M. Maeir et al., "A Late Iron Age I/Early Iron Age II Old Canaanite Inscription from Tell eṣ-Ṣâfī/Gath, Israel: Palaeography, Dating, and Historical-Cultural Significance," *BASOR* 351 (2008): 62; see also Byrne, "Refuge of Scribalism," 17–22.

52 Schiedewind, *How the Bible*, 58–63; Carr, *Writing*, 114, 163–64.

53 See, e.g., Carr, *Writing*, 111–73, esp. here 112–15; and Christopher A. Rollston, "Scribal Education in Ancient Israel: The Old Hebrew Epigraphic Evidence," *BASOR* 344 (2006): 47–74, esp. 48–50.

centuries have tended to do so on the basis of Israel's and Judah's failure to obtain full-blown statehood during this period. For example, in a fairly technical conclusion to *Scribes and Schools in Monarchic Judah*, Jamieson-Drake argues that Judah under David and Solomon did not attain the status of statehood—according to sociological indices such as population, craft specialization, etc.—but could be classified as a chiefdom at most.[54] I do not dispute here Jamieson-Drake's analysis on this point, nor do I consider the minimal nature of scribal activity that follows from this assertion problematic. I disagree, however, with Jamieson-Drake's assumption that the dominant usage of writing and literacy in ancient Israel was centered on information management and administrative documentation.[55] Schniedewind also seems to accept this limited function of scribalism, if only tacitly, with his assertion that "[i]t is difficult to assume that royal or temple scribes would have engaged in the composition of large literary works," and his concomitant relegation of literary promulgation to the oral sphere.[56] On the contrary, argues Carr, "a small-scale writing-education system does not preclude the creation of longer works. All that is required is a few scribes and the felt need to create and perpetuate a writing-stabilized cultural tradition that marks off the emergent hierarchy from others."[57] This short response to Schniedewind is practically hidden in a footnote, but it triggers a significant question concerning the location—both geographic and social—of such scribal specialists as Carr describes. A proposal may be offered that answers both this question and the related query concerning the intended audience of the posited "royal apologies" of §4.2.

If we consider the ultimate purpose of writing (and with it, literacy) to have been—and to remain—more than merely pragmatic information management, we arrive at a much more broadly-construed function of scribal education. Recent analyses have demonstrated that writing served to consolidate corporate identity[58] and that systems of scribal education tended to focus on the *enculturation* of students as well as their formal education in literacy.[59] These observations—combined with the recognition that scribal services were utilized primarily by elites and also conferred at least the appearance of prestige upon the client—suggest that scribalism need not have been strictly limited to the palace or temple func-

54 Jamieson-Drake, *Scribes and Schools*, 138–45.

55 Ibid., 152–57.

56 Schniedewind, *How the Bible*, 63.

57 Carr, *Writing*, 163 n. 191.

58 For discussion of scholarship on the issue, see, e.g., Seth L. Sanders, "What Was the Alphabet For? The Rise of Written Vernaculars and the Making of Israelite National Literature," *Maarav* 11 (2004): 25–56; and Byrne, "Refuge of Scribalism," 2.

59 Carr, *Writing*, 3–14, esp. 12, for an introductory discussion of "education-enculturation."

tions: in short, the large institutions associated, according to Jamieson Drake, with full-blown statehood. Rather, scribal education may have remained entirely peripheral during the Iron I, or at most only nominally related to and supported by emergent power structures. On this model, the scribe found some economic benefit in what might be considered akin to "freelancing" prestige inscriptions for wealthy—and perhaps somewhat presumptuous—clientele: "The *affectation* of the prestige inscription... might have provided the Iron I scribe a hook to diversify his commissions (if not his clientele, provided the pretentious patron does not also commission inscriptions for his retainers)."[60] As certain powerful individuals increased in political stature (along with the attendant wealth), they would presumably have trended towards greater expressions of self-aggrandizement in the form of propagandistic and apologetic texts. Having been displaced to the periphery with the collapse of centralized governments at the end of the Bronze Age, the position of scribal training in the Iron Age I Levant would gradually have moved back towards the center as a result of this patronage, no matter how unsavory the commissioning individual. As Byrne writes, "[w]arlordism ranks far below the ideal form of intellectual patronage, but it does afford survival. The scarcity of the craft, moreover, inflated the value of the scribal retainer and the prestige that accrued to the sybarite with wherewithal to retain one...."[61] Contrary, then, to previous assertions that scribalism was dependent upon the formation of the state for its own emergence and support, the model that Byrne and Sanders have developed presupposes a more modest view of a small-scale scribal economy in which scribes rented their services to tribal chieftains or petty kings (such as we might reasonably assume the historical Saul and David to have been) but did not necessarily serve solely at the behest of the despot. Moreover, when they *did* act according to the wishes of the regnant chieftain or warlord, the action did not *depend on*, but rather *facilitated*, the consolidation of corporate identity and thus of the nascent state. Sanders has eloquently summarized the process: "[t]he view required...is not that an Israelite state established writing but that writing was recruited by an Israelite state to establish itself, in order to argue publically that it existed."[62]

60 Byrne, "Refuge of Scribalism," esp. 19; the decentralized nature of scribalism in Iron Age Israel was first brought to my attention by Robert R. Wilson ("The Hebrew Bible as a Scribal Artifact: Reflections on the Current Discussion" [paper presented at the Columbia Hebrew Bible Seminar, New York, N.Y., 20 September 2006], citing Michel Tanret, "The Works and the Days...On Scribal Activity in Old Babylonian Sippar-Amnānum," *RA* 98 (2004): 33–62.

61 Byrne, "Refuge of Scribalism," 22.

62 Sanders, "Writing," 107; however, cf. David M. Carr, "The Tel Zayit Abecedary in (Social) Context," in *Literate Culture and Tenth-Century Canaan: The Tel Zayit Abecedry in Context*

We might add to this model the observation that scribal training throughout the ANE included the memorization and internalization of various genres, including narrative literature and political-enculturational material.[63] Given the prevalence of the memorization of texts in antiquity, it was commonplace for advanced scribes to have committed to memory vast textual corpora that could then be cited verbatim or modulated and reworked in order to be fitted into new contexts and shapes:

> ...having learned such precise, verbatim memorization in a text-supported oral educational system, Israelite authors were able—like non-Israelite authors taught in similar systems—to echo their own writing. Their training in verbatim memorization in a text-supported environment gave them tools for exact or semiexact repetition that allowed them to produce works that featured remarkably precise parallels. They could author multiple speeches and other narrative elements that closely paralleled earlier speeches and narratives in their own composition.[64]

It is, I suggest, within this confluence of the oral-textual milieu and the emergent monarchy in Israel that the apologetic texts of Saul's and David's reigns would have first been composed. The models for those compositions would have lain at hand or, rather, had already been memorized by the trained scribes that each petty tyrant hired to lend legitimacy to his nascent rule. Working from these memorized models or templates drawn from their educational backgrounds, the scribal retainers would presumably have composed royal apologetic for the benefit and self-satisfaction of the patron's small court and cadre of hangers-on: it is unlikely that this apologetic was intentionally distributed much further than this environment, although given Sanders's insistence that the nascent state mobilized scribalism as its forays into self-legitimization, we might expect there to have been some "trickle-down" effect of this newly-established corporate identity among the semi- and non-literate populace.[65] One suspects that it is quite improbable that the narratives themselves circulated in writing far beyond the scribal-educational system in which these retained scribes

---

(ed. Ron E. Tappy and P. Kyle McCarter Jr.; Winona Lake, Ind.: Eisenbrauns, 2008), 113–29, esp. 122–26.

63 See, e.g., Carr, *Writing*, 20–30.

64 Ibid., 160; see also 31–46, esp. 40–42, for Mesopotamian exemplars, and 124–73, esp. 159–64, for Israelite scribal education. Sanders points out that there was a cuneiform-based scribal tradition in Israel, "stretching from the Middle Bronze age through the Hellenistic period" ("Alphabet," 28; see also Wayne Horowitz, Takayoshi Oshima, and Seth Sanders, "A Bibliographical List of Cuneiform Inscriptions from Canaan, Palestine/Philistia, and the Land of Israel," *JAOS* 122 [2002]: 753–66).

65 By "trickle-down" I intend to indicate a process of informal interactions between those enculturated with the established court's textualized rhetoric and the general populace, whereby the values of the court are transferred to the populace without the latter ever having heard—much less, read—the apology's text.

would have operated and in which they presumably taught, but those texts may conceivably have functioned as educational exercises to be memorized and recited by upper-level trainees.

If the model of 10th century Israelite and Judahite scribalism I have developed here is correct, then the term "texts" as it is used throughout the remainder of this study takes on a peculiar—and not immediately self-evident—meaning: a text was composed orally, intended primarily for oral recitation, and circulated only in written form in an exceptionally limited educational context. Moreover, a brief sketch of the developmental process whereby the DtrH took shape is warranted here: the implied and assumed audiences of the earliest apologetic "texts" hypothesized in the following chapters were minimal and comprised mainly of the subject's courtiers and adjutants. The original purpose of the texts' recitation in such small circles was to affirm the audience's choice of liege (although one suspects "choice" very rarely factored into the equation), to encourage enduring loyalty to the individual, and to foster the audience's self-identification as members of a single and united corporate group. Only with the increased centralization of scribal education under the developing monarchies of the 9th cent. did these texts acquire a more public character. For the most part, this expanding "publication" would have been directed towards encouraging Israelite and Judahite society to re-envision the overarching commonalities between the increasingly politically-divergent polities.[66] However, the publication of the emergent scribal tradition simultaneously allowed its promulgation to and subversion by disaffected—or at least disenfranchised—prophetic and Levitical groups at the social periphery.[67] Because of their broad-based support by wealthy clientele (e.g., 2 Kgs 4:8–10; 5:1–5), these groups were able to afford the services of a scribe on at least a part-time basis and—at the latest by the mid-8th cent.—had the wherewithal and motivation to craft a larger narrative corpus, an

66 Sanders, "Alphabet," 28–31, 47–49, and esp. 50–54.

67 For the disenfranchisement or peripheralization of religious functionaries, see, e.g., Frank Moore Cross, *Canaanite Myth and Hebrew Epic: Essays in the History of the Religion of Israel* (Cambridge, Mass.: Harvard University Press, 1973), 195–215; Baruch Halpern, "Sectionalism and the Schism," *JBL* 93 (1974): 519–32; idem, "Levitic Participation in the Reform Cult of Jeroboam I," *JBL* 95 (1976): 31–42; John R. Spencer, "Priestly Families (or Factions) in Samuel and Kings," in *The Pitcher is Broken: Memorial Essays for Gösta W. Ahlström* (ed. Steven W. Holloway and Lowell K. Handy; JSOTSup 190; Sheffield: Sheffield Academic Press, 1995), 387–400; Ziony Zevit, *The Religions of Ancient Israel: A Synthesis of Parallactic Approaches* (London: Continuum, 2001), 449; Jeremy M. Hutton, "The Levitical Diaspora (I): A Sociological Comparison with Morocco's Ahansal," in *Exploring the* Longue Durée*: Essays in Honor of Lawrence E. Stager* (ed. David Schloen; Winona Lake, Ind.: Eisenbrauns, 2009), 223–34; idem, "Southern, Northern, and Transjordanian Perspectives," in *Religious Diversity* (ed. John Barton and Francesca Stavrakopoulou; London: T&T Clark, forthcoming).

anthology of sorts, utilizing extant traditions and assuring themselves (and perhaps even the communities they served) of their own divine mandate to participate in the checks-and-balances system of the monarchy that Yahweh had established over Israel (and, by extension, Judah). As with the earlier court-produced apologetic, this Prophetic Record presumably had as its primary intended audience none other than the northern prophetic community producing the document in the first place; a secondary—and perhaps unintended, although not unwanted—audience would have been the various lay communities who formed the clientele of these holy lineages. Despite the limited nature of the intended audience, it was precisely these disaffected Levitical factions that fled south upon the destruction of the northern kingdom in 720 and that comprised the kernel of the Deuteronomistic movement in Judah.[68] To speak in the following chapters, then, of a proto-Deuteronomistic PR is not outside the realm of plausibility. In fact, to do so is to treat seriously and critically the evidence supplied by the biblical text, while at the same time reconstructing a viable social and historical context for the hypothesized scribal work on the basis of cultural cognates.

68 The theory of Deuteronomy's northern origins, consolidated by E. W. Nicholson (*Deuteronomy and Tradition* [Philadelphia: Fortress, 1967], 58–82) is currently undergoing renewed interest; see, e.g., Jeffrey C. Geoghegan, "'Until This Day' and the Preexilic Redaction of the Deuteronomistic History," *JBL* 122 (2003): 201–27, esp. 217–20, 226; idem, *The Time, Place, and Purpose of the Deuteronomistic History: The Evidence of "Until This Day"* (BJS 347; Providence: Brown University, 2005), 84–88; Mark Leuchter, "The Literary Strata and Narrative Sources of Psalm xcix," *VT* 55 (2005): 20–38; idem, "'The Levite in Your Gates': The Deuteronomic Redefinition of Levitical Authority," *JBL* 126 (2007): 417–36; idem, "Why Is the Song of Moses in the Book of Deuteronomy?" *VT* 57 (2007): 295–317; and Mark A. Christian, "Revisiting Levitical Authorship: What Would Moses Think?" *ZAR* 13 (2007): 194–236, esp. 219–21.

5. Of Success and Succession

5.1. Rost's "Succession Narrative," Briefly Described

In his detailed consideration of the Succession Narrative (siglum SN), L. Rost proceeded from the basic assumption that 1 Kings 1 contained the kernel of the story's thematic thrust: a concern as to who would rule over the United Monarchy once David had died. Rost traced this concern throughout 2 Samuel 9–20 and 1 Kings 1–2.[1] Although the theme did not permeate—or at least, was not immediately obvious in—that entire textual span, smaller units could be found whose themes, once integrated into the whole, supported the posited project of the SN. Adducing the inclusion of earlier traditions in the SN, Rost considered the boundaries of that full text of the SN to extend backward through those verses of Nathan's oracle to David (2 Sam 7:11b,16) that supported the legitimacy of Solomon. Within the SN itself, the originally independent Davidic-era account of the wars against the Ammonites (2 Sam 10:1–11:1; 12:26–31) formed a suitable framework for the birth-narrative of the hero Solomon (11:2–12:25); thus, the two traditions were combined and placed in the SN as part of the narrative's superstructure.[2] Similarly, the vignette concerning Amnon's rape of Tamar and the ensuing vengeful acts of Absalom (2 Samuel 13–14) provided the necessary conflict that would leave the succession in doubt, thereby supplying the narrative tension. But Rost's hypothesized SN encompassed an additional, extant set of material: he suggested the Ark Narrative (AN), an earlier text dating to the time of David and comprising 1 Sam 4:1b–18a,19–21; 5:1–11b,12; 6:1–3b,4,10–14,16; 6:19–7:1; 2 Sam 6:1–15,17–20a, was "dovetailed" into the SN through the addition of the "Michael scene in 2 Sam 6[:16,20–23]."[3] Thus, the unified original text of the AN, which was "to be regarded as an independent, self-contained

---

1 Rost's study, despite its relative antiquity, remains the benchmark study for the delineation of the boundaries of the narrative (*The Succession to the Throne of David* [trans. Michael D. Rutter and David M. Gunn, with an introduction by Edward Ball; HTIBS 1; Sheffield: Almond, 1982]; trans. of *Die Überlieferungen von der Thronnachfolge Davids* [BWANT 42; Stuttgart: Kohlhammer, 1926]).

2 Rost *Succession*, 57–62. This may be the case, but cf. the argument below (§5.3.2.2) that the entirety of 2 Sam 10:1–12:25 should be dated *later* than the reign of David.

3 Rost, *Succession*, 13. For Rost, the History of David's Rise (HDR) ends in 5:10 with David's accession to the throne, and therefore the AN cannot possibly belong to that complex (*Succession*, 8–9; cf. below, §6.5.2).

source which has been preserved in its entirety," and which "relate[d] the fate of the ark from its removal from Shiloh up until its installation in Jerusalem," served as a dynasty-legitimizing preface to the newly composed SN.[4] According to Rost, this complex served as a description and legitimization of Solomon's succession to the throne of David.

Several valuable summaries of the issues at stake and the secondary literature handling those problems have appeared in the last two decades,[5] and it is quite clear even from a cursory glance at these *Forschungsberichten* that the puzzles posed by the SN are labyrinthine and myriad. The main issues, however, are usually classified into three categories: the date of the narrative, its limits and unity (or disunity), and its *Tendenz*.[6] These issues will be summarized schematically here in reverse order. Because the problems are interrelated, it will be necessary to discuss all three before reaching a final conclusion regarding any one of them. Moreover, while a detailed discussion of the narrative's full developmental history would require much more space than is available here (as is evidenced by the magnitude of the recent studies by Seiler, Vermeylen, and Rudnig[7]), such a study is unnecessary in the context of the present project. Because my primary project concern is to demonstrate the compositional stratification of the Transjordanian Motif's constituent typologies, the current chapter must craft only a logical argument for the compositional relationship between the monarch-type vision of Transjordan and its complementary prophet-type vision. (The separation of the monarch-type from the deliverer-type will occur over the course of chs. 6 and 7.) In §3.5, I suggested that the paradigmatic instances of the prophet-type vision of Transjordan (Joshua 3–4; 2 Kings 2) were most plausibly traced to the pre-exilic Deuteronomistic redaction (Dtr[1]). If a plausible argument can be sustained that the narrative framework of David's flight to

4 Ibid., 26.

5 See, e.g., Walter Dietrich and Thomas Naumann, *Die Samuelbücher* (EdF 287; Darmstadt: Wissenschaftliche Buchgesellschaft, 1995), 169–295; Stefan Seiler, *Die Geschichte von der Thronfolge Davids (2 Sam 9–20; 1 Kön 1–2): Untersuchungen zur Literaturkritik und Tendenz* (BZAW 267; Berlin: de Gruyter, 1998), 3–26; most recently, see Thilo Alexander Rudnig, *Davids Thron: Redaktionskritische Studien zur Geschichte von der Thronnachfolge Davids* (BZAW 358; Berlin: de Gruyter, 2006), 1–14.

6 E.g., Albert de Pury and Thomas Römer, "Einleitung: Zu den wichtigsten Problemen der sogenannten Thronnachfolgegeschichte," in *Die sogenannte Thronfolgegeschichte Davids: Neue Einsichten und Anfragen* (ed. Albert de Pury and Thomas Römer; OBO 176; Fribourg: University Press; Göttingen: Vandenhoeck & Ruprecht, 2000), 1–3.

7 By way of comparison, Seiler's monograph (*Geschichte*) spans over 320 pages (excluding bibliography and indices), Rudnig's (*Davids Thron*) over 360, and J. Vermeylen's (*La loi du plus fort: Histoire de la rédaction des récits davidiques de 1 Samuel à 1 Rois 2* [BETL 154; Leuven: University Press, 2000]) nearly 700 (although, to be fair, the last is a study of 1 Samuel 8–1 Kings 2).

and return from Transjordan was already incorporated into the PR, then the separation of the two types of Transjordanian geographic attachment may be maintained.

5.2. The *Tendenz*: For or Against Solomon?[8]

5.2.1. Challengers to a Rostian pro-Solomonic Document

Many commentators have accepted the essentially pro-Solomonic stance of the SN that Rost proposed,[9] but the assessment is hardly unanimous. Despite the large measure of support for the pro-Solomonic character of the document(s) encompassing or underlying 2 Samuel 9–20; 1 Kings 1–2, however, Rost's position has also been challenged. Some commentators view the pro-Solomonic interpretation as a matter of incorrectly perceived *Tendenz*,[10] while others challenge the nature of *Tendenz* as a viable criterion on which to base an analysis of the extent of the SN. For example, D. M. Gunn perceives both pro- and anti-Solomon sentiments but argues that the narrative's complexity prohibits its identification as mere propaganda;[11] J. S. Ackerman followed Gunn in this assessment.[12] This

8 The question underlying the title of this section was first posed as such by François Langlamet ("Pour ou contre Salomon? La rédaction prosalomonienne de 1 Rois i–ii," parts 1–2, *RB* 83 [1976]: 321–79, 481–528).

9 Those accepting the pro-Solomonic tendencies of 2 Samuel 9–20; 1 Kings 1–2 include: T. C. G. Thornton, "Solomonic Apologetic in Samuel and Kings," *CQR* 169 (1968): 159–66; R. N. Whybray, *The Succession Narrative: A Study of II Samuel 9–20; I Kings 1 and 2* (SBT II/9; Naperville, Ill.: Allenson, 1968), 19–47; Tryggve N. D. Mettinger, *King and Messiah: The Civil and Sacral Legitimation of the Israelite Kings* (ConBOT 8; Lund: Gleerup, 1976), 30; P. Kyle McCarter, "'Plots, True or False': The Succession Narrative as Court Apologetic," *Int* 35 (1981): 355–67; Seiler, *Geschichte*, 299–313, esp. 306; James W. Flanagan, "Court History or Succession Document? A Study of 2 Samuel 9–20 and 1 Kings 1–2," *JBL* 91 (1972): 172–81, with modifications; and, to some extent, Harry Hagan, "Deception as Motif and Theme in 2 Sm 9–20; 1 Kgs 1–2," *Bib* 60 (1979): 301–26, esp. 322.

10 Lienhard Delekat, "Tendenz und Theologie der David-Salomo-Erzählung," in *Das ferne und nahe Wort: Festschrift Leonard Rost zur Vollendung seines 70. Lebensjahres am 30. November gewidmet* (ed. Fritz Maass; BZAW 105; Berlin: Töpelmann, 1967), 26–36; Ernst Würthwein, *Die Erzählung von der Thronfolge Davids—theologische oder politische Geschichtsschreibung?* (ThSt B 115; Zurich: Theologischer Verlag, 1974), 7–59, esp. 11–31, 43–47; Timo Veijola, *Die ewige Dynastie: David und die Entstehung seiner Dynastie nach der deuteronomistischen Darstellung* (AASF B 193; Helsinki: Suomalainen Tiedeakatemia, 1975), 16–30; Langlamet, "Pour ou contre...," 321–79, 481–528.

11 David M. Gunn, *The Story of King David: Genre and Interpretation* (JSOTSup 6; Sheffield: JSOT Press, 1978).

12 James S. Ackerman, "Knowing Good and Evil: A Literary Analysis of the Court History in 2 Samuel 9–20 and 1 Kings 1–2," *JBL* 109 (1990): 41–60. For other approaches leery of assigning a particularly pro- or anti-Solomonic valence to the narrative, see R. A. Carlson, *David the Chosen King: A Traditio-Historical Approach to the Second Book of Samuel*

concern has generated a series of arguments in which practitioners stress the *form* of the narrative over its apparent *content*. Those who apply a more literary-sensitive or form-critical methodology argue that only by examining the external structure of the narrative,[13] including elements such as patterns, themes, and *Leitwörter*, can one gain an accurate appreciation of the extent of the SN. Instead of a simple political theme, Gunn proposed "intrigue, sex and violence" as major patterns within the SN; H. J. L. Jensen also maintained these basic categories but softened their expression to *desire*, *rivalry*, and *collective violence*.[14] One must object here: surely the broad themes proposed by Gunn and Jensen can be traced outside the boundaries of the SN. Moreover, the narrative does seem to have as its primary goal a description of how it is that David (and Solomon after him) was able to "secure monarchic power."[15] Although "intrigue, sex and violence" certainly play significant roles in the narrative, they are subsidiary themes to the establishment and maintenance of the Davidic dynasty's power.

5.2.2. Methodological Complications

E. Ball objected to Rost's method because, he argued, it first delineated the *theme* and only subsequently used that datum as a criterion for understand-

(trans. Eric J. Sharpe and Stanley Rudman; Stockholm: Almqvist & Wiksell, 1964); Hannelis Schulte, *Die Entstehung der Geschichtsschreibung im Alten Israel* (BZAW 128; Berlin: de Gruyter, 1972), 169–70; Charles Conroy, *Absalom Absalom! Narrative and Language in 2 Sam 13–20* (AnBib 81; Rome: Biblical Institute Press, 1978); Jan P. Fokkelman, *King David (II Sam. 9–20 & 1 Kings 1–2)*, vol. 1 of *Narrative Art and Poetry in the Books of Samuel* (Assen: Van Gorcum, 1981), 418–19; John Van Seters, *In Search of History: Historiography in the Ancient World and the Origins of Biblical History* (New Haven: Yale University Press, 1983; repr., Winona Lake, Ind.: Eisenbrauns, 1997), 277–91; Gillian Keys, *The Wages of Sin: A Reappraisal of the "Succession Narrative"* (JSOTSup 221; Sheffield: Sheffield Academic Press, 1996), 43–54; Steven L. McKenzie, "The So-Called Succession Narrative in the Deuteronomistic History," in *Die sogenannte Thronfolgegeschichte Davids: Neue Einsichten und Anfragen* (ed. Albert de Pury and Thomas Römer; OBO 176; Freiburg: Academic Press; Göttingen: Vandenhoeck & Ruprecht, 2000), 123–35.

13 The appreciation of literary criteria as "external"—i.e., formal—is perhaps biased toward the content (internal data) of the text. The terms are those of Rost (*Succession*, e.g., 70) and are not meant to be absolute here.

14 Gunn, *Story*, 89; Hans J. L. Jensen, "Desire, Rivalry and Collective Violence in the 'Succession Narrative'," *JSOT* 55 (1992): 39–59, esp. 43–44.

15 For the "Sicherung königlicher Macht" as the primary motivation of 2 Samuel 9–20; 1 Kgs 1–2, see Klaus-Peter Adam, "Motivik, Figuren und Konzeption der Erzählung vom Absalomaufstand," in *Die deuteronomistischen Geschichtswerke: Redaktions- und religionsgeschichtliche Perspektiven zur "Deuteronomismus"-Diskussion in Tora und Vorderen Propheten* (ed. Markus Witte et al.; BZAW 365; Berlin: de Gruyter, 2006), 183–211, esp. 186–92.

ing the limits of the piece.[16] Ball argued that Rost's description of the narrative's *content* is "a rather loose statement of *theme*," which, when used as a criterion for delineating the boundaries of a narrative, may lead to a false understanding of the text's composition:

> ...there is a methodological difficulty in too great a reliance on the thematic method of defining the boundaries of a narrative such as this, since it entails a large risk that the crucial definition of the theme will be arrived at *before* the boundaries of the material are known. This is in fact what happens in Rost's analysis. Yet strictly speaking (though one cannot be rigid in this matter) the reverse procedure ought to be followed. How can a critic be to any degree certain that he has accurately characterized the theme of a piece of literature, at any time a delicate and intricate business, unless he knows what that piece of literature consists of?[17]

One may wholeheartedly agree with Ball (and Gunn) that the a priori assumption of a unified theme throughout a text before the delineation of that text's boundaries artificially privileges *content* over *form* in a way that disrupts both *form* and *content*. P. R. Ackroyd raised similar questions about the methodology implied in a search for the "succession narrative" as such, wondering to what extent the themes of the SN—the rejection of the Saulides, the succession of the Davidic lineage, the building of the temple, and the participation of Yahweh in the life of Israel—can be isolated from the DtrH as a whole.[18]

While one must remain sensitive to the concerns raised by Ackroyd, it is not so easy to dismiss the often-compartmentalized (and therefore somewhat-separable) nature of certain themes within the DtrH. Most critics would agree that the Deuteronomistic corpus functioned (and continues to function) in its entirety with a highly nuanced theological goal: the portrayal of God's self-revelation to the nation of Israel, as the constituent political units perceived it. But this overarching *telos* of the text should not encumber a discussion of the smaller, nested themes within each of its constituent parts, chapters, or episodes. To argue that the SN exemplifies themes common to the whole of the historical project is to argue a tautology, to make a case for the selection's inclusion in an anthology with demonstrably similar—or even identical—concerns in which the selection has been included *precisely* because it shares and participates in those larger concerns.

Furthermore, it is possible to propose an equally valid argument set in opposition to Ball's methodological objection: all too often, literary-critical

16 Edward Ball, introduction to *The Succession to the Throne of David*, by Leonhard Rost (trans. Michael D. Rutter and David M. Gunn; Sheffield: Almond, 1982), xxiii–xxiv.

17 Gunn, *Story*, 81, cited in Ball, "Introduction," xxiv.

18 Peter R. Ackroyd, "The Succession Narrative (so-called)," *Int* 35 (1981): 383–96, esp. 390–96.

investigations of the type espoused by Gunn and others prematurely adduce large structural complexes and minute lexical links where none should be recognized or may be recognized only as the product of textual development. An example of this criticism—and of the type of studies against which it is leveled—may be found in D. Edelman's critique of W. L. Humphreys's complex structuring of the Saul-David story.[19] According to Edelman, Humphreys imposed an artificial and ultimately indefensible schema on the Rise of Saul narrative,[20] creating a systematic structure where, in fact, none should be recognized. Edelman's suggestion that simpler patterns and themes—e.g., Saul's Demise and David's Rise—were more appropriate for the delineation of the narrative is surely correct, but her implementation of this methodology is itself somewhat problematic in its overreliance on structuring principles chosen as reified markers of textual coherence. In 1 Samuel 9–31, for example, Edelman claimed to be able to discern three "patterns": (a) a three-part kingship ritual (designation-testing-confirmation),[21] (b) the regnal account pattern, and (c) the division of Saul's career into two segments (rise and fall). Moreover, she found a "theme" (Jonathan's covenant with David) and a *Leitwort* (יד). My responses to Edelman's solution are three-fold: (a) The application of the first "pattern" to Saul's rise in 1 Samuel 9–12 is suspect (see below, ch. 7). Furthermore, the text displays no explicit narration in Jonathan's case of the first element of the kingship—the designation. One then must assume it was implied, but this supposition casts the reader on unsafe ground. (b) The standard regnal account, despite the fact that it is split (1 Sam 13:1; 31:1–2 Sam 2:11), is moot since 1 Sam 13:1 was potentially added later. Therefore, it is not really a "pattern" unless one is already looking outside of the David-Saul narratives for analogues. (c) The only real "pattern" to be conceded to Edelman is the diptych-form "rise and downfall" motif. However, one wonders how diagnostic this motif is in

19 Diana Edelman, "The Deuteronomistic Story of King Saul: Narrative Art or Editorial Product," in *Pentateuchal and Deuteronomistic Studies* (ed. C. Brekelmans and J. Lust; BETL 94; Leuven: Leuven University Press, 1990), 207–20; W. Lee Humphreys, "The Tragedy of King Saul: A Study of the Structure of 1 Samuel 9–31," *JSOT* 6 (1978): 18–27; idem, "The Rise and Fall of King Saul: A Study of an Ancient Narrative Stratum in 1 Samuel," *JSOT* 18 (1980): 74–90; idem, "From Tragic Hero to Villain: A Study of the Figure of Saul and the Development of 1 Samuel," *JSOT* 22 (1982): 95–117. For a review of Humphreys's schematic reading of the HDR, see below, §6.2.2.

20 Humphreys discerned a structure to the pericope 1 Samuel 9–31 in which Saul's successes and failures alternate, building towards the climax in ch. 31 in which his greatest success—taking back control of his own fate—is at the same time his greatest failure—his death ("Tragedy," esp. 19).

21 Edelman cites here Mettinger, *King and Messiah*, 72, 79, 86–87; and Baruch Halpern, *The Constitution of the Monarchy in Israel* (HSM 25; Chico, Calif.: Scholars Press, 1981), 51–148.

actuality; indeed, the narrative would hardly be dramatic if there were not some sort of conflict, and the rise and fall motif is merely indicative that the author or compiler understood Saul's kingship to have been supervened. Edelman briefly discusses a fourth pattern, "the rise of the lowly and the fall of the mighty,"[22] but she dismisses Saul's protestations in 1 Sam 9:21 as "a requisite part of the kingship pattern." Undoubtedly, Saul's protestations of humility and low standing are more formulaic than a statement of narrative reality, but one should notice in 1 Samuel 11—a source Edelman does not separate from 1 Sam 9:1–10:16 (cf. §7.3, below)—that Saul *is* supposed to be a farmer, if already one possessing land (see §7.3.1.1). Furthermore, this pattern of "the rise of the lowly and the fall of the mighty" is established throughout the Bible as a major structuring element in nearly every narrative and serves as the undercurrent to all the stories in which the younger son experiences success over the elder. One may also agree with Edelman in her recognition of the theme of the covenant between Jonathan and David,[23] but she has missed an equally powerful theme: David's use and abuse of the women in his life, particularly Michal.[24] Finally, Edelman's *Leitwort* cannot be as diagnostic as she claims, for the word יד is so often merely an idiom that one must doubt whether it can really be applied as a *Leitwort*. Far more probable is the existence of the *Leitwort* "to ask" (שׁאל), since that root appears everywhere from 1 Samuel 1, which at the very least presages Saul's appearance, to 1 Samuel 28 (which is the prediction of Saul's demise).[25] In 1 Sam 14:19, Saul cuts off a priest giving an oracle, at which point God stops answering Saul's queries (1 Sam 14:37; 28:6) and begins to answer David (23:2; see also 23:4; 30:8; 2 Sam 2:1; 5:19, 23). Finally, Saul is driven to "ask" by illicit means. He is able only to contact Samuel, who seems to be quite annoyed that Saul has disturbed him (1 Sam 28:16). Edelman's restructuring of the Saul story thus shows significant deficiencies and suggests a wary reception of her suggested methodology. Therefore, I disagree substantially with her conclusion that "[a]ny judgments about the content and format of the postulated 'History of Saul' or HDR must be made on the basis of a preliminary, detailed literary analysis of the

22 Edelman, "Deuteronomistic Story," 212 and n. 11.

23 See below, §6.4.1; and David Jobling, "Jonathan: A Structural Study in 1 Samuel," in *The Sense of Biblical Narrative: Three Structural Analyses in the Old Testament (I Samuel 13–31, Numbers 11–12, I Kings 17–18)* (JSOTSup 7; Sheffield: JSOT Press, 1978), 4–25.

24 See e.g., Jo Ann Hackett, "1 and 2 Samuel," in *The Women's Bible Commentary* (ed. Carol A. Newsom and Susan H. Ringe; London: SPCK, 1992), 85–95; and §6.5 below.

25 See, e.g., Marsha C. White, "'The History of Saul's Rise': Saulide State Propaganda in 1 Samuel 1–14," in *"A Wise and Discerning Mind": Essays in Honor of Burke O. Long* (ed. Saul M. Olyan and Robert C. Culley; BJS 325; Providence: Brown Judaic Studies, 2000), 287–88.

canonical form of the narrative complex so that structural elements and literary devices can be used as markers to untangle the narrative's stages of growth."[26] This solution is ultimately unacceptable because it fails to take into account the fact that structural elements of earlier strata may be appropriated by later glossators to link their own redaction with the extant text (see, e.g., the situation of Mephibosheth and David's promise to Jonathan, described below, §5.3.4.1). In the end, Edelman's criticism that Humphreys adduces an arbitrary and ultimately unsubstantiable structure (i.e., *form*) on the basis of *content* suggests that Ball's criticism of Rost is perhaps also one-sided and ineffective.

Claims that studies foregrounding thematic structures arbitrarily privilege content over form similarly lack the necessary nuance with which to draw out the fact that narrative structure is a human imposition on the text and that the perception of larger-scale literary structures (and themes) is a *subjective* enterprise that necessarily interacts with the given extent of the text. Neither content (theme) nor form can ultimately serve as the sole criterion by which textual unities are discerned; instead, the two must support one another mutually, and we must admit that human subjective judgment plays a large role in the description of both content and form. There is an inherent danger in the methodological use of either form or content as an overriding concern: the a priori delimitation of a passage based on internal evidence (content) will support the "discovery" of certain themes and patterns, which, when used as criteria by which to analyze the unit, will naturally confirm the "unity" of the piece. By the same token, the a priori assumption that certain themes *must* persist throughout a piece will condition the possible outcome (*form*) discoverable by such an analysis. This artificial delimitation of the passage will only serve to confirm the analytical suspicions that, in fact, served to define the text's limits in the first place. In both cases, circularity is inescapable and tends to bear itself out.[27] Methodologically, both solutions are problematic because they both proceed from within the world of the analysis itself.[28] The only

26 Edelman, "Deuteronomistic Story," 217.

27 See also the complaints of Halpern on the same issue, as the issue of circularity is applied to the "pro-" and "anti-monarchic" sources of Saul's rise (*Constitution*, 150–51), as proposed by Wellhausen (see also below, §7.1.1).

28 This discussion is not, however, an attempt to dismiss the *validity* of literary- and earlier tradition-critical methodologies. I admire greatly the work of Ackerman, who argues for the thoroughgoing cohesion of themes and motifs in the Solomonic Succession Narrative (perceived to be found in 2 Samuel 2–4; 9–20; 1 Kings 1–2; "Knowing Good and Evil," 41–60). Insofar as he is examining the "Solomonic Succession Narrative," he is correct in his perception of those themes. However, epistemologically, the presence and coherence of those themes proves nothing more than that those chapters had all been examined as one unit; there is no criterion external to the examiner's perception of the text that permits or clarifies a possible historical development behind the present state of the text.

possible way to escape this hermeneutical circle is to define the limitations of a text—and its function(s)—on the basis of an analysis whose fundamental suppositions remain *external* to the text itself, although even here the matching of text to generic model is a somewhat subjective enterprise.

5.2.3. Royal Apology in the Succession Narrative: A Prospectus

In the preceding chapter, I appealed to the form-critical analysis of royal apology as a unit defined by a limited and quantifiable set of criteria (§4.2). These criteria are demonstrably present in the texts examined by Hoffner, Tadmor, and Ishida.[29] Although this "demonstrable presence" remains a subjective perception of the relative parallelism between the elements in the texts, a form-critical study remains the most useful way to demonstrate the correspondences that most commentators would agree are present.

Many interpreters—both historical critics and literary critics—seem to agree that the bulk of the text of 2 Samuel 9–20, as well as of the first two chapters of 1 Kings, comprises a narrative unit.[30] Consideration of this unit's *Tendenz* as pro-Solomonic, anti-Solomonic, or simply "a story told for the purpose of serious entertainment"[31] may safely be set aside for the moment. It will be addressed again below in §5.4. In the next section (§5.3), the unity and boundaries of the SSN will be examined. Typically, two types of arguments have been utilized to demonstrate the unity of the

29 Harry A. Hoffner, "Propaganda and Political Justification in Hittite Historiography," in *Unity and Diversity: Essays in the History, Literature, and Religion of the Ancient Near East* (ed. Hans Goedicke and J. J. M. Roberts; JNHES; Baltimore: The Johns Hopkins University Press, 1975), 49–62; Hayim Tadmor, "Autobiographical Apology in the Royal Assyrian Literature," in *History, Historiography and Interpretation* (ed. H. Tadmor and M. Weinfeld; Jerusalem: Magnes, 1983), 36–57; Tomoo Ishida, "'Solomon Who is Greater than David': Solomon's Succession in 1 Kings i–ii in the Light of the Inscription of Kilamuwa, King of Yᵓ DY-Śamᵓal," in *Congress Volume: Salamanca, 1983* (ed. J. A. Emerton; VTSup 36; Leiden: Brill, 1985), 145–53; idem, "Solomon's Succession to the Throne of David—A Political Analysis," in *Studies in the Period of David and Solomon and Other Essays* (ed. Tomoo Ishida; Winona Lake, Ind.: Eisenbrauns, 1982), 175–87.

30 See in particular the through summaries of scholarship in K. K. Sacon, "A Study of the Literary Structure of the 'Succession Narrative'," in *Studies in the Period of David and Solomon and Other Essays* (ed. Tomoo Ishida; Winona Lake, Ind.: Eisenbrauns, 1982), 27–29; Ackerman, "Knowing Good and Evil," 55–60; and Serge Frolov, "Succession Narrative: A 'Document' or a 'Phantom'?" *JBL* 121 (2002): 81–83. See also the important collection of essays in Albert de Pury and Thomas Römer, eds., *Die sogenannte Thronfolgegeschichte Davids: Neue Einsichten und Anfragen* (OBO 176; Fribourg: University Press; Göttingen: Vandenhoeck & Ruprecht, 2000).

31 Gunn, *Story*, 62.

"Solomonic Succession Narrative." Practitioners of the literary methodology have argued for this unity on the basis of recurrent themes, *Leitwörter*, and patterns in the text,[32] while those who use the historical-critical methodology have often operated from the standpoint of the text's content. In addition, some adduce the document as pro-Solomonic apology, based on a sociological consideration of the document's thematic function, while others argue for the text's origin as an anti-Solomonic historical narrative.

Ishida has most saliently argued for the text 2 Samuel 9–20; 1 Kings 1–2 as a unity on the basis of its comparison with the genre "royal apologetic."[33] I argue below that Ishida's form-critical application of the structure of royal apologetic is flawed in that it faultily perceives much of 2 Samuel 9–20 to be correlated to the category *Rival Princes' Evil Acts*. I argue that this correlation need not apply and that a more succinct passage (namely, 2 Sam 11:2–27; 1 Kings 1–2*) contains all the elements needed to fulfill the structure of ancient Near Eastern royal apologetic, as outlined by Hoffner and Ishida. This containment of the Solomonic apologetic biography in only three chapters of the 17, or so commonly considered to form the SN (2 Samuel [2–4]; 9–20; 1 Kings 1–2), suggests that the SN may, in fact, be a figment of our imagination—at least, as the extensive, unified document that scholarship had considered it to be until the mid-1970's or so—a theory still pervasive in non-technical treatments of the subject. In other words, I find it highly unlikely that 2 Sam (10:1–19); 11:1–12:25,(26–31) + 1 Kings 1–2 were originally composed along with the rest of chapters formerly understood as comprising the SN.[34] Rather, it is preferable to consider the SN to have been one medial step on the path of development from a "Court-History of David" (siglum CH; see §5.3.1 for clarification)—itself probably a composite document—to the larger PR, which, as we have seen above (§§3.4–5), constituted an intermediate step towards the development of the DtrH.

32 E.g., Whybray, *Succession Narrative*, 19–50, esp. 25–34; Sacon, "Literary Structure," 27–54; Ackerman, "Knowing Good and Evil," 41–60.

33 Ishida, "Solomon's Succession"; see above, §4.2.

34 In this regard, I am in basic accordance with Flanagan, "Court History," 172–81; P. Kyle McCarter, "'Plots, True or False': The Succession Narrative as Court Apologetic," *Int* 35 (1981): 361–64; P. Kyle McCarter, *II Samuel: A New Translation with Introduction and Commentary* (AB 9; New York: Doubleday, 1984), 9–16; and a number of other commentators.

5.3. The Whole or the Sum of Its Parts? The Unity of the SN

5.3.1. Court History (CH) or Succession Narrative (SN)?

Sacon's detailed description of the SN finds structural parallelism between 1 Kings 1–2 and 2 Samuel 9, as well as the appearance of several themes appearing elsewhere in 2 Samuel:

> Salient features in the epilogue [1 Kings 1–2] are the recapitulations of the motifs appearing in the preceding chapters. The depiction of David's advanced age and sexual impotence (1 Kgs 1:1–4) is set in ironical contrast to his vigor and sexual potency (2 Sam 11:2–5). Adonijah's preparation of rebel forces (1 Kgs 1:5) and his sacrificing (1 Kgs 1:9, etc.) are parallel with those of Absalom's rebellion (2 Sam 15:1 and 12). A note about Adonijah's handsome appearance (1 Kgs 1:6) is also parallel to that of Absalom in 2 Sam 14:25. Adonijah's expectation of good tidings in 1 Kgs 1:42 reminds us of that of King David in 2 Sam 18:25, 26, and 27.[35]

While all of these allusions to earlier motifs could have been crafted by a careful Solomonic apologist in order to provide an already extant description of the Davidic dynasty's troubles (2 Samuel 9–20) with a fitting and historically motivated ending (1 Kings 1–2),[36] the number of the motifs picked up in the latter chapters of the SN and the general narrative style of the text throughout both suggest to Sacon that no significant source-critical break is to be made between the two units 2 Samuel 9–20 and 1 Kings 1–2. This section examines the likelihood of Sacon's (and others') assessment that 2 Samuel 9–20 + 1 Kings 1–2 was originally composed as a single document. By comparing the function and dating of ancient Near Eastern royal apology to that what appear to be pro-Solomonic additions (2 Sam 11:2–12:25*; 1 Kings 1–2*[37]) to the CH, I will argue below that the Solomonic Succession Narrative (siglum SSN)[38] was not originally unified but took the basic form of its present shape at latest by the mid-8th cent.

35 Sacon, "Literary Structure," 30.

36 For instance, the beauty of Absalom (2 Sam 14:25) and Adonijah (1 Kgs 1:6) could also be related to the notice of Saul's good looks (1 Sam 9:2), but that literary connection has not been made by Sacon. Why not? The answer, for Sacon, lies in the *clustering* of the motifs.

37 I recognize here the heterogeneous nature of 1 Kings 1–2; the issue will be taken up below, §5.3.2.3.

38 I use the siglum SSN henceforth to distinguish my own understanding of the Succession Narrative—as a late-9th to mid-8th cent. composite of an earlier CH augmented by the addition, among other things, of a specifically Solomonic Apology (SA)—from previous understandings of the Succession Narrative (SN) as an originally unified document. This differentiation, therefore, should not be taken as an outright refutation of those schemas that discuss a "Succession Narrative" but argue for the secondary development of that composite document.

(as part of the PR), suggesting that an even earlier date (ca. early- to mid-9th cent.) for the CH is appropriate. While its wholesale inclusion in the late-9th to mid-8th cent. PR gives the latest probable *terminus ante quem* for the formation of the composite SSN, it is more likely—judging from a comparison with the function and dating of other ancient Near Eastern royal apology—that the bulk of these pro-Solomonic additions (2 Samuel 11:2–12:25*; 1 Kings 1–2*) had already been composed and interpolated into the rest of the developing CH as early as the late-10th cent.

5.3.2. The Argument for the Division of 2 Samuel 9; 13:1–20:26 from 2 Sam 11:2–27; 12:15b–25; 1 Kings 1–2*

5.3.2.1. Basis for the Division

As noted above, the purportedly pro-Solomonic stance of the SN that Rost proposed is inextricably intertwined with the literary judgment concerning the boundaries of that text.[39] Those who read the SN synchronically have typically maintained Rost's limits of the text, at least at the end. One may point here to figures such as R. N. Whybray, who considered the SN a unified novel in which could be found features such as (a) thematic unity, (b) cohesive structure, (c) competent use of dialogue, (d) complex characterization, and finally (e) consistency and elevation of style.[40] According to Whybray, this novel was written early in the reign of Solomon in order "to rally support for the régime by legitimizing Solomon's position…."[41]

Many subsequent commentators have proceeded along similar trajectories functioning from the supposition that, taken as a whole, the SN was remarkably unified. However, many more have adduced source-critical fractures in the narrative that, it is supposed, point to a more complex composition history than previously assumed. For example, P. K. McCarter, working in the wake of J. Blenkinsopp and J. W. Flanagan, among others, advanced the view that 1 Kings 1–2 "should be described as court apologetic," which, while presupposing 2 Samuel 9–20, did not derive from the same author.[42] Yet within 2 Samuel 9–20, a few other cohesive narratives could be discerned. McCarter considered chs. 13–20 a cohesive

39 Otto Kaiser, "Beobachtungen zur sogenannten Thronnachfolgeerzählung Davids," *ETL* 44 (1988): 5–20, esp. 6.

40 Whybray, *Succession Narrative*, 19–47.

41 Ibid., 54.

42 McCarter, "'Plots, True or False'," 361; J. Blenkinsopp, "Theme and Motif in the Succession History (2 Sam. xi 2ff) and the Yahwist Corpus," in *Volume du Congrès, Genève, 1965* (ed. G. W. Anderson et al.; VTSup 15; Leiden: Brill, 1966), 44–57, esp. 47–48; Flanagan, "Court History," 172–81.

unit, following Conroy, but assigned ch. 9 to a separate, independent text comprising 2 Samuel 21:1–14 + 2 Samuel 9,[43] and, following Flanagan, he allowed that 2 Samuel 11–12 and 1 Kings 1–2 comprised "a secondary addition to the older narrative, a contribution of a writer or editor who employed an old account of David's Ammonite campaign as a vehicle for telling a story with a prophetic perspective…."[44]

To complicate matters, even among those who espouse the original independence of 2 Samuel 11–12*; 1 Kings 1–2*, the inclusion of the Ammonite war material exclusive of the David-Bathsheba-Uriah story (10:1–11:1, 12:26–31) in the apologetic additions to the Court History of David is not agreed upon. On the one hand, Rost considered this narrative earlier material reused by the author of the SN to frame the David-Bathsheba story and thus as part of the original SN.[45] On the other hand, Flanagan argued the framework was "more deeply embedded in the [surrounding] narrative than [was] the David-Bathsheba-Uriah triangle."[46] Recently, and in opposition to both parties, Frolov has argued on the basis of syntactic clues that the entire complex 2 Sam 10:1–12:31 should be considered part of the secondary transformation of the "Court History" into the "Succession Narrative."[47] Such arguments are capable of engendering a wide array of factions and splinter-factions; the limitations of the present study do not permit participating in this particular debate with full vigor. Therefore, although I leave unexamined the exact relationship between 10:1–11:1 and 12:26–31, I am inclined to agree with Frolov that the framework supplied by the narrative of David's wars with Ammon provides a fitting exposition for the Bathsheba story's inclusion, although, as will be seen shortly, I understand the diachronic development of the text much differently. As a result, I cannot agree with Frolov's reconstruction of many of the diverse episodes as "Deuteronomistic" and of the additions in 2 Samuel 10–12, 1 Kings 1–2 as "post-Deuteronomistic supplements."[48] Despite a thorough methodology and tight argumentation, Frolov has reached what I consider to be an incorrect conclusion concerning dating.

43 Ibid., 363.
44 Ibid., 364.
45 Rost, *Succession*, 57–62.
46 Flanagan, "Court History," 176. See also McCarter, *II Samuel*, 12.
47 Frolov, "Succession Narrative," 95, 102–3.
48 Ibid., 104.

5.3.2.2. The Relationship Between 2 Sam 10 and 2 Sam 11–12**

It should be noted that 2 Sam 10:1–11:1; 12:26–31 corresponds to a large extent with 1 Chr 19:1–20:1; especially important here is the parallel formed by 2 Sam 11:1 and 1 Chr 20:1. Some commentators have attempted to use the relatively late context of 2 Sam 11:1 (with its spring New Year) as evidence for the lateness of the entirety of 2 Sam 11:1–12:31.[49] This assessment is not entirely accurate.[50] More recent research of Chronicles' relationship with Samuel-Kings has suggested a model attributing the synchronic portions to reliance on a common source.[51] This interpretation stands in contradistinction to the older assumption that the Chronicler depended on Samuel-Kings for the base narrative but omitted those sections that exposed David's foibles and character flaws. An indication of the relevance of this newer model comes already in 2 Sam 10:1: the Chronicler's addition of the name of the Ammonite king (נחש; 1 Chr 19:1) contrasts with the Deuteronomist's addition of his successor's name (חנון; 2 Sam 10:1); both names were presumably added from the genealogical material received in the *Vorlage* of each account (חנון בן־נחש; v. 2). Further examination of the two passages reveals that they are replete with what D. M. Carr has termed "cognitive" or "non-essential variants,"[52] which surely would not have occurred if the Chronicler had been cribbing off the Deuteronomist's work.

If one follows this newer model of interaction between Chronicles and Samuel-Kings, the date of the inclusion of 2 Sam 10:1–11:1*; 12:26–31* could potentially be much later than the composition (and corresponding interpolation) of 11:2–12:25* and would presumably date to the earliest Deuteronomistic level at which Samuel and Kings were tied together. The question as to whether this redactional joint would have happened as early as a posited Hezekian-era redaction (see §3.3), at the time of the Josianic

49 E.g., McCarter, *II Samuel*, 285; Kaiser, "Beobachtungen," 18–20, and bibliography there. Equally troublesome are the attempts of some commentators to interpret the phrase לתשובת השנה as evidence of a fall campaign season.

50 However, in favor of the inclusion of 10:1–19 and 12:26–31 in the CH, one may point to David's capture of Rabbah (12:26–31), which does provide a fitting explanation of the support provided by Shobi ben-Nahash during David's exile (17:27–29). Moreover, David's desire to renew treaty obligations with Hanun (אעשה־חסד; 10:2) picks up the same vocabulary from 9:1. These two connections to the basic CH might suggest that 12:26–31 was initially part of that text.

51 Most recently, see David M. Carr, "Empirische Perspektiven auf das Deuteronomistische Geschichtswerk," in *Die deuteronomistischen Geschichtswerke: Redaktions- und religionsgeschichtliche Perspektiven zur "Deuteronomismus"-Diskussion in Tora und Vorderen Propheten* (ed. Markus Witte et al.; BZAW 365; Berlin: de Gruyter, 2006), 1–17.

52 Ibid., 2.

redaction (Dtr[1]), or later, is left open here.[53] It is unnecessary, however, to follow Rost in assuming that 2 Sam 10:1–11:1* + 12:26–31 comprise a framework necessarily combined with 2 Sam 11:2–12:25 at the time of the latter passage's introduction.[54] Because both texts begin with a *waw* + prefix-conjugation introducing a temporal clause (ויהי אחרי־כן; 2 Sam 10:1; cf. ויהי לעת הערב; 2 Sam 11:2), they each bear the same relationship to the foregoing episode, no matter what passage that is taken to be. And while it is true that no stylistic difference separates 11:1 from 11:2 (compare the identical temporal construction: ויהי לתשובת השנה; cf. also the opening line of ch. 13: ויהי אחרי־כן),[55] this objection hardly constitutes proof of the two passages' unity in the face of the evidence from 1 Chronicles 19–20.

Synchronically, the Ammonite war provides an excellent framework for David's dalliance with Bathsheba in 2 Samuel 11. Several interpreters have noted the importance of David's continuing residence in Jerusalem.[56] In fact, without v. 1, in which Rabbah is named, the story presupposes only the ongoing siege of an unnamed city (designated only as העיר in vv. 16,17, and 20), initiated before the beginning of the passage at hand. It is common to attribute the initiative of synchronizing the Ammonite battle report with David's adulterous affair with Bathsheba to the author of the latter passage (2 Sam 11:2–12:25*).[57] However, Because 2 Sam 11:2–12:25* can be read entirely independently of 2 Sam 10:(1–6a),6b–11:1 + 12:26–31, it is equally possible that a later editor arranged an extant and

---

53 One ought not overlook, though, the common use of תחתיו in 1 Chr 19:1 and 2 Sam 10:1 to indicate that the son reigns "in his [i.e., the father's] place." This phrase is normally taken as an indication of Deuteronomistic (i.e., Dtr[1] or DtrG) authorship (see, e.g., Vermeylen, *Loi du plus fort*, 286), but the evidence from Chronicles here may point to its origination in a proto-Deuteronomistic (and simultaneously proto-Chronistic) milieu (see already François Langlamet, review of E. Würthwein, *Die Erzählung von der Thronfolge Davids—theologische oder politische Geschichtsschreibung?* and T. Veijola, *Die ewige Dynasty*, *RB* 83 [1976]: 119 n. 2). In short, this feature alone might occasion a rethinking of the Hezekian redaction of the DtrH, yet equally intriguing is Vermeylen's point that the name "Hanun" is otherwise unknown except as a king of Gaza during the 8th cent. (*Loi du plus fort*, 287, and bibliography n. 114).

54 Rost, *Succession*, 73–74: the story "could not have existed without the framework of the Ammonite war report to which it is connected." Rost considers 2 Sam 10:1–5(6a) of a different source from 2 Sam 10:6b–11:1 (ibid., 60, 73), but the recurrence of vv. 1–6a in 1 Chr 19:1–6a—a few non-essential variations notwithstanding—seems to indicate a common source containing the entirety of 2 Sam 10:1–11:1.

55 Kaiser, "Beobachtungen," 19 n. 51.

56 E.g., Gunn, *Story*, 70; Timo Veijola, "Solomon: Bathsheba's Firstborn," in *Reconsidering Israel and Judah: Recent Studies on the Deuteronomistic History* (ed. G. N. Knoppers and J. G. McConville; trans. Peter T. Daniels; SBTS 8; Winona Lake, Ind.: Eisenbrauns, 2000), 349; originally published as "Salomo: Der Erstgeborene Bathsebas," in *Studies in the Historical Books of the Old Testament* (ed. J. A. Emerton; VTSup 30; Leiden: Brill, 1979), 230–50.

57 See, e.g., McCarter, *II Samuel*, 285.

independent Ammonite battle report, comprising 2 Sam 10:(1–6a),6b–11:1 + 12:26–31, around an episode of the developing SN that had no real exposition of its own (2 Sam 11:2–12:25*).[58] In short, I propose, the story concerning David, Bathsheba, and Uriah could have already been incorporated into the evolving SN by the time a later editor inserted the Ammonite battle report in order to provide a more explicit framework for the story; therefore, no *terminus post quem* dating of 2 Sam 11:1; 12:26–31 necessarily applies equally to 11:2–12:25*.

The unity of the latter passage is also questionable. Already in 1926 Rost referred to "the doubtful place of the Nathan pericope" (roughly, 2 Sam 12:1–15a, perhaps also including 11:27b and 12:25) in the context of 2 Samuel 11–12.[59] In the context of the present argument, it is unnecessary to offer a detailed critical reading of this passage, but a few salient observations must be made. Rost pointed (correctly) to the composite nature of the episode. He included vv. 1–7a and possibly vv. 11–15a in the original text of the SN.[60] Even if we dismiss Rost's hypothesis of a completely uniform SN in favor of the one espoused here, in which 2 Samuel 11–12* + 1 Kings 1–2* are decidedly pro-Solomonic interpolations, the divine claim in v. 7b to have anointed David as king over Israel (משחתיך למלך על־ישׂראל אנכי) refers to 1 Sam 16:1–13, which A. F. Campbell has plausibly argued was part of a pre-Deuteronomistic PR (see also below, §6.3.1.2). Although Campbell did not include 2 Samuel 9–20 in the PR, he did allow 1 Kgs 1:1a,5–15a,16–48; 2:1a,10,12 to be included in that document.[61] It should be remembered, however, that Campbell's list of the PR's constituent verses comprises a minimal text; moreover, Campbell's student and sometime collaborator, M. A. O'Brien, maintained the SN *was* part of the DtrH.[62] Regardless of whether 2 Sam 12:7b is an insertion (with Rost) or part of the base text around which other verses were inserted later, the themes of the PR—such as the divinely-mandated confrontation of monarchic power and the prophetic prerogative to instate and impeach kings—are evident in 2 Samuel 12*. It seems quite likely, therefore, that the latter passage should be considered a heretofore unrecognized

58 For a similar assessment, see Vermeylen, *Loi du plus fort*, 284–94. Vermeylen attributes 10:1–11:1; 12:26–31 to several different Deuteronomistic and post-Deuteronomistic redactors—which is difficult, given the overlap with 1 Chronicles 19–20—but the basic thrust remains the same.

59 Rost, *Succession*, 59.

60 Ibid., 74–75.

61 Antony F. Campbell, *Of Prophets and Kings: A Late Ninth-Century Document (1 Samuel 1–2 Kings 10)* (CBQMS 17; Washington DC: Catholic Biblical Association of America, 1986), 81–84.

62 Mark A. O'Brien, *The Deuteronomistic History Hypothesis: A Reassessment* (OBO 92; Fribourg: University Press; Göttingen: Vandenhoeck & Ruprecht, 1989), 139–41, and 139 n. 31.

passage in a PR containing much more material from 2 Samuel than even Campbell claimed.[63] This identification would supply a *terminus ante quem* of the pro-Solomonic additions in 2 Sam 11:2–12:24(25)* + 1 Kings 1–2* at the time of the formation of the PR sometime between the late-9th and mid-8th centuries. Of this material, the prophetic addition(s) in 12:1–15a* may be safely excised from the hypothesized earlier material, leaving as the probable maximal extent of the earliest pro-Solomonic additions 2 Sam 11:2–27*;[64] 12:15b–24(25)*[65] + 1 Kings 1–2*. This early material, it would seem, bears significant formal commonalities to the royal apologetic material adduced by Hoffner and Ishida (§4.2), as demonstrated in the next section.

5.3.2.3. The Solomonic Additions (2 Samuel 11:2–27; 12:15b–24[25]* + 1 Kings 1–2*) as Royal Apology*

A form-critical examination of the SN as an instance of ancient Near Eastern royal apology can provide a template against which the internal structuring of the SN can be measured. Several authors have previously compared the "Succession Narrative" to other works of ancient Near Eastern royal apology. T. Ishida has been the most explicit in this comparison, having described both Esarhaddon's apology and the SN using a

63 For the similarity between 12:1–15a and other passages of the designation of a king by the prophet, see Vermeylen, *Loi du plus fort*, 304. However, Vermeleyn does not operate with the assumption of a PR and so attributes the *Grundschrift* of this passage (vv. 1a,9abα,10a, 13abα,15a) to DtrG and the remaining additions (vv. 1b–8,9bβ,10b–12,13bβ–14) to DtrN (ibid., 310–19). Given the passage's thematic similarity to passages that he would have to consider quintessentially DtrP (1 Sam 10:1; 16:1–13), this attribution seems to odd in my judgment.

64 Vermeylen puts forth a compelling case for the secondarity of 11:10–12bα,19–25,27aβb (*Loi du plus fort*, 296–310), but the recognition of these verses as Deuteronomistic is relatively unimportant in the following discussion.

65 I leave here undecided the originality of 12:15b–23, which has been challenged with good cause. The nameless (and characterless) child's historical existence is doubtful, and it is more likely that he was a literary construct invented to protect Solomon's birthright to the throne. Timo Veijola argues that the historical Solomon's true heritage may have been in doubt, pointing to the conundrum brought about by the name שלמה, "His Replacement" ("Solomon," 345–47; see also Würthwein, *Erzählung*, 31–32; and Vermeylen, *Loi du plus fort*, 294–322, esp. 319–20). Accordingly, by "killing off" the "first child" of David and Bathsheba, the narrator ensures Solomon's Davidic heritage. In this reading, Solomon is more likely the "replacement" of his true father, Uriah, whom Bathsheba had recently lost, than the "replacement" of some non-existent first child (although cf. Mettinger, *King and Messiah*, 30). Although this passage's originality or lack thereof has direct bearing on the overall *Tendenz* of the claimed Solomonic additions, its usefulness for dating the passage is not so clear. In the following sections, I assume the passage's originality in what I consider pro-Solomonic additions, but I also incline towards its historical implausibility.

modified version of Hoffner's structure of Hittite royal apology.[66] The seven elements of Ishida's modified version of Hoffner's six-stepped structure and their corresponding biblical textual elements of the SN are:[67]

1. *Introduction: the legitimate successor's divine election as future king in his youth* (the implications of Solomon's election in 2 Sam 12:24b–25 and the confirmation of this election in 1 Kgs 1:48b).
2. *Preliminary remark: the reigning king's designation of a legitimate successor despite his inferior position in the order of succession* (the explicit declarations of Solomon's kingship in 1 Kgs 1:13,17,30,33–35; see also the action of seating Solomon on the throne of the king in 1 Kgs 1:46).
3. *Preliminary remark: comparison between the just past and the subsequent deterioration* (2 types):
   3a. *Noble antecedent or solemn decision* (not found in 2 Samuel–1 Kings).
   3b. *Evil acts of an unworthy predecessor and/or rival princes* (the actions of David and of Solomon's rivals Amnon, Absalom, and Adonijah throughout 2 Samuel 9–20 + 1 Kings 1–2; esp. 1 Kgs 1:5–27[68]).
4. *Rebellion: rival princes' attempt to usurp the throne against the divine will* (Adonijah's crowing; 1 Kgs 1:5–11).
5. *Legitimate successor's counter-attack and victory* (the court intrigue serving the purpose of establishing Solomon's rule; 1 Kgs 1:11–31).
6. *Establishment of the kingship* (the anointing of Solomon; 1 Kgs 1:32–40; see also Adonijah's recognition of his kingship in 1:53; see also 2:46b).
7. *Punishment of the rebels* (Solomon's punishment of Adonijah, Abiathar, and Joab; 1 Kgs 2:13–46a[69]).

Despite the aptitude of most of the correlations made by Ishida, it is not clear to me that *all* the manifestations of illicit behavior by the royal family

66 Tomoo Ishida, "The Succession Narrative and Esarhaddon's Apology: A Comparison," in *Ah, Assyria...: Studies in Assyrian History and Ancient Near Eastern Historiography Presented to Hayim Tadmor* (ed. M. Cogan and I. Ephᶜal; Jersalem: Magnes, 1991), 166–73.

67 The titles of the elements are those of Ishida (ibid., 167). I have inserted in parentheses the descriptions of the biblical passages Ishida correlated to the elements therein (ibid., 169–73). As discussed in ch. 4, Ishida recasts the sevenfold structure at the end of his article, and that restructuring has been integrated here. The augmented schema adds elements 3a (pushing what had formerly been designated element 3 into the sub-motif 3b) and reverses the order of elements 6–7. In its essentials, it remains ostensibly the same as Hoffner's original schema. For a more detailed description of the contents of each of these categories, as they were originally conceived by Hoffner and as they came to be understood by Ishida, see above, §4.2.

68 Ishida cites as the constituents parts of this element "David's committing adultery with Bathsheba and murdering Uriah, her husband (II Sam. 11:2–25); Amnon's committing rape upon Tamar and Absalom's murder of Amnon (II Sam. 13:1–29); Absalom's rebellion (II Sam. 15:1–18:15); Adonijah's attempt to usurp the throne (I Kings 1:5–27)" ("Succession Narrative," 171).

69 Despite the fact that David had ostensibly commanded Solomon to deal harshly with Joab while on his death bed ("So do what you find wise, but don't send that codger down to Sheol in peace"; ועשׂית כחכמתך ולא־תורד שׂבתו בשלם שאל; 1 Kgs 2:6), such textual reminiscence of a private communication provides a convenient mandate for Solomon's securing of his kingdom.

necessarily qualify as the "evil acts of an unworthy predecessor"[70] within the purview of the apologetic structure. It seems sufficient to me that *only* David's dalliance with Bathsheba and subsequent murder of Uriah (2 Sam 11:2–27*) need qualify as the exemplification of this element.[71] Given that the same element, "evil acts of rival princes," in Esarhaddon's apology consists only of his brothers' actions against him *after* he has been designated king, it seems unlikely that the possibility of Solomon's kingship was considered very long before the death of David was imminent. While reticence is called for in determining whether David actually had designated Solomon as his successor, I tend to side with those who believe he had not and that the claim was made by Nathan and perhaps Bathsheba in order to take advantage of David's senility as a means of solidifying their own power.[72] This means, however, that Da-

---

70 Ishida, "Succession Narrative," 173.

71 We may wonder why Solomon would have implicated his own father as the perpetrator of "evil acts," but as Ishida himself has noted, as a pro-Solomonic document, the SN had to be somewhat anti-Davidic ("Solomon's Succession," 181–85). To the extent that the document was, in fact, targeting David's failures (particularly the mismanagement of the Absalom and Sheba revolts), cognates in other royal apologetic writings may be adduced; Ishida has pointed to the similarity of the SN to the Kilamuwa stele in which Kilamuwa notes that he has performed works that his predecessors had not ("Solomon," 149).

72 See e.g., Ishida, "Solomon's Succession," 186–87. J. W. Wesselius has argued that Bathsheba's participation in the plot was an act of revenge for David's coercion of her sexuality and subsequent murder of her husband ("Joab's Death and the Central Theme of the Succession Narrative [2 Samuel ix–1 Kings ii]," *VT* 40 [1990]: 347–48). This may especially be the case if, historically speaking, Solomon were not David's biological son (see n. 65 above), and Bathsheba—knowing a bit about the vicissitudes of the royal court—knew that both her own life and the life of her son were in jeopardy. Her participation in what might be considered Nathan's ruse may then be read as an act of survival. This possibility provides yet another layer of ambiguity to Bathsheba's willingness to relay Adonijah's request for Abishag to Solomon: assuming Bathsheba's court-savvy intellect, she would have known that such a request would have been a dangerous one for Adonijah to make, and presumably Adonijah knew, too (which was why he asked Bathsheba to intercede for him; 1 Kgs 2:13–17). The real question for the reader, then, is with what degree of glee Bathsheba conveys (or even fabricates?) Adonijah's request, knowing that Solomon would use it as a pretense for disposing of his rival. Cf. the reconstruction of Tomoo Ishida, "Adonijah the Son of Haggith and His Supporters: An Inquiry into Problems about History and Historiography," in *The Future of Biblical Studies—The Hebrew Scriptures* (ed. Richard Elliot Friedman and H. G. M. Williamson; Atlanta: Scholars Press, 1987), 177–79. Although a more thorough reading of the narrative in light of the composition history of 1 Kings 1–2 is warranted before any firm decisions as to historicity are made, the text *presents* the claim as historical, despite the obvious allusions here to the contrary. Iain Provan has argued that whatever the form and content of the text may *appear* to be, and whatever our eventual understanding of the accessibility of the authorial intent, the text invites the reader to apply a hermeneutic of suspicion with regards to the claim of Solomon's legitimacy ("Why Barzillai of Gilead [1 Kings 2:7]? Narrative Art and the Hermeneutics of Suspicion in 1 Kings 1–2," *TynBul* 46 [1995]: 103–16).

vid's coercive tryst with—or rape of—Bathsheba and his ruthless murder of her husband Uriah must comprise an "evil act of a predecessor."[73]

It is my contention, then, that the structure of royal apologetic writings applies to the specifically Solomonic passages found only in 2 Sam 11:1–12:25* + 1 Kings 1–2*.[74] While Ishida has argued that the seven constituent elements are to be found scattered through 2 Samuel 9–20; 1 Kings 1–2, I argue that a proper schematization of the structure limits the "Solomonic royal apology" *only* to 2 Sam 11:2–27; (12:15b–25) + 1 Kings 1–2*. Clearly, five of the seven basic elements are to be found clustered in 1 Kings 1–2: there one finds elements 2 (e.g., 1 Kgs 1:13,17,30,33–35,46), 4 (1 Kgs 1:5–11*), 5 (1 Kgs 1:11–31*), 6 (1 Kgs 1:32–40*,53; 2:46b), and 7 (1 Kgs 2:13–46a*).[75] But Ishida's designation of the bulk of 2 Samuel 9–20 as "rival princes' evil acts" assumes a category that *need not* comprise the various sins of the Davidic family there. Ishida's second formulation of the category as the "evil acts of an unworthy predecessor"[76] suggests that the category (element 3b) may just as easily comprise only the atrocities committed by David in the David-Bathsheba-Uriah narrative in 2

73 I am hesitant to indict Adonijah's attempt to secure the crown so quickly as the text seems to want us to. As has often been pointed out, Adonijah should have expected to succeed his father to the throne, since he was the oldest living heir (e.g., Ishida, "Solomon's Succession," 178–79; idem, "Adonijah," 174–77). While the crowning of the prince is cast as an act of treachery in the present text, that need not serve as an indication of the historical meaning (or even historicity) of the action; in all likelihood, Adonijah—along with Abiathar and Joab—considered it the natural progression of political events and could be forgiven (at least, publicly; 1 Kgs 1:49–53). Furthermore, it is possible that Adonijah's request for Abishag (1 Kgs 2:13–21)—if at all historical (see n. 72)—is to be considered as a secondary component of the initial rebellion comprising the crowing of Adonijah (1:5–11) or a second attempt at the throne. Once Solomon had ascended to the throne, Adonijah's request for Abishag's hand—whether innocent or not—could be recast textually as far more dangerous to the stability of the kingdom, since the political ramifications of the transfer of the king's harem were well-known. If this is the case, the retaliation of Solomon against Adonijah's request for Abishag (1 Kgs 2:23–25) also seems likely as a second iteration of "the punishment of the rebels."

74 See also the similar observation of Rudnig (*Davids Thron*, 91–119).

75 The range of verses here overlaps with various layers of redactional work, judging from cursory comparison with a few of the proposed models. Veijola found secondary additions of varying antiquity in 1 Kgs 1:30,35–37,46–48; 2:1–11,24,26b–27,31b–33,37b,42a*,43*, 44–45 (*Ewige Dynasty*, 16–26); Vermeylen distinguished additions scattered throughout these two chapters (1:5abβ,6a,6bβ,7–8,12aβb,21,30aαb,35,37,46–48,51abβ; 2:2a,3,4aβ,7–9, 11,26–27,28aβ,33,37b,42a*,43b*,44–45) (*Loi du plus fort*, 439–65); Langlamet's division is even more complex ("Pour ou contre…?" 524–25). I leave unanswered here the question of the relationship of 1 Kings 1–2 to the following chapters. Ackroyd has suggested the final verse of chapter 2 (v. 46) may have served as a temporal introduction to 3:1: "Now when the kingdom was established under the control of Solomon, Solomon made a marriage alliance…" ("Succession Narrative," 384, Ackroyd's translation); cf. Ernst Würthwein, *Die Bücher der Könige: 1. Könige 1–16* (ATD 11/1; Göttingen: Vandenhoeck & Ruprecht, 1985), 25.

76 Ishida, "Succession Narrative," 173.

Sam 11:2–27*; 12:15b–25*. The final element, the "Introduction," appears within that narrower unit as well, in the brief notice of Solomon's birth and divine election (2 Sam 12:24b[25]). This revision of Ishida's correlation of elements forces a reduction of the seven-part structure into a fairly compact and tightly-knit textual unit in which, though several elements be out of their "normal" order (as exhibited by both the Assyrian and Hittite models), all seven remain present in a narrower section of the received text.

This condensed apology, then, would comprise only 2 Sam 11:2–27; 12:15b–25* + 1 Kings 1–2*. This form-critical reevaluation of what constitutes the "Succession Narrative" supports dividing that document into an original "Court History" (siglum CH) and the pro-Solomonic apology (siglum SA), which comprises both the exposition in 2 Sam 11:2–27*; 12:15b–25*,[77] as well as the bulk of the apology in 1 Kings 1–2*.[78] This apology was overlaid on the extant CH (comprising roughly 2 Sam 9:1–13*; 13:1–20:26*), forming an authentically *Solomonic* Succession Narrative (hence, SSN). This document did not just record history; it *argued* for it.

5.3.2.4. The Lamb Motif

The question arises whether the SA ever existed independently of the CH or was composed as an intentional addition to the CH. If it can be shown that the pro-Solomonic additions never existed independently of the CH, then the date of composition of the SA provides a *terminus ante quem* in the same way that the PR demarcated the Solomonic Apology's latest point of composition. Despite the separate origins of the CH and the SA, literary connections between the two texts do exist. These connections have generally been taken to demonstrate the essential unity of the SN (2 Samuel 9–20; 1 Kings 1–2), but I will argue here that the additions comprising the Solomonic Apology were skillfully crafted such that they played on motifs already present in the CH and created a unifying structure to the SSN that had not previously existed in the CH.

One of the most often cited pieces of evidence for a purported connection between 2 Samuel 9–20 and 1 Kings 1–2 is the theme of retribution, discerned throughout the narrative by J. Fokkelman.[79] David's decree that the rich man in Nathan's "court-case" should repay the poor

77 See, e.g., Frolov, "Succession Narrative," 95, 102–3.

78 Flanagan, "Court History," 172–81; see also McCarter, *II Samuel*, 9–16.

79 Fokkelman, *King David*, 413–14.

man's sheep fourfold (ארבעתים; 2 Sam 12:6) is paralleled narratively by the loss of four sons: the first son of Bathsheba, Amnon, Absalom, and Adonijah.[80] J. S. Ackerman notes further that in the stories of Amnon and Absalom (and of Adonijah as a typological figuration of Absalom), the text contains hints of a "lamb motif." Amnon's murder occurs at a sheep-shearing festival (2 Sam 13:23–29), and Absalom himself apparently takes on the characteristics of sheep, being "without blemish" (לא־היה בו מום) and having his long hair shorn once a year (14:25–27). Finally, Absalom's death bears a striking resemblance to that of the ram caught in the thicket in Genesis 22.[81] These correspondences are too subtle and too elegant to have been merely accidental, argues Ackerman, and they point to a unity of story in the narrative 2 Samuel 9–20; 1 Kings 1–2. According to these two literary arguments, the ending of the SN (1 Kings 1–2) is tied both structurally and thematically to the bulk of the document (2 Samuel 9–20).

Two problems prohibit the immediate acceptance of Ackerman's argument for the SN's posited original unity. First, McCarter notes that Rabbinic literature had long ago pointed to the fourfold schema of retribution but that it replaced the death of Adonijah with the emotional loss of Tamar.[82] Such a schematization would effectively divorce the two sections of the narrative,[83] since it considers the fulfillment of the retribution to have occurred with Absalom's death in 2 Samuel 18 rather than with Adonijah's in 1 Kings 2. While one may wonder whether this replacement of Adonijah is indeed a valid substitution,[84] it seems clear from the Rabbinic tradition's recognition and variation of the motif that

80 Ackerman followed Fokkelman and Carlson in this observation ("Knowing Good," 48–51). While the narrative space opened up by Nathan's parable is not strictly analogous to the situation—i.e., it is difficult to tell whether Uriah corresponds to the poor man or the lamb!—the general consensus among those who have pointed to this motif seems to be that creating a strictly representative tale was not the point for the character of Nathan. The parable had to be conceived as a juridical case brought before the king and could therefore not imply too much guilt on the part of David. For a thorough discussion of the problem of calling the story a *parable*, see George W. Coats, "Parable, Fable, and Anecdote: Storytelling in the Succession Narrative," *Int* 35 (1981): 368–82. While he argues that Nathan's *parable* should in fact be called a *fable*, the observation that the story need not act on a strictly one-to-one correspondence remains supported by Coats's piece; see recently Jeremy Schipper, "Did David Overinterpret Nathan's Parable in 2 Samuel 12:1–6?" *JBL* 126 (2007): 383–407.

81 Ackerman, "Knowing Good," 50.

82 McCarter, *II Samuel*, 299.

83 As noted above, McCarter's argument actively works toward this divorce (ibid., 9–16).

84 In opposition to her four brothers, Tamar lives—albeit as a "destroyed woman" (שֹׁמֵמָה) in her brother Absalom's house (2 Sam 13:20). David never seems to show much remorse for his daughter's rough treatment, as opposed to the cries of anguish for the son of Bathsheba (12:17), the grief of David for Amnon and his other sons (13:31), and his unseemly weeping for Absalom (19:1). Furthermore, in the short episode involving Tamar (13:1–20) I find no allusions to the sheep motif as Ackerman has outlined it.

Ackerman's supposition is, albeit not incorrect, a subjective—rather than objective—description of the theme's expression.[85]

The second problem for Ackerman's model is posed by the fact that several textual witnesses read "sevenfold" (שׁבעתים).[86] Reading with this variation destroys any coherence of a "fourfold" scheme across the longer narrative and renders the Rabbinic understanding of a fourfold retribution obsolete in the process.[87] In short, nothing about the schema of fourfold recompense *necessitates* its position as an overarching structuring element of the SN, since the very foundation of the motif (the prophetic pronouncement) lies within a section of the narrative whose origin is demonstrably later than the earliest narrative. By arguing from a position within the world created by the text, Ackerman's postulation of the fourfold schema of retribution (following Fokkelman) proves only that within the SN—conceived a priori as 2 Samuel 9–20; 1 Kings 1–2—the schema functions as a structuring element. Because it makes no direct reference to criteria external to the passages under debate,[88] Ackerman's solution can by no means constitute an argument for the primary incorporation of 2 Sam 11:2–27*; 12:15b–25*; 1 Kings 1–2* in a document comprising a "Solomonic Succession Narrative." However, the presence of the motif in what appears in the developmental schema assumed here to be a composition by the author or compiler of the PR (2 Sam 12:1–15a*), and its application across the breadth of the CH, strongly suggests that the bulk of the CH had already been compiled by the time this passage was added. This coherence of imagery will be picked up again in the following section.

The textual development proposed above can provide an adequate and reasonable reconstruction of the developments that led to the motif of fourfold retribution. In the original Davidic-era or early Solomonic-era document (the CH—which *lacked* at least 2 Samuel 10–12; 1 Kings 1–2 and many secondary passages throughout 2 Samuel 9*; 13–20*), only two of David's sons died: Amnon and Absalom. The "sheepish" demeanor of these two sons was not particularly meaningful in the context of the CH.

85 Furthermore, one wonders to what extent Adonijah fits into the "sheep-motif" as Ackerman has described it. While Adonijah certainly is presented as a second Absalom with respect to his haughty pretensions to the throne, does this really qualify him for participation in the motif? As with the case of Tamar (see the preceding note), I see little reason to extend Absalom's sheer (or "shear"?) appearance to Adonijah.

86 Several LXX manuscripts, including the OG (represented by LXX^{B}), provide this reading; see, e.g., Carlson, *David*, 156; and McCarter, *II Samuel*, 294.

87 These challenges to Ackerman's schema of retribution may explain the text's ambivalence to the unnamed child of Bathsheba. After all, the child—the subject only of two verbs: "he became sick" (ויאנשׁ; 12:15), and "he died" (וימת; v. 18)—receives little characterization.

88 The text's appeal to the system of recompense espoused by Exod 21:37 cannot be considered external justification of the motif, since the structure has been appropriated and internalized by the additions; see below.

However, two events forever changed the meaning and text of that document, as well as the political milieu in which the text was read. The first event was historical: Solomon came to power unexpectedly and eliminated his primary rival, Adonijah. The second event was the development of a broader literary-historical situation: the impending succession of Rehoboam required a royal apologetic text explaining the unexpectedness of Solomon's reign. The king's scribe(s) grafted a correspondingly pro-Solomonic apology (the SA) onto the extant CH. Because there had been concerns raised about Solomon's parentage, the apology presented a history in which the identity of Solomon's progenitor could not be doubted. This may have occurred with or without the original presence of 2 Sam 12:15b–23.[89] After the earlier insertion of Adonijah's death (1 Kings 2:25), usually considered to play an integral role in the earliest report of Solomon's accession, the literary invention of this first child of Bathsheba and David (2 Sam 12:15b–23) brought the number of David's *sons* who had died to four. This numeration suggested a parallel to the juridical ruling of fourfold recompense for a stolen sheep in Exod 21:37.[90] Sheep imagery was already present in the CH as well and had provided a convenient motif for the PR-level's parable of Nathan.

It is impossible to know whether Nathan's parable (or "fable"[91]) was an accurate and authentic reminiscence of a historical prophetic rebuke; given that I have reconstructed it above (see §5.3.2.2) as a constituent episode of the PR, presumably composed by that document's author, we might presume that it is at best a shadow of a memory. But the textual ambiguity between the readings "sevenfold" and "fourfold" (2 Sam 12:6) militates against the reification of the pronouncement at either level. How then can we understand the textual variation? I would propose the following reconstruction, assuming that the basic text of Nathan's confrontation with David (2 Sam 12:1–15a*) was, in fact, secondarily added by the compiler of the PR: the parable originally read "sevenfold," but with the later insertion of 2 Sam 12:15b–23 and the corresponding arrival of the death-toll at four (the first son of David and Bathsheba, Amnon, Absalom, and Adonijah), the *Vorlage* of the MT changed its figure to "fourfold" to reflect this development's correspondence with Exod 21:37, while the *Vorlage* of the OG retained the original "sevenfold." However one chooses to interpret the textual anomalies of Nathan's parable, it is clear that

89 Vermeylen argues that vv. 15b–23 were not originally part of the Solomonic redaction but that the original pro-Solomonic redaction nonetheless contained enough hints to suggest David's paternity was uncontestable (*Loi du plus fort*, 296–98, 309–10).

90 This order of events assumes, of course, that Exod 21:37 is based upon authentically old juridical standards.

91 Coats, "Parable," 377–80.

even though the pro-Solomonic additions (and the Prophetic reformulations thereof) were written subsequent to the formation of the CH, they picked up the themes and motifs already hinted at in that document, such that the SSN could be crafted to feature a unique structure governing the whole. In short, this overarching motif, discernable only through a more synchronic literary-critical stance, came about thanks to the skillful use of the imagery extant in what redaction-criticism can demonstrate to comprise earlier strata.

An even closer relationship of the SA (2 Samuel 11–12*; 1 Kings 1–2*) and the body of the CH (2 Samuel 13–20*) would be reached if Wesselius's argument concerning the interrelatedness of 2 Samuel 10–12 and 13–14 could be proven.[92] He argued that Bathsheba's connivance in 1 Kings 1 was intended as a form of retaliation for David's murder of her husband.[93] Likewise, Ahitophel's participation in Absalom's revolt was motivated not just by friendship towards the new king but by his animosity toward David occasioned by the slights to his granddaughter Bathsheba (reading with 2 Sam 23:34). A similar motivation would be apparent for Jonadab's churlish recommendation to Amnon (2 Sam 13:5), if his brother Jonathan were the same Jonathan of David's men (2 Sam 21:21) and had been involved in the Uriah incident in which men other than Uriah had been killed (2 Sam 11:17,24). While this last point is quite difficult to substantiate, the connections Wesselius drew do point to the possible existence of a tightly-knit cohesion between 2 Samuel 11–12; 13–14 and the "additions" in 21–24. This cohesion would not necessarily negate the reconstruction of a multiple-staged development of the SSN, but it could provide a foundation and *terminus post quem* for the inclusion of 2 Samuel 21–24. That is to say, although it is doubtful that Bathsheba was purely a literary creation, one need not consider the mimetic presentation of her character in the SSN as absolute. The redactor who appended the apologetic elements 2 Sam 11:2–27*; 12:15b–25* + 1 Kings 1–2* onto the CH could easily have included some of the "additions" in 2 Samuel 21–24* as well, thereby implying—or even fabricating—a false genealogical connection between Bathsheba and Ahitophel. Further, this implication suggests motivations for the historical Ahitophel that may or may not have been real. In a similar vein, one need not trust any implied connection between Jonadab's brother Jonathan and the havoc wreaked upon the order of succession by Jonadab's actions. The project of the historian is to reconstruct life-worlds in which motivations are realistic and understand-

92 Wesselius, "Joab's Death," 349–51.

93 Cf. Baruch Halpern, *David's Secret Demons: Messiah, Murderer, Traitor, King* (Grand Rapids, Mich.: Eerdmans, 2001), 406.

able. That does not necessarily make the historian correct. As will be argued below (§5.3.4), the account of David's provision for Mephibosheth may be a complete fabrication on the part of the "court historian" or later author, using characters known from other material grafted together into a fictional account of David's generosity and designed to serve as an indicator of the king's benevolence towards the Saulide family.

Although this section has not engaged in a detailed redaction-critical study of 2 Samuel 11–12*; 1 Kings 1–2*—an endeavor that will undoubtedly prove to be a necessity for any thoroughly substantiated study of the Court History's development—it has pointed to the results of a few redaction-critical studies. Those studies support the same relative ordering of the addition of texts here, though they argue for later dates of each inclusion than suggested here. Nonetheless, if it is possible to link the base text of Nathan's oracle (2 Sam 12:1–15a) to a pre-Deuteronomistic stratum rather than to a prophetically-concerned Deuteronomist's editorial work (DtrP), then we have here evidence for the pre-Deuteronomistic compilation of the SN, and hence for the pre-Deuteronomistic juxtaposition of the monarch-type and deliverer-type visions of Transjordan. This pre-Deuteronomistic composition of the SN is not unanimously held, however, and requires further defense.

5.3.3. Further Fractures: Separating the Transjordanian Flight (2 Sam 15:7–17:29*; 19:9b–20:13*) from a Narrative of Absalom's Rebellion (2 Sam 18:1–19:9a*)

Over the last decade, commentators have increasingly called into question the unity of the episodes concerning David's Transjordanian flight (2 Sam 15:7–17:29*; 19:9b–20:13*) with the actual battle-narrative in which David's troops dispatch of Absalom (18:1–19:9a). Because of its obviously schematic structure and manifest connections to Gilgal (2 Sam 19:16, 41)—and thus to the Elijah-Elisha complex (2 Kgs 2:1–18; see §1.2.2) and the narrative of Israel's entry into Canaan (Joshua 3–4)—these interpreters have tended to consider the structural frame of David's Transjordanian flight to be late Deuteronomistic (DtrS). Accordingly, the redactor(s) who effected this literary interpolation had in view the Judahite departure into the Babylonian captivity and the imminent or recent return of the *gôlâ*-community in a "homecoming" narrative parallel to David's double-movement across the Jordan River.[94] If this posited history of 2 Samuel's composition were to hold true, it would effectively collapse the monarch-

94 See especially the recent discussion of Rudnig (*Davids Thron*, 315–17).

type and prophet-type views of Transjordan posited in §1.2.4 above, and date this combined "monarch-prophet-type" view to the late-exilic or perhaps even post-exilic eras. However, as was already seen to be the case with Römer's exilic dating of the AN to the exile, the too-hasty attribution of the loss-return motif solely to an exilic-era Deuteronomist may not fully account for the possibilities of the Deuteronomistic (and, specifically, exilic) reinterpretation of earlier, extant, and already-received traditions (§3.4.4.5, above). Integral to the position holding an exilic provenance of the DtrS origin of 2 Sam 15:7–17:29* + 19:9b–20:13 are the various mentions of Gilgal in 2 Sam 19:16 and 19:41. Rudnig has recently cited the "Traditionen von Jordanübergang und Landnahme"[95] as the primary influence here:

> Der Aufenthalt außer Landes ist somit für das Volk die Zeit von Gefahr und Bewährung. Dies entspricht deutlich einem in golaorientierter Theologie vertretenen Gedanken: Nur diejenigen, die durch das Gericht des Exils geläutert worden sind, dürfen den Anspruch erheben, das wahre Israel zu sein. Und wenn mit Rückkehr über den Jordan bei Gilgal das Paradigma von Exodus und Landnahme zitiert wird, liegt folgende Idee zugrunde: Nach der Überwindung der Krise kommt David ins Land, gerade so, wie das aus Ägypten befreite Volk das ihm verheißene Land in Besitz nimmt. Wie etwa Jes 40,3f.10; 41,18f; 42,13; 43,19f; 49,10; 52,12 zeigen, ist die Idee eines neuen Exodus ein Theologumenon frühestens der exilischen, plausibler aber der nachexilischen Zeit. Der Gedanke an einen neuen Eintritt ins Land und eine neue Landnahme hat in den Landtexten Ez 47,13–23; 48,1–29 seine theologische Parallelen.[96]

This identification of David's flight and return with Israel's entry into Canaan is made here without pausing to contemplate whether, perhaps, the mentions of Gilgal in 2 Sam 19:16b,41aα* are secondary insertions *modeled on* Joshua 3–4. It must be admitted that neither mention is syntactically necessary to its context and both appear in contexts that are generally agreed to be literary-critical seams on other grounds.[97] It remains equally possible—and equally unconsidered by Rudnig[98]—that it was the tradition in 2 Samuel currently under discussion that brought about the localization of the conquest narrative in Joshua 3–4. Already in the 8th

95 Ibid., 315.

96 Ibid., 316.

97 Verse 16b anti-climactically anticipates the descent of the Judahites with Shimei in tow (v. 17b) and doubles the apparently corrupted notice in v. 19 that Ziba had arrived with a group of Benjaminites to bring the king across the river.

98 Rudnig envisions the "artful" insertion of vv. 39,40b around v. 40a (ibid., 315). However, v. 39 follows naturally on vv. 32–36,37b–38, and v. 41 advances v. 40b, with or without הגלגלה in v. 41aα. It is likely that two traditions have been dovetailed here; see François Langlamet, "David et Barzillaï. 2 Samuel 19:32–41a: le récit primitif et sa 'forme'," in *Isac Leo Seeligman Volume: Essays on the Bible and the Ancient World* (ed. Alexander Rofé and Yair Zakovitch; 3 vols.; Jerusalem: Magnes, 1983), 154–58; Vermeylen, *Loi du plus fort*, 631.

cent., Micah knew of a tradition in which the Israelite conquest occurred at Gilgal (Mic 6:5), and while it may be the case that the *theologumenon* of the "New Exodus" is at earliest a 6th cent. invention, forged in response to the Babylonian exile, Rudnig's too facile identification of David's flight with the exile begs the question of the propriety of that identification. The *conquest* motif was current already by the 8th cent., and it is manifestly *that* motif in which David's return partakes. There is, therefore, nothing prohibiting an earlier development of that motif; in fact, if the argument in this and the following chapters is correct in its essentials, then the triumphant return after a purifying exile is merely a derivative of the earlier conquest motif, the unintended result of redactional accretions that began forming long before the purifying exile's paradigmatic expression during the 6th cent. Deutero-Isaiah's *conflation* of the "purifying exile" motif and the conquest motif is one exemplar of a larger movement within Judahite thought and cannot be taken as the *first* expression of its type.

At the more text-oriented level, it is difficult to argue effectively against the source-critical separation of David's Transjordanian flight from the original account of the suppression of Absalom's Rebellion; as will be seen, I find some features of this theory compelling. Therefore, in light of the foregoing discussion, a survey of and response to the Continental commentators favoring the particularly late-dating of 2 Sam 15:7–17:29* + 19:9b–20:13* is warranted in the following pages.

5.3.3.1. Kratz, Fischer, and Aurelius

Although R. G. Kratz was not the first to offer the proposal of a secondary interpolation of 2 Samuel 15–17; 19–20*,[99] it is through his initiative that the discussion has been rekindled in recent years. In his 2000 volume, *Die Komposition der erzählender Bücher des Alten Testaments*, Kratz dismissed what he claimed was only an apparent reliance of 2 Samuel 15–20 on the literary prehistory of the SN in 2 Samuel 2–9:

> The narratives of the revolts of Absalom and Sheba in 2 Sam. 15–19 and 20 are most strongly woven into the context; they hardly ever seem to have a life of their own, but continue the Absalom narrative in 2 Sam. 13–14. I see the main difficulty of these narratives in their presupposition that David was king over Israel and Judah, which could hardly have been said before there were two states, and that he

---

99 According to Alexander A. Fischer ("Flucht und Heimkehr Davids als integraler Rahmen der Abschalomerzählung," in *Ideales Königtum: Studien zu David und Salomo* [ed. Rüdiger Lux; ABG 16; Leipzig: Evangelische Verlagsanstalt, 2005], 49), that distinction goes to Hugo Winckler, who made the proposal nearly a century ago (*Geschichte Israels in Einzeldarstellung* [2 vols.; Leipzig: Pfeiffer, 1895–1900], 2:233–35).

> operates in the region of the Benjaminite sons of Saul (Mahanaim), which clearly requires the literary connection with the prehistory in 2 Sam. 2–9. However, as is shown by the indication in 18.6, which is usually neglected or explained away by exegetes, this does not seem to be original. The battle against Absalom does not take place in Transjordan but in Ephraim, that is, west of the Jordan (cf. also 18.23). The gate of the city where according to 18.4 and 19.9 David stands and receives the people is therefore not in Mahanaim (thus according to 17.24); it is the same gate as that at which according to 15.1–6,13 Absalom steals the hearts of the Israelites going to Jerusalem. 19.6 seems to know nothing (yet) of the appropriation of the concubines in Jerusalem (12.11f.; 15.16; 16.21–23). Now that means that the whole account of the flight from [*ab*, i.e., beginning with] 15.14 in chs 15–17 and 19.9b, 10ff. must have been added later. The narrative originally comprised only 15.1–6, 13; 18.1–19.9a, and has been handed down largely intact.[100]

Because of the terseness with which Kratz's argument was made, the reasons for source-critical separation are not immediately intelligible to the reader. Thus, the argument for the literary integrity of a *Grundbestand* in 2 Sam 15:1–6,13; 18:1–19:9 required some additional explanation and defense; A. A. Fischer provided that elaboration in 2005, although he had been anticipated in some respects by Erik Aurelius already in the preceding year.[101] The points of clarification outlined by Fischer are five-fold; I will respond to each in order:

(1) Proceeding from the recognition that 2 Sam 18:1–19:9 nowhere mentions the name Mahanaim, but refers only to "the city" (see 18:3; 19:4 [Eng. v. 3]), Fischer noted the ambiguity of the episode's location and proposed to investigate whether "the city" could indicate Jerusalem, rather than Mahanaim. Admittedly, the indication that the battle took place in the "Forest of Ephraim" (יער אפרים; 18:6) has proved to be a *crux interpretum* over the years, and a relocalization of the forest to Cisjordan eases matters considerably. As Fischer pointed out, 2 Sam 13:23 mentions a locale named Ephraim in the area of Baal Hazor, where Absalom's sheep-shearers are stationed. This Ephraim seems to be the same town known to Josephus as Εφραιμ (*J.W.* 4.9.9 [=4.551]) and to Eusebius as Αφρα (*Onom.* 28.4).[102] Accordingly, the decisive battle in the "Forest of Ephraim" was fought ca. 20 km north of Jerusalem, not in Transjordan.[103]

100 Reinhard G. Kratz, *The Composition of the Narrative Books of the Old Testament* (trans. John Bowden; London: T&T Clark, 2005) 175–76; trans. of *Die Komposition der erzählenden Bücher des Alten Testaments* (Göttingen: Vandenhoeck & Ruprecht, 2000). My interpretive addition, based on the German original, is bracketed.

101 Fischer, "Flucht und Heimkehr," 43–69, esp. here 49–55. Fischer includes v. 9b in the original text, for reasons that will become clear below.

102 Cf. those who take "Ephraim" in 2 Sam 13:23 as the tribal name: Yoel Elitzur, *Ancient Place Names in the Holy Land: Preservation and History* (Jerusalem: Magnes; Winona Lake, Ind.: Eisenbrauns; Jerusalem: Magnes, 2004), 269 n. 5 and bibliography there. In this case, I agree with Fischer that the syntagm GN_1 + עם + GN_2 indicates that GN_2 was a locality and not a tribal designation (Flucht und Heimkehr," 50 n. 27, citing Otto Thenius, *Die Bücher Samuels*

The identification of biblical Ephraim (2 Sam 13:23), Ephron (עפרון; 2 Chr 13:19, cf. *qere*: עֶפְרַיִן), or Ophrah (עָפְרָה; Josh 18:23—not to be confused with the Ophrah of the Abiezrites in Manasseh) with modern *aṭ-Ṭay(yi)be* (178.151) is typically an important element in the argument over the location at which 2 Samuel 18–19 plays out.[104] Although Fischer recognized this location of Ephraim as a possibility, he did not trace the linguistic evidence provided by the modern name. Aside from the other biblical references to the locality, both of which use *ayin* to represent the first consonant of the name, the witnesses are indeterminate in indicating this consonant. The Greek sources naturally represent the name with the decidedly undiagnostic smooth breathing mark (e.g., John 11:52; Josephus's *J.W.* 4.9.9; *Onom.* 28.4; 86.1; 90.18), and at both 2 Sam 13:23 and 18:6, we find אפרים in *Tg. Jon.*, which took these indicators from MT (glossing in 18:6 that the battle had occurred in the "Forest of the *house of* Ephraim" [בחורשא דבית אפרים]). However, LXX^{L} contains the variant Γοφραιμ at 2 Sam 13:23, and the Syriac translation of the *Treatise on Weights and Measures* by Epiphanius uses a *heth*.[105] One must then reckon here with the probability that MT preserves a corrupted or intentionally emended form of the original name, which began with *ayin*. Folk narratives in the area explain the subsequent shift of the name from *ʿEphraim* or the like to *Ṭaybe* as a result of Saladin's campaigns,[106] and enough evidence exists to link this shift to toponymic replacement sometime after the period of Arab entry into the southern Levant: the Hebrew root עפר (< Proto-Semitic **ĠPR*), denoting a type of quadruped (e.g., Heb. עֹפֶר, "young hart, stag") was homophonous with the Arabic root *ʿFR*, negatively valued because of its derivative nouns such as *ʿifrît* ("demon or evil spirit"), *ʿifr* ("tremendous, wicked, mischevous"), *ʿifriyâ* ("disaster or misfortune"), and so on.[107] The name was changed euphemistically to *Ṭaybe* (meaning "good").[108] According to Elitzur, the number of toponyms

[3d ed.; EHAT; Leipzig: Hirzel, 1898], 165; see also S. R. Driver, *Notes on the Hebrew Text of the Books of Samuel* [Oxford: Clarendon, 1890], 233).

103 Fischer, "Flucht und Heimkehr," 50–51. Fischer did not include the reference to Eusebius (for which, see, e.g., Elitzur, *Ancient Place Names*, 268), which would have strengthened his argument slightly.

104 See, e.g., Albrecht Alt, "Das Institut im Jahre 1927," *PJ* 24 (1928): 32–41, and, for further bibliography, Elitzur, *Ancient Place Names*, 269 n. 5.

105 For documentation of the name in these and later sources, see ibid., 269–71.

106 The change is obviously not a natural linguistic progression but is given a folk etiology in locally remembered narratives; see ibid., 277.

107 Vocabulary here cited according to ibid., 272; see also Edward William Lane, *An Arabic-English Lexicon* (8 vols.; London: Williams & Norgate, 1865): I/5:2089c–2090a.

108 This theory was originally proposed by Richard Hartmann, "Zum Ortsnamen aṭ-Ṭajjiba," *ZDMG* 65 (1911): 536–38; for a modern clarification and elaboration, see Elitzur, *Ancient Place Names*, 272–90.

in modern-day Israel based on the Arabic *ṭaybe* is "more than ten,"[109] and there are at least two locations bearing that name in modern-day Jordan: (a) one in southern Jordan (1939.9627)[110] and (b) one west of Irbid—formerly known as *ʿefre*—which G. Hölscher identified as the Εφρων of 1 Macc 5:46–52; 2 Macc 12:27 and the Γεφρους of Polybius (*Hist.* 5.70.12).[111] One wonders whether this latter Ephron might not be identified as the namesake of the (incorrectly spelled) יער אפרים.[112] Furthermore, the name may be related to the Hapharaim (*ḥ*ʾ*-pw-rw-m-*ʾ) of the Shishak inscription,[113] which occurs—according to Y. Aharoni's arrangement—along with the unknown Adoraim and the enigmatic *p.ʿmq* (= "the Valley"?) between Zaphon (no. 20) and Rehob (no. 17).[114] If correct, this conjecture would locate the city somewhere near the Jordan Valley, probably on the eastern side of the Jordan.[115]

---

109 Elitzur, *Ancient Place Names*, 272.

110 Wolfgang Zwickel, *Eisenzeitliche Ortslagen im Ostjordanland* (BTAVO B81; Wiesbaden: Reichert, 1990), 32; Nelson Glueck, *Explorations in Eastern Palestine, II* (AASOR 15; New Haven: ASOR, 1935), 37 no. 16.

111 G. Hölscher, "Bemerkungen zur Topographie Palästinas, 1: Die Feldzüge des Makkabäers Judas (1. Makk. 5)," *ZDPV* 29 (1906): 142; the town is mentioned also by Hartmann, "Zum Ortsnamen," 536; F.-M. Abel, *Géographie de la Palestine* (3d ed.; 2 vols.; Paris: Gabalda, 1967), 2:318–19; compare also two towns of the identical name (*Taiyibet Lism* or simply *eṭ-Ṭayibeh*) in the Golan: one just west of the *Jebel Druze* noted by G. Schumacher, *Across the Jordan* (New York: Scribner & Welford, 1886), 221; idem, "Das südliche Basan," *ZDPV* 20 (1897): 167; and the other east of modern Irbid and southeast of *Derʿā*, mentioned by Jan Jozef Simons, *Geographical and Topographical Texts of the Old Testament: a Concise Commentary in XXXII Chapters* (Nederlands instituut voor het Nabije Oosten; Studia Francisci Scholten memoriae dicata 2; Leiden: Brill, 1959), 425.

112 Because of the demonstrated confusion between the אפרים of MT 2 Sam 13:23; 18:6 and the עפרה/עפרון of 2 Chr 13:19 and Josh 18:23, it is unnecessary to postulate an eastward migration of Ephraimites, as do Martin Noth ("Das Land Gilead als Siedlungsgebiet israelitischer Sippen," *PJ* 37 [1941]: 68–69, 73; idem, *The History of Israel* [2d ed.; trans. P. R. Ackroyd; London: Adam & Charles Black, 1960], 60–62; trans. of *Geschichte Israels* [2d ed. Göttingen: Vandenhoeck & Ruprecht, 1958]) and Hans Joachim Stoebe (*Das zweite Buch Samuelis* [KAT 8/2: Gütersloh: Gütersloher Verlagshaus, 1994], 399).

113 Benjamin Mazar, "The Campaign of Pharaoh Shishak to Palestine," in *Volume du Congrès: Strasbourg, 1956* (ed. G. W. Anderson et al.; VTSup 4; Leiden: Brill, 1957), 62.

114 Yohanan Aharoni, *The Land of the Bible: A Historical Geography* (rev. ed.; trans. A. F. Rainey; Philadelphia: Westminster, 1979), 323–27; cf. K. A. Kitchen, who contests the identification of no. 20 as Zaphon and locates—or at least mentions—Haparaim between Rehob and Beth-shean (*The Third Intermediate Period in Egypt [100–650 B.C.]* [Warminster: Aris & Phillips, 1986], 298–99). Kitchen also identifies *pa-ʿemeq* as "the valley… *par excellence*," the Jezreel Valley. While possible, it is difficult for me to see how the Jezreel Valley and not the Jordan Valley would be considered as such.

115 Mazar identifies the city as *Tell eṣ-Ṣaʿidiye*, although I find this postulation not entirely convincing ("Campaign," 62). Cf., though, Martin Noth, who identifies Hapharaim as the same city mentioned in Judg 19:19 in the boundary description of Issachar ("Die Wege der Pharaonenheere in Palästina und Syrien, IV: Die Schoschenkenliste," *ZDPV* 61 [1938]: 283); so also James Henry Breasted, *Ancient Records of Egypt* (5 vols.; London: Histories & Mysteries of Man, Ltd., 1988), 4:350, §712; and Kevin A. Wilson, *The Campaign of*

Thus, the evidence locating the "Forest of Ephraim" in the Cisjordan is ambiguous. Although I concede the existence of an "Ephraim" ca. 20 km north of Jerusalem, and would even allow that it is to this Ephraim that 2 Sam 13:23 and 18:6 originally referred, we must be quite explicit in stating that the locality's name was most likely not אפרים but rather עפרון or the like and that it was changed in the MT because of confusion. Any later transfer of the battle eastward (such as that posited by Kratz, Fischer, and Aurelius) would have been plausible precisely because a town by the same name existed in Transjordan. Therefore, the corresponding implicit claim made by Kratz that "Israel" here represents only the northern tribes does not necessarily fail, but it, along with the suggestion that the "Forest of Ephraim" *must* be located in Cisjordan, requires interpretive argumentation and cannot be put forth merely as an already-established fact.[116]

(2) Fischer argued the *de facto* footrace between Ahimaaz and the Cushite in 2 Sam 18:19–32, usually understood to encompass the former's traversing of a path through the Jordan Valley, need not indicate a Transjordanian location. Instead, the Versions exhibit a good deal of confusion concerning the location of the path: LXX^{B} (OG) and Origen understood דרך הַכִּכָּר in v. 23 as a proper name (ὁδὸν τὴν τοῦ Κεχὰρ), while Aquila, Symmachus, and Theodotian translated it as "short-cut" (ὁδὸν τὴν διατέμνουσαν).[117] Morever, examination of the term in Neh 3:22 and 12:28 suggests that הככר more accurately designates the surrounding area and could thus refer simply to a local road. Finally, D. A. Dorsey was unable to find any examples of a road named after the region through which it ran; accordingly, the road is not the longitudinal road running the length of the Jordan Valley.[118] Hence, whereas the Cushite tried to fight

---

Pharaoh Shoshenq I into Palestine (FAT II/9; Tübingen: Mohr Siebeck, 2005), 107. A fuller exploration of the precise route (and nature of the campaign) must before undertaken before certainty may be approached (see, e.g., Siegfried Herrmann, "Operationen Pharao Schoschenks I. im östlichen Ephraim," *ZDPV* 80 [1964]: 55–79). For example, Frank Clancy has argued recently that Shishak never campaigned east of the Jordan ("Shishak/Shoshenq's Travels," *JSOT* 86 [1999]: 3–23).

116 Compare the use of the broader term "Israel" to indicate Absalom's constituency in 2 Sam 16:3,15,18,21,22; 17:4,10,11,13,15; 18:6,7,16,17, as well as 2 Sam 19:9b–11, where each man of "Israel" flees to his respective "tents" (לאהליו; cf. 2 Sam 20:1; 1 Kgs 12:16) and recognizes his share in the guilt of Absalom's insurrection.

117 See Fischer, "Flucht und Heimkehr," 52, presumably citing Frederick Field's *Origenis Hexaplorum* (1867–1875; repr., Hildesheim: Olms, 1964), in which this variant can be found. A. E. Brooke and Norman McLean list only διατεταγμενην and διατεταμενην "with might, earnestly" (*The Old Testament in Greek: According to the Text of Codex Vaticanus* [Cambridge: Cambridge University Press, 1917–1940]). For the translation "short-cut," see also Vulg. *per viam compendii/conpendii*.

118 Fischer, "Flucht und Heimkehr," 52, citing David A. Dorsey, *The Roads and Highways of Ancient Israel* (Baltimore: The Johns Hopkins University Press, 1991), 49–50; for the Shiloh-Jerusalem road running through Ophrah of Benjamin (= Ephraim), 136–38, N15.

his way cross-country, Ahimaaz made his way to the highway running between Shiloh and Jerusalem.

The criticism that no road is named for the region through which it travels is fair, if difficult to know with certainty, but the comparison of the uses of הככר in Nahum does not do justice to the overwhelming usage of the term to indicate the Jordan River Valley in monarchic and exilic literature (e.g., Gen 13:10–12; 1 Kgs 16:24). Fischer's argument here is not really an argument *for* the Cisjordanian theater of 2 Sam 18:1–19:9, merely an argument against the traditional localization of that passage in Transjordan. Moreover, although I find the Cisjordanian interpretation plausible, the citation of 18:23—with its mention of the דרך הככר as further evidence of the episode's western provenance—fails to convince when one carefully scrutinizes the topographical assumptions of the claimed eastern location of the story at Mahanaim, which are equally (and perhaps better) suited to the data in the passage.[119] Fischer was unable to determine what the phrase דרך הככר would indicate:

> Entweder muss man den Ausdruck als einen nicht näher erklärbaren Straßennamen nehmen, der hier nur erwähnt ist. Oder man versteht das *nomen rectum* הַכִּכָּר gar nicht als festen geographischen Begriff, sondern als einen *Genetivus qualitatis*. Danach käme man—abgeleitet von der Grundbedeutung *Scheibe*—auf eine Bedeutung wie etwa *Bogen(-weg)*.[120]

But neither of Fischer's solutions is particularly compelling: if the name does not indicate a road running through the Jordan Valley (as most commentators interpret it), then it must indicate either (a) a road running *to* an otherwise unnamed "District," or (b) a generally described "round-about way." The first solution is patently useless; if anything, one would have to argue that the road was the one running from Jerusalem parallel to the *W. Qilt* into Jericho (i.e., *to* the Jordan Valley).[121] This road is called the דרך הערבה elsewhere (2 Sam 4:7; 2 Kgs 25:4 = Jer 52:7; see also Jer

119 I am currently beginning work on a monograph-length study on the location of Mahanaim. At present, two components have been completed and can be found in publication: Jeremy M. Hutton, "Mahanaim, Penuel and Transhumance Routes: Observations on Genesis 32–33 and Judges 8," *JNES* 65 (2006): 161–78; and idem, review of Y. Elitzur, *Ancient Place Names in the Holy Land*, *Maarav* 14 (2007): 77–97, esp. 84–96 (i.e., the section entitled "מחנים ~ μαναειμ ~ [*al-muġanni*]: A Proposal"). Further studies will include a source-critical discussion of Genesis 32, a study of Mahanaim's location from the standpoint of the geographical texts in Joshua, and—of particular importance here—an exegetical reading of 2 Samuel 18, with particular attention paid to geography. Although such a reading cannot *prove* the event's occurrence at one historical location over another, it will show that the narrative is constructed in such a way that the topography surrounding biblical Mahanaim (most likely *T. aḏ-Ḏahab al-Ǵarbīya*) conforms to the basic topographic assumptions of the literary episode.

120 Fischer, "Flucht und Heimkehr," 52.

121 See, e.g., Dorsey, *Roads and Highways*, 204–6, J32.

39:4), and although the nomenclature does not seem problematic in itself, it is difficult to see exactly how finding this road would permit Ahimaaz a faster return to Jerusalem from a battle waged well north of the city; the route is nearly perpendicular to the expected direction of travel.[122] The second solution is just as difficult and no more specific than the first. If, however, ככר indicates the southern portion of the Jordan Valley (i.e., that portion north of the Dead Sea as far north as the "Vale of Sukkoth"; Gen 13:10–11; 1 Kgs 7:46; 2 Chr 4:17; for the Vale, see Ps 60:6; 108:7), then the nomenclature of paths wherein the road's *destination* sits in the position of the *nomen rectum* would pertain perfectly to the longitudinal highway running the length of the Jordan River Valley—as it would have been named by someone in the northern sector of that valley (from which direction Ahimaaz was running).

(3) According to Fischer, although the ambiguous nature of "gate" and "wall" do not serve to narrow the pool of potential locales at which 2 Sam 19:1–9 takes place (*contra* Kratz), other phraseological indications of David's environs do not adequately localize him anywhere other than Jerusalem: not only does Joab find David at "his house" (*in seinem Haus*; הבית) in v. 6,[123] but the text also mentions David's "sons and daughters, ... wives and...concubines." Fischer, following Kratz, interpreted this locution as an indication that the *Grundbestand* (found in 18:1–19:9) does not yet know that the concubines have been left behind in Jerusalem in 15:16; 16:21–22.[124] Although it may be pointed out that Fischer has inserted the 3.m.s. possessive pronoun here on "house," a feature not appearing in the MT, this interpretive clarification does bear some weight: there is no indication in 19:1–9 that David is anywhere *other* than in Jerusalem, and the appearance of Joab at "the house" omits a significant amount of detail if we are expecting any mention of the house being the site of David's exile. Indications exist, however, that this portion of the narrative may itself be secondary to the battle-scene in 2 Sam 18:1–17* (with its proper ending in v. 18). The claim that 19:6 does not know of the concubines' humiliation in 16:21–23 may—if 19:6 is not simply a typical list of those in the king's household who were in danger during a popular uprising or military insurrection (cf. 2 Kings 10)—register some disparity between the

---

122 Nevertheless, this is not to say that a reasonable reconstruction is impossible. If the battle had taken the armies down the eastward escarpment of the hill country, then Ahimaaz may have found it easier to continue south-eastward to Jericho on Dorsey's J29 route, running from Ephraim/Ephron to Jericho (ibid., 202). This, however, would preclude a battle in a forest so thick that the forest itself seemed to defeat the enemy (2 Sam 18:8).

123 Fischer, "Flucht und Heimkehr," 52.

124 Ibid., 53.

two sets of verses, but again, that this disparity necessitates a source-critical separation requires further investigation and defense.

Most problematic in this regard is the redaction-critical division performed by E. Aurelius, who attempted to bolster Kratz's argument. Aurelius plausibly adduced a pro-Davidic (and anti-Joabite) redaction in 2 Sam 18:10–15a; 18:19–9:9. As part of this argument, he pointed to the transparent close of the battle-account in 18:17 and the somewhat tragic failure of Absalom to leave behind progeny, capping the story in v. 18a (although cf. 14:27).[125] The notice that the stele is called יד אבשלם "to this day" (v. 18b) was predictably (and plausibly) assigned to a Deuteronomistic editor, and the entire remaining portion of Kratz's and Fischer's posited *Grundbestand* is reckoned to a pro-Davidic secondary redaction. Aurelius considered himself to be working in support of Kratz's argument—notice, e.g., the omission of all of the Transjordanian flight passage in Aurelius's reconstructed "original story" encompassing 13:1–29,34a, 37aβ,38b–39; 14:33aβγb; 15:1–6,13; 18:1–2a,4b,6–9,15b–18.[126] But the omission of 18:19–19:9 consequently removes nearly all of the markers that Kratz and Fischer adduced as indicators of the story's occurrence in Cisjordan. No longer is there a footrace along the דרך הככר in 18:23; no longer does Joab redress David in "the house" (19:6); no longer is there mention of David's concubines in 19:6, which purportedly conflicted with 16:21–23 to such an extent that it warranted removing the entire "flight and homeward return" framework to begin with. In fact, Aurelius has shown convincingly, in my opinion, that 16:21–23 is itself a secondary interpolation on the basis of the doubled advice of Ahitophel narrated in 16:21 (along with its fulfillment in vv. 22–23) and the immediately following 17:1–3.[127] The latter answer is assumed in vv. 4–23; the former is not. In short, the diligence with which Aurelius has handled the various conflicting traditions of 2 Samuel 15–20 makes it *less* likely that the original battle narrative (now limited to 18:1–2a,4b,6–9,15b–18) must be divorced from the surrounding material detailing David's flight to Transjordan and his triumphant return. The *only* indicator left intact by Aurelius's argument is the location of the battle, which has already been shown above to be ambiguous and therefore indeterminate.

(4) With Kratz, the meaning and importance of David's appearance "at the gate" (בשער; vv. 9a,9bα) is well-received in light of the fact that it was

---

125 Erik Aurelius, "David's Unschuld: Die Hofgeschichte und Psalm 7," in *Gott und Mensch im Dialog: Festschrift für Otto Kaiser zum 80. Geburtstag* (ed. Markus Witte; BZAW 345; 2 vols.; Berlin: de Gruyter, 2004), 1:391–412, esp. 396–400.

126 Ibid., 402; this division was followed by Adam, "Motivik," 188. For the removal of 18:2b–4a,10–14, see already Würthwein, *Erzählung*, 65–66.

127 Aurelius, "David's Unschuld," 394–95.

precisely here that Absalom had laid the foundation of his own legitimacy. But in opposition to Kratz, Fischer included v. 9b—or at least v. 9bβ: "All the people came before the king" (ויבא כל־העם לפני המלך). Fischer was *required* to make this interpretive move because it allowed him to juxtapose the purportedly natural ending of the base narrative to the supposedly artificial *communitas* of the secondarily interpolated homeward journey in 19:10–44.[128] The ambiguity of referent engendered by the mention of "Israel" in 18:6, however, renders Kratz's observation concerning the irony of David's weeping at the same gate that served as the site of Absalom's preparations for his *coup d'état* both important and literarily meaningful, but certainly not redaction-critically *necessary*. The scene "at the gate" may have been the intended literary motif of the original author, without requiring the added specificity of both scenes' location in Jerusalem. Moreover, as we have just seen, Aurelius's relegation of this passage to a secondary redaction renders the comparison a moot point.

(5) Finally, Fischer argued that Joab plays a central role in 2 Sam 18:1–19:9 but disappears from view in the surrounding processional passages detailing the movements of David's entourage out of (15:14–17:29*) and back into Cisjordan (19:10–44). Fischer deduced that this occlusion of Joab signals a switch in compositional layers, borne out in the shift from a *Grundbestand* narrative concerned primarily with the military's role in the maintenance of monarchic power (18:1–19:9) to a redactional framework eager to emphasize the role of "priests and counselors, who, with God's help, pull the strings."[129] This thematic variation is, I would suggest, the strongest of Fischer's various arguments for the source-critical separation of 2 Samuel 15–17; 19:10–20:22 from an "original" battle-report in 18:1–19:9*, which—if working from a strictly observant redaction-critical stance—should probably be confined to 18:1–2a,4b,6–9,15b–18a. Yet the disappearance of Joab from 2 Samuel 15–17; 19:10–44 may only be ephemeral, as an investigation of earlier redaction-critical work will show.

5.3.3.2. Würthwein and Langlamet

The disappearance of Joab is countered by the reappearance of his brother Abishai in 16:9, who offers to do away with the offensive Shimei. David rebukes the petulant officer with the phrase "What have I to do with you,

128 Fischer, "Flucht und Heimkehr," 54.
129 Ibid., 54–55, quote from 55, my translation.

you *sons of Zeruiah*?" (מה־לי ולכם בני צריה; v. 10).[130] Because Asahel has already been killed in 2 Sam 2:23, the use of the plural here can only refer to both Abishai and Joab. While the use of this phrase is undoubtedly schematic (appearing also in 2 Sam 19:23; the castigating use of בני צריה occurs again in 3:39), its presence here constitutes evidence of a large anti-Joabite redactional layer, the intent of which was to exonerate David and to pin the blame for several murders on Joab. Passages related by virtue of similar vocabulary or anti-Joabite rhetoric—2 Sam 3:38–39; 15:24–26; 16:10; 19:23—all comprise doublings of other speeches (cf. 3:35–37; 15:27–28; 16:11; 19:24).[131] This same trend may be shown for other passages in what Würthwein and Langlamet have isolated as a redactional stratum. The former included two of these passages (2 Sam 15:24–26,29; 16:9–12), along with a few others (2 Sam 14:2–22; 18:2b–4a,10–14; 20:4–5,8–13; 1 Kgs 2:5–9) in his "joabfeindliche Überarbeitung,"[132] which—if all connected to 1 Kgs 2:5–9—he effectively attributed elsewhere to a post-DtrH Deuteronomistic redactor (i.e., DtrP?).[133] Langlamet included all of these passages in his "pro-Solomonic redaction" but did not adequately distinguish the clearly secondary insertions from their contexts, including large swaths of material instead. For example, rather than excising the rather obvious secondary intrusions in 2 Sam 15:24–26; 16:10[12]; 19:23, Langlamet included much of 2 Samuel 15 (vv. [8],16b–17a,24*,25–26,31,34aβγδεb,35aα); 16:1–14*; 19:17–40*, and so on.[134] Although Veijola and Langlamet each recognized elements of both support and antipathy—thus suggesting an originally anti-Solomonic tractate or pamphlet (to use Vermeylen's image) had been overlaid with pro-Solomonic material—their respective datings comprise the primary point of friction between these two schemas. On the one hand, for Würthwein, the redaction was late-Deuteronomistic, which might be termed "DtrS" in the terminology of Kratz and Fischer. On the other hand, Langlamet considered the redaction to date no later than Hezekiah or Josiah.[135] Each

---

130 Translation NSRV, my italics.

131 See, e.g., Schulte, *Entstehung*, 148–54, esp. 152–54; and Kaiser, "Bebachtungen," 14 (who adds 16:12). Schulte assigned all these passages discrediting the "sons of Zeruiah" to a pre-Deuteronomistic redactor whom one "must locate in chronological proximity [to the original text]" (*Entstehung*, 154).

132 Würthwein, *Erzählung*, 43–47.

133 Idem, *1. Könige 1–16*, 5–6, 20. See also Fischer, *Hebron nach Jerusalem*, 108–116.

134 Langlamet, "Pour ou contra…," 350–56; see also idem, "David et la Maison de Saül: Les épisodes 'benjaminites' de II Sam. ix; xvi, 1–14; xix, 17–31; 1 Rois ii, 36–46," parts 1–5, *RB* 86 (1979): 194–213, 385–436, 481–513; 87 (1980): 161–210; 88 (1981): 321–22; and Timo Veijola, "David und Meribaal," *RB* 85 (1978): 338–61.

135 Ibid., 524–28, esp. here 528. Vermeylen attributes these passages to several different redactional stages: 2 Sam 3:38–39 belong to the "Solomonic Story of David"; 16:10 to the

date effectively denies the possibility of its composition anywhere nearly contemporaneous with the events it purports to describe; nonetheless, in both theories the posited redaction's major thrust is the divine election of Solomon, and the redaction's purpose seems therefore to be to the legitimization of the Davidic lineage.

Both solutions to the problematic date of the redaction strike me as odd. Langlamet's Hezekian dating would, of course, substantiate the claim defended here that the bulk of the SSN—with its schematized flight to and return from Transjordan—had already been compiled by the time Dtr received that source. However, even a date as late as Hezekiah's reign makes little sense from a functionalist standpoint. The crises facing Hezekiah and Josiah were externally-imposed. In neither case was the Davidic monarch in a position in which his throne was threatened from within the community (and would therefore need to be defended by referring the audience to Solomon's legitimacy and deflecting the blame for Solomon's draconian treatment of his rivals onto the scheming Joab). Far more likely, it would seem, is that the need to defend Solomon's legitimacy would have arisen during that monarch's own reign or during the early years of Rehoboam's, in which the legitimacy of Davidic rule over the northern kingdom was ardently challenged and successfully cast off. In other words, *if* there were a "pro-Solomonic" redaction of an earlier "anti-Solomonic" writing—a conclusion of which I am not convinced—its relevance would have diminished as the Davidic lineage became increasingly ensconced in the Judahite power structure. But granted the supposed existence of such a redactional stratum, and the inherence in it of those verses Kaiser adduced as markers of an anti-Joabite redaction (2 Sam 3:38–39; 15:24–26; 16:10[12]; 19:23), then the case becomes all the more compelling that at least 2 Samuel 9–20*; 1 Kgs 1–2* had been brought together sometime before the formation of the DtrH, even if 2 Sam 18:1–2a,4b,6–9,15b–18a formed a very early traditional core of that composition.[136] We might note

"Second Solomonic Edition"; 19:23 to DtrP; and 15:24–26 to Persian Period additions (*Loi du plus fort*, 548–672). This distribution is not convincing, in my mind.

136 This assessment stands in a great deal of agreement with that of Sophia K. Bietenhard, who, following primarily F. Langlamet, argued that 2 Samuel 2–3; 9–20; 1 Kings 1–2 had come together in its basic form already by her S2 edition, well before the work of Dtr (*Des Königs General: Die Heerführertraditionen in der vorstaatlichen und frühen staatlichen Zeit und die Joabgestalt in 2 Sam 2–20; 1 Kön–2* [OBO 163; Fribourg: University Press; Göttingen: Vandenhoeck & Ruprecht, 1998], esp. 250–52, 320–31); and, to some extent, that of Seiler, who dates the SN to the Solomonic period, at least three years into his reign (*Geschichte*, 314–21). Seiler's conclusion is perhaps too optimistic, though, in its assumption of a fairly uniform SN. Cf. Rudnig, who argues for an early redaction encompassing 2 Samuel 10–12*; 1 Kings 1–2, which was placed around the narrative of Absalom's revolt at the time of its inception but into which was introduced the "itinerary" of 2 Samuel 15–19* only at a post-Deuteronomistic level (*Davids Thron*, 334–37).

in addition that Langlamet's secondary "Benjaminite Episodes" in 2 Sam 16:1–14*; 19:17–40* appear to have been overlaid with the "anti-Joabite" materials in 16:10(12) and 19:23. We thus have evidence of the periodic pre-Deuteronomistic development of the SN punctuated by the redactional additions of first "Benjaminite" material and then "anti-Joabite" material. This recognition has direct bearing on where we find the beginning of this expanded CH.

5.3.4. The Beginning of the CH and Its Relationship to the HDR($_2$)

In the previous sections, I argued that Rost's "Succession Narrative" should be divided at least into a "Court History" and the "Solomonic Apology," which supplemented the CH and augmented its meaning to support the reign of Solomon. Accordingly, the CH originally did not include 2 Samuel 10–12*; 1 Kings 1–2*. Moreover, the remaining chapters of the classically-construed SN display indications of a developmental history not easily penetrated, although it would seem the bulk of 2 Sam 15–17*; 18:19–20:25* had coalesced with the earliest battle-report in 18:1–2a,4b,6–9,15b–18a, forming the CH already by the time of the addition of the Solomonic Apology. In this section, I will briefly address the suspicion that the CH did not begin with 2 Sam 6:20b–23, which Rost argued had been used to incorporate the Ark Narrative (AN) into the SN, nor did the CH begin with 2 Samuel 9 (another popular opinion). Instead, I side here with those who find that the beginning of the CH can be traced as far back as 2 Sam 2:8[137] and that the text shows evidence of having been combined with some of the surrounding material at a relatively early stage.

137 See, e.g., M. H. Segal, "The Composition of the Books of Samuel," *JQR* 55 (1964–1965): 318–39, esp. 322–24; Schulte, *Entstehung*, 138–78; Gunn, *Story*, 63–84; Kaiser, "Beobachtungen," 8–15; Bietenhard, *Königs General*, 134; cf., however, Dietrich and Naumann, *Samuelbücher*, 177–79; and Veijola, *Ewige Dynastie*, 94. Rolf Rendtorff argued that the author of 2 Sam 3:6–4:12 may have belonged to the same "circle" (*Kreis*) as the author of the SN ("Beobachtungen zur altisraelitischen Geschichtsschreibung anhand der Geschichte vom Aufstieg Davids," in *Probleme biblischer Theologie: Gerhard von Rad zum 70. Geburtstag* [ed. H. W. Wolff; Munich: Kaiser, 1971], esp. 430–32). Gunn argues that beginning at least from 2:8 or 2:12, "we have...what is generally recognized as a long, coherent, and flowing story of how David came to be in a position to receive the crown of Israel, with only a few passages...that might be considered extraneous...." This small group of about three chapters (chs. 2–4) shares three important stylistic and thematic continuities with 2 Samuel 9–20 + 1 Kings 1–2: "it is relatively extensive and elaborated, its primary focus is upon the characters involved and their inter-relations..., and it makes superb use of direct speech" (*Story*, 67–68). Ackerman seems to follow this delineation, allowing that these scholars "are certainly correct that there are elements in the Court History in 2 Samuel 9–20 and 1 Kings 1–2 that presuppose knowledge of earlier material" ("Knowing Good," 56). Ackerman points out as well that the inclusion of this block of text provides David with

5.3.4.1. The Redactional Resurrection of Mephibosheth

Rost argued an already extant Ark Narrative (comprising 1 Sam 4:1b–18a,19–21; 5:1–11b,12; 6:1–3b,4,10–14,16; 6:19–7:1 + 2 Sam 6:1–15,17–20a) and the core of an old prophecy by Nathan to David (2 Sam 7:11b,16) had been built upon by the Solomonic apologist who connected the bulk of his work (for Rost, 2 Sam 9–20 + 1 Kgs 1–2) to these preexistent texts, using the Michal passage in 2 Sam 6:20b–23.[138] We may permit a date prior to Solomon's reign for the composition and circulation of the bulk of the Ark Narrative (with Rost), but it is quite likely that 1 Samuel 4–7 originally stood quite separate from its "ending" in 2 Samuel 6. The latter section was composed later with the original tradition at hand and with the memory of David's transfer of the ark to Jerusalem in the background.[139] While we must ultimately reject an original connection between the AN and the CH for reasons to be discussed below (see further, §6.5.2), we must acknowledge that 2 Samuel 9 forms an awkward and illogical beginning to the latter document.[140] In this chapter, neither David nor Jonathan receives an introduction commensurate with the beginning of a narrative:

> ויאמר דוד הכי יש־עוד אשׁר נותר לבית שׂאול ואעשׂה עמו חסד בעבור יהונתן
> And David said, "Is there yet anyone remaining of the House of Saul for whom I may perform *ḥesed* on behalf of Jonathan?" (2 Sam 9:1).[141]

---

further moral pretext for ordering Joab's execution in 1 Kgs 2:5, since Joab's brutal murder of Abner takes place in 2 Sam 3:26–27, an action itself predicated on Abner's slaying of Joab's brother Asahel in 2 Sam 2:18–23. Sacon has argued through a study of smaller literary elements, mostly what he calls "micro-contextual narrative patterns," that the boundaries of the traditional SN should be pushed forward to include 2 Samuel 2–4 as well ("Literary Structure," 30–31, 44–47, 52). These "micro-contextual narrative patterns" include "various types of repetition of words and sentences constituting inclusio, chiasmus, or concentric structure." I have excluded 3:12–16 as redactional elements below (see §6.5.2). For a recent challenge to the conventional interpretation of 2 Samuel 2–5, see Alexander A. Fischer, *Von Hebron nach Jerusalem: Eine redaktionsgeschichtliche Studie zur Erzählung von König David in II Sam 1–5* (BZAW 335; Berlin: de Gruyter, 2004).

138 Rost, *Succession*, 6–64.

139 See, e.g., Patrick D. Miller, Jr. and J. J. M. Roberts, *The Hand of the Lord: A Reassessment of the "Ark Narrative" of 1 Samuel* (JHNES; Baltimore: The Johns Hopkins University Press, 1977; repr., Atlanta: SBL, 2008), 34–35. Miller and Roberts allow for an early dating for the narrative's core (ibid., 93–94) but give no explicit notice of an exact point at which the ending in 2 Samuel 6 may have been crafted to fit the extant portion of the narrative.

140 Schulte, *Entstehung*, 139. The relationship of 2 Samuel 7–8 to the CH is difficult and will not be addressed here. For a detailed discussion of ch. 7 and its interpretations subsequent to that of Rost, see McCarter, *II Samuel*, 209–31. The length of McCarter's comment is indicative of the complexity of the issue. Rost did not include ch. 8 in his SN, and the chapter is not normally included in subsequent studies of that document.

141 I take *ḥesed* here (as elsewhere) to mean something along the lines of "covenant loyalty." For discussions of the "love" between David and Jonathan in 2 Sam 18:1 as political terminology, see below, p. 241, n. 58.

Shortly, Ziba introduces Mephibosheth, the Saulide heir, to David in vv. 3–4 as the son of Jonathan, even though the reader has been informed of Mephibosheth's existence in 4:4:[142]

> ויאמר ציבא אל־המלך עוד בן ליהונתן נכה רגלים...הנה־הוא בית־מכיר בן־עמיאל בלו דבר (9:3b, 4bβ)
>
> And Ziba said to the king, "There is yet a son of Jonathan's, handicapped in the legs, . . . who is in the home of Machir ben-Ammiel in Lo-debar."

While this introduction to Mephibosheth remains integral to the larger SN (including the Benjaminite episodes in 2 Sam 16:1–14*; 19:17–40*; etc.), Veijola has shown convincingly, in my opinion, that the addition of 9:1,7b, 10aβγb,11b,13 (as well as the phrase [בן־/בעבור] יהונתן [אביך] in vv. 6,7a and the emendation of a hypothesized original לשאול to ליהונתן in v. 3) occurred as part of a larger redactional reworking of the Succession Narrative.[143] This redaction encompassed at least 1 Sam 20:12–17,42b; 23:16–18; 24:18–23a; 2 Sam 4:2b–4; 9:1,3*,6*,7a*,7b,10aβγb,11b,13; 19:29; 21:2b,7, and was most likely attributable to DtrG.[144] For the most part, this division is presupposed in the present study. With the omission of 9:1 from the *Grundbestand*, the unsuitability of 9:2 to serve as the opening of a narrative complex brings into sharper relief the necessity of tracing the beginning of the CH earlier in 2 Samuel. In terms of the continuity of theme, the original narrative of 2 Samuel 9* demands the recent cataclysmic demise of the Saulide family as a backdrop against which David's offer to "perform *ḥesed*" stands in sharp contrast.

Along with others holding a similar position, McCarter argued that 2 Samuel 9 presupposes David's slaughter of the remaining Saulides at the behest of the Gibeonites in 2 Sam 21:1–14 most expediently, since 9:1

---

142 Ziba is introduced naturally in v. 2 (ולבית שׁאול עבד ושׁמו ציבא), but this is expected since he has not yet appeared in Samuel. See, e.g., Kaiser, who argues that the story in 2 Samuel 9 conveys all the information needed without reference to 4:4 ("Beobachtungen," 10–11; cf. McCarter, *II Samuel*, 260). We should appreciate Ackroyd's assessment that even if 4:4 is an insertion, the narrative style with which it was incorporated shows skill on the part of the narrator ("Succession Narrative," 389).

143 Veijola, "David und Meribaal," 344–49.

144 Ibid., esp. 360–61. Veijola concludes that it is historically unlikely that David's desire to include Mephibosheth in his court was an innocent display of favor. Had Mephibosheth actually existed, the move to bring Mephibosheth into the court would most likely have been motivated as a way to keep him under control; see also, e.g., John Bright (*A History of Israel* [4th ed.; Louisville, Ky.: Westminster John Knox, 2000], 208); and Leo G. Perdue, who regards this as one reading of the text, while at the same time pointing to the latent ambiguity of David's motivations ("'Is There Anyone Left of the House of Saul...?' Ambiguity and the Characterization of David in the Succession Narrative," *JSOT* 30 [1984]: 72, 75). Cf. McCarter, who argues that David's actions here are only honorable—even if it *did* benefit David to have Mephibosheth within arm's reach (*II Samuel*, 265). However, this solution is proposed along with McCarter's concomitant juxtaposition of 2 Samuel 21; see below.

"implies that Saul's house is threatened with extinction, not merely that one Saulid [i.e., Ishbosheth], however prominent, has died."[145] However, Veijola's redaction-critical division of 2 Samuel 9 served already to divorce that chapter from 2 Samuel 21*. Although it is not impossible that both a son and a grandson of Saul bore the same name,[146] there are indications even within 2 Samuel 9–20 that the Mephibosheth of the CH was not Jonathan's son, but Saul's. Veijola pointed to two passages of the CH (outside of ch. 9) in which Mephibosheth is mentioned.[147] In the first, David asks Ziba, "And where is the son of your master?" (ואיה בן־אדניך; 2 Sam 16:3). Since Ziba had served as *Saul's* steward during that monarch's lifetime, the clear implication of this verse is that Mephibosheth was Saul's child. In the second, David is greeted upon his return from Transjordan by Mephibosheth, who is there explicitly called "son of Saul" (מפבשת בן־שאול; 19:25).[148] It is possible, of course, that both of these

145 McCarter, *II Samuel*, 263–65, 443; idem, *I Samuel: A New Translation with Introduction and Commentary* (AB 8; Garden City, N.Y.: Doubleday, 1980), 263. For this interpretation, see also Karl Budde, *Die Bücher Samuel* (KHC 8; Tübingen: Mohr, 1902), 244, 304–7; Hans Wilhelm Hertzberg, *I & II Samuel: A Commentary* (OTL; trans. John S. Bowden; London: SCM, 1964; repr., Philadelphia: Westminster, n.d.), 299, 381; Carlson, *David*, 198–203; and George Auzou, *La danse devant l'arche: Étude du livre de Samuel* (ConBib 6; Paris: Éditions de l'orante, 1968), 363–69, esp. 364–65.

146 Cf. McCarter, *II Samuel*, 124–25. The name of Mephibosheth requires much interpretation; it is probably derived from מִפִּי בַּעַל ("From the Mouth of Baal"), as its Greek reflex throughout LXX[L] would attest (μεμφιβααλ/μεμφειβααλ; cf. μεμφιβοσθε of LXX[B]). But the same son of Jonathan goes by a different name in 1 Chr 9:40 (מְרִי־בַעַל) and 8:34 (מְרִיב בַּעַל); cf. LXX μαρειβααλ/μεριβααλ. *Tg. Jon.* reads מפיבשת in all cases in 2 Samuel and is therefore unhelpful. For discussion of these names, see McCarter (ibid., 128). The former would mean "Rebelliousness of Baal" and the latter "One who contends with Baal," both intended insultingly, although it is not entirely clear that בעל was intended to indicate a deity other than Yahweh (J. Andrew Dearman, "Baal in Israel: The Contribution of Some Place Names and Personal Names to an Understanding of Early Israelite Religion," in *History and Interpretation: Essays in Honour of John H. Hayes* [JSOTSup 173; Sheffield: Sheffield Academic Press, 1993], 189; Gordon J. Hamilton, "New Evidence for the Authenticity of *bšt* in Hebrew Personal Names and for Its Use as a Divine Epithet in Biblical Texts," *CBQ* 60 [1998]: 237; Richard S. Hess, *Israelite Religions: An Archaeological and Biblical Survey* [Grand Rapids, Mich.: Baker, 2007], 242–43). McCarter suggests alternatively מֵרִיב בַּעַל ("The lord [Yahweh] is advocate") or מְרִי־בַעַל ("The lord [Yahweh] is my master"). McCarter takes the alternation as a sign of two different characters whose identities have been confused: a son of Saul by his concubine Rizpah, Mephibosheth/Mephibaal (2 Sam 21:8), and the son of Jonathan, Meribbaal (the Mephibosheth of 2 Sam 4:4; 9; 16; 19; and 21:7a). The confusion, then, occurred because of the presence of Rizpah in both 2 Sam 3:7 and 21:8,10–11, such that "the name Mephibosheth/Mippibaal is shuffled onto a son of Jonathan with a similar sounding name, Meri(b)baal" (*II Samuel*, 125). I find McCarter's argument quite difficult. The obvious confusion with respect to the paternity of Mephibosheth requires a more adequate solution.

147 Veijola, *Ewige Dynastie*, 108 n. 14; idem, "David und Meribaal," 338–61.

148 Cf. the harmonizing readings of Syr., "Mephibosheth son of Jonathan, son of Saul" (*wmpybšt br ywntn br š'wl*) and of LXX, "Mephibosheth son of the son of Saul" (μεμφιβοσθε υιος υιου

remarks refer to Mephibosheth's status as a *descendant*, rather than a son, of Saul. But the confusion posed by the various passages surrounding the appearances of Mephibosheth suggests something more is at stake. Over the course of these appearances the following situation arises:

(a) In the CH outside of ch. 9, Mephibosheth appears to be Saul's son (16:3; 19:25).
(b) In the CH in ch. 9, Mephibosheth is reckoned as Jonathan's son (9:3).
(c) Throughout the CH, Mephibosheth's situation and actions are those of the last remaining Saulide.
(d) 2 Sam 21:7 (like 9:3) reckons Mephibosheth as Jonathan's son.
(e) 2 Sam 21:8 (like 16:3 and 19:25) recognizes Mephibosheth to be Saul's child.
(f) However, 21:8—in opposition to the situation obtaining in the CH—affirms the existence of several *other* Saulides.
(g) The text of 2 Sam 21:7 is linked to 9:1–3*, as well as to 1 Sam 20:11–17,23,40–42; 23:16–18.

Out of this textual tangle, Veijola was able to demonstrate decisively that only *one* Mephibosheth existed in the original text—Mephibosheth ben-Saul—and that 2 Sam 21:7 was a redactional insertion designed only to alleviate the tension between the secondary redactional stratum recalling David's oath to Jonathan (comprising, in my judgment, 1 Sam 20:11–17, 23,40–42; 23:16–18; 2 Sam 4:4; 9:1,3 [לשאול → ליהונתן],6* [בן־יהונתן],7a* [בעבור יהונתן אביך],7b,10aβγb,11b,13; 19:29) and the notice in 21:8 that Mephibosheth ben-Saul was one of the seven Saulides given over to the Gibeonites to satisfy his father's blood-guilt.[149] Veijola argued, therefore, that 2 Samuel 21 necessarily followed 2 Samuel 9 sequentially, since Mephibosheth could not be killed in 21:8 only to appear as the object of David's grace in 9:6–11.[150] But Veijola's sequential solution, which he did not extrapolate to its full extent, poses problems as well: specifically, it does not take into consideration the varying levels of familiarity David exhibits in each chapter with the location of the Saulides.

Rost long ago pointed to this discrepancy in the context of his refutation of Budde's rearrangement (2 Samuel 21:1–14 + 9:1–13),[151] and the argument works just as effectively against the overly-simplistic sequentiality apparently espoused by Veijola (2 Sam 9:1–13* + 21:1–6*,8–14). Rost argued the two chapters diverged dramatically in their respective presentations of the character of David. In 2 Sam 9:1, David must ask

---

σαουλ). The textual variation, while not direct evidence of intentional emendation one way or the other, provides witness to the confusion occasioned by two "different" Mephibosheths.

149 Veijola, "David und Meribaal," 338–61; see earlier idem, *Ewige Dynastie*, 108. My delineation of the redaction here omits a few of Veijola's claimed passages (e.g., 2 Sam 4:2b–3; 21:2b). For further discussion of redactional work in 2 Samuel 21, see below, §6.6.

150 Veijola, "David und Meribaal," 353.

151 Rost, *Succession*, 65–66; see also Langlamet, "Maison de Saül," part 1, 204–6.

Ziba the whereabouts of any remaining Saulides, but by 21:1–14* he has evidently learned the location of six others. It does not seem enough to explain David's ignorance in ch. 9 as coyness, however: while the text does not explicitly state whether Mephibosheth was the *only* remaining descendent of Saul, we must explain why Ziba would not have presented the other seven remaining descendants of Saul noted in 21:8. Assuming he took David's offer to do *ḥesed* for the remaining Saulide(s) at face value, might we argue that Ziba especially favored Mephibosheth and wanted him alone to inherit Saul's property? Or perhaps Ziba—who for some reason bore a grudge against Mephibosheth—perceived David's offer as a thinly veiled death sentence and sought to get rid of the young heir by divulging his hiding place in Transjordan? This latter suggestion would explain the battle of deception waged by Ziba and Mephibosheth against one another in the following chapters at the synchronic level (2 Sam 16:1–4; 19:25–31). Unfortunately, the text does not provide an explicit motivation of Ziba's deliverance of his deceased master's descendant, and any explanation we might provide for the steward's omission of the other six Saulides is conjectural at best. But the fact that David evidently knows exactly where to find these Saulides in 2 Samuel 21 suggests Ziba *should* have known as well and, for whatever reason, does not say. One might argue that, within the literary horizon of ch. 9, Ziba himself does not know where (or whether) other Saulides might be found. But that he would have no knowledge of his master's living children is a difficult assumption to make: would Saul's major-domo not have known the fate of the other son of Saul by Rizpah (Armoni) or of Saul's five grandsons through Merab, who were most likely to be found living rather openly in the court of the well-known Barzillai, their grandfather (see, e.g., 1 Sam 18:19; 2 Sam 21:8)?

The reason for Ziba's reticence or inability to disclose the location of the remaining Saulides, I suggest, is as follows: Ziba *does not* know where Saul's remaining descendants (other than Mephibosheth ben-Saul) were in hiding precisely because no other Saulide dynasts existed in the literary horizon of the extended CH and its constituent traditions, in which ch. 9 plays a dominant role in the characterization of David's relationship to the remaining household of the Saulide dynasty. This conclusion then demands that we divorce 2 Samuel 9 and the rest of the CH from 2 Samuel 21, which—in the span of one original verse (v. 8)—lists nine members of Saul's court (Rizpah and her two sons, and Merab and her five sons). Thus, we may in fact agree with McCarter's assessment, cited above, that 2 Samuel 9 is concerned with the extinction of the Saulide dynasty without subscribing to his evaluation of 2 Samuel 21 as the necessary precursor to ch. 9. Rather, the concern of 2 Samuel 9 is not merely with the deaths of

Ishbosheth and Abner but presumably with the multiple deaths of the dynasty ensuing from the battle with the Philistines at Gilboa: both Saul and the presumptive heir Jonathan die (2 Sam 1:4–5,12,17,22–23,26; also 1 Sam 31:2), as do Saul's other sons Abinadab and Malki-shua (1 Sam 31:2).[152] This devastation is merely compounded by the ensuing deaths of Abner (3:27) and Ishbosheth (4:6–7). After 2 Samuel 4, we hear nothing more of any of Saul's household (other than Mephibosheth) until 2 Samuel 21.[153]

These difficulties can be solved adequately through the following reconstruction: the two texts, the first from the extended CH and fleshed out with the Benjaminite episodes, and the other from 2 Sam 21:1–6*,8–14*, originally existed independently of one another. In both, Mephibosheth was a son of Saul. In the source from which 21:1–6*,8–14* was drawn, David executes the hapless Mephibosheth along with several relatives (v. 8). As a story of the elimination of rivals to the throne, 2 Samuel 21 would provide a fitting conclusion to a hypothetical History of David's Rise (provisionally, HDR_1), in which David's concern over Yahweh's punishment of Saul's breaking of covenant loyalty against the Gibeonites (21:1b) becomes the pretext for the elimination of the remaining members of the Saulide lineage. This action is comparable to Jehu's slaughter of the remaining Omrides in 2 Kgs 10:1–11, itself justified through Jehu's devotion to Yahweh (vv. 15–27). In the other source (the CH), Mephibosheth also figured originally as the son of Saul (2 Sam 9:2,3* [with לשאול],4–5, 6*,7a*,8–10aα,11a,12; see also 16:3a). Only with extreme difficulty could we argue that this textual complex ever began with the circumstantial phrase introducing 9:2 (ולבית שאול עבד ושמו ציבא); instead, the chapter must have followed immediately on an event that would precipitate v. 3. That event, as suggested above, must have been the combined Saulide deaths of 2 Samuel 2:8–4:12*, the entirety of which at least presupposes the deaths of Saul and Jonathan in 2 Samuel 1, although it does not neces-

152 The importance of this battle in dividing the two Histories of David's Rise will become apparent below (§6.4–5). For now, it is enough to point out that Jonathan appears in one (the HDR_1; 1 Samuel 31) as only one child of three, the other two of whom we have never yet heard. In the other (HDR_2; 2 Samuel 1), he is the only son of Saul mentioned, and thereby becomes the focal point around whom the narrative revolves. This vast variation in the position of Jonathan will be a major criterion upon which to base the division. As Gunn notes, Ishbosheth is only the *last* Saulide to die who had any political standing and whose whereabouts was known (*Story*, 68).

153 See §6.5.2. Both of Michal's appearances in 2 Sam 3:12–16 and 6:20–23 show signs of being redactional units designed to unite two complexes of materials. Rizpah's position in 2 Sam 3:7 may be the result of a fabrication on the part of the author of the CH, who had the tradition preserved in 2 Samuel 21 at hand. It would have been simple enough for the author of the CH to invent a reason for the dispute between Abner and Ishbosheth, inserting Saul's concubine Rizpah into the role of the *casus belli*.

sarily require us to assume that 2 Samuel 1 was firmly connected to the CH at its earliest stage.[154]

After the combination of these two variant textual complexes (2 Sam 21* over against 2 Sam 2:8–4:12* + 9*; etc.), the father-son relationship between Saul and Mephibosheth was effaced or obfuscated when an editor harmonized these traditions with a series of redactional insertions recasting Mephibosheth as an otherwise unknown son of Jonathan and utilizing that character as the object of David's grace (comprising ca. 1 Sam 20:11–17,23,40–42; 23:16–18; 2 Sam 4:4; 9:1,3 [לשאול → ליהונתן],6* [בן־יהונתן],7a* [בעבור יהונתן אביך],7b,10aβγb,11b,13; 19:29; 21:7). In short, the literary apparition named Mephibosheth ben-Jonathan serves in both complexes—now interwoven—as the vehicle whereby David fulfills his oath sworn to Jonathan. Both this oath-motif and a series of anti-Joabite diatribes (2 Sam 3:38–39; 15:24–26; 16:10[12]; 19:23) have been attributed to DtrG (= Dtr^1?) with good cause.[155] The interweaving of the two textual complexes is thus at latest a Deuteronomistic innovation, although it may be earlier, if the evidence suggesting the overarching work of an early Prophetic Record is not ignored.

5.4. The Development of 2 Samuel: A Sketch

5.4.1. Stages of Development: A Retrospective Glance

Although a thorough investigation of the relationship between the developing SSN and the PR is not possible in the context of the present study, I have now sketched enough of the extended CH's macrostructure to make a plausible conjecture that it achieved a relatively early skeleton comprising at least 2 Samuel 2–4*+ 9*+ 11:1–12:25* + 13–20* + 1 Kgs 1–2* already at a pre-Deuteronomistic node of its development, for it is throughout these chapters that the various overlays of redactional insertions commonly attributed to DtrG have been made. Moreover, if my assignment of 12:1–15a* to the PR is accurate, then a complex extending already at least through 11:1–12:25* + 15:1–37* + 16:15–19:16*; (20*) + 1 Kgs 1–2* was possibly intact as early as the late-9th cent., but at least by

154 Frolov, "Succession Narrative," 95.

155 Similarly, Kaiser has argued for the beginning of the CH at 2 Sam 2:8 on the basis of a network of pro-Davidic insertions in 2 Sam 1:10–11a; 4:10–11a; 1 Kings 1:29b; and 2:31b–33 ("Beobachtungen," 11–12). Although the text does not read entirely smoothly when these omissions have been made, Kaiser's composition-critical argument was primarily directed at refuting Van Seters's extreme late dating of the CH, and it may thus require some additional refinement before total agreement is warranted.

the mid-8th cent. Tracing this complex's development back further, the excision of the Solomonic Apology in 11:1–12:25* + 1 Kgs 1–2* leaves a somewhat schematic Transjordanian exile of David in ca. 15:1–37* + 16:15–19:16*; (20*). If we follow several recent Continental commentators, this itinerary could itself be a secondary elaboration of an original short battle report in 13:1–29,34a,37aβ,38b–39; 14:33aβγb; 15:1–6,13; 18:1–2a,4b,6–9,15b–18. In chronological order then, a rough outline of the development of 2 Samuel might be schematized as such:

(a) The earliest kernel of tradition was an early, concise battle report (ca. 13:1–29,34a,37aβ,38b–39; 14:33aβγb; 15:1–6,13; 18:1–2a,4b,6–9,15b–18bα).[156]

(b) The battle report was elaborated by the addition of a "Transjordanian Exile" framework, such that the text now encompassed 15:1–37* + 16:15–19:16*; (20*).

(c) The addition of a Solomonic Apology (SA) comprising 2 Sam 11:1–27*; 12:15b–25*; 1 Kings 1–2* brought about a change in the function of the document, which now for the first time may legitimately be termed a "Solomonic Succession Narrative" (SSN)

(d) The addition of a series of so-called "Benjaminite episodes" (2 Samuel 2–4*; 9*; 16:1–14*; 19:17–41* but *not* including 2 Samuel 21) was introduced into the SSN.

(e) At some point, a prophetic redactor added 2 Sam 12:1–15a*. Further sets of additions followed, spanning larger textual complexes: a system of connections interlacing several "Jonathan" narratives of 1 Samuel with the "Mephibosheth ben-Jonathan" passages of 2 Samuel (e.g., 1 Sam 20:11–17,23,40–42; 23:16–18; 2 Sam 4:4; 9:1,3*,6*,7a*,7b,10aβγb,11b,13; 19:29; 21:7), a network of anti-Joabite insertions (2 Sam 3:38–39; 15:24–26; 16:10[12]; [18:2b–4a,10–15a,19–32; 19:1–9]; 19:23),[157] and possibly a complex of insertions arguing for the sanctity of the Lord's anointed (2 Sam 1:10–11a; 4:10–11a; 1 Kings 1:29b; and 2:31b–33).

The exact order of these sets of additions in stage (e) is not accessible at this juncture, but the span over which they are introduced indicates at least two significant observations to be made. First, the "Jonathan" and "Mephibosheth ben-Jonathan" passages point to the thematic linkages already established between several passages in the History of David's Rise and the SSN. Secondly, they indicate the interpolation of an entirely different tradition (or, as will be seen below, *set* of traditions) that did not share the same characters or same explicit concerns with the SSN but is present in 2 Samuel 21*. A closer examination of the ideological thrust of a few of these stages will illuminate this discrepancy.

156 With, e.g., Kratz, *Composition*, 175–76; Fischer, "Flucht und Heimkehr," 43–69; Aurelius, "David's Unschuld," 396–400.

157 See, e.g. Langlamet, "Maison de Saül," part 3, 482–85.

5.4.2. The Date and Function of Each Stage

It was suggested above that the SSN (stage [c]) had as one of its functions the legitimization of Solomon at least in its earliest instantiation. We might begin now to flesh out that suggestion a bit further. The insertion of the so-called Benjaminite episodes presupposes a historical milieu in which the Davidic dynasty was attempting to secure its grasp over the area formerly ruled by the Saulide dynasty. Presumably, this area was Benjamin but may have comprised the larger Israelite hill-country, consolidated into a single—but quite heterogeneous—polity. The insurgence to which the SSN was immediately addressed was probably fueled by reminiscence of the Saulide dynasty so harshly dealt with by David and Solomon (commemorated in two sets of traditions, one comprising 2 Samuel 21 and the other ch. 20 and 1 Kgs 2:36–44*). Although the SSN (which now explained why Solomon had gained the kingship, as opposed to any other of David's sons) had been built on a Court History of David, neither the CH nor the expanded SSN could adequately address the issue of the Saulide counter-movement on its own. The document (SSN) therefore had to be grounded philosophically on yet another text that provided a much more explicit discussion of why David's family, and not Jonathan's, ruled over the northern tribes.

The theological foundation of the anti-Saulide sentiment wanting in the SSN was to be found in an idealistic History of David's Rise in which the onus of the action fell on only a few characters. This document specifically featured David's friendship with Jonathan as its primary vehicle for the transfer of the kingdom to the Judahite monarch (see below, §6.4). This ideational History of David's Rise (provisionally the HDR_2) provided an adequate basis for the desired anti-Saulide thrust of the (at first) loosely-conjoined HDR_2 + SSN complex. It shared with the SSN a few major characters—David, Saul, and Abner—and the SSN was easily grafted onto the HDR_2 through the relatively minor redactional addition of the Benjaminite episodes and the addition of 2 Samuel 9 in particular. These relatively minor additions served to solidify the already substantial narrative connections between the HDR_2 and SSN (characters, etc.), while at the same time producing a large complex of traditions that defended the kingship of Solomon (and therefore the kingship of his son Rehoboam) against the charges leveled by rabble-rousers of the north, modeling themselves on figures such as Shimei and Sheba. This developing text would have carried the greatest degree of political cachet around the time of Solomon's death and Rehoboam's accession.[158] It narrated events that

158 For this suggestion, see Tadmor, "Autobiographical Apology," 36–57; and above, §4.2.

had purportedly taken place as long as eight decades before, but the fracturing of the kingdom during the early part of Rehoboam's reign and the centrifugal return of many non-Judahite elements to their segmentary social structures not only prove a need for a Solomonic defense of Davidic legitimacy but also suggest the Judahite court's attempt at political apology ultimately failed.

I hypothesize that the later unification of these two large narrative complexes (HDR_1 and HDR_2 + SSN) was apparently occasioned by the circumstances surrounding the formation of the PR, which sought either to legitimize Jehu's rule over Israel (in the late-9th cent.) or to anticipate the downfall of the Jehuite dynasty because of a failure to maintain "religious purity" (as late as mid-8th cent.). In either case, those who wanted or needed to legitimize Jehu's overthrow of the Omride dynasty had to prove first of all that it was Jehu, rather than one of the scores of Omride dynasts (2 Kgs 10:1), whom Yahweh had nominated to rule the north. This proof was accomplished by the gathering of independent and disparate prophetic materials in support of Jehu and in opposition to the validity of the Omrides' claims to the throne. But secondly, the Jehuite apology had to justify the separation of Israel from Judah in the first place. Here, the addition of a tradition concerning the prophetic legitimization of Jeroboam's revolt against Solomon (1 Kgs 11:29–39*), along with a prophetic denunciation of Solomon's paternity (2 Sam 12:1–15a) to the already extant Solomonic materials (HDR_2 + SSN), enabled the redactors to recast Solomon's reign in a negative light without changing a single word of the extant SSN. Solomon's biographer had attempted to portray the king in the best light possible at the time. However, the intervening years of Davidic oppression of the north (registered in the complaints to Rehoboam in 1 Kings 12) and of continual factional struggle between the two kingdoms added a patina of disgrace to the figure of Solomon presented in his own Apology. Herein lies the solution to the variation between the respective *Tendenzen* of both the PR and the SSN: without needing to change a word of the developing SSN structure itself, the framework around the SSN could indicate prophetic disappointment in the Solomonic reign, justifying the schism brought about by Jeroboam's rebellion. Although the SSN had been pro-Solomonic originally, its inclusion in the PR (and the PR's concomitant vilification of Solomon) cast a shadow over the figure of Solomon, who had appeared ruthless enough at the time of his accession.

No matter the process of its formation, the SSN's function may be understood with reference to Hittite and Assyrian royal apologetic documents of similar form. For some scholars, the perceived negative portrayal of Nathan and Bathsheba's coup suggests that the Solomonic "apologist" was not an apologist at all, but rather was trying to indict the king as a fraud and a scoundrel, a despot whose usurpation of the throne was falsely justified by public reports of a Davidic promise that had never been made and that was concocted in a back-room deal between the prophet Nathan and the king's mother, who felt her own position in the court threatened.[159] For others, the political coup and deception of the ailing David launched by Solomon was justified as a necessary action taken to maintain the unity of the kingdom.[160] Insofar as the SSN exemplifies the genre of ancient Near Eastern royal apology, it provides a rationalization for the deceptive practices of Solomon's court officials and explains them as real-life actions performed not out of malice but as an attempt to stabilize an inherently unstable political situation. In short, apology attempts to come to grips with admittedly unsavory political realities—the dirt and grit of everyday life.

If Tadmor is correct in his assertion that the autobiographical apology of Esarhaddon was the product of royalist attempts to secure a peaceful transition of power from the Assyrian monarch to his son Assurbanipal—again, a crown-prince whose reign was unexpected by the norms established by primogeniture—we may propose an analogous second (and perhaps equally important) function that the author/redactor of the SSN had in mind: namely, the smooth transition of Judahite power over Israel from Solomon to his son Rehoboam. The further developing SSN, with the addition of the Benjaminite episodes, apparently attempted to hold in check a socio-political situation in which the remaining members of Saul's Benjaminite clan challenged the legitimacy of the Davidic lineage. Signs of this contention between the two dynastic houses are myriad. For instance, we may point to the military engagement between the Saulides and Davidides (2 Sam 2:12–28), the attempts of the Davidide court to present a favorably-portrayed alternative version of the king's dealings with Mephibosheth (2 Sam 9:1–13*), the charges leveled at David by Shimei (2 Sam 16:5–8), the call of Sheba for a separation, "everyone to his tent, O Israel" (איש לאהליו ישראל; 2 Sam 20:1)[161]—which is mirrored by Jeroboam's cry in 1 Kgs 12:16—and finally, the narrative of David's treatment of the remainder of Saul's house (2 Sam 21:8–9).[162]

159 See above, n. 72.

160 E.g., Ishida, "Solomon's Succession," 166–73; McCarter, "'Plots, True or False," 364–67.

161 Frolov ("Succession Narrative," 99) astutely points to the irony of this cry of rebellion, which echoes the earlier military failures of Israel in which the army fled, "every one to his tent" (2 Sam 18:17; 19:9).

162 McCarter (*II Samuel*, 263–65, 443) has argued that this episode originally served as the precursor to David's "rescue" of Mephibosheth, but this solution is both unnecessary (since that pericope only assumes the death of Saul and Jonathan) and untenable (because the

S. Frolov has argued that one of the episodes detailing this internecine struggle for power—namely, Shimei's murder in 1 Kgs 2:39–46—clears the way for the consolidation of power within the Davidic household, but he claims that this function of the story operates despite the fact that "Saul's dynasty is never presented as a feasible alternative to David and his perverse and rebellious brood."[163] Frolov concludes from Shimei's remarks in 2 Sam 16:7–8 that Shimei welcomed the reign of Absalom (over against that of David) and therefore had no objections to David's dynasty, only to David himself. Similarly, he argues, the claim of Ziba that Mephibosheth desired the kingdom (2 Sam 16:3) turns out to be false,[164] proving that the Saulides did not consider themselves a viable alternative to the Davidic dynasty.[165] For Frolov, "Shimei's failure even to mention the possibility that Saul's house might be restored to the throne speaks volumes about the author's mindset."[166] I concur that this is the case but that the "volumes" spoken about the author's mindset are not the indications Frolov hears. The act of placing the composition of the whole during the period of Dtr, as Frolov does, naturally foists an unimpeachably pro-Davidic stance on the author; history had borne out the success of the Davidic dynasty, at least through the period under investigation. But if we recognize—*contra* Frolov—the early composition of the PR and the inherence of the SSN within it, we recognize a less absolutized reading of the Benjaminite episodes. Written at a time in which the Saulide dynasty (and its congeners) may still have held some degree of social stature, the Davidide defensive documents could do naught but outright deny the recognized legitimacy of any perceived Benjaminite contenders. Frolov's excessively literalistic argument that not even the Saulides recognized their own dynastic legitimacy thus fails to take into account the theologizing tendencies of the text, reifying the speech of the characters (an action which can, admittedly, be fruitful in a synchronic study of the text) and neglecting the historically-conditioned reading that the establishment of a diachronically oriented reading of the text demands. While the theological truth of the various characters' speeches was eventually proved by the contingencies of history (and thus served as programmatic and normative for the Deuteronomistic compiler)—and despite the apparent dearth of any recognition of a real Saulide threat—there remains some indication that

mention of Mephibosheth in 2 Sam 21:7 is redactional rather than necessary to the plot; see below, §6.6).

163 Frolov, "Succession Narrative," 99–100.

164 This tends to be the predominant reading of historical critics, but cf. recently Jeremy Schipper, "'Why Do You Still Speak of Your Affairs?' Polyphony in Mephibosheth's Exchanges with David in 2 Samuel," *VT* 54 (2004): 344–51.

165 Frolov, "Succession Narrative," 100.

166 Ibid., 100 n. 58.

this presentation of the text is indeed idealist. The ambiguity of Mephibosheth's protestations points to a situation in which the *threat* of Mephibosheth's legitimacy to the throne was real—even if the literary character were now only a figuration of northern anti-Davidic sentiments as a whole.[167] Therefore, the narrative recollection of Mephibosheth's speech would necessarily have had to support some Davidic claim to the throne. Whether that mimesis was intended to be historically accurate is irrelevant. The SSN was composed as a document whose ideational power structure was threatened and potentially compromised. Consequently, David's embattled flight to and successful return from Transjordan—whether historically accurate or not—inaugurated a new expression of the Transjordanian Motif.

167 Schipper, "Polyphony," 344–51.

6. The Mystery of the History of David's Rise

6.1. The Manifold Problems of the HDR

In the previous chapter, I discussed the composition of the Solomonic Succession Narrative (SSN), its reconstructable function(s) during the waning years of the United Monarchy as well as the early stages of the Divided Monarchy (until the reign of Jehu), and its relationship to the later History of David's Rise (HDR_2). In the process, I referred to two Histories of David's Rise: an earlier, more historical form (HDR_1)[1] and a later, more intentionally sculpted form (HDR_2). In this context, I presented the SSN as intimately associated with the latter, grounding its initially pro-Solomonic sentiments in the pro-Davidic and anti-Saulide thrust of the HDR_2, while utilizing a fabricated motif of the fulfillment of the vow of friendship between David and Jonathan—instantiated in the figure of Mephibosheth—as the vehicle of the transfer of monarchic legitimacy between the two families. These two complexes of traditions concerning the interactions of David and Saul were woven together only *after* the independent coagulation of the larger complexes consisting of (a) the Narratives of Saul's Rise (NSR_{AB}) and the earlier History of David's Rise (HDR_1; see §7.4) and (b) the later History of David's Rise and the Court History/ Succession Narrative complex (HDR_2 + SSN).

The present chapter investigates several problematic aspects of the HDR. In the following section (§6.2) appears a discussion of the nature of the text's doublets as the product of a process whereby two originally independent collections of traditions were intertwined. Both collections initially supported the Davidic family over against the Saulide government. This understanding of the History of David's Rise is, in some respects, a combination of the two major models for understanding the first book of Samuel since the late-19th cent. CE: the conjoined-documents model

1 My designation of this version as "more historical" should not be taken as an assertion that this version was entirely reliable historically. Most of the episodes are, at the very least, unverifiable (e.g., David's marriage to Michal) and, for the most part, probably legendary (e.g., David's slaying of Goliath). For the purposes of this study, my designation of the HDR_1 as the "more historical" of the two should be taken to mean that the author composed the piece with the intention to create a document that spoke to its original audience in a manner that purported to address its contemporary situation by providing an apology for David's reign.

(§6.2.1) and the loose-collection-of-materials model (§6.2.2). However, the observations of the first model have, to the best of my knowledge, never been adequately incorporated into a system consistent with the bulk of the observations made by L. Rost and those who have followed him in arguing for a loose collection of traditional materials comprising a single History of David's Rise, over against the more monolithic Succession Narrative. A fully detailed discussion of this interweaving of the textual traditions would be superfluous here, since none of our Transjordanian texts falls within the scope of the HDR, generally recognized to extend from ca. 1 Samuel 16–2 Samuel 5 or 6.[2] Instead, a basic discussion and separation of the two proposed collections will have to suffice in order to serve as support for the argument that the matrix of Transjordanian traditions contained in the SSN text (and specifically, the CH substratum of that text) originally stood separately from those traditions in which Saul featured. This separation will highlight the variation in the meaning of trips to Transjordan between those stories clustered in the CH (i.e., the monarch-type vision of Transjordan) and those consonant with Saul's rebuff of the Ammonite invasion in 1 Samuel 11 (i.e., the deliverer-type vision of Transjordan). Therefore, it is necessary in §6.2 to establish the criteria by which the variant traditions of the HDR may be reconstructed. In §§6.3–6, I will attempt to furnish a provisional separation of the two Histories based on those criteria.

Following an initial separation of the two Histories (§6.3) comes a clarification of the boundaries of the two texts. The span of the HDR_2 collection has already been discussed to some extent above (§5.3.4), but the mechanisms through which it was appropriated as the ideational support of the SSN require clarification. In particular, its foundational motif of the friendship between David and Jonathan will be elucidated (§6.4). I suggested above that the SSN was loosely appended to the ending of the HDR_2 after the beginning of that collection's consolidation and solidification, allowing an originally smooth transition between the two. Below, I postulate an ending of the HDR_2 (2 Samuel 1) on the basis of the study above. This hypothesis yields an ending we might expect given the

2 Usually, the document is held to have begun at 1 Sam 16:14 and ended at 2 Sam 5:10; e.g., Peter Mommer, *Samuel: Geschichte und Überlieferung* (WMANT 65; Neukirchen-Vluyn: Neukirchener Verlag, 1991), 176–80. However, some schemas extend the document's reach further into 1 Samuel: Artur Weiser envisioned 1 Sam 16:1–13 as part of the document ("Die Legitimation des Königs David: Zur Eigenart und Entstehung der sogen. Geschichte von Davids Aufstieg," *VT* 16 [1966]: 325–54, esp. 325–29), and 15:1 was selected as the document's beginning by both Jakob H. Grønbaek (*Die Geschichte vom Aufstieg Davids [1. Sam. 15–2. Sam. 5]: Tradition und Komposition* [ATDan 10; Copenhagen: Munksgaard, 1971], 25–29) and Tryggve N. D. Mettinger (*King and Messiah: The Civil and Sacral Legitimation of the Israelite Kings* [ConBOT 8; Lund: Gleerup, 1976], 33–47).

function of the text as a legitimization of David's rule over against that of the Saulides. This hypothesis comes with the caveat that the SSN and the HDR_2 were so intimately linked at such an early stage that any discussion of the boundary between the two is purely heuristic. The original ending of the HDR_2 + SSN complex melts quickly into the larger traditions of Solomon's reign following on 1 Kings 2. Unfortunately, the beginning of the HDR_2 is just as difficult to locate as its ending, although, as will be seen, 1 Sam 17:12 offers an adequate point of departure for that narrative complex.

The HDR_1 poses similar problems with respect to its beginning, but it has apparently had no complex of traditions appended at its end until its combination with the larger HDR_2 + SSN complex. In §6.5 I argue that the original traditional collection of the HDR_1 ended with David's accession to kingship over Israel, his annexation of Jerusalem, and the establishment of the royal family in that city (2 Sam 5:4–16). This narrative was eventually augmented with yet another chapter that denied the legitimacy of any remaining Saulides (e.g., 2 Samuel 6*).[3] The beginning of the early Davidic History is much less stable and self-contained, however, since many of its elements depend directly on the tradition's early appropriation of the independent narratives of Saul's Rise.[4] The beginning of the HDR_1, therefore, cannot be fully analyzed without some understanding of its reliance upon and references to the originally independent body of narratives concerning Saul's monarchy (for which see ch. 7).

The goal of this chapter, therefore, will be to demonstrate the following two points: First, the loose conglomeration of chapters extending from 1 Samuel 15–2 Samuel 5(6)*, commonly referred to as the History of David's Rise, is in fact the product of the combination of two different cohesive narrative complexes of traditions about David. Second, while the apparently later History of David's Rise (HDR_2) can be identified as the theoretical basis and political justification of the claims made by the SSN, the earlier History (HDR_1) was the only one that made direct reference to the narratives concerning Saul's political ascendency.

---

3 I have suggested above (§5.3.4.1) that 2 Samuel 21 also played some role in the final stages of David's takeover of the formerly Saulide kingdom; see §6.6.

4 See, e.g., Anton van der Lingen, *David en Saul in I Samuel 16–II Samuel 5: verhalen in politiek en religie* ('s-Gravenhage: Boekencentrum, 1983), 108, English summary, 242; and Marsha White, "'The History of Saul's Rise': Saulide State Propaganda in 1 Samuel 1–14," in *"A Wise and Discerning Mind": Essays in Honor of Burke O. Long* (ed. Saul M. Olyan and Robert C. Culley; BJS 325; Providence: Brown Judaic Studies, 2000), 271–92.

6.2. The Nature of the History of David's Rise

6.2.1. Doublets in the HDR as Continuations of Pentateuchal Sources

During the late nineteenth century, scholars began to recognize two or three potentially independent and continuous strands of narrative in 1 Samuel. Several scholars argued that these sources could be connected to the familiar Pentateuchal sources,[5] while others proposed they had originally been preserved at specific cult centers.[6] The presence of three apparently independent narratives of Saul's Rise necessarily caused some consternation. The problem was alleviated to some extent in 1 Sam 8–12 with Wellhausen's proposal that the evidently tripartite structure of those chapters was best accounted for by partitioning them into an early "pro-monarchic" and a later "anti-monarchic" source.[7] This aspect of the solution will be examined further in ch. 7 below, but Wellhausen's proposal did not adequately answer the Pentateuchal source theory with regard to the remainder of 1 Samuel; it simply became too laborious to try to correlate the doublings and treblings of episodes found throughout the book. The conundrum posed below will illustrate the dilemma: how does one account for the many sets of doublets (e.g., 1 Sam 18:10–11 // 19:9–10) when a theory of continuous sources collides with the three introductions to David (1 Sam 16:1–13; 16:14–23; 17:12–14)?

---

5 C. H. Cornill, "Zur Quellenkritik der Bücher Samuelis," *Königsberger Studien*, vol. 1 (Königsberg: Hübner & Matz, 1887), 23–59; Karl Budde, "Saul's Königswahl und Verwerfung," *ZAW* 8 (1888): 223–48; idem, *Die Bücher Richter und Samuel, ihre Quellen und ihre Aufbau* (Giessen: Ricker, 1890), 169–210, esp. 208–10; idem, *Die Bücher Samuel* (KHC 8; Tübingen: Mohr, 1902), xii–xxi; Paul Dhorme, *Les Livres de Samuel* (Paris: Gabalda, 1910), esp. 6; Wilhelm Caspari, *Die Samuelbücher* (KAT 7; Leipzig: Deichert, 1926), 6–19; Otto Eissfeldt, *Die Komposition der Samuelisbücher* (Leipzig: Hinrichs, 1931); Robert North, "David's Rise: Sacral, Military, or Psychiatric?" *Bib* 63 (1982): 524–44; cf. Hans Joachim Stoebe, *Das erste Buch Samuelis* (KAT 8/1; Gütersloh: Mohn, 1973), 47 (abbreviated below as *EBS*). More recently, Blenkinsopp has pointed to the commonalities with J displayed by many of the episodes in 1–2 Samuel ("Jonathan's Sacrilege," *CBQ* 26 [1964]: 423–49, esp. 445–49; see also 445 n. 80 for a review of the literature).

6 E.g., Hans Wilhelm Hertzberg, *I & II Samuel: A Commentary* (trans. John S. Bowden; OTL; London: SCM, 1964; repr., Philadelphia: Westminster, n.d.), 130–34; Klaus-Dietrich Schunk, *Benjamin: Untersuchungen zur Entstehung und Geschichte eines israelitischen Stammes* (BZAW 86; Berlin: Töppelman, 1963), 80–108, esp. 107. For discussion, see Baruch Halpern, *The Constitution of the Monarchy in Israel* (HSM 25; Chico, Calif.: Scholars Press, 1981), 149, 339 n. 2. Budde began his source division by connecting various traditions to specific cult centers but argued that each could ultimately be connected to one of the Pentateuchal sources (*Richter und Samuel*, 169–210). For a more detailed presentation, see Stoebe, *EBS*, 32–52, esp. 46–47.

7 Julius Wellhausen, *Die Composition des Hexateuchs* (4th ed.; Berlin: de Gruyter, 1963), 240–46; more recently, Nadav Na'aman, "The Pre-Deuteronomistic Story of King Saul and Its Historical Significance," *CBQ* 54 (1992): 638–58.

6.2.2. The HDR as a Single, Loose Traditional Collection

During the 20th cent. CE, these variations of a two-source theory lost much of their relevance in the face of L. Rost's analysis of the composition of the books of Samuel.[8] Throughout much of the past seventy years or so, the History of David's Rise has been argued to be a loose compilation of traditional narratives that originally bore little coherent relationship to one another. The classic treatment in this regard is J. Grønbaek's *Die Geschichte vom Aufstieg Davids*. Therein, Grønbaek lays out the narrative structure of the HDR, spanning 1 Sam 15:1–2 Sam 5:10. This literary unit, which was composed of disparate traditional materials, was purportedly compiled in Jerusalem in the years following the portioning of the so-called United Monarchy (ca. 906–883 BCE).[9]

Over the next two decades or so, Grønbaek's model held sway, and challenges to it tended to come most often in the form of elaborations on the composition history of the HDR. As an example of this trend, one may point briefly to the work of W. L. Humphreys, who, in a three-part series of articles, proposed and clarified a schematization of the compilation of the various Saul and Samuel stories with the narratives describing David's accession to power.[10] Humphreys envisioned a narrative tradition about Saul that had been "swallowed up" by additions about Samuel and David.[11] The narrative contained in the present text follows a series of up-and-down movements in Saul's fortunes; successes alternate with failures until finally the two merge in the episode of Saul's death: in taking his own life, Saul's death becomes the one action that could demonstrate his control of his own destiny.[12] But this final form of the text is not without a significant historical development. Originally, Humphreys argued, there had been "an older body of carefully structured Saul material being secondarily utilized and partially broken by later circles in the service of quite distinct

8 Leonhard Rost, *The Succession to the Throne of David* (trans. Michael D. Rutter and David M. Gunn, with an introduction by Edward Ball; HTIBS 1; Sheffield: Almond, 1982).

9 Grønbaek, *Aufstieg*, 259–78, esp. 277–78; see also Hans-Ulrich Nübel, "Davids Aufstieg in der frühe israelitischer Geschichtsschreibung" (Ph.D. diss., Bonn, 1959), esp. 124; and Weiser, "Legitimation," esp. 330–31, 351.

10 W. Lee Humphreys, "The Tragedy of King Saul: A Study of the Structure of 1 Samuel 9–31," *JSOT* 6 (1978): 18–27; idem, "The Rise and Fall of King Saul: A Study of an Ancient Narrative Stratum in 1 Samuel," *JSOT* 18 (1980): 74–90; idem, "From Tragic Hero to Villain: A Study of the Figure of Saul and the Development of 1 Samuel," *JSOT* 22 (1982): 95–117.

11 Idem, "Tragedy," 18.

12 Humphreys structured his understanding of the text's narrative dynamics such that Samuel appeared at the beginning of each "act" (ibid., 19).

interests."[13] Three layers of redaction worked the initial form of the narrative into its present state. The first recension of the early Saul tradition, overlaid upon chs. 9–15, was that of a northern prophetic school and was composed of loosely associated additions in 1 Sam 10:17–25; 12, a reworking of 13:8–15a, and a recasting of ch. 15,[14] possibly around the mid-8th cent. in response to the failure of the northern monarchy. This edition recast Saul as the tragic hero.[15] The second recension was carried out by a southern, Judahite (and ostensibly pro-Davidic) group whose work appears throughout chapters 16–31, specifically the addition of chapters 21–22; 23; 27:1–28:2; 29–30 and the reworking of 17–20; 24; 26; and 28.[16] This group of additions was derived from a more coherent cycle of Davidic traditions[17] and may have been added during the time of Hezekiah "when renewed Davidic claims upon the now fallen northern kingdom were asserted."[18] This edition focused on Saul as the rejected king.[19] The basic structure remained that of the oldest (Saul) narrative,[20] although "the figure of the first king was essentially recast by being set in a new context, and the tragic thrust of the older narrative was blunted."[21] A third redaction (i.e., the fourth stratum) of the text originated during the 7th cent. as a result of Deuteronomistic editing (found, for example, in 7:3–4,13–14; 13:1; 20:11–17,23,40–42; 25:28–31; and the bulk of 1 Samuel 8:8–22; 12:6–25[22]). As components of the overlay, the episodes added by the second (pro-Davidic) redactor thus did not comprise a separate, independent, and continuous tradition. In his formulation of this diachronic reconstruction of the text's development, the primary criterion upon which Humphreys based his source division was the text's view of the monar-

13 Humphreys, "Rise and Fall," 75. This older layer was comprised of "1 Sam 9:1–10:16; 11:1–11; 13–14; 15 (although now recast); 17–22 (again recast); 26; 28; 31" (ibid., 76). According to Humphreys, the Greek and Hittite connotations of the earliest stratum suggest the dating of that narrative should be during the United Monarchy, probably during the reign of Solomon (ibid., 87).

14 Ibid., 75, 85; idem, "Tragic Hero," 103, 107.

15 Ibid., 110.

16 Idem, "Rise and Fall," 76; idem, "Tragic Hero," 103.

17 Idem, "Tragic Hero," 107.

18 Idem, "Rise and Fall," 85.

19 Idem, "Tragic Hero," 110.

20 Idem, "Rise and Fall," 85.

21 Ibid., 86. Notice that this dating assumes that the argument about the structure was original to the Saul narrative and therefore demands the ending be known in advance of the composition of the narrative. "With the prophetic recasting of the material through the notice of the rejection of Saul's dynasty, however, attention is already focussed on Jonathan in a new and distinct way, and this is capitalized upon by the royalist circle in the manner demonstrated by Jobling to legitimize Davidic claims over all of Israel..." (Rost, *Succession*, 109, see also 110).

22 Humphreys, "Tragic Hero," 111.

chy,[23] a criterion not unlike the one Wellhausen had employed in his early separation of the pro- vs. anti-monarchic sources in 1 Samuel 7–12 (see §7.1.1).

Such early dating schemas for the "original" or "preliminary" edition of the HDR have not remained in vogue. A bevy of studies has emerged in recent years, challenging the pre-Deuteronomistic dating of an independent HDR.[24] In a seminal study of Israelite historiography, J. Van Seters argued for the identification of the compiler of the HDR as Dtr on the premise that the framing texts in 1 Sam 14:47–16:13 and 28:3–25 could be securely attributed to Dtr.[25] Unfortunately, Van Seters does not provide a comprehensive discussion of how he has arrived at this identification.[26] Although I am in full agreement with the identification of 1 Sam 15:1–25; 16:1–13 as secondary texts that an editor had either elaborated or composed in order to knit together the HDR with the foregoing material, it is not at all clear that the identification of that editor with Dtr is necessary.

Some discussion has already been given to R. Kratz's reconstruction of the HDR's composition history (§3.4.4.4), but a slightly longer discussion is warranted here. Kratz has discerned a "pre-Deuteronomistic bridge" (1 Sam 14:52; 16:14–23 + 18:17–27 + 19:9–10,11–12 + 21–31 + 2 Samuel 2–5 [8–10]) between the early Saul traditions (1 Samuel 1–14*) and the composite Court History (2 Samuel 11–1 Kings 2*). This bridge, composed after the fall of the northern kingdom, was later taken up by Dtr and supplemented with Deuteronomistic and post-Deuteronomistic additions.[27] Two concerns mitigate the force of this argument. First, I disagree strenuously with the omission of the entirety of 1 Samuel 17* on the basis of its claimed tensions with 16:14–23; as will be shown below (§6.3.1.2), the introduction of David and David's entry into Saul's orbit in 17:12–31 stands separately, source-critically speaking, from vv. 1–11, which comprise the direct continuation of 16:14–23. To claim that the introduction to David in 1 Samuel 17 stands in total conflict with his introduction in 16:14–23 underestimates the value of the versional evidence here. Second, the attribution of 1 Samuel 21–31 to a single compositional layer omits a

---

23 E.g., ibid., 107.

24 See most recently Klaus-Peter Adam, *Saul und David in der judäischen Geschichtsschreibung* (FAT I/51; Tübingen: Mohr Siebeck, 2007).

25 John Van Seters, *In Search of History: Historiography in the Ancient World and the Origins of Biblical History* (New Haven: Yale University Press, 1983; repr., Winona Lake, Ind.: Eisenbrauns, 1997), 264–71, esp. 264–65.

26 Ibid., 261–64; Van Seters apparently relies solely on the authority of Klaus-Dietrich Schunk here (ibid., 263 n. 59, citing Schunk, *Benjamin*, 84–85).

27 Reinhard G. Kratz, *The Composition of the Narrative Books of the Old Testament* (trans. John Bowden; London: T&T Clark, 2005); trans. of *Die Komposition der erzählenden Bücher des Alten Testaments* (Göttingen: Vandenhoeck & Ruprecht, 2000).

medial step in the development of the HDR; Kratz himself discusses the difficulties involved in reading these chapters sequentially,[28] yet he seems to ignore the possibility of breaking these chapters into two more-or-less parallel units, each of which was itself a loosely conjoined compilation of traditional materials, and each of which would have presented a cohesive narrative of David's life on the lam.

6.2.3. Rediscovering Doublets in the HDR: Halpern, Langlamet, and Willi-Plein

B. Halpern has pointed to the problems attendant to a purely redaction-critical approach such as Humphreys'[29] and has suggested a more practicable methodology for source-critical separation. The doublet, Halpern argues, is "the only strong indication of the presence of more than a single source."[30] Furthermore, Halpern argues that 1 Samuel demonstrates the presence of multiple doublets which—when separated from the corresponding doublet and appended to previous episodes—form longer, continuous sources.[31] In the present form of the text, these sources have been combined together to form a single long narrative. Accordingly, the consequent source-critical separation of the book of 1 Samuel divides the book cleanly into two coherent and continuous sources.

The first of Halpern's reconstructed sources (A) comprises 1 Sam 9:1–10:13; 13:(2–3),4–14:51(52); 17:12–30(31),41,48b,50,55–58; 18:1–5(6a), 10–11,17–19,30; 20:1b–42; 21:1–24:23; 28:3–25; 31.[32] This source, which Halpern reconstructs as the earlier of the two, ends with Saul's death on Gilboa and the Jabeshites' provision for the bodies of Saul and his sons. Its portrayal of Saul seems to be consistent with that of the deliverers in the book of Judges (Ehud, Deborah and Barak, Gideon, and Jephthah), and it reproduces the basic call-narrative form of those stories.[33] According to this narrative, Saul is a tragic figure through and through, while David is explicitly said to have had political relations with the Philistines, a situation for which no apology is given. Finally, here it is Yahweh who com-

28 Ibid., 178–79.

29 See especially Halpern, *Constitution*, 150–51. I have discussed the circularity of such an approach above (§5.2.2).

30 Ibid., 151.

31 "A consistent, variant narrative is the only sure criterion for establishing the existence of more than one original source" (ibid., 151–52).

32 For the complete argument supporting this breakdown, see ibid., 152–71.

33 Ibid., 155, 171–72. Cf. my own analysis below (§7.3.1), which finds more continuity between 1 Samuel 11 and Judges 3; 6–8; 11–12 than between the former passage and 1 Sam 9:1–10:16.

mands the anointing of Saul, thrusting the relatively unknown figure into the geopolitical stage and providing Israel with a king.

The second source (B) postulated by Halpern comprises 1 Samuel 8; 10:17–27; 11; 12; 15; 16; 17:1–11,32–40,42–48a,49,51–54; 18:(6a),6b–9, 12–16,20–29; 19; 25; 26; 27; 28:1–2; 29; 30; 2 Samuel 1–2; etc. Its ending does not follow Saul's death immediately but continues to be interested in the life and kingship of David. Samuel figures much more prominently in this version than in the A source, and he bridges the gap between Saul's kingship and David's kingship. Saul's kingship is an abortive attempt at the fulfillment of the monarchic institution, while David endures as the paradigmatic king, in comparison to whose reign other kings' tenures will be judged. As part of this glorification of David, his association with the Philistines—taken for granted in the A source—is denied outright in this narrative, to the extent that David is even given an alibi for Saul's death on Gilboa (1 Samuel 31). Although this narrative also maintains a thoroughly Yahwistic character, here it is the people Israel who have demanded the institution of the monarchy, which God only begrudgingly sanctions.

A. van der Lingen also divided the HDR into two separate sources, apparently without awareness of Halpern's recently published study.[34] He divided the text into two thematically unified documents: one (the A-source) narrated the story of David's Rise, seeking to demonstrate "the legitimate kingship of David";[35] the other source (B) sought to explain Saul's demise in spite of his early divinely ordained successes.[36] Insofar as it finds the beginning of the B-document in Saul's rescue of Jabesh-gilead (1 Samuel 11), van der Lingen's thesis attributes a much larger span of Samuel to the HDR than to do most other schemas (besides Halpern's). These documents were eventually combined and overlaid with two strata of redaction (RII and RIII),[37] a process essentially completed during the 7th cent., before the formation of the DtrH.

---

34 Van der Lingen, *David en Saul*, 240–43.

35 Ibid., 111, 242. The A-source comprises 1 Sam 17:12–15,17–23aα,24,25aαb,26a,27–30, 39aα,40aβbα,48aα,48b,49,51abα,55–58; 18:2,9,17a,19–20,22–27,28b,29b; 19:1–7*,11–18a; 22:1–3a,4–5; 23:1–4a,5,7a,8–9,10aα,11aβ,11bβ–13,14aα,19abα,20–25aα,25b–26; 24:4,5bβ, 6,8bβ–10,12,15,17,23b; 25:2–20, 23a, 24a, 25a, 27, 35, 36–37, 39–44; 27:2–3,5–6a,8–10,12; 28:1b–2; 29:1–4,6–11; 30:1–6a,8–10a,11–20,26–31*; 2 Sam 1:1b–4,11–12; 2:1–4a,8–9ab, 12–17,24–28a,29–31,32b; 3:12a,14–16,20,21b,22–27b,31–36; 4:1a,2a,5–6,7c,8a,12; 5:3, 17–21*,22–23,25,6–9,10a.

36 Ibid., 108, 241–42. Van der Lingen accounted to this source 1 Sam 11:1,2abα,3–8aα,9–11, 15; (13:1b–2,16–18,23; 14:1,6a,7–8,11–12abα,13–17,20–22,23b–31,36abα,37a, 37bβ,38, 39b–40,41b–45a,45bβ,46–48,52); 16:15–18b,19–23; 17:1–9*,11,32–36a,37bα,38,39b,40aα, 40bβ,42–44,48aβ,50bα,51bβ–53; 18:3–4,6aβ–8bα,10–12a,13–14a; 19:9*–10,19,20aαb,21, 22*,23–24*; 20:1–3,18–22abα,24–39; 21:2–11a*; 22:6–17bα,18b; 26:2–5a,6,7*,12abα–14aα,16aβb*,17,21,22,25b; 28:4–5,6–8a,8bα,9,13,14a,15aαbβ,16aα,19aβ,20–25; 31:1–13.

37 Ibid., 242.

Working backwards from the Succession Narrative, F. Langlamet arrived at a schema very much like van der Lingen's, in which two independent documents were edited together.[38] At a medial stage in the text's development, a short history of "David, son of Jesse"[39] was attached to the developing SN through the addition of the "Benjaminite scenes."[40] Another layer of redaction added an entirely separate story in which Jonathan featured.[41] Although Langlamet had originally supposed that the Jonathan texts comprised a layer of redaction (S3) subsequent to the one that had incorporated the earlier tale of David (S2), he was forced afterwards to emend this view because of his recognition that the indicators of S3 do not appear definitively in any S2 texts and that the two sets of texts may have been in competition with one another rather than sequentially ordered.[42] Although Langlamet did not go on in that article (or in its immediate successor[43]) to clarify his suggestion of competing texts, that recognition has not received adequate consideration in subsequent scholarship.

Contrary to van der Lingen's and Langlamet's respective visions of two independent documents, more recent composition-critical proposals tend to emphasize the primary nature of one set of texts and to relegate the other to secondary insertions. For example, O. Kaiser has suggested viewing the passages featuring Jonathan in 1 Sam 18:1–21:1* as the foundational text into which several passages—especially those in which Michal appears—have been inserted.[44] For Kaiser, this foundational text was

38 François Langlamet, "De 'David, fils de Jessé' au 'Livre de Jonathan': Deux editions divergentes de l''Ascension de David' en 1 Sam 16–2 Sam 1?" *RB* 100 (1993): 321–57, esp. 343–54; idem, "'David—Jonathan—Saül' ou le 'Livre de Jonathan': 1 Sam 16,14–2 Sam 1,27*," *RB* 101 (1994): 326–54.

39 This stage comprised roughly 1 Sam 17:12–31*; 18:2,5cd,6–9*, 20–27*; 19:8 (+ 18:6–9*), 11–17; 25:44; 27:1a–d,2,3,5–12; 28:1–2; 29:1–5,6a–e,7–11; 30:1–31*; 2 Sam 1:1–4,11–12; 2:1a,2a*,3*,4a.

40 François Langlamet, "Pour ou contre Salomon? La redaction prosalomonienne de 1 Rois i–ii," parts 1 and 2, *RB* 83 (1976): 321–79, 481–528; idem, "Absalom et les concubines de son père: Recherches sur II Sam., xvi, 21–22," *RB* 84 (1977): 161–209; idem, "David et la Maison de Saül: Les épisodes 'benjaminites' de II Sam. ix; xvi, 1–14; xix, 17–31; 1 Rois ii, 36–46," parts 1–5, *RB* 86 (1979): 194–213, 385–436, 481–513; 87 (1980): 161–210; 88 (1981): 321–22; idem, "David, fils de Jessé: Une edition prédeutéronomiste de l''Histoire de la Succession'," *RB* 89 (1982): 5–47.

41 Idem, "De 'David' au 'Livre'," 348–49. This document was composed of 1 Sam 16:14–23; 18:1*,3–4,10–12; 19:1–4,5f,6–7,9–10d,10e*; 20:1b–39; 21:1–8; 22:1–4,6–23*; 23:1–28; 24:1–23; 25:2–43; 26:1–25; 31:1–13; 2 Sam 1:2–16,17,18a*,19–27; 2:1–7; it will be noted that in the sections from 2 Samuel 1–2, Langlamet's two sources overlap.

42 Idem, "De 'David' au 'Livre'," 350.

43 Idem, "'David—Jonathan—Saül'," 326–54.

44 Otto Kaiser, "David und Jonathan. Tradition, Redaktion und Geschichte in I Sam 16–20: Ein Versuch," *ETL* 66 (1990): 281–96. As his *Grundschrift*, Kaiser suggests 16:14–23; 18:1aβb, 5; 19:8; 18:6aα*b,7,8aα^{2}β,9; 19:9–10ab^1; 20:1b–7,9–10,18–22,24–39; 21:1a* (ibid., 289).

already the product of some artistic combination and revision of earlier traditions. One of the central themes of this composite text was the friendship between Jonathan and David, the first mention of which (18:1*) had been composed with the extant narrative at hand in which Jonathan aids David's escape from Saul (1 Samuel 20*). It did not, however, include any mention of a covenant between the two, which was crafted only at the time of the Deuteronomistic editorial superimposition in an effort to legitimize Davidic claims to the northern kingdom.[45]

The most recent exemplar of a schema recognizing the presence of doublets in 1–2 Samuel is that of I. Willi-Plein.[46] Although she eschewed the somewhat standard demarcation between the HDR and the "Succession Narrative" or "Court History," preferring instead to focus on the larger unit of the "History of David's House" (*Davidshausgeschichte*; siglum DHG here), Willi-Plein proposed the differentiation between those passages in which Michal features and those in which Jonathan features. The Michal passages, she argued, were tightly interwoven with the rest of the DHG and were therefore foundational to that corpus, which comprised an extensive portion of 1 Sam 14:47–1 Kgs 4:6* and was composed during the 9th cent.[47] In Willi-Plein's reconstruction, the author of the DHG compiled a document that focused on the theme "Monarchy over Israel" and that knew of a nascent Israelite state in which Israel and Judah were not separate political entities but rather geographic ones, and thus not diametrically opposed to one another. The monarchy was assumed as the paradigmatic form of political leadership, but it was not taken for granted that the institution was hereditary; for this reason, the primary source of tension in the DHG is the familial struggle between David and the potential Saulide

---

See also idem, "Beobachtungen zur sogenannten Thronnachfolgeerzählung Davids," *ETL* 44 (1988): 9–10.

45 Ibid., esp. 288–89, 294–96.

46 Ina Willi-Plein, "ISam 18–19 und die Davidshausgeschichte," in *David und Saul im Widerstreit—Diachronie und Synchronie im Wettstreit: Beiträge zur Auslegung des ersten Samuelbuches* (ed. Walter Dietrich; OBO 206; Fribourg: University Press; Göttingen: Vandenhoeck & Ruprecht, 2005), 138–71; idem, "Michal und die Anfänge des Königtums in Israel," in *Congress Volume, Cambridge, 1995* (ed. J. A. Emerton; VTSup 66; Leiden: Brill, 1997), 401–19, here 407, n. 18; and idem, "Frauen um David: Beobachtungen zur Davidshausgeschichte," in *Meilenstein: Festgabe für Herbert Donner* (ed. S. Timm and M. Weippert; Wiesbaden: Harrassowitz, 1995), 349–61.

47 Willi-Plein, "ISam 18–19," 166–68; the full text of the DHG comprises 1 Sam 14:47–52; 17:55–58; 18:2,5–9,16–30; 19:8–17; 21:2–4,7–10; 21:11–16; 22:1–2,6,9–23; 23:6–15,(16–18),19–20,25–28; (24:9*,10aα,14–15,17aβb–18aα,21–23; 25:1b); 25:2–44; (26:1–8,10,12–15,17–22,25); 27:1–28:16,19–25; 29–31; 2 Sam 1:1–4,11–12,17–27; 2:2–9,12–32; 3:1–8,11–16,19–39; 4:1,5–12; 5:3,6–10,13–18,25; 6:10,12b–14,16–23; 7:1–3,16; 8:1–2,15–18; 9:2–9,11–13; 10:1–13*; 11*; 12:1–6a,9aβ,10a,13a,15–31; 13:1–33*; 14; 15:1–23,27–28,30–37*; 16:1–10,13b–23; 17:1–29; 18:1–17; 18:19–19:9; 19:10–44; 20:1–25; (21:8–11); 21:12–14,(15–18),19,(20–22); 1 Kgs 1; 2:1–46; 3:1; 4:1–6.

heirs.[48] However, the Jonathan passages (e.g., 1 Sam 18:1; 23:16–18) display indications of having been added later—perhaps at the time of the formation of the "Court Narrative" (*Höfische Erzählwerk*) in the 8th or 7th centuries.[49] In these passages, the hereditary monarchy is taken to be the norm, and it is this conception that the redactor who added these passages had to address.[50]

6.2.4. Methodological Principles: Diachronic Study of Doublets

6.2.4.1. The Nature of Doublets

Insofar as Halpern reconstructs two reasonably continuous narratives of David's rise—both concurrent with Saul's downfall, and only one continued by the Court History in 2 Samuel—our respective reconstructions of the formation process of 1 Samuel are similar. However, three problematic assumptions, all of which are interrelated, permeate Halpern's argument. First, Halpern assumes that doublets are the most secure criterion by which to divide a text, an assumption I do not deny. However, I find problematic the reification of an (admittedly subjective) "most secure" criterion to the position of the *only* secure criterion, as well as the consequent progression whereby *more* doublets provide even *more security*. What happens when there seem to be *three* separate episodes that might comprise a set of "doublets" (e.g., three ways in which Saul comes to power over Israel)? Because of Halpern's relatively synchronic examination of the interwoven narrative strands, his model does not—and *cannot*—take into account the diachronic development of the two constituent traditions.[51] Halpern's model does not, in my mind, adequately account for the pre-history of each narrative strand as a loose collection of traditional materials. Furthermore, there is no necessary reason to assume that *every* member of a doublet (or a triplet) has a corresponding counterpart in the posited parallel narrative strand, even if that member appears to be "duplicated." This caution is particularly relevant when we adopt a hypothesis of developing texts such that two growing traditions could be combined and interwoven with one

48 Ibid., 153–63.

49 Ibid., 166; see also Walter Dietrich, "Das Ende der Thronfolgegeschichte," in *Die sogenannte Thronfolgegeschichte Davids: Neue Einsichten und Anfragen* (ed. Albert de Pury and Thomas Römer; OBO 176; Fribourg: University Press; Göttingen: Vandenhoeck & Ruprecht, 2000), 38–69.

50 Willi-Plein, "ISam 18–19," 163–66.

51 Halpern's model does *allow* for this contingency, admitting that 1 Samuel 11 may have been a secondary addition into the complex 1 Sam 8; 10:17–27 (*Constitution*, 156–57), but this possibility receives inadequate consideration throughout the study, in my opinion.

another at an early stage into one single text, upon which were added not only the subsequent episodes of the composite narrative, but also additional redactional episodes in the larger narrative complex. In the model proposed here, only the first series of episodes would potentially have corresponding actual doublets, while the redactional episodes written subsequent to the combination of the two may have the appearance of being one member of a doublet, but which would in fact not point to any extant continuous narrative strand.

6.2.4.2. The Quantification of Doublets

Halpern's study raises questions concerning the qualification and quantification of doublets. He juxtaposes the earlier attempt of H. Seebass to discern doublets in the story of Saul's anointment against his own,[52] noting "rather than a fine division founded on key words and minute repetitions, a perception of the more general structure is the aim."[53] Again, I agree with the principle proposed by Halpern that minute studies of word repetition may be flawed (since the repetition may be redactional or attributable to scribal accident)[54] and should thus play a diminished role, subservient to impressions of the functions and thrusts of the larger episodes. But the crux of the issue is contained precisely in Halpern's use of the word *perception*. What, exactly, constitutes a doublet? While I will not replicate Halpern's source-division in its details, a quick comparison of our respective divisions should suffice to show that he and I differ markedly on those episodes actually constituting doublets. For instance, I perceive 1 Samuel 11 as incontrovertibly divorced from 1 Sam 10:17–27 by virtue of both its structure (which, I argue in §7.3.1, stands alone as an independent and coherent narrative) and its theme (which parallels that of the deliverers). Halpern, on the other hand, argues for the sequentiality of the two passages, observing that 1 Samuel 11 gives no introduction to Saul, and therefore demands the familial introduction in 10:17–27.[55] Our respective assessments are reversed with respect to the kindnesses shown by the

---

52 Horst Seebass, "Die Vorgeschichte der Königserhebung Sauls," *ZAW* 79 (1967): 155–71.

53 Halpern, *Constitution*, 152. For a discussion of the problematic nature of Seebass's suggestion, see below, §7.3.2.1, and Bruce C. Birch, "The Development of the Tradition on the Anointing of Saul in 1 Sam. 9:1–10:16," *JBL* 90 (1971): 55–68.

54 See also the intentional variety discussed by J. T. Willis as "comprehensive anticipatory redactional joints" ("The Function of Comprehensive Anticipatory Redactional Joints in 1 Samuel 16–18," *ZAW* 85 [1973]: 294–314).

55 Halpern, *Constitution*, 155. It is precisely this *lack* of introduction in 1 Samuel 11 that I perceive to be fundamentally important in determining the genre of the narrative as a deliverer-type story.

Jabeshites to Saul's body (along with those of his sons) in 1 Sam 31:11–13; 2 Sam 2:4b–7; and 21:12–13a*,14aα* (see §6.6). Halpern views the two scenes as doublets differing in narrational voice and lexical usage,[56] while I regard the lexical variation between אנשי יביש גלעד (2 Sam 2:4b,5) and ישבי יביש גלעד (1 Sam 31:11) as a relatively minor variation and the putative change in narrator as an apparition, concocted by the juxtaposition of two sources. In my view, 1 Sam 31:11–13; 2 Sam 2:4b–7; and 21:12–13a*,14aα* form a logically sequential pair of episodes, although 2:4b–7* has undergone a bit of elaboration and 21:12–13a*, 14aα* has been displaced from its original position. A second, indirectly narrated account of Saul's death has been inserted between these passages.

Perhaps the most dramatic variation between our respective understandings of doublets is the size and extent of doublets we each assume. Halpern, who is very thorough in his method, apportions most of the episodes in which Jonathan figures prominently to his A source (18:1–5; 20:1b–21:1; 23:16–18); however, a significant scene involving Jonathan has been attributed to the B source (2 Samuel 1). It is unclear to me how Halpern could have made this assignment of 2 Samuel 1, unless he has simply missed what appears to me to be the most over-arching set of doublets in the entire History of David's Rise: the privileging of Jonathan in one of the sources and the privileging of Michal in the other.

In 2 Samuel 1, Jonathan is the only son of Saul mentioned (eight times: vv. 4,5,12,17,22,23,25,26). Compare, in opposition, the single mention of Jonathan in 1 Sam 31:2, in conjunction with his brothers Abinadab and Malki-shua. Thereafter, the three sons of Saul are grouped together and referred to only as "his sons" (בניו; vv. 2,6,7,8,12). Furthermore, in each and every one of the sections in which Jonathan appears as a main character (i.e., *not* 1 Samuel 31), he does so as the *only son* of Saul whom the text knows. By the same token, those passages that know of Michal (1 Sam 18:20–30; 19:8–17; 25:43–44; 2 Sam 3:12–16; 6:20–23) know *only* of Michal; it is almost as though the siblings' paths never cross.[57] Furthermore, the relative structure of each interpersonal relation of Saul's children with David follows the same path: the two become intimates (Michal: 18:20,27; Jonathan: 18:1–5);[58] Saul's child uncovers the king's

56 Ibid., 169–70.

57 The only possible exception is the episode in which David demands Michal back from Abner before he will treat with the Israelite general (2 Sam 3:12–16). This episode is redactional, I argue, and will be discussed below (§6.6).

58 The notice that "Jonathan loved David" (18:1) need not be taken to indicate anything other than a purely platonic relationship. J. A. Thompson argues that the word "love" (אהב) throughout 1 Samuel is used with political overtones ("The Significance of the Verb *Love* in the David-Jonathan Narratives in 1 Samuel," *VT* 24 [1974]: 334–38, pointing to William L. Moran, "The Ancient Near Eastern Background of the Love of God in Deuteronomy," *CBQ*

plot to kill David and, showing loyalty to the latter, assists in an escape while exhibiting devious behavior towards the betrayed father (Michal: 19:11–17; Jonathan: 20:1–21:1). That Halpern did not recognize this function of each of Saul's children (Michal and Jonathan) strikes me as odd but is due, perhaps, more to the finely-grained scope of his study than to any real failure in method.

Inasmuch as Kaiser and Willi-Plein have adduced the literary function of each of the two children of Saul as a valid criterion for compositional study, I find their respective schemas more compelling than Halpern's and worthy of much further study. Additionally, Willi-Plein's description of the developing attitudes toward the hereditary monarchy in early monarchic Israel is both intriguing and credible, if not fully convincing. However, I cannot agree that either the Michal passages or the Jonathan passages are the product of a later redactional stratum; these passages are all simply too integral to the HDR to excise completely. Moreover, Willi-Plein's schema does not adequately account for the parallel traditions in which Merab and Michal are each promised to David. Kaiser's relegation of Merab to secondary status similarly underestimates the import of 1 Sam 18:17–19* for the composition-critical breakdown of the HDR. In effect, although I believe that Kaiser and Willi-Plein have correctly adduced the single most important criterion of source-critical separation of 1 Sam 16:14–2 Samuel 5* and also have put forth cogent discussions of the

25 [1963]: 77–87). Peter R. Ackroyd seconds this assessment and points to the political overtones of the verb "to bind" (קָשַׁר) in 1 Sam 18:1 ("The Succession Narrative [so-called]," *Int* 35 [1981]: 383–96). Katharine Doob Sakenfeld also follows this political viewpoint. She considers the storyline around David and Jonathan to be arguing for the legitimate nature of David's kingship: the "combination of personal friendship and political allegiance allows Jonathan to function as a bridge figure in David's rise to kingship" ("Loyalty and Love: The Language of Human Interconnections in the Hebrew Bible," *Michigan Quarterly Review* 22 [1983]: 190–204; see also David Jobling, "Jonathan: A Structural Study in 1 Samuel," in *The Sense of Biblical Narrative: Three Structural Analyses in the Old Testament [I Samuel 13–31, Numbers 11–12, I Kings 17–18]* [JSOTSup 7; Sheffield: JSOT Press, 1978], 4–25). By noting the exact vocabulary used (and in particular, the word חסד), she points to the public nature of the term (Sakenfeld, "Loyalty," 222). Both David and Jonathan ask חסד from the other. The Syriac, she says, does not offer much help since it uses the term "goodness" (טבתא). But if this is the case, it may carry the political overtones of Akkadian *ṭābūta epēšum*, "to make a treaty of friendship" (Delbert R. Hillers, "A Note on Some Treaty Terminology in the Old Testament," *BASOR* 176 [1964]: 46–47). In all this, I do not discount the fact that there are significant affective overtones of the verb, even when used with this more political sense: Susan Ackerman, "The Personal Is Political: Covenantal and Affectionate Love (*ʾāhēb*, *ʾahăbā*) in the Hebrew Bible," *VT* 52 (2002): 437–58; Jacqueline E. Lapsley, "Feeling Our Way: Love for God in Deuteronomy," *CBQ* 65 (2003): 350–69; Ellen White, "Michal the Misinterpreted," *JSOT* 31 (2007): 451–64, esp. 452–54. Affective love need not be read as homosexuality: Yaron Peleg, "Love at First Sight? David, Jonathan, and the Biblical Politics of Gender," *JSOT* 30 (2005): 171–89; cf. Marcus Zehnder, "Exegetische Beobachtungen zu den David-Jonathan Geschichten," *Bib* 79 (1998): 153–79.

attitudes prevalent in each group of texts described, both models suffer from a certain myopic restraint with respect to the amount of Samuel to be apportioned to earlier sources. If Halpern was too liberal with his qualification and distribution of doublets, and thus unable to account for multiple exemplars of a given tradition, Kaiser and Willi-Plein have erred too conservatively by not perceiving the full extent to which doublets run throughout the *entirety* of 1 Samuel 16–2 Samuel 5*.

More satisfying in this regard are the more broadly attempted studies of Langlamet and van der Lingen, each of whom studied the full span of the HDR. However, Langlamet's series of studies was published over the span of two decades; the theory was constantly in development, and despite its relatively secure anchorage in 2 Samuel, it had to become increasingly complex as Langlamet worked his way back into 1 Samuel. Because of his periodic publication, Langlamet eventually had to revise a significant portion of the schema. Moreover, Langlamet's consideration of 1 Samuel 16–18—a key text in the development of Samuel, as will be seen below—is inadequate, and the result does not inspire overwhelming confidence. Van der Lingen's schema similarly displays a real ingenuity, beginning from the text-critical observation of 1 Samuel 16–18, but after a cogent analysis of chs. 16–17, the schema runs aground on the shoals of ch. 18, where van der Lingen began to proceed on the basis of a thematic analysis rather than a text-critical scrutiny.[59] This shift means that very early in van der Lingen's analysis the children of Saul are no longer matched with their respective constituent stories of introduction to David in ch. 17 and the various continuations of their stories in the following chapters of 1 Samuel. Moreover, while van der Lingen's B-source maintains Jonathan as the only known child of Saul, his A-source juxtaposes in the same source what I consider to be the doublets of Saul's daughter to be married (Merab: 18:17a,19; Michal: 18:22–27), and it permits the simultaneous appearances of Michal and Jonathan (19:1–7*).[60] Yet overall, van der Lingen's schema is the closest to the one I have offered here.

6.2.4.3. Structural Analysis of Narrative as Subjective

The third assumption Halpern makes in his source-critical breakdown of 1 Samuel is that both sources must demonstrate the tripartite structure of designation–testing–confirmation that he has established in the earlier chapters as the way in which kings are chosen and ratified. Whether or not

59 Van der Lingen, *David en Saul*, 28.
60 Ibid., 108–11.

this systematization of the structure holds up under scrutiny is an issue that will not be decided here. Not only does Halpern apply the structure as confirmation of his source-division of the Narratives of Saul's Rise somewhat arbitrarily (since it is difficult to perceive the structure operating in David's favor in the A source),[61] though, the application of the structure is itself a subjective process as well. This observation is borne out by the fact that Edelman has recognized the three-fold structure of kingship recognition, proposed by Halpern, to apply to the passage 1 Samuel 9–12 as a whole.[62] In short, the applicability of the hypothesized structure even as *confirmation* of the proffered division of sources is questionable and subject to debate.[63]

With the inherent subjectivity of the project in mind, let us begin the division of sources with the observation made above: there seem to be at least two groups of texts distributed throughout the composite HDR, one recognizing Jonathan as its hero and "bridge figure" (i.e., the mediator of the Israelite kingdom from Saul to David)[64] and the other holding Michal to fill this same role. D. Jobling has argued for this role of Jonathan most explicitly, pointing to the rising dramatic tension in the Jonathan-David episodes (18:1–5; 19:1–7; 20:1–21:1; 23:15b–18), interspersed with interludes of exposition and characterization (the "Saul-David" sections in 16:14–17:58; 18:6–30; 19:8–24; 21:2–23:15a; 23:19 onward).[65] The transfer of the kingdom progresses by a series of identifications: first of Saul with Jonathan and then of Jonathan with David.[66] Since he does not analyze the text with source-critical implications in mind, Jobling's conclusions apply primarily to the present text. However, the excision of the Michal-related passages leaves a continuous source-narrative in which much, if not all, of Jobling's analysis remains productive, despite the new

---

61 Halpern's statement that "the A source appears to have had a 'David block' shoved into it" (*Constitution*, 171) may be an attempt to account for this deficiency, since such a secondary insertion presumably would not have been able to work out the full expression of the ritual. But what does this say about the applicability of the ritual structure to begin with? The reader may notice that, like Halpern's method, the source-critical division of the present study is motivated by and ultimately geared towards a project whose results will, in turn, confirm the division itself. In that regard, it would be methodologically unsound to criticize Halpern's method.

62 Diana Edelman, "Saul's Rescue of Jabesh-Gilead (I Sam 11 1–11): Sorting Story from History," *ZAW* 96 (1984): 195–209; see §7.1.4, below.

63 Undoubtedly, the present schematization will gather its own supporters and critics; we can only point to the subjectivity of the exercise and make the case for division.

64 For the terminology of the "bridge figure," see Sakenfeld, "Loyalty," 224, quoted in n. 58, above. See also Walter Brueggemann, "Narrative Coherence and Theological Intentionality in 1 Samuel 18," *CBQ* 55 (1993): 228.

65 Jobling, "Jonathan."

66 Ibid., 18.

character of the text.[67] Furthermore, as will be shown below (§6.3.2), this same process of separation produces a Michal-based counter-narrative to the story featuring Jonathan, in which Michal plays the role of Saul's child through whom the kingdom is delivered to David. Before the contours of this counter-narrative are explored fully, the sources themselves must be fully separated. This process begins most easily in 1 Samuel 17–18, where the contingencies of textual transmission have left us a situation worthy of further study: the apparently complete separation of two seemingly independent narratives of David's battle with the Philistine Goliath and his introduction into Saul's court.

6.3. 1 Samuel 17–18 as Test-Case

6.3.1. The Text-Critical Complexity of 1 Samuel 17–18

6.3.1.1. The Text Common to LXX^B and MT

In the text-critical study of 1 Samuel 17–18, it has long been noted that the Old Greek account, usually considered to have been preserved most fully in the manuscript LXX^B,[68] omits a significant portion of the text. Roughly 45 percent of the MT text is missing in LXX^B and its congeners, which preserve a text nearly identical in scope to MT 1 Sam 17:1–11,32–40,42–48a,49,51–54; 18:6aβb*–8a,9,12a,13–16,20–21a,22–26a,27–29a.[69] Yet de-

67 Jobling himself notes, "one may reasonably doubt whether there is any traditio-historical link... between Michal and Jonathan" (ibid., 20). A complete review of how Jobling's thesis would function within the newly reconfigured separation would be beneficial, but is impractical here for purposes of space. In its essence, Jobling's analysis of the narrative action remains substantially undisrupted by the source separation proposed here.

68 J. Lust provides a convenient list of manuscript witnesses beyond the basic LXX^B and MT ("The Story of David and Goliath in Hebrew and in Greek," in *The Story of David and Goliath: Textual and Literary Criticism* [ed. Dominique Barthélemy et al.; OBO 73; Fribourg: University Press; Göttingen: Vandenhoeck & Ruprecht, 1986], 6).

69 The list here has been compiled with the help of Emanuel Tov's chart displaying the full text of LXX ("The Nature of the Differences between MT and the LXX in 1 Sam. 17–18," in *The Story of David and Goliath: Textual and Literary Criticism* [ed. Dominique Barthélemy et al.; OBO 73; Fribourg: University Press; Göttingen: Vandenhoeck & Ruprecht, 1986], 24–33; see also idem, "The Composition of 1 Samuel 16–18 in the Light of the Septuagint Version," in *Emperical Models for Biblical Criticism* [ed. Jeffrey H. Tigay; Philadelphia: University of Pennsylvania Press, 1985], 97–130). I differ from Tov only in a few places, where his chart indicates that further refinement may be necessary (i.e., inclusion of 18:8a, exclusion of 18:26b). When discussing this passage, the precise limits of the shared text usually diverge between individuals; some, like Lust, treat the text a bit more schematically in considering 17:32–54 a block ("Story," 11), rather than specifying the two text-types share only vv. 32–40,42–48a,49,51–54; I take this, however, as a time-saving device and not an indication that Lust considers vv. 41,48b,50 part of the shared text. Others treat the text more

spite the apparent omissions, LXX^B relates here a cohesive story in which David is already a fixture in Saul's court, albeit only as a young shepherd who knows how to play the harp and is at the very beginning of his introduction into the warrior class.[70] Despite numerous objections to the contrary, the narrative thus follows immediately, easily, and naturally on 16:14–23. When David hears the Philistine's[71] challenge (17:8–11), he asks to fight against the giant (v. 32). After an exchange with Saul in which David details his qualifications (vv. 33–37), Saul girds the boy with armor (v. 38). However, the armor does not allow David enough movement (v. 39), so he elects to fight the Philistine with nothing but a sling and the protection of Yahweh (v. 40). David wins the battle, removing the Philistine's head in the process and delivering a great victory to Israel (vv. 42–48a,49,51–54). While Saul is praised for his success, it is the young David who is recognized by the women of Israel (18:6aβb*) as the real victor of the day: "Saul has killed his thousands, but David his myriads" (v. 7).[72] Jealous of this recognition, Saul begins to harbor hatred for David

---

precisely; see, e.g., Simon J. De Vries, who gives the text's extent as 17:1–11, 32–40,42–48a, 49,51–54; 18:6aβ–7,8aα^2,9,12a,13–16,20–21a,22–26a,27–29a ("David's Victory over the Philistines as Saga and as Legend," *JBL* 92 [1973]: 23–36); and Tov, who differs from De Vries only in omitting 18:6aβ and including all of 18:8,26b,29a in his statement of the shared text ("Nature," 19; see also Halpern, *Constitution*, 161–65).

70 Although cf. the assessment of Julio Trebolle (Barrera) ("The Story of David and Goliath [1 Sam 17–18]: Textual Variants and Literary Composition," *BIOSCS* 23 [1990]: 28), quoted below in n. 110.

71 That this Philistine's name was Goliath of Gath is recounted here, in a circumstantial verbless clause in v. 4aβ: גלית שמו מגת. Cf. the similarly circumstantial presentation of the Philistine's identity in the MT-only text (17:23): גלית הפלשתי שמו מגת ממערכות פלשתים (with Q ממערכות). Many interpreters have treated this identification skeptically, preferring an anonymous Philistine and citing the notice in 2 Sam 21:19 that it was Elhanan who killed Goliath (e.g., Wellhausen, *Composition*, 248; P. Kyle McCarter, *I Samuel: A New Translation with Introduction and Commentary* [AB 8; Garden City, N.Y.: Doubleday, 1980], 291; Alexander Rofé, "The Battle of David and Goliath: Folklore, Theology, Eschatology," in *Judaic Perspectives on Ancient Israel* [ed. Jacob Neusner, Baruch A. Levine, and Ernest S. Frerichs; Fortress: Philadelphia, 1987], 127–28; Baruch Halpern, *David's Secret Demons: Messiah, Murderer, Traitor, King* [Grand Rapids, Mich.: Eerdmans, 2001], 7–8, 148; Steven L. McKenzie, *King David: A Biography* [Oxford: Oxford University Press, 2000], 75–76; J. Vermeylen, *La loi du plus fort: Histoire de la rédaction des récits davidiques de 1 Samuel à 1 Rois 2* [BETL 154; Leuven: University Press, 2000], 95–96; A. Graeme Auld, "The Story of David and Goliath: A Test Case for Synchrony *plus* Diachrony," in *David und Saul im Widerstreit—Diachronie und Synchronie im Wettstreit: Beiträge zur Auslegung des ersten Samuelbuches* [ed. Walter Dietrich; OBO 206; Fribourg: University Press; Göttingen: Vandenhoeck & Ruprecht, 2005], 126). Although I find this observation persuasive, it is relatively unimportant in the context of the present argument.

72 McCarter, Brueggemann, and others argue that the poem here should be read merely as an example of parallelism, in which *both* Saul and David are honored, but that as the second member of the pair, David is naturally credited with the larger sum. The women of Israel, then, did not intend the slight that Saul experiences, and the king's insecurity is brought into even sharper relief (McCarter, *I Samuel*, 312; Brueggemann, "Narrative Coherence," 228–

(v. 8a), and David's successes proliferate, winning him support from the people (vv. 12a,13–16). There is no direct mention of a potential marriage to one of Saul's daughters for the victor of the battle with the Philistine—as there is in the text not preserved by LXX^{B} (cf. MT 17:25)—but Michal does appear. Her amorous feelings towards David are made known to Saul, who decides to use them as an excuse for doing away with David (vv. 20–21a). Saul sends the young hero on a suicide mission: the collection of one hundred Philistine foreskins in place of a bride price (vv. 22–26a). David collects the number handily, delivering a double payment and winning the hand of Michal in the process (vv. 27–28; cf. LXX there and 2 Sam 3:14, which only gives David credit for 100 Philistine foreskins).[73]

This narrative is concise, logical, and easily integrated into the surrounding narrative episodes, in which David has already been brought into Saul's court in order to calm the king during his violent mood-swings (16:14–23) and is later rescued by Michal from her father's wrath (19:8–17).[74] It bears none of the frequently cited tensions and inconsistencies that pervade the full text of the MT version, in which, for example, Saul and Abner must be introduced to the young victor (17:55–58) shortly after having equipped him with the king's armor (vv. 38–40). It is tempting, therefore, to hold to the commonly asserted textual supremacy of LXX^{B} in Samuel and to relegate the remainder of MT to the dustbin of random interpretive glosses, exegetical comments, and generally secondary fea-

29). Because a battle ensues after the single combat (17:52–53), it is unnecessary to hypothesize with Wellhausen, Grønbaek, McCarter, and others that an original battle narrative has been replaced here by the story of David's single combat (so Wellhausen, *Composition*, 250; Grønbaek, *Aufstieg Davids*, 90–92; McCarter, *I Samuel*, 296; Kaiser, "David und Jonathan," 285; McKenzie, *King David*, 78; Willi-Plein, "ISam 18–19," 145–46; cf. Ralph W. Klein, *1 Samuel* [WBC 10: Waco: Word Books, 1983], 173). As Vermeylen points out, it is nearly impossible to separate the themes developed here (the conflict between Saul and David and the transfer of royal power) from the remainder of 1 Samuel 18–2 Samuel 1 (*Loi du plus fort*, 96). Instead, we may deduce from here that the Goliath episode has been used as an opportunity to introduce an early traditional couplet celebrating the Israelites' victories in skirmishes against the Philistines.

73 De Vries points out correctly that the whole narrative is designed to focus on the magnificent victory of Yahweh—not David—over Goliath ("David's Victory," 32). Cf. the imagery of Goliath flat on his face, familiar to the reader of the Ark Narrative, in which the statue of Dagon is forced onto its face in the presence of the Ark of the Covenant (1 Sam 5:3,4; see Mark K. George, "Constructing Identity in 1 Samuel 17," *BibInt* 7 [1999]: 389–412, esp. 406 and bibliography therein). Saul recognizes that "Yahweh was with David" only in 18:28, even though the story itself introduces David as one in God's favor in 17:18. The story is similar to other tales of Yahweh's victory ("quasi-" or "modified" holy-war narrative) and accordingly, argues De Vries, seems to derive from a school of northern prophets (e.g., Elijah and Elijah), from sometime "during the post-Solomonic period" ("David's Victory," 34).

74 For the connection to 16:14–23, see, e.g., Hans Joachim Stoebe, "Die Goliathperikope 1 Sam. xvii 1–xviii 5 und die Textform der Septuaginta," *VT* 6 (1956): 405–10. McKenzie notes that 19:11–17 takes place on the wedding night and should follow immediately on 18:20–25 (*King David*, 81).

tures.[75] It is perhaps equally tempting to insist on the textual priority of the longer MT tradition and to recognize in the LXX the effects of editorial omissions that removed tensions latent in the longer text;[76] recently, D. Rudman has opined that "[i]t is difficult to see why an editor would add extra material when it is so obviously contradictory, and correspondingly difficult to escape the conclusion that the OG textual tradition represented by the LXX^B reflects an attempt to harmonise the two conflicting stories of David's arrival at Saul's court by eliminating contradictory material."[77] Further reflection on the verses not preserved in LXX^B should give us pause before such a hasty dismissal of the data.

75 See, e.g., Henry Preserved Smith, *A Critical and Exegetical Commentary on the Books of Samuel* (ICC; New York: Scribner, 1899), 150–51; Caspari, *Samuelbücher*, 199; Hans Joachim Stoebe, "David und Mikal: Überlegungen zur Jugendgeschichte Davids," in *Von Ugarit nach Qumran: Beiträge zur alttestamentlichen und altorientalischen Forschung* (ed. J. Hempel et al.; BZAW 77; Berlin: Töpelmann, 1958), 224–43, esp. 26; idem, "Goliathperikope," 397–413, esp. 404; idem, *EBS*, 312–15; Klein, *1 Samuel*, 174–75; A. Graeme Auld and Craig Y. S. Ho, "The Making of David and Goliath," *JSOT* 56 (1992): 19–39; Trebolle, "Story," 16–30, esp. 28–30; McKenzie, *King David*, 71–73; Auld, "Story," 124–125 (Auld proposed that the MT additions were inspired by other passages of 1 Samuel); Adam, *Saul und David*, 143–50. For extensive bibliography before ca. 1970, see Stoebe, "Goliathperikope," 398 n. 2; and idem, *EBS*, 312–15.

76 E.g., Budde, *Richter und Samuel*, 212–14; idem, *Samuel*, 121; Dhorme, *Samuel*, 167–68; Grønbaek, *Aufstieg Davids*, 80–91, esp. 84–88; De Vries, "David's Victory," esp. 23–24 and 23 n. 2; Heda Jason, "The Story of David and Goliath: A Folk Epic?" *Bib* 60 (1979): 36–70; Dominique Barthélemy, "La qualité du Texte Massorétique de Samuel," in *The Hebrew and Greek Texts of Samuel: 1980 Proceedings of IOSCS, Vienna* (ed. Emanuel Tov; Jerusalem: Academon, 1980), 19–20; idem, "Trois niveaux d'analyse (à propos de David et Goliath)," in *The Story of David and Goliath: Textual and Literary Criticism* (ed. Dominique Barthélemy et al.; OBO 73; Fribourg: University Press; Göttingen: Vandenhoeck & Ruprecht, 1986), 47–54; David W. Gooding, "An Approach to the Literary and Textual Problems in the David-Goliath Story: 1 Sam 16–18," in *The Story of David and Goliath: Textual and Literary Criticism* (ed. Dominique Barthélemy et al.; OBO 73; Fribourg: University Press; Göttingen: Vandenhoeck & Ruprecht, 1986), 55–86; Stephen Pisano, *Additions or Omissions in the Books of Samuel* (OBO 57; Fribourg: University Press; Göttingen: Vandenhoeck & Ruprecht, 1984), 78–86; Rofé, "Battle," 117–51; Arie van der Kooij, "The Story of David and Goliath: The Early History of Its Texts," *ETL* 68 (1992): 118–31; Walter Dietrich, "Die Erzählungen von David und Goliat in 1Sam 17," *ZAW* 108 (1996): 172–91; Halpern, *David's Secret Demons*, 7; Erik Aurelius, "Wie David ursprünglich zu Saul kam (1 Sam 17)," in *Vergegenwärtigung des Alten Testaments: Beiträge zur biblischen Hermeneutik* (ed. Christoph Bultmann, Walter Dietrich, and Christoph Levin; Göttingen: Vandenhoeck & Ruprecht, 2002), 44–68. For earlier sources, see Stoebe, "Goliathperikope," 397 n. 4.

77 D. Rudman, "The Commissioning Stories of Saul and David as Theological Allegory," *VT* 50 (2000): 527.

6.3.1.2. The Text of the MT-pluses/OG-minuses

Claims that the OG harmonized the obvious tensions of the longer MT text by omitting much of the offending material beg the question of why the tensions were there to begin with.[78] This criticism is in no way eliminated or alleviated by the admission that the supposedly prior MT was already composite.[79] Moreover, when placed under scrutiny, these verses add up to a linear, reasonable folktale, although a few of the phrases may be excised, as they are clearly redactional linkages of the two independent narratives.[80] While a thorough discussion would demand its own monograph, it is necessary to engage in a substantive—although still somewhat schematic—analysis of the literary coherence of this second version.

In this alternative account, David is introduced in 17:12: "Now, David was the son of an Ephrathite from Bethlehem (in) Judah, whose name was Jesse, and who had eight sons. In the days of Saul, the man [Jesse] was very old." (ודוד בן־איש אפרתי הזה מבית לחם יהודה ושמו ישי ולו שמנה בנים והאיש בימי שאול זקן בא באנשים). Although D. W. Gooding has challenged the propriety of this introduction, preferring the far sounder ויהי איש אחד of 1 Sam 1:1; 9:1 to the opening ודוד בן־איש אפרתי הזה of the verse under discussion, his grammatical observations directed at separating vv. 12–31 from the surrounding narrative do not carry much weight.[81] For example, his insistence that the notice that Jesse's sons "went after Saul to *the* battle" (הלכו אחרי־שאול לַמִּלְחָמָה; v. 13) presupposes a previously indicated battle is a misreading of the Hebrew definite article, which can often denote an abstract or immeasurable noun (hence, "went after Saul into battle"; cf. Isa 1:22 בַּשֶּׁמֶן "with oil")[82] or even an

78 Auld and Ho, "Making of David and Goliath," 38; Dietrich, "Erzählungen," 179.

79 So, e.g., Barthélemy, "Trois niveaux," 47–54; van der Kooij, "Story," 126–28; Dietrich, "Erzählungen," 180–84, 189; Aurelius, "David," 44–68.

80 E.g., Eissfeldt, *Komposition*, 12–13, 57; McCarter, *I Samuel*, 306–9; van der Lingen, *David en Saul*, 12–22; Lust, "Story," 11–14; idem, "David dans la Septante," in *Figures de David à travers la Bible: XVIIe congrès de l'ACFEB (Lille, 1er–5 septembre 1997)* (ed. Louis Desrousseaux and Jacques Vermeylen; Paris: Cerf, 1999), 243–63, esp. 245–52; Tov, "Composition," 118 ("independent and coherent," although cf. p. 121: "partial [or partially preserved]"); Antony F. Campbell, "From Philistine to Throne (1 Samuel 16:14–18:16)," *ABR* 34 (1986): 35–41; idem, *1 Samuel* (FOTL 7; Grand Rapids: Eerdmans, 2003), 171–91; William Boyd Nelson, Jr., "1 Samuel 16–18 and 19:8–10: A Traditio-Historical Study" (Ph.D. diss., Harvard University, 1992), reviewed in *HTR* 85 (1992): 499–500; Vermeylen, *Loi du plus fort*, 89–101, esp. 100.

81 Gooding, "Approach," 57. For further discussion of the introductory phrase ויהי איש (אחד), see recently Mark Leuchter, "'Now There Was a [Certain] Man': Compositional Chronology in Judges–1 Samuel," *CBQ* 69 (2007): 429–39.

82 E.g., Campbell, *1 Samuel*, 178.

otherwise unknown noun (thus, "went after Saul to a battle"; cf. 1 Sam 17:34; Amos 5:19: הארי...הדב "*a* lion...*a* bear").[83]

Even more troublesome for Gooding's attempt to read vv. 12–31 as immediately and naturally sequential to vv. 1–11 is the handling of the enigmatic הזה of v. 12. Proponents of a primary LXX text have almost unanimously explained the word as a harmonizing addition to the MT-only text, connecting this passage to the foregoing story of 16:1–13.[84] Gooding attempted to refute this argument with the observation that if this were indeed the opening line of an entirely separate narrative, one would expect instead here ויהי איש אפרתי...ושמו ישי. Gooding is correct and, ironically, may have unwittingly proposed the solution for those who view 1 Sam 17:12–31 as the opening scene of a separate narrative. J. Lust quickly observed that an editor could easily have made such a minor emendation to provide the developing composite narrative with the appearance of continuity.[85] Indeed, the application of this emendation would bring the structure of 17:12–14a fully into line with that of 1 Sam 9:1; with the rather innocuous supposition that 17:12 initially read ויהי איש אפרתי...ושמו ישי, both 9:1 and 17:12–14a would then exhibit the following features: (a) introductory formula ויהי איש; (b) statement of origin (GN + מן); (c) name of the father (PN + ושמו); (d) father's situation, including the notice that he had a son or sons (ולו ... בן / בנים); (e) name of the son(s) who will be the story's protagonist(s) (PN + ושם). Similarly, the introduction to Micah in Judg 17:1 displays elements (a), (b), and (e). Moreover, the structure is played upon in the introduction to Manoah (Judg 13:2), which bears elements (a), (b), and (c), as well as an explicit negation of (d), which eliminates the possibility of (e). Therefore, Gooding's observation works at cross-purposes to the remainder of his argument: every other text in which the phrase ויהי איש (אחד) appears forms the introduction to a new source-critical unit (Judg 13:2; 17:1; 19:1b; 1 Sam 1:1; 9:1; cf. 2 Sam 21:20 = 1 Chr 20:6?). If one assumes for the time being that vv. 12–31 indeed came from a separate source, then it is possible to posit an independent existence of vv. 12–14a as David's introduction into a longer story in which he was not yet known and perhaps the opening lines of this separate narrative. Upon that narrative's combination with the other version found in LXX^{B}, the editor deftly rewrote the first few words of v. 12 in order to

83 See GKC 406, 407 §§126n,r, respectively; S. R. Driver, *Notes on the Hebrew Text of the Books of Samuel* (Oxford: Clarendon, 1890), 112.

84 E.g., Hertzberg, *I & II Samuel*, 149; Tov, "Composition," 123; idem, "Nature," 43; Rofé, "Battle," 121.

85 See J. Lust, "Second Thoughts on David and Goliath," in *The Story of David and Goliath: Textual and Literary Criticism* (ed. Dominique Barthélemy et al.; OBO 73; Fribourg: University Press; Göttingen: Vandenhoeck & Ruprecht, 1986), 90–91.

present the already familiar David anew to the audience. In short, claims of the aboriginal unity of 17:1–11 + 12–31 on the basis of the introduction to David in v. 12 are unfounded.

A second difficulty for our argument, perhaps, is that the number of sons ascribed to Jesse in 17:12 seems to conflict with the four sons of v. 14, of whom David is the youngest. Although it is conceptually possible that four sons remain unaccounted for in the text (cf. 1 Chr 2:13–15)[86]—after all, the verse mentions only the three oldest sons (שלשה הגדלים; see also שלשת בני־ישי הגדלים in v. 13)—this interpretation is unnecessary, if we may accept the emendation proposed by S. De Vries, who suggested that this discrepancy merely signals that the introduction to David in v. 12 has been reworked on the basis of 16:10 (שבעת בניו): that is to say, originally Jesse had only four sons, all of which are named in both 16:6–10 and 17:13—Eliab, Abinadab, and Shammah.[87] Clearly, 16:6–10 and 17:13 are related in some way, but how are we to understand this relationship? Is this connection original, or should we recognize here the harmonizing work of a redactor? Halpern argued that 16:1–13 must form the prologue to 16:14–23,[88] which would thus clear the way for 17:12 to be harmonized with 16:10. However, the introduction David receives in 16:18 as "a son of Jesse the Bethlehemite who knows how to strum" (בן לישי בית הלחמי ידע נגן) is already introduction enough to the lad, whose self-characterization continues then in his monologue 17:34–36. On the other hand, Vermeylen proposed that 16:1–13* and 17:12–31 derive from the same redactional stratum and may be read sequentially.[89] But this proposal is contradicted by the recognition above that vv. 17:12–14a originally provided an independent introduction to David. In my mind, the most compelling solution is Campbell's assertion that 16:1–13 stands separate from vv. 14–23.[90] Since 16:1–13 bears significant commonalities to several other passages of presumably prophetic origin (e.g., the prophetically-emended narrative concerning the anointing of Saul in 1 Sam 9:1–10:16, esp. 10:1; and the anointing of Jehu in 2 Kgs 9:1–13), it may thus be

86 Mommer, *Samuel*, 181.

87 De Vries, "David's Victory," 28; see also Hertzberg, *I & II Samuel*, 149.

88 Halpern, *Constitution*, 160–61; cf. already Stoebe, "Goliathperikope," 399–400.

89 Vermeylen, *Loi du plus fort*, 98.

90 Campbell, *Of Prophets and Kings*, 126; see also Theodor Seidl, "David statt Saul: Göttliche Legitimation und menschliche Kompetenz des Königs als Motive der Redaktion von I Sam 16–18," *ZAW* 98 (1986): 39–55; and Barthélemy, "Trois niveaux," 47–48. Stoebe allows at most that 17:12–31 followed loosely on 13:7–15a ("Goliathperikope," 400). Literary studies have recognized the dramatic break between these two passages as well, despite reading them as parts of an integrated whole; see David M. Howard, "The Transfer of Power from Saul to David in 1 Sam 16:13–14," *JETS* 32 (1989): 473–83; and Brueggemann, "Narrative Coherence," 228.

considered a tertiary introduction to David added at some point by the author-editor who compiled the Prophetic Record (over against the introduction in 16:18, which leads directly into the common text of LXX^B and MT; and that in 17:12,14).[91]

Thus, there are signs of three independent introductions to David: (a) the anointing of David by Samuel in 16:1–13 (PR); (b) the introduction of David into Saul's court in 16:14–23, continued in 17:1–11,32–40 (i.e., what Tov has called Version 1); and (c) the coincidental arrival of David at the battlefield and subsequent participation in battle against a Philistine warrior, narrated in the story presently under scrutiny (17:12–31, etc.; Tov's Version 2). Regardless of the direction of the harmonizations, it is safe to claim that 16:10–16 and 17:12–14a have been brought into alignment with one another subsequent to the combination of these three traditions and that the latter forms the introduction to David belonging to an independent narrative and quite possibly comprises the opening lines of that narrative.

Whether the eighth (v. 12) or fourth in line (with vv. 13–14?), David remains in this narrative strand the youngest of Jesse's sons and therefore bears the onerous task of delivering supplies from home to his three older brothers who are camped with the army of Israel at the battle-front (vv. 13–14,16–18). When David arrives at the Israelite battle-lines, he finds his brothers in order to deliver the provisions and ask how they are faring (vv. 20–22). But while he is speaking with them, a Philistine warrior[92] steps forward into the space between the two armies (v. 23aβ), and the Israelites flee from fear (v. 24). The man is already well-known to the Israelites, since he has commonly stepped forward to taunt them (although the exact wording of that taunting goes unspoken). He is so well known, in fact, that Saul has offered the hand of his daughter to any man who will face the Philistine (v. 25). When David asks who the man is, he is told of the marital arrangements offered by the king (vv. 26–27). Although David's brother Eliab tries to talk David out of such foolishness (v. 28), David seems intrigued at the prospects of marrying the king's daughter (vv. 29–30). As the Philistine approaches, David rushes out to meet him (vv. 41, 48b). The youth quickly dispatches the Philistine, being better (literally "stronger") with the sling and stone than the professional warrior was with

91 Campbell, *Of Prophets and Kings*, 17–23; idem, "From Philistine to Throne," 40 n. 1; cf. Mommer, who attributes 16:1–13 to the author-compiler of the HDR (*Samuel*, 177–86, esp. 183). Seidl recognizes that 16:14–23 has usually been deemed the older of the two passages and that it bears significant thematic and theological commonalities with 1 Sam 9:1–10:16; this assessment is consistent with the schema presented here and in the following chapter ("David statt Saul," 47, 52; see also Vermeylen, *Loi du plus fort*, 82–87, esp. 84).

92 See n. 71 above.

his more sophisticated weaponry (v. 50). When Saul sees David's feat, he inquires as to the hero's identity, but even Abner, the commander of the army, does not know who the boy is (v. 55). The general brings the boy before Saul, introducing the two to one another (vv. 56–57). When David arrives in the presence of Saul, Saul's son Jonathan becomes fast friends with David, making a covenant with him and dressing him in the princely robes (18:1–4).[93] In this version, as in the first version, David becomes the commander of the army (v. 5).

The narrative arc of this second version's account of the battle and introduction of David into Saul's court is ostensibly the same as that of the first, and—when we take account of those verses that seem to harmonize the two passages—this version reads just as smoothly as does the other, with one exception: as E. Tov has noted, this version "lacks an account of the duel itself."[94] It seems plausible to me that v. 50 originally served as the second version's narration of the individuals' battle,[95] although it would admittedly comprise an extremely thin narration of the duel. However, the terse nature of v. 50 does not necessitate considering the LXX minuses as text simply removed from the longer, original account or as freely composed expansions on the part of the MT. It is logical that an editor who was combining two distinct traditions would omit the most obvious discrepancies or duplications, no matter how many other tensions and conflicts were apparent. In short, while problematic, the omission of an explicit narration of the duel does not constitute *a priori* grounds for consideration of the LXX^B text as inferior.[96]

Finally, two short episodes conclude the version of the narrative omitted from LXX^B. Predictably, those who claim the unity and primacy of the MT version frequently cite these passages as either obvious doublets or conflicting passages that required removal by an editor in order to

---

93 This serves as the instigating episode in Jonathan's self-identification with David, which sets the tone for the remainder of the story (Jobling, "Jonathan," 12). Barbara Green has argued that this scene (and particularly the notice in v. 2 that "Saul did not allow him to return to the house of his father") is one of the episodes detailing Saul's "adoption" of David (*Mikhail Bakhtin and Biblical Scholarship: An Introduction* [SemeiaSt 38; Atlanta: Society of Biblical Literature, 2000]: 67–134). Since both scholars analyze the text as a literary unity, neither would make the explicit source-division for which I have argued here. However, both observations are instructive for the present discussion. My response to Jobling has been made above; it is clear to me as well that Green's analysis of the story's theme in which Saul attempts to be David's father is an element common to both the HDR_1 (by becoming David's father-in-law) and the HDR_2 (by bringing David into his court).

94 Tov, "Nature," 41.

95 So also Campbell, "From Philistine to Throne," 36–37; and Dietrich, "Erzählungen," 183.

96 For example, compare my reading of Gen 31:44–33:20, in which the composite text allows several tensions to remain and omits *only* the duplication of Jacob's meeting with Esau (Jeremy M. Hutton, "Mahanaim, Penuel and Transhumance Routes: Observations on Genesis 32–33 and Judges 8," *JNES* 65 [2006]: 164–70, esp. 168).

render a more streamlined text. First, there is a short notice that Saul, in a rage, tried to kill David with a spear while David was playing the lyre for the king (18:10–11). This passage is a clear doublet of 19:9–10.[97] Since the latter follows much more naturally upon David's introduction into Saul's court, as a result of David's increasing popularity and Saul's corresponding degeneration into paranoia, that passage seems to be much more logically integrated in its context.[98] Although this circumstance certainly permits the excision of 18:10–11 as unnecessary in the larger context of 1 Sam 17–18,[99] in my opinion it does not necessarily prevent the assignment of 18:10–11a to a posited second version,[100] although that solution does seem improbable. More likely, the repetition indicates that vv. 10–11 were composed as a redactional insertion designed to weave together the posited alternate narrative strand (Version 2) with the account of David's introduction into Saul's court in the text common to LXX^B and MT (Version 1). It is additionally significant that the phrase used to narrate Saul's attempt on David's life (ויטל שאול את־החנית "Saul hurled the spear"; 18:11) anticipates the usage of the same phrase in 21:33 (with Jonathan as the target), a passage that cannot be related to the common text (17:1–11, etc.; see below).

Second, in this variant sequence Saul offers David the hand of his daughter Merab but withdraws the offer, instead giving her as a wife to Adriel the Meholatite (vv. 17–19).[101] Again, proponents of the MT as the primary text explain the omission of this passage in LXX^B as an editor's careful removal of a passage that stood in obvious conflict with David's marriage to Michal (18:20–21a,22–26a,27).[102] Yet the notice in v. 21b that

---

97 Kaiser, "David und Jonathan," 286; cf., though, Campbell, who does not recognize 9:10–11 as the second time mentioned in 18:10–11 (*1 Samuel*, 184).

98 See Willis, "Function," 308–10; Tov, "Nature," 42. I prefer to handle these passages redactionally rather than metabolically; cf. Yonathan Ben Nahum, "What Ailed the Son of Kish?" *JBQ* 19 (1991): 244–49; and Vladimir M. Berginer and Chaim Cohen, "The Nature of Goliath's Visual Disorder and the Actual Role of His Personal Bodyguard: נֹשֵׂא הַצִּנָּה (I Sam 17:7,41)," *ANES* 43 (2006): 27–44.

99 E.g., Tov, "Nature," 42.

100 Verse 11b ("But David eluded him twice" [NRSV]; ויסב דוד מפניו פעמים) seems quite clearly to be a harmonization of this tradition with 19:9–10. However, whether 18:11b was composed at the same time as vv. 10–11a or as a harmonizing supplement to those verses is difficult to discern.

101 For discussions of the political role of marriage in the Bible, see Jon D. Levenson and Baruch Halpern, "The Political Import of David's Marriages," *JBL* 99 (1980): 507–18; Peter D. Miscall, "Michal and Her Sisters," in *Telling Queen Michal's Story: An Experiment in Comparative Interpretation* (ed. D. J. A. Clines and T. C. Eskenazi; JSOTSup 119; Sheffield: Sheffield Academic Press, 1991), 246–60; Jo Ann Hackett, "1 and 2 Samuel," in *The Women's Bible Commentary* (ed. Carol A. Newsom and Susan H. Ringe; London: SPCK, 1992), 85–95; Ken Stone, "Sexual Power and Political Prestige," *BRev* 10.4 (1994): 53; Willi-Plein, "ISam 18–19," 144–47.

102 E.g., Rofé, "Battle," 120–21.

"Saul said to David *a second time* (בשתים),[103] 'You shall become my son-in-law today,'' which is similarly missing from the common text, suggests deliberate harmonization between two originally separate accounts. With an eye for detail, the editor has crafted a verse that is not inconsistent with the notice given earlier in the verses missing from LXX^B^ that the king had offered his hand in marriage to the warrior who could defeat the menacing Philistine (17:25); in fact, it recognizes that a promise has been made but that Saul reneged on that promise (18:19).[104] In the context of the longer (combined) text, that restitution may now come in the form of a political marriage to the king's daughter Michal. The phrase "a second time" has parallels in several texts in which deliberate harmonization between two previously independent sources has been accomplished; see, for example, 1 Sam 18:11b (discussed above) and, in particular, Samuel's proposal to "renew" the kingship in 1 Sam 11:14 (חדשׁ *piel*; see below, §7.3.1.5). Rather than supporting the claim that an editor removed these verses because of the perceived conflict, the explicit claim that Saul proposed a political marriage of one of his daughters to David a second time indicates that a variant tradition has been interpolated here at some point.

6.3.1.3. Theoretical Considerations

Two more theoretical points may be adduced as part of the larger argument that an original text close to the *Vorlage* of LXX^B has been combined with a single, cohesive tradition that now forms the bulk of MT 17:12–30,41, 48b,(50),55–58; 18:1–5,8b,(10–11a),12b,17–19,26b,29b–30, rather than shortened from a longer *Vorlage* identical to MT. First, Tov's study has shown that the translator of LXX "remained, as a rule, loyal to his parent text, and it is therefore not conceivable that he would have omitted some 45% of the text."[105] Second, although one cannot conclusively exclude the possibility that an earlier Hebrew tradent (instead of the Septuagintal

103 E.g., NRSV; the phrase may also mean "through the second (daughter)," with KJV and JPS, or provide a "second opportunity" to be the king's son-in-law, with ASV and NIV.

104 McCarter's impression that David turned the offer down is odd (*I Samuel*, 306). Similarly injudicious is McKenzie's assertion that "Merab's hand is a reward for future gallantry, not past deeds" (*King David*, 80). In fact, the text suggests that David's acceptance of Merab's hand introduces him inextricably into the army as a permanent fixture; it is in no way a condition of the marriage.

105 Tov, "Composition," 115; idem, "Nature," 38; but cf. the methodological criticism put forth by van der Kooij ("Story," 123–24). Auld points out that "the rendering…of the MT pluses" in LXX^A "was made by a different translator from the one who created the main Greek text" ("Story," 122; see also Michel Lestienne, *Premier Livre des Règnes*, vol. 9.1 of *Le Bible d'Alexandrie* [Paris: Cerf, 1997], 40–42, esp. 40).

translator) had made the decision to shorten the text,[106] Tov makes a compelling case that "there are no cogent reasons for assuming a large scale shortening of the original text."[107] In fact, "[i]t is highly unlikely that the Hebrew text would be revised only in chapters 17–18 and not in other chapters in 1 Samuel which contain obvious contradictions and doublets of stories…."[108] Aside from the implausibility of several purported shortenings (e.g., 18:1–4 does not conflict with anything in the common text), the omission of text as a rule is not nearly so common in the oral-textual interface as what D. Carr has called a "Trend toward Expansion" (*Trend zur Expansion*).[109] These arguments serve to diminish the probability that MT provides the earliest "complete" form of the text of 1 Samuel 17–18. Rather, the more archaic text is to be found in the passages common to LXX^B and MT. Moreover, a critical reading of the additional material in MT suggests it was at one time an independent tradition and has been interpolated into the common text through the evident addition of several harmonizing verses (e.g., 17:15,19).[110]

---

106 This idea was defended by Avraham Kuenen, *Historische-kritische Einleitung in die Bücher des Alten Testaments* (trans. Th. Weber; Leipzig: Reisland, 1890), 1.2:61–62; trans. of *Historisch-kritisch onderzoek naar het ontstaan en de verzameling van de boeken des Ouden Verbonds*; Leiden: Engels, 1861). Admitted also by, e.g., Dhorme (*Samuel*, 167–68), Dominique Barthélemy and David Gooding (both essays named "Response," in *The Story of David and Goliath: Textual and Literary Criticism* [ed. Dominique Barthélemy et al.; OBO 73; Fribourg: University Press; Göttingen: Vandenhoeck & Ruprecht, 1986], 96 [Barthélemy]; cf. 99–100 [Gooding]).

107 See Tov for explicit argumentation of this point ("Nature," 38–39); see also McCarter, *I Samuel*, 307.

108 Tov, "Composition," 118.

109 David M. Carr, "Empirische Perspektiven auf das Deuteronomistische Geschichtswerk," in *Die deuteronomistischen Geschichtswerke: Redaktions- und religionsgeschichtliche Perspektiven zur "Deuteronomismus"-Diskussion in Tora und Vorderen Propheten* (ed. Markus Witte et al.; Berlin: de Gruyter, 2006), 1–17, esp. 6–8; so also Vermeylen, *Loi du plus fort*, 91.

110 The number and nature of harmonizing additions is, of course, widely debated. The verses in 1 Sam 17:15,19 are reasonably understood as redactional additions designed, respectively, to deliver David back to his father's house and to unite this passage with Tov's Version 1, which specifies the site of the battle (17:1–2), and the current passage, which does not; for v. 15, see, e.g., Seidl, "David statt Saul," 41. Other apparently redactional passages not discussed above include 17:23b,31; and 18:6aα*,(8aα^2),26b. The notice in 18:19 may be redactional as well; see below. De Vries has also adduced expansions in 17:8–9,34–36,43,46aβ^2 ("David's Victory," 23–36); several of these suggested expansions seem logical, but one must clarify they are all represented in the LXX^B tradition as well. It is unnecessary to hypothesize with Brueggemann that the "distinct elements [of 1 Samuel 18] … existed independent of each other as floating units of tradition" ("Narrative Coherence," 226). Cf. also Trebolle, who doubts that either version ever comprised a unified account: "The episodes collected in [Version 1] appear never to have comprised a continuous and complete narrative strand. Likewise, it is not certain that, by collecting all the material added in [Version 2] (17:12–31,41,48b,50), we are in fact able to reconstruct a second version of the story of David and Goliath" ("Story," 28).

6.3.2. The Textual History of 1 Samuel 17–18

6.3.2.1. Initial Considerations

Despite the plausibility of the combination of two entirely independent narrative versions of David's entry into Saul's court, the date at which those two versions were combined remains obscure. At first, the commonsense *terminus post quem* of the combined text (MT) would seem to be the Hellenistic Period, after the translation of the LXX occurred.[111] Indeed, most solutions allowing for the MT's interweaving of two distinct traditions have made the translation of the LXX the centerpiece of the argument; usually this aspect of the solution is combined with a replace ment/integration element. For example, Lust suggested that 1 Samuel 17–18 displays indications of two variant traditions, one having entirely replaced the other at some point in the transmission history of the text: after the original "romantic tale" (Version 2) had been entirely replaced by the "heroic epic," the translation into Greek took place. "At the same time, or later, the 'romantic epic' concerning David's victory was reinserted and combined with the 'heroic epic'. The result was the Vorlage of the MT."[112] De Vries conceptualizes the order of events slightly differently. Along with others who allow for the composite nature of the MT text before it was abridged to form the shorter version now found in LXX^B,[113] De Vries argued the original introduction to David took place in the "saga" (1 Sam 17:12–31, etc.), which the "accession historian" (i.e., the Davidic apologist) used as the basis of this account.[114] Then, a pro-Davidic and anti-Saulide redactor added the introduction to David in 16:1–23 to show—already at the beginning of the HDR—that God supported David. A separate hero narrative (1 Sam 17:1–11, etc.) arose independently and replaced the saga-based text in the *Vorlage* of LXX^B (=OG) but was only interpolated into the Hebrew version.

I find both of these solutions improbable, however. First, Lust's proposal relies on what I would consider to be the rather tenuous premise of complete replacement or suppression and subsequent reinsertion. It seems extremely unlikely that, once excised from the tradition, a passage would be reintroduced. Moreover, against both Lust and De Vries, it is not clear why the "saga" or "romantic tale" should be considered the original beginning and the "heroic epic" the secondarily introduced one. Second,

111 E.g., McKenzie, *King David*, 71; Adam, *David und Saul*, 150.

112 Lust, "Story," 14.

113 See, e.g., Barthélemy, "Trois niveaux," 47–54; van der Kooij, "Story," 126–28; Dietrich, "Erzählungen," 180–84, 189; Aurelius, "David," 44–68.

114 De Vries, "David's Victory," 36.

De Vries's solution seems almost coincidental in the precision with which a later editor would have excised from an extended MT-type narrative exactly those passages that belonged originally—in this model—to a single, unified account. But at least De Vries allows that what remained had likewise originally been a similarly unified account. Even more problematic than De Vries's model are those that hypothesize the compilation of a congeries of narratives and the subsequent omission of the passages that purportedly create tensions, such that a cohesive narrative is whittled out of what was once accounted as a mélange of disparate traditions, rife with tensions.

Furthermore, neither solution is based on any demonstrable textual situation that obtained over the course of the text's transmission history. Although the presence of manuscripts apparently closely related to LXX^{B} at Qumran (4QSam^{a} and 4QSam^{b})—a relationship demonstrated only in passages other than 1 Samuel 17–18[115]—alongside of a manuscript more closely related to, but still superior to, MT (4QSam^{c})[116] indicates the variety of text types in which the book of Samuel appeared in late antiquity, no texts containing only 1 Sam 17:12–31,etc., have been found. Finally, neither schema takes into account the material and geographical limitations of a textualized account; because lengthening presumably occurred in one manuscript and its daughter manuscripts (i.e., those manuscripts copied directly from it or within the same community or interrelated communities) or, more likely, in the oral tradition of one scribal lineage, the *terminus post quem* after which the longer text was created is a moving target that cannot be determined with sufficient exactitude.

The *Vorlage* text of the LXX (or perhaps we ought to speak here already of antecedent oral traditions committed to memory within certain communities) may have diverged at the earliest immediately after the formation of the tradition or, at latest, shortly before the book of Samuel's

115 Frank Moore Cross et al., *1–2 Samuel* (vol. 12 of *Qumran Cave 4*; DJD 17; Oxford: Clarendon, 2005), 25–27, 223–24. However, in that recently released publication of 4QSam^{a}, 4QSam^{b}, and 4QSam^{c} by Cross et al., the extant passages on 1 Sam 17–18 provide no direct evidence as to whether 4QSam^{a} or 4QSam^{b} contained the shorter text (ibid., 78–80, 228). In fact, judging from the presence of 18:4–5 in Fragment 17 of 4QSam^{a} (ibid., 80), it would appear that that manuscript may have contained the longer account. Although Lust reckoned 18:1b,(3),4 to the Old Greek on the authority of Hippolytus (*De David et Goliat* 10,2–4), supposing that those verses had dropped out of LXX^{B} by parablepsis ("Story," 7–9), I do not find this solution compelling. I would suggest that Hippolytus may have been incorporating a well-known tradition here not present in his own source text, but which he knew from at least passing familiarity with the MT to have been a major motif of this episode. This may thus be a case of what might be called "oral-textual contamination" of the OG (still best represented by LXX^{B}) under influence from MT or one of its congeners (see more technically Barthélemy, "Response," 97; and Cross et al., *1–2 Samuel*, 25).

116 Cross et al., *1–2 Samuel*, 252–54.

translation into Greek. There are very few linguistic indicators suggesting incontrovertibly that Version 2 was composed as late as other texts in Late Biblical Hebrew;[117] rather, most of the features exhibited are consistent with Standard Biblical Hebrew (e.g., orthography of דוד instead of LBH דויד, etc.). Those features that Rofé has argued point to a 4th cent. dating are questionable;[118] a few of those that are reasonably well attested as

---

117 LBH as described by, e.g., Avi Hurvitz, *A Linguistic Study of the Relationship between the Priestly Source and the Book of Ezekiel: A New Approach to an Old Problem* (CahRB 20; Paris: Gabalda, 1982); Robert Polzin, *Late Biblical Hebrew: Toward an Historical Typology of Biblical Hebrew Prose* (HSM 12; Missoula, Mont.: Scholars Press, 1976); Mark F. Rooker, *Biblical Hebrew in Transition: The Language of the Book of Ezekiel* (JSOTSup 90; Sheffield: JSOT Press, 1990); idem, "Diachronic Analysis and the Features of Late Biblical Hebrew," *BBR* 4 (1994): 135–44. See also the assessment of Auld, "Story," 125: "Linguistically, [the Hebrew pluses] blend perfectly into the context .... Linguistically at least, the MT pluses are not an alien intrusion (like the pluses in A and L), but a careful development of the existing text in its own terms."

118 Rofé has argued that the entire passage of 1 Samuel 17–18 should be dated to "the fourth century B.C.E., at the end of the Persian period" ("Battle," 125–34, quote from 134). This assertion was made on the basis of several indicators in ch. 17, such as (a) the anomalous length of the account and its "paradigmatic" nature; (b) the lack of any further mention of the episode in Samuel, complete omission of the episode in Chronicles, and allusions to the episode in late material; (c) the Philistine hero appearing to have been only secondarily associated with Goliath; (d) linguistic evidence, including *orthographic indicators*, (d_1) the *plene* spelling of דוב in vv. 34,36, (d_2) the spelling קליא in v. 12; *lexical indicators*, (d_3) the presence of the verb ברר (repointing בְּרוּ as בֹּרוּ) in v. 8, (d_4) the Rabbinic nature of ערב *hiphil* in v. 16; *idiomatic indicators*, (d_5) the diachronic chiasmus ירא + חתת in v. 11; *semantic indicators*, (d_6) the semantic innovation of רע לבב in 17:28; *morphological indicators*, (d_7) the unexpected form יהושיע for יושיע in v. 47; *syntactic indicators*, (d_8) the "pleonastic phrase" מעל ל instead of על in v. 39, (d_9) the unexpected use of הזה with an indefinite noun in v. 17, (d_{10}) the appearance of *waw*-copulative (see *IBHS* §32.1.1) in consecution with a clear *way-yiqtol* consecutive form (ויקם), i.e., where *waw*-relative is expected in vv. 34–35, (d_{11}) the temporal use of ב + *inf. const.* without a preceding ויהי in vv. 55,57, and 58; and finally, (e) *realia* such as (e_1) the meaning of the term חפשי in 17:25, (e_2) the description of Goliath's armor in vv. 5–7, (e_3) the exact type of battle implied by vv. 4,23 (i.e., simple single or representative combat?). Auld did not discuss Rofé's linguistic arguments, but I find most of them unconvincing. Although a full refutation of Rofé's argument is impossible here, the following brief responses may be given: (a) The unconventional length of the David and Goliath episode (60 verses total) is a product of Rofé's interpretive decision to analyze 17:1–58; 18:2,5 as a whole, and the figure is cut nearly in half when either constituent version is examined on its own. Relatedly, the "paradigmatic" nature that Rofé describes is a function of the doubling of many of the episodes. (b) A similar argument with respect to the absence of the episode elsewhere in Samuel could be made for several episodes in which David features and need not indicate an extreme late dating of the passage. Moreover, the argument itself neglects the references to Goliath's sword and the attribution of its delivery to Nob by David in 1 Sam 21:10; 22:10. (c) The clearly secondary nature of the glosses identifying the Philistine hero as Goliath only testify to the fact that the episode is not necessarily historical and that the glosses are later than the base text; they have little, if any, bearing on the date of the base text. (d) Most of the *kinds* of arguments that Rofé has used here have been qualified elsewhere, primarily because they tend to overemphasize the presence of Aramaizing features without analyzing the possible reasons for Aramaism and do not sufficiently prove linguistic contrast between SBH and LBH (e.g. Gary A. Rendsburg, "Some False Leads in

features of later Hebrew are found in passages that De Vries had earlier and cogently deemed to be potentially late additions (17:8–9,34–36,43,46aβ²).[119] Furthermore, Hellenistic period combination of the two versions does not preclude that the additional material was as old as the common text of LXX^B and MT.[120] How far back in time, then, might the existence of two different texts—one shorter and one longer—extend? Finally (and relatedly), neither solution takes into account the process of combination and redaction evident in the remainder of the HDR beyond the confines of 1 Samuel 17–18. The process and full duration of the variant biforms' formations are therefore uncertain but must at least take into account those literary features of the complete HDR that may provide confirmation of the hypothesis defended here: 1 Samuel 17–18 evinces traces of two separate narrative collections that comprised relatively continuous and independent Histories of David's Rise.

6.3.2.2. Sibling Rivalry: Division on the Basis of Saul's Children

The source division performed on the basis of Saul's children, a tactic suggested above, can already be seen as consistent with the bifurcation of 1 Samuel 17–18 into two originally independent narratives. In Version 1, a component of what is designated below as the HDR_1, only Michal appears (18:20–21a,27–28); in Version 2, the beginning of what will be called the HDR_2 below, only Jonathan appears (18:1–4). Yet a successful defense of the two-source theory necessitates an adequate explanation of the variation in the two traditions between the daughter whom David married—Michal in the common text and Merab in the MT-only text. Although Michal is a

---

the Identification of Late Biblical Hebrew Texts: The Cases of Genesis 24 and 1 Samuel 2:27–36," *JBL* 121 [2002]: 23–46, esp. 24–35; idem, "Hurvitz Redux: On the Continued Scholarly Inattention to a Simple Principle of Hebrew Philology," in *Biblical Hebrew: Studies in Chronology and Typology* [ed. Ian Young; JSOTSup 369; London: T&T Clark, 2003], 104–28; Avi Hurvitz, "Hebrew and Aramaic in the Biblical Period: The Problem of 'Aramaisms' in Linguistic Research of the Hebrew Bible," in *Biblical Hebrew: Studies in Chronology and Typology* [ed. Ian Young; JSOTSup 369; London: T&T Clark, 2003], 24–37). (e) It is unclear to me that sufficient information is given in the text to enable Rofé's interpretation of the *realia* assumed by 1 Samuel 17–18. I hope to devote a fuller study to the final two aspects of Rofé's argument in the future; see cursorily Vermeylen, *Loi du plus fort*, 95.

119 De Vries, "David's Victory," 23–36.

120 Trebolle, "Story," 29: "The material added in [Version 2], which was probably transmitted in a very loose composition before its insertion in [Version 1], ... may be as old as what was collected in the shorter form of the text." Campbell suggests that Version 2 may be the older of the two and that one or both may have a setting in the Davidic Kingdom (*1 Samuel*, 186). McCarter dates the combination to the fourth century (*I Samuel*, 308); so also McKenzie, who sets the *terminus post quem* of the MT-only text at 200 BCE (*King David*, 71).

fixture in the HDR, and especially (or exclusively, as will be argued below, §6.5) in the traditions most closely connected to the common text of LXX^{B} and MT (i.e., the HDR$_{1}$), the only places in which Merab appears again are in the presumably harmonizing 1 Sam 14:49[121] and in the LXX^{L} and *Tg. Jon.* of 2 Sam 21:8, in which David delivers into the hands of the Gibeonites "the five sons of Merab whom she bore to Adriel, the son of Barzillai the Gileadite." Notwithstanding this severe affront to David's onetime purveyor of succor in Transjordan, this latter verse is noteworthy for textual reasons: the MT has here "Michal" rather than "Merab." Which takes text-critical precedence? W. Dietrich claims that "[t]he Septuagint replaces 'Michal' with 'Merab' [in 2 Sam 21:8] in order to avoid the tension."[122] But this solution seems to be overreaching the evidence in an attempt to harmonize what may prove to be two vastly different traditions and only serves to introduce more tension here: the information concerning Michal's marriage given in MT 21:8 ("the five sons of Michal the daughter of Saul that she bore to Adriel ben-Barzillai the Meholatite") is inconsistent with the information provided elsewhere in the biblical record, where she has been married to "Palti ben-Laish who was from Gallim" (1 Sam 25:44; cf. 2 Sam 3:15).[123] Thus, for Dietrich's emendation of LXX^{L} to be correct, he would have to argue that either (a) not only the daughter's name had been emended in the presumably independent LXX^{L}, *Tg. Jon.*, and two late Hebrew manuscripts,[124] but the details of her husband's identity as well or (b) MT 1 Sam 18:17,19 has secondarily emended an original "Michal" to "Merab" in order to avoid the same tension that occasioned the emendation in LXX^{L} 2 Sam 21:8.

121 For 1 Sam 14:49 as part of the secondary summary in 14:47–52, see Peter Mommer, "David und Merab—eine historische oder eine literarische Beziehung?" in *David und Saul im Widerstreit—Diachronie und Synchronie im Wettstreit: Beiträge zur Auslegung des ersten Samuelbuches* (ed. Walter Dietrich; OBO 206; Fribourg: University Press; Göttingen: Vandenhoeck & Ruprecht, 2005), 197.

122 Walter Dietrich, *The Early Monarchy in Israel: The Tenth Century B.C.E.* (trans. Joachim Vette; SBLBibEnc 3; Atlanta: SBL, 2007), 70 n. 24; compare also Stoebe, "David und Michael," 229; Kaiser, "David und Jonathan," 291–92 and nn. 38–39; and Eveline van Staalduine-Sulman, *The Targum of Samuel* (Studies in Aramaic Interpretation of Scripture 1; Leiden: Brill, 2000), 618. Van Staalduine-Sulman claims that *Tg. Jon.* added the name of Merab, but the syntax of the verse—both in Aramaic and in van Staalduine-Sulman's translation—would suggest that in fact it is Michal who has been inserted here parenthetically in order to harmonize the tradition received by the Targumic translator with the MT: וית חמשא בני מירב דרביאת מיכל בת שאול דילידת עדראל "and the five sons of Merab—whom Michal the daughter of Saul raised—, whom she bore to Adriel…"

123 For a longer discussion of the difficulties inherent in these passages, consult Mommer, "David und Merab," 196–204, esp. 202–3. It is unnecessary to assume with Mommer that Saul did, in fact, have two daughters and that 18:17–19 were composed to explain why David was not married to the elder one; cf. also Stoebe, "David und Mikal," 240–42.

124 E.g., *BHS*, ad. loc. See also the discussion in P. Kyle McCarter, *II Samuel: A New Translation with Introduction and Commentary* (AB 9; New York: Doubleday, 1984), 439.

Several scholars have noted that the tradition contained in 18:17–19 may be taken as parallel with David's marriage to Michal in 18:20–21a,22–26a,27–29a.[125] Clearly, there was a tradition in which David had been offered one of Saul's daughters, but David's claim to the daughter's hand in marriage was preempted or delayed when Saul realized David's machinations were directed towards the kingship. One possible explanation for the existence of parallel daughter-marriage stories would be that both were the fabricated products of Davidic assertions that the king had at some point married into the Benjaminite royal family. But there is equally the possibility of an authentic memory of such a marriage. The daughter's name in the HDR_1 was Michal, but in the alternate tradition, the daughter's identity is not so clear. One could speculate that the HDR_2 initially contained only the short notice in 18:17–18 that David was supposed to marry an unnamed daughter of Saul's, omitting only the two words מרב הגדולה from v. 17 (and consonant with 17:25, where the daughter is similarly unnamed). This daughter may have been understood to be Michal, but the marriage itself was unimportant in the context of this tradition because in this narrative it was Jonathan who was to serve the function of the "bridge figure."[126] Then, at the time of the intertwining of the HDR_2 with the HDR_1 (the latter of which included 21:8 towards its end and read מרב, an otherwise unknown daughter of the royal family), the redactor wanted to retain this portion of the text mentioning either Michal or simply a daughter of Saul (18:17–18) and had to harmonize it with the newly introduced HDR_1 story featuring Michal in an extended role. Through the addition of two words in v. 17 (the identity of the girl as the "elder daughter") and of vv. 19,21b, the redactor was able to provide an introduction to the character of Merab, an otherwise unexplained figure in HDR_1 (2 Sam 21:8). For some reason, Michal was inserted into the *Vorlage* of MT 21:8 at a later date.

To summarize, a far simpler solution than Dietrich's, and one which does not assign two different husbands to Michal (other than David), is to assume the "correct" reading is that of LXX^L, and a few other witnesses at 21:8 ("Merab"), which is an authentic remnant of tradition (although not necessarily historical), preserved within the loose group of texts collectively identified here as the HDR_1.[127] The schematic offer of marriage to David in the HDR_2 (1 Sam 18:17–18*) originally mentioned only the king's unnamed daughter: הנה בתי אתה אתן־לך לאשה. But with the com-

125 E.g., Robert B. Lawton, "David, Merob, and Michal," *CBQ* 51 (1989): 424 n. 6; Stoebe, "David und Mikal," 227; Hertzberg, *I & II Samuel*, 160.

126 See above, n. 58. For the possible identification of Paltiel and Adriel, see Stoebe, "David und Mikal," 230–33.

127 So also Willi-Plein, "ISam 18–19," 157–58 n. 86; and Mommer, "David und Merab," 202–3.

bination of the two Histories of David's Rise, the editor had to specify that this daughter was not the same one as Michal; finding another daughter of Saul already mentioned in the HDR_1, the editor imported that biographic datum into the present episode, inserting 18:19 as a harmonizing gloss.[128]

6.3.3. Concluding Remarks and a Proposal for the Development of MT vs. LXX^B 1 Samuel 17–18

After this analysis of potential harmonizations between the two traditions, the source-critical separation of the HDR can begin along the following lines, to which the text-critical difference between MT and LXX^B provides some oblique corroboration:

HDR_1: 1 Sam 16:14–23; 17:1–11,32–40,42–48a,49,51–54; 18:6aβb*–8a*,9,12a, 13–16,20–21a,22–26a,27–29a.[129]

HDR_2: 1 Sam 17:12* (with beginning emended to ויהי איש אפרתי...ושמו ישי, and with original ארבעה),13–14,16–18,20–23a,24–30,41,48b,(50),55–58; 18:1–2,(3),4–5,[130] 8b,(10–11a),12b,17–18*,29b–30.

Redactional harmonizations include: 1 Sam 17:12* (rewriting of beginning, and ארבעה → שמנה),15,19,23b,31,(50); 18:3,6aα*,8aα*,17 (+ הגדולה מרב),19, 21b,26b.

Thus, what has been proposed as a relatively objective basis for source division—the child of Saul's who figures as the bridge-character for the transfer of Saul's kingdom to David—both helps to confirm the identification of Versions 1 and 2 in 1 Samuel 17–18 as continuous and independent narratives and paves the way for a new breakdown of the larger traditional narrative collections associated with those two episodes (the HDR_1 and HDR_2, respectively). It remains, however, to propose a process of development explaining the fact that the OG preserved the proposed composite text of HDR_1 + HDR_2 (or HDR_{1+2}) throughout 1 Samuel 19–2 Samuel 6* but not in 1 Samuel 17–18. It is difficult to account for the absence of the beginning of the HDR_2 in OG alongside the presence there of apparent additions to the HDR_1 text of 1 Samuel 17–18 that must have been made

128 Kaiser reaches a similar conclusion ("David und Jonathan," 292); cf. Willi-Plein, "ISam 18–19," 156–58.

129 It is recognized that these passages contain a number of the extant LBH features in 1 Sam 17:1–18:30 and that one or more levels of editorialization have occurred here; see, e.g., Vermeylen, *Loi du plus fort*, 92–93; but cf. Aurelius, "David," 44–68. Without a fuller analysis, which would be impractical for the purposes of the present study, it is difficult to make this division with any more precision.

130 For the possible omission of v. 3, see below.

subsequent to the combination of the full HDR_{1+2} (e.g., 17:8–9,34–36, etc.[131]). I can surmise three ways that the omission occurred:

(a) It seems a remote possibility that the HDR_2 introduction to David (1 Sam 17:12–30*,55–58*,18:30*) was not combined with the rest of the text of Samuel until *after* the combination of the HDR_{1+2}, its subsequent inclusion in the PR and DtrH, and the subsequent separation of textual traditions that led to the variations between the MT and OG. The problem with this solution, however, is that it divorces the addition of the HDR_2 account of David's introduction from the rest of the claimed HDR_2 text, shoving its interpolation into the now composite HDR_1 + HDR_2 text much later. The OG shows no other such obvious signs that its *Vorlage* separated from that of the MT any time before the final redaction of the DtrH (although cf. 3 Kgdms 11–12). This *terminus post quem* forces the insertion of the HDR_2 introduction (1 Sam 17:12–31*, etc.) into some versions of the text (*Vorlage* of MT)—but not others (*Vorlage* of OG)—well into the Persian period, much too late for stories about Jonathan to have been politically productive.

(b) A second option would be to suggest that somehow, the *Vorlage* of the OG had been corrupted by the physical loss of a section of the text. This loss was supplemented with material that lay at hand, but that material was derived from a *very* early text or oral tradition of Samuel containing only the HDR_1 material. While this solution seems preposterous at first glance, a similar situation of manuscript replacement seems to have obtained in the section 2 Sam 11:2–1 Kgs 2:11.[132] For some reason, that section of LXX^B shows signs of being *kaige*, an alternative and later textual tradition rather than the expected OG. Similarly, the *same* section in the sixth column of the Hexapla, which normally presents the *kaige* reading, seems to follow the OG.[133]

(c) Finally, a third possibility exists. If we allow for divergent traditions already at the level of the oral-textual interface, we might propose that the variant *Vorlagen* of MT and OG were preserved in two different

131 See De Vries, "David's Victory," 23–36.

132 James Donald Shenkel has extended this textual span to include 2 Sam 10:1–11:1 (*Chronology and Recensional Development in the Greek Text of Kings* [HSM 1; Cambridge, Mass.: Harvard University Press, 1968], 117–20).

133 H. St. John Thackeray, *The Septuagint and Jewish Worship: A Study in Origins* (London: Oxford University Press, 1921), 16–28,114–15. It is almost as if the pages of each manuscript had been ripped out and swapped between codices! Richard Saley has pointed out to me (personal communication) that it is possible Origen sought to supplement his sixth column (normally *kaige*) with a translation that was a variant to that of column 2 (normally the OG, but *kaige* here), using whatever variant was at hand. Thus, he managed to find an extant exemplar of the OG. But this supposition does not answer exactly how LXX^B came to contain a section of *kaige* to begin with.

communities valuing their own respective inherited (and memorized) tradition over the other.[134] In this model, the community that preserved the *Vorlage* of the OG as its idiosyncratic version of Samuel did not admit (or make judgment as to) the authority of the HDR_2 introduction but allowed into its textual or oral tradition most of the emendations and theological elaborations eventually introduced into the portion of text it shared in common with the community or communities that preserved the longer text.[135] In short, this model would allow for the selective updating of two different oral-textual traditions by communities that remained distinct from—but in conversation with—one another.

Disagreement is sure to persist among students of the formation of the book of Samuel, particularly as pertains to these chapters, and the three proposals made here are only the barest sketches of schemas that would permit early combination of these two distinct narrative corpora, while at the same time taking account of the available manuscript data. Of these three suggested schemas for the development of 1 Samuel 17–18, I favor the third, tentatively. This model eschews previous arguments dedicated to recovering the "original" text and instead prefers to identify both LXX^B and MT as authentic representatives of nearly contemporaneous—and equally authoritative—competing textual traditions. Accordingly, the variance between the two manuscripts should be attributed to the exigencies of the simultaneous preservation of variant textual traditions and not simply to overly simplistic schemas of textual omission or supplementation in sequential stages of development.

In the following two sections (§§6.3–4), I continue to examine the original forms of the two Histories of David's Rise and propose a series of hypothetical redactional combinations that served to retain a consistent level of social meaning within the politico-historical milieu within which each developed. Finally, at beginning of the conclusion (§8.1), I lay out the brief schema of the redactional history whereby the complex formed by the early Saul narratives (NSR_{AB}) and the HDR_1 was combined with its counterpart complex HDR_2 + SSN.

134 I rely here on the oral-textual interface and the memorization and preservation of texts within scribal "families" as described by David M. Carr, *Writing on the Tablet of the Heart* (Oxford: Oxford University Press, 2005). In this regard, I believe that we can move beyond Barthélemy's objection to the hypothesis that in LXX^B we find evidence of a literary stage of 1 Samuel 17 before the stage at which Version 2 was added ("Trois niveaux," 49).

135 Cf., however, Jürg Hutzli, who has documented some emendations made to the shared portion of the MT not represented in LXX^B ("Mögliche Retuschen am Davidbild in der masoretischen Fassung der Samuelbücher," in *David und Saul im Widerstreit—Diachronie und Synchronie im Wettstreit: Beiträge zur Auslegung des ersten Samuelbuches* [ed. Walter Dietrich; OBO 206; Fribourg: University Press; Göttingen: Vandenhoeck & Ruprecht, 2005], 103–9).

6.4. The Relationship of HDR_2 to Its Surrounding Material

6.4.1. Doublets within the HDR_2 Complex

The recognition that Michal and Jonathan play significant dramatic roles in the HDR_1 and HDR_2, respectively, can aid in the attribution of various passages of 1 Samuel to each literary collection. It is not surprising that the relatively small role played by Michal in the HDR_1 has not classically been viewed as a narrative doublet to the position played by Jonathan in the HDR_2. Following the introduction of David to Saul's court in chs. 17–18, Michal appears in only one scene before Saul's death (1 Sam 19:8–17, belonging to the HDR_1). In contrast, Jonathan appears in no less than three: (a) There is an initial expository scene in which Jonathan convinces Saul—with David eavesdropping—that David, who had slain "the Philistine," was an innocent man and deserved no such harsh treatment as Saul plotted against him (1 Sam 19:1–7); (b) there follows a medial scene in which the narrative tension rises. David comes to Jonathan and asks why Saul is trying to kill him. The two make a covenant with one another and then formulate a plan in which David will skip dinner with the king. Jonathan informs David of Saul's violent reaction by an elaborate sign involving a young servant fetching the arrows that Jonathan shoots from his bow, and David runs away (20:1–21:1). (c) The last scene in which David and Jonathan appear together narrates Jonathan's journey to meet David in the wilderness. Jonathan predicts David's rule over Israel and makes a covenant with David. The two part ways, never to see one another again (23:16–18).

The fact that doublets seem to appear even within the Jonathan passages contributes to the neglect of Michal's rescue of David as a doublet of Jonathan's protection of the same. The first scene of the doublet (19:1–7), in which Jonathan tells David to hide in a field while Jonathan talks to Saul about David, seems parallel to the second scene (20:1b–4,18–39; 21:1).[136] In both, David hides in a field, while Jonathan susses out Saul's intentions. In the first, the conversation between Saul and Jonathan occurs at the field in which David is hiding within earshot; in the second, the conversation occurs elsewhere, and Jonathan's instructions to David are conveyed through the use of the prearranged sign.[137] Therefore, in both

136 For the omission of vv. 11–17,23,40–42 from this scene, see, e.g., McCarter, *I Samuel*, 342–44; Kaiser, "Beobachtungen," 11; and idem, "David und Jonathan," 287–88.

137 If the omission of vv. 40–42 in this scene from the original account is a valid emendation, then David hears Jonathan giving the instructions to the servant and, knowing that the command "Run! Hurry! Don't just stand around!" (v. 38a) is meant for him, David takes flight (21:1). It is possible that v. 38 is an addition, since the words spoken by Jonathan in v.

stories the instructions are given to David secretly. Yet neither one directly contradicts the other in the order given. Indeed, Saul promises that he will allow David to live in the earlier scene, but given the portrayal of Saul's irrational behavior in the HDR_2, it need not be the case that this promise precluded the continuation of his attempts to kill David. Halpern took this as an indication that the two scenes served as what might be called *external doublets* (that is, as doublets designating the presence of variant source texts),[138] but 19:1–7 and 20:1b–10,18–39; 21:1 can more readily be explained as sequential episodes in the original form of HDR_2, either occasioned by their original independence and secondary juxtaposition within the loose collection or explained as *internal doublets*, that is, as doublets formed by the addition of one of the members at the time of the story's inclusion into a larger narrative complex (here, at the time of the HDR_2's combination with the SSN).

Similarly, there are two accounts of a covenant made between David and Jonathan outside of 18:3. Both 20:11–17,23,40–42 and 23:16–18 speak of a pact made between the two. The second episode (23:16–18) is quite short and has the feel of an explanatory intrusion, designed to solidify the reader's belief that Jonathan bore no ill will against David, whom he considered to be the proper heir of the kingship (v. 17). In all respects, it seems to be a secondary insertion designed only to reiterate the earlier covenant.[139] As noted above (§5.3.4.1), the first pact made between David and Jonathan (20:11–17,23,40–42) *also* shows signs of being an intruding secondary insertion. In theory, these outward and explicit manifestations of Jonathan's love for David indicate the presence of two narrative traditions, but that need not be the case. For some reason, Halpern does not separate these two from one another, instead attributing both scenes to his B source.[140] In this case, I agree with Halpern's assessment that both episodes of covenant may be (loosely) attributed to the same narrative complex.

An adequate and reasonable explanation for the presence of multiple and diverse scenes presenting Jonathan and David can be given. The various duplications and explanatory passages mentioned here can be read

---

37 complete the agreed-upon sign. However, it seems equally plausible to me that Jonathan's command for the boy to hurry in v. 38a is an added note of urgency in the secret message to David.

138 Halpern, *Constitution*, 164; for the dismissal of 19:1–7 as secondary, see Kaiser, "David und Jonathan," 283 and n. 11.

139 Cf. Langlamet, "De 'David' au 'Livre'," 353. For a vastly different understanding of the passages concerning the pact that David and Jonathan make, see Jerzy Woźniak, "Drei verschiedene literarische Beschreibungen des Bundes zwischen Jonathan und David," *BZ* n.s. 27 (1983): 213–18.

140 Halpern, *Constitution*, 168, 171.

as providing mounting evidence that although the SSN document had been appended onto the HDR_2 *before* the combination of that complex with the complex of the HDR_1, several strengthening filaments were added at the same time as or—more likely, *after*—the complexes' combination in order to solidify the text's assertions of David's copacetic handling of Jonathan's descendant (2 Samuel 9*). Therefore, in light of the supposed redactional priority of a HDR_2 + SSN complex, it seems logical that we should consider both 20:11–17,23,40–42 and 23:16–18 as *internal doublets* serving to unite the HDR_2 with the SSN.[141] An explicit notice of Jonathan and David's *covenant* to one another would have been improbable in a story in which the death of Jonathan at his father's side on Gilboa (2 Sam 1:1–17) concludes Jonathan's appearances in that narrative, without the extension of the covenantal obligations to the other's family (בית דוד; 1 Sam 20:16).[142] In the original and independent HDR_2 collection, with its end limited by 2 Sam 2:4a,[143] David's escape was occasioned by Jonathan's friendship, and concern for the Bethlehemite's life, but not necessarily anything more.[144] After their departure, the two never see one another again, with David spending his time hiding out in the wilderness of Judah and in the Philistine territories. The deaths of Saul and Jonathan—the only heir known by the HDR_2—on Gilboa allowed the transfer of the kingdom to David. With the addition of the Benjaminite episodes into the SSN (and particularly 2 Samuel 9*) and the increasingly close connection between the SSN and the consolidated HDR_2, David's grace shown to Mephibosheth took on a new overtone. As described above (§5.3.4.1), the figure of Mephibosheth was later reframed to function as the vehicle for David's

141 See similarly Timo Veijola, "David und Meribaal," *RB* 85 (1978): 338–61; and Willi-Plein, "ISam 18–19," 149.

142 Timo Veijola accounted both 1 Sam 20:12–17,42b and 23:16–18 along with 24:18–23a to DtrG (*Die ewige Dynastie: David und die Entstehung seiner Dynastie nach der deuteronomistischen Darstellung* [AASF B 193; Helsinki: Suomalainen Tiedeakatemia, 1975], 81–93). This is not entirely consistent with the schema presented here, but it may be possible that these covenental obligations may be partitioned further between those sections that assure a unidirectional promise made by Jonathan (18:3; 20:11–16, MT v. 17) and those that present a reciprocal covenant (LXX 20:17; 23:16–18). Thus, it may be overstepping the available evidence to claim Deuteronomistic authorship for the entirety of these passages.

143 2 Sam 2:4a can be established as a maximal limit of the HDR_2 because of the recognition that the CH picked up as early as 2 Sam 2:8 (see §5.3.4) and the attribution of 2:4b–7 to HDR_1 (see below, §6.5.1). However, the logical ending of a story of the battle between David and Saul ends with Saul's death and with David's accession to the *Israelite* throne concomitant with his reception of the signs of kingship, the diadem and armband of Saul (2 Sam 1:10). David's movement to Hebron in 2 Sam 2:1–4a seems to assume the limitation of his kingdom only to Judah and therefore anticipates the ensuing battle with the "remaining" house of Saul (whose existence, outside of the apparently resurrected Joab, is only first mentioned in the CH). I would therefore attribute 2 Sam 2:1–4a to the redactional joint between the HDR_2 (which originally ended at 1:27) and the CH/SSN (which begins in 2:8).

144 So also Kaiser, "David und Jonathan," esp. 288–89, 294–96.

gace to the remaining Saulide family. Several stories of the HDR_2 detailing the relationship between David and Jonathan had to be adjusted such that they provided adequate explanation of the "promise" made to Jonathan that served as the foundational reason for bringing Mephibosheth into David's court. This literary feature, possibly attributable to Dtr, continued to defend David and his dynasty against the accusations of the disenfranchised Benjaminites (see §5.4.2). It would have been at this time that the covenant passages in 20:11–17,23,40–42; 23:16–18; and possibly 18:3 were added to the substrate level of the HDR_2.[145] If my reconstruction of the varied natures of all the episodes involving Jonathan is correct, the original form of the loose HDR_2 collection would have appeared approximately as follows.

6.4.2. The Extent of the HDR_2

The HDR_2:

[1 Sam 13–14 (now revised)]*[146] The story begins with little direct narration of the process whereby Saul came to be king. In opposition to the HDR_1, which had to account for the introduction of kingship in Israel, the HDR_2 *assumed* the kingship in Israel and proceeded from the assumption that Saul held that position.[147] The traditions in 13–14 have been so thoroughly redacted (see, e.g., my interpretation of 14:6–15 in §7.3.2.3) that any search for the obvious beginning of the HDR_2 comes up emptyhanded. For this reason, the present study begins with the appearance of

---

145 The strength of this argument is increased when we realize both additions were made within contexts that can be shown definitively to have been original scenes in the HDR_2 (see below); cf. Veijola, *Ewige Dynastie*, 85–86.

146 Many of the textual traditions in 1 Samuel 13–14 *cannot* be attributed to the HDR_2. 1 Sam 13:1–7 is a mixture of redactional notes designed to unite the various traditions in the current biblical text (e.g., v. 7) and of comprehensive structural notes (such as v. 1) appended to the text as a fairly late stage of redaction. 13:8–15 seems to be a similarly late text (Campbell, *Of Prophets and Kings*, 54 and n. 79). The first set of verses that can be reasonably attributed to the HDR_2, then, are 13:19–23, which provide an exposition of the impending battle between the Israelites and the Philistines and describe the intolerable situation in which the Israelites must make their way to Philistia to sharpen any metal tools or weapons. This passage seems familiar with the Philistines of history and is at the very least consistent with most of the other biblical notices concerning the Philistines that attribute metallurgical skills to that group (Peter B. Machinist, "Biblical Traditions: The Philistines and Israelite History," in *The Sea Peoples and Their World: A Reassessment*, [ed. E. D. Oren; Philadelphia: University Museum, University of Pennsylvania, 2000], esp. 58–59).

147 I do not attribute any of the three rises of Saul (1 Sam 9:1–10:16; 10:17–27; 11:1–15) to the HDR_2. Halpern considered there to be only two Narratives of Saul's Rise (*Constitution*, 152–60), but cf. my arguments against the limitation of that number to two (see §7.1) and against the identification of those pericopes in general (see §§7.2–3).

the HDR_2 in its first traceable location, 1 Samuel 17 (the verses omitted by the LXX[B]; see above).

[1 Sam 17:12,13–14,16–18,20–23a,24–30,41,48b,(50),55–58; 18:1–2,4–5, 8b, (10–11a), 12b, 17–18*, 29b–30; 19:1–7; 20:1–4, 18–22, 24–39; 21:1]* The HDR_2 story of David's slaying of the Philistine and of his introduction into Saul's court has already been discussed above (§6.2.2), as have the narratives of Jonathan's rescue of David. In this regard, the narrative action of the HDR_2 moves quite similarly to that of the HDR_1 (see §6.5), since both exhibit a tight structure of (a) David's defeat of the Philistine and subsequent introduction into Saul's court, (b) the formation of a relationship between David and Saul's child, and (c) the discovery by the child of Saul's plot to kill David and the ensuing rescue of David by that progeny. From the time of David's escape, the wanderings begin.

[23:14aβ–15; 23:19–28]*[148] David moves to Ziph, where the inhabitants of the region discover him. Saul is informed of the refugee's location and surrounds the area, but before he can capture David, he receives word that the Philistines are attacking "the land" (presumably the territory of Benjamin) and leaves. *[26:1–25*]*[149] A second narrative occurs in the wilderness of Ziph. Again, the Ziphites inform Saul that the fugitive David is hiding out in their land (v. 1). This notification is constructed in a manner quite similar to their initial notice in 23:19:

הלוא דוד מסתתר עמנו במצדות בחרשה בגבעת החכילה אשר מימין הישימון (23:19)

"Isn't David hiding among us, in the fortified areas, in Horsha, in the hill of Hakilah, which is south of Yeshimon?

הלוא דוד מסתתר בגבעת החכילה על פני הישימון (26:1)

"Isn't David hiding among us, in the hill of Hakilah, which is across from Yeshimon?

This similarity suggests one of the episodes is a later addition, possibly deriving from the same time as the additions discussed above (20:11–17; etc.), which belong to the level of redaction in which the SSN was combined with the HDR_2.[150] At best, we can say only that the Ziph-based narratives in the HDR_2 form a pair of what appear to be internal doublets.[151]

---

148 This episode must be considered the doublet of the Qeilah episode of the HDR_1 (23:1–13), in which David moves into the area and is discovered by the inhabitants who inform Saul.

149 I attribute 1 Sam 25:2–42 to neither History of David's Rise. It bears some degree of continuity with both stories but insufficient elements to link it to either one.

150 While 26:1–25 serves as a doublet to 1 Sam 24, it is possible that the latter is the secondary text (see n. 172). The scene in 23:19–28 also has its corresponding doublet in the HDR_1, namely, David's near entrapment in 23:1–13.

151 However, F. H. Cryer ("David's Rise to Power and the Death of Abner: An Analysis of 1 Samuel xxvi 14–16 and Its Redaction-Critical Implications," *VT* 35 [1985]: 385–94) has

[27:1–28:2]*[152] From Ziph, David escapes to the Philistine territories—an apparent external doublet of the tradition preserved in 21:11–16[153]—and dwells there for quite some time with his entire family.[154] The notice in v. 4 points to the fact that Saul ceases to chase David after the preservation of the monarch's life in ch. 26, forming a doublet with 24:17–22. In both sources, then, the confrontation in the wilderness is the last time David and Saul ever meet face to face. David thrives in Achish's court, becoming the master of Ziklag and conducting raids against those tribes and ethnic groups surrounding the Judahite hill-country (vv. 5–8). David leaves none alive to bring word to his master Achish that he has, in fact, not been plundering the ethnically Israelite areas (vv. 9–12). Thus,

---

argued that certain links in the narrative (and particularly in vv. 14–16)—namely, (a) the condemnation of Abner for not guarding the "anointed" of Yahweh; and (b) the condemnation of the sons of Zeruiah for being hotheads—link this pericope to the redactional stratum proposed by Ernst Würthwein, which sought to absolve David of his complicity in Abner's death and to condemn Joab (*Die Erzählung von der Thronfolge Davids—theologische oder politische Geschichtsschreibung?* ThSt B 115 [Zurich: Theologischer Verlag, 1974]: 7–59, here 17, 43–47). Cryer dates this redaction (combining HDR and SN) to the time of Solomon on the basis of incidentals. If Cryer's understanding of the narrative is to be followed, this may suggest an attribution of ch. 26 to the redaction combining the HDR_2 with the SSN. It may further suggest an original theme of the SSN, namely, David's innocence and Joab's guilt. In that regard, this suggestion is certainly consistent with other scenes in the SSN that seem to emphasize Joab's brutality and Machiavellian nature (e.g., 2 Sam 3:27; 18:15; 20:9–10). Since the SSN had already picked up on this theme and used it as a justification for Solomon's murder of Joab (Cryer, "David's Rise," 391)—an event implicitly integral to the political stabilization of the kingdom—the redactor who combined the HDR_2 with the SSN complex surely had its imagery at his disposal. I disagree, however, with Cryer that vv. 14–16 are necessarily an insertion. The assumption Cryer makes—that the "good" Joab material must be from an earlier stratum (ibid., 389)—is unnecessary, since it could foreshadow his ultimate demise (1 Kgs 2:28–35). The irony of a hero who falls from the dynasty's graces may have been an intentional literary device, used to explain how David's head general became such a *persona non grata* within the Solomonic court. Also, Cryer's assessment that "the 'Yahweh's anointed' topos presupposes knowledge of Saul's [secret] anointing" (ibid., 391) strikes me as misguided as well. As opposed to the early prophetic redaction of the NSR_{AB} with the HDR_1, it is simply *assumed* throughout the SSN that the king has been anointed (e.g., 1 Kgs 1:34). Nor do I agree that the "Yahweh's anointed" topos "is a piece of pure dynastic propaganda supporting the Davidic line" (ibid., 391), because it bears resonations with the mode of Yahwistic legitimization also claimed by the Jehuite line (2 Kgs 9:1–13; Campbell, *Of Prophets and Kings*, 17–23). Rather, it strikes me as a *prophetic* legitimization of the dynasty.

152 Although there is no clear indication at beginning of this scene that it belongs inherently to the HDR_2, its natural continuation throughout the latter part of 1 Samuel and ultimate culmination in 2 Samuel 1 firmly establish this tradition's inherence to the narrative tradition of HDR_2.

153 It is not clear to me that 21:12–16 belongs inherently to the HDR_1. However, the clear rooting of 27:1–28:2; 29:1–30:31 in the HDR_2 provides some cause for that attribution. See also n. 166.

154 Verse 3 knows of David's marriages to Ahinoam and Abigail, apparently incorporating ch. 25 into the narrative horizon of the HDR_2 (if it were not original to that structure).

David earns the trust of his liege to such an extent that he is called to the battle of Gilboa with Achish (28:1–2).

[29:1–30:31]*[155] As the Philistines are amassing for war with the Israelites, David's ethnicity raises doubts with the other commanders, so Achish is forced to send David back to Ziklag. David and his men return to their hometown while the Philistines march on to Jezreel (29:1–11). Arriving home, they find that a marauding band of Amalekites has destroyed the city and plundered their wives and children. David and his men fly in hot pursuit, ultimately catching the raiding party, putting it to the sword, and returning safely with the spoils of the battle (30:1–31). As Halpern (among others) has pointed out, this episode provides David with a perfect alibi for the battle at Gilboa, alleviating any concern for allegations of impropriety in his dealings with the Saulide dynasty.[156]

[2 Sam 1:1–27; (2:1–4)] Because David has not gone to the battle (and because the narrator of the HDR_2 is not omniscient, speaking instead from David's point of view),[157] we are informed only indirectly of the deaths of Saul and Jonathan on Mt. Gilboa by an Amalekite runner who claims to have killed Saul at the king's bidding (vv. 1–10). David, mourning the deaths of the anointed king of Israel and of his friend Jonathan, rends his garments and has the messenger killed (vv. 11–16). The remainder of the narrative comprises David's composition of a song for Saul and Jonathan (vv. 17–27). I see no reason to doubt that the HDR_2 initially ended with this song, since it laments the deaths of the Benjaminite royals, thereby implicitly clearing the way for David's reign. This chapter, as noted above, serves with the omitted text of 1 Samuel 17–18 as a benchmark for the separation of the two Histories of David's Rise, since *only* a single son of Saul—Jonathan—is of concern throughout the chapter. In this regard, the style and content of David's lament is consistent with its identification as an original part of the HDR_2. The maximal limit of the HDR_2 should probably be considered 2 Sam 2:4a, but it is not clear that 2:1–4a do, in fact, belong to this collection.

155 Despite the intervening chapter (28:3–25), it is clear from the storyline that this passage continues the concerns of David's loyalty generated and problematized in 27:1–28:2. The presence of Abiathar, known elsewhere from the HDR_1, in two verses whose originality is spurious (30:7–8), may point to the secondarity of those verses.

156 Halpern, *Constitution*, 172.

157 The narrator of the HDR_1, in contrast, tends to take a stance of omniscience, narrating from the points of view both of David and of Saul (see, e.g., 1 Sam 28:3–25).

6.4.3. The Date and Function of the HDR_2

A brief discussion of the original intended function of this narrative is warranted here. As I have argued throughout the preceding discussion, the Solomonic apologist was able to construct a reasonable (although not necessarily successful) piece of royal apology at the end of the apparently pro-David CH (i.e., the SA narrative in 1 Kings 1–2, as well as its exposition in 2 Sam 11:1–12:25). If we may take Würthwein's and Cryer's observations on the material in the SSN demonizing Joab as applicable to the present source-critical division,[158] then it is fully possible that the author of the SSN used motifs of Joab's violence as a disguise and justification of that figure's political murder. The motif was retrojected frequently into the SSN, but almost no mention is made in the HDR_2: other than the brief note in 1 Samuel 26 (see discussion above), Joab receives no such textual treatment in the HDR_2 when that text's substratum is divorced from its later accretions. The text apparently seeks only to justify David over against the Saulide Jonathan.[159] But if this observation is correct, then the text of the HDR_2 was written at a time when Jonathan was widely recognized to have been no threat (having been killed on Gilboa), and this circumstance forces us to expand the probable horizon of intent to include all the remaining Saulides—or perhaps even Benjaminites—who may have had a claim to the Israelite throne, which David now occupied. The schematic presentation of Jonathan as the *only* son of Saul, and as a bridge figure,[160] suggests that the narrative was composed with an eye toward the relevant topic of the day: why it was the Davidic family and not the heirs of Saul who controlled the northern part of the kingdom. The relative independence of this text with respect to the SSN complex belies the heavy thematic stress it exerted on the latter, especially with respect to the recognition of the only possible heir through whom the Saulide crown could pass—Jonathan. While the two narratives or narrative collections (HDR_2 and SSN) existed separately until the time of their combination, they were hardly independent of one another. The HDR_2 collection was prior to and informed the worldview of the CH (and the SSN, which was founded upon the CH). I therefore suggest a dating of the HDR_2 sometime around the end of David's reign.

158 Würthwein, *Erzählung*, 43–47; Cryer, "David's Rise," 385–94. Würthwein suggests the following episodes as insertions utilizing this motif: 2 Sam 15:24–29; 16:5–14; 18:2b–4a,10–14; 20:4–5,8–13; 14:2–22.

159 In short, it was not until the addition of the SA to the CH that Joab's behavior was portrayed as worthy of his death.

160 With Jobling, "Jonathan," 4–23; and Sakenfeld, "Loyalty and Love," 220–26.

6.5. The Relationship of HDR_1 to Its Surrounding Material

6.5.1. The Extent of the HDR_1

The clarification of the HDR_2 in the preceding section allows for a much simpler discussion of the HDR_1. As noted above, the diagnostic criterion upon which the present separation of paired episodes has progressed is the identity of Saul's deceptive child. In the case of the HDR_1, that child is Michal, whom David marries after his bout with the Philistine. As with the preceding section, the description of the narrative begins after the marriage of David to Michal:

The HDR_1:

[1 Sam 19:8–17]* David's marriage to Michal and Saul's recognition that Yahweh was with David (18:27–28) lead directly to the episode surrounding Saul's attempt on David's life (19:9–10)—an almost word for word repetition of what Willis has argued is a comprehensive anticipatory redactional joint in 18:10–11.[161] Michal saves David from her father's henchmen through trickery (19:11–16), and when questioned, Michal protests her own innocence, claiming that David had threatened her with violence (v. 17).[162] This is the last contact David and Michal have in the HDR_1, because in 25:44 Saul gives his daughter to another man.[163]

---

161 Willis, "Function," 308–10. See n. 54, above; for this connection, see Willi-Plein, "ISam 18–19," 151. Divorcing the HDR_1 from the HDR_2 alleviates the tension held by McKenzie's claim that 19:11–17 has been displaced and should follow immediately on 18:20–25 (*King David*, 81).

162 The ensuing episode in 19:18–24, a doublet of 1 Sam 10:10–13, comes from unspecified origin. In this passage, Samuel appears in his hometown of Ramah, where David takes temporary refuge from Saul. Stylistically and thematically, 19:18–24 fits well with 16:1–13, since the two pericopes show no language typical of Dtr (Peter Mommer, "Ist auch Saul unter den Propheten? Ein Beitrag zu 1 Sam 19,18–24," *BN* 38/39 [1987]: 59). Mommer therefore attributes 19:18–24 to the author of the HDR. But in my opinion, it is also possible that the etiological pericope in 19:18–24 belongs neither to the HDR_1 nor to the HDR_2, but rather is to be considered part of the redactional material of the Prophetic Record, precisely because of its continuity with 16:1–13. It may equally be of much later date (Christophe Nihan, "Saul among the Prophets," in *Saul in Story and Tradition* [ed. Carl S. Ehrlich with Marsha C. White; FAT I/47; Tübingen: Mohr Siebeck, 2006], 88–118). Mommer (ibid.) argues that this passage was based on the ostensibly pro-Saulide tale in 10:10–13 and a reversal thereof. Cf., however, John Sturdy ("The Original Meaning of 'Is Saul among the Prophets [1 Samuel x 11, 12; xix 24]?'" *VT* 20 [1970]: 209), who argued that the existence of two forms of this story suggests that "[t]he second can only have been composed by people who did not know the first, but had the proverb on its own." The true origin of the saying, Victor Eppstein argues, is the way in which Saul handled his exercise of authority, using Samuel as a model: in fact Saul was more like the judge-prophets in his exercise of power. A subsequent diminution of the status of the prophet also led to confusion about the saying. The narrative origin of the episode used in 1 Sam 10:10–13 to etiologize the saying is drawn from common folkloristic stock ("Was Saul also among the Prophets?" *ZAW* 81 [1969]: 299–301). Con-

[21:2–16]*[164] David arrives in Nob, where he meets Ahimelek the priest, who allows David to eat the showbread, believing that Saul had sent the Bethlehemite on a secret mission (vv. 2–7). But Doeg the Edomite overhears this exchange (v. 8) and relays the news of David's whereabouts to Saul in a future episode. David also requests the use of a weapon of some kind, but the only weapon available is the sword of Goliath the Philistine, whom David slew in the Valley of the Terebinth[165] (vv. 9–10). From here, David flees either to Gath, where he feigns madness to ensure he will be left alone (21:11–16),[166] to the cave at Adullam (22:1–2),[167] or to

---

trary to Eppstein's attempt to root the "original" usage of the proverb in Saul's admirable (and historical) emulation of Samuel, Sturdy attempts first to figure out what the saying means in the context of the two stories. In both, he argues, it was seen by the author of the narrative as a good thing to be a prophet, but Saul is viewed negatively, thereby suggesting supporters of a Davidic monarchy composed the narrative ("Is Saul?" 210–11). No doubt, both narratives are secondary and later than the existence of the saying. In light of this, Sturdy suggests the original meaning of the saying was "Saul is no prophet." This interpretation seems to me more likely than that of Eppstein.

163 For the later appropriation of Michal by a redactor in 2 Sam 3:12–16* and 6:1–23*, see §6.5.2.

164 It is unclear from the joint in 21:2 ("David came to Nob") that this passage, rather than another (e.g., 23:14aβ–15), initially followed David's escape from Saul with the help of Michal immediately. This attribution is reconstructed on the basis of Ahimelek's speech to David (see the following note).

165 This reference creates another point of connection within the HDR_1, since the Valley of the Terebinth was the site of the battle with the Philistine in 17:2. Whether Goliath was the name of the Philistine or not (see n. 71), this incidental reference to the earlier scene seems authentic. However, the Nob-centered section of the narrative shows signs of being overlaid with redaction (see n. 164), and it is possible this notice is not authentic but rather a redactional insertion to combine this narrative unit with the HDR_1 in 17:2. Obviously, once the redaction of HDR_{1+2} had been completed, the Valley of the Terebinth was the only recognized site of David's battle with the Philistine, since the tradition reconstructed for the HDR_2 did not originally preserve a location. It may be pointed out that in neither narrative was there preserved a tradition that David brought Goliath's *sword* to Nob: HDR_1 notes only that "David took the head of the Philistine and brought it to Jerusalem, but he put his gear in his tent" (17:54), while HDR_2 does not specifically note any despoiling of the Philistine's body.

166 It is possible that this passage belongs authentically to the HDR_1, in which case Nob served as the medial point in David's journey to Gath. The connection between the scene at Nob and that at Gath (v. 11) is itself not sure, but the narrative logic of Saul's sack of Nob (22:6–23) assumes David had stopped only briefly at the sanctuary and then moved on. In short, it is not *illogical* that David would have moved on quickly to Gath. If this is the case, 21:11–16 functions as an external doublet to David's journey to Gath in 1 Sam 27:1–12; 28:1–2; 29:1–11; 30:1–31—all clearly from HDR_2, since this series provides an explanation for David's absence from the battle of Gilboa, itself united thematically to 2 Sam 1:1–27, one of the anchor-points of the HDR_2.

167 As was the case with 21:11–16 (see the previous note), it is difficult to know whether this scene originally fit with the HDR_1 because of the ambiguity of the originating point ("David went from there..."), but it is consistent thematically with the presumed narrative contours of that story. Halpern (*Constitution*, 166) notes that the segment in 22:1–2 bears a tight connection to 2 Samuel 23, in which the cave at Adullam is mentioned again and that a tight

Moab, along with his family (22:3–5).[168] It is difficult to know which of these passages followed directly on the scene at Nob, but all potentially provide the HDR_1 with a reasonable itinerary of David's flight. The plurality of available traditions here is indicative of the HDR_1's development from an originally loose collection of traditions or of the aggregation of independent traditions onto the skeletal structure of the nascent HDR_1.

[22:(6–8),9–23]* No matter where David has fled from, Doeg the Edomite delivers the news of David's whereabouts to Saul, who calls the priests of Nob into account (9–11). Saul demands to know why Ahimelek has rebelled against him by providing David with a sword and provisions (vv. 12–13). But, like Michal earlier, Ahimelek protests his own ignorance, arguing he had no knowledge that David—who is Saul's son-in-law and one of Saul's best warriors—was not telling him the truth (vv. 14–15). Saul decrees the entire family of priests at Nob will die (v. 16), but when none of the Benjaminite soldiers agrees to follow through on Saul's orders, Doeg massacres the entire city on his own (vv. 17–19). Of the priestly family, only Abiathar ben-Ahimelek survives and goes to live with David (vv. 20–23).

[23:1–13]* Having presumably consulted the oracular ephod with which Ahimelek escaped (23:6), David is instructed to relieve Qeilah from the Philistine onslaught (vv. 1–4).[169] David does so, and Saul hears of the Bethlehemite's victory (vv. 5,7a). Thinking he might be able to trap David in the city with no means of escape, Saul plots to close in on the city with David in it, but David escapes yet again (vv. 8–14aα).[170]

[24:1–23]* Even though they have moved to the rocky crags around Ein-gedi, David and his men are again found out by Saul, who makes a foray into the wilderness to trap the outlaw (vv. 1–3).[171] In this member of the well-known doublet (vis-à-vis ch. 26), Saul enters a cave to relieve himself—the same cave in which David and his men are hiding. David stealthily cuts off the hem of Saul's garment, and Saul leaves the cave (vv.

---

connection might also be suggested between this tradition and the tradition in 1 Samuel 24, which also takes place at a cave.

168 The flight to Moab seems odd, as does David's movement in v. 5 to the Forest of Hareth. Hareth is not mentioned again in the narrative, and this episode seems to stand outside of either History of David's Rise narrative tradition. The presence of the prophet Gad might support this assessment, suggesting an origin of the passage in the PR.

169 Verses 2b–4a seem to be an identical tradition inserted into the story.

170 Verse 14aα is probably a redactional insertion since the next episode of the HDR_1, 24:1–23, begins with "David went up from there...."

171 Verse 2a is a redactional insertion that relates the present episode to the preceding story in 23:27–28. The scene functions just as well with the omission of this notice and slight reworking of the remainder of v. 2b.

4–8).[172] As Saul makes his way back to his troops, David calls to the departing king. He protests his innocence, arguing God had delivered Saul into his hand that day but David had not committed treachery (vv. 9–16). In return, Saul recognizes the goodness with which David has treated him, and, realizing David will someday rule, Saul asks only that David allow his progeny to live (vv. 17–22; possibly a late insertion in the vein of 1 Sam 20:11–17, etc.). David makes that pledge, and Saul goes his way in peace. This is the last time that the two have any personal contact whatsoever.

[28:3–25]* The next time Saul appears in this narrative, we are prepared for his demise. Samuel has died (25:1;[173] 28:3), and Saul's Israelite forces are amassing at Gilboa to fight a battle with the Philistines (vv. 4–5). Saul must seek the assistance of the medium of En-dor, having lost all access to other forms of oracular divination from the Lord (vv. 6–13). The medium conjures up the ghost of Samuel, who declares Saul and his sons will soon join Samuel (vv. 14–19). Saul steels himself for the battle to come and returns with his men to the Israelite camp to prepare for battle (vv. 20–25).

[31:1–13]* On the day of battle, the Israelites are soundly defeated by the Philistine masses on the slopes of Gilboa (v. 1). The Philistines kill the three sons of the king, Jonathan, Abinadab, and Malki-shua (v. 2). Sorely wounded and sensing imminent defeat, Saul asks his armor bearer to kill him, but the man refuses. Saul commits suicide on the field of battle rather than be taken alive, and the remaining Israelites retreat (vv. 3–7). The Philistines find the bodies of the Benjaminite royal family on the field of battle and hang them from the walls of Beth-shean, mutilated (vv. 8–10). The inhabitants of Jabesh-gilead hear of the atrocities performed upon the bodies of Saul and his sons and retrieve the corpses, bringing them to Jabesh and performing proper burial rites (vv. 11–13). In the same trajectory as this passage, we may include 2 Sam 2:4b–7*, although it is probable that those verses have replaced an earlier episode in which the inhabitants of Jabesh-gilead feature (see §6.6). In that passage, David hears

172 The present text now describes how David almost immediately felt guilty because of his actions toward Yahweh's anointed (vv. 6–8a). It is possible that these verses are later interpretive additions stressing the importance of the "anointed of the Lord" (cf. 2 Sam 1:14), but it is clear that both traditions (HDR_1 and HDR_2) knew of Saul's position as "the anointed of Yahweh," and the omission of these verses is not necessary. McCarter argues this narrative is secondary to its doublet in ch. 26 (*I Samuel*, 386). If this is the case, it would not be original to the HDR_1.

173 It seems probable to me, though, that 25:1 (the notice of Samuel's death) is a redactional joint, since it has little relation to its immediate context and anticipates the bulk of 28:3. Initially, the HDR_1 would have moved directly from David's promise to Saul and Saul's departure in 24:23 to the scene beginning in 28:3, which knows of Samuel's death. Perhaps only the notice in 25:44 intervened, stating that Saul gave Michal to Palti ben-Laish from Gallim.

of the Jabeshites' beneficent actions towards the deceased king and sends word to the Gileadite residents, extolling their treatment of Saul and his sons and implicitly inviting them to join the ranks of his subjects.[174] The residents of Jabesh have responded to Saul's death with the proper respect for a king and with concerns for proper ritual burial. The presence of the Jabeshites at this juncture recollects their close affinity to Saul and the royal family based upon Saul's defeat of the Ammonites and rescue of the city (1 Sam 11:1–15), thereby providing evidence for an initial relationship between this first narrative of Saul's Rise (see below, §7.3.1) and the HDR_1.

Halpern argues that the episode concerning David's overtures towards the inhabitants of Jabesh-gilead (2 Sam 2:4b–7) forms a doublet—narrated indirectly—of the directly narrated scene in 1 Sam 31:11–13.[175] But this argument neglects the natural movement the story should take; with the death of Saul, the narrator must make the switch from direct narration concerning Saul to direct narration concerning David. This direct narration can only include a report from messengers concerning Saul's death, since David was, at least implicitly, not present at the battle of Gilboa. No literary markers in the report of 2 Sam 2:4b–7 demand it be considered anything less than the natural narrative continuation of 1 Sam 31:11–13, although a few indicators point to its secondarity in the HDR_1.

[2 Sam 5:(4–5),6–6:23]* On the basis of comparison with Tadmor's schematization of ancient Near Eastern royal apology, we may postulate the HDR_1 originally ended with the establishment of the kingdom. Both the HDR_2 and the HDR_1—and particularly the latter—contain elements corresponding closely to Tadmor's six-part schema of royal apologetic, discussed in §4.2.[176] In the HDR_1, I would suggest the following correspondences: (a) the introduction (1 Sam 17:14–23); (b) the historical survey: noble antecedents (Samuel and the favored Saul in 9:1–10:16; 11:1–15); (c) the historical survey: the unworthy predecessor (the rejected Saul in 13:7b–15*); (d) the coup d'état (HDR_1 beginning in 19:8 and ending with Saul's death and burial in 31:13); (e) the merciful victor (2 Sam 2:4b–7 or, preferably, 2 Sam 21:12–13a*,14aα* [see §6.6]); (f) the edict (or at least the establishment of the kingdom; 2 Sam 5:[4–5],6–6:23). It is this close correspondence of the HDR_1 to the formal structure of ancient Near Eastern royal apologetic that allows a reconstruction of the present

174 I agree with Edelman, who considers this scene an attempt by David to gain favor with staunch supporters of the Saulide regime ("Saul's Rescue," 202).

175 Halpern, *Constitution*, 170.

176 Hayim Tadmor, "Autobiographical Apology in the Royal Assyrian Literature," in *History, Historiography and Interpretation* (ed. H. Tadmor and M. Weinfeld; Jerusalem: Magnes, 1983), 36–57.

passage as the original end of the story. Yet the original ending of the HDR_1 has most likely undergone some degree of revision, since this entire passage seems to assume David was living in Hebron (e.g., vv. 5,13), as opposed to the Judean wilderness, which is the last place David had been living, so far as the reader knows. Nonetheless, the narrative probably concluded with David[177] and his men taking over the city of Jerusalem and establishing rule from that location (vv. 6–10). Verses 13–16 note the king's household and may also be authentic.

6.5.2. The Relationship of the Ark Narrative to the HDR_1

The position of the Ark Narrative (siglum AN; ca. 1 Sam 4:1–7:1; 2 Sam 6:1–23) within the book of Samuel—and indeed, its coherence as a unit—remains the subject of much debate. Literary judgments concerning the narrative's full extent, its theological function(s), and its compositional history have been handled extensively elsewhere, and these topics need not be taken up here in detail.[178] Because Michal features in what is commonly recognized as the Ark Narrative's final scene (2 Sam 6:1–23),[179] it is necessary to comment briefly on the apparent relationship of the AN to the HDR_1. The claim to any supposed literarily unified AN is directly contin-

177 2 Sam 5:6 of MT reads המלך—a position David did not yet occupy in this reconstruction of the HDR_1, but LXX^B renders "David," and Syriac gives "King David." The change from the personal name to the political title would have been an easy and natural correction for the redactor to make, given this passage's position immediately following David's accession to the kingship in 5:1–3.

178 See, e.g., Franz Schicklberger, *Die Ladeerzählungen des ersten Samuel-Buches: Eine literaturwissenschaftliche und theologiegeschichtliche Untersuchung* (FB 7; Würzburg: Echter Verlag, 1973); Antony F. Campbell, *The Ark Narrative (1 Sam 4–6; 2 Sam 6): A Form-Critical and Traditio-Historical Study* (SBLDS 16; Missoula, Mont.: Scholars Press, 1975); Patrick D. Miller and J. J. M. Roberts, *The Hand of the Lord: A Reassessment of the "Ark Narrative" of 1 Samuel* (JHNES; Baltimore: The Johns Hopkins University Press, 1977; repr., Atlanta: SBL, 2008); C. L. Seow, *Myth, Drama, and the Politics of David's Dance* (HSM 44; Atlanta: Scholars Press, 1989); Robert Rezetko, *Source and Revision in the Narratives of David's Transfer of the Ark: Text, Language, and Story in 2 Samuel 6 and 1 Chronicles 13, 15–16* (Library of Hebrew Bible/Old Testament Studies 470; New York: T&T Clark, 2007), esp. 234–85. For a recent survey of the secondary literature, see Erik Eynikel, "The Relation between the Eli Narratives (1 Sam. 1–4) and the Ark Narrative (1 Sam. 1–6; 2 Sam. 6:1–19)," in *Past, Present, Future: The Deuteronomistic History and the Prophets* (ed. Johannes C. de Moor and Harry F. van Rooy; *OtSt* 44; Leiden: Brill, 2000), 88–106.

179 Those who reckon some or all of 2 Samuel 6 to the independent AN include: Rost, *Succession*, 6–34, esp. 13 (only vv. 1–15, 17–20a); Campbell, *Ark Narrative*, 170–72 (vv. 2–23); but cf. idem, *2 Samuel* (FOTL 8; Grand Rapids, Mich.: Eerdmans, 2005), 68–69. Eynikel also apparently makes the connection ("Relation," esp. 100). Cf. those who deny the original connection of 1 Sam 4:1–7:1* to 2 Samuel 6*: e.g., Schicklberger, *Ladeerzählung*, 235; Miller and Roberts, *Hand of the Lord*, 32–36; McCarter, *II Samuel*, 182–84.

gent on the existence of the passage found in 2 Sam 3:12–16: from the perspective of the narrative found in the first chapters of 2 Samuel, David has not seen Michal since his escape from the Saulide court. Only with Michal's forcible removal from Paltiel, and consequent reintroduction to her estranged husband David in 2 Sam 3:12–16, are the two reunited. The reunion proves to be an unhappy one for both parties, although not without political benefit for David.

At first glance, 2 Sam 3:12–16 appears to be lodged firmly in the beginning of the SSN. However, the surrounding episode functions just as well—if not better—with the excision of vv. 12–16.[180] Not only is the passage in vv. 12–16 somewhat textually corrupt (particularly v. 12),[181] but it is also self-contradictory. Abner sends a message to David, inviting a treaty, to which David responds that Abner need only return Michal to see David face to face (vv. 12–13). But in v. 14, David sends word to Ishbosheth demanding the return of his sister to David; she is taken forcibly from her husband Paltiel, who follows her as far as Bahurim (vv. 15–16a).[182] These notices seem to derive from two different sources, but their respective origins are unclear. Kaiser notes the anomalous switch from Abner to Ishbosheth that occurs between vv. 13–14 and the reverse in v. 16b, and he cites this discrepancy as validation of his assertion that 1 Sam 18:20–27 is redactional.[183] I agree that these verses do not sit well in their context; it seems to me most likely that vv. 12–14,16b comprise a later addition to the already secondary vv. 15–16a. But regardless of the precise delineation of emendations and additions here, the clear secondarity of vv. 12–16 does not necessitate Kaiser's relegation of the earlier passage (1 Sam 18:20–27; cf. also 25:44) to redactional status. If one accepts that the demand for the return of Michal in 3:12–16 is ostensibly secondary and unnecessary to its present position, has been secondarily inserted into the substrate layer here (possibly part of an already developing SSN), and cannot be attributed to the primary material of the HDR_1 because of the integral role(s) played by Abner (and Ishbosheth?), then the first stratum of

180 The transition between the surrounding phrases is fluid and natural. After Abner has sworn to deliver the throne of Israel to David, "(v. 11) [Ishbosheth] could not reply to Abner because of fear for him. (v. 17) But Abner spoke to the elders of Israel, saying...."

181 Aramaic provides a smooth translation, glossing over the difficult MT תחתו לאמר למי־ארץ. LXX shows confusion, translating the GN Θαιλαμ (LXX[B]) or Χεβρον (LXX[L]). See Cross et al., *1–2 Samuel*, 110–11. If Cross, Parry, and Saley are correct in their reconstruction of 4QSam[a], 2 Sam 3:12 also omitted the difficult portion.

182 Notice that Bahurim seems to be a Saulide stronghold in the southern part of Benjamin throughout the CH. E.g., it is Shimei's home in 2 Sam 16:5; but cf. 2 Sam 17:18, where Ahimaaz and Jonathan, serving as spies for David, take refuge in the city. This may point to a certain ambivalence about the city, or it may have been intentional irony: even in a Saulide stronghold, David gains the upper hand.

183 Kaiser, "David und Jonathan," 291; idem, "Beobachtungen," 9–10.

the passage (i.e., vv. 14–16a?) must be attributed to the combination of the HDR_1 complex with the HDR_2 + SSN complex. Because the presence of the Michal episode in 6:16,20b–23 is predicated upon the prior or concurrent insertion of 3:12–16*, its insertion should also be attributed to the redactional combination of the two major complexes, regardless of whether 6:16, 20b–23 are of a piece with the remaining verses of ch. 6 or comprise a secondary elaboration of an original ending to the AN.[184] But when, exactly, did that combination occur?

A. D. H. Mayes traces the insertion of the AN to a Deuteronomistic editor who inserted 1 Sam 7:2 and 2 Samuel 6 in order to effect the transition between the older substratum and the added material, a judgment he seems to ground thematically: "The editor…has used the ark story to illustrate the consequences of cultic corruption…and indeed also to point over the house of Saul to the Davidic dynasty as the time when Yahweh, through his ark, was again present with his people."[185] Mayes was followed in this assessment by Campbell and O'Brien, both of whom excluded 1 Sam 4:1–7:1; 2 Samuel 6 from the Prophetic Record.[186] Their argument for the AN's exclusion from the PR requires some analysis here, since its conclusion has important ramifications for the present argument. O'Brien points out that Nathan's prediction in 2 Sam 7:13 is fulfilled in 1 Kgs 8:15–21, in which "Solomon clearly identifies the installation of the ark in the temple as an essential part of the fulfillment of Nathan's prophecy…."[187] That both 2 Sam 7:13 and 1 Kgs 8:15–21 are products of Dtr is nearly indisputable, but O'Brien's claim that the ark's installation plays an "essential part" in Solomon's speech is specious. Admittedly, the ark appears in a clear Deuteronomistic context, signaled by the notice that the ark was where the covenant of Yahweh was kept (לארון אשר־שם ברית יהוה; 1 Kgs 8:21; see also ארון ברית יהוה in 8:1,6[MT]). But this appearance occurs only in the final verse of the passage at hand (v. 21; although cf. 8:1–11[188]), where it seems a virtual afterthought to the primary

184 Without a fuller examination of the intricate interweaving of the narratives contained in 2 Samuel 2–8, it would be foolhardy to claim anything more than that 6:16,20b–23 are attributable to the redactor who joined the two large complexes. Although I suspect these verses are, in fact, secondary to their present context (with, e.g., Rost, *Succession*, 13; McCarter, *II Samuel*, 189; and Seow, *Myth*, 136), this assertion is tangential to the present argument.

185 Mayes, *Story*, 84.

186 Campbell, *Of Prophets and Kings*, 67–68; Mark A. O'Brien, *The Deuteronomistic History Hypothesis: A Reassessment* [*DHH*] (OBO 92; Fribourg: University Press; Göttingen: Vandenhoeck & Ruprecht, 1989), 136–37; cf. Van Seters, *In Search of History*, 347–52.

187 O'Brien, *DHH*, 136.

188 O'Brien considers 1 Kgs 8:1–11 to be pre-Deuteronomistic (a minimal text of the narrative framework being vv. 2a,3a,4aα,5,6,62,63b) without any Deuteronomistic reworking (ibid., 152–53). But that assumption is belied by the literary connection between v. 9 and v. 21

thrust of the prayer, namely, that Solomon has completed work on the Temple itself, for the phrase בנה בית occurs a total of six times in differing inflections—and with varying definiteness—of the object in the passage (vv.16,17,18,19[2x],20)! It seems far more likely that v. 21 was constructed by Dtr to create literary space for the ark in a cognitive system that considered the ark nearly peripheral to its central concern, which was the Temple. The need for this literary space, we may deduce, was occasioned by the ark's relative centrality in one of Dtr's received texts. This literary judgment is supported by the pairing in the quintessential prophecy-fulfillment pattern of 1 Kgs 8:15–21 with 2 Sam 7:13, which itself contains no mention of the ark but stresses that Solomon "will build a Temple" (יבנה־בית). Furthermore, one may contrast the designation of the ark in 1 Kgs 8:21 with the pre-Deuteronomistic 2 Sam 6:2: "the ark of God, which is called by the name of the Lord of Hosts who is enthroned on the cherubim" (NRSV; ארון האלהים אשר־נקרא שם שם יהוה צבאות ישב הכרבים עליו). The two designations of the ark have completely different understandings of its importance, as illustrated by the Deuteronomistic insistence in 1 Kgs 8:9 that "[t]here was nothing in the ark except the two tablets of stone that Moses had placed there at Horeb" (NRSV; אין בארון רק שני לחות האבנים אשר הנח שם משה בחרב). It is not simply enough to argue that Dtr was appropriating older material in the text generated by the insertion (1 Kgs 8:21), since one would expect that the author would have tried more diligently to bring the two in line with one another. This discrepancy suggests, then, that the older material was not simply reworkable traditional oral stock, but a text that by necessity maintained its own integrity, to some degree, throughout the process of editorial addition. The Historian was working with a document that already included the narrative of David's transfer of the ark to Jerusalem (2 Samuel 6*) and therefore needed to accommodate the former war-palladium's received literary importance in David's kingship to the Deuteronomists' privileging of the Temple in Solomon's kingdom. Moreover, it is unclear that the assertion of Deuteronomistic editing in 1 Sam 7:2 and 2 Samuel 6 is entirely accurate, much less necessary, since neither 1 Sam 7:2 nor the bulk of 2 Samuel 6 contains language diagnostic of Dtr.[189] Although the latter theme

(e.g., Ernst Würthwein, *Die Bücher der Könige: 1. Könige 1–16* [ATD 11/1; Göttingen: Vandenhoeck & Ruprecht, 1985], 88). See also below in this section.

189 See also Mettinger, *King and Messiah*, 42. Moshe Weinfeld finds Deuteronom(ist)ic language only in 2 Sam 6:2 (קרא שם על) and 6:21 (לצוות נגיד). But the first case, he allows, is an ancient usage of language subsequently appropriated by the Deuteronomist (*Deuteronomy and the Deuteronomic School* [Oxford: Clarendon Press, 1972], 325), and the second case may be challenged as an unrecognized sign of prophetic redaction; see Campbell, *Of Prophets and Kings*, 56–57; and Friedrich Mildenberger, who includes 6:16, 20–23 in his

found by Mayes—Yahweh's presence with the people—is admittedly central to the passage, it must be stressed that the former theme—cultic corruption—can only be obliquely read into the passage when the assumption of Deuteronomistic authorship has already been made and the text contextualized correspondingly.

The thematic dynamic of 2 Sam 6:20b–23 also works towards a pre-Deuteronomistic date for the insertion of that passage: several scholars have argued the notice in vv. 20b–23 that Michal did not bear any children was meant to indicate there were no other Saulides.[190] In this regard, the passage fits perfectly with its surroundings, upholding both (a) the HDR_1's primary assertion that after Saul's death on Gilboa, David could expect no more competition from the Saulides and (b) the predominant concern of the HDR_2 + SSN complex with the legitimization of the Davidic scion Solomon over against both the other Davidides, as well as potential Saulide rivals (see §5.4). But if the reconstruction of the relative dating of this passage's insertion at the time of the prophetic editor's combination of these two major source complexes is correct, the scene was written well after the period in which concern for the possibility of a rival Saulide heir would have been most prevalent and was therefore purely a well-employed redactional tool.

The only possible way for us to read 2 Sam 6:20–23 as original to the HDR_1 would be to attribute the first redactional layer of 2 Sam 3:12–16 (i.e., vv. 14–15[16a], in which David requests Michal directly from Ishbosheth) to the HDR_1 collection and to attribute the secondary redactional insertion featuring Abner (vv. 12–13,[16a],16b) to the PR. Accordingly, the entire passage of 2 Samuel 6:1–23 would comprise the culminating episode of the HDR_1 collection. This alternative attribution has the benefit of providing David's kingdom not only with the political legitimacy of remarrying Saul's daughter (3:14–15,16a; 6:20–23), but also with the theological legitimacy garnered by moving the Ark into Jerusalem (6:1–19). It has the detriment, however, of adding yet another bit character to the HDR_1 (i.e., Ishbosheth in 3:14). The obscurity of Ishbosheth in the HDR_1 would be accounted for in his qualification as בן־שׁאול in 3:14, but I find this solution unlikely.

prophetic redaction ("Die vordeuteronomistische Saul-Davidüberlieferung" [Ph.D. diss., Tübingen, 1962], 29).

190 E.g., Campbell, *Of Prophets and Kings*, 56–57; Hackett, "1 and 2 Samuel," 91; Katharine Doob Sakenfeld, *Just Wives? Stories of Power and Survival in the Old Testament and Today* (Louisville, Ky.: WJKP, 2003), 82; Willi-Plein, "ISam 18–19," 157–59; and most recently, Jeremy Schipper, "Disabling Israelite Leadership: 2 Samuel 6:23 and Other Images of Disability in the Deuteronomistic History," in *This Abled Body: Rethinking Disabilities in Biblical Studies* (ed. Hector Avalos, Sarah J. Melcor, and Jeremy Schipper; SemeiaSt 55; Atlanta: SBL, 2007), 103–13. The exact cause of Michal's childlessness is irrelevant here.

Thus, having challenged the Deuteronomistic-era incorporation of the AN into the surrounding material as too late a proposal, we must reach the conclusion that the AN was joined to the HDR_1 and HDR_2 + SSN complexes already at or by the time of the combination of those two complexes, although it seems unlikely that the AN had been attached to the HDR_1 any earlier. It is reasonable to conclude that the relative dating of the inclusion of the AN points to that corpus's inclusion—and to the joining of the HDR_1 and HDR_2 + SSN complexes in the PR.

6.6. Reconstructing the Combination of the HDR_1 and HDR_2

If the reconstruction presented here is correct in its broad strokes, if not in its particulars, the composition history of 1–2 Samuel may be outlined as follows: The members of the prophetic guild among which the PR took shape had two complexes of traditions available for use in their composition of a history of the formation and dissolution of the United Monarchy. The shorter and earlier of the two, the loosely conjoined traditions of the HDR_1 complex, detailed David's rise and Saul's concurrent destruction through the prophetic mediation of Yahweh's will (ca. 1 Sam 9:1–2 Sam 5:10,[13–16]*). Earlier tradents had already gathered together with the loose collection of the HDR_1 a few traditions concerning Saul's Rise (the NSR_{AB}; see §7.3, below). Aside from the traditions surrounding Saul's accession to the kingship, which were not paralleled in the HDR_2 complex, the plot of this first collection was quite similar to that of the other. Many episodes of the first collection had analogues in the second. The later loose collection of traditions concerning David's rise (i.e., the HDR_2) had already been combined with the SSN to provide a longer account of David's reign, from the time he was introduced to Saul's court until his death and Solomon's succession (ca. 1 Sam 17:12–1 Kgs 2*). Because the two traditions told ostensibly the same story in very different ways, the redactors could not place them end-to-end but had to interweave the two narrative complexes, such that a preponderance of nearly contiguous doublets resulted.

In comparing the two traditions, our attention is drawn immediately to the fate of the ending of the HDR_1. This earlier historiographic work was familiar with many of the historical figures of Saul's court. It knew of Saul's three sons who died with him on Mt. Gilboa (1 Sam 31:2); it knew of Saul's intimate connection with the inhabitants of Jabesh-gilead (1 Sam 11:1–5; 31:8–13); it knew also of Saul's daughter, Michal, who—it was claimed—had been married to David (1 Sam 18:20).[191] But it did not know much of Merab, Saul's elder daughter who had married the son of a Transjordanian chieftain; at most, it knew only that she had been the mother of five sons who had been killed in David's purge of the Saulide court upon his succession to the throne (if 2 Sam 21:1–6*,8–14* LXX^L is to be attributed to the HDR_1). Nor did it know at all of Saul's general Abner, known only by the HDR_2. Similarly, the later collection knew only of Jonathan—and possibly of Merab—as Saul's progeny.

While most of the combination of the NSR_{AB} + HDR_1 complex with the HDR_2 + SSN complex could be performed almost seamlessly by interposing the various episodes of each, a few small redactional additions had to be made in order to produce a cogent whole. Among these small additions were the notices of David's compassion shown to Mephibosheth and to the remains of Saul and Jonathan, both of which were added to the narrative of the purge of the Saulides (2 Sam 21:7,12–14*). In a trenchant analysis of 2 Sam 21:1–14, S. Chavel recently adduced vv. 12–13a,14a as the most original traditum in which the remains of Saul and of his son Jonathan were shown respect. This short notice of the reinterment of their bones was at some point woven together with the Gibeonite narrative (comprising vv. 1–11,13b,14aβb).[192] Chavel correctly notes the complexity of the traditions surrounding the removal of the royal family's remains to Jabesh-gilead:

> …the text in 1 Sam 31:1–2 Sam 2:7 seems to have undergone a process of expansion from a story exclusively about Saul's death and remains, to one that in 1 Sam 31:8, 12–13 includes those of his three sons (probably because in 1 Sam 31:1–7 the three fight and fall beside him), and then to one that in 2 Sam 1:4, 5, 12, 17–27 puts the spotlight on Saul and Jonathan (probably under the impact of the addition of David's lament, in 2 Sam 1:17–27). In the final result, it appears that, while David focuses in on Saul and Jonathan, the Philistines have absconded with, and the Jabeshites have returned, the remains of Saul's sons Abinadab and Malkishua as well. The reinterment story in 2 Sam 21:12–13a, 14aα, though, speaks exclusively of Saul and Jonathan, creating the impression that the people of Jabesh-gilead do not have the bones of any other members of the royal family.[193]

Because he was working without explicit reference to a larger diachronic framework of Samuel's composition history, Chavel did not pursue these variations further but suggested that in its original form, 2 Sam 21:12–13a,14aα had comprised an alternative tradition to the other passages featuring the inhabitants of Jabesh-gilead in 1 Sam 31:8–13 and 2 Sam 2:4b–

191 It is possible (but unlikely) that HDR_1 knew of Ishbosheth (2 Sam 3:14) and of Michal's return to David and subsequent childlessness (2 Sam 3:14–15, [16a?]; 6:20–23).

192 Simeon Chavel, "Compositry and Creativity in 2 Samuel 21:1–14," *JBL* 122 (2003): 23–52, esp. 32, 48–49.

193 Ibid., 48–49.

7. But in light of the recognition made above that two nearly continuous traditional collections narrating David's rise may be discerned in 1 Samuel 15–2 Sam 5*, this judgment may be modified.

Chavel's observation that the original story (assumed here to be the HDR_1 account in 1 Sam 31:1–13) was concerned only with "Saul's death and remains" is borne out by examination of 1 Sam 31:8–13, which narrates Saul's death in battle alongside his three sons. Although vv. 8 and 12–13 include the sons as beneficiaries of the Jabeshites' beneficence, the intervening verses describe the Philistines as concerned only with *Saul's* head (ראשו; v. 9), *Saul's* accoutrements (כליו; vv. 9,10), and *Saul's* body (גויתו; v. 10). Similarly, the people of Jabesh-gilead hear only about *Saul* (אליו and לשאול; v. 11). Despite the objection that one can only expect the narrator's concern over Saul's demise (and not that of his sons), the overwhelming use of the 3.m.s. suffix throughout the passage is eye-catching and suggests the secondarity of the references to Saul's sons in vv. 8,12–13. Similarly, 2 Sam 2:4b–7 demonstrates a concern only with the fate of Saul: the Jabeshites bury *Saul* (v. 4b); David recognizes their kindness to *Saul* (v. 5); it is *Saul* who has died (v. 6). Yet a few indicators in 2 Sam 2:4b–7 point to the oddity of those verses. Once in the passage the relative pronoun אשר is used as a nominalizing particle that introduces a subordinate clause (v. 4b),[194] a usage that increased in LBH.[195] Two more times (vv. 5,6) the word is used to introduce a causal clause ("...*because* you have done this thing").[196] The omission of v. 6 in LXX^B is striking as well.[197] All in all, no specific evidence points to a judgment irrevocably eliminating any or all of 2 Sam 2:4b–7 from its current position, but one wonders whether the traditum Chavel isolated in 2 Sam 21:12–13a,14aα did not originally belong here at the beginning of 2 Samuel.[198] On this theory, the narrative originally would have followed a structure that looked something like the following:

194 GKC §157c; Reginald Williams, *Hebrew Syntax: An Outline* (2d ed.; Toronto: University of Toronto Press, 1976), 76 §464 (although cf. the recititive usage to introduce direct speech, 76–77 §467, with McCarter, *II Samuel*, 81); *IBHS*, 644 §38.8b. Originally, the word most likely occurred immediately after or instead of לאמר (where it is rendered in LXX^B) but was transferred to its present position in MT in order to retain relative rather than subordinating force—i.e., "[It was] the men of Jabesh-gilead *who*..." rather than "said *that* 'the men of Jabesh-gilead...'" (McCarter, *II Samuel*, 81).

195 E.g., Rooker, *Biblical Hebrew*, 111–12; but cf. 1 Sam 18:15, which I have argued above is a fairly early usage.

196 See GKC §158b; *IBHS*, 640 §38.4a; Williams, *Hebrew Syntax*, 77 §468; see, e.g., 1 Kgs 3:19.

197 McCarter, *II Samuel*, 81.

198 Because of David's implied stature as not yet being king, Chavel plausibly suggests that "the report belongs to the period prior to Abner's defection, or at least to the texts depicting that period" ("Compositry," 45).

(1 Sam 31:13) They took his bones (assuming עצמתיו) and buried (them) under the tamarisk in Jabesh, and they fasted seven days. (2 Sam 2:4b) When it was told to David that the men of Jabesh had buried Saul, (21:12*) David went and took the bones of Saul from the town nobles of Jabesh-gilead (בעלי יביש גלעד) who had stolen them from the wall (reading του τείχους with LXX^L and שורא with *Tg. Jon.*) of Beth-shean where the Philistines had hung them (repointing MT as תְּלוּם) on the day the Philistines struck Saul at Gilboa. (v. 13a*) He brought up from there the bones of Saul, (v. 14aα*) and he buried them (emending to ויקברם) in the land of Benjamin, at Zela, in the grave of Kish his father.

The editor who removed the last few sentences and connected them with 2 Sam 21:1–11,13b,14aβb supplemented these verses with the name of Saul's son Jonathan in vv. 12aα,13aβ,14aα*. That story was itself displaced to the collection of random material, gathered after the bulk of the Davidic tradition contained in the CH but before those chapters narrating Solomon's succession (the SA). All that was necessary to alleviate problems posed by the odd juxtaposition of two figures named Mephibosheth (2 Sam 9:3; 16:3; 19:25; 21:8) was the subsequent addition of a single sentence (v. 7) clarifying that David had done away with Mephibosheth the son of Saul (who was named in v. 8 [HDR_1]), while at the same time preserving the life of Mephibosheth the son of Jonathan (taken over from 9:3 and the other covenant passages between David and Jonathan and understood to be the "Saulide"—בן־שאול—of 16:3 and 19:25 [HDR_2 + SSN]).[199]

In short, it was the compiler of the PR who accomplished this combination of the two traditions and possibly Dtr who inserted the later connective link in 2 Sam 21:7. Not only were historical notices of the kingdom under Solomon and his northern and southern successors included in the PR, but several independent episodes were also introduced in the late-9th or early- to mid-8th cent. redaction, including the explicitly prophetic rejection of Saul (1 Sam 15:27–28), the anointment of David (1 Sam 16:1–13), and the prophetic narratives taking place after Solomon's reign, including both the Ahijah-Jeroboam story (1 Kgs 11:31–39)[200] and parts of the Elijah-Elisha complex. This redaction probably incorporated the bulk of the loosely conjoined Samuel materials as well.[201] Composed

199 See, e.g., Veijola, "David und Meribaal," 351.

200 For this delineation, see Campbell, *Of Prophets and Kings*, 25–32.

201 As John L. McKenzie points out, there seem to be four distinct roles that Samuel plays throughout his lifetime; it is difficult to believe that all of these originated in one source ("The Four Samuels," *BR* 7 [1962]: 3–18). We may compare the schema presented here to that proposed by D. J. McCarthy, who argued that the development of 1 Samuel 8–12 occurred in phases, which progressed from the existence of independent narratives, through clusters of narratives, and finally to the completed text ("The Inauguration of Monarchy in Israel: A Form-Critical Study of I Samuel 8–12," *Int* 27 [1973]: 401–12).

of various types of documents—prophetically overlaid folktales, hero legends, royal apologies, and relatively neutral historiography—this composite text related its vision of the history of Israel and Judah: a history in which Yahweh acted through the prophets to bring about the institution of the monarchy (albeit somewhat reluctantly) and to establish the kingship in the hands of his servants. At the hypothesized time of the codification of the PR, those servants were firmly entrenched in power: the Jehuite dynasty in Israel and the Davidic dynasty in Judah.

If the sitting Davidide was the recently crowned Joash, then both dynasties had recently defeated the Baalist (or syncretistic) movements pushed by the Omride dynasty (and its scion Athaliah in the south) and established (or *reestablished* in the case of Joash) Yahwistic religion in their respective kingdoms. If the document's date should be traced into the 8th cent., a slightly different set of historical conditions obtains. At this time, the increasingly international character of the Jehuite dynasty began to come under attack from opponents in the northern kingdom who resented the dynasty's apparent failure to maintain the strict adherence to Yahweh's rule presaged in or promised by Jehu's revolt (e.g., the prophet Hosea). Because the PR was a document that authentically established prophetic authority as a counter-measure to the abuse of the kingship and claimed to prove the root of that authority in God's action within Israel, it could therefore have served as a foundational, authoritative text within both the Jehuite court controlling Israel and the entrenched Davidic dynasty ruling Judah, whether composed as late as the mid-8th cent. (with the impending downfall of the northern kingdom already clearly in view) or as early as the late-9th cent. Moreover, although the PR contained distinctively northern elements, it would not necessarily have been out of place or unappreciated in certain southern circles. The composite document's thrust was sufficiently broad to justify both dynastic groups (or to proclaim judgment against the Jehuites), depending on the reader's hermeneutic, while at the same time explaining the existence of an independent Israel. The ability to account for both the redactional development and the continuing normativity of both Histories of David's Rise lends credence to the evolutionary model I have proposed here, which divorces the two Histories of David's Rise. One (the HDR_1) was inextricably linked to the NSR_{AB} (see §§7.4; 8.1) and held a view of Transjordan quite distinct from that of the other (the HDR_2 + SSN complex).

7. The Narrative(s) of Saul's Rise

7.1. Composition History of 1 Samuel 8–14

Because 1 Samuel 11 is the only chapter of the PR which displays the deliverer-type vision of Transjordan, it is necessary to engage here in a preliminary discussion of the composition history of 1 Samuel 8–14. Unfortunately, limitations of space preclude a detailed analysis of the formation history of these seven chapters, a project that must await future study. I will seek to demonstrate in this chapter only that the narrative of Saul's rise through his military victory at Jabesh-gilead (1 Sam 11:1–15; hereafter dubbed the NSR_A) was originally separate from both of the other passages detailing his elevation to a position of authority, 1 Sam 9:1–10:16 (designated by the siglum NSR_B) and 1 Sam 10:17–27 (the NSR_C). That 1 Sam 9:1–10:16 originally derived from a source independent of 1 Sam 11:1–15 is, of course, not a new argument, as will be surveyed further below. However, it is necessary to reiterate the argument since contrary appraisals abound. The literary and thematic connections between 1 Sam 10:17–27 and 11:1–15 have only relatively recently been adduced as markers of the original consecution of those two stories, but in this case too there are indications that the juxtaposition of the two passages has been effected redactionally and was not original. In turn, this composition-critical analysis will provide a rough model that describes the process whereby 1 Samuel 8–14 developed into its current shape and gathered its connections to the following materials (1 Samuel 15–1 Kings 2). As will be seen, this process was a long and complex one, with several intermediary stages, at each of which the combined tradition displayed a remarkably coherent unity of purpose.

7.1.1. The Classical Model

J. Wellhausen is credited with the classical articulation of the solution to this problem.[1] In the narrative tapestry of Israel's transition from a loose

1 J. Wellhausen, *Prolegomena to the History of Israel* (trans. J. S. Black and Allan Menzies, with a preface by W. Robertson Smith; 1885; repr., with a foreword by Douglas A. Knight; Atlanta: Scholars, 1994), 247–56; idem, *Die Composition des Hexateuchs* (4th ed.; Berlin: de Gruyter, 1963), 240–46.

confederation of tribal entities to a monarchy united under a solitary figure who had been designated by Yahweh, Wellhausen discerned two originally independent narratives now intricately interwoven. One was, on the whole, "pro-monarchical" insofar as it recognized the monarchy as an improvement over the previous socio-political system, which had been reliant on an essentially ad hoc and potentially corrupt leadership. This source he considered to have been the earlier of the two, ostensibly comprising 1 Sam 9:1–10:16 + 11:1–15* + 13–14. It displays no "hostility or incompatibility between the heavenly and the earthly ruler" but rather envisions the institution as a gift from YHWH.[2] Wellhausen recognized in the other, later source (1 Samuel 7–8 + 10:17–27 + 12) an essentially "anti-monarchical" impulse that, once threaded through its predecessor, curbed the joy with which the institution was received by the Israelites. Wellhausen attributed the inclusion of this later material to the Deuteronomistic Historian, though he recognized the presence of earlier traditions the historian had only reused. By juxtaposing passages from each source next to one another, and with the careful insertion of the suture at 1 Sam 11:12–14,[3] the Deuteronomistic author provided a coherent presentation of Saul's inauguration as king. In the newly knit narrative, Saul's clandestine designation and commission at the hands of Samuel (1 Sam 10:1–8) precedes the young king's public selection and acclamation in 10:17–27. Yet despite the publicity of this designation, "Saul is at this point only king *de jure*; he does not become king *de facto* until after he has proved himself" in the victory over the Ammonites in 1 Samuel 11.[4] Thus, although Wellhausen understood 1 Sam 11:1–11,15 as an integral part of the older story, he also recognized its importance as the bridge through which that narrative complex was combined with the later account.[5] The date of the Deuteronomistic addition—and hence, of the combined text as a whole—could be fixed, according to Wellhausen, because the later sequence's high degree of anti-monarchic sentiment could "only have arisen in an age which had no knowledge of Israel as a people and a state, and which had no experience of the real conditions of existence in these forms; in other words. [*sic*] it is the offspring of exilic or post-exilic Judaism."[6]

In his own comprehensive survey of the origins and composition history of the DtrH, M. Noth reached substantially similar conclusions.[7]

2 Wellhausen, *Prolegomena*, 254.

3 Even in other models, 1 Sam 11:12–14 are commonly considered to be redactional insertions designed to situate this episode in its context. See below, §7.3.1.5.

4 Wellhausen, *Prolegomena*, 250.

5 Ibid., 251–52; idem, *Composition*, 241–43.

6 Wellhausen, *Prolegomena*, 255.

7 Martin Noth, *The Deuteronomistic History* [*DH*] (trans. J. A. Clines et al.; JSOTSup 15; Sheffield: Sheffield Academic Press, 2001), 78–85.

Although Noth allowed Dtr to have included a few scattered, earlier local traditions, he argued the later source was so infused with the author's own ideological outlook that its composition must ultimately be attributed to the historian. The influence exerted on the field by Wellhausen and Noth is evident in the continuing influence of this model bifurcating an older, pro-monarchic source and a later, anti-monarchic one. However, a barrage of resistance in the years since Noth's initial statement on the DtrH has fragmented the once nearly unanimous assessment of 1 Samuel's composition history, and several different positions have been taken. This bewildering variety of schemas may be roughly consolidated into three groups, at least with respect to the posited original position of 1 Samuel 11.[8]

7.1.2. Those in Favor of the Original or Secondary Unity of 1 Sam 9:1–10:16* + 11:1–15*

The first group is comprised of those who retain Wellhausen's classical attribution of 1 Samuel 11 to a larger "old, pro-monarchic" or "pro-Saulide" complex[9] but temper that attribution with an appreciation of Noth's recognition that an assortment of earlier traditions had been incorporated into this source in its earliest formation. Although a sub-set of this first group does not explicitly differentiate between the origins of 9:1–10:16* and 11:1–15*, this unclarified position is normally taken by those most concerned with later stages of the development of 1 Samuel or with separate concerns entirely, and therefore the position's lack of refinement does not constitute a difficulty.[10] More often, scholars recognize the divergent origins of the passages 9:1–10:16* and 11:1–15*, even though they are held to have been joined at some point prior to the Deuteronomistic Historian's reception of the whole complex. Only with the crystallization of the remainder of the DtrH was the surrounding and intervening material introduced (1 Samuel 7–8 + 10:17–27 + 12). Beginning with the work of A. Weiser and his student F. Mildenberger, a strong

8 Since the following discussion overlaps with that provided in §3.4.1, the discussion here proceeds at a much quicker pace; the reader is referred to the earlier discussion for more precise statements of each individual's scholarship.

9 My use of the term "pro-monarchic" here is not an indication that most of these scholars make such a division on the basis of the text's perceived stance towards the monarchy. I merely pick up the basic description that Wellhausen bestowed on the sequence.

10 See, e.g., Nadav Na'aman, "The Pre-Deuteronomistic Story of King Saul and Its Historical Significance," *CBQ* 54 (1992): 638–58, esp. 642–45; Marsha White, "'The History of Saul's Rise': Saulide State Propaganda in 1 Samuel 1–14," in *"A Wise and Discerning Mind": Essays in Honor of Burke O. Long* (ed. Saul M. Olyan and Robert C. Culley; BJS 325; Providence: Brown Judaic Studies, 2000), 271–92, esp. 275, 279–80.

component of this theory has recognized the reworking of the traditions within what are generally construed as "prophetic circles," that is, groups of prophets and prophets' apprentices who somehow maintained the textual traditions of earlier polities and political factions and then adapted them for use both within their own community and in the larger Israelite and Judahite kingdoms.[11]

The basic tenets of this position have been modified somewhat since its earliest proposals. Closely related to the "limited prophetic edition" (hereafter LPE) camp of this first group are those who argue for a much more extensive pre-Deuteronomistic prophetic edition (hence, proponents of an "extended prophetic edition," EPE).[12] Fundamental to this position is Weiser's cogent argument that the classical source-critical division of 1 Samuel 7–15 on the basis of any perceived valence for or against the monarchy was a false dichotomy and could not properly constitute a basis for division.[13] Rather, a careful source- and redaction-critical division could only proceed on the basis of close readings of the individual traditions. Several others have subsequently followed Weiser in this assessment;[14] indeed, it was the observations of Weiser that prepared the

---

11 Artur Weiser, *The Old Testament: Its Formation and Development* (trans. Dorothea M. Barton; New York: Association, 1961), 166–70, esp. 169–70; idem, *Samuel: Seine geschichtliche Aufgabe und religiöse Bedeutung* (FRLANT 81; Göttingen: Vandenhoeck & Ruprecht, 1962), 46–94, esp. 47–48, 69–70; Friedrich Mildenberger, "Die vordeuteronomistische Saul-Davidüberlieferung" (Ph.D. diss., Tübingen, 1962), 17, 29; J. Maxwell Miller, "Saul's Rise to Power: Some Observations Concerning 1 Sam 9:1–10:16; 10:26–11:15 and 13:2–14:46," *CBQ* 36 (1974): 157–74, esp. 171; Antony F. Campbell, *Of Prophets and Kings: A Late Ninth-Century Document (1 Samuel 1–2 Kings 10)* (CBQMS 17; Washington DC: Catholic Biblical Association of America, 1986), 18–21, 102; idem, *1 Samuel* (FOTL 7; Grand Rapids, Mich.: Eerdmans, 2003), 128; see also, recently, Reinhard Müller, *Königtum und Gottesherrschaft: Untersuchungen zur alttestamentlichen Monarchiekritik* (FAT II/3; Tübingen: Mohr Siebeck, 2004), 148–58, esp. 157–58.

12 E.g., Weiser, *Old Testament*, 166–70, esp. 169–70; idem, *Samuel*, 46–94, esp. 69–79; Georg Fohrer, *Introduction to the Old Testament* (trans. David E. Green; Nashville: Abingdon, 1968), 218–25, esp. 219–20; Bruce C. Birch, *The Rise of the Israelite Monarchy: The Growth and Development of 1 Samuel 7–15* (SBLDS 27; Missoula, Mont.: Scholars Press, 1976), 54–63, and esp. 121 nn. 96–98; Volkmar Fritz, "Die Deutungen des Königtums Sauls in den Überlieferungen von seiner Entstehung I Sam 9–11," *ZAW* 88 (1976): 346–62, esp. 359–60; Tryggve N. D. Mettinger, *King and Messiah: The Civil and Sacral Legitimation of the Israelite Kings* (ConBOT 8; Lund: Gleerup, 1976), 80–98, esp. 96; P. Kyle McCarter, *I Samuel: A New Translation with Introduction and Commentary* (AB 8; Garden City, N.Y.: Doubleday, 1980), 14–30, 205–7; Peter Mommer, *Samuel: Geschichte und Überlieferung* (WMANT 65; Neukirchen-Vluyn: Neukirchener Verlag, 1991), 192–202, esp. 195. Contrary to Fritz ("Deutungen," 346), I do not see the assertion that 9:1–10:16* and 11:1–15* were originally independent traditions to be mutually exclusive with the claim that they had both been incorporated into a larger textual complex already at an earlier level.

13 E.g., Weiser, *Samuel*, 25.

14 See, e.g., Hans Jochen Boecker, *Die Beurteilung der Anfänge des Königtums in den deuteronomistischen Abschnitten des I. Samuelbuches: Ein Beitrag zum Problem des "Deuteronomistischen Geschichtswerks"* (WMANT 31; Neukirchen-Vluyn: Neukirchener

way for Mildenberger's own thesis (see above, §§3.4.1.2–3), and so the proponents of the LPE owe much to the methodological observations of the EPE camp. In general, the latter group argues that most of 1 Samuel 7–15 had achieved its present form by the time Dtr received it. The historian, then, supplied only a light veneer of redactional work to the whole complex and certainly could not be credited with the composition of 10:17–27*, a passage that in recent scholarship has been almost exclusively associated with Dtr.

The EPE proponents' line of inquiry encounters a significant objection when a close examination of the surrounding material is performed: there do seem to be significant indicators of Deuteronomistic involvement in the classically construed "late tradition" in 1 Samuel 7–8 + 10:17–27 + 12. However, the relatively early dating, which the EPE camp suggests for much of the traditional material (e.g., the names and positions of Samuel's sons in 1 Sam 8:1–3), is not necessarily precluded by the attribution of the traditions' assembly to Dtr rather than an earlier tradent. F. Crüsemann deftly melded the observations of the two groups by arguing a pre-Deuteronomistic kernal could be found in certain portions of the so-called "late source" (1 Sam 8:1–3,11–17; 12:3–5), not to mention the constituent traditions of the clearly pre-Deuteronomistic early source (to which he accounted 9:1–10:16*; 10:21–23,24aβb,26b,27a; 11:1–15*). Yet Crüsemann argued—wisely and, for the most part, consistent with the LPE group—that these two corpora remained separate until their combination by Dtr.[15]

Although I consider Crüsemann's position a strong one, it is not my intention in the course of this study to decide on the Deuteronomistic or pre-Deuteronomistic provenance of 1 Samuel 7–8; 10:17–27; 12. Because I do not assume a pre-Deuteronomistic provenance of these chapters, the present study bears the greatest affinities with the LPE camp. It is this position that will be defended in the following pages; thus, further refinement is not necessary here.

Verlag, 1969), 4–6, 35, 58–61, 76–77, 87–88, and esp. 89–99; Frank Crüsemann, *Der Widerstand gegen das Königtum: Die antiköniglichen Texte des Alten Testamentes und der Kampf um den frühen israelitischen Staat* (WMANT 49; Neukirchen-Vluyn: Neukirchener Verlag, 1978), esp. 54–84, 194–95; A. D. H. Mayes, *The Story of Israel between Settlement and Exile: A Redactional Study of the Deuteronomistic History* (London: SCM, 1983), 101–2. Müller has recently argued against the preservation of any specifically antimonarchic texts in monarchic-era biblical texts, although he does allow for the antimonarchic impulses of later texts such as 1 Samuel 8; 10:17–27, which he considers Persian-era (*Königtum*, esp. 237–49).

15 Crüsemann, *Widerstand*, 54–66.

7.1.3. Those in Favor of the Deuteronomistic Combination of 11:1–15* with 9:1–16* and 10:17–27*

The second group finds three distinct narratives in the stories of Saul's accession to the kingship. In the early days of this theory's propagation, the combination of these three distinct traditions was posited to have occurred only at the relatively late Deuteronomistic stage of the book's composition history. In this schema, all three were brought together simultaneously, if a specific redactional context was proposed at all.[16] A paradigmatic exemplar of this theory is A. D. H. Mayes, who suggested the inclusion of 1 Samuel 11 came only with the formation of the Josianic edition of the DtrH.[17]

If this Deuteronomistic dating were indeed the proper reconstruction of the text's redaction history, the thesis of the present study would be much affected, because it would delay the time of the Transjordanian Motif's earliest collation until the first Deuteronomistic edition of the DtrH. However, such a late date of combination with the other narratives of Saul's Rise is not necessary. As M. C. White has eloquently articulated,

> The most reasonable explanation for this pattern [i.e., the alternation of non-Deuteronomistic 'pro-monarchic' material with Deuteronomistic 'anti-monarchic' material] is not that a Deuteronomist brought together originally independent positive stories about Saul's kingship and placed them in a remarkably logical order. Rather, a coherent positive history of Saul preexisted negative Deuteronomistic commentary on Saul and the kingship.[18]

Although I do not fully agree with White's attribution of several chapters to Dtr, this statement accurately encapsulates the spirit behind an early,

16 E.g., Otto Eissfeldt, *The Old Testament: An Introduction* (trans. Peter R. Ackroyd; New York: Harper & Row, 1965), 271–81; idem, *Die Komposition der Samuelisbücher* (Leipzig: Hinrichs, 1931); Hans Wilhelm Hertzberg, *I & II Samuel: A Commentary* (trans. John S. Bowden; OTL; London: SCM, 1964; repr., Philadelphia: Westminster, n.d.), 93, 130–34, esp. 132; trans. of *Die Samuelbücher* (2d ed.; DATD 10; Göttingen: Vandenhoeck & Ruprecht, 1960); Isac Leo Seeligmann, "Hebräische Erzählung und biblische Geschichtsschreibung," *TZ* 18 (1962): 313; J. Alberto Soggin, *Das Königtum in Israel: Ursprünge, Spannungen, Entwicklung* (BZAW 104; Berlin: Töpelmann, 1967), 31–45, esp. 41–42; Gerhard Wallis, *Geschichte und Überlieferung: Gedanken über alttestamentliche Darstellungen der Frühgeschichte Israels und der Anfänge seines Königtums* (AzTh 2/13; Stuttgart: Kohlhammer, 1968), 61–62, 67–87; R. E. Clements, "The Deuteronomistic Interpretation of the Founding of the Monarchy in I Sam. viii," *VT* 24 (1974): 398–410, esp. 398; Robert R. Wilson, *Prophecy and Society in Ancient Israel* (Philadelphia: Fortress, 1980), 172–80; A. D. H. Mayes, "The Rise of the Israelite Monarchy," *ZAW* 90 (1978): 1–19; idem, *Story*, 86–101, esp. 88–89; Steven L. McKenzie, "Saul in the Deuteronomistic History," in *Saul in Story and Tradition* (ed. Carl S. Ehrlich with Marsha C. White; FAT I/47; Tübingen: Mohr Siebeck, 2006), 60.

17 Mayes, *Story*, 88–89, 105; for fuller discussion, see above, §3.4.2.3.

18 White, "'History of Saul's Rise'," 280.

pre-Deuteronomistic stage of 1 Samuel 9–14*, which I envision as fundamental to the formation process of the DtrH, as will be seen in the remainder of this chapter.

7.1.4. Those in Favor of the Original or Secondary Unity of 10:17–27* and 11:1–15*

A third, and much more loosely-knit, group is constituted by those who argue for a composition history of 1 Samuel in which either originally or at an intermediate stage of composition 11:1–15* followed in direct consecution on a passage other than 9:1–10:16. In opposition to the position espoused by the LPE camp, which based its conclusions on the observations of the EPE camp, this position has its roots in the work of the earlier members of the second group. Fundamental in this regard is the work of O. Eissfeldt, who had argued earlier that 1 Sam 10:21bβ–27a was the continuation of a tradition comprising 1 Samuel 4*; 6*; 13–14*, and served as the immediate preparation for 1 Sam 11:1–5,6b–15.[19] In that sequence, he argued, Israel's king is to be recognized by his extreme height, head and shoulders above the rest of the people, and none of the assembled people matches that description until a second oracle is delivered and Saul is found hiding in the baggage. Once Saul has been designated as king, he is provided almost immediately with an opportunity to prove his critics wrong (10:27; cf. 11:12–13).[20]

Although this particular insight of Eissfeldt's is compelling and worthy of additional consideration,[21] the fundamental assumption on which it is based—namely, that there existed three extensive sources running the length of Samuel—is tenuous at best, and the associated source-critical schema can no longer command the position it once did. Nevertheless, attempts to salvage the possibility of the unity between 10:17–27* and 11:1–15* have not been in short supply. For example, B. Halpern states that the attempt to postulate a third independent source for 1 Samuel 11 "has not commanded a consensus, partly due to the conservative nature of the scholarly enterprise, and partly, no doubt, because of the difficulty of tracing three continuous, intelligible, literarily unified sources throughout

19 Eissfeldt, *Komposition*, 7–8, 10–11, 56.

20 Ibid., 10.

21 See, e.g., the fruitful use of Eissfeldt's recognition in the schema worked out by Mommer, who proposes to find in reality *four* pre-Deuteronomistic narratives of Saul's rise, in which he divides 10:20–21abα from vv. 21abβ–24 (*Samuel*, 69–91, 194–95).

the book of Samuel."[22] Instead, he argues, closer analysis of the assumptions leading up to the now widely accepted tripartite division of 1 Samuel 8–12, and a concomitant source-division on the basis of doublets alone, suggests that 1 Sam 11:1–15* fits well within the sequence 1 Samuel 8; 10:17–27; 11; 12.[23] Halpern notes several points of continuity between 11:1–15* (NSR_A) and 10:17–27 (NSR_C):

(a) Both passages recognize Gibeah as Saul's hometown (10:26; 11:4).
(b) 1 Samuel 11 gives no indications of Saul's patrimony, provided in 10:20–21.
(c) Saul does not need to "demonstrate his 'charisma'" during the tribal muster in 1 Samuel 11 because he has already been designated as king.

Halpern's concern to do away with the reified assumptions of past paradigms is well placed, especially insofar as it builds on the growing dissatisfaction with the early attempts of Eissfeldt and others to trace three continuous traditions through 1–2 Samuel and with the overly simplistic source-division predicated on the passage's perceived valence towards the monarchy. However, I must disagree with Halpern's assessment on methodological grounds. We need not puzzle too long over the lack of a third continuous narrative strand in the HDR. The assumption underlying Halpern's argument is that a continuous filament running through the HDR and deriving from 1 Samuel 11 is necessary for that episode to comprise an "independent source"; this assumption is indicative of the inherent problems of source-critical textual divisions that do not attribute a great deal of importance to the diachronic reconstruction of the text's compositional and redactional development. It is this assumption itself that affects Halpern's reconstruction of 1 Sam 11:1–15 as the sequel to 10:17–27, since he bases his division of 1 Samuel 8–12 on the division of the rest of the book of 1 Samuel. To assume 1 Sam 9:1–10:16; 10:17–27; and 11:1–15 do not comprise a doublet (or, more accurately, a "triplet") is an over-reliance on the a priori assertion that "it is the doublet, *and preferably the consistent presence of doublets*, that indicates the participation of a second source in any given narrative."[24] While this assertion may indeed serve as a general maxim, it should not be reified as an impenetrable law: if a pair of doublets is combined at an early stage and used as the grounding of a single narrative, Halpern's method would be theoretically unable to recognize the pair of doublets! Moreover, each of the indicators of continuity between 10:17–27 and 11:1–15* that Halpern adduced may be challenged:

---

22 Baruch Halpern, *The Constitution of the Monarchy in Israel* (HSM 25; Chico, Calif.: Scholars Press, 1981), 150 with bibliography at 340 n. 8.

23 Ibid., 149–58, esp. 154–55.

24 Ibid., 151–58, quote from 151 (my emphasis).

(a) The correspondence of Gibeah as Saul's hometown—a memory that goes challenged by other traditions (see below, §7.3.2.2)—is not necessarily a sign of continuity of story, merely continuity of traditional characterization.

(b) As I suggest below (§7.3.1), the story in 1 Samuel 11 was a reused deliverer-type narrative and may not have belonged to Saul originally. In fact, I find it likely that Saul was only secondarily added as the hero of the story. This suggests that any lack of patronymic for Saul is due to scribal redaction rather than the consequence of 1 Samuel 11 immediately after 10:17–27.

(c) A rigid distinction between "charismatic" and "institutional" authority among Israel's judges is no longer a universally recognized dichotomy.[25] Instead, the muster and defeat of the Ammonites comprise the same elements of authorizing action as those of comparable deliverers, as I demonstrate below (§7.3.1).

A few years after the publication of Halpern's schema, W. Dietrich published a more moderate source- and redaction-critical approach, apparently without knowing of Halpern's work.[26] In his study of the Prophetic traditions incorporated into the already-formed book of Samuel by DtrP, Dietrich concluded that there were some very old original traditions contained within the book and that the bulk of 1 Samuel 11 (specifically, vv. 1–11,15) should be understood as an originally independent tradition.[27] In this regard, Dietrich was in concurrence with the members of the first two groups discussed above. In opposition to the first group of scholars, however, Dietrich asserted that the literary connections between 1 Samuel 11* and the original old tradition comprising 1 Samuel 7 + 8:1–5,20b + 10:17,18aα^{1},19b–21a,24–25 were prior to any connection between the former passage and 9:1–10:16; 13–14. Dietrich claimed here that 11:1–11, 15 had been incorporated into the "Book of Saul's Rise" through the insertion of several redactional sutures throughout chapters 10 and 11: 10:21b–23a,26–27; 11:7* (ואחר שמואל), 12–14.[28] Only with Dtr's combination of this "Book of Saul's Rise" with the "Book of David's Rise" (which included 9:1–10:16; 13–14) was 1 Samuel 11* brought together with the rest of Wellhausen's so-called "old source."[29]

Dietrich's solution here is compelling. He constructs a valuable argument for accepting Eissfeldt's ingenious observation concerning the source-critical divide at 10:21abβ, while at the same time mitigating the force of Noth's attribution of 10:20–21abα to the late stages of the text

25 See Rodney R. Hutton *Charisma and Authority in Israelite Society* (Minneapolis: Fortress, 1994), 43–70.

26 Walter Dietrich, *David, Saul und die Propheten: Das Verhältnis von Religion und Politik nach den prophetischen Überlieferungen vom frühesten Königtum in Israel* (BWANT 122; Stuttgart: Kohlhammer, 1987). For the divorce between 1 Samuel 11 and 9:1–10:16, see 92–94; for the discussion uniting 1 Sam 10:17–27 with 11:1–15*, see 131–50, esp. 145–50.

27 Ibid., 146.

28 Ibid., 147–48.

29 Ibid., 150.

introduced by Dtr (on comparison with the evidently derivative Joshua 7).[30] This argument in turn permits a thorough reevaluation of Wellhausen's so-called "late source," such that its constituent early traditions may now be examined independently from one another and reconceptualized as forming the backbone of an early, pre-Deuteronomistic source spanning 1 Samuel 7–14 (with, e.g., Weiser, Birch, Fritz, Mettinger, etc.). However, a few details of Dietrich's solution require further scrutiny.

Foremost among the inconsistencies in Dietrich's schema is the well-attested observation that the verses of the so-called "late, anti-monarchic source" immediately abutting the constituent traditions of Wellhausen's "early, pro-monarchic source" all display some evidence of intentional crafting, specifically to coordinate the two complexes. This transparent attempt at redaction, effected by the author who joined the two bodies of literature, has been examined recently by R. Müller, who notes that the beginning and ending verses of each of the "late" episodes accounts for the geographic assumptions of each intervening scene.[31] That is to say, 1 Sam 8:4 provides a transition from Mizpah (the site of 1 Samuel 7) to Ramah. The notice that Samuel sent the people of Israel home (8:22b) then accounts for Saul's beginning his journey at home (9:1–3) and for Samuel's apparent arrival at the unnamed city of 1 Samuel 9 as well. After the breakdown of the donkey-narrative in 10:13–16 (which will be handled in greater detail in §7.3.2), 10:17 once again provides the unifying redactional material that acts to frame the setting for the selection of Saul. Before the evidently self-standing deliverer-type narrative in 1 Samuel 11 (for this assessment, see §7.3.1), the transition occurs in 10:25b–26a. Finally, the transition in 11:15–12:1 moves Saul and the people to Gilgal and locates Samuel's corresponding farewell speech such that Saul has faithfully carried out Samuel's orders to go to Gilgal (10:8), thereby setting the scene for 13:7b–15. The clustering of so many transitional verses at the outermost limits of the "late source," and particularly in the closing verses of chapter 10, is suggestive of the imprecision of Dietrich's schema.

Second, and perhaps just as important, is the recognition gained in the previous chapter that of the two Histories of David's Rise, one (the HDR_1) presupposed *both* the folktale in 1 Sam 9:1–10:16 *and* the story of Saul's military campaign in 1 Samuel 11, while the other (HDR_2) required no knowledge of either narrative. In the context of the HDR discussion, that reconstruction was a rejection of the early Pentateuchal-source theories of Samuel's composition held by Budde, Eissfeldt, and others and, at the same time, a confirmation of the value of some of their observations

30 Ibid., 137–40.

31 Müller, *Königtum*, 148–76, esp. 149.

(§6.2.1). In the context of the present discussion, that recognition acquires further value. Once the texts forming the bulk of the two Histories of David's Rise have been distinguished and once it is recognized that at least the earlier of the two (HDR_1) was not composed separately from Wellhausen's "early story" of Saul's Rise but was rather appended to an already extant Saul tradition (which seemed on the face of it to comprise at least 1 Sam 9:1–10:16* + 11:1–15* + 13–14), we gain some leverage on the composition history of the Narrative(s) of Saul's Rise—not to mention the historio-political and socio-theological motivations for that composition.

Further consideration of the function and dating of the received Narrative of Saul's Rise (NSR; 1 Samuel 8–14) must take into account the severe discontinuities between immediately abutting episodes of the NSR.[32] The source division of the NSR will therefore consider these tensions and operate with them in immediate view. Whenever one proposes a source-critical schema, however, one must do so with the tacit or explicit proviso that the differentiation of the sources of the text at hand is dependent to a large degree on the assumptions from which such a source-critical project proceeds. Therefore, a central criterion of the following attempt at a source- and redaction-critical division of 1 Samuel 8–14 will proceed with the intention of reconstructing a plausible and reasonable compositional development of the book of Samuel.

As will be demonstrated, attentiveness to the diachronic development of the text permits a reasonable reconstruction of the developmental history of the book of Samuel. The following discussion will account for the essentially threefold nature of the NSR in 1 Samuel 8–14, arguing for the original independence of the NSR_A (1 Sam 11:1–15*) from the NSR_B (1 Sam 9:1–10:16*), as well as the discernable secondary stages of their combination and redaction. Because it is the consensus of most scholars

32 Contrast the burgeoning secondary literature of the literary-critical approach(es) seeking to read the NSR as a unified narrative. While I admit there is much about this approach to praise, its goals are inconsistent with those of the present study and are thus treated only sparingly; it is the process of development whereby that literary reading came about that is currently under investigation. Cf., e.g., Lyle Eslinger, "Viewpoints and Point of View in 1 Samuel 8–12," *JSOT* 26 (1983): 61–76; Robert Polzin, *Samuel and the Deuteronomist* (San Francisco: Harper & Row, 1989); Diana Vikander Edelman, *King Saul in the Historiography of Judah* (JSOTSup 121; Sheffield: JSOT Press, 1991); Sarah Nicholson, *Three Faces of Saul: An Intertextual Approach to Biblical Tragedy* (JSOTSup 339; Sheffield: Sheffield Academic Press, 2002); Barbara Green, *How Are the Mighty Fallen? A Dialogical Study of King Saul in 1 Samuel* (JSOTSup 365; Sheffield: Sheffield Academic Press, 2003); Serge Frolov, *The Turn of the Cycle: 1 Samuel 1–8 in Synchronic and Diachronic Perspectives* (BZAW 342; Berlin: de Gruyter, 2004); idem, "The Semiotics of Covert Action in 1 Samuel 9–10," *JSOT* 31 (2007): 429–50; and Joachim Vette, *Samuel und Saul: Ein Beitrag zur narrativen Poetik des Samuelbuches* (BVB 13; Münster: LIT Verlag, 2005).

that Samuel's selection of Saul by lot in 1 Sam 10:17–27 (what may be designated the NSR_C, along with 1 Samuel 7–8; 12) is in its present form relatively late and because that narrative by its very nature stands outside the present discussion, the status of the NSR_C will not be considered in detail here but only insofar as it is necessary to support the thesis that the NSR_A and the NSR_B had been brought together (hence, NSR_{AB}) already at the time of the composition of the HDR_1 in order to form the prologue to that narrative body, and thus part of the earliest Davidic Apology. This early Davidic Apology was designated in ch. 6 as the HDR_1 complex (= NSR_{AB} + HDR_1). Moreover, I find it most probable that the HDR_1 complex was brought together with the HDR_2 complex (= HDR_2 + SSN) at the time of the formation of the PR, and hence well before the incorporation of Wellhausen's so-called "late-source" (NSR_C), whether or not that document's inclusion was pre-Deuteronomistic, Deuteronomistic, or (partially) post-Deuteronomistic.

7.2. The Function and Dating of the NSR_{AB} (1 Sam 9:1–10:16*; 11:1–11*,15*; sections of 13 and 14)

Before a full-scale investigation of the original independence of the two constituent narratives of the NSR_{AB} may begin, a few words concerning the function and dating of that composite document must be offered. By the same principle outlined above in §4.2.2, we may suggest the hypothesis that the early narratives of Saul's rise were committed to memory or to writing—and received further publication—as an attempt to legitimize the presumptive Saulide heir.[33] The heir to the hereditary kingship whom the tradition was meant to legitimize remains dependent upon the precise dating of the text, which is, of course, impossible to reconstruct with certainty. Yet if we can be so bold as to date some of the traditions to the 10th century[34] and to assume that the biblical prosopography of the Saulide

33 With Hayim Tadmor, "Autobiographical Apology in the Royal Assyrian Literature," in *History, Historiography and Interpretation* (ed. H. Tadmor and M. Weinfeld; Jerusalem: Magnes, 1983), 36–57.

34 For recent studies that suggest such an early date of at least some of the *traditions* in 1–2 Samuel—if only oral—see Mommer, *Samuel*, 103, 108–9; White, "'History of Saul's Rise'," 271–92; Mark Leuchter, "The Literary Strata and Narrative Sources of Psalm xcix," *VT* 55 (2005): 20–38, esp. 30–36; idem, "Something Old, Something Older: Reconsidering 1 Sam. 2:27–36," *Journal of Hebrew Scriptures* 4 (2003): art. 6 (www.jhsonline.org); idem, "Samuel, Saul, and the Deuteronomistic Categories of History," in *From Babel to Babylon: Essays on Biblical History and Literature in Honour of Brian Peckham* (ed. Joyce Rilett Wood, John E. Harvey, and Mark Leuchter; Library of Hebrew Bible/Old Testament Studies

family is reasonably accurate, the following possibilities arise: Jonathan would have been the intended beneficiary if the oral traditions had been composed before the battle of Gilboa at which he (and most of his brothers) are said to have perished; Ishbosheth may have been the ideal candidate if the tradition formed after that battle.[35]

Insofar as M. White argued that the complex comprising the episodes in the Samuel-Saul narratives served as Saulide political propaganda[36] and was later appropriated to serve as the foundational prologue to David's own apologetic texts, my argument here is substantially in line with hers.[37] However, I must disagree with White in several specifics of her presentation. First, the valence of the narratives in chapters 9–14 is not so clear as one might hope and cannot be demonstrated without a good deal of hermeneutical interpretation on the part of the reader.[38] Second, I find it quite doubtful that the constituent traditions of White's "History of Saul's Rise" came together as early as the end of Saul's reign. No matter the literary correspondences between 1 Samuel 1 and 9–14, a connection between those chapters at the source level is unnecessary; ch. 1 may have been composed with 9–14* in view at a later date. Third, I find White's terminological designation of the complex as a "history" uncompelling, although I admit their potential use (independently of one another) as propagandistic material during Saul's reign. Fourth, White's assumption that 1 Sam 9:1–10:16—with its episode of Saul's anointing in 10:1—is a compositional unity[39] does not take into account the demonstrable redaction history that the text underwent at a stage subsequent to the

455; London: T&T Clark, 2006), 101–110; idem, "'Now There Was a [Certain] Man': Compositional Chronology in Judges–1 Samuel," *CBQ* 69 (2007): 429–39.

35 It is unlikely that the narrative would have been aimed at preserving Mephibosheth's reign since, as I have suggested above, that Saulide was probably not historically a survivor of the Davidic purge of the Saulides. For discussions of the historical implications of this text, particularly with respect to its legitimizing function, see previous studies such as: Crüsemann, *Widerstand*, 59–60; William E. Evans, "An Historical Reconstruction of the Emergence of the Israelite Kingship and the Reign of Saul," in *Scripture and Context II: More Essays in the Comparative Method* (ed. William W. Hallo, James C. Moyer, and Leo G. Perdue; Winona Lake, Ind.: Eisenbrauns, 1983), 61–77; J. W. Flanagan, "Chiefs in Israel," *JSOT* 20 (1981): 47–73.

36 White claims that this propagandistic text included 1 Sam 1:1–28 + 2:11a; 2:11b–34 + 3:1a; 3:1b–4:1a; 4:1b (LXX)–18a; 4:19–5:4; 5:6–6:14; 6:16; 1 Sam 9:1–8; 9:10–10:7; 10:9–10,13–16; 1 Sam 10:27b (4QSam^{a})–11:11; 11:15; 13:2–7a,15b–20; 13:22–14:46; 14:47–48 ("'The History of Saul's Rise'," 291).

37 Ibid., 282–84; see also idem, "Saul and Jonathan in 1 Samuel 1 and 14," in *Saul in Story and Tradition* (ed. Carl S. Ehrlich with Marsha C. White; FAT I/47; Tübingen: Mohr Siebeck, 2006), 119–38.

38 Weiser, *Samuel*, 25; Boecker, *Beurteilung*, 4–6, 35, 58–61, 76–77, 87–88, and esp. 89–99; Crüsemann, *Widerstand*, 54–84, 194–95. For a good synthesis of these studies, see Mayes, *Story*, 86–96.

39 Ibid., 284–87.

complex's combination with the HDR_1 and with the HDR_2 complex (see §7.3.2 below). Finally, I remain unconvinced of White's assertion that Jonathan is the only candidate for the text's support (see below, §7.4).[40]

Despite these disagreements with some of the specifics of White's argument, I hope to demonstrate in the following pages that the LPE and EPE common view of a pre-Deuteronomistic compilation of (at least) 1 Sam 9:1–10:16* + 11:1–15* + 13–14* is correct in its fundamental assertions and that any proposed Deuteronomistic dating of the combination of those portions of Samuel is unnecessary. This early source, I suggest, had been formed at the latest by the time of the composition of the HDR_1, which, as I demonstrated in ch. 6, knew of the combined traditions. It underwent a long process of development that cannot be confined only to the two periods of (a) its initial formation and (b) its inclusion in the DtrH. Rather, I will argue that it is possible to trace the independent traditions' developments into the present text through at least two intermediary stages: their combination into the prologue of the HDR_1[41] and the resultant complex's inclusion in the PR.

I argued in the previous chapter that although the HDR does not necessarily present an accurate record of real historical events, the fact of its composition does indicate the existence of a sociological niche available for a matrix of apologetic texts defending the legitimacy of the Davidide kings—David, Solomon, and Rehoboam—over against that of the Benjaminite Saulide dynasty. Human emotional responses and motivations in much of both HDR_1 and HDR_2 seem realistic, easily understandable within their historical context.[42] The same cannot be said for the Narrative of Saul's Rise. In 1 Samuel 8–14, events are narrated in a manner that seems less humanly motivated than divinely mandated or coincidentally prescient. Saul's journey throughout the southern Ephraimite hill-country (9:4–5) is ostensibly a folkloristic account of how Saul's peregrinations anticipate his future control over the same area.[43] As will be

---

40 This assertion of White's is predicated on the recurrence of the verb נתן in 1 Samuel 1 ("Saul and Jonathan," 119–38; see also idem, "'The History of Saul's Rise'," 284–88). But even in White's presentation, that chapter so schematically alludes to Saul and Jonathan that the sheer ingenuity of the allusions calls into question the unity of White's claimed early propagandistic narrative: nowhere else in 9:1–10:16; 11; 13–14 does the author display such literary playfulness.

41 Here again, I am in basic agreement with White, who draws attention to the function of 1 Sam 10:8; 13:7b–15a as effecting the transition between her "History of Saul's Rise" and the "History of David's Rise," although I am unconvinced that this transition was effected so early as White argues (1 Sam 14:49–2 Sam 8:15; "'History of Saul's Rise'," 280–81).

42 E.g., J. A. Wharton, "A Plausible Tale: Story and Theology in II Samuel 9–20, I Kings 1–2," *Int* 35 (1981): 341–54.

43 Joseph Blenkinsopp, "The Quest of the Historical Saul," in *No Famine in the Land: Studies in Honor of John L. McKenzie* (ed. J. W. Flanagan and A. W. Robinson; Claremont: Scholars

argued later in this chapter (§7.3.1), the presentation of Saul's campaign to save Jabesh-gilead (1 Samuel 11) has more in common structurally with the narratives of the book of Judges than with the other stories of Saul's legitimization to the Israelite kingship. The battle at Michmash (1 Samuel 14), a prolix scene with several distinct episodes, again seems to narrate supernaturally effected events in the context of the formation of the Israelite kingship, but it gives little indication of the emplotment of historical events related to human motivations and emotional responses. In other words, the style of the NSR bears little resemblance to that of either HDR; for this reason I have avoided White's use of the term "history" to describe the complex of Saul-related traditions and instead have designated the matrix of early stories found scattered throughout 1 Samuel 9–14 as the *Narrative* of Saul's Rise.

This is not to argue, on the other hand, that the function of the NSR was not analogous to the respective functions of the HDR and the SSN. Clearly, the narratives of Yahweh's anointment of Saul through the prophet Samuel (9:1–10:16) and Yahweh's support in the battle with the Ammonites (11:1–11) have as their primary function a support of Saulide authority. While the kingship *qua kingship* may not originally have been a concern of the narratives (this will be discussed below), it must be admitted that the narratives have as their primary concern a legitimization of Saulide leadership during a period of relatively scattered Israelite

---

Press, 1975), 96 n. 32; Diana Edelman, "Saul's Journey through Mt. Ephraim and Samuel's Ramah (1 Sam. 9:4–5; 10:2–5)," *ZDPV* 104 (1988): 57; idem, *King Saul in the Historiography of Judah* (JSOTSup 121; Sheffield: JSOT Press, 1991), 43–44; J. Vermeylen, *La loi du plus fort: Histoire de la redaction des récits davidiques de 1 Samuel 8 à 1 Rois 2* (BETL 154; Leuven: University Press and Peeters, 2000), 31. This reading is not inconsistent with the more outmoded reading of Christian A. Hauer, who suggests that each of Saul's coronation narratives preserves an account of the extension of Saul's control over the area in which each respective tradition was preserved ("Does I Samuel 9 1–11 15 Reflect the Extension of Saul's Dominions?" *JBL* 86 [1967]: 306–10). Miloš Bič proposed an entirely different reading of the narrative of the search for the asses ("Saul sucht die Eselinnen," *VT* 7 [1957]: 92–97). Bič argued that the story was a metaphorical representation of a cultic ritual in which Saul—the son of a temple guardian—performs a procession motivated by a desire to find the dying-and-rising-god Baal. When he runs into Samuel, he is shown the error of his ways by the old prophet who is at the time searching for a man who could be accepted as a king by the people. Because of his fine looks (1 Sam 9:2), Saul *is* that man. His inclusion into the Yahwistic social structure is indicated by Saul's honorific treatment at the banquet (9:22–24). Hans Joachim Stoebe responded quickly to this presentation with a solidification of the classical treatment of the story as a narrative about a search for asses. The main point of this story, according to Stoebe, is to confirm Saul's status as an איש חיל ("Noch einmal die Eselinnen des *Kîš* [1 Sam ix]," *VT* 7 [1957]: 362–70; cf. also Birch, *Rise*, 115–16 n. 57). While I do not agree with many of the details of Stoebe's argument (for criticism of both Stoebe and Bič, cf. Weiser, *Samuel*, 49 n. 4; D. Rudman, "The Commissioning Stories of Saul and David as Theological Allegory," *VT* 50 [2000]: 519–20), his insight into the personally transformative nature of Saul's journey is foundational for the argument throughout the remainder of this section.

loyalties.[44] The fact that a reconstruction of a politico-historical rift between the ruling houses of two supposedly agnatically related tribal units (Judah and Benjamin) might plausibly be made for the versions of the HDR allows for a similar reconstruction of the socio-political function of the three versions of the NSR. However, the distinction between the two documents (HDR vs. NSR) is drawn with respect to the *alternatives* to the authorized power. Both versions of the HDR legitimized *Davidic* rule over Judah and Israel (and the document's consequent elevation of the Davidic dynasty over at least the central Israelite hill country) over against potential *Saulide* rule in the form possibly of Jonathan or Ishbosheth (or Abner?); a similar political challenge was issued by Benjaminites who were not Saul's descendants, such as Shimei ben-Gera and Sheba ben-Bikri, both of whom, the biblical text claims, were involved with anti-Davidic activities (2 Sam 16:5–9; 20:1–2). In contradistinction to this concern with lineage, the biblical presentation of the composite NSR_{AB} seems to have legitimized Saul's *kingship* over against a system of *non-hereditary authority* in which only Yahweh could serve as Israel's king and savior. Insofar as a defense of *kingship* continued to be necessary in the face of opposition during the time of David's reign, the HDR was dependent upon the Saulide propaganda of 1 Samuel 9–14. White cogently writes that the HDR "was composed as an extended update of Saul's story and introduction of David, and was created to be attached to Saul's history. The purpose of David's history, as attached to Saul's history, was to draw on the establishment of kingship (1 Sam 9:1–10:16; 10:27b [4QSam[a]]–11:11,15) and to overturn the choice of the dynasty."[45]

Given the picture of the Israelite social structure presented for the period immediately preceding the inauguration of the monarchy with Saul's reign, we should expect nothing less. The most explicit declarations of this process are external to Samuel (e.g., Gideon's refusal of the kingship in Judg 8:22–23)[46] or most likely stem from later editorial

---

44 See, e.g., the similar assessments of Charles Ted Vehse ("Long Live the King: Historical Fact and Narrative Fiction in 1 Samuel 9–10," in *The Pitcher is Broken: Memorial Essays for Gösta W. Ahlström* [ed. Steven W. Holloway and Lowell K. Handy; JSOTSup 190; Sheffield: Sheffield Academic Press, 1995], 435–44, esp. 441); and Marsha White, "Searching for Saul: What We Really Know about Israel's First King," *BRev* 17.2 (2001): 22–29, 52–53.

45 White, "'History of Saul's Rise," 282.

46 But cf. G. Henton Davies, who reads Judg 8:22–23 not as an outright refusal of the kingship by Gideon but rather a monarchic contract with Israel: "While I am king, I will rule as if Yahweh were king." This is an interesting attempt to come to grips with the fact that Gideon was offered the dynastic kingship, but I doubt that Davies is correct in her suggestion "that Gideon's words were spoken by him," i.e., that the episode is historical ("Judges viii 22–23," *VT* 13 [1963]: 154). Cf. Barnabas Lindars, who argued that editorial shaping of the Gideon/Jerubbaal saga has produced a final form in which "Gideon's refusal [of the kingship] is

juxtaposition (e.g., 1 Samuel 8 and 12).[47] However, we do have a few seemingly early indications in 1 Samuel 9–14 that assume a more traditional social structure to which Saul's kingship was viewed as directly antagonistic: (a) the presentation of Saul at the feast in 1 Sam 9:22–24 seems originally to have presupposed a structure of authority depending on the prospective leader's recognition by community notables, rather than the dynastic control of the systems and structures of authority;[48] (b) Samuel's anointing of Saul as *nāgîd* (נגיד; 1 Sam 10:1) seems to be a title designating an "uncrowned leader" in its earliest usage;[49] (c) the similarities between the NSR_A (1 Sam 11:1–11*, esp. 6–7) and the independent narratives of the deliverers (§7.3.1) apparently suggests that the former, like the latter, assumes non-dynastic principles of leadership in Israel. The movement from a social structure based upon non-dynastic leadership (as portrayed in the book of Judges and early in the book of 1 Samuel) towards a bureaucratically supported dynastic kingship (as presented during the reign of Solomon in 1 Kings 3–11, but which probably reached its fullest expression only during the early 9th cent. under the Omride dynasty in the north) would probably not have occurred at one time, no matter the Deuteronomistic portrayal of the process in 1 Samuel. Rather, we may reasonably suspect that Israel's recognition of Saul's "kingship" (whatever

---

expressed according to the narrator's own ideals" ("Gideon and Kingship," *JTS* n.s. 16 [1965]: 321–22 and 322 n. 1).

47 For chs. 8 and 12 as anti-monarchic interpolation, see Wellhausen, *Composition*, 240–46; Noth, *DH*, 77; but cf. Boecker, *Beurteilung*, 10–35, 64–88; and Halpern, who argues that 1 Samuel 8 and 10:17–27 are decidedly *not* Deuteronomistic (*Constitution*, 154 and 343 n. 42). He bases this conclusion on the work of Artur Weiser ("Samuel und die Vorgeschichte des israelitischen Königtums: 1. Samuel 8," *ZTK* 57 [1960]: 141–61 = idem, *Samuel*, 25–45), who, along with I. Mendelsohn ("Samuel's Denunciation of Kingship in Light of the Akkadian Documents from Ugarit," *BASOR* 143 [1956]: 17–22), argues that ch. 8 is potentially historical and most likely significantly older than a Deuteronomistic dating would allow. Recently, Mark Leuchter has argued that Assyrian cognates comprise the most accurate parallel of 1 Sam 8:11–17 ("A King Like All the Nations: The Composition of I Sam 8,11–18," *ZAW* 117 [2005]: 543–58).

48 E.g., Ludwig Schmidt, *Menschlicher Erfolg und Jahwes Initiative: Studien zu Tradition, Interpretation und Historie in Überlieferungen von Gideon, Saul und David* (WMANT 38; Neukirchen-Vluyn: Neukirchener Verlag, 1970), 85; K. A. van der Jagt, "What Did Saul Eat When He First Met Samuel? Light from Anthropology on Biblical Texts," *BT* 47 (1996): 226–30; and recently, Mark W. Hamilton, "The Creation of Saul's Royal Body: Reflections on 1 Samuel 8–10," in *Saul in Story and Tradition* (ed. Carl S. Ehrlich with Marsha C. White; FAT I/47; Tübingen: Mohr Siebeck, 2006), 144–45.

49 Campbell, *Of Prophets and Kings*, 47–61, esp. 59–60; although cf. recently Alexander A. Fischer, "Die Saul-Überlieferung im deuteronomistischen Samuelbuch (am Beispiel von I Samuel 9–10)," in *Die deuteronomistischen Geschichtswerke: Redaktions- und religionsgeschichtliche Perspektiven zur "Deuteronomismus"-Diskussion in Tora und Vorderen Propheten* (ed. Markus Witte et al.; BZAW 365; Berlin: de Gruyter, 2006), 163–81, esp. 169–71; idem, *Von Hebron nach Jerusalem: Eine redaktionsgeschichtliche Studie zur Erzählung von König David in II Sam 1–5* (BZAW 335; Berlin: de Gruyter, 2004), 217–21.

that constituted) was but one medial step in a long socio-historical process to which the stories of Gideon, Abimelek, and David also bear witness—no matter their mimetic accuracy.[50] We should take into serious consideration the biblical presentation of that development. In doing so, the socio- and politico-historical function of the Narrative of Saul's Rise gains clarity, and we find that while the basic thrust of the HDR may be articulated as "*David*, rather than *Saul*, as king," the NSR's can legitimately be summarized as "Saul as *king*, rather than *deliverer*."[51]

This treatment of the basic argument of each composite text suggests a dating of the constituent traditions of the $\mathrm{NSR}_{\mathrm{AB}}$ earlier than that proposed by the majority of scholars. However, in opposition to White's claim, the formation of that composite text need not have occurred as early as the end of the reign of Saul (see §§7.4; 8.1).[52] I suggest that each of the two early Narratives of Saul's Rise ($\mathrm{NSR}_{\mathrm{A}}$ and $\mathrm{NSR}_{\mathrm{B}}$; see §7.3 for their separation) was composed at the latest during the early years of David's reign over both Judah and Israel, when the forces of *Realpolitik* exerted on the Israelite population came to an impasse, forcing a choice between the lesser of two evils (as they would have been perceived by traditionalists espousing the ideological view expressed in Judg 8:22–23): (a) take the side of the dynasty begun by the Benjaminite Saul, who had been successful, at least early in his career, in unifying the nascent Israelite identity,[53] but whose descendants were lobbying for the dynastic

---

50 Jo Ann Hackett, "'There Was No King in Israel': The Era of the Judges," in *The Oxford History of the Biblical World* (ed. Michael D. Coogan; New York: Oxford University Press, 1998), 201; see also recently Robert D. Miller, *Chieftains of the Highland Clans: A History of Israel in the 12th and 11th Centuries B.C.* (Grand Rapids, Mich.: Eerdmans, 2005).

51 The apparent ambivalence of the divine sanction for the kingship achieved in the literary juxtaposition of 1 Samuel 8 with the following material is typically understood as the product of constraints placed upon the later editors: "by using [the narrative of the Rise of David], it had become impossible for the Deuteronomists to deny the divine origin of Saul's kingship without also denying that of David" (R. E. Clements, "Deuteronomistic Interpretation," 407–8). In this regard, I disagree with Halpern's assessment of the putative narrative in 1 Sam 9:1–10:16; 11:1–15 as taking "an anomalous departure from league traditions as though [the institution of kingship] were a reasonable occurrence in everyday life. Kingship is not an issue [in 1 Sam 9:1–10:16; 11:1–15], it is a premise" (*Constitution*, 153). The monarchy in *both* 9:1–10:16 *and* 11:1–15 is an institution that, while clearly in place, requires renewed justification.

52 Cf. White, "History of Saul's Rise," esp. 283.

53 Saul's kingdom probably never included the Galilee, nor did he ever control most of Judah. If we regard the territorial description of Ishbosheth's territory in 2 Sam 2:8–9 as accurate, Saul's kingdom probably encompassed the central Israelite hill country from the border with Judah as far as the Jezreel Valley and the central Gileadite highlands from Heshbon as far north as the *W. Yabīs*. See e.g., Kurt Möhlinbrink, "Sauls Ammoniterfeldzug und Samuels Beitrag zum Königtum des Sauls," *ZAW* 58 (1940/1941): 61; Diana Edelman, "The 'Ashurites' of Eshbaal's State (2 Sam 2:9)," *PEQ* 117 (1985): 85–91; idem, "The Asherite Genealogy in 1 Chr 7:30–40," *BR* 33 (1988): 13–23; idem, "Saul's Journey through Mt. Ephraim and Samuel's Ramah (1 Sam. 9:4–5; 10:2–5)," *ZDPV* 104 (1988): 48–49. I

continuation of Saul's kingship in opposition to the long-held ideal of Yahweh's kingship, or (b) side with the charismatic usurper David ben-Jesse who, though apparently supported even by Yahweh, was unfavorable as a king because of his status as quasi-Israelite or even foreigner (i.e., Judahite) and the rumors of his political dealings with the Philistines. The alternative of having a non-dynastic, popularly-recognized leader was no longer available to the Israelite population, as was later implicitly recognized in the purported record of Samuel's final farewell to the Israelites (1 Sam 12:1–2,11–13).

Those who chose the first, pro-Saulide alternative became the hypothetical audience(s) of the NSR$_A$ and NSR$_B$; the group(s) who chose the latter would presumably have been one of the many demographics later targeted by the HDR$_1$ as that text tried to legitimize the Davidic dynasty over against the House of Saul (see §6.6). There is thus a secondary function of the HDR$_1$ that may be discerned because of its reuse of the traditions contained in the NSR$_{AB}$, a function not directly recognized in the analysis above: the HDR$_1$ sought not only to legitimize David's family over against Saul's, but that text was still equally susceptible to the not-yet-antiquated challenge that dynastic kingship was not suitable; the composers of the HDR$_1$ therefore had to reuse the NSR$_{AB}$ specifically to make the case for the very existence of Yahweh's support for dynastic kingship in Israel to begin with! No matter Saul's moral stature in the ensuing conflict between the two royal houses, his legacy thus quickly became that of the first of Israel's leaders to whom divine permission for dynastic kingship had been granted, in effect clearing the way for David's ultimate seizure and proliferation of that institution.

7.3. The Source-Critical Separation of NSR$_A$ and NSR$_B$

The central project of this section will be a source-critical separation of the two earliest (and most intimately intertwined) narratives of Saul's rise, the NSR$_A$ and NSR$_B$. In order to make the distinction between these two accounts of the rise of Saul, a separation not easily performed on the basis of linguistic features, the methodology proceeds here primarily based on differences of style and structure.

As it currently stands, the biblical text portrays the following series of events in the early life of Saul: the young man Saul, the son of a property-

---

disagree, however, with Edelman's distinction between being king "על-GN" and being king "אל-GN" as matters of political status, which is an insufficiently substantiated differentiation ("Ashurites," 88; cf. also Mommer, *Samuel*, 116 n. 326).

owning Benjaminite, is sent on a mission with a servant (*naʿar*; נער) of the household to find some of the family's asses that have gone missing. After making an exploratory jaunt into the southern hill-country of Ephraim[54] and finding nothing, Saul suggests they turn around before his father begins to worry about them (9:1–5). But the servant has another suggestion: while they are in the area, they ought to visit the seer[55] who resides in a nearby city (v. 6). When they reach the (unnamed) city, they are met first by a group of women who direct them to the house of the seer, and then the seer himself, whom the reader recognizes from ch. 8 as the famous Samuel (vv. 11–19; Saul does not seem to recognize the man, immediately, at least). After reassuring Saul that the donkeys have been found, Samuel invites Saul and his servant to a feast, at which Saul is given the seat of honor as well as a specially reserved portion of the meal (vv. 20–24). After the feast, he returns home with Samuel, where he spends the night (v. 25). In the morning, Samuel anoints Saul *nāgîd* (נגיד) over Israel and gives him three signs by which he will recognize this as an authentic elevation of status (9:26–10:7). The first two occur without significant narration, but the third—the ecstatic prophesying of Saul after meeting a band of prophets—is given three full verses (10:10–12). After meeting his uncle, who asks him where he has been, Saul informs him of the meeting with Samuel (who had informed them that the donkeys had been found) but does not tell him about "the matter of the kingship" (vv. 13–16). Samuel then convenes the Israelites at Mizpah with a brief review of their request for a king (vv. 17–19), and a lot-drawing ceremony ensues that makes explicit the divine choice of Saul (vv. 20–21a). But after Saul's selection, he cannot be found until Samuel delivers an oracle (vv. 21b–23). Saul is then established as king among the people before they are sent to their respective homes (vv. 24–27). After he has been at home for a while in Gibeah, Saul hears word of the Ammonite oppression of the Jabeshites, to which he responds immediately (11:1–6). He carves up his yoke of oxen, sending the pieces throughout Israel as an open threat against those who do not attend the battle (v. 7). Saul rallies the troops in Bezek, a city across the Jordan Valley from Jabesh. The Israelites march throughout the night, taking the Ammonite camp by surprise in the morning, and inflict a great defeat upon them (vv. 8–11). In reaction to this military victory, the Israelites proceed to Gilgal where they anoint Saul king (vv. 12–15), and Samuel delivers a long oration introducing the period of the monarchy

54 For the trajectory of this journey as a counter-clockwise circle through the southern territory of Ephraim, see Edelman, "Saul's Journey."

55 While the biblical text of 1 Sam 9:6 uses the term "man of God" (איש אלהים), I have leveled the term "seer" throughout, for reasons which will become clear below.

(12:1–25). After the brief notices of Saul's reign, the Israelites are called out to their leader, now officially recognized (13:1–4). When they hear that the Philistines have taken Michmash (v. 5), however, many of the Israelites begin to slip away from Saul's camp at Gilgal, hiding in the countryside (vv. 6–7). Saul waits seven days in Gilgal (abiding by Samuel's command given in 10:8), but when so many of his troops have slipped away that he can wait no longer, Saul finally makes the sacrifices himself (vv. 8–9). Almost as if on cue, Samuel appears and chastises Saul for not waiting. In transgressing the Lord's command, Saul has cost himself an "eternal kingship" (vv. 10–15). Despite Saul's rejection by Yahweh, the Philistine threat to Israel remains, and Saul proceeds into the highlands to recover the land that the Philistines had taken (vv. 16–17).[56] It is not Saul who becomes Israel's hero in the ensuing battle with the Philistines, but his (apparently full-grown) son Jonathan, who, along with his *naʿar*, attacks the Philistine garrison at Michmash, causing a panic amid the camp and turning the garrison against itself (14:1–16). Saul rushes into battle without fully consulting Yahweh (vv. 17–20), inspiring those Israelites who had defected to the Philistines to return to their original allegiances and those who had earlier hidden themselves to join in the fray (vv. 21–22). Despite God's action in battle against the Philistines (v. 23), the battle is not an unmitigated success, for Saul foolishly declares a curse on anyone who eats that day (v. 24). But Jonathan has not heard the curse, and only when he tastes some honey that he has found in the forest (being hungry from his exertion in battle) is he informed of the prohibition (vv. 25–28). Jonathan's reply, moderate in tone and content in opposition to his father's all-consuming zealousness, is that the slaughter would have been even greater if the Israelites had been allowed to eat (vv. 29–31). After an odd interlude in which the Israelites *do* take the spoils of war and in which Saul is forced to build an altar in order to keep his subjects from sinning by eating inappropriately from the slaughtered animals (vv. 32–35), Saul inquires of God whether he should pursue the Philistines further. The oracle gives no answer (vv. 36–37). Saul assembles the people in order to figure out what sin was committed that has prevented God's answer, with the threat that whoever is at fault will die, even if it is his own son Jonathan (v. 39). When he discovers that it *is* Jonathan who is at fault, Saul attempts to carry out his vow, but the people stop him. They ransom Jonathan's life, since the prince has performed so well in battle (vv. 40–45).

56 I skip here the explanatory note in vv. 19–23 detailing the lack of metalworking technology in the highlands. Although the tradition has the appearance of being authentic (and thus, part of the early stratum of NSR_{AB}), it does not further the narrative and may hence be excluded from the discussion for the moment.

While 14:52 seems out of place and somewhat superfluous to the record of battles fought in vv. 47b–48, the rest of the summary paragraph of ch. 14 (vv. 46–51) seems to form the end of the narrative selection. Three major points are made here: (a) Saul has established his kingship (לכד המלוכה על־ישׂראל; v. 47a); (b) Saul now has a court and, perhaps more importantly, three sons through which the dynasty may continue (vv. 49–51); and (c) Saul fights battles with neighboring countries all around (vv. 47b–48). The first two concerns may be distinguished—albeit in a more fully developed manner—in 2 Samuel 5, the summary of David's accession to power: (a) David has established his kingship over both Judah and Israel (וימשׁחו את־דוד למלך על־ישׂראל; vv. 1–3); and (b) David has fathered many sons, any one of whom could rule the kingdom (vv. 13–16). But Saul's insecurity as king over Israel is juxtaposed to David's capture of Jerusalem (vv. 6–8) and subsequent transformation of that city into his new capital, complete with cedar beams sent by King Hiram of Tyre (vv. 9–12). Just as 2 Sam 5:1–16 seems to have served as the summary of David's rise in HDR_1, so too does 1 Sam 14:46–51 serve as the summary of Saul's rise. Although the style cannot be compared favorably (and therefore should probably not be considered to originate from the same hand), the concerns provided for by each are analogous.

Thus, as the biblical text currently stands, the narratives centered on Saul's early career up to the time of his utter rejection by Yahweh through the prophet Samuel (1 Sam 15:27–30) can be found in a section of 1 Samuel that comprises a scant seven chapters, a total of only 195 verses (9:1–15:26). In this relatively short section of text, the narrative is tight, and we are given three stories of Saul's recognition by either Yahweh or the Israelites as king (9:1–10:16; 10:17–27; 11:11,15), three battle sequences (11:1–11; 14:1–45; 15:2–7), one story describing Jonathan's disobedience of a vow imposed on the Israelites by Saul (14:24–29,36–45), several minor (and unexpected) explanatory or etiological episodes (10:10–12; 13:19–23), a long oration by Samuel (12:1–25), and two distinct narratives of Saul's rejection (13:7b–15; 15:10–35). In trying to determine the earliest traditions collected here, we may eliminate several of these episodes.

First, we may exclude from the present discussion Wellhausen's so-called "anti-monarchic strain" (1 Samuel 7–8 + 10:17–27a + 12), which has been designated as the NSR_C below. Although several commentators in the EPE camp have argued for the early origins of this textual sequence, its current form is most plausibly associated with the various Deuteronomistic revisions. Although the passage in 1 Samuel 12 was written significantly later than the period I am proposing for the origin of the

NSR_{AB}, that chapter provides a viewpoint seemingly plausible for the time period it intends to replicate. Together with the final Deuteronomistic arrangement of the DtrH in its entirety, the plausibility of 1 Samuel 12 implies an authentic and historically faithful understanding on the part of the historian that Saul's reign was the beginning of the end of the traditional way of life for those opposed to dynastic systems of authority. Unfortunately, despite the fact that the separation of the NSR_C and a reconstruction of the conditions of its independent existence and ultimate inclusion in what later became the biblical text are significant issues in the structure and development of the book of Samuel as a whole, they are subsidiary issues to the current discussion and will thus be treated rather superficially here.

Second, because the HDR_1 narrative of David's anointing presumes Saul's prior rejection as an intimately related part of the story, most of 1 Samuel 15 may be reasonably included in the material added to the NSR_{AB} either by the author of the HDR_1 or subsequently by the compiler of the PR, who needed to connect the NSR_{AB} + HDR_1 complex with the HDR_2 + SSN complex.[57] Furthermore, the function of the NSR_{AB} posited above suggests that as a pro-Saulide document, it should not contain any indications of a rejection of Saul. This recognition would mitigate the probability that 13:7b–15 also formed part of the early text and suggests instead that the earliest possible date of the passage's incorporation was the time at which the author of the HDR_1 appropriated both extant versions of the NSR.[58] The NSR_C was introduced only later.

The foregoing analysis grounds the NSR_{AB} coupling in its historical context as an explanation of and apology for Saul's kingship, with the resultant contextualization suggesting that the NSR_A and the NSR_B may

57 With Campbell, *Of Prophets and Kings*, 68–69; Campbell divides 1 Samuel 15 into an original narrative of rebuke (15:1aα,2–9,13–15,17a,18–22,24–25,31–35a) and the PR overlay of the rejection (15:1aβ,10–12,16,17b,19b[?],23b[?],26–30,34). Campbell allows only verse 23a to be from the hand of Dtr, as argued earlier by A. Tosato ("La colpa di Saul [1 Sam 15,22–23]," *Bib* 59 [1978]: 251–59). Cf. Veijola, who argued that 1 Samuel 15 was unknown by DtrG, who had inserted 14:47–52 to conclude the reign of Saul and prepare for the reign of David (beginning with 16:14; Veijola, *Das Königtum in der Beurteilung der deuteronomistischen Historiographie: Eine redaktionsgeschichtliche Untersuchung* [AASF B 198; Helsinki: Suomalainen Tiedeakatemia, 1977], 79–81). The problem with this assessment, however, is that it assumes DtrG, rather than some earlier editor, was the one to link the NSR with the HDR through the insertion of 14:52; if my reconstruction here is correct, though, this connection had already been forged at an earlier period so that v. 52 linked NSR_{AB} with the HDR_1, either before the prophetic editor inserted 1 Samuel 15 or through the old tradition retained in that chapter.

58 For a close approximation of my position, compare that of White, "'History of Saul's Rise'," esp. 281–82.

reasonably be examined as components of an authentically archaic stratum of 1 Samuel.

7.3.1. The NSR_A as a Unit Fully Separate from the NSR_B

In the present state of the text, the Ammonite battle seems to form the military action "which [Saul's] hand will find" (אשׁר תמצא ידך), predicted by Samuel in 10:7b.[59] Since the battle narrative seems to be "untouched by polemic,"[60] it (along with 9:1–10:16 and 13:2–14:52) has often been considered instrumental in reconstructing the historical Saul, although this view is encountering increasing opposition.[61] Whether or not the biblical text is held to be reasonably accurate in its portrayal of the historical events surrounding Saul's rise,[62] the general consensus of many historians is that the story of the Ammonite battle in 1 Sam 11:1–11 has been recast in the model of a deliverer-type narrative,[63] at least if it was not, in fact,

59 Blenkinsopp, "Quest," 84; Campbell, *Of Prophets and Kings*, 20; Na'aman, "Pre-Deuteronomistic Story," 643. For this phrase as designating a specifically military endeavor, see Schmidt, *Menschlicher Erfolg*, 74–80, esp. 80; David Wagner, *Geist und Tora: Studien zur göttlichen Legitimation und Delegitimation von Herrschaft im Alten Testament anhand der Erzählungen über König Saul* (ABG 15; Leipzig: Evangelische Verlagsanstalt, 2005), 54; however, cf. Hertzberg, who interprets the phrase as a general statement of Saul's preparedness for any opportunities that may arise (*I & II Samuel*, 85).

60 Blenkinsopp, "Quest," 78.

61 E.g., Mommer, *Samuel*, 114–15.

62 For the problems associated with the assumption, see Diana Edelman, "Saul's Rescue of Jabesh-Gilead (I Sam 11 1–11): Sorting Story from History," *ZAW* 96 (1984): 195–209; Patrick M. Arnold, *Gibeah: The Search for a Biblical City* (JSOTSup 79; Sheffield: JSOT Press, 1990), 95–97; J. Maxwell Miller and John H. Hayes, eds., *Israelite and Judaean History* (OTL; Philadelphia: Westminster, 1977), 324–25; and recently, Siegfried Kreuzer, "Saul—Not Always—at War: A New Perspective on the Rise of the Kingship in Israel," in *Saul in Story and Tradition* (ed. Carl S. Ehrlich with Marsha C. White; FAT I/47; Tübingen: Mohr Siebeck, 2006), 39–58, here 40–41. To this doubt concerning the historicity of the Saulide traditions, Miller adds the caveat that the historicity of 1 Samuel 11 could be plausible only if Saul had *already* chased the Philistines from the highlands (as is narrated in ch. 14); chapter 11 may thus post-date 1 Samuel 14 historically ("Saul's Rise," 167). But this solution overlooks or ignores the indications in 13:5 that the Philistines invaded Michmash while Israel was gathered in Gilgal, the biblical text's implicit explanation of the order of events. The presence or absence of the Philistines in Cisjordan during Saul's campaign is an accident of textual redaction, and not a historical situation. A sizeable bibliography of those who read the story historically is available in Edelman, "Saul's Rescue," 195 n. 1.

63 For this comparison, see Edelman, "Saul's Rescue," 205–9 (citing Mettinger, *King and Messiah*, 72, 79, 86–87; and Halpern, *Constitution*, 51–148); Miller, "Saul's Rise," 165, esp. n. 22; and McCarter, *I Samuel*, 205–6: "a development in the category of the story of the deliverer." Although many have argued 1 Samuel 11 preserves "unquestionably…the most reliable and informative" historical account, the framing of the narrative in a deliverer-type format may speak against that assumption (for quote, see Clements, "Deuteronomistic

originally a deliverer narrative on the order of those of Ehud, Gideon, and Jephthah.[64] In his classic treatment of the deliverer narratives, W. Richter argued that 1 Samuel 11 displays stylistic and thematic affinities to the passages narrating the military successes of Ehud and Gideon (respectively, Judges 3; 6).[65] Subsequently, J. Blenkinsopp compared the traditions surrounding Saul with the narrative of Jephthah's success in battle, and several of the similarities he adduced may be applied as well to the deliverer-tales of Ehud and Gideon, a task undertaken in §§7.3.1.1–4.[66]

7.3.1.1. The Elevation of the Hero to a Position of Leadership (Despite Protestations of Humble Social Location)

Every one of the four heroes in these deliverer-type stories begins his career as a member of a lower class, or as a simple landowner. They are never of the lowest classes, but neither do they seem to be particularly wealthy, since they are performing the work themselves rather than having it done by servants.[67] At his introduction in 1 Samuel 11, Saul is found plowing a field behind a yoke of oxen (1 Sam 11:5). Contrary to Jephthah, who is said to have been a journeyman who surrounded himself with

---

Interpretation," 398; also Weiser, *Samuel*, 70–71; Miller, "Saul's Rise," 165; and Fritz, "Deutungen des Königtums," 356–58).

64 For Saul as taking on the office of the savior in Israel, see Wilhelm Caspari, *Die Samuelbücher* (KAT 7; Leipzig: Deichert, 1926), 12; Hans Wildberger, "Samuel und die Entstehung des israelitischen Königtums," *TZ* 13 (1957): 467–69; Martin Noth, *The History of Israel* (2d ed.; trans. P. R. Ackroyd; London: Adam & Charles Black, 1960), 168; trans. of *Geschichte Israels* (2d. ed.; Göttingen: Vandenhoeck & Ruprecht, 1958); Weiser, *Samuel*, 71–73, 76; Seeligmann, "Hebräische Erzählung," 313; J. Alberto Soggin, *Das Königtum in Israel: Ursprünge, Spannungen, Entwicklung* (BZAW 104; Berlin: Töpelmann, 1967), 41–45; Wallis, *Geschichte und Überlieferungen*, 55; Birch, *Rise*, 56–58; Klein, *1 Samuel*, 108–9; Fritz, "Deutungen," 358; Mommer, *Samuel*, 103, 118; and Leuchter, "'Now There Was…'," 433; idem, "Samuel," 106–8.

65 Wolfgang Richter, *Traditionsgeschichtliche Untersuchungen zum Richterbuch* (BBB 18; Bonn: Heinstein, 1963), 177–80.

66 Blenkinsopp, "Quest," 85–86. I do not deal with Deborah's narrative here because no part of it takes place in Transjordan. Jo Ann Hackett has pointed out to me that Ehud's story may similarly occur entirely on the western bank of the Jordan (personal communication), but in Ehud's story, the battle solidifying his position as a leader in Israel does take place at the Jordan River.

67 I take as rhetorical and formulaic the protestations of both Gideon and Saul that the clan of each is the smallest in their respective tribe, that the nuclear family of each is the smallest in the clan, and/or that the individual under question is the smallest in the family (Judg 6:15; 1 Sam 9:21; cf. the assumption and acting out of the protest in 1 Sam 16:6–16 and a similar protest in 18:18). The assumed marginalization of these figures is not borne out by the fundamental structure of the hero-tales. More recent sociological analysis than Weber's has disproved the close connections normally assumed between the economically or ethnically marginalized and charismatic authority (R. Hutton, *Charisma and Authority*, 68).

"worthless men" (Judg 11:3) because his half-brothers would not allow him to inherit their father's estate (Judg 11:2), Saul owns land and therefore has at least some status in the Israelite social system, though he does not seem to be any better off than other independent land-owners initially.[68] The same is probably true of Gideon ben-Joash, whom the reader meets while he is threshing wheat (חבט חטים) in a wine-pressing installation (בגת) to hide the process from Midianite marauders (Judg 6:11). While we are given no specific indications of Ehud's social position, he serves as a messenger to Eglon, bearing Israel's tribute (Judg 3:17), which suggests that he did not yet belong to a position of elite social standing.

Without exception, the text claims that the character's position is raised through success in battle. Ehud garners specific mention as the one who rallies the Israelites and leads them into battle (וירדו עמו, v. 27; the command רדפו אחרי, v. 28). But beginning in v. 28b, the Israelites become the subject(s) of the actions of war: they "(v. 28b) went down... seized... did not allow... (v. 29) struck..." (וירדו...וילכדו...ולא־נתנו...ויכו). Ehud's social standing in the wake of the battle is not explicitly mentioned, but the juxtaposition of the structural notices that "the land was quiet for eighty years" (3:30b) and that "after [Ehud] was Shamgar ben-Anat" (3:31aα) suggests that even prior to the later reframing of the episode, Ehud was considered to have attained some enduring stature through the success of the battle.

The case of Jephthah's elevation has already been pointed to above, but the details deserve mention here. When the Ammonites besiege the Gileadites, the elders send to Jephthah, asking him to become a military leader (קצין; 10:6) so they may fight against the Ammonites. It is unclear why they immediately extend this position to him, but the answer may lie in Jephthah's previous experience with a leadership role in his band of outlaws and ne'er-do-wells (v. 3). It is similarly unclear to Jephthah, and he responds to the request by pointing out that the Gileadites had earlier expelled him, so why now should they want him to be "like a lord" (צר כאשר; v. 7) to them. Their second offer to Jephthah is that he shall be made "head" (ראש; v. 8) over them, an offer to which he agrees on the condition that Yahweh delivers the Ammonites to him in battle (v. 9). Oddly, the elders immediately set him up as both ראש and קצין over the army (v. 11), despite the fact that the battle has not yet been fought. After an attempt at a peaceful solution is spurned by the king of the Ammonites (vv. 12–28), the "spirit of the Lord" washes over Jephthah and he rallies

68 E.g., Campbell, *1 Samuel*, 116.

his troops (v. 29), bringing a quick destruction upon the Ammonites (vv. 32–33). While the elders of Gilead had set him up as a leader *before* his military victory, the very conditions under which he had agreed to accept the title (v. 9) have now been fulfilled.[69]

The long narrative of Gideon's rise to prominence contains three episodes of conflict: the destruction of his father Joash's altar (6:25–32), the Cisjordanian battle against the Midianite coalition (7:9–25), and the Transjordanian pursuit of the remainder of the invaders (8:4–21). Not only does Gideon gain a formalized position of prominence within the community through his leadership on the battlefield, but the Israelites also offer to Gideon the dynastic kingship: "Rule over us, not only you, but your son, and the son of your son" (משל־בנו גם־אתה גם־בנך גם בן־בנך; vv. 22). Gideon, however, turns down the offer, stating, "I will not rule over you, nor will my son rule over you; *Yahweh* will rule over you" (לא אמשל אני בכם ולא־ימשל בני בכם יהוה ימשל בכם; v. 23). Whether this episode attempts to render a historical event is immaterial, but the theological upshot is clear:[70] Gideon's series of military victories has made him sufficiently respectable in the eyes of his peers that they wish to elevate him to a stature of prominence.

In the case of Saul, the movement to crown him king is likewise only undertaken *after* the battle with the Ammonites at Jabesh. Regardless of whether vv. 12–14 (and particularly v. 15) are deemed to be integral to the original form of the tradition (see §7.3.1.5), it is clear on analogy with other deliverer-type narratives that Saul's success in battle would have occasioned his elevation in status. As the text presently stands, the confirmation of Saul's increased authority follows immediately on his victory. In v. 12, those faithful to Saul from the beginning demand the lives of those who challenged his ability to deliver Israel (cf. 10:27a), but Saul

69 Two more episodes occur in the narrative of Jephthah's rise to prominence: (a) the tragic episode in which he must fulfill the vow he made to Yahweh (vv. 30–31) by sacrificing his daughter and its etiological upshot (vv. 34–40), and (b) the battle with the Ephraimites (12:1–6). While Jephthah has previously been elevated to a position of authority within the Gileadite social structure (v. 11) and confirmed by his victory in battle against the Ammonites, it is only subsequent to the battle with the Ephraimites that the framing elements conclude Jephthah's rise to judgeship—an elevation over all Israel, which occurs immediately following the battle-narrative.

70 Davies argued that the episode *was* historical and that Gideon's response constituted a tacit acceptance of the kingship couched in a theological denial ("Judges viii 22–23," 151–57; see also John Gray, ed., *Joshua, Judges and Ruth* [NCB; London: Nelson, 1967], 313). Cf. C. F. Burney, who attributed Gideon's response to "the later eighth century stage of prophetic thought" (*The Book of Judges with Introduction and Notes and Notes on the Hebrew Text of the Books of Kings with an Introduction and Appendix* [Library of Biblical Studies; 1903; repr., New York: KTAV, 1970], 235; previously, George Foot Moore, *Judges* [ICC; New York: Scribner, 1895], 230).

graciously denounces the threat of revenge, for "[that] day Yahweh [had] given salvation in Israel" (היום עשה־יהוה תשועה בישראל; v. 13), and in v. 15, Saul's kingship is confirmed through sacrificial rituals. This validation provides a fitting ending to the deliverer narrative of 1 Samuel 11 but also to the somewhat non-linear development of institutionalized authority as described through the passages discussed here (Judges 3; 6–8; 11:1–12:5; and 1 Samuel 11), as well as to the legitimate institutionalization (cf. Judg 8:22–23) of the dynastic monarchy in Israel.

7.3.1.2. Privately Undertaken Muster of Available Tribal Forces

Blenkinsopp points out the parallels between the actions of Saul and Jephthah immediately after each has been endowed with the "spirit of the Lord."[71] Jephthah "passed through (עָבַר) Gilead and Manasseh, and he passed through (עָבַר) Mizpeh-gilead, and from Mizpeh-gilead to the side of (לְעֵבֶר)[72] the Ammonites" (Judg 11:29). While Blenkinsopp observes that this locution implies a levying of troops, this reading is dubious. Nowhere does the text explicitly state as much; moreover, a tribal muster would be redundant, since the Israelites are already gathered at Mizpah in defense of the border with the Ammonites (Judg 10:17). Furthermore, Jephthah has already arrived at Mizpah (whence he has sent messengers to the king of Ammon; 11:11b–12a). The logical narrative force of v. 29 thus seems lost in the shuffle, because it is unclear why Jephthah must "pass through" the various territories once he has received the divine commission. Saul's commission, on the other hand, clearly comprises a widespread levying of troops, which gathers in Bezek "as one man" (1 Sam 11:7; see below).[73] Like Saul's call to arms, Ehud's blast on the *shofar* (Judg 3:27) has the effect of summoning the Israelites[74] to battle against

71 Blenkinsopp, "Quest," 85–86.

72 I follow here LXX's εἰς τὸ πέραν (לְעֵבֶר) rather than MT's עָבַר.

73 The exaggerated numbers of troops who gathered in Bezek (11:8) notwithstanding, it seems probable—further divorcing the hero-tale in 1 Samuel 11 from the surrounding environment—that only the troops of "Israel" were included in the original story (with Birch, *Rise*, 55; see also Mommer, *Samuel*, 115–16; Vermeylen, *Loi du plus fort*, 41–42). The men of Judah, who number exactly one tenth of the number of the men of Israel, were probably included secondarily and schematically as the story became increasingly geared towards an audience of both Israelites and Judahites—that is, at the time of the appropriation of the NSR_{AB} by the writer of the HDR_1 *at earliest*.

74 It would seem as though the story in its original form probably only assumed the participation of the Benjaminites and possibly the Ephraimites (this assumption is a common one; see, e.g., Baruch Halpern, *The First Historians: The Hebrew Bible and History* [University Park: Pennsylvania State University Press, 1988], 66). The locus of the call in v.

the Moabites. Judg 6:34 presents a less ideational picture of the call to arms and thus probably an earlier one: "The spirit of the Lord clothed Jephthah, and he gave a blast on the shofar, and Abiezer was called out after him." Here, the levy gathers only the capable men of Abiezer, the hero's own clan, and it is not until Gideon sends out messengers to the surrounding clans and tribes—"all Manasseh," Asher, Zebulon, Naphtali—that those tribes appear.[75] But the addition of these tribes to Gideon's force disrupts the theological intentions of the passage, since now "the army which was with [Gideon] was too large for [God's] giving Midian into their hand, lest Israel glorify itself over [God], saying '*my* hand has saved me!'" (Judg 7:2).[76] In any case, we have in these four passages a similar narrative element in which the hero seems to levy the troops of "(all) Israel" himself. However, upon closer inspection, it would appear: (a) that Jephthah's "levy" is superfluous since the troops were already stationed in Mizpah; (b) that Gideon's levy of Abiezer precedes narratively and logically the levy of the northern tribes, who are then disbanded through the test at the river; and therefore that (c) Ehud's and Saul's respective levies of "Israel" are stylized and theologically motivated such that neither actually would have been able to call upon the forces of "all Israel" but

---

27, Mt. Ephraim, need designate only the central hill country and not necessarily only the Ephraimite homeland.

75 It goes almost without saying that the tribes whom Gideon calls in this story are *only* those whose territory was placed in immediate danger by the encampment of the invading force in the Valley of Jezreel (6:33). That he could have reasonably expected the members of Benjamin or Judah (not to mention Reuben, Gad, etc.) to participate is doubtful, especially if we recall the "failure" of some tribes to join in the campaign against Sisera in Judg 5:16–17, 23. See especially Lawrence E. Stager, "Archaeology, Ecology, and Social History: Background Themes to the Song of Deborah," in *Congress Volume: Jerusalem, 1986* (ed. J. A. Emerton; Leiden: Brill, 1988), 221–34. Clearly, the expectation of Gad to join in such a conflict as Gideon's would have been misplaced. Furthermore, whether the addition of the Galilean tribes would reasonably have been expected—if, that is, the story is historical!—is also debatable, but the call to arms does lend some insight into the more probable function of the hero-narratives. Rather than being leaders of all Israel (as Ehud and Saul were purported to be), the "deliverers'" initial calling was one that would have been limited to a few tribes at most (i.e., those tribes immediately threatened) and most probably to a single tribe (e.g., Jephthah's Gilead) or even a single clan (e.g., Gideon's Abiezer).

76 Na'aman has cited the depletion of Saul's forces in 1 Sam 13:6–7 as confirmation of the integrity of 1 Samuel 11 within the "old-story" ("Pre-Deuteronomistic Story," 645). Accordingly, argues Na'aman, the deliverer-character Saul must suffer a depletion of forces parallel to that of Gideon's culling of troops (Judg 7:2–7) so that God may save Israel by a number so low as to prove that the salvation was not the people's own doing, but God's. However, the text does not present the attrition under Saul as such, but rather as the justification of Saul's impatience with respect to the sacrifice. The passage is therefore linked *only* (a) *narratively* to the immediately following pericope in vv. 7b–15a; and (b) *lexically* to the observation of the Philistine guards at Michmash that "The Hebrews are coming out from the foxholes where they've hidden themselves" in 1 Sam 14:11b. 1 Sam 13:6–7 may appear theologically-oriented in the present state of the text, but its immediate effects point to a redactional orientation in its original usage.

would have rather relied at most upon the collective fear of those tribes under immediate pressure, and more probably only upon their own patrilineal segment.[77]

7.3.1.3. Similarities in Socio-Political Milieu

The conclusion of the preceding element of narrative structure leads directly into the last common element of the four narratives: the sociological models of agnatic relation, social structure, and mode of production assumed by each hero-story, as well as the identity of the enemy. Simply stated, the social structures of the Israelite tribal system, as presented in each of these four narratives, were founded upon principles of non-dynastic charismatic assumption of temporary authority in a primarily subsistence-based agrarian economy. Jephthah's story gives the least indication of this economic presupposition, if we assume Jephthah could potentially have been given an inheritance (possibly in the form of land?), had his half-brothers allowed him to remain in Gilead. Once exiled, Jephthah and his men "go out" (יצא), probably an indication of raiding. Ehud's narrative likewise leaves much to the imagination, mentioning only the Israelites' loss of the "City of Palms" (עיר התמרים)—Jericho, presumably a production center of date honey[78]—in 3:13 and a tributary gift to Eglon (מנחה) in vv. 15,17, and 18. The modes of production discernable in Gideon's story are perhaps the most plentiful: Gideon is first met (Judg 6:11) while threshing *wheat* (suggesting the presence of grain agriculture) in a *winepress* (indicating viticulture). Gideon prepares a goat kid (גדי־עזים), indicating the husbandry of ovines, for Yahweh's messenger along with flour (קמח) in 6:19. The presence of ovines is further substantiated by the "wool fleece" (גזת הצמר) Gideon uses to confirm his calling in 6:37–40.[79] Gideon sacrifices one of his father's bulls (פר / שור) on his new altar to Yahweh in vv. 25–26, confirming the presence of cattle (bovines). Saul's situation is very similar to that of Gideon. The reader meets Saul in 1 Samuel 11 when he is coming back "from the field" (מן־השדה; v. 5) with a "yoke of cattle" (בקר צמד; v. 7), confirming the exploitation not only of bovines but also of arable land for farming, since one would presumably have a "yoke of cattle" in a "field" for that purpose. In other words, all

77 See similarly Mommer, *Samuel*, 115–16; Müller, *Königtum*, 151.

78 E.g., Philip J. King and Lawrence E. Stager, *Life in Biblical Israel* (LibAncIsr; Louisville, Ky.: WJKP, 2001), 103–4.

79 These verses also confirm further the presence of grain agriculture, since the experiment is performed at a "threshing floor" (גרן).

indications here point to the employment of a variety of agricultural subsistence strategies on the part of Gideon's family and the Abiezrites, as well as of Saul's family—i.e., even those families whose status in society was relatively high.

While this situation of subsistence farming as the economic backdrop of the hero-narratives in Judges and in 1 Samuel 11 may not be differentiated effectively from that of the base narrative of the NSR_B (in which Saul's family owns donkeys), it may easily be distinguished from the later appropriations and expansions by the later editors of the HDR_1 complex, who assumed a hierarchical structure of kingship endowed with the power to bring people to the court at the will of the king (cf. the removal of David to the court of Saul in 16:14–23).[80] Even further removed from this economic model is the HDR_2, which assumes a static divide between the agricultural subsistence class and the bureaucratically-supported royalty with a permanent, standing army, rather than an army mustered through the optional commitment of each tribal organization (e.g., 1 Sam 18:5).

Yet not only are the social structure and the modes of production assumed to be similar across these deliverer narratives: the enemies with which each hero does battle also repeatedly come from the east. This fact remains in contradistinction to the enemies of Deborah and Barak (native Canaanites), Samson and the Saul of the NSR_B (the Philistines), not to mention both Histories of David's Rise (Philistines and, in the HDR_2 and PR redaction, Amalekites). In each of the narratives of Ehud, Gideon, Jephthah, and Saul (NSR_A), the enemy comes primarily from the eastern side of the Jordan River. Ehud fends off the Moabites who have come north from the Moabite *Kerngebiet* to cross the Jordan River at its fords (Judg 3:28), rather than taking the longer track around the southern edge of the Dead Sea. Gideon is pitted against "(all) Midian and Amalek, and the sons of the East" (6:3,33) who "crossed over" (ויעברו; v. 33) to Cisjordan. Despite the normal location of the Amalekites and the Midianites far to the south, the identification or coalition of these groups with the "sons of the East" (בני קדם; 6:3,33; 7:12; 8:10) suggests that the author(s) understood the origination of these peoples in Transjordan,[81] at least for the purposes of the narrative. Camels seem to be the primary form of livestock associat-

80 See above (§6.3.1.2) for the distinction between the base-narrative (1 Sam 16:14–23) and its prophetic expansion (1 Sam 16:1–13).

81 Cf. the journey of Jacob that takes him to the land of the "sons of the East" (Gen 29:1). The בני קדם appear as participants in circles of wisdom in 1 Kgs 5:10 and Job 1:3, but as marauding enemies from the east synonymous with Moab, Edom, and Ammon in Isa 11:14; Jer 49:28; Ezek 25:4,10. Judg 8:24 identifies these camel-based nomads as "Ishmaelites." In that regard, these Ishmaelites may be compared favorably to the Ishmaelites of Gen 37:25, who are coming from Gilead.

ed with these polymorphic groups, evidenced by the Gideon story (Judg 6:5; 7:12; 8:21,26).[82] Indeed, once Gideon has routed the invaders, he pursues them back into the Transjordanian highlands and slaughters them there.

Both Jephthah and Saul confront the Ammonites in Transjordan, although in neither scene are camels mentioned, and neither are the Ammonites identified or associated with the "sons of the East." Rather, they seem to belong to a society whose mode of production is not camel-based full nomadism but is now a sedentarized hierarchy with a royal component, and what appears to be a standing campaigning army.[83] The Jephthah narrative recognizes a king of the Ammonites (Judg 11:12–14, 28), as does the Saul tradition (Nahash appears in 1 Sam 11:1–2), but while the Ammonite campaign against the southern Gilead makes geopolitical sense (since the two polities abut one another and each conceivably exerted pressure on the other), the campaign against Jabesh-gilead is more difficult to explain as a strictly historical event. Sitting in the *W. Yabīs*, Jabesh lay quite far to the north to have come into contact with a sedentary Ammonite population whose *Kerngebiet* lay in the southern extension of the Jabbok Valley. Hence, there is scattered evidence in some textual versions that there may have been—either as part of the original narrative or as an explanatory addition thereto—a concern to explain the presence of the Ammonite army so far north.[84]

82 The traditions of the HDR portray the camel as a primary form of livestock to the Amalekites (1 Sam 15:3; 1 Sam 30:17) and the Geshurites and Girzites (1 Sam 27:9).

83 For a discussion of the historicity of camel-based nomadism, see William F. Albright, "Prolegomenon," in *The Book of Judges with Introduction and Notes and Notes on the Hebrew Text of the Books of Kings with an Introduction and Appendix*, by C. F. Burney (Library of Biblical Studies; New York: KTAV, 1970), 1–38, esp. 11–12, 16–19.

84 See 4QSam[a]; P. Kyle McCarter, *I Samuel* (AB 8; Garden City, N.Y.: Doubleday, 1980), 199; Frank M. Cross, "The Ammonite Oppression of the Tribes of Gad and Reuben," in *History, Historiography and Interpretation: Studies in Biblical and Cuneiform Literature* (ed. Hayim Tadmor and Moshe Weinfeld; Jerusalem: Magnes, 1983), 148–58; Eugene Charles Ulrich, *The Qumran Text of Samuel and Josephus* (HSM 19; Missoula, Mont.: Scholars Press, 1978), 166–70; Frank Moore Cross et al., *1–2 Samuel* (vol. 12 of *Qumran Cave 4*; DJD 17; Oxford: Clarendon, 2005), 65–67; Ralph W. Klein, *1 Samuel* (WBC 10; Waco, Tex.: Word Books, 1983), 102–3. This Qumran manuscript, in accord with Josephus (*Ant.* 6.68–70), provides the rationale for the far northern extension of Ammonite military power: Nahash had chased a group of Reubenites and Gadites who had fled to the city from further south (see esp. Cross, "Ammonite Oppression," 152). Cross has argued for the originality of the "addition" on the basis of linguistic, versional, and stylistic evidence. McCarter shares this assessment, despite the fact that the omission "apparently was not haplographic—there seems to be nothing in the text to have triggered it" (*I Samuel*, 199). Even Birch, working without the benefit of Cross's data, followed LXX here (*Rise*, 43). However, Alexander Rofé has rightly impugned the originality of the paragraph, arguing that the text has the appearance of a late addition with midrashic tendencies ("The Acts of Nahash According to 4QSam[a]," *IEJ* 32 [1982]: 129–33). For this assessment, refinements thereof, and reactions thereto, see also Stephen Pisano, *Additions or Omissions in the Books of Samuel* (OBO 57; Fribourg: Univer-

The groups against which the Israelite heroes act in Judges 3; 6–8; 11 and 1 Samuel 11 were recognized to have been Transjordanian groups outside the purview of Israelite ethnicity. This situation may be contrasted to that in the remainder of the NSR, in which the primary enemy comprises the Philistine invaders from the west (cf. 1 Samuel 13–14), and from the HDR_1 and HDR_2, in which the Israelites' principal enemies were the Philistines (e.g., 1 Samuel 17–18). The (southern-dwelling) Amalekites, divorced from any connection to the peoples of the eastern desert region, figure prominently as well in the HDR_1 and HDR_2 traditions (1 Samuel 15; 30). It is not until the beginning of the CH's supplement to HDR_2 that we again hear of a major battle fought against any of the polities found east of the Transjordanian Israelite territory (2 Samuel 10; 12:26–31), but here the Ammonites are clearly correlated with a sedentary urbanized society—centralized at a city Rabbath-ammon (2 Sam 10:1–3,14; 11:16–24)—with realistic geopolitical motivations and international modes of interaction. The Ammonites of the CH are quite distinct, sociologically speaking, from the "sons of the East" who go out raiding with the Midianites and Amalekites in Judges 6–8, nor can they be compared favorably to the Ammonites of Judges 10–11 and of 1 Samuel 11 who play the role of invaders. These distinctions contained in the biblical texts themselves suggest a fine differentiation is in order between the NSR_A (isolated only in 1 Samuel 11) and the other Narratives of Saul's Rise (comprising the remainder of the pericope in 1 Samuel 9–14) and between the NSR_A and both traditions of the HDR.

7.3.1.4. Geographic Considerations

One further point of differentiation between the NSR_A and the NSR_B may be made. This observation revolves around the assumed geography of the NSR_A, and of Saul's action in a territory that seems to have been well outside the boundaries of the early stages of his kingdom consisting of

sity Press; Göttingen: Vandenhoeck & Ruprecht, 1984), 91–98, and bibliography therein; Dominique Barthélemy, *Critique textuelle de l'ancien testament, vol. 1: Josué, Juges, Ruth, Samuel, Rois, Chroniques, Esdras, Néhémie, Esther* (OBO 50/1; Fribourg: University Press; Göttingen: Vandenhoeck & Ruprecht, 1982), 166–72; Terry L. Eves, "One Ammonite Invasion or Two? 1 Sam 10:27–11:2 in the Light of 4QSam[a]," *WTJ* 44 (1982): 308–26, esp. 323–24; Zecharia Kallai, "Samuel in Qumrān: Expansion of a Historiographical Pattern (4QSam[a])," *RB* 103–4 (1996): 581–91; Edward D. Herbert, "4QSam[a] and Its Relationship to the LXX: An Exploration in Stemmatological Analysis," in *IX Congress of the International Organization for Septuagint and Cognate Studies, Cambridge, 1995* (ed. Bernard A. Taylor; SBLSCS 45; Atlanta: Scholars Press, 1997), 37–55; Na'aman, "Pre-Deuteronomistic Story," 643.

Benjamin and southern Ephraim.[85] Bezek—directly west across the Jordan Valley from Jabesh-gilead—sat well to the north of Shechem and the boundary between Ephraim and Manasseh. Even if D. Edelman's assumption that the Jabeshites established a treaty of sovereignty with the petty king Saul is correct,[86] Jabesh would have been quite far for him to campaign abroad, especially if Manasseh (and therefore Bezek) were not under his control at the time. Not only are the Ammonites of a different socio-political cast than the enemies of Saul in the other NSR traditions, the NSR$_A$ envisions a completely distinct theater of battle from that presumed by the NSR$_B$.[87]

7.3.1.5. The NSR$_A$ (1 Sam 11:1–11) as a Separate Tradition*

The extent of the original NSR$_A$ within 1 Sam 11:1–15 remains the subject of frequent debate. Although the appearance of dissenters in 10:27a and 11:12–13 might be understood as an indicator of the original or early unity of 10:17–11:15,[88] this explanation of the current textual arrangement is not the most expedient. As the preceding argument has made clear, the two

85 See Blenkinsopp, "Quest," 96 n. 32; Edelman, "Saul's Journey," 57; but cf. Kreuzer, who assumes the veracity of Saul's campaign in 1 Samuel 11 ("Saul—Not Always—at War," 46–50).

86 Edelman, "Saul's Rescue," 195–209. Cf. the suggestion of Möhlinbrink that the Jabeshites could not approach Manasseh and Ephraim for help because those two tribes were already indisposed in their own battles against the Philistines ("Sauls Ammoniterfeldzug," esp. 62).

87 It is tempting to speculate wildly that the deliverer narrative of 1 Samuel 11 originally belonged to Bedan, the otherwise unknown deliverer from Transjordan mentioned in MT 1 Sam 12:11 and 1 Chr 7:17. This proposal was recently approached—but never stated outright—by Serge Frolov ("Bedan: A Riddle in Context," *JBL* 126 [2007]: 164–67, esp. 166). Accordingly, the author of 1 Sam 12:11 would have playfully interpolated an older list of deliverers into Samuel's speech to subvert what both the author and the implied audience knew to have been the secondary attribution of the narrative to Saul (compare the well-known example of the secondary attribution of Goliath's defeat to David). Contrast, of course, the more conventional claims that "Bedan" should be identified as an alternative name of one of the judges already known (e.g., Y. Zakovitch, "יפתח = בדן," *VT* 22 [1972]: 123–25; Howard Jacobson, "The Judge Bedan [1 Samuel xii 11]," *VT* 42 [1992]: 123–24; idem, "Bedan and Barak Reconsidered," *VT* 44 [1994]: 108–9); or as a scribal error for, or authentic linguistic realization of, the name Barak, which is attested in LXX (respectively, John Day, "Bedan, Abdon or Barak in 1 Samuel xii 11?" *VT* 43 [1993]: 261–64; D. T. Tsumura, "Bedan, a Copyist's Error? [1 Samuel xii 11]," *VT* 45 [1995]: 122–23). Christophe Lemardelé's recent linkage of Saul's deliverer-type behavior in 1 Samuel 11 with his supposed designation as a נזיר in 1 Sam 1:11,22 would of course cast doubt on my proposal ("Saül le *nazir* ou la Légende d'un roi," *SJOT* 22 [2008]: 47–62). But Lemardelé includes too much of the present text in his reconstructed early narrative (e.g., 1 Sam 10:10–13), and his proposal is not particularly convincing.

88 E.g., Halpern, *Constitution*, 155; Dietrich, *David*, 147–48; cf. Crüsemann, *Widerstand*, 54–58.

episodes in 10:17–27 and 11:1–15 need not have been joined from the outset, since at least the latter stands alone thematically as a self-contained unit.[89] However, if 10:27a; 11:12–13 are viewed as redactional insertions methodically introduced in order to link the two passages at a later time, the juncture between the episodes disintegrates. Consideration of 10:27; 11:12–14 suggests this option is the preferable one.

As Weiser noted, if we consider the framework of the deliverer-narrative (10:27; 11:12–15) to have been transmitted together with 11:1–11, but independently of 10:17–26, we are confronted with an irreconcilable tension. On one hand, the framework assumes Saul has been made king, or at least has been endowed with some authority (and therefore that the central episode demands a prologue in which his status has been elevated). On the other hand, the narrative proper eschews any such Saulide claim to power preceding the opening of the story.[90] As discussed above, it is unlikely that Saul should be viewed as coming from humble means, but it is equally unlikely that his status in 1 Sam 11:1 is that of an extremely wealthy or powerful land-owner (§7.3.1.1); this suggests, then, that the thematic connection wrought by the addition of 11:12–13 and 10:(26),27a ought to be attributed to the hand of a later redactor, rather than an authentic tradition.[91] This connection was made at earliest in the presumably Deuteronomistic-era redactional level, combining the NSR_A with the NSR_C (1 Sam 10:17–25*), since it assumes the presence of the detractors of Saul's kingship.[92] Verse 10:27b LXX, 4QSam[a] (כמו ויהי חדש) must also be assigned to a secondary redactional level,[93] though it need not be so late as 10:27a; 11:12–13. Instead, it may have originally connected the NSR_A to the NSR_B,[94] yet a connection to 10:26–27a; 11:12–13 cannot be ruled out. The position of 10:27b 4QSam[a] remains ambiguous, but I consider the presence of that manuscript's plus in the earliest form of the NSR_A tradition unlikely.[95]

89 See also here Mettinger, *King and Messiah*, 83–87; Mommer, *Samuel*, 110–22, esp. 111.

90 Weiser, *Samuel*, 73–74.

91 Mettinger, *King and Messiah*, 84–85; Crüsemann, *Widerstand*, 56–58; Klein, *1 Samuel*, 104, 108; Fritz, "Deutungen," 350; Vermeylen, *Loi du plus fort*, 42. For the necessity of the coherence of at least vv. 26–27a, see Boecker, *Beurteilung*, 57–58.

92 Cf. Crüsemann, who attributes to a pre-Deuteronomistic redactor the combination of 9:1–10:9* and 11:1–11*,15 through the addition of an old tradition (10:21bβ–23,24aβb) and the accompanying redactional verses (9:2b; 10:13b–16,26b,27a; 11:12–13; *Widerstand*, 54–58).

93 Mommer, *Samuel*, 111; and Vermeylen, *Loi du plus fort*, 41. Cf. the bibliography of those who argue for the verse's inherence in the original form of the tradition in Mommer, *Samuel*, 111 n. 292. This attribution seems irreconcilable, however, with the conclusion that the NSR_A was originally independent; the temporal clause "After about a month" presupposes a prior episode.

94 Klein, *1 Samuel*, 104–5.

95 With Mommer, *Samuel*, 111; and Campbell, *1 Samuel*, 111.

The clearly superfluous mention of Samuel in v. 7 (ואחר שמואל) and his enigmatic appearance in v. 14 are best considered redactional as well.[96] In the case of the former, the phrase constitutes a doubling of the preceding prepositional phrase אחרי שאול.[97] In the case of the latter, the prophet—who appears here for the first time since 10:25—arrives suddenly and only with the intention of moving "the people" collectively to Gilgal in order to "renew" (חדש piel) the kingship.[98] In short, given the obvious secondarity (and ambivalent function) of Samuel in vv. 7,14, it seems clear that the priest/prophet did not feature in the original NSR_A but was introduced only at a later stage of textual development, yet when exactly this later stage was achieved remains open for debate.

Although vv. 12–14 and the small insertion in v. 7 are most often recognized as Deuteronomistic additions,[99] Birch found reason to attribute these embellishments to his prophetic redactor and thereby defended the inclusion of much of 10:17–27 in his prophetic edition.[100] This ascription of 10:27; 11:12–14 to the compilers of the EPE would not be inconceivable, were one able to demonstrate that 10:17–27 had been interpolated prior to the formation of the DtrH. However, the linguistic data corre-

96 Mettinger, *King and Messiah*, 84; McCarter, *I Samuel*, 203; Klein, *1 Samuel*, 104, 109; Mommer, *Samuel*, 113; Vermeylen, *Loi du plus fort*, 41, 43.

97 Mommer points to the clear distinction between the original form אחרי and the secondary form אחר. The former occurs as the usual localizing preposition, while the latter is primarily a temporal preposition. But, notes Mommer, the latter is used as the localizing preposition in a few texts (Gen 22:13; 37:17; Num 25:8; 1 Sam 12:14; 2 Kgs 23:2; 25:5; *Samuel*, 113 n. 303; see also Klein, *1 Samuel*, 104), all which of which appear to be late monarchic or exilic, at the earliest.

98 For חדש as "renew," see Isa 61:4; Ps 51:12; 104:30; Job 10:17; Lam 5:21; 2 Chr 15:8; 24:4,12 (Mommer, *Samuel*, 112 n. 299; for further discussion, see also Birch, *Rise*, 56, 60). Hertzberg avoids the philological conundrum with the implication that the word has been emended to reflect the new situation occasioned by the combination of this passage with the preceding episode: "originally it will have been no 'renewal', but an *institution* of the kingship" (*I & II Samuel*, 94, my emphasis; see also McCarter, *I Samuel*, 205; but cf. Mettinger, *King and Messiah*, 84).

99 E.g., Veijola, *Königtum*, 77, 82, 102, and esp. 116 and 118; Mayes, *Story*, 89; Vermeylen, *Loi du plus fort*, 41–43, esp. 43; cf. Klein, *1 Samuel*, 104; Müller, *Königtum*, 148. Vermeylen actually attributes the additions in 1 Samuel 11 to two different Deuteronomistic strata: to DtrG he credits 10:27b; 11:7a*,14, and he assigns vv. 7b–8,12–13 to DtrP (*Loi du plus fort*, 43). The omission of vv. 7b–8 seems unnecessary to me, although I agree that the inclusion of Judah and the schematic numbers of v. 8bβ may be omitted safely (although cf. Mommer, *Samuel*, 119). At the very least, vv. 7a–8a(bα) stand as original. Furthermore, the assignment of vv. 12–13 to a separate layer of redaction than that of v. 14 is possible (see also ibid., 119–21), but not entirely necessay.

100 Birch, *Rise*, 55–56. Similarly, Mettinger claims that the redactional juncture of the NSR_C (10:17–25*) and the NSR_A (11:1–11*,15) through the addition of 10:26–27; 11:12–14 occurred prior to the formation of the DtrH (*King and Messiah*, 85; see also Crüsemann, *Widerstand*, 54–58; and Mommer, *Samuel*, 119). However, this argument relies on the addition's valence with respect to the monarchy and may not be the most reliable guide to interpretation.

sponding to the insertion of Samuel in vv. 7,14 (אחר and חדשׁ piel) point to a relatively late date of composition, favoring a late monarchic or exilic date, at earliest. Here, the more moderate LPE camp, which would allow the classical attribution of 11:12–14 to the Deuteronomistic Historian, stands in better stead. In any case, we may conclude that it is extremely unlikely for the original deliverer-type narrative of Saul to have included vv. 12–14.[101]

Just as the NSR_A can be divorced from the preceding textual episodes through this bracketing of vv. 7*,12–14, so too can the web of its interconnections with the following chapters be cleared away without damaging the inherent hero-tale structure of Saul's rescue of Jabesh. Many scholars recognize 1 Sam 11:15 as authentic to the original form of the story related by the NSR_A,[102] but the circumstantial data leading to this conclusion are not entirely convincing.[103] As Müller recently demonstrated, the coronation itself is a plausible ending to the tradition (cf. Judg 8:22–23), if one accounts for the various repetitions and tensions in v. 15, which bears two references to Gilgal, two indications that the ceremony was carried out "before Yahweh" (לפני יהוה), and the conflict between "all the people" (כל־העם) and "all the men of Israel" (כל־אנשׁי ישׂראל). From this overfull and chiastically-organized verse, Müller teases out a plausible original form of the verse, in which "All the people went to Gilgal, and there they made Saul king before Yahweh" (וילכו כל־העם הגלגל וימלכו שׁם את־שׁאול לפני יהוה).[104] Yet Müller is not entirely convinced that even this short conclusion is original to the NSR_A. This minimal report not only envisions too broad a scope to Saul's leadership of "all Israel," but it also introduces a natural geographical link between the battle against the Ammonites at Jabesh and the campaigns against the Philistines in the Benjaminite and Ephraimite highlands, narrated in 1 Samuel 13–14. The cultic center of Gilgal lay directly on the way between the two regions, if one were to travel through the Jordan Valley, and thus served as a convenient site for the redactor to locate Saul's crowning.[105]

Müller's argument against the originality of 11:15 is persuasive, though it should be pointed out that there was likely a second Gilgal in the

---

101 Mommer, *Samuel*, 112–13; Müller, *Königtum*, 148. This attribution of 11:12–14(15*) to a later editor is by no means a denial of Weiser's suggestion that the framework of the NSR_A (10:27; 11:12–15) may itself preserve an authentically ancient tradition (*Samuel*, 73), although such a view is hardly necessary.

102 E.g., Veijola, *Königtum*, 91, 116; Crüsemann, *Widerstand*, 56; Mayes, "Rise," 15; idem, *Story*, 88; Klein, *1 Samuel*, 104; Vermeylen, *Loi du plus fort*, 43.

103 E.g., Fritz, "Deutungen," 357–58; Mommer, *Samuel*, 117–18.

104 Müller, *Königtum*, 149–151.

105 Ibid., 151–53.

highlands near Shechem.[106] If my insinuation offered above is correct—in which case the NSR$_A$ did not originally narrate the story of Saul's success in the Transjordan but rather that belonging to one of Israel's early deliverers from Manasseh—this highland location near Shechem may have been the original locus of the hero's recognition of authority and thus integral to the earliest form of the tradition (which, according to this model, comprised 1 Sam 11:1–11*,15aα*).[107] Moreover, it must be noted that if 15aα* is secondary, it must have been added at an earlier point than were vv. 12–14, since we should otherwise expect to see Samuel more intimately involved in the proceedings. As the text currently stands in MT, it is the people who crown (וַיַּמְלִכוּ) Saul king, as opposed to the more interpretive LXX, in which it is Samuel who anoints the newly ascendant king (καὶ ἔχρισεν Σαμουηλ ἐκεῖ τὸν Σαυλ εἰς Βασιλέα).[108]

Despite any possible alternate identifications of Gilgal, however, Müller has correctly recognized that the present reference in 11:15 is to the Gilgal of Benjamin in the Jordan River Valley, just west of the Jordan River at *Ḫ. Mufǧir* (193.143), or *Ġalǧala* (196.139), both of which are near Jericho.[109] So how is it that the location of Saul's crowning came to be commemorated at this site? From a literary standpoint, the localization fits well with the necessary movement of Saul's army between the two theaters of operation appearing in chapters 11 and 13 and should most likely be recognized as the product of redactional work designed to stitch together

106 See, e.g., F.-M. Abel, *Géographie de la Palestine* (3d ed.; 2 vols.; Paris: Gabalda, 1967), 2:336–38; and Jeremy M. Hutton, "Topography, Biblical Traditions, and Reflections on John's Baptism of Jesus," in *Proceedings of the Princeton-Prague Symposium on the Historical Jesus* (ed. J. H. Charlesworth; Grand Rapids, Mich.: Eerdmans, forthcoming).

107 This solution is to be preferred over that of Mommer, who suggests Saul's deliverance of a beleaguered city occurred originally at Gilgal rather than Jabesh (*Samuel*, 118). Although I agree with Mommer that this passage has been connected with 2 Sam 2:4b–7 redactionally (ibid., 116; see §6.6 above), I argue 2 Sam 2:4b–7 constitutes the later passage, which was crafted to take up the traditions of the NSR$_A$.

108 Mettinger, *King and Messiah*, 84; Müller, *Königtum*, 149. Mommer finds a similarly interpretive attribution of the initiative to Samuel already in v. 14 (*Samuel*, 119).

109 For Gilgal's identification with the former, see, e.g., Yohanan Aharoni, *The Land of the Bible: A Historical Geography* (rev. ed.; trans. A. F. Rainey; Philadelphia: Westminster, 1979), 435; Denis Baly, *The Geography of the Bible: A Study in Historical Geography* (New York: Harper & Brothers, 1957), 202, following James Muilenburg, "The Site of Ancient Gilgal," *BASOR* 140 (1955): 11–27; cf. Abel, *Géographie*, 2:336–37; for the latter, see A. Alt, "Das Institut im Jahre 1924," *PJ* 21 (1925): 5–58, here 27, and bibliography in 27 n. 1; Yoel Elitzur, *Ancient Place Names in the Holy Land: Preservation and History* (Jerusalem: Magnes; Winona Lake, Ind.: Eisenbrauns, 2004), 146 and n. 9; and Jeremy M. Hutton, "'Bethany Beyond the Jordan' in Text, Tradition, and Historical Geography," *Bib* 89 (2008): 305–28, esp. 322–23. Jan Jozef Simons (*Geographical and Topographical Texts of the Old Testament: A Concise Commentary in XXXII Chapters* [Nederlands instituut voor het Nabije Oosten; Studia Francisci Scholten memoriae dicata 2; Leiden: Brill, 1959], 139–140, §314) and Abel (*Géographie*, 2:48; cf. 2:336–37) place Gilgal at *Ḫān es-Sahl* (*Ḫān al-aḥmar*).

those two chapters; this suture has the effect of moving Saul's army to that ritual center in preparation for his rejection in 1 Sam 13:7b–15 (for which 13:4b also prepared) and at the same time of comprising a demonstration of obedience to Samuel's command to go straight to Gilgal in 10:8 after doing "what his hand finds to do" (10:7). In short, both 10:8 and 13:4b, 7b–15 display indications of belonging to the same narrative horizon as 11:15. Yet regardless of whether 11:15 was original to the text in part or in whole, or was composed specifically as a redactional joint, a solution to the question posed above remains wanting. If the identification of Gilgal (of Benjamin) as the site of Saul's crowning has either been forged redactionally or displaced geographically, it stands to reason that there was some other precipitant factor than mere narrative convenience to occasion the localization of the episode precisely here. That precipitating factor can only have been the developing tradition of Gilgal as the site where literary characters or historical personages most often crossed back into Cisjordan and where their newly found authority was first recognized. In this regard, 2 Samuel 19 provides the nearest touchstone, establishing the period of the combination of the HDR_1 and HDR_2 + SN complexes as the *terminus post quem* of the introduction of 1 Sam 10:8; 13:7b–15 and as the concomitant relocalization (if original) of 11:15aα*.

A similarly geographic riddle is posed by the mention of "Gibeah of Saul" (גבעת שׁאול) in v. 4. As Mommer recognized, and as will be discussed in greater detail below (§7.3.2.2), Saul's hometown was likely not Gibeah, but rather Zela (cf. 2 Sam 21:11–14).[110] Therefore, the mention of Gibeah of Saul constitutes a secondary relocalization of Saul's hometown, most likely predicated on the author's knowledge of the tradition that Gibeah was Saul's base of power. This geographic displacement, which seems to have occurred already at the earliest stage of the NSR_A's formation, may constitute an additional datum supportive of the assertion made above that the NSR_A did not originally belong to Saul but was rather attributed to him already at a very early stage in its development. The textual and geographic confusion throughout 1 Samuel 11–15, therefore, betrays an extremely prolix interaction between developing texts and the same theological traditions that seem to have developed alongside them.[111]

---

110 Mommer, *Samuel*, 116–17.

111 At the very least, Mic 6:5 knows the tradition of "what happened from Shittim to Gilgal" and plays on the movement as a trope by which he may effectively insinuate the very foundations of the downfall of the Israelite monarchy (Rodney R. Hutton, "What Happened From Shittim to Gilgal? Law and Gospel in Micah 6:5," *Currents in Theology and Mission* 26 [1999]: 94–103, esp. 99–100). This is not to say, however, that the deliverer narrative of 1 Sam 11:1–11* definitely did not end with v. 15 or that Saul's leadership was not recognized formally in

Without establishing a model for the introduction of the various traditions in 1 Samuel 13, it is difficult to provide a full accounting of the stages of development whereby the NSR_A was incorporated into the burgeoning corpus that eventually became 1 Samuel. Nonetheless, it is clear that this deliverer-type hero-narrative of Saul (the NSR_A) may reasonably be cut loose from its narratological moorings to the surrounding textual tradition. As I have argued in the preceding sections, nothing inherent to the self-contained story in 1 Samuel 11 necessarily links it to the surrounding episodes. The conclusion reached here, then, is as follows: The self-contained unit in 1 Sam 11:1–11*,(15aα*) originally provided not merely one episode in the larger narrative of Saul's rise to power, but rather one complete version—NSR_A—which, no matter how idealized or unhistorical it may be, came to serve as a legitimizing force for Saul's reign (and for the benefit of his progeny), most likely during the latter part of his reign.

7.3.2. The NSR_B as a Complete Literary Unit

Like the NSR_A, the NSR_B functions as a complete and independent story once we have recognized the fact that it bears several traces of subsequent reworking. In this section I argue that the NSR_B consisted of both the folktale in 1 Sam 9:1–10:16 and an ending in which Saul and his *naʿar* take over a Philistine garrison in Gibeah.[112] This story, however, has been broken apart and overlaid with a series of revisions, evident from a study of the tensions within the text. Once these tensions have been identified and the extent of the revision explained (§7.3.2.1), it will be possible to hypothesize the original shape of the folktale complete with its ending (§§7.3.2.2–4) and, finally, to propose a redaction history whereby the NSR_B was combined with the NSR_A, supplemented with the HDR_1, and

---

certain areas of the Israelite hill country; it is simply to argue that in the juxtaposition of the NSR_A with its prelude in the NSR_B, probably at the time of the two traditions' incorporation in the HDR_1, this passage was adapted to its context through the localization in Gilgal.

112 For the genre of 9:1–10:16 as a folktale (*Sage* or *Märchen*—both are used), see Hugo Gressmann, who is usually credited with this assessment (*Die Schriften des Alten Testaments* [1910; 2d. ed.; Göttingen: Vandenhoeck & Ruprecht, 1921], II/1:34–35). However, Gressmann had been preceded in this description by Eichhorn, as was pointed out by W. A. Irwin ("Samuel and the Rise of the Monarchy," *AJSL* 58 [1941]: 120 n. 25). For a list of similar assessments, see Boecker, *Beurteilung*, 12–13. Fritz contests this generic description, preferring instead to describe the story as a "prophetic narrative" (*Prophetenerzählung*) ("Deutungen," 350–51). White also rejects the description of this story as a "folktale," as part of her argument against multiple successive layers of redaction ("'The History of Saul's Rise'," 284).

intertwined with the HDR_2 + SSN complex to form the heart of the PR (§§7.4; 8.1).

7.3.2.1. Tensions within the Unit

Several tensions in 1 Sam 9:1–10:16 disrupt the unity of that passage. Many earlier scholars argued that those discrepancies suggest the presence of two source texts. Often, this argument was predicated on the theory that the text displayed evidence of the continuation of the Pentateuchal sources.[113] Others simply argued for the presence of two traditions so thoroughly interwoven as to be presently inseparable.[114] H. Seebass went so far as to argue that two complete sources could be fully separated, but his analysis is belabored, and one must agree with Birch's criticism that "in doing so [Seebass] is forced to a minute division of materials that stretches the limits of credulity."[115]

The most economical reading of the tensions within 1 Sam 9:1–10:16 is to posit a core story that has been augmented by later accretions.[116] Although it is normally L. Schmidt to whom credit is given for having isolated the earliest stages of the folktale in 9:1–10:16, it must be pointed out that he was working contemporaneously with W. Richter, who arrived

113 E.g., Karl Budde, *Die Bücher Richter und Samuel, ihre Quellen und ihr Aufbau* (Giessen: Ricker, 1890), 203–10; Ernst Sellin, *Introduction to the Old Testament* (trans. W. Montgomery; London: Hodder & Stoughton, 1923), 108–16; Otto Eissfeldt, *The Old Testament: An Introduction* (trans. Peter R. Ackroyd; New York: Harper & Row, 1965), 271–80; idem, *Komposition*, 6–11, 56–57.

114 E.g., Ivar Hylander, *Der literarische Samuel-Saul-Komplex (1. Sam. 1–15) traditionsgeschichtlich untersucht* (Uppsala: Almqvist & Wiksell; Leipzig: Harrassowitz, 1932), 133–54, esp. 148; Hertzberg, *I & II Samuel*, 78–86, esp. 79.

115 Horst Seebass, "Die Vorgeschichte der Königserhebung Sauls," *ZAW* 79 (1967): 157–165; cf. Birch, *Rise*, 30 = idem, "The Development of the Tradition on the Anointing of Saul in I Sam 9:1–10:16," *JBL* 90 (1971): 56; and Schmidt, *Menschlicher Erfolg*, 81–82.

116 E.g., Wildberger, "Samuel," esp. 452–55 (*contra* Birch's assessment [*Rise*, 115 n. 52 = idem, "Development," 55–56 n. 4]; cf. also the criticism of Wildberger lodged by Schmidt [*Menschlicher Erfolg*, 60–61]); Georg Christian Macholz, "Untersuchungen zur Geschichte der Samuel Überlieferungen" (Th.D. diss., Heidelberg, 1966), 137–46, according to Boecker, *Beurteilung*, 14–15; Schmidt, *Menschlicher Erfolg*, 58–102; Wolfgang Richter, *Die sogenannten vorprophetischen Berufungsberichte: Eine literaturwissenschaftliche Studie zu 1 Sam 9,1–10,16, Ex 3f. und Ri 6,11b–17* (FRLANT 101; Göttingen: Vandenhoeck & Ruprecht, 1970), 13–56, esp. 13–29; Hans Joachim Stoebe, *Das erste Buch Samuelis* [*EBS*] (KAT 8/1; Gütersloh: Mohn, 1973), 200–201; Birch, *Rise*, 29–42 = idem, "Development," 55–68; Mettinger, *King and Messiah*, 64–79; Campbell, *Of Prophets and Kings*, 19–20; idem, *1 Samuel*, 106–9; Christophe Nihan, "Du voyant au prophète: Royauté et divination en Israël selon 1 Samuel 9,1–10,16," *Foi & Vie* 38 (1999): 7–25; Vermeylen, *Loi du plus fort*, 21–33; Mommer, *Samuel*, 92–110; Fischer, "Saul-Überlieferung," 66–69. Weiser's presentation follows a somewhat similar model but differs markedly in its conclusions (*Samuel*, 46–61; see below for specific points of divergence).

at a significantly similar conclusion. Both argued for the revisions to the NSR_B to have been made at a pre-Deuteronomistic level, within prophetic circles.[117] In recent Continental scholarship, these later accretions are most often claimed as Deuteronomistic (i.e., exilic DtrG and DtrP) and post-exilic additions.[118] But there are several indications that the additions were made earlier than such an attribution would allow. Although a full response to the attempts to attribute the revisions to the Deuteronomistic period is not possible in the confines of the present study, I will attempt to discuss those proposals where possible and to show that while the indicators of Deuteronomistic origin may apply to portions of verses, they are not diagnostic of the entire revision.[119]

For the purposes of the present study, the most convenient point of departure is B. Birch's *The Rise of the Israelite Monarchy*. There, Birch identified five discrepancies that can be found quite readily in the text of 9:1–10:16.[120] Although these tensions have been cited as evidence for the two-source hypothesis, closer inspection reveals they are adequately (and better) analyzed as the products of successive layers of redaction.

(1) The use of the phrase "man of God" (איש אלהים; 9:6–8,10) alternates seemingly unpredictably with the name Samuel (9:14–15,17–19,22–24,26–27; 10:1,9,14–16) and with the term "seer" (ראה) in the

117 Schmidt, *Menschlicher Erfolg*, 58–102; Richter, *Berufungsberichte*, 56; see also Birch, *Rise*, 140–53; Mettinger, *King and Messiah*, 74–79; Campbell, *Of Prophets and Kings*, 19–20; idem, *1 Samuel*, 106–9; cf. Mommer, who dates the traditions early but removes them from a specifically prophetic context (*Samuel*, 92–110). Hans-Christoph Schmitt argues for a date between 722 and 587 in prophetically-inspired "Elohistic" circles, in spite of his recognition that the motif of anointing by a prophet is apparently dependent on (or consequent with) 2 Kings 9 ("Das sogenannte vorprophetische Berufungsschema: Zur 'geistigen Heimat' des Berufungsformulars von Ex 3,9–12; Jdc 6,11–24 und I Sam 9,1–10,16," *ZAW* 104 [1992]: 202–13, esp. 210–13); in this regard, he appears not to have been familiar with Campbell's *Of Prophets and Kings*. Equally troublesome for the identification of this group as specifically "Elohistic" is the fact that it is the original narrative which uses אלהים (e.g., 9:27; 10:3,7) while the secondary additions associated with the anointing overwhelmingly use יהוה (9:15,17; 10:1,6).

118 E.g., Nihan, "Du voyant au prophète," 14–25; idem, "Saul among the Prophets," in *Saul in Story and Tradition* (ed. Carl S. Ehrlich with Marsha C. White; FAT I/47; Tübingen: Mohr Siebeck, 2006), 93–95; Vermeylen, *Loi du plus fort*, 21–33; Fischer "Saul-Überlieferung," 169–77; with these Europeans may be classified the view of McKenzie, "Saul," esp. 60, 69; and idem, "The Trouble with Kingship," in *Israel Constructs Its Identity: Deuteronomistic Historiography in Recent Research* (ed. A. de Pury, T. Römer, and J.-D. Macchi; JSOTSup 306; Sheffield: Sheffield Academic Press, 2000), 286–314, here 297; trans. of "Cette royauté qui fait problème," in *Israël construit son histoire: L'historiographie deutéronomiste à la lumière des recherches récentes* (ed. A. de Pury, T. Römer, and J.-D. Macchi; *MdB* 34; Geneva: Labor et Fides, 1996), 267–95.

119 See also the incisive criticism of this position offered by Schmitt, "Berufungsschema," 208–10.

120 Birch, *Rise*, 30 = idem, "Development," 56–57.

explanatory gloss of 9:9[121] and in verses that contain direct speech by Saul or Samuel (9:11,18,19[122]). One of the more recent proponants of the two-source hypothesis is Terry L. Fenton, who attempted to correlate the history of Israelite prophecy with the presumed development of 9:9–11. Following Dhorme, Hylander, and others, Fenton argued that the discrepancy between איש אלהים and ראה should be recognized as an indicator of a literary seam. Moreover, Fenton held that the text displays evidence of the Deuteronomistic addition or emendation of v. 9b and of the concomitant displacement of v. 9a before v. 10 (which, on this view, originally read לכה ונלכה <עד הראה>, reconstructed on the basis of v. 9), where it originally appeared as an explanation for the shift from איש אלהים (v. 8) to ראה (v. 10, reconstructed).[123] Fenton's argument is intricate and in places elegant; support may be voiced in favor of the latter conclusion, namely, that a Deuteronomistic editor crafted v. 9b such that it brought the folktale within the scope of Deuteronomistic theological thought about the nature of prophets and prophecy by replacing the former term, איש אלהים, with the Deuteronomistically-preferred term, נביא.[124] However, Fenton's former conclusion that the discrepancy betrays a literary seam is not compelling in my judgment.

This reticence to embrace Fenton's proposal proceeds from two concerns with the text. First, there are, properly speaking, *three* designations of Samuel: not only does he appear as "seer" and "man of God," but he is mentioned by name as well. Any attempt to recover the two purported constituent traditions must also reckon with this difficulty. Now already in 1971 Birch argued this discrepancy was only apparent and that

121 Verse 9b identifies the term "seer" with "prophet" (נביא). Supposing the latter term's homophonous relationship to the verb נביא in v. 7, John Briggs Curtis argued that v. 9 was in fact not secondary but the conclusion of a folk etiology ("A Folk Etymology of *nābîʾ*," *VT* 29 [1979]: 491–93). This argument fails to take into account the widespread distribution of the terms cognate to Hebrew נביא in the ancient Near East and may be ignored safely. Shemuel Shaviv suggested that the passage meant to utilize the paronomasia itself ("*nābîʾ* and *nāgîd* in 1 Samuel ix 1–x 16," *VT* 34 [1984]: 108–110; see also Leuchter, "Samuel," 106), but this line of argumentation is forced as well.

122 Although the narrator has already made the identification implicitly in this transition between the use of "man of God" and "Samuel" with the appearance of the prophet (והנה שמואל יצא לקראתם; v. 14), it is not until v. 19 that the narrator allows Samuel to identify himself to Saul: אנכי הראה. It is only at that point, then, that the transition from "man of God" to "Samuel" (through the mediating term "seer") has been completed.

123 Terry L. Fenton, "Deuteronomistic Advocacy of the *nābîʾ*: 1 Samuel ix 9 and Questions of Israelite Prophecy," *VT* 47 (1997): 23–42; see previously Paul Dhorme, *Les livres de Samuel* (Paris: Gabalda, 1910), 77; Hylander, *Samuel-Saul-Komplex*, 139–42; Seebass, "Vorgeschichte," 158.

124 Fenton, "Deuteronomistic Advocacy," esp. 36–39; for Deuteronomistic authorship of the entire verse, see Veijola, who attributed the entire verse to DtrG (*Königtum*, 73); and Vermeylen, who attributes v. 9 to DtrP (*Loi du plus fort*, 23).

the shift from "man of God" to "Samuel" points to the dramatic moment in v. 14, which reveals to the reader the identity of the "man of God." Accordingly, this was not a sign of redaction but rather the narrative technique of the author to heighten the drama of the first encounter between two of the main characters in the book of Samuel.[125] Presumably, this literary argument could also be expanded to account for the discrepancy in terminology between v. 8 and v. 10. But as Stoebe has pointed out, it seems odd to think that Saul and his servant would have had access to knowledge of a "man of God" without knowing the identity of Samuel, the famous prophet who had been operative in the area for some time (cf. 1 Samuel 8).[126] Indeed, Saul's uncle seems to be familiar with the figure (10:15), a state of affairs presupposed by Saul's simple statement, "we came to Samuel (ונבוא אל־שמואל)" in the preceding verse.[127] As it stands, Birch's argument does not sufficiently handle the problem of the use of ראה in vv. 9,11,18,19. Moreover, it is extremely difficult to reconstruct a complete plot (much less a *point*) for a hypothesized second source delineated along the lines of this terminology.[128]

A second problem that Fenton's solution encounters is the widespread late use of the expression איש אלהים. As Noth pointed out long before, a "man of God" often appears when the Deuteronomistic Historian needed to justify sacrifices not performed in Jerusalem in concordance with the Deuteronomic law.[129] In the remainder of the Deuteronomistic History outside of 1 Samuel 9:1–10:16, the use of the term "man of God" is overwhelmingly used in passages attributable to Dtr^1 or a later, possibly prophetically-inspired editor (see Deut 33:1; Josh 14:6; Judg 13:6,8; 1 Sam 2:27; 1 Kgs 12:22; 17:18,24; 20:28; 2 Kgs 1:9–13; 13:19; 23:16–17; and ubiquitously in 1 Kings 13; 2 Kings 4–8).[130] I therefore find it far more probable that the original term "seer" (רֹאֶה), used throughout the passage, was "corrected" by a Deuteronomistic editor to "man of God" in 9:6–8 and possibly inserted along with the rest of v. 10bβ, concurrent with or

125 Birch, *Rise*, 34 = idem, "Development," 60; also Schmitt, "Berufungsschema," 208; see previously Weiser, *Samuel*, 49–50.

126 E.g., Stoebe, "Noch einmal," 363; Schmidt, *Menschlicher Erfolg*, 59; Richter, *Berufungsberichte*, 19–20, 35; Mommer, *Samuel*, 97; Campbell, *1 Samuel*, 106.

127 See also Hertzberg, *I & II Samuel*, 86.

128 Campbell, *Of Prophets and Kings*, 19–20.

129 Noth, *DH*, 141; although cf. Leuchter's claim that the man of God "occupied an important juridical position in pre-Monarchic and early Monarchic Israel" ("Samuel," 105; further, idem, "Something Old," §2.3). In reality, I agree with Leuchter that there were such individuals, but I currently remain unconvinced they went by the title "man of God." However, although I am presently unable to demonstrate this conjuncture, this title may be a literary feature of the PR rather than a historical datum, in which case Leuchter's claim may stand with only minimal reformulation.

130 I remain open to the possibility of a more limited analogue of the Smend school's DtrP.

subsequent to the introduction of the figure of Samuel into the story. For some reason, the gloss in v. 9 and the use of רֹאֶה in vv. 11, 18, 19 escaped the correction.

A related tension in the folktale, which a two-source theory such as Seebass's purports to alleviate, is the discrepancy between the apparently resident "man of God" in 9:6 and the peripatetic seer who happens to have arrived in town on business just before Saul. Yet again, a redactional model is better than a two-source model. When asked if there is a seer in the town (הֲיֵשׁ הָרֹאֶה בָּזֶה; 9:11), the girls (נערות) whom Saul has met respond, "There is—he is just up ahead; hurry now, because he has come/is coming to the city today because the people have a sacrifice today at the high place" (יֵשׁ הנה לפניך מהר עתה כי היום בא לעיר כי זבח היום לעם בבמה; 9:12aβb). The two-source hypothesis seeks to attribute these verses (roughly, vv. 12–13) to the same tradition in which Saul and his servant hope to obtain information from the resident man of God.[131] But already here, both the terminology and the presumed location of the clairvoyant fall into disharmony. Moreover, the girls' assumption of a peripatetic seer runs at variance with Saul's question to the man in the gate ("where is the house of the seer?"), which must, by the logic of differentiating sources on the basis of terminology for cultic personnel, belong to the purported "Seer-source."[132] On the other hand, the supplement model asks whether the function and originality of the girls may be called into question. If the answer they give does not function within the logical parameters of the story that have already been established in the earlier, presumed original verses of the narrative, their correspondence to the original form of the story may legitimately be denied.[133] Upon inspection, it appears that the girls' answer has been elaborated in vv. 12b and 13b and that the simplest form of their answer, "There is—he is just up ahead" (יֵשׁ הנה לפניך; v. 12aβ) directly anticipates the natural continuation of the narrative in vv. 14abα and 18:[134] "[14a]...and they went up to the city. [14bα] As they

131 Hylander, *Samuel-Saul-Komplex*, 149; Seebass, "Vorgeschichte," 162. The reconstruction of Hylander is incredibly complex and improbably arranged.

132 E.g., Schmidt, *Menschlicher Erfolg*, 69; Mommer, *Samuel*, 97.

133 For this solution, see Stoebe ("Noch einmal," 364–65; idem, *EBS*, 203); and recently Fischer, who omits the entirety of vv. 11–13 ("Saul-Überlieferung," 172); but cf. Schmidt, *Menschlicher Erfolg*, 70.

134 An elimination of the explanatory note in vv. 15–17 on the basis of its overriding concern with Samuel's vision is possible since it does not disrupt the flow of the action; e.g., Mommer, *Samuel*, 99–100. Verse 14bβγ may also be excised fairly easily, since it seems to assume the traveling mendicant Samuel who has come to town specifically for the sacrifice (cf. v. 12b) rather than the stationary seer who lives there.

were coming into the city,[135] [18] Saul approached <the man>[136] in the gate, and said, 'Tell me, where is the house of the seer?'"[137] In short, the first part of the girls' response to Saul (v. 12aβ) is a grammatically adequate answer to Saul's question in its own right, although apparently not so informative so as to prevent Saul from asking for directions from yet another interlocutor. There is nothing in the answer that directly or indirectly assumes the seer does not live in the town permanently. This short answer, therefore, does not conflict with 9:6.[138] The girls are plausibly considered original to the pericope; only the secondary elaboration of their answer in vv. 12b, 13b (and possibly 13a; see below) is not.

(2) There seems to be some discrepancy in the present text as to whether Samuel sends Saul and his servant ahead, saying, "Go up before me to the high place" (עלי לפני הבמה; 9:19a), or accompanies Saul to the hall (ויביאם לשכתה; v. 22a). Birch considers there to be no real conflict between 18–19 and 22–24,[139] but one must admit that the juxtaposition of the two different loci of the communal meal seems odd (לשכה vs. הבמה).

---

135 McCarter reads this "into the midst of the gate" with MT's v. 18 (בתוך השער; cf. LXX and 4QSam^a "in the midst of the city"), despite the fact that "[a]ll major witnesses" read "into the midst of the city" with MT in v. 14 (המה באים בתוך העיר; *I Samuel*, 169; cf. Schmidt, *Menschlicher Erfolg*, 72; and Richter, *Berufungsberichte*, 20). While possible, I see no inherently obvious reason to make the correction, since the gate would have been precisely the point at which one enters into the city. In one of my few quibbles with Mommer, I see no reason why v. 14bα should be considered secondary (*Samuel*, 99). Furthermore, I think it is possible that 14bβ (reading "a man" instead of "Samuel"; Schmidt, *Menschlicher Erfolg*, 72) should also be read as part of this stratum, since it shares a participial construction of past progressive action with 14bα.

136 If the hypothesis is correct that Samuel was subsequently written into the source (*contra* Birch, *Rise*, 34–35 = idem, "Development," 60–61; and with Schmidt, *Menschlicher Erfolg*, 71–72; and Campbell, *I Samuel*, 107), then another noun must have stood in the position where we now read את־שמואל. I substitute here "the man" merely because it is the most generic description of the person whom Saul would have seen standing in the gate.

137 Even v. 13aαb fits into this scenario and may be original: "(v. 12aβb) There is—he is just up ahead. Hurry now, for the people have a sacrifice today at the high place. (v. 13aαb) As soon as you go into the city you will find him before he goes up to the high place to eat. So hurry now, for you will find him today." Mommer allows that the second phrase beginning with כי ("because there is a sacrifice at the high place today"; v. 12bβ) is original to the story, and he thus omits only v. 12bα^2 and 13aβ (*Samuel*, 99; cf. Schmidt, who omits only v. 13aγ [*Menschlicher Erfolg*, 70–71]). There remain a few redundancies in this schema that may have crept in as the exchange expanded.

138 Cf. Weiser, who finds no conflict between the claim that Samuel lives in the city but has just returned, since 7:16 notes that Samuel regularly traveled on a circuit. Rather, he insists, the coincidence of Saul's unanticipated arrival at the city with the day of Samuel's return demonstrates the fateful circumstances of their meeting (*Samuel*, 50).

139 Birch, *Rise*, 34 = idem, "Development," 60. Campbell also apparently recognizes the two sites of the meal as unproblematic, since he has included both v. 19 and v. 22 in his earlier stratum of the story (*Of Prophets and Kings*, 19–20), and neither does McCarter seem troubled by the pair of terms, noting only that the לשכה was "a room associated with the high place where sacrificial meals were eaten" (*I Samuel*, 180).

The term במה appears twice earlier in the apparent addition to the women's answer to Saul (vv. 12b*, 13*), and we should therefore be wary of its presence here.[140] However, the narrative flow is not interrupted in such a way that we may discern a significant break between either of these usages; this discrepancy may be a figment of the reader's imagination.

The presence of the lexeme לִשְׁכָּה has occasioned some recent debate concerning the date of the overlay as a whole; A. Fischer, for instance, has observed that the term does not appear in pre-exilic texts.[141] However, part of this claim is based on the supposed exilic dating of 2 Kgs 23:11, which remains under heated debate, and it is therefore possible that the term is attested in the late monarchic period at the earliest. This late monarchic dating would, of course, still indicate a Deuteronomistic origin of v. 22aβ (if not more of the text) rather than a pre-Deuteronomistic provenance. One wonders, though, whether the use of κατάλυμα in LXX[B]—a word that renders several Hebrew nouns having to do with dwellings (מלון, לון, אהל, מִשְׁכָּן)—does not indicate lexical confusion on the part of a later scribe here, who unintentionally adapted a phrase that had originally indicated Saul's introduction to the seer's domicile. In short, I do not find Fischer's Deuteronomistic dating of the redaction to be overwhelmingly convincing.

Campbell adds here a significant point of tension: he finds the "chance nature of Saul's visit to the man of God" to stand in contrast to "the invitations (9:13) that have been issued for a banquet in Saul's honor."[142] Although the chance meeting of Saul and the seer seems without doubt to have been a central element of the folktale's structure, it is not clear to me that this by necessity conflicts with the presence of "invitees" (קְרֻאִים) in 9:13a,22b (see above) or with the seer's having "invited" them (קָרָאתִי; v. 24a). If, however, it is the case that these verses are to be read as consequent to the knowledge that Samuel received in his auditory experience (vv. 15–16), then perhaps all these verses (vv. 15–17,22b–24a) are to be attributed to the later overwriting, with Schmidt and Campbell.[143]

140 Although, cf. Mommer's allowance that vv. 12bα[1]β, 13aαb are original (*Samuel*, 99).

141 Fischer, "Saul-Überlieferung," 174.

142 Campbell, *1 Samuel*, 107. For the issue of divine direction as a narrative technique, see Ferdinand Deist, "Coincidence as a Motif of Divine Intervention in 1 Samuel 9," *OTE* n.s. 6 (1993): 7–18; and Jonathan Jacobs, "The Role of the Secondary Characters in the Story of the Anointing of Saul (1 Samuel ix–x)," *VT* 58 (2008): 495–509.

143 Schmidt, *Menschlicher Erfolg*, 68–69; Campbell, *Of Prophets and Kings*, 19–20; cf. Richter, *Berufungsberichte*, 24. Following Veijola, the "deliverer-formula" of v. 16b would be attributed to DtrG; this attribution does not significantly affect the argument here (*Königtum*, 73–74); see also Nihan, "Saul," esp. 93; and Steven L. McKenzie, "The Trouble with Kingship," in *Israel Constructs Its Identity: Deuteronomistic Historiography in Recent Research* (ed. A. de Pury, T. Römer, and J.-D. Macchi; JSOTSup 306; Sheffield: Sheffield Academic Press, 2000), 286–314, here 297; trans. of "Cette royauté qui fait problème," in *Israël construit son histoire: L'historiographie deutéronomiste à la lumière des recherches*

(3) There is a sharp contrast between Samuel's words in which he informs Saul that he will tell him "all that is in [his] heart" in the morning (ושלחתיך בבקר וכל אשר בלבבך אגיד לך; 9:19b) and those in the immediately following verse in which Samuel divulges to Saul the fact that the donkeys have been found (v. 20a).[144] Verse 20a contrasts as well with the prophet's fulfillment of the promise, found in 10:2 (which repeats word for word the concerns expressed by Saul in 9:5; see below[145]). There the prophet apparently prognosticates Saul's meeting with two men who will inform him the donkeys have been found and that his father has begun to worry about *Saul*. This information seems from the immediate context of 10:2–3 as though it should be news to Saul (thus confirming the problematic nature of the premature divulgence of this datum in 9:20a). Yet not only does 9:20 contrast with the most logical plot of the folkloristic donkey-narrative, it also anticipates Saul's accession to the kingship with Samuel's glorification: "To whom belongs all the worth of Israel, if not to you and to the house of your father?" (ולמי כל־חמדת ישראל הלא לך ולכל בית אביך; 9:20b). Saul protests this enigmatic statement with a stereotyped response (v. 21), uniting that verse in a redactional pair with v. 20.[146]

As in the case above, Fischer claims a Deuteronomistic origin for 9:20–21 on the basis of the "late" linguistic context of חמדה and the apparent allusion to the lot-selection process of 1 Sam 10:20–24.[147] The linguistic datum is compelling enough to warrant seeing a Deuteronomistic origin of some of 9:20–21*, although the appearance of the term in pre-exilic prophetic contexts (Isa 2:16; Jer 3:19; 12:10; 25:34) supports a late

---

récentes (ed. A. de Pury, T. Römer, and J.-D. Macchi; *MdB* 34; Geneva: Labor et Fides, 1996), 267–95). I am generally unconcerned with the precise delineation of the redactional layers in these verses; for a reasonable discussion, see Mommer, *Samuel*, 100–101.

144 Birch, *Rise*, 30 = idem, "Development," 56; Mommer, *Samuel*, 98; Campbell, *1 Samuel*, 107. Vermeylen argues that 9:20–21 are original to the story and that 10:2–4 is a Deuteronomistic addition (*Loi du plus fort*, 24–27). This reading is hardly convincing. First, it requires that Vermeylen then omit 9:19aβb as secondary, despite the close relationship of v. 19b to vv. 25–26a. Second, it entirely disregards the connections between the crises in 9:3 (loss of asses) and v. 7 (lack of bread) on the one hand and 10:2 (reassurance that the asses have been found) and 10:4 (provision of bread) on the other. Vermeylen's odd attributive schema is directed entirely at elucidating the parallel structures of 1 Sam 9:1–10:16 and 1 Samuel 28. But these parallels would be equally strong at the level of the PR, were Vermeylen to allow the insertion of several additions prior to the Deuteronomistic redaction.

145 Stoebe, "Noch einmal," 366–67; Schmidt, *Menschlicher Erfolg*, 67–68; Richter, *Berufungsberichte*, 21. Weiser credited this redundancy to the secondary nature of 10:2–3*, but that assessment is predicated on his assumption that the anointing of Saul was the central concern of this folktale, a specious claim at best. Weiser's reading of the "signs" predicted in 10:2–4 is belabored and too quickly dismisses those episodes as secondary, based on faulty reliance on the outdated assumption that traditions were necessarily preserved at the sanctuary mentioned in them (e.g., *Samuel*, 57–59).

146 E.g., Mommer, *Samuel*, 100.

147 Fischer, "Saul-Überlieferung," 173; following Klein, *1 Samuel*, 89.

monarchic date, as opposed to Fischer's exilic *terminus post quem*. Additionally, Fischer's observation is founded on the frequently cited Deuteronomistic provenance of 10:20–21abα*, although this attribution has more often than not been assumed only on the authority of Noth and remains somewhat conjectural in my opinion.[148] Moreover, the claims to Deuteronomistic authorship do not necessarily apply to v. 20a, which stands apart from vv. 20b–21 grammatically. The syntactic disjunction indicated by וּלְמִי at the beginning of v. 20b has been preserved textually as well: 4QSam[a] contains a sizeable *vacat* between v. 20a and v. 20b.[149] While this datum indicates only that there was some scribal attempt to preserve the (perceived) disjuncture here, it may bolster the proposal made here that v. 20a derives from an earlier stratum of redaction than vv. 20b–21, which seem to be Deuteronomistic.

Regardless of its precise origins, the redactional addition in vv. 20–21 both disrupts the narrative flow of the original folk-tale and casts a shadow of illicit motivation over what is "in Saul's heart" in v. 19. Since v. 20 negates the possibility that desire to find his father's missing donkeys was what concerned Saul and since the episode in the morning is driven in the present text by the plot-twist of the anointment of Saul (10:1)—clearly the goal of the earliest overwriting[150]—the clear reference of "what is in Saul's heart" (v. 19) has now become concern for the kingship. One may certainly agree with Schmidt and Birch that the prophetic reworking of the folktale background narrative has woven in a "modified call-narrative,"[151] and this assessment is compatible with the equally compelling observation by R. Klein that this call narrative was crafted intentionally to insinuate that something else was already on Saul's mind when he went to the city.[152] As a result, the revision encompassing 9:20a and 10:1 seems to

148 Noth, *DH*, 81–82. I disputed this claim in a recent lecture, which I hope to publish soon ("'Long Live the King!' 1 Sam 10:17–27 in Light of Ahansali Intra-Tribal Mediation," [paper presented at the annual meeting of the SBL, Boston, Mass., Nov. 23, 2008]).

149 Cross et al., *1–2 Samuel*, 61.

150 Schmidt, *Menschlicher Erfolg*, 68; Richter, *Berufungsberichte*, 50–53; Birch, *Rise*, 37–38 = idem, "Development," 68; Campbell, *Of Prophets and Kings*, 20; Na'aman, "Pre-Deuteronomistic Story," 642; Schmitt, "Berufungsschema," 208–9.

151 Birch, *Rise*, 35–41 = idem, "Development," 61–67; see previously Schmidt, *Menschlicher Erfolg*, 88–90; Richter, *Berufungsberichte*, 45–52, esp. 50–51; and Mettinger, *King and Messiah*, 66. Birch uses the structure of call narratives as proposed by Ernest Kutsch and refined by Wolfgang Richter and Norman Habel (Ernest Kutsch, "Gideons Berufung und Alterbau Jdc 6,11–24," *TLZ* 81 [1956], 75–84; Richter, *Berufungsberichte*; Norman Habel, "The Form and Significance of the Call Narratives," *ZAW* 77 [1965]: 297–323; for summary, Schmitt, "Berufungsschema," 202–4). Peter Ignatius argues that this use of the call schema is meant as a derogation of Saul's status ("1 Sam 9,1–10,16: Have the Davidic Propagandists Capitalized on the Folktales about Saul to Enhance the Image of David?" *BiBh* 28 [2002]: 648–49).

152 Klein, *1 Samuel*, 89; but cf. Stoebe, *EBS*, 204.

have been motivated by a concern to show that Saul was somehow concerned with something *more* than the recovery of familial property, but to what extent this insinuation was perceived as a negative evaluation of Saul's character cannot be judged from the literary remains. This insinuation was subsequently developed into a full-blown accusation of improperly seeking the kingship with the Deuteronomistic insertion of vv. 20b–21, concomitant with the insertion or elaboration of 10:17–27*.

(4) The number of signs Samuel gives to Saul in the morning fluctuates between the singular (τὸ σεμεῖον; 10:1 LXX)[153] and the plural (10:7,9). Indeed, the earlier stratum seems to presume at least two "signs," predicted in 10:2–4 (although they are not called such here). Saul will meet two men who will tell him that the donkeys have been found (v. 2), and then he will meet three men who will provide him with sustenance (vv. 3–4). The first, as noted above, is narrated in such a way that it repeats word for word Saul's concern for his father's donkeys (9:5):

Saul (9:5):

לכה ונשובה פן־יחדל אבי מן־האתנות ודאג לנו

"Come on; let's return before my father stops (worrying) about the donkeys, and starts worrying about us."

Samuel (10:2):

והנה נטש אביך את־דברי האתנות ודאג לכם לאמר מה אעשה לבני

"Look, your father has left off about the asses and is (now) worried about you, saying, 'What have I done to my son?'"

Furthermore, the forecasted delivery of two loaves of bread to Saul and his companion (10:4) will alleviate the problem the two travelers had faced, according to 9:7—namely, the lack of any bread to bring as a gift for the seer, much less with which to sustain themselves on the journey home![154] Since both of these signs fulfill Saul's concerns from earlier in the narrative—and specifically from that part of the narrative for which no revision can fruitfully be suggested—it is likely that the original folktale encompassed these prognostications as well.[155] However, v. 9 is more

153 LXX preserves a passage that has dropped out of the MT due to haplography. See McCarter for a discussion (*I Samuel*, 171; also Mettinger, *King and Messiah*, 66–67).

154 E.g., Hertzberg, *I & II Samuel*, 85; Stoebe, *EBS*, 206. Stoebe's reading is perhaps somewhat overdrawn in arguing that these episodes provide Saul with the necessary accoutrements for his status as an איש חיל ("Noch einmal," 362–70; although see below). Weiser viewed the bread as an honorarium given unwittingly to the newly anointed and ascendant king of Israel (*Samuel*, 58), but this too seems an over-interpretation on the assumption that the men on pilgrimage were planning to deliver the bread as an offering at Bethel.

155 See Schmidt, *Menschlicher Erfolg*, 66–67; Richter, *Berufungsberichte*, 16. Mettinger included the bestowal of the spirit (10:5–6) in his original tradition, but this judgment is predicated on his perception of the importance of the number three throughout the narrative (this being the *third* sign; *King and Messiah*, 71, 73; see also Fischer, "Saul-Überlieferung," 168) and is hardly necessary. I accept the validity of the observation insofar as v. 5a itself lays out a

intimately related to the obvious narrative intrusion in 10:5b–6,10–13, since it brings to a close any concern with the original signs and prepares for the fulfillment of the secondary elaboration.[156] It is tempting to think that his association of v. 9 with the addition suggests v. 7, which also mentions "signs" (אתות), should be attributed to the addition as well; however, the multiple signs of v. 7 concur with those predicted by the seer in vv. 2–4. Therefore, the association of v. 7 with the original narrative is preferable, in distinction to the single sign of LXX 10:1, which may be related positively to the "modified call-narrative" of the prophetic revision.[157] If Birch is correct in his application of Habel's schema to the revised pericope, "the sign" of LXX 10:1b must refer to the commission itself. That Saul will deliver Israel *is* the single sign in the revision, Birch argues. On this understanding, v. 9 would have to be secondary to the base text, introduced by an editor different from the one who introduced the modified call narrative, with its single "sign."[158] Instead, v. 9 picked up on the plural "signs" of the extant v. 7 and may have been composed at the time of the introduction of vv. 5b–6,10–13.[159] However, it should be noted that v. 9 uses אלהים instead of יהוה (with 9:27; 10:3,7; over against 10:1; etc.).[160]

---

circumstance in need of rectification, but to attach vv. 5b–6 to the original narrative is to belabor the importance of Richter's insight.

156 Campbell, *1 Samuel*, 109; cf. the divisions proposed by Schmidt and Richter (Schmidt, *Menschlicher Erfolg*, 63–66, 73; Richter, *Berufungsberichte*, 21–22). Victor Eppstein makes the distinction between the base narrative and the prophetic narrative of 10:5–6,10–12 (to which we may add v. 13 as a redactional insert if not an original part of the intrusion) on the basis of their respective concerns ("Was Saul also among the Prophets?" *ZAW* 81 [1969]: 287–303). Despite the difficulties in substantiating many of the specifics of Eppstein's argument, his assessment that this episode serves here as an etiology (ibid., 297) for the common saying "Is Saul also among the prophets?" may go unchecked. See also John Sturdy, "The Original Meaning of 'Is Saul Also among the Prophets (1 Samuel x 11, 12; xix 24)?'" *VT* 20 (1970): 206–13; Peter Mommer, "Ist auch Saul unter den Propheten? Ein Beitrag zu 1 Sam 19,18–24," *BN* 38/39 (1987): 53–61; idem, *Samuel*, 95–97; Nihan, "Saul," 90–92. Hertzberg split ch. 10 into two narratives maintained at different cultic sites, one of which contained this passage about Saul and the band of prophets (*I & II Samuel*, esp. 79–80).

157 E.g., Mettinger, *King and Messiah*, 68–69, 73; Schmitt, "Berufungsschema," 209–10. Cf. Veijola, who attributed v. 1b LXX to DtrG (*Königtum*, 75–76); as with 9:16b, this does not significantly affect the argument here. Some have challenged the authenticity of the LXX plus, and the reading is thus not entirely secure: see, e.g., Pisano, *Additions*, 166–69; but cf. McCarter, *I Samuel*, 171. Vermeylen doubts the authenticity of much of the addition, but he does allow the originality of καὶ τουτό σοι τὸ σημεῖον... (*Loi du plus fort*, 25–26).

158 Schmidt found the end of the original narrative in v. 9, because all of the folktale's complications had been solved (*Menschlicher Erfolg*, 73). As will be seen in the following discussion, the assessment is problematic.

159 Birch, *Rise*, 39–40 = idem, "Development," 64–66; see similarly Mettinger, *King and Messiah*, 69; cf. Schmidt, *Menschlicher Erfolg*, 63–64, 73. Birch made the assessment that 10:1 may be derived from a source separate from 10:7,9, but the variation between the singular and plural "sign(s)" leads one to question his presentation of the relative chronology of the text's development. Birch argued there were originally two narratives: (a) the folktale and (b) the etiology of the proverb. These two narratives were redacted together by a pro-

(5) Closely related to the preceding discrepancy, Birch points out that although several signs are predicted (vv. 2–8), only one is narrated explicitly (v. 10),[161] which indicates at least some rewriting of the end of the narrative. Although Schmidt argued for the end of the folktale in Saul's commissioning (10:7,9),[162] this solution cannot be sustained, since it leaves unfinished a large proportion of the conflicts built up in the course of the passage. Miller has argued more cogently that the reader expects something more than the end of the donkey narrative in 10:16, specifically an indication that Saul was successful at "what his hand found to do."[163] Presently, 1 Samuel 11 serves as the conclusion to this command,[164] yet the reader nonetheless expects a much tighter structure of prediction and fulfillment in which Saul's carrying-through of Samuel's instructions occurs more immediately.[165] Furthermore, a reasonable reconstruction of

---

phetic editor who framed his work in the style of a modified call narrative. However, one wonders, if this were the case, whether the "sign" referred to in the prophetic addition in 10:1 (LXX) would indeed have been considered to be Saul's rescue of the people. Compare, e.g., the translation of McCarter: "this will be the sign for you that Yahweh has anointed you prince over his estate: [v. 2] when you depart from me today..." (*I Samuel*, 166). Here, the foretold events of the folktale are collapsed into a single "sign," a solution requiring none of the hypothetical gerrymandering of the text present in Birch's reconstruction. If we operate with McCarter's translation, then the prophetic revision makes sense without the concomitant utilization of an extant etiology for the proverb about Saul's prophethood. Furthermore, without knowing the precise time of inclusion of the redactional material surrounding vv. 5b–6 and vv. 10–13, it is difficult to substantiate the claim that the etiology was part of an early prophetic redaction rather than a late inclusion, after a redactor had already included 1 Samuel 11 as the fulfillment of Samuel's commands in 10:1–5a,7b. This may be the most convincing evidence to be mustered in favor of a prophetically concerned Deuteronomist (roughly akin to the Smend school's DtrP).

160 Mommer, *Samuel*, 101–2; Schmidt argued that this discrepancy betrayed the divergent composition histories of the original etiological narrative (vv. 10–13) and the redactional origin of the verses composed to incorporate that tradition (vv. 5b–6; *Menschlicher Erfolg*, 63–66; see also Richter, *Berufungsberichte*, 22–23).

161 See also Seeligmann, "Hebräische Erzählung," 320; and Hertzberg, *I & II Samuel*, 86.

162 E.g., Schmidt, *Menschlicher Erfolg*, 73, 86, and esp. 101.

163 Miller, "Saul's Rise," 159–65; see also Stoebe, "Noch einmal," 369; Blenkinsopp, "Quest," 83; Fischer, "Saul-Überlieferung," 168–69.

164 See, e.g., Campbell, *1 Samuel*, 117.

165 Nihan has proposed an altogether different ending to the folktale, in which the seer divulges to Saul information as to how to find the asses so that he may return home with them, in effect only alluding to the future mighty acts of the king ("Du voyant," 13–15; see also Mommer, *Samuel*, 94). However, a severe criticism dulls the ingenuity of this supposed ending. Although Nihan never carries out this proposal to its logical conclusion, ending the story at 10:9, the solution assumes that the seer's prediction of Saul meeting two men who will tell him that the asses have been found (10:2) is either not part of the original story or that the statement "the asses have been found (נמצאו האתנות)" refers to a third party as the finder and not to Saul's own father. On this second understanding, Saul would presumably then procure the donkeys from the third party and head for home. This is much like the conclusion of Stoebe that Saul's social standing is granted or confirmed by the finding of the asses ("Noch einmal," 268–70) but without the important qualification that Saul then is

the original tradition must supply an ending to this folkloristic narrative in which Saul does not go from a position of relative youth and vigor (9:2) to that of a lethargic father of a son whose age qualifies him for battle (13:4–14) in the span of approximately two weeks (or five weeks, if reading 10:27b–11:1 with LXX^B καὶ ἐγενήθη ὡς μετὰ μῆνα and 4QSam^a ויהי כמו חדשׁ).[166] As was demonstrated in §7.3.1, the narrative in 1 Samuel 11 stands alone structurally, with more elements in common with deliverer narratives than with the folkloristic tale of Saul's search for missing donkeys. Therefore, an ending to the donkey narrative must be reconstructed such that it provides a fitting conclusion to the folktale, explaining how Saul came to be an important personage in Benjamin and Israel. Without such an ending, the original narrative would have been anti-climactic and therefore an extremely unlikely entity. The journey throughout Benjamin and the southern part of Ephraim seems to anticipate Saul's future control of the territories.[167] It is logical to surmise that the original ending of the folktale would have provided at least some indication as to how that control came about. For example, Mayes argued that the truncated end of the folktale could be found in the recognition of Saul's stature in 10:23b,24aβb, which refers back to 9:2.[168] This solution too readily assumes a necessary link between the height notices of 9:2b and 10:23, which concurrently assumes the former *must* be original in its context. To be preferred is Eissfeldt's suggestion that 10:21bβ–24 preserves an independent tradition in which the pre-designated king, unknown even to Samuel, would be revealed to the people by his extreme height. This tradition was secondarily linked to 9:1–10:16* by the insertion of 9:(2aβ),2b.[169] Moreover, Mayes's solution only serves to postpone the premature ending of the folktale; no kingdom corresponding to the itinerary of 1 Sam 9:4–5aα is granted to Saul in the course of 10:17–27, and the only logical fulfillment of Samuel's instruction in 10:7, namely 1 Samuel 11, is not combined with the folktale until the formation of the

---

prepared to go to battle as a recognized warrior. Moreover, this solution neglects to consider the fact that it is not Saul who finds the asses! If taken to its extreme conclusion, Nihan's proposal comprises such a banal ending to the folktale as to be virtually meaningless.

166 Blenkinsopp, "Quest," 84; Dietrich, *David*, 99.

167 Blenkinsopp, "Quest," 96 n. 32; Edelman, "Saul's Journey," 57.

168 Mayes, *Story*, 100, 167 n. 18; see also idem, "Rise," 13. Previously, Crüsemann had argued that 10:23–24aβb,26bα comprised a supplementary addition to the story in 9:1–10:9* and had formed the bridge between that passage and 11:1–15* through the addition of 9:2b; 10:26a, 26bβ,27a; 11:12 (without אל־שׁמואל)–13 (*Widerstand*, 54–58).

169 Eissfeldt, *Komposition*, 7–8; see also Hertzberg, *I & II Samuel*, 88–89; Richter, *Berufungsberichte*, 25; Mommer, *Samuel*, 94–95 (see bibliography at 95 n. 214); Campbell, *1 Samuel*, 112–13; Fischer, "Saul-Überliefering," 171–72 (who omits v. 2aβ as well); cf. Noth, *DH*, 81; and Stoebe, *EBS*, 218. According to Eissfeldt, however, 10:21bβ–27 found its sequel in 1 Samuel 11 (without v. 6aα); 13 (without vv. 3bα,4b–5,7b–15a); 14 (*Komposition*, 11).

Josianic edition of the DtrH, in Mayes's schema.[170] A logical ending to the story is still missing.

7.3.2.2. Saul's Uncle as a Key to the Ending of the NSR$_B$

Finding the key to this dilemma requires a thorough rereading of the narrative with a keen eye towards logical story-telling methods, specifically towards the fulfillment of unanswered predictions. In this regard, one datum no commentator has adequately addressed—to the best of my knowledge—is the function of Saul's uncle in the heavily edited episode in 10:14–16.[171] The appearance of Saul's uncle in these verses is odd, since he has not previously figured as a character in the story.[172] We expect Saul's father Kish instead, since he has already made an appearance himself, albeit a brief one (9:3).[173] I suggest that the prediction of Saul's meetings in 10:2–4 offers another alternative: a choice that may very well explain the unexpected presence of a member of Saul's family in the pericope.

A few clues in the story suggest that Saul's uncle (Ner?; cf. 1 Sam 14:51) originally figured in the earlier, unedited version of the story, but a tangential approach to those clues must be taken here. Miller notes that attention to the assumed geography of the narrative may be instructive.[174]

170 Mayes, *Story*, 81–105, esp. 88–89, and 117–20.

171 Campbell argues a prophetic redactor has clearly edited this episode, since it presumes Samuel, rather than a nameless seer, as a major character of the pericope (vv. 14–16; cf. above), as well as Samuel's anointment of Saul, elliptically described as the "matter of the kingship" in 10:1 (דבר המלוכה; v. 16) (*Of Prophets and Kings*, 19–20). Cf. Miller, who argued that the Deuteronomistic Historian had inserted vv. 13–16 ("Saul's Rise," 160). Mommer supposes a pre-Deuteronomistic formation of vv. 14–16, since those verses refer to all the major motifs of the passage, despite the fact that they derive from various redactional layers; moreover, he claims, the episode prepares for 10:17–27 (*Samuel*, 94–95; see also Crüsemann, *Widerstand*, 57). It is not entirely clear to me, however, that the episode does not simply prepare for the continuation of the early NSR$_{AB}$ complex in 11:1–11*. The only possible indicator of later date is the מלוכה, working from the assumption that the kingship was introduced only with the insertion of 1 Samuel 8 + 10:17–27 + 12, which Mommer claims already occurred at the pre-Deuteronomistic level.

172 Schmidt, *Menschlicher Erfolg*, 59; Richter, *Berufungsberichte*, 22.

173 McCarter, *I Samuel*, 184; cf. Stoebe, *EBS*, 211–12. D. R. Ap-Thomas suggested that "Saul's uncle" actually referred to the Philistine governor of the region ("Saul's 'Uncle,'" *VT* 11 [1961]: 241–45), but this solution seems unlikely as well. Cf. the equally unlikely solution, proposed by Karel van der Toorn, that Saul's uncle was some sort of ritual functionary ("Saul and the Rise of Israelite State Religion," *VT* 43 [1993]: 521 n. 9). Vermeylen understands the "uncle" (דוד) as a "discrete allusion to the kingship of David" (*Loi du plus fort*, 31); while this reading works well at the synchronic level, Vermeylen has not adequately explained how it is relevant in a diachronic model.

174 Miller, "Saul's Rise," 159–61.

Most interpreters have assumed on the basis of "Gibeat-ha-Elohim" (גבעת־האלהים) in 10:5[175] and "Gibeat-Saul" (גבעת שאול) in 11:4 that either of the well-known cities, Gibeah or Gibeon, was Saul's hometown.[176] However, this supposition contrasts with indications of Saul's historical hometown external to the NSR and may, in fact, be related to the secondary (prophetic) identification of the unnamed city of the seer to Samuel's Ramah.[177] In 2 Sam 21:13–14, the bones of Saul and Jonathan are exhumed from their grave in Jabesh-gilead and reinterred in Zela (צֵלַע), a city of Benjamin, in the grave of Saul's father Kish. If this notice may serve as a reliable historical datum, it would indicate that Saul's family was based not at Gibeah, but at Zela.[178] With this datum in mind, the signs predicted by the seer come into clearer relief. The first of the seer's predictions was:

---

175 Na'aman argued that the relative clause "where the Philistine garrison is" (אשר־שם נצבי פלשתים) used to describe Gibeah-ha-Elohim in 10:5aβ was a later addition because it anticipates the presence of a Philistine garrison (מצב) in 13:3 ("Pre-Deuteronomistic Story," 640–42; see also McCarter, *I Samuel*, 182). But I do not believe this needs to be the case (with Miller, "Saul's Rise," 159). While the narrative reasons for this judgment will become clear below, it may be said at this juncture that none of the versional evidence suggests the removal of this relative clause as a secondary insertion.

176 Cf. H. W. Hertzberg, "Mizpa," *ZAW* 47 (1929): 179–81; Aaron Demsky, "Geba, Gibeah, and Gibeon: An Historico-Geographic Riddle," *BASOR* 212 (1973): 26–31, esp. 27–28; J. Maxwell Miller, "Geba/Gibeah of Benjamin," *VT* 25 (1975): 145–66; Klein, *1 Samuel*, 91; van der Toorn, "Saul," 520–25. I make no definitive decision here regarding the prolix nature of the Geba-Gibeah-Gibeon debate but concur with those commentators who locate Saul's hometown elsewhere.

177 Blenkinsopp, "Quest," 83, 96 n. 29; cf. the idiosyncratic suggestion of Serge Frolov and Vladimir Orel that the unnamed city of 1 Sam 9:1–10:16 is Bethlehem ("A Nameless City," *JBQ* 23 [1995]: 252–56). Their argumentation here is quite specious, and the solution is predicated on the assumption that, "[s]ince Samuel was not an Ephraimite but a Levite, the land of Zuph must be somehow connected with Ephrath." This logic conflates the folkloristic Samuel of 1 Sam 9:1–10:16 with the Chronicler's portrayal of the same individual as a Levite; cf. 1 Chr 6:18–20 (Eng. v. 33–35). For the malleable nature of genealogy in support of one's credentials to serve as a Levite, see Jeremy M. Hutton, "The Levitical Diaspora (I): A Sociological Comparison with Morocco's Ahansal," in *Exploring the* Longue Durée*: Essays in Honor of Lawrence E. Stager* (ed. David Schloen; Winona Lake, Ind.: Eisenbrauns, 2009), 223–34.

178 Cf. Wellhausen's proposed emendation of 1 Sam 9:1 to איש מגבעת בנימין (*Composition*, 242), accepted by, e.g., Kittel (*BHK*, ad loc.); Hertzberg, *I & II Samuel*, 75, 80; and Richter, *Berufungsberichte*, 14 and n. 5. The proper recognition of Saul's hometown makes this emendation superfluous in the context of the original folktale. Avraham Faust suggests the historical Saul's movement from Zela to Gibeah may be correlated to the trend observable in the archaeological record whereby the population of the southern Samarian and Benjaminite highlands abandoned smaller villages in favor of larger cities ("Settlement Patterns and State Formation in Southern Samaria and the Archaeology of [a] Saul," in *Saul in Story and Tradition* [ed. Carl S. Ehrlich with Marsha C. White; FAT I/47; Tübingen: Mohr Siebeck, 2006], 14–38).

> When you leave me today, you will find two men at the grave of Rachel on the border of Benjamin, in Zelzah (בְּצֶלְצַח), and they will say to you, "The donkeys that you have gone to seek have been found, but now your father has left off the matter of the donkeys and worries about you, saying, 'What have I done to my son?'" (10:2)

Miller has noticed that the location of this encounter (Zelzah) sounds suspiciously similar to the name of Saul's presumed hometown Zela, and—assuming some sort of textual confusion[179]—suggests the sign was expected to have taken place at Saul's hometown.[180] This possibility that the first sign was to occur near Saul's hometown suggests further that the men who informed Saul of the donkeys' finding and of Kish's subsequent worries concerning Saul's fate was nothing miraculous or extraordinary—since that quality was reserved for the seer's correct prediction of the sign—but rather came about due to the men's familiarity with Saul and his father. The story assumes Saul will be informed of his father's concern by a third party, rather than by Kish himself (in which case, one might have expected Samuel to have disclosed this to him in 10:2). Clearly, 10:2 presupposes that Kish's concern persists after Saul's meeting with the men; Kish therefore was not one of the two men. However, I suggest that one of the men predicted by Samuel in v. 2 was revealed in the original form of the folktale to be precisely Saul's uncle, who would have been quite familiar with the everyday workings of his brother's household. The words predicted by the seer fit perfectly in the mouth of Saul's uncle: "The donkeys that you have gone to seek have been found, but now your father has left off the matter of the donkeys and worries about you, saying, 'What have I done to my son?'" The odd presence of Saul's uncle in the

---

179 It is not clear to me exactly how the textual confusion might have worked, though. Clearly, the suggestion would require a reduplication of the first radical <ṣ> and a devoicing of the final radical *^{c} > /ḥ/ if one were to suppose a strictly genetic development of the name *ṣelṣaḥ* (צלצח) from an original *ṣēla*^{c} (צלע). We should remain cognizant of the possibility, however, that the episode in 2 Sam 16:5–8,13b—in which Shimei of the house of Saul (v. 5) disparages David from a rock rib above the road (ושמעי הלך בצלע ההר לעמתו; v. 13b)—contaminated the town's name in 2 Sam 21:13–14 and that צלצח was the original name of the town (although cf. Josh 18:28, which preserves the name צלע). This conjecture may be somewhat substantiated by the description of the men whom Saul will meet in 10:2 LXX^{B} as ἁλλομένους μεγάλα "jumping greatly." The verb ἅλλομαι was used in a few other places to render Heb. צלח (Judg 14:6,19; 15:14; and, nearer at hand, 1 Sam 10:10), and the LXX may therefore indicate either confusion, lexical contamination from, or—most probable, in my opinion—deliberate paronomasia with, the "leaping" of the spirit in v. 10. In either case, both names (צלצח and צלע) bear similarity to the name of the tell *Ḫ. Ṣalah* which lies quite close to *el-Jîb*, commonly identified with Gibeon, and *Nebi Samwil*, a site that—regardless of its authenticity—has classically been identified with the prophet Samuel's base of operations and indeed preserves the prophet's name (Blenkinsopp, "Quest," 90; see also idem, "Did Saul Make Gibeon His Capital?" *VT* 24 [1974]: 1–7).

180 Miller, "Saul's Rise," 159–60.

present state of the text can be explained quite easily if we suppose he originally figured as a character in the folktale, whose presence was perfectly reasonable in the narrative's logic. Only with the subsequent inclusion of the NSR_A tradition (1 Samuel 11) and the concomitant prophetic rewriting of the NSR_B (see the reconstruction below, §§7.4; 8.1) did this character need to be overwritten so that Saul knew of a matter of the kingship but did not tell anyone.[181]

Two hypotheses have been proposed here: (a) that Saul's uncle may originally have figured in the fulfillment section of the folktale (NSR_B), and (b) that Saul's hometown was not Gibeah, Geba, or Gibeon, but rather Zela. These assertions provide mutual support and give an indication that the folktale as it now stands in combination with the larger NSR—truncated in favor of a different military victory and disfigured by subsequent redaction—suffers from a deficiency of explanatory and narrative power in its independent presentation of the rise of Saul that is *not* solved by the elevation of Saul over the Israelites in 1 Samuel 11. The lack of any specific description of the events comprising the fulfillment of the remaining signs and of the ultimate goal of the narrative—Saul's consolidation of power over Benjamin and southern Ephraim—suggests we should postulate one immediate goal towards which the folktale may have worked: the solidification of Saul's power at the city ever subsequently recognized as the center of his power, Gibeah, Geba, or Gibeon. This hypothesized ending of the folktale would probably have appeared in a form quite analogous to the story of David's taking of Jerusalem in 2 Sam 5:6–10: a battle performed under the auspices of Yahweh, in which individual honor leads to the establishment of a dynasty at the chosen location. Let us state this hypothesis for the moment thus: the taking of Gibeah-Elohim, whether identified with Gibeah or Gibeon (or even Geba), with its Philistine garrison or prefect (10:5), originally comprised the military victory that Saul's "hand found to do," forming a suitable ending to the folktale in which all the loose narrative threads are tied together.

Two difficulties with this solution present themselves immediately. First, we have no pericope in the books of Samuel that might qualify, even

---

181 Presumably, Saul's meeting with his uncle would have had to be rewritten at the stage of the combination of the NSR_{AB} in order to include Samuel (and to reduce the appearance of this pericope as the fulfillment of one of the signs, since now "what Saul's hand would find to do" had been deferred until the separate story included as 1 Samuel 11). However, it is possible that the final notice, "Saul did not tell him the matter of the kingship..." (v. 16b), was added only at the time of the inclusion of the NSR_C in order to draw out the secretive and esoteric nature of that selection scene. As noted above, the word מלוכה appears to be late monarchic or exilic (Mommer, *Samuel*, 94–95). This linguistic datum might indicate that 10:16b could be a specifically Deuteronomistic addition, although vv. 14–16a may derive from an earlier redactional hand.

remotely, as a fulfillment of the second sign predicted by the seer (10:3–4). It appears that along with truncation of the folktale's ending in order to make room for the NSR_A, and with the contemporaneous revision of the original episode featuring the fulfillment of seer's first prognostication (i.e., the present text's 10:14–16) in order to serve as a redactional anticipation of the Ammonite battle and Saul's subsequent coronation, the redactor also jettisoned the fulfillment of the seer's second sign.[182]

Second, the present text now includes only a brief indication that Saul was successful in the taking of an unnamed military base—the ending of the folktale hypothesized above: "All Israel heard: 'Saul struck the garrison of the Philistines (נציב פלשתים),[183] and Israel has even become odious to the Philistines...'" (1 Sam 13:4).[184] But even this indication is problematic, because in the immediately preceding verse it is Jonathan, not Saul, who is given the credit for striking "the garrison of the Philistines which was in Geba" (נציב פלשתים אשר בגבע; 13:3). Not only is the person to whom the victory is credited not clear, but the city Gibeah which was hypothesized above to have been the ultimate goal of the folktale also fails to appear here, apparently superseded by a city whose name was based on the same root: Geba. It would appear that, like the disappearance of the fulfillment of the second sign (10:3–4), the original fulfillment of the seer's order, "Do what your hand finds to do" (10:7), has been scuttled in favor of Saul's Ammonite campaign.[185] After the addition of the NSR_A provided the "true" basis for Saul's coronation (and the fulfillment of the seer's command in 10:7), the original ending was then not only superfluous, but unfulfilling as well; it told only of Saul's seizure of a city, not of his successful defense of Israelite interests. The more magnanimous version of Saul's rise has prevailed.[186]

Yet there remains something intriguing about the relic of the hypothesized original ending found in 13:3–4. The recognition that the historian attributes the seizure of Geba to Jonathan (v. 3) while at the time

182 For this caveat, see van der Toorn, "Saul," 525–26.

183 This phrase should be compared to the similar phrase in 10:5: נצבי פלשתים. The versional evidence of 10:5 supports the singular, and the consonantal text should probably be read as נציב (identical to the MT of 13:4) rather than as MT's נצבי.

184 For 13:3–4 as the remnant of the original narrative's ending, see Stoebe, *EBS*, 207; Gregory Moberly, "Glimpses of the Heroic Saul," in *Saul in Story and Tradition* (ed. Carl S. Ehrlich with Marsha C. White; FAT I/47; Tübingen: Mohr Siebeck, 2006), 86; and Fischer, "Saul-Überlieferung," 168–69. Moberly advances the improbable theory of Edelman that "Saul in 1 Sam 9:27–10:14 posed as a member of the prophetic guild in order to gain access to a Philistine prefect for the purpose of assassinating him" (Moberly, "Glimpses," 85, see also 86–87; Edelman, *Saul*, 54).

185 E.g., Stoebe, "Noch einmal," 368.

186 Cf. David G. Firth, "The Accession Narrative (1 Samuel 27–2 Samuel 1)," *TynBul* 58 (2007): 61–81.

the victory was credited to Saul (v. 4) deserves further exploration. Does this discrepancy simply mean that Saul was given accolades for the deeds of his army and that—however much the individual hero of the day was Jonathan—Saul's military savvy demanded recognition? Surely, this is one possible reading of the text. However, if this is the case, we must remember that Jonathan's victory over the Philistine garrison (מצב) narrated in 14:1–15 came not at Geba but at Michmash, the town across the valley from Geba, and 13:3–4 and 14:1–15 therefore describe two different battles.[187] Furthermore, the MT textual tradition preserving "Geba" (גבע) in 13:3 does not go unchallenged by the versional evidence. The previous verse, which details where Jonathan's troops were stationed, reads Gibeah-Benjamin (גבעת בנימין; 13:2). The LXX text of 13:2 remains ambiguous,[188] but 13:3 "on the hill" (εν τω βουνω) most likely supports an original גבעה.[189] The confusion is perpetuated throughout the MT of 1 Samuel 13–14, in which the names Gibeah (13:2,[190] 15;[191] 14:2,[192]

187 It is tempting to argue that these were two distinct battles. Jonathan took Geba, reinvigorating Israelite faith in Saul, but Michmash was subsequently lost while Saul tarried in Gilgal. This turn of events necessitated a reassertion of Israelite domination in the Benjaminite hill country and resulted in the battle of Michmash. But in opposition to this overly historical reading of the biblical text, Blenkinsopp ("Quest," 87) has suggested that the notice in 13:2–4 and the story in 14:1–23 may be considered "alternate versions of the uprising." This is the far more likely solution and the assumption from which I operate in the following argument.

188 LXX^L: γαβαα; LXX^B: γαβεε; McCarter takes both as probably rendering גבע (*I Samuel*, 225). *Tg. Jon* reads "in the Hill of the House of Benjamin" (בגבעתא דבית בנימין), except for one manuscript which reads בגבעתא דבנימין (Eveline van Staalduine-Sulman, *The Targum of Samuel* [Studies in Aramaic Interpretation of Scripture 1; Leiden: Brill, 2000], 302 and n. 809). Syr. places Jonathan on the Hill of Benjamin (*brmtᵓ dbnymyn*), perhaps indicating an original גבעה. The confusion exhibited by MT and LXX here is a prelude to, and indicative of, the long history of confusion and conflation of these names with one another and with Gibeon; see Barthélemy, *Critique textuelle* 1:122–24, 300; Demsky, "Geba, Gibeah and Gibeon," 27–28; Arnold, *Gibeah*, 19–38; Sebastian P. Brock, *The Recensions of the Septuagint Version of I Samuel* (Quaderni di Henoch 9; Turin: Silvio Zamorani editore, 1996), 326–28; Ching-Wen Chen, "Gibeon and Saul in the Power Transition of the Early Monarchy," in *From East to West: Essays in Honor of Donald G. Bloesch* (ed. Daniel J. Adams; Lanham, Mary.: University Press of America, 1997), 23–50, esp. 36–37; and Eyal Regev, "Josephus on Gibeah: Versions of a Toponym," *JQR* 89 (1999): 351–59. For the conflicting views of Saul's relationship to Gibeon, see Blenkinsopp, "Did Saul Make Gibeon," 1–7; S. Yeivin, "The Benjaminite Settlement in the Western Part of Their Territory," *IEJ* 21 (1971): 141–54, esp. 150–54; Stanley D. Walters, "Saul of Gibeon," *JSOT* 52 (1991): 61–76.

189 McCarter, *I Samuel*, 225; Aramaic renders the same: בגבעתא, but Syriac gives *bgbᶜ*, apparently referring to Geba.

190 But cf. the preceding note.

191 Again, LXX^B may support the reading גבע with its ambiguous γαβαα. However, LXX^L adds βουνον, suggesting that גבעה may be intended. *Tg. Jon.* reads בגבעתא דבית בנימין (see n. 188) and is of little help here, since the confusion has been eliminated through leveling. Syr. supports גבעה (*bgbᶜtᵓ dbnymyn*)

16[193]) and Geba (13:3,[194] 14:5[195]) alternate almost interchangeably. While many scholars have emended the text to conform to the obvious geographical situation of the cities Geba and Michmash,[196] Stoebe's excellent and thorough discussion of the versional evidence for each occurrence of both names and of the geographical issues involved with each points to a combination of two traditions. In a tradition featuring Saul as the major character, the name Gibeah was used as the name of the seized city. In the tradition centering on Jonathan, the city was known as Geba.[197] Miller has picked up Stoebe's recognition of the composite nature of the text in 1 Samuel 13–14 and suggested that "two parallel versions of a tradition have been combined (or dovetailed) in chapters 13–14."[198] For Miller the sites were the same (Gibeah = Geba), and the two traditions may both have had their bases in a single historical event.[199] No matter how the relationship between the two cities is to be understood, both Stoebe and Miller agree that Saul's liberation of Gibeah, presently narrated as the liberation of Michmash in ch. 14, fulfills the seer's command that Saul is to do "what his hand finds to do" (10:7).[200] This solution takes seriously the textual history of the notices that both Saul and Jonathan liberated a city formerly in the possession of the Philistines (13:3–4), while at the same time collapsing the historical background of the traditions into a more concise understanding of the historical basis of each tradition. Yet this solution does not deal adequately with the relative dating of the traditions and

---

192 McCarter emends to גבע because of topological concerns in the face of the versional evidence, most of which (particularly all manuscripts of LXX) supports MT גבעה (*I Samuel*, 235).

193 εν γαβεε of LXX^B may again support reading the name as גבע, but LXX^L has γαβαα (see n. 191). Cf. *Tg. Jon.*'s leveled בגבעתא דבית בנימין.

194 See n. 188 above.

195 This reading is supported by both LXX^B and LXX^L, as well as by Syr.

196 E.g., McCarter, *I Samuel*, 235; cf. Campbell, *1 Samuel*, 137–38.

197 Hans Joachim Stoebe, "Zur Topographie und Überlieferung der Schlacht von Mikmas, 1. Sam. 13 und 14," *TZ* 21 (1965): 269–80, esp. 277. The only problematic occurrence of the city's name, then, is 13:2, in which Jonathan is based in Gibeah-Benjamin (see also n. 188) and Saul at Michmash, which will be [re?-]taken in 1 Samuel 14! However, since 13:2 (along with vv. 3–4) seems to be a redactional anticipation of the battle yet to be narrated in 1 Samuel 14 (which already bore the traces of the combinatory conflation), Gibeah was used rather than the expected Geba, a battle that had not yet taken place (ibid., 278). Campbell finds Stoebe's solution uncompelling (*1 Samuel*, 138), but he has not taken full account of the passage's history of composition.

198 Miller, "Saul's Rise," 162; see also Blenkinsopp, "Quest," 87; a similar conclusion is reached in Dietrich, *David*, 99–101.

199 Miller, "Saul's Rise," 163–64. It is not entirely clear to me how Stoebe understands the relation between the cities Gibeah and Geba, but if I have read his work correctly, he does not assume that competent Israelite readers ever recognized the two as the same city.

200 Stoebe, "Topographie," 273; Miller, "Saul's Rise," 162–65.

neglects to postulate the developmental process whereby the biblical authors arrived at the present text.

In order to provide the NSR_B with an adequate ending teased out from the seizure of the Philistine garrison in 1 Samuel 14, we must first of all answer these questions: (a) What part of 1 Samuel 14 may we reasonably attribute to a hypothetical, rewritten, or reformulated ending to the folktale contained in 9:1–10:16 in which Saul (and his companion?) figure as the heroes? (b) How should we then understand the relationship between the hypothesized *Urtext* in which Saul storms the city and the present text in which the feat is attributed to Jonathan? And (c) what reasons might we postulate for the reattribution of the story to Jonathan, such that the action is legitimately motivated, and not simply a capricious mucking about with the texts by a whimsical editor? In short, *how* and *why* did the present text develop, if, in fact, it displays the dismembered remains of the original ending to the NSR_B?

7.3.2.3. 1 Sam 14:6–16 as the Ending to 1 Sam 9:1–10:16

The first task in reconstructing the hypothetical ending of the folktale is to delineate the passage such that it address two concerns: namely, (a) that a reasonable ending to the folktale must encompass a specific and lexically similar fulfillment of the predictions and implied promises of the seer, and (b) that any additional episodes not advancing the folktale's plot are superfluous and therefore probably not original to what otherwise appears to have been a tightly-constructed folkloristic narrative. An episode that would complete the concerns raised by the folktale and preserve the narrative integrity of that text must be governed by the following criteria:

(a) The episode presumably must describe Saul's "doing what his hand finds to do" to a garrison (root נצב) at a city or site name Gibeah or Gibeat-Elohim (10:7). While the extension of Saul's authority may be broadened over Benjamin and southern Ephraim in the last passages of the story (an ending assumed by the circumambulation of precisely those territories in 9:4–5[201]), the story may have been etiological with respect to Saul's already extant kingship, in which case the extension of authority over Benjamin and Ephraim would have been presumed rather than explicitly stated.

(b) Because the episode should follow directly after the fulfillment of the seer's two signs in which Saul's *naʿar* still figures (assumed by the men's proffering of *two* loaves of bread in 10:4; see also 10:14), we should expect the *naʿar* to be present—if not active[202]—in the conclusion of the story. Concomitantly,

201 See Blenkinsopp, "Quest," 96 n. 32; Edelman, "Saul's Journey," 57; and above.

202 The *naʿar* plays a major role in the early part of the story, since he is the one who suggests visiting the seer in the first place (vv. 6–8). Far from being a passive tag-along in the

we should expect Jonathan to be absent from the folktale's ending, since Saul himself seems to be a young man.

(c) The etiological nature of the story most likely attempted to legitimize Saul's raised authority in Benjamin (and perhaps much of Ephraim), but not likely much more. I find it highly unlikely, therefore, that any new issues were raised once the concerns prevalent in 9:1–10:16 were adequately handled. That is to say, it is probable that no new topics were broached once Saul had witnessed the fulfillment of the seer's prognostications and performed his single military act.

In this regard, we may dismiss Miller's inclusion in the folktale ending of all the material in 1 Sam 13:4–18; 14:20–23; and 31–35,[203] because the inclusion of these episodes does not adequately fulfill the criteria that I have just outlined.[204]

1 Sam 13:4–18. Verses 13:4,5, and 6 each mentions Israel, a gentilic substantive that occurs only four times in 9:1–10:16. Three of these occurrences appear in verses already set aside above as part of the prophetic redaction or as even later explanatory glossing (e.g., 9:9,20–21). The other, which compares Saul's good looks to the rest of the Israelites (9:2aβ), may be related more easily to the notice of Saul's extreme height in v. 2b, which anticipates the similar notice in 10:23, than to the folktale, in which Saul's height is otherwise inconsequential (and therefore also most likely secondary).[205] Verse 13:4 also narrates those Israelites loyal to Saul gathering at Gilgal, a shrine that—outside of the clearly redacted 10:8[206]—does not figure at all in the NSR_B and which, as discussed above, is also likely secondary. While 13:4 does echo the נציב פלשתים of 10:5, the brief notice that Saul is given credit for its capture cannot constitute a reasonable fulfillment of the first criterion suggested above.[207] Therefore the verse must be classified as a redactional joint between 10:5 and the newly reworked ending of the pericope. Yet since it seems to presume a

---

narrative, he functions as the instigating force that—once applied—drives the remainder of the story.

203 Miller, "Saul's Rise," 162. Cf. also Birch, who puts forward an argument for the essential unity of 1 Sam 14:1–46 and suggests that "the collection of materials in chapters 13–14 functions...as the partial fulfillment of the commission in 9:16..." (*Rise*, 85–94, quote from 91).

204 I develop here arguments against the inclusion of these various pericopes in the ending of the folktale whose beginning is found in 9:1–10:16. The arguments are extensive but by no means exhaustive.

205 E.g., Eissfeldt, *Komposition*, 7–8; Mommer, *Samuel*, 94–95; Fischer, "Saul-Überlieferung," 171–72. Important to note, however, is that ישראל occurs in 9:2a, while it is 9:2b that contains the suspect clause. Cf. the enigmatic reading of Vermeylen, who considers 10:21bβ–23 a Deuteronomistic addition based on 9:2 (*Loi du plus fort*, 22).

206 E.g., Weiser, *Samuel*, 59 n. 27; Richter, *Berufungsberichte*, 19, 25–26; Birch, *Rise*, 84; Mettinger, *King and Messiah*, 64; Veijola, *Königtum*, 73; Mommer, *Samuel*, 95; Campbell, *1 Samuel*, 140; Fischer, "Saul-Überlieferung," 175; cf. Vermeylen, *Loi du plus fort*, 27.

207 *Contra*, e.g., Moberly, "Glimpses," 86; Fischer, "Saul-Überlieferung," 168–69.

connection with 1 Samuel 14, rather than with the initial intrusion of 1 Samuel 11, it probably should be dated significantly later than the combination of ch. 11 (the NSR_A) with 9:1–10:16 (the NSR_B). Neither can the rejection of Saul in 13:7b–15 be considered original to the NSR_B, since it displays a marked thematic contrast to that story.[208] Similar arguments may be adduced to disentangle the rest of 13:5–18 from the NSR_B.[209]

1 Sam 14:20–23. Certain portions of this passage are much harder to dismiss than those in the previous discussion. The confusing tumult (מהומה) of v. 20 to which Saul and "the people" are called out is a frequent motif in early battle literature and could potentially figure into a folklore-styled narrative or holy-war tradition. The "Hebrews" (עברים) who had formerly sided with the Philistines may be an authentic recollection by the ending of the folktale,[210] but their reversion to faithfulness toward Israel, Saul, and Jonathan (v. 21b) violates two of the criteria posed above (namely, that Jonathan not be present and that no new issues be raised).[211] Verse 22 picks up the theme of those highland inhabitants who had hidden themselves, but here the term "Israelite" is used rather than "people" or "Hebrew" (see v. 20 above). Not only is this redundant, but the repetition is made in an entirely different vocabulary.[212] Verse 23 remains a possible original notice in the passage, despite its specific mention of Beth-aven (MT) or Beth-horon (LXX^L). In the end, it is possible that most of vv. 20–21,23 were somehow attached to the folktale, but it remains impossible to determine exactly the context in which they would have appeared. This passage, therefore, will remain outside of our argument.

---

208 E.g., Birch, *Rise*, 74–85; cf. Dietrich, who argues 10:8 and chs. 13–14 (esp. 13:8–15) were original to the folktale and formed the bridge between the Saul and David narratives (*David*, 90–91).

209 The only portion of this passage I find difficult to dismiss is vv. 6b–7a, which bears some connection to 14:11, noted below. Although "the Hebrews" did not feature in 9:1–10:16, I find the ethnicon much less problematic than the political designation "Israel." One wonders, furthermore, if the reader is meant to contrast "the people" who go into hiding (in Cisjordan?) from "the Hebrews" (עברים = "other-siders"?) who flee to Transjordan. Notice, however, that if this is the case, the connection of 13:6b–7a with 14:11b disintegrates because in the latter it is precisely "the Hebrews" who have hidden (in Cisjordan). Redactional contamination of any of these passages remains a distinct possibility. Some have suggested the identification of the Hebrews with the Apiru of Egyptian records (e.g., Stoebe, *EBS*, 247–49; George E. Mendenhall, *The Tenth Generation: The Origins of the Biblical Tradition* [Baltimore: The Johns Hopkins University Press, 1973], 135–38), but it seems to me that a different distinction is offered here.

210 See n. 209 above and 13:7a, which also discusses the "Hebrews."

211 It is entirely possible, however, that the verse has been secondarily emended to include both Israel and Jonathan. If this is the case, the verse would have originally read something like: וגם־המה להיות עם שאול.

212 Cf. 13:6b and its resumption in 14:11bβγ: הנה עברים יצאים מן־החרים התחבאו־שם.

1 Sam 14:31–35. Not only does the initial mention of Michmash as the site of the battle in v. 31 immediately cast a shadow of suspicion over the originality of that verse, but the notice that the people were exhausted (ויעף העם מאד; v. 31b) also aligns the verse more assuredly with the episode of Saul's prohibition of eating. The remainder of this episode—in which the people slaughter the animals despoiled from the fleeing Philistines and eat the slaughter inappropriately, to which Saul responds by building an altar and forcing the proper execution of kosher law (vv. 32–35)—is simply not available as a concern contemporaneous to a document legitimizing Saul's reign. The law prohibiting this action is preserved in the Deuteronomic (12:23–27) and Priestly (Lev 19:26) codes.[213]

The foregoing discussion has made clear the fact that the ending of the folktale in 9:1–10:16, properly considered, cannot comprise a large chunk of 1 Samuel 13–14, as has often been suggested or assumed in studies that deal uncritically with Wellhausen's so-called "early source" (9:1–10:16*; 11:1–15*; 13–14). However, Miller's proposal that Jonathan's storming the Philistine garrison (מצב) at Michmash comprised a tradition parallel to that of Saul's storming the Philistine garrison (נציב) at Gibeah is a notable suggestion that may further our understanding of the likely form of the end of the NSR$_{B}$. Not only does this lexical similarity between the Michmash pericope (14:1–15) and the hypothesized ending to the NSR$_{B}$ suggest a dovetailing of the traditions, but the characterization of Jonathan and his armor-bearer betrays yet another point of connection between the actual text and the hypothesized one as well. As Blenkinsopp has noted, "[o]f the armor-bearer who accompanies [Jonathan] we hear only the barest essentials, as in the story of Gideon and Purdah his servant.... He follows his master with the same anonymous loyalty as shown later by Saul's armor-bearer in the battle of Mount Gilboa."[214] While this anonymous loyalty is certainly present in the episodes indicated, Blenkinsopp has left out the most poignant parallel to the anonymous but active side-kick: Saul's anonymous *naʿar* in the NSR$_{B}$. Even though Saul has given up hope of success, saying to "his servant who was with him (נערו אשר־עמו), 'Come on, let's head back before my father stops (worrying) about the donkeys and starts worrying about us'" (9:5), the servant suggests rather that they make one last-ditch effort to find the donkeys by visiting a seer in the town near which they find themselves (9:6). This faith mirrors almost perfectly the faithfulness of Jonathan's intrepid armor-bearer in 14:1–15.

Yet not only are the personalities of the two main characters in the NSR$_{B}$ and in 14:1–15 similar; rather, several lexical commonalities unite

213 See McCarter, *I Samuel*, 249.

214 Blenkinsopp, "Jonathan's Sacrilege," *CBQ* 26 (1964): 425.

the two as well. The first (and most obvious) is the designation of each hero's sidekick. The servant of Saul's household[215] is described variously as "his servant who was with him" (נערו אשׁר־עמו; 9:5) or simply "his/the servant" (הנער / נערו; 9:7,8,10,22).[216] Many discussions of the passage in 14:1–15 have described Jonathan's side-kick as an "armor-bearer," accurately picking up on the designation of the servant as "[the one] carrying his armor" (נשׂא כליו) in vv. 7,12(2x),13,14, but this description fails to take seriously the designation of the man as "the servant/boy carrying his armor" (הנער נשׂא כליו) in vv. 1 and 6. The use of the term נער in the Jonathan passage draws attention to the possible parallels between that text and the NSR_B. Admittedly, the circumstantial clause of v. 1 (ויהי היום) and the fact that vv. 2–5 give no immediately valuable data to further the plot of the narrative draw some suspicion to the use of the term נער. In that regard, Jonathan's suggestion in v. 1, "Come on, let's cross over to the garrison of the Philistines..." (לכה ונעברה אל־מצב פלשׁתים) seems to anticipate the same suggestion in v. 6: "Come on, let's cross over to the garrison of the these uncircumcised ones..." (לכה ונעברה אל־מצב הערלים האלה). The circumstantial data of vv. 2–5 has probably been recast by the anticipatory framing of v. 1 as to what the situation was "on the day when Jonathan said to his servant...."[217] If this is the case, vv. 1–5 may therefore be eliminated from the discussion, in which case we are dealing only with a short version of the story concerning Jonathan's storming of Michmash, comprising 14:6–15.[218]

The use of the term נער in 14:6 therefore deserves some comment. Certainly, its occurrence could be explained as an entirely capricious

215 The term *naʿar* is a difficult one to translate, since it designates not only a household slave but also a companion—an idealized image, perhaps—who accompanies the lord of the household (or in this case his son); see the large study by Carolyn S. Leeb (*Away from the Father's House: The Social Location of* naᶜar *and* naᶜarah *in Ancient Israel* [JSOTSup 301; Sheffield: Sheffield Academic Press, 2000]).

216 I disregard here the presence of לנער in v. 27 because of its probable origination from the hand of the later redactor.

217 Notice that vv. 1–5 are precisely those verses containing the topological data that many interpreters use to reconstruct a historically verisimilitudinous report, even in those verses (vv. 6–15) integral to the tradition of the storming of the citadel but completely devoid of specific topographic indicators (e.g., Hertzberg, *I & II Samuel*, 111–13; Campbell, *I Samuel*, 145). For an enigmatic, and perhaps overly precise, identification of the rock formations mentioned in 1 Sam 14:4, see N. Wyatt, "Jonathan's Adventure and a Philological Conundrum," *PEQ* 127 (1995): 62–69.

218 This episode feeds directly into the remainder of 1 Samuel 14 fairly naturally, and in this regard my delineation of the passage at v. 15 is unnatural and arbitrary. However, the delineation of the episode is consistent with the first criterion posed above as to what should be expected from the ending of the NSR_B. In v. 15, the downfall of the garrison is apparent and expected. The specific inclusion of any further verses in a reconstructed ending of the NSR_B would violate the third criterion imposed upon the reconstructive process.

addition, in which the editor, redactor, or scribe unintentionally drew a comparison between this pericope and 9:1–10:16. However, the consistent use of the solitary phrase נשׂא כליו throughout the remainder of the narrative casts doubt upon this dismissive answer and draws even sharper attention to the combination of that phrase with נער in 14:6. Why has the self-sufficient designation "armor-bearer" been augmented there by the term "servant"? The answer, I submit, lies in an implicit—even if unintentional—authorial acknowledgment that Jonathan's faithful "armor-bearer" bears many of the same traits as Saul's servant in 9:1–10:16. Unfortunately, the lexical communion of the two passages can only be pointed to. Without further evidence an intentional scribal connection drawn between the two cannot be substantiated.

Similarly, the phraseology used by the characters in both texts may be compared favorably, even though no direct correlation between the passages may be substantiated. In the initial exchange between Saul and his servant, five utterances are made (vv. 5–8,10), three of which are paralleled structurally by the speech of Jonathan and his servant in 14:6–15. Beyond those three parallels, two more lexical features bridge the two texts, bringing the total number of lexical or structural similarities—other than the common use of the term נער—between the two passages to five:

(1) initial use of the series לְכָה וְ + 1.c.pl. cohortative[219] to instigate action:

Saul (9:5):
לְכָה וְנָשׁוּבָה פֶּן־יחדל אבי מן־האתנות ודאג לנו
"Come on, let's return[220] before (literally, *lest*) my father stops (worrying) about the donkeys and starts worrying about us!"

Jonathan (14:6aα):
לְכָה וְנַעְבְּרָה אל־מצב הערלים האלה...
"Come on, let's cross over to the garrison of these uncircumcised ones..."

(2) hopeful use of אולי + 3.m.s. imperfect (with Yahweh or Yahweh's representative as subject) to strengthen the character's resolve, thereby continuing the action:

---

219 With the 1.c.pl. cohortative, we normally expect the m.pl. לְכוּ rather than the singular לְכָה form: לְכוּ appears in Gen 37:20, 27; 1 Sam 9:9; 11:14; 2 Kgs 7:4, 9; Isa 1:18; 2:3; Jer 18:18 (2x); 48:2; Hos 6:1; Jon 1:7; Mic 4:2; Ps 83:5; 95:1 (without וְ); Neh 2:17. Other than forms already listed here, לְכָה + 1.c.pl. cohortative appears with וְ in Neh 6:2,7 and without וְ in Gen 19:32; 31:44; 1 Sam 9:10; 2 Chr 25:17. The series לך (וְ) + 1.c.pl. cohortative was apparently unproductive throughout the entire lifespan of Biblical Hebrew, since it occurs nowhere in the Bible and may therefore be safely ignored in this discussion.

220 Cf. the second such phrase, לכה ונלכה preserved in 9:10 in many manuscripts (but not in MT[L]). McCarter makes no mention of this discrepancy (*I Samuel*, 169). It would appear that the conjunction is not present in 4QSam[a], but the text is poorly preserved (see Cross et al., *1–2 Samuel*, 60), and the witness it provides in this case is not particularly compelling.

the servant (9:6b):

...עתה נלכה שם אולי יגיד לנו את־דרכנו אשר־הלכנו עליה

"...Now let's go there; perhaps he [the seer] will tell us which way we should go."

Jonathan (14:6aβ):

...אולי יעשה יהוה לנו...

"...Perhaps Yahweh will act for us...."

(3) the formulation of the plan using הנה + verb + qualifications:

Saul (9:7):

(ו)הנה נלך ומה־נביא לאיש כי הלחם אזל מכלינו[221]

"If we go,[222] what will we bring to the man, because the bread is gone from our packs?"

Jonathan (14:8):

הנה אנחנו עברים אל־האנשים ונגלינו עליהם

"Alright, we're crossing over to the men, and we will reveal ourselves to them."

(4) the required openness of Saul and Jonathan to a sign (אות) or signs whereby they will know that God is with them:[223]

the seer (i.e., Samuel; 10:7):

והיה כי תבאנה (*qere*) האתות האלה לך עשה כל[224] אשר תמצא ידך כי האלהים עמך

"And when these signs occur, do all that your hand finds (to do), because God is with you."

Jonathan (14:10):

ועם־כה יאמרו עלו עלינו ועלינו כי־נתנם יהוה בידינו וזה־לנו האות

"And if they say to us, 'Come up to us!' then we will go up because Yahweh has given them into our hand, and this will be the sign for us."

---

221 A few manuscripts omit the *waw*, but it is preserved in 4QSam[a].

222 I use here the translation of Dennis J. McCarthy, who describes this use of והנה: "*w[e]hinnēh* introduces a condition with yiqtol where there is no question of a verb of perception....It might be called a concessive statement, a subdivision of the condition, but in any case it is a kind of condition..." ("The Uses of *w[e]hinnēh* in Biblical Hebrew," *Bib* 61 [1980]: 336). Clearly, if one distinguishes between הנה and והנה, then this lexical connection falls away. However, the construction is not so unique as to carry much weight in any event.

223 Shimon Bakon separates Jonathan's sign from those he deems "prophetic," i.e., "a pledge that an event will occur in the future which will confirm the authenticity of the prophecy uttered" ("Sign—אות," *JBQ* 18 [1990]: 241–250, quote from 249). In opposition, Bakon considers Jonathan's sign to be "neither an 'omen' nor a 'heads or tails' decision" (ibid., 247) but rather "a 'hint' interpreted by the beholder as divinely inspired" (ibid., 250). It is not clear, however, that the immediate consecution of 1 Sam 9:1–10:16* + 14:6–15 permits or necessitates the proposed divergence of semantic value. If these two passages are interpreted within the same narrative horizon, the sign proposed by the protagonist in 14:10 may simply be seen as an additional, ad hoc qualification to the seer's command in 10:7, which, upon completion of the signs given by the seer previously, serves simply to verify that the hero's hand has "found something to do."

224 Reading כל with LXX rather than לך with MT. The corruption was most likely caused by the word לך two words before.

(5) Finally, the structure עֲשֵׂה כל אשר + verb + body part in the command given by the seer (noted already in the preceding case) resembles structurally the reassurance given by Jonathan's armor-bearer who is of the same mind with respect to the method of attack:

Samuel (10:7):

והיה כי תבאנה האתות האלה לך עֲשֵׂה כל אשר תמצא ידך כי האלהים עמך

"And when these signs come true, do all that your hand finds (to do), because God is with you."

the armor-bearer (14:7):

עֲשֵׂה כל אשר לבבך נטה לו[225]

"Do all that your heart inclines to."

The speech patterns and lexical choices of the characters in these two stories show many similarities. Although such a solution is ultimately unsubstantiable, there is a possibility that the story of Jonathan's seizure of Michmash is an appropriation and rewriting of the original ending of the NSR_B in which Saul seized not the מצב פלשתים at Michmash (opposite Geba) but the נציב פלשתים at Gibeah. Such a suggestion requires not only the comparison of textual data but also a critical understanding of the proposed relationship between the two texts—one actual, the other unfortunately only hypothesized—both temporally and narratively. Would one text have preceded the other in the developing corpus, or did the traditions develop simultaneously?[226] If the former, how did the process of writing and rewriting affect the two texts? Or is it a mistake to believe that there were *ever* two individual texts? If the latter, is establishing a sequence of the traditions' origins justified, or even possible? Finally, what motivations—political, ideological, or historical—may be hypothesized for including one but not the other, or for overwriting the one to form the other? Clearly, since we are working with a hypothetical text reconstructed only on the basis of what we subjectively *expect* from the folktale whose truncated and already-reworked beginning is found in 1 Sam 9:1–10:16, the following discussion is entirely speculative. However, its ultimate goal is to show that there is much to be said for the history of the development of the text of 1 Samuel within the historical period of the early Israelite monarchy. Furthermore, the discussion is organized to demonstrate the high probability that the NSR_A tradition contained in 1 Samuel 11 originally developed independently of the NSR_B. Only with the redaction of the NSR_B associated with its inclusion in the HDR_1 was the

225 McCarter reconstructs the passage on the basis of LXX^L: עשה אשר לבבך נטה לו כלבבי כלבבך (*I Samuel*, 235–36). LXX^B and MT provide support for the insertion of כל, although McCarter apparently does not consider that the original reading.

226 With Miller, "Saul's Rise," 164.

NSR_A added and modified to support the validity of Saul's early dynastic kingship further—over against charismatic and temporary leadership.

7.3.2.4. The Relationship between the NSR_B Ending and Jonathan's Attack on Michmash

In the preceding section, I reconstructed the most likely ending of the original form of the donkey narrative on three assumed criteria: (a) that even in the original form of the narrative the accession of Saul to a position of prominence in the Cisjordanian hill-country was of primary importance, (b) that the tale remained consistent in its presentation of characters and their narrated personalities, and (c) that the missing end of the folktale completed narrated promises or predictions but did not pose any more problems within the narrative's horizon. Picking up on cues from Miller and Blenkinsopp, I argued that the episode of Jonathan's storming the Philistine garrison at Michmash (limited to 14:6–15*)—with the name of the hero changed to Saul and the designation of the side-kick appropriately corrected to הנער—would have formed a suitable ending to the beginning of the folktale now found overlaid and incomplete in 9:1–10:16*. But this suggestion poses several problems with respect to the relationship between the hypothesized Saul-based narrative and the Jonathan-based story preserved in the text.

Specifically, we must question whether there ever existed two completely independent stories, one centered on Saul and the other concerning the exploits of Jonathan. If there *were* indeed two such independent but related texts, we must examine the historicity of the two: were they two stories ultimately based on the same historical event and only secondarily attributed to different protagonists? Or were they based on two distinct events whose respective tradition histories and textual witnesses were both so well known that the manner in which they ultimately were narrated converged? If there were *not* originally two distinct texts, then we must offer a reasonable reconstruction of how the later edition derived and diverged from the earlier. Was the original version of the story already somewhat authoritative before its appropriation by the later version? Did the original remain known or preserved after its appropriation? Or can we reasonably suggest that its existence was forgotten soon after the appropriation?

Miller argued that the two stories existed independently and contemporaneously as "parallel traditions" that "dovetailed" in chs. 13–14.[227] This

227 Miller, "Saul's Rise," 162–65.

solution to the problem takes seriously the attribution of the victory over the Philistine garrison in Geba[228] (נצ׳ב פלשתים אשר בגבע; v. 3, see also the similar locution in v. 4) to both Jonathan (v. 3) and Saul (v. 4). He argues that the sites named in both traditions, Geba in the present text and Gibeah in the hypothetical tradition, were actually the same city and therefore that the parallel traditions were probably based on the same recollected historical event.[229] However, Miller's proposal does not take into account the very close correspondence in the lexicology and phraseology of the NSR_B with the present text of 14:1–15. Nor does it take into consideration the tradition- and redaction-history of the surrounding textual material, evidence that can under no circumstances be left out of a critical study of the "dovetailed" traditions.

I have demonstrated above that in at least five instances the Jonathan tradition(s) in 1 Samuel 14 (even when limited to the scant 11 verses: vv. 6–15) uses lexemes or verbal locutions that appear, often identically, in the demonstrably original elements of the folktale concerning Saul in 9:1–10:16*. In fact, two of the lexical and formal similarities between the two texts I discerned above are quite rare in biblical Hebrew. In the DtrH, the series (וְ) לְכָה + 1.c.pl. cohortative appears four times in the verses mentioned above (9:5,10; 14:1,6) and only once more:

ויאמר יהונתן אל־דוד לְכָה וְנֵצֵא השׂדה...
"Jonathan said to David, 'Come on, let's go out to the field....'" (1 Sam 20:11)

This verse is part of a larger episode, 1 Sam 20:11–17, that seems to be a secondarily inserted internal doublet of the story in which Jonathan informs David of Saul's impending wrath by shooting an arrow over David's head (20:1–10,18–42), wrought by a redactor subsequent to the combination of the HDR_2 and SSN.[230] If I am correct in the relative dating of all these texts, the author of 20:11 would presumably have had both 9:1–10:16 and 14:6–15 (and possibly 14:1, which itself is derivative of v. 6) available, although not necessarily contained in the text of that author's own creation. The fact that the only original uses (9:5,10; 14:6) of this sequence in the entire DtrH appear in precisely the texts under investigation is indicative of the strong lexical relationship between them. Furthermore, the structure עֲשֵׂה כל אשׁר + verb + body part that was found in 10:7 and 14:7 appears in only three other places in the Bible (two of which are the nearly identical: 2 Sam 7:3 and 1 Chr 17:2):

---

228 But see n. 191 above, suggesting that this should be read גבעה.

229 Miller, "Saul's Rise," 163–64.

230 See §5.4.1. Notice the long orthography used in Jonathan's name in 1 Samuel 14: (i.e., יהונתן over against the shorter יונתן); Campbell expressed confusion over this circumstance (*1 Samuel*, 145); see below for its explanation.

כל אשׁר בלבבך לך עֲשֵׂה כי יהוה עמך (2 Sam 7:3 = 1 Chr 17:2[231])
"Go, do all that is in your heart because the Lord is with you."[232]

כל אשׁר תמצא ידך לעשׂות בכחך עֲשֵׂה... (Eccl 9:10)
"Do with your strength[233] all that your hand finds to do...."

The first of these, the oracle in support of the Davidic dynasty, would obviously have had the NSR_B command in 10:7 at hand as its confirmation of divine support.[234] The second, clearly an adage, shared popular imagery with 1 Sam 10:7 (cf. Lev 12:8; 25:28; 1 Sam 25:8; Judg 9:33; Isa 10:10[235]) but is most likely only distantly related and need not be studied further in this context. Even if we loosen the restriction of those passages in which the word כל may reasonably be reconstructed, yielding the sequence עֲשֵׂה אשׁר + verb + body part, we add only two more occurrences:[236]

עשׂה לי כאשׁר יצא מפיך...
"Do to me that which came out of your mouth...." (Judg 11:36)

...ועשׂה־לו את אשׁר־טוב בעיניך...
"...and do to him what is good in your eyes." (2 Sam 19:38).

Yet, both of these remove the named bodily organ from the position of the subject and force both "eyes" and "mouth" into prepositional phrases. The structure here differs too greatly to be included with 1 Sam 10:7 and 14:7, which remain the only apparently original (i.e., excluding the derivative 2 Sam 7:3) passages employing the sequence עֲשֵׂה כל אשׁר + verb + body part in the DtrH. The folktale in 9:1–10:16* prepares the reader for an episode much like 14:6–15: the protagonist's single-handed siege (with a single side-kick) of a Philistine garrison. Not only do the two passages fit

---

231 1 Chr 17:2 uses האלהים rather than the tetragrammaton. Cf. 1 Sam 10:7.

232 The presence of the imperative לך in this passage may give some indication as to the corruption in 14:7, which resulted in the sequence עשׂה כל־אשׁר בלבבך נטה לך rather than the Vorlage of LXX^L reconstructed by McCarter (*I Samuel*, 235–36; see n. 225 above): עשׂה אשׁר לבבך נטה לו. LXX^B preserves an original כל, but this may also have been a mistake for לך somewhere in the command. The situation would have been even more complicated if both כל and לך were to be found in the command, given the preponderance of כ's and ל's in the reconstructed *Vorlage*: לך עשׂה כל אשׁר לבבך נטה לו כלבבי כלבבך.

233 For "with your strength" as an adverbial modifier of the imperative "Do," see Choon-Leong Seow, *Ecclesiastes: A New Translation with Introduction and Commentary* (AB 18C; New York: Doubleday, 1997), 302.

234 Notice, however, that 10:7 uses האלהים rather than the tetragrammaton (cf. 1 Chr 17:2 and n. 231 above).

235 Seow, *Ecclesiastes*, 302, 306.

236 The command form of וְ + 2.m.s. imperfect found in Judg 9:33 (ועשׂית לו כאשׁר תמצא ידך) is a pertinent comparison for most exercises. It also lends credence to the assumption that Saul's task is a military one, since its reference is to destroying an army in a hostile engagement. However, the form of Judg 9:33 departs too greatly from the current inquiry to be of diagnostic value. See also 1 Sam 25:8; Isa 10:10.

together thematically, but they even stand apart from the remainder of the DtrH lexically and syntactically.

In response to Miller's postulation of two independent but similar traditions that have been dovetailed, we may, then, say the following: it is certainly possible that the supposed parallel traditions of Saul's and Jonathan's respective attacks on a Philistine garrison were both popular enough that the way in which they came to be written down was dramatically similar. It would, in fact, be very difficult to disprove this solution conclusively, given the fluidity with which traditions may develop and influence one another before their commitment to a solidified text, for even after texts have been written down they remain malleable, and one can easily speculate on the reasons that the biblical authors may have cited when discarding the tradition of Saul's seizure of Gibeah. But several arguments mitigate the probability of two independent stories. First and foremost, the redactional insertion of the NSR_A (Saul's rescue of Jabesh), in which Saul's kingship is justified by his own heroic action and confirmed by the people (rather than simply predicted by a nameless seer and witnessed by no one), could only have been made at some point prior to the hypothesized ending of the NSR_B (which, if I have properly reconstructed the broad plot of the text, features Saul's seizure of Gibeah to act as the capital of his new kingdom). However, in its comportment with the traditional location of Saul's dynasty at Gibeah, the NSR_A already featured that city as Saul's hometown (11:4), making its seizure in the original ending of the NSR_B quite problematic. According to the viewpoint that posits a conflate text of two independent traditions, this problem would necessarily have been solved by the omission of the Saul-tradition and the concomitant rewriting of the extant Jonathan tradition towards the linguistic style of the Saul text. But although this proposition establishes a sequence of textualization providing an adequate relative chronology for the conflation of the respective Saul and Jonathan traditions, it does not effectively deal with the problem of the source division of the remainder of the DtrH.

The source division of that corpus that has been proposed in this study can provide a more compelling answer: the reconstructed ending of the NSR_B based solely upon the portions of the folktale that remain in the present text of 9:1–10:16* anticipates both the themes and the lexical and syntactic structures found in 14:6–15, and there are orthographic indications in the latter passage that a later editor has identified the protagonist as Jonathan rather than Saul. To begin with, the original ending of the folktale, which has been crystallized as 14:6–15, would have needed very few textual adjustments in order to reshape the narrative around Jonathan and his armor-bearer:

(a) the emendation of נער to נשׂא כליו in vv. 6 (in which נער remained for some reason),7,12(2x),13(2x),14.
(b) the change of נצ׳ב to מצב in vv. 6,11,12 (המצבה),15.[237]
(c) the probable change to כי־נתנם יהוה ביד ישׂראל from an original כי־נתנם אלהים בידנו in v. 12.

And, most importantly,

(d) the emendation of the protagonist's name from Saul to Jonathan in vv. 6,8,12 (2x),13 (2x),14.

It is possible that evidence of this last emendation is to be discerned in the alternate spellings of Jonathan's name in 1 Samuel 13–2 Samuel 21. The shorter form יונתן is the less common spelling of this individual's name, occurring in 1 Sam 13:2,3,16,22(2x); 14:1,3,4,12(2x),13(2x),14,17,21,27, 29,39,40,41,42(2x),43(2x),44,45(2x),49; 19:1a. This comprises 31 of the 90-some times that Jonathan son of Saul is mentioned in 1 Samuel 13–2 Samuel 21. It is striking that nearly all the occurrences of this shorter form of Jonathan's name are located in 1 Samuel 13–14,[238] precisely those chapters that seem to be a congeries of traditions compiled with the purpose of discrediting Saul and elevating Jonathan so that the latter's recognition of David in the ensuing chapters may supply legitimacy to the upstart Bethlehemite king.

In short, I find it quite doubtful that the respective Saul (9:1–10:16* + ending) and Jonathan (14:6–15) traditions existed independently. I therefore suggest that the ending of the original donkey-folktale, i.e., Saul's storming of a Philistine garrison at Gibeah, has been secondarily emended to be a story concerning Jonathan's attack on a Philistine post at Michmash. I suggest the appropriation of an original (featuring Saul) by careful textual editing to fulfill a new purpose.[239] The redactional history must have occurred in a relatively constrained series of events and can be related to the development of the remainder of the books of Samuel as sketched out here.

237 This is, however, more likely the product of an inadvertent transposition because of the oral-written interface during the development of the text and is thus most likely a non-essential cognitive variant; see David M. Carr, "Empirische Perspektiven auf das Deuteronomistische Geschichtswerk," in *Die deuteronomistischen Geschichtswerke: Redaktions- und religionsgeschichtliche Perspektiven zur "Deuteronomismus"-Diskussion in Tora und Vorderen Propheten* (ed. Markus Witte et al.; BZAW 365; Berlin: de Gruyter, 2006), 1–17.

238 Compare the mere two times in those chapters (14:6,8) that the name appears in its longer spelling יהונתן.

239 *Contra* Miller's suggestion of "parallel traditions" ("Saul's Rise," 162–65).

7.4. The Development of 1 Samuel 13–14*: A Summary

Important to consider is the clear division of themes with respect to the HDR_1 and its near-mirror-image HDR_2. The former demonstrates a heavy reliance upon the NSR_{AB} to fuel the legitimacy of any dynastic monarchy—even a monarchy rooted in Davidic stock. In order to transfer the legitimacy garnered by the Saulide family to the Davidide rulers of Judah, the HDR_2 used David's friendship with Jonathan (1 Sam 18:1) as a literary construct that most likely had little basis in historical events (§6.4). The two traditions (HDR_1 and HDR_2) clearly arose independently of one another and remained separate until sometime after the division of the kingdom.

The question then arises as to whether a source-critical reconstruction might alleviate the problem posed by Miller's theory of "parallel traditions." On a theory of early dovetailing, an episode relating Saul's seizure of Gibeah at the end of the NSR_B became superfluous at the time of that text's combination with the NSR_A and was jettisoned shortly thereafter in favor of an independent story narrating Jonathan's attack on Michmash (now found in 1 Samuel 14*). But this source-critical reconstruction poses a serious problem to the posited bifurcation of sources in that it incorporates a Jonathan-based narrative into the early formative text of the NSR_{AB} (and consequently, into the HDR_1 from which Jonathan's other appearances may be safely omitted with no ill effects on the integrity of the text). Obviously, this reconstruction is difficult: if David's fidelity to Mephibosheth ben-Saul (2 Samuel 9*) was merely a literary construct introduced along with Langlamet's other Benjaminite episodes (e.g., 2 Sam 16:1–14;* 19:17–41*; see §5.3.4.1) and Jonathan himself completely integral to the HDR_2 (2 Samuel 1*) but entirely superfluous to the HDR_1 (1 Samuel 31*; see §§6.3–4), then any solution arbitrarily introducing a heroic Jonathan into the independent NSR_{AB} + HDR_1 complex interpolates that character into the wrong complex. In opposition, Jonathan's appearance in 1 Samuel 13–14* must continue to be grouped with episodes belonging to the HDR_2, which features substantially the same courageous character of high stature. As was seen in §6.3.1.2, though, 1 Sam 17:12* (emended) comprises an adequate introduction the HDR_2, which does not presuppose more than passing acquaintance with the characters of Saul and Abner. Equally problematic is the fact that this attribution would leave the NSR_{AB} still without a suitable ending until the combination of the NSR_{AB} + HDR_1 and HDR_2 + SSN complexes.

Far more likely is the scenario in which the original ending of the NSR_B—in which Saul and his *naʿar* stormed Gibeah—underwent the redactional transfer of the narrative's protagonist from Saul to Jonathan, perhaps as early as the introduction of the other Benjaminite episodes in the SSN and thus possibly at the hands of the editor who combined the HDR_1 and HDR_2 + SSN, since only the latter complex knew of Jonathan as anything more than one of Saul's three sons with whom he died on Gilboa. Alternatively, this shift of 1 Samuel 13–14's hero from Saul to Jonathan occurred at the time when the later editor, identified above as Dtr (= DtrG/Dtr^1), added the Covenant passages (1 Sam 20:11–17, etc.). Since 1 Samuel 13–14* does not seem to anticipate any covenant between David and Jonathan, the former attribution seems the more likely. If we collapse the number of redactors to the minimum number possible, this assignment of the pro-Jonathan emendations of 1 Samuel 13–14* would suggest that it was the editor of the PR who also combined the two major textual complexes (NSR_{AB} + HDR_1 over against HDR_2 + SSN) and simultaneously added the Benjaminite episodes. I find it more plausible, however, that the Benjaminite episodes of 2 Samuel had already been incorporated in the HDR_2 + SSN complex by the time of its inclusion in the PR, for reasons which will become clear in the fuller reconstruction of 1–2 Samuel's composition history presented in the following chapter.

8. Conclusion: A Composite Motif

8.1. Composition History of 1 Samuel 9–1 Kings 2*

The preceding chapters have provided a hypothesis of the development of the book of Samuel. Despite the length of the study, it can only be said that this has been a sketch of the hypothesis. Books of similar length dealing with much more narrowly defined sections of the corpus will naturally have handled those sections in greater detail and with greater attention to the previous secondary literature. Several important passages remain unexamined in the present work (e.g., the rejection passages in 1 Samuel 13:7b–15; 15:1–25); without a thorough examination of such passages as these, the present study remains somewhat provisional in nature. Moreover, as an attempt at a larger synthetic offering that also seeks to engage a range of theoretical and methodological perspectives, this book will undoubtedly appear overly elaborate to some and hopelessly simplistic to others. Nonetheless, I hope that I have been able to craft a reasoned and sustainable argument for the early genesis of the traditions now preserved in 1 Samuel 9–1 Kings 2, as well as the long process of transmission, redaction, and reinterpretation these traditions underwent as part of the larger development of the Deuteronomistic History as a whole. If the various principles and attributions I have outlined here may be taken as proscriptive, it is possible to trace the developmental stages through which the traditions of 1–2 Samuel passed.

The first stage was comprised of relatively short, independent traditions constituting small anecdotes supporting certain political or religious regimes. Only towards the end of this stage did larger collections of material begin to take shape (e.g., the HDR_1 and HDR_2). If my dating of each constituent tradition is correct, the following constituent texts developed in the predominantly text-supported oral milieu of the early- to mid-10th cent.:

(a) *Deliverer-Narrative of Saul's Rise (NSR_A)*: The earliest traditions to have developed were short narratives relating the successes of a Benjaminite hero named Saul. One of these stories was a deliverer-type narrative of Saul's rise (the NSR_A; §7.3.1; 1 Sam 11:1–11*, [15aα*]). As is typical of other deliverer narratives, the protagonist learns of a foreign threat and acts decisively to alleviate that menace. In this case, the threat occurs in the northern portion of Israelite

Transjordan, and the muster occurs in northern Cisjordanian Manasseh. Thus, the geography of the narrative does not sit well in a Benjaminite hero-tale, no matter how thoroughly Saul (e.g., vv. 5,6, etc.) and his hometown Gibeah (v. 4) seem to feature in it. Instead, it seems more probable that the story originated as an originally oral deliverer-narrative of an unknown, Manassite hero of the so-called pre-monarchic period and was only secondarily applied to Saul sometime after that tribal dignitary (or warlord) had secured power over a swath of the central Israelite high country.

(b) *Narrative of Saul's Rise (NSR$_B$)*: The other narrative (§7.3.2) developed as an etiological folktale telling the story of how a young man on an errand inadvertently traverses the territory he will someday control and then meets a seer who convinces him to perform an act of heroism (ca. 1 Sam 9:1–2a,4–8,10–12aβ,14abα,18*,19,22–24,25–27*; 10:2–5a,7,14–16*; 14:6–16*). This tradition would presumably have developed in an oral setting sometime during Saul's reign, given its reminiscence of that king's heroism. These two stories continued to exist independently throughout the reign of the king they were meant to legitimize.

(c) *Ark Narrative (AN)*: Sometime during the 10th cent., the Shilonite lineage of local holy men, or a closely related lineage at least, produced a tale involving the peregrinations of the cultic implement serving as the central object of veneration in their patrilineal community. This tale has not been examined in detail above but in its basic scope underlies 1 Sam 4:1–7:1*. It remained tied to the Shilonite lineage and, thus, remained independent for some time.

(d) *First History of David's Rise (HDR$_1$)*: The rise of a rival warlord in Judah occasioned the formation of a competing body of laudatory literature. A loose collection of stories—all of which potentially hung together as part of a whole but none of which was entirely indispensable in a recitation—gathered around the figure of David (the HDR$_1$). This collection of episodes featured the youth's introduction to Saul's court as a harpist (1 Sam 16:14–23), his defeat of a Philistine warrior (17:1–11,32–40,42–48a,49,51–54), and his marriage to the king's daughter (18:6aβb*–8a*,9,12a,13–16,20–21a,22–26a,27–29a). A cycle of stories concerning his escape from an attempt on his life (19:8–17*) and his time in the desert (21:2–16*; 22:[6–8],9–23; 23:1–13*; 24:1–23*; 28:3–25*; 31:1–13; 2 Sam 2:4b + 21:12,13a*,14aα*; 5:[4–5],6–10[13–16]; 21:1–6*,8–11,13b,14*) was also available for recital. Already at an early stage in this collection's growth, it knew of both the NSR$_A$ and the NSR$_B$, possibly already combined together as a diptych-type tradition in which two separate heroic portrayals augmented one another. It is unclear when, exactly, the combination of these two independent sources would have been made; it is likewise unclear whether the combined source of the NSR_{AB} (9:1–10:16* + 11:1–11*,15* + 14:6–16*) would ever have existed independently of the HDR_1 in this order; it is quite probable that it did not, although the opening scenes of the HDR_1 ending (1 Sam 31:11–13 + 2 Sam 2:4b + 21:12,13a*,14aα*) assumed the integral connection between Saul's family and Jabesh-gilead.

(e) *Second History of David's Rise (HDR_2)*: By the late-10th cent., another loose collection of pro-Davidic material had entered the political arena. This collection presented David in a much more positive light than had the relatively ambivalent HDR_1. This narrative corpus also told of David's defeat of Goliath (1 Sam 17:12*[emended],13–14,16–18,20–23a,24–30,41,48b,[50],55–58), but this narrative introduced David as the protagonist in its first lines (vv. 12–14) and did not presuppose any previous material in 1 Samuel. This loose collection included episodes in which David and Jonathan become fast friends (18:1–2,[3],4–5,8b), David is promoted to the head of the army (vv. 12b), and David is offered—and then loses—the hand of Saul's daughter in marriage (vv. 17–18*,[29b–30]). Here, too, David escapes into the wilderness and remains there until Saul's death on Gilboa (e.g., 19:1–7; 20:1–4,18–22, 24–39; 21:1; 23:14aβ–15; 23:19–28*; 26:1–25*; 27:1–28:2*; 29:1–30:31*; 2 Sam 1:1–27; [2:1–4a]).

(f) *Report of Battle Against Absalom*: By the time the Solomonic Court had established itself, a short report of the battle between David's forces and Absalom's was in circulation (2 Sam [13:1–29,34a,37aβ, 38b–39; 14:33aβγb; 15:1–6,13]; 18:1–2a,4b,6–9,15b–18). This report may have detailed a battle in Cisjordan initially (see §5.3.3 for discussion), but if so, it was soon overlaid with a framework shifting the location of the battle eastward into Transjordan (2 Sam 15:7–12*,14–37* + 16:15–17:29* + 18:19–19:16*). In this combined version, David now responded to the gathering threat posed by Absalom by leaving Jerusalem and taking refuge in Mahanaim. Unfortunately, it is nearly impossible to know whether this addition is a historically accurate reminiscence of an exile imposed upon the king—even if originally unrelated to and only secondarily conflated with Absalom's rebellion—or merely a literary construct framed through communal memory of Ishbosheth's similarly imposed exile in Transjordan.

The second stage of growth, consisting of the combination and elaboration of these primary traditions, overlapped to some extent with the first phase, insofar as the NSR_{AB} + HDR_1 complex had already coagulated by the end of the 10th cent. At the same time, the Report of the Battle Against Absalom was undergoing a series of successive elaborations, reinterpretations, and reframings. Toward the end of the 10th cent., the addition of the Solomonic Apology (SA), comprising 2 Sam 11:1–27*; 12:(15b–23),24–25*; 1 Kings 1–2*, transformed an already developing pro-Davidide CH into a document of political advantage for Solomon. Circulation of the document must have been minimal, but its argument was essential to the continued constitution of the Judahite hegemony over Benjamin and the tribes of the central hill country: the text argued for the legitimacy of Solomon over against his brothers and the resurgent Benjaminite, Ephraimite, and Manassite lineages vying for political autonomy. This autonomy may already have been *de facto*, although not *de jure*. Several additions were plausibly made in the face of the polity's impending or increasing fragmentation, including a series of episodes providing Absalom with further cause for revolution (2 Samuel 13 + 14*) and Sheba with a fitting ending (2 Samuel 20*). By hearkening back to several earlier conflicts, the text now served as a transparent threat to those both within and outside of the Judahite lineage system who would seek a greater level of independence from the unstable crown. I find it most likely that the Benjaminite episodes (2 Samuel 2–4*; 9*; 16:1–14*; 19:17–41*) would have been introduced at this time, such that the burgeoning complex now comprised an authentic Court History (CH) that continued to grow around the SA, much as a tree, constrained by an encroaching fence or sign post, will eventually begin to grow around the obstruction. This textual aggregate was by necessity joined conceptually with the HDR_2, which detailed the lives of many of the same figures and provided a rationale for the transfer of Jonathan's rightful inheritance of the crown to the Davidic dynasty. This HDR_2 + SSN complex presented a much more refined David than the one to be examined shortly. This complex lionizes a David whose good fortune brings him to the battlefield, where, coincidentally, he hears a Philistine warrior's imprecations and engages the warrior in a duel. Afterwards, the hero experiences a dramatic rise and is met with good fortune at every turn. Foremost among his fortunate encounters is the one wherein he and his soldiers are told to turn back from the Philistine column upon their approach to the battle at Mt. Gilboa (1 Sam 29:2–11*): this insulting dismissal provides David with a necessary and convenient alibi for Saul's death. Because of his close personal relationship with the deceased crown prince Jonathan, David's claim to the throne is equally strong as that of Ishbosheth—argues the text—who is next in line to the throne. After securing the throne, David and his court suppress two rebellions and, finally, are subjected to an agonizing civil dispute between rival claimants to the throne. This text, all told, encompassed a large swath of 1–2 Samuel: 1 Sam 17:12*(emended),13–14,16–18,20–23a,24–30, 41,48b,(50),55–58; 18:1–2,(3),4–5,8b; 19:1–7*; 20:1–4*,18–22*,24–39*; 21:1; 23:14aβ–15; 23:19–28*; 26:1–25*; 27:1–28:2*; 29:1–30:31*; 2 Sam 1:1–27*; 2–4*; 9*; 11:2–27*; 12:(15b–23),24–25; 13–14*; 15–20*; 1 Kings 1–2*

The earlier of the two narrative complexes, the NSR_{AB} + HDR_1 aggregations, contained roughly 1 Sam 9:1–10:16* + 11:1–11*,15* + 14:6–16* +14:52 + 17:1–11,32–40,42–48a,49,51–54; 18:6aβb*–8a*,9,12a,13–16, 20–21a,22–26a,27–29a; 19:8–17*; 21:2–16*; 22:(6–8),9–23; 23:1–13*; 24:1–23*; 28:3–25*; 31:1–13; 2 Sam 2:4b + 21:12,13a*,14aα*; 5:(4–5),6–10(13–16); 21:1–6*,8–11,13b,14*. In addition, there was most likely an early form of Saul's rejection, as hypothesized by A. F. Campbell (ca. 1 Sam 15:1aα,2–9,13–15,17a,18–22,24–25,31–35a).[1] This complex detailed first the rise and fall of the Benjaminite strongman Saul. The insertion of the NSR_A into the NSR_B justified openly to the people Saul's chieftaincy in the familiar terms of the deliverer narratives and simultaneously rendered Saul's storming of Gibeah extraneous and redundant (§§7.3.2.4; 7.4; cf. his location at Gibeah in 11:4). The episode concerning the storming of Gibeah (14:6–15*) was displaced until after the acclamation of the new king in 11:15aα* because it no longer had any bearing on the events of the HDR_1 at that time. Whether it remained an account of the "storming of Gibeah" is uncertain, but the passage, isolated as the minimal unit forming the conclusion to the NSR_B, contains no geographic references that would definitively identify the city. The site of the battle could therefore have remained anonymous.[2] This large complex also related Saul's fall and the chronologically overlapping ascendance of the Judahite chieftain David and, finally, ended with the latter's solidification of power over the Judahite tribal possession—an admittedly vague and nebulous concept—and his elimination of Saulide rivals. This narrative was gritty, emphasizing the hero's derring-do and providing meager apology for his ruthless liquidation of those opposed to his rule (e.g., 2 Sam 21:1–6,8–11,13b,14*). The composite text (NSR_{AB} + HDR_1) was most likely assembled during the late stages of David's reign in order to legitimize the Davidic successor to the throne, whether that was intended to be Solomon or Adonijah, and would have existed as such throughout Solomon's reign, even after the composition of the much more monolithic HDR_2 + SSN complex. At the beginning of the 9th cent., therefore, two relatively large textual complexes

1 Antony F. Campbell, *Of Prophets and Kings: A Late Ninth-Century Document (1 Samuel 1–2 Kings 10)* (CBQMS 17; Washington DC: Catholic Biblical Association of America, 1986), 68–69.

2 Compare the lack of explicit (and familiar) geographical references postulated for the pre-redaction stratum of 9:1–10:16.

justifying the now entrenched Davidite monarchy were circulating in Judah, albeit most likely among only a few scribal lineages.

The third and final pre-Deuteronomistic stage was the consolidation of what has been deemed so far the "Prophetic Record." This section of the total corpus resulted from the combination and redactional interpretation of the two main complexes discussed so far, as well as an initial attempt at incorporating the Ark Narrative (thus, AN + NSR_{AB} + HDR_1 + HDR_2 + SSN), and extended throughout 1 Samuel 4–1 Kings 2*. If Campbell's hypothesis is correct in its fundamentals, and I believe it is, then the full document reached from 1 Samuel 1 as far as 2 Kings 9 or 10. A full list of the small emendations superimposed on or threaded into the constituent texts would be too cumbersome for the scope of the present chapter, but they include the prophetic overlay in 1 Sam 9:1–10:16* (especially, 10:1); 15*; and 28*. Moreover, this redactor-compiler also crafted several episodes specifically for their context: among these are 1 Sam 16:1–13; 1 Kgs 12:1–15a*; and possibly 2 Samuel 6*, although the redactor's work may be limited to 6:16,20–23 if an earlier document was appropriated.

In any case, the redactor was fairly limited in the creativity that could be displayed while still preserving the basic form of the two HDR traditions as they had been received. The doublets fell naturally and easily into several pairs: the introduction of David into Saul's court; the gradual failure of their relationship and the rescue of David by one of Saul's children; David's flight in the wilderness and Philistine sojourn; and finally, the death of Saul. Yet the narratives of Saul and Jonathan preceding the introduction of the usurper David into the Benjaminite court (i.e., the episodes that now form 1 Sam 14:1–52) had little cognate material in the HDR_1 and were not so easily placed in the tight structuring in which Saul was anointed, led a successful attack against the Ammonites, was recognized as king, and almost immediately rejected as king. These narratives of Saul's military successes against the Philistines, mitigated in retrospect by the ultimate failure of the dynasty over against the Davidides, could only logically be placed before Saul's rejection at the hands of the prophet Samuel (1 Samuel 15*), the position in which the original ending of the NSR_B, Saul's seizure of the Philistine garrison (the original stratum of 1 Sam 14:6–15), had already fallen. Given the proclivity of the HDR_2 to elevate Jonathan's integrity over that of his father Saul,[3] it was hardly problematic to reconstruct the already extant 14:6–15 in such a way that it was recast as Jonathan's victory at Michmash. The later addition of topo-

3 E.g., David Jobling, "Jonathan: A Structural Study in 1 Samuel," in *The Sense of Biblical Narrative: Three Structural Analyses in the Old Testament (I Samuel 13–31, Numbers 11–12, I Kings 17–18)* (JSOTSup 7; Sheffield: JSOT Press, 1978), 4–25.

logical and geographical data in 14:1–5 served to relocate the tradition to Michmash and later—because of confusion, perhaps—from there to Geba (13:3). This transference of the tradition also provided a more concrete reason for Jonathan's disobedience to his father's ridiculous prohibition of eating on the day of a battle: he had not been present to hear his father's oath (14:27a). While Jonathan's storming of the garrison has now been fully incorporated into the oath and hunger-based story (14:24–31a), it seems odd that Saul should levy such a heavy penalty (i.e., death) upon "the man who eats food before the evening when [Saul has] been avenged upon [his] enemies" (האיש אשר־יאכל לחם עד־הערב ונקמתי מאיבי; v. 24), knowing that his son was not present to hear the prohibition (v. 17).[4] To summarize, the thorough reworking of the joint between the respective beginnings of the two Histories of David's Rise is apparent in the awkward and much-discussed complex of variant traditions found in 1 Samuel 9–14. As part of the prophetic redactor's reinterpretation of Saul's position within the nascent Israelite monarchy, the truncated and displaced tradition in 1 Sam 14:6–15*—which had not sat well in its context for a long time—was reworked such that Jonathan became the hero, replacing his father. This reformulation crafted a narrative that stood in greater continuity with later episodes of the HDR and prepared the reader for the transfer of the monarchy to David through Jonathan.

This large document theologized history to an extent not yet attempted during the transmission history of the text, and it explicitly subjugated the institution of kingship to God's sovereignty. However, while the themes and goals of the document described here remain in line with the model laid out by A. F. Campbell in *Of Prophets and Kings*, the document's moniker might not be fully accurate. The traditions Campbell attributed to composition of the prophetic redactor not only envision the peripatetic prophet as arbiter of the divine command (e.g., 2 Kings 9*) but also locate some of these figures at specific locales (e.g., the reworking of 1 Sam 9:1–10:16* to insinuate that the city was Ramah and the identification of Ahijah as a Shilonite in 1 Kings 11:39–49*). The geographic fixity of all the PR traditions outside of the inherited Elijah-Elisha Cycle suggests that the "prophetic" redactor was working within the confines of a priestly-prophetic lineage based at Shiloh, and perhaps a derivative filial branch in Kirjath Jearim (cf. 1 Sam 7:1). The apparent addition of the AN through

4 Of course, one may easily compare this to the vow made by Jephthah (Judg 11:30b–31). It appears that among the early charismatic leaders of Israel, it was not uncommon to have made foolish vows that needlessly jeopardized the members of one's family. But 1 Samuel 14 shows the joints of seemingly inept redaction (e.g., the odd insertion of vv. 31b–35 in which the entire people Israel breaks Saul's prohibition!), and we may therefore be justified in looking to these redactional joints as the cause of the vow in Jonathan's absence.

the formulation of at least 2 Sam 6:16,20–23 (if not the bulk of 2 Samuel 6) may confirm this judgment, if we follow B. Halpern's explicit identification of the Elide lineage at Shiloh as a local expression of Yahwism predicated on the importance of cherubim-based iconographic representation.[5] As suggested above (§4.3), these priestly lineages considered themselves instrumental in the theological-political machinery of the kingship and sought, through the formulation of the PR, to textualize and encode their particular vision of the ideal kingdom. While perhaps a minority report in late-9th and early- to mid-8th cent. Israel, it was this document that was brought south at the end of the 8th cent. following the destruction of Samaria and the concomitant collapse of the northern monarchy: the very institution on which this priestly-prophetic lineage depended for its own limited expression of power.

8.2. The pre-Deuteronomistic *Bricoleur* and the Transjordanian Landscape as Palimpsest

At the beginning of the preceding section, I laid out my understanding of the origin and compilation of sources that eventually formed the Deuteronomistic History. The process whereby these sources came to be the expression of that history may be described as an endeavor to write a historiographical text rooted in the sociopolitical situations of its diverse authors, comprising everything from folktales to royal apologetic literature and from prophetic narratives to authentic attempts at objective historiographical representation. This huge complex schematizing the span of Israelite history was thus infused with a Cisjordanian world-view that ultimately utilized the symbolic detritus of earlier sources. Moreover, cutting across the grain of the history itself and rooted precisely in the contingencies of that history (see §2.3), were three major systems of representation of the Transjordanian landscape that can be tracked in the Deuteronomistic History and correlated with specific source documents:

Individual Deliverer-Narratives. The short individual deliverer-narratives (Judges 3; 8; 12; and 1 Samuel 11) view Transjordan as a hinterland from which enemies come and back to which they must be pursued. The battles fought east of the Jordan—or even more fully developed by the narratives,

5 Baruch Halpern, "Sectionalism and the Schism," *JBL* 93 (1974): 519–32; idem, "Levitic Participation in the Reform Cult of Jeroboam I," *JBL* 95 (1976): 31–42; and Jeremy M. Hutton, "Southern, Northern, and Transjordanian Perspectives," in *Religious Diversity* (ed. John Barton and Francesca Stavrakopoulou; London: T&T Clark, forthcoming).

at the fords of the Jordan—occasion increased authority for the head figure but are not otherwise seen as metaphysically transformative. The common outlook of these stories views the journey to Transjordan in solely pragmatic terms, at the most phenomenological levels of consciousness, "typified experience" and "pragmatic motive."[6] Ehud uses the fords of the Jordan defensively, allowing them to serve as a natural fortification of his position as part of his mission to relieve Israel from Eglon's tyranny (Judg 3:15–23, esp. vv. 28–29). Like Ehud, Jephthah uses the fords of the Jordan to ensnare the retreating Ephraimites in a deadly trap snapping shut at the slip of the tongue (Judg 12:4–6). Gideon and Saul each cross the Jordan River to retaliate against the depredations of marauding Midianites and Ammonites (respectively, Judg 7:24–8:21; 1 Sam 11:1–11). In none of these cases does the narrator explicitly recognize any intentional crossing of the Jordan for any purpose *other than* military strategy. There is no hint that any of these figures had designs on the Israelite monarchy or its early precursors. Furthermore, the journey past the Jordan River does not seem to have been conceived of as transformative in and of itself; rather, it is the military victory of each figure that occasions the subsequent or correlative elevation in status.

This vision of the landscape may be correlated to the historical preeminence of small, segmentary social groups in the Iron Age I Levant. The fragmented and tribe-based corporate groups that rally to the cause of war throughout the book of Judges (and by implication in 1 Sam 11, although cf. v. 8) finds its best analogue in the period before the centralization of Israel's monarchy and most likely derives from that period—or at least remembers it with nostalgia. The systems of production and social organization that characterize the narratives exhibiting the deliverer-type vision of Transjordan are the same systems that can reasonably be reconstructed as normative for the agropastoralist highland villages (§2.1.2).

The Court History. This collection of texts presents Transjordan as a politically autonomous yet supportive region to which political figures could escape in exile, externally- or self-imposed. Historically, the exile in Transjordan seems to have served a practical purpose for the figure, and in

6 Stefan Bekaert, "Multiple Levels of Meaning and the Tension of Consciousness: How to Interpret Iron Technology in Bantua Africa," *ArchDial* 5 (1998): 6–29. The level of the typified experience is the most phenomenological level in Bekaert's model. It is at this level of operation that the subject states simply, "That's just the way it is!" Events here are conceived of as completely normal, and culture at this level designates merely an "enormous repertoire of typified experiences" (ibid., 17). The level of the pragmatic motive differs from the typified experience only insofar as the level of typified experience can be described neutrally ("I went to the store"), whereas at the level of the pragmatic motive, the subject describes the event with an outcome in mind ("I went to the store to buy food").

this regard, that landscape plays a pragmatic role in the symbolic system of the extended Court History, much as it does in the preceding category. But two concerns mitigate the similarity of this symbol system to the previous one.

First, the nuanced meaning in the Court History of Transjordan as a place of exile differs substantially from the landscape's meaning in the stories of the Judges. Ishbosheth operates his rump government from Mahanaim (2 Sam 2:8–9), and Mephibosheth is sequestered in Lo-debar for safety (9:3–5). Absalom escapes to Geshur (13:38). David flees to Mahanaim when ousted from Jerusalem (15:16–16:13; 17:27–29). In each of these cases, the exile in Transjordan permits the prospective king to live through a difficult and tumultuous time, but the outcomes of each sojourn vary. In all cases but David's, the effect of the Transjordanian incubation is illusory at best. A pair of assassins kills Ishbosheth in his bed (4:5–8). Mephibosheth is supposedly repatriated to his familial holdings but gathers little political authority, regardless of whether he desired it (9:6–13; 16:1–4; 19:25–31). Absalom returns to Jerusalem (14:23) and becomes king for a short while, but the coup becomes his undoing, and his monarchy does not endure (15:10–18:18). Only David returns from Transjordan with renewed and lasting political legitimacy, but even that triumphant return is but a Pyrrhic victory, since he has lost his own son in the battle for the kingship. This synchronically read monarch-type vision of Transjordan contained in the Court History suggests two more episodes from the Court History/Solomonic Succession Narrative complex might display a recognition of this component of the Transjordanian Motif, no matter their respective dates of composition. First, in the exile-and-return framework of the CH, Sheba flees before David's troops to Abel Beth-maakah at the very source of the Jordan River and meets his demise there (20:7,13–22). In one of the later additions to the CH, Shimei is forbidden only to cross the Kidron Valley (1 Kgs 2:37*), but he is executed for leaving town westward to chase two of his slaves who had fled to Gath (2:39–46). No matter our judgment concerning the fairness of Solomon's treatment of Shimei, the initial threat not to cross the Kidron Valley (i.e., eastward) can only be understood as a reference to the developing historical conception of Transjordan as a place of safe exile.

Second, while the return to the Cisjordan could be accompanied by ignominious death or unqualified wealth and power, there is no evidence to suggest the historical figures themselves ever envisioned a transformative element to the Transjordanian sojourn: the exile, if historical, was always pragmatic. I have argued above that the formation of the CH/SSN might be located within the historical events that occasioned the necessity of each layer of redaction (e.g., §2.3). In short, Ishbosheth's historical flight to

Transjordan may have occasioned the historiographic, narrated flight of David. This narrative emplotment of the Transjordanian sojourn already recognized some degree of transformation that seemed to have occurred during David's literary stay in Mahanaim. David's desperate act of flight was ripe for a reinterpretation by the historian or novelist as a momentous occasion in the life of the community at large. This recognition on the part of the authors of that document is evidenced by the intentional structuring of the CH as a whole and of 2 Sam 15:7–17:29* + 19:9b–20:13 in particular (see above §1.2), such that David's exile in and return from Transjordan became the centerpiece of the document. The centrality of that sojourn in subsequent understandings of David's reign could no longer be understood on the purely quotidian plane and therefore garnered recognition of a stay in Transjordan as incubative. This understanding of exile in Transjordan thus went beyond the view of that landform espoused by the early individual tales of Israel's deliverers, approaching an understanding of Transjordanian exile as functioning at Bekaert's level of "Metaphysical Intervention."[7]

While the authors of the CH and SSN need not have known the stories of Gideon and Saul, the resonations between those stories and the narrative of David's return from Mahanaim become all the more pronounced in light of the metaphysically transformative nature now attributed to the journey to Transjordan. Exactly *when* the deliverer-tales were finally combined with the SSN is a matter of little consequence. Whenever this juxtaposition of the three texts occurred, the intertextual relationships between them would have occasioned new readings of all three. Whereas previously it had been the military victory that occasioned the leader's rise to power in the deliverer-tales, the new recognition of Transjordan as a place of incubative transformation provided added confirmation of the leader's legitimacy: the military victory *in Transjordan* occasioned the accession to authority. Conversely, the resonations of Saul's and Gideon's respective victories in Transjordan under the guidance of the "spirit of the Lord/God" (Judg 6:34; 1 Sam 11:6) must have brought a hint of theological consonance to Joab's victory in the Forest of Ephraim and David's successful return from Mahanaim.

Individual Legends in the Prophetic Record. Concomitant with Shishak's invasion and destruction of Mahanaim and Penuel was the conceptual failure of Transjordan as a place of exile and refuge. The tradition of Jeroboam's flight to Egypt—rather than Transjordan—shortly before this

---

7 According to Bekaert's model, explanations that rely on the working of secret or invisible beings, and in which observing the traditional rules yields the desired results, fall into the level of (meta)physical intervention ("Multiple Levels," 18).

event also would have complicated the cognitive and emotional relationships existing between the Cisjordanian population and the Transjordanian landscape. Forced to re-envision and reinvent Transjordan's narrative function known from the earlier sources, the authors and compilers of the DtrH found an answer to their problem in the prophetic material inherited from a source concerned with the prophets Elijah and Elisha, which portrayed the crossing of the Jordan itself as transformatively significant.

Jehu's anointing in the Transjordanian city of Ramoth-gilead (2 Kgs 9:1–13), inherited from the PR and a partaker in the monarch-type vision of Transjordan, seems at first to take place only at the level of the pragmatic: he is stationed there with Israel's army, fending off the Aramaeans. In this regard, Jehu's anointing seems no different than the typified experience and pragmatic motivation of the deliverer-narratives or of the metaphysical intervention seen above in David's transformation. But this impression of the function of Jehu's sojourn in Transjordan is augmented and elaborated through its juxtaposition with the prophetic narratives of Elijah and Elisha.

Elijah's initial call sends the prophet to the *W. Cherith*, a cleft on the eastern bank of the Jordan near his hometown of Tishbe. There the waters of the river quench his thirst, and even the ravens feed him (1 Kgs 17:2–6). Elisha's mystical relationship with the Jordan River is narrated in a series of scenes in which the water of the river heals skin disease (2 Kgs 5:14) and supports an iron axe-head (2 Kgs 6:6). These stories all attest to the conception in the Elijah-Elisha cycle of the liminal nature of the Jordan River's waters.[8] These stories operate on several of Bekaert's levels of consciousness: the "Gestalt" experienced by the prophetic disciple who had borrowed the faulty axe revolves around the characteristics of strength and potency exhibited by the river;[9] Na'aman's bathing in the river serves as a "metonymy" or "metaphor," using the imagery of mundane washing to express deeper notions of ritual cleansing and renewal;[10] "Codic

---

8 Rachel S. Havrelock, "The Jordan River: Crossing a Biblical Boundary" (Ph.D. diss., University of California, Berkeley, 2004).

9 Bekaert, "Multiple Levels," 19. This type of experience "occurs when a cultural unit derives its meaning partly through other cultural units with which it shares 'family resemblances'." An experiential gestalt may be a metaphor that has lost its effectiveness as such, or a metaphor may be an experiential gestalt made explicit. As an example of this category, Bekaert points to the strength of the blacksmith: "this 'strength'...is not experienced as an abstract category. Rather, strength is like a plant holding its leaves and branches up firmly, like hard and dry wood, like bitter taste, like a fist, like muscles and tendons" (ibid.). A comparative metaphor is not made explicit in this category, but the same qualities—in this case, strength—are considered to be recognizable in all members of the group.

10 Bekaert, "Multiple Levels," 20–21. Metonymy and metaphor are cases of, respectively, less or more explicit comparison of two aspects of life. The more explicit of the two, metaphor, attributes the characteristics of one thing to another: the degree to which this comparison is

Oppositions" are especially prevalent in the story of Elijah's assumption and Elisha's empowerment (2 Kgs 2:7–14).[11] The two characters cross the Jordan River at Gilgal, and Elijah's assumption to heaven is the only event narrated while on the eastern bank of the river. Afterwards, Elisha crosses westward, fully empowered through his inheritance of Elijah's mantle and two portions of the prophet's spirit. The Jordan River and Transjordan serve as undeniable liminal spaces in these stories. In this regard, the stories pick up and continue the imagery of David's crossing in 2 Samuel 19 but symbolically encode the crossing in an obvious set of codic oppositions.

No longer is the authority figure—Elijah, Elisha, or Jehu—merely the *mediator* and the *mediated* within the human community (as David was during his crossing); he is now mediated across the Jordan River through the power of God. The river itself is cut in two, and the prophets cross the riverbed dry-shod. It is now agents of the divine who mediate Elijah's ascension to heaven ("a chariot of fire and horses of fire"; 2 Kgs 2:11), and the same divine spirit mediated through Elijah's mantle enables Elisha's return to the mundane western bank. It is God's prophet Elisha whose disciple anoints Jehu in Transjordan, sanctioning the bloody coup against the Omrides.

The conjoining of the sources forming the PR juxtaposed the bulk of the episodes that together inform the Transjordanian Motif. Presumably, it was Dtr who finished the job with the addition of 2 Kings 2 and at least one version of the entry into Canaan in Joshua 3–4*. Therefore, at the time of the first edition of the DtrH, David's sojourn in Mahanaim would have been read in light of Elijah's incubation in the *W. Cherith*; Saul's campaign against the Ammonites in light of Elisha's reception of authority at the fords of Gilgal; Absalom's attempt to usurp the Judahite kingship after his stay in Geshur in light of Jehu's divine election in Ramoth-gilead. After the event of the exile, the narratives of flight and return would have provided hope for the Judahite community and probably influenced the prospective hope of Deutero-Isaiah.

If the schema I have presented in this study is correct, then the independent but complementary visions of Transjordan had been overlaid upon one another already by the end of the 7th cent., a palimpsest of signifying strata melded together in the Cisjordanian worldview. This

---

explicit (or available) is dependent upon the familiarity of the subject with the culture: "The member is never wrong."

11 Bekaert, "Multiple Levels," 21–22. Codic opposition is the realm of the explicit, objectivized system of signification from which we derive meaning by analyzing the units of opposition. This level works by positing systems of structural relationships and fitting cultural units into that system.

compilation was in effect a synthesis and flattening of several distinct systems that had all used the same polysemous *signifier* (i.e., the Transjordanian landscape) in their respective symbolic systems, but which had matched that signifier with a slightly different historically motivated *signified*. The historiographical and literary endeavor practiced by several authors in Israel's history—which only *culminated* in the work of Dtr—fused together these originally independent texts. In so doing, these three prominent symbolic conceptions of the "historical" function of the Transjordanian landscape were also spliced together to form a singular conception of that topographic and geo-political feature. By using the historical texts at hand, each Israelite redactor—perhaps even unintentionally—played the role of the *bricoleur*,[12] constructing a single developing symbolic system from earlier meaningful sets of signs. This product of *bricolage*, the landscape of Transjordan, evinces the traces of past cognitive etchings and emotive inscriptions long since dissipated. Further inspection of these pocks and scratches, however, reveals a panoply of affective engagements with the land, superimposed on one another, and only barely legible. Truly remarkable, perhaps, is the persistence of this emotional attachment to Transjordan in modern Christian and Jewish communities. Most unexpected of all is the unintended melding and transformation of various incidentally juxtaposed cognitive encounters with a place into a single whole that informs and conditions our deepest theological instincts.

12 For the *bricoleur*, see Claude Lévi-Strauss, *The Savage Mind* (Chicago: The University of Chicago Press, 1966), 17–35. Part packrat, part handyman, part jack-of-all-trades, the *bricoleur* uses materials with different original meanings (i.e., *uses*) to construct or maintain an object with a meaning other than that for which the material was originally intended. This *bricoleur*, argues Lévi-Strauss, is like the mythmaker who constantly searches the repertoire of signifier-signified sets for "useful" (i.e., *meaningful*) pairings. The new use of the pairings to which the *bricoleur* wants to adapt the materials at hand is necessarily constrained by their present form (which, itself, is derived from their previous usage): "they are drawn from the language where they already possess a sense which sets a limit on their freedom of manoeuvre" (ibid., 19). Thus, the *bricoleur* or mythmaker in this model pairs already meaningful *signifiers* with new *signifieds*, such that the sign bears a *new* meaning, *new* connotations.

Bibliography

Abel, F.-M. *Géographie de la Palestine*. 3d ed. 2 vols. Paris: Gabalda, 1967.

Ackerman, James S. "Knowing Good and Evil: A Literary Analysis of the Court History in 2 Samuel 9–20 and 1 Kings 1–2." *JBL* 109 (1990): 41–60.

Ackerman, Susan. "The Personal Is Political: Covenantal and Affectionate Love (*ʾāhēb, ʾahăbā*) in the Hebrew Bible." *VT* 52 (2002): 437–58.

Ackroyd, Peter R. *Exile and Restoration: A Study of Hebrew Thought of the Sixth Century B.C.* Philadelphia: Westminster, 1968.

________. "The Succession Narrative (so-called)." *Int* 35 (1981): 383–96.

Adam, Klaus-Peter. "Motivik, Figuren und Konzeption der Erzählung vom Absalomaufstand." Pages 183–211 in *Die deuteronomistischen Geschichtswerke: Redaktions- und religionsgeschichtliche Perspektiven zur "Deuteronomismus"-Diskussion in Tora und Vorderen Propheten*. Edited by Markus Witte et al. BZAW 365. Berlin: de Gruyter, 2006.

________. *Saul und David in der judäischen Geschichtsschreibung*. FAT I/51. Tübingen: Mohr Siebeck, 2007.

Adams, Robert McC. "The Mesopotamian Social Landscape: A View from the Frontier." Pages 1–20 in *Reconstructing Complex Societies: An Archaeological Colloquium*. BASORSup 20. Edited by Charlotte B. Moore. Cambridge, Mass.: ASOR, 1974.

Aharoni, Yohanan. *The Land of the Bible: A Historical Geography*. Rev. ed. Translated by A. F. Rainey. Philadelphia: Westminster, 1979.

Albright, William Foxwell. "The Biblical Period." Pages 1:3–69 in *The Jews: Their History, Culture, and Religion*. 2 vols. Ed. Louis Finkelstein. New York: Harper, 1949.

________. "The Israelite Conquest in the Light of Archaeology." *BASOR* 74 (1939): 11–22.

________. "Prolegomenon." Pages 1–38 in *The Book of Judges with Introduction and Notes and Notes on the Hebrew Text of the Books of Kings with an Introduction and Appendix*, by C. F. Burney. Library of Biblical Studies. New York: KTAV, 1970.

Alcaina Canosa, Celso. "Panorama crítico del circlo de Eliseo." *EstBib* 23 (1964): 217–34.

________. "Vocación de Eliseo (1 Re 19,19–21)." *EstBib* 29 (1970): 137–51.

________. "Eliseo secede a Elias (2 Re 2, 1–18)." *EstBib* 31 (1972): 321–36.

Al-Eisawi, Dawud M. "Vegetation in Jordan." Pages 45–57 in *Studies in the History and Archaeology of Jordan* 2. Edited by Adnan Hadidi. Amman: Jordanian Department of Antiquities, 1985.

Alt, Albrecht. "Das Institut im Jahre 1924." *PJ* 21 (1925): 5–58.

Alt, Albrecht. "Das Institut im Jahre 1927." *PJ* 24 (1928): 5–74.

________. "Erwägungen über die Landnahme der Israeliten in Palästina." *PJ* 35 (1939): 8–63. Repr., pages 1:126–75 in *Kleine Schriften zur Geschichte des Volkes Israel* [*KS*]. 2 vols. Munich: Beck, 1953.

________. "The Monarchy in the Kingdoms of Israel and Judah." Pages 239–60 in *Essays on Old Testament History and Religion*. Translated by R. A. Wilson. Oxford: Blackwell, 1966. Translation of "Das Königtum in den Reichen Israel und Juda." *VT* 1 (1951): 2–22. Repr., pages 2:116–34 in *KS*.

________. "The Settlement of the Israelites in Palestine." Pages 172–221 in *Essays in Old Testament History and Religion*. Translated by R. A. Wilson. Garden City, N.Y.: Doubleday, 1968. Translation of "Die Landnahme der Israeliten in Palästina." Pages 1:89–125 in *KS*.

Alter, Robert. *The David Story: A Translation with Commentary of 1 and 2 Samuel*. New York: Norton, 1999.

Ap-Thomas, D. R. "Saul's 'Uncle.'" *VT* 11 (1961): 241–45.

Arnold, Patrick M. *Gibeah: The Search for a Biblical City*. JSOTSup 79. Sheffield: JSOT Press, 1990.

Auld, A. Graeme. *Joshua, Moses and the Land: Tetrateuch-Pentateuch-Hexateuch in a Generation since 1938*. Edinburgh: T&T Clark, 1980.

________. "The Story of David and Goliath: A Test Case for Synchrony *plus* Diachrony." Pages 118–28 in *David und Saul im Widerstreit—Diachronie und Synchronie im Wettstreit: Beiträge zur Auslegung des ersten Samuelbuches*. Edited by Walter Dietrich. OBO 206. Fribourg: University Press; Göttingen: Vandenhoeck & Ruprecht, 2005.

________, and Craig Y. S. Ho. "The Making of David and Goliath." *JSOT* 56 (1992): 19–39.

Aurelius, Erik. "David's Unschuld: Die Hofgeschichte und Psalm 7." Pages 1:391–412 in *Gott und Mensch im Dialog: Festschrift für Otto Kaiser zum 80. Geburtstag*. Edited by Markus Witte. BZAW 345. 2 vols. Berlin: de Gruyter, 2004.

________. "Wie David ursprünglich zu Saul kam (1 Sam 17)." Pages 44–68 in *Vergegenwärtigung des Alten Testaments: Beiträge zur biblischen Hermeneutik*. Edited by Christoph Bultmann, Walter Dietrich, and Christoph Levin. Göttingen: Vandenhoeck & Ruprecht, 2002.

________. *Zukunft jenseits des Gerichts: Eine redaktionsgeschichtliche Studie zum Enneateuch*. BZAW 319. Berlin: de Gruyter, 2003.

Auzou, George. *La danse devant l'arche: Étude du livre de Samuel*. ConBib 6. Paris: Éditions de l'orante, 1968.

Avioz, Michael. "The Book of Kings in Recent Research." Parts 1–2. *CurBR* 4 (2005): 11–55; 5 (2006): 11–57.

Baena, Gustavo. "El vocabulario de II Reyes 17, 7–23. 35–39." *EstBib* 32 (1973): 357–84.

________. "Carácter literario de 2 Reyes 17, 7–23." *EstBib* 33 (1974): 5–29.

________. "Carácter literario de II Reyes 17, 13. 35–39." *EstBib* 33 (1974): 157–79.

Bakon, Shimon. "Sign—אות." *JBQ* 18 (1990): 241–50.

Ball, Edward. Introduction to *The Succession to the Throne of David*, by Leonhard Rost. Translated by Michael D. Rutter and David M. Gunn. Sheffield: Almond, 1982.

Baly, Denis. *The Geography of the Bible: A Study in Historical Geography*. New York: Harper & Brothers, 1957.

________. "The Nature of Environment, with Special Relation to the Country of Jordan." Pages 19–24 in *Studies in the History and Archaeology of Jordan* 2. Edited by Adnan Hadidi. Amman: Jordanian Department of Antiquities, 1985.

________. "The Pitfalls of Biblical Geography in Relation to Jordan." Pages 123–24 in *Studies in the History and Archaeology of Jordan* 3. Edited by Adnan Hadidi. Amman: Jordanian Department of Antiquities, 1987.

Barré, Lloyd M. *The Rhetoric of Political Persuasion: The Narrative Artistry and Political Intentions of 2 Kings 9–11*. CBQMS 20. Washington DC: Catholic Biblical Association of America, 1988.

Barrick, W. Boyd. "On the Removal of the 'High Places' in 1–2 Kings." *Bib* 55 (1974): 257–59.

Barth, Fredrik. "A General Perspective on Nomad-Sedentary Relations in the Middle East." Pages 11–21 in *The Desert and the Sown: Nomads in the Wider Society*. Edited by Cynthia Nelson. Berkeley: Institute of International Studies, University of California at Berkeley, 1973.

________. "Introduction." Pages 9–38 in *Ethnic Groups and Boundaries: The Social Organization of Cultural Difference*. Edited by Fredrik Barth. Boston: Little, Brown, 1969.

Barthélemy, Dominique. *Critique textuelle de l'ancien testament, vol. 1: Josué, Juges, Ruth, Samuel, Rois, Chroniques, Esdras, Néhémie, Esther*. OBO 50/1. Fribourg: University Press; Göttingen: Vandenhoeck & Ruprecht, 1982.

________. "La qualité du Texte Massorétique de Samuel." Pages 1–44 in *The Hebrew and Greek Texts of Samuel: 1980 Proceedings of IOSCS, Vienna*. Edited by Emanuel Tov. Jerusalem: Academon, 1980.

________. "Response." Pages 95–98 in *The Story of David and Goliath: Textual and Literary Criticism*. Edited by Dominique Barthélemy et al. OBO 73. Fribourg: University Press; Göttingen: Vandenhoeck & Ruprecht, 1986.

________. "Trois niveaux d'analyse (à propos de David et Goliath)." Pages 47–54 in *The Story of David and Goliath: Textual and Literary Criticism*. Edited by Dominique Barthélemy et al. OBO 73. Fribourg: University Press; Göttingen: Vandenhoeck & Ruprecht, 1986.

Bartlett, J. R. "Sihon and Og, Kings of the Amorites." *VT* 20 (1970): 257–77.

Bateson, Mary Catherine. "Ritualization: A Study in Texture and Texture Change." Pages 150–65 in *Religious Movements in Contemporary America*. Edited by Irving I. Zaretsky and Mark P. Leone. Princeton, N.J.: Princeton University Press, 1974.

Becker, Uwe. *Richterzeit und Königtum: Redaktionsgeschichtliche Studien zum Richterbuch*. BZAW 192. Berlin: de Gruyter, 1990.

Becking, Bob. "Did Jehu Write the Tel Dan Inscription?" *SJOT* 13 (1999): 187–201.

Bekaert, Stefan. "Multiple Levels of Meaning and the Tension of Consciousness: How to Interpret Iron Technology in Bantua Africa." *ArchDial* 5 (1998): 6–29.

Bell, Catherine. *Ritual Theory, Ritual Practice*. New York: Oxford University Press, 1992.

Ben-Barak, Zafrira. "Meribaal and the System of Land Grants in Ancient Israel." *Bib* 62 (1981): 73–91.

Ben Nahum, Yonathan. "What Ailed the Son of Kish?" *JBQ* 19 (1991): 244–49.

Ben Zvi, Ehud. "The Account of the Reign of Manasseh in II Reg 21,1–18 and the Redactional History of the Book of Kings." *ZAW* 103 (1991): 355–74.

________. *Hosea*. FOTL 21A/1. Grand Rapids, Mich.: Eerdmans, 2005.

Bender, Barbara. "Introduction." Pages 1–18 in *Contested Landscapes: Movement, Exile and Place*. Edited by Barbara Bender and Margot Winer. Oxford: Berg, 2001.

________. "Introduction: Landscape—Meaning and Action." Pages 1–17 in *Landscape: Politics and Perspectives*. Edited by Barbara Bender. Oxford: Berg, 1993.

________. "Theorising Landscapes, and the Prehistoric Landscapes of Stonehenge." *Man* 27 (1992): 735–55.

________, Sue Hamilton, and Christopher Tilley. "Leskernick: The Biography of an Excavation." *CornArch* 34 (1995): 58–73.

________. "Leskernick: Stone Worlds; Alternative Narratives; Nested Landscapes." *PPS* 63 (1997): 147–78.

Benzinger, Immanuel. *Jahvist und Elohist in den Königsbüchern*. BWANT 27. Berlin: Kohlhammer, 1921.

Berginer, Vladimir M., and Chaim Cohen. "The Nature of Goliath's Visual Disorder and the Actual Role of His Personal Bodyguard: נֹשֵׂא הַצִּנָּה (I Sam 17:7,41)." *ANES* 43 (2006): 27–44.

Bernhardt, Karl-Heinz. "Natural Conditions and Resources in East Jordan According to Biblical Literature." Pages 179–82 in *Studies in the History and Archaeology of Jordan* 2. Edited by Adnan Hadidi. Amman: Jordanian Department of Antiquities, 1985.

Berque, Augustin. "There is Only Mount Jingting." *ArchDial* 4 (1997): 22–23.

Betts, Alison. "Pastoralism." Pages 615–19 in *The Archaeology of Jordan*. Edited by Burton MacDonald, Russell Adams, and Piotr Bienkowski. Sheffield: Sheffield Academic Press, 2001.

Bič, Miloš. "Saul sucht die Eselinnen." *VT* 7 (1957): 92–97.

Bickert, Rainer. "Die Geschichte und das Handeln Jahwes: Zur Eigenart einer deuteronomistischen Offenbarungsauffassung in den Samuelbüchern." Pages 9–27 in *Textgemäß: Aufsätze und Beiträge zur Hermeneutik des Alten Testaments*. Edited by A. H. J. Gunneweg and Otto Kaiser. Göttingen: Vandenhoeck & Ruprecht, 1979.

________. "Die List Joabs und der Sinneswandel Davids: Eine dtr bearbeitete Einschaltung in die Thronfolgeerzählung: 2 Sam. xiv 2–22." Pages 30–51 in *Studies in the Historical Books of the Old Testament*. VTSup 30. Leiden: Brill, 1979.

Bienkowski, Piotr. "The Iron Age and Persian Periods in Jordan." Pages 265–74 in *Studies in the History and Archaeology of Jordan* 7. Edited by Ghazi Bisheh. Amman: Jordanian Department of Antiquities, 2001.

________. "The North-South Divide in Ancient Jordan: Ceramics, Regionalism and Routes." Pages 93–107 in *Culture Through Objects: Ancient Near Eastern Studies in Honour of P. R. S. Moorey*. Edited by Timothy F. Potts, M. Roaf, and Diana Stein. Oxford: Griffith Institute, 2003.

Bietenhard, Sophia K. *Des Königs General: Die Heerführertraditionen in der vorstaatlichen und frühen staatlichen Zeit und die Joabgestalt in 2 Sam 2–20; 1 Kön–2*. OBO 163. Fribourg: University Press. Göttingen: Vandenhoeck & Ruprecht, 1998.

Biran, Avraham, and Joseph Naveh. "An Aramaic Stele Fragment from Tel Dan." *IEJ* 43 (1993): 81–98.

________. "The Tel Dan Inscription: A New Fragment." *IEJ* 45 (1995): 1–18.

Birch, Bruce C. "The Choosing of Saul at Mizpah." *CBQ* 37 (1975): 447–57.

________. "The Development of the Tradition on the Anointing of Saul in 1 Sam. 9:1–10:16." *JBL* 90 (1971): 55–68.

________. *The Rise of the Israelite Monarchy: The Growth and Development of 1 Samuel 7–15*. SBLDS 27. Missoula, Mont.: Scholars Press, 1976.

Blenkinsopp, Joseph. "Did Saul Make Gibeon His Capital?" *VT* 24 (1974): 1–7.

________. "Jonathan's Sacrilege." *CBQ* 26 (1964): 423–49.

________. "The Quest of the Historical Saul." Pages 75–99 in *No Famine in the Land: Studies in Honor of John L. McKenzie*. Edited by J. W. Flanagan and A. W. Robinson; Claremont: Scholars Press, 1975.

________. "Theme and Motif in the Succession History (2 Sam. xi 2ff) and the Yahwist Corpus." Pages 44–57 in *Volume du Congrès, Genève, 1965*. Edited by G. W. Anderson et al. VTSup 15. Leiden: Brill, 1966.

Boecker, Hans Jochen. *Die Beurteilung der Anfänge des Königtums in den deuteronomistischen Abschnitten des I. Samuelbuches: Ein Beitrag zum Problem des 'deuteronomistischen Geschichtswerks.'* WMANT 31. Neukirchen-Vluyn; Neukirchener Verlag, 1969.

Böhl, F. M. T. *Palestina in het licht der jongste opgravingen en onderzoekingen*. Amsterdam: Paris, 1931.

Boling, Robert G. *The Early Biblical Community in Transjordan*. SWBA 6. Sheffield: Almond, 1988.

________. *Judges: Introduction, Translation, and Commentary*. AB 6b. Garden City, N.Y.: Doubleday, 1975.

________. "Levitical History and the Role of Joshua." Pages 241–61 in *The Word of the Lord Shall Go Forth: Essays in Honor of David Noel Freedman in Celebration of His Sixtieth Birthday*. Edited by Carol L. Meyers and M. O'Connor. ASORSVS 1. Winona Lake, Ind.: Eisenbrauns, 1983.

Borger, Riekele. *Die Inschriften Asarhaddons Königs von Assyrien*. AfOB 9. Osnabrück: Biblio-Verlag, 1956. Repr., 1967.

Bourdieu, Pierre. *Outline of a Theory of Practice*. Translated by Richard Nice. Rev. and expanded ed. Cambridge: Cambridge University Press, 1977.

Braudel, Fernand. *The Mediterranean and the Mediterranean World in the Age of Philip II*. 1949. Rev. ed. Translated by Siân Reynolds; New York: Harper & Row, 1972.

Braulik, Georg. "Spuren einer Neubearbeitung des deuteronomistischen Geschichtswerkes in 1 Kön 8,52–53.59–60." *Bib* 52 (1971): 20–33.

Breasted, James Henry. *Ancient Records of Egypt*. 5 vols. London: Histories & Mysteries of Man, Ltd., 1988.

Bright, John. "The Book of Joshua: Introduction." *IB* 2:541–50.

________. *A History of Israel*. 4th ed. Louisville, Ky.: WJKP, 2000.

Brock, Sebastian P. *The Recensions of the Septuagint Version of I Samuel*. Quaderni di Henoch 9. Turin: Silvio Zamorani editore, 1996.

Brodsky, Harold. "The Jordan—Symbol of Spiritual Transition." *BRev* 8.3 (1992): 34–43, 52.

Bronner, Ethan. "Find of Ancient City Could Alter Notions of Biblical David." *New York Times*. Oct. 30, 2008. Accessed online at: http://www.nytimes.com/2008/10/30/world/middleeast/30david.html?_r=2&ref=world&oref=slogin

Brooke, A. E. and Norman McLean. *The Old Testament in Greek: According to the Text of Codex Vaticanus*. Cambridge: Cambridge University Press, 1917–1940.

Brueggemann, Walter. "The Kerygma of the Deuteronomistic Historian: Gospel for Exiles." *Int* 22 (1968): 387–402.

________. "Narrative Coherence and Theological Intentionality in 1 Samuel 18." *CBQ* 55 (1993): 225–43.

Buccellati, Giorgio. *Cities and Nations of Ancient Syria: An Essay on Political Institutions with Special Reference to the Israelite Kingdoms*. Studi Semitici 26. Rome: Instituto di Studi del Vicino Oriente, Università di Roma, 1967.

Budde, Karl. *Die Bücher Richter und Samuel, ihre Quellen und ihr Aufbau*. Giessen: Ricker, 1890.

________. *Die Bücher Samuel*. KHC 8. Tübingen: Mohr, 1902.

________. "Saul's Königswahl und Verwerfung." *ZAW* 8 (1888): 223–48.

Budry, Edmond. "Thine Is the Glory." Hymn #145 in *Lutheran Book of Worship*. Translated by R. Birch Hoyle. Minneapolis: Augsburg, 1978.

Burney, C. F. *The Book of Judges with Introduction and Notes and Notes on the Hebrew Text of the Books of Kings with an Introduction and Appendix*. Library of Biblical Studies. 1903. Repr., New York: KTAV, 1970.

Byrne, Ryan. "The Refuge of Scribalism in Iron I Palestine." *BASOR* 345 (2007): 1–31.

Campbell, Antony F. *1 Samuel*. FOTL 7. Grand Rapids, Mich.: Eerdmans, 2003.

________. *2 Samuel*. FOTL 8. Grand Rapids, Mich.: Eerdmans, 2005.

________. *The Ark Narrative (1 Sam 4–6; 2 Sam 6): A Form-Critical and Traditio-Historical Study*. SBLDS 16. Missoula, Mont.: Scholars Press, 1975.

________. "From Philistine to Throne (1 Samuel 16:14–18:16)." *ABR* 34 (1986): 35–41.

________. "Martin Noth and the Deuteronomistic History." Pages 31–62 in *The History of Israel's Traditions: The Heritage of Martin Noth*. Edited by S. L. McKenzie and M. P. Graham. JSOTSup 182. Sheffield: Sheffield Academic Press, 1994.

________. *Of Prophets and Kings: A Late Ninth-Century Document (1 Samuel 1–2 Kings 10)*. CBQMS 17. Washington DC: Catholic Biblical Association of America, 1986.

________, and M. A. O'Brien. *Unfolding the Deuteronomistic History: Origins, Upgrades, Present Text*. Minneapolis: Fortress, 2000.

Carlson, R. A. *David, the Chosen King: A Traditio-Historical Approach to the Second Book of Samuel*. Translated by Eric J. Sharpe and Stanley Rudman. Uppsala: Almqvist & Wiksell, 1964.

Carr, David M. "Empirische Perspektiven auf das Deuteronomistische Geschichtswerk." Pages 1–17 in *Die deuteronomistischen Geschichtswerke: Redaktions- und religionsgeschichtliche Perspektiven zur "Deuteronomismus"-Diskussion in Tora und Vorderen Propheten*. Edited by Markus Witte et al. BZAW 365. Berlin: de Gruyter, 2006.

________. "The Tel Zayit Abecedary in (Social) Context." Pages 113–29 in *Literate Culture and Tenth-Century Canaan: The Tel Zayit Abecedry in Context*. Edited by Ron E. Tappy and P. Kyle McCarter Jr. Winona Lake, Ind.: Eisenbrauns, 2008.

________. *Writing on the Tablet of the Heart: Origins of Scripture and Literature*. Oxford: Oxford University Press, 2005.

Casey, Edward S. "How to Get from Space to Place in a Fairly Short Stretch of Time: Phenomenological Prolegomena." Pages 13–52 in *Senses of Place*. Edited by Steven Feld and Keith H. Basso. Santa Fe, N.M.: School of American Research, 1996.

Caspari, Wilhelm. *Die Samuelbücher*. KAT 7. Leipzig: Deichert, 1926.

Certeau, Michel de. *The Practice of Everyday Life*. Translated by Steven Rendall. Berkeley and Los Angeles: University of California Press, 1984.

Chavel, Simeon. "Compositry and Creativity in 2 Samuel 21:1–14." *JBL* 122 (2003): 23–52.

Chen, Ching-Wen. "Gibeon and Saul in the Power Transition of the Early Monarchy." Pages 23–50 in *From East to West: Essays in Honor of Donald G. Bloesch*. Edited by Daniel J. Adams; Lanham: University Press of America, 1997.

Christian, Mark A. "Revisiting Levitical Authorship: What Would Moses Think?" *ZAR* 13 (2007): 194–236.

Clancy, Frank. "Shishak/Shoshenq's Travels." *JSOT* 86 (1999): 3–23.

Clements, R. E. "The Deuteronomistic Interpretation of the Founding of the Monarchy in I Sam. VIII." *VT* 24 (1974): 398–410.

________. Review of B. C. Birch, *The Rise of the Israelite Monarchy*. *JTS* 29 (1978): 507–8.

Coats, George W. "Parable, Fable, and Anecdote: Storytelling in the Succession Narrative." *Int* 35 (1981): 368–82.

Cogan, Mordechai. *I Kings: A New Translation with Introduction and Commentary*. AB 10. New York: Doubleday, 2000.

________. "Israel in Exile—The View of a Josianic Historian." *JBL* 97 (1978): 40–44.

________, and Hayim Tadmor. *II Kings: A New Translation with Introduction and Commentary*. AB 11. New York: Doubleday, 1988.

Cohen, Martin A. "The Rebellions During the Reign of David: An Inquiry into Social Dynamics in Ancient Israel." Pages 91–112 in *Studies in Jewish Bibliography, History and Literature in Honor of I. Edward Kiev*. Edited by Charles Berlin. New York: KTAV, 1971.

Cohn, Robert L. "Convention and Creativity in the Book of Kings: The Case of the Dying Monarch." *CBQ* 47 (1985): 603–16.

Conroy, Charles. *Absalom Absalom! Narrative and Language in 2 Sam 13–20*. AnBib 81. Rome: Biblical Institute Press, 1978.

Cornill, Carl Heinrich. *Einleitung in das Alte Testament*. GTW 2/1. Freiburg: Mohr Siebeck, 1891.

________. "Zur Quellenkritik der Bücher Samuelis." Pages 23–59 in *Königsberger Studien*, vol. 1. Königsberg: Hübner & Matz, 1887.

Cortese, Enzo. "Lo schema deuteronomistico per i re di Giuda e d'Israele." *Bib* 56 (1975): 37–52.

Cosgrove, Dennis E. "Geography is Everywhere: Culture and Symbolism in Human Landscapes." Pages 118–35 in *Horizons in Human Geography*. Edited by Derek Gregory and Rex Walford. Totowa, N.J.: Barnes & Noble, 1989.

________. "Inhabiting Modern Landscape." *ArchDial* 4 (1997): 23–28.

________. "Place, Landscape, and the Dialectics of Cultural Geography." *CanGeogr* 22 (1978): 66–72.

________. *Social Formation and Symbolic Landscape*. Madison, Wis.: The University of Wisconsin Press, 1984.

Coughenour, Robert A. "Preliminary Report on the Exploration and Excavation of Mugharat el Wardeh and Abu Thawab." *ADAJ* 21 (1976): 71–78, 186–89.

________. "A Search for Maḥanaim." *BASOR* 273 (1989): 57–66.

Crenshaw, J. L. "Method in Determining Wisdom Influence upon 'Historical' Literature." *JBL* 88 (1969): 129–42.

________. *Prophetic Conflict: Its Effect upon Israelite Religion*. BZAW 124. Berlin: de Gruyter, 1971.

Cross, Frank M. "The Ammonite Oppression of the Tribes of Gad and Reuben." Pages 148–58 in *History, Historiography and Interpretation: Studies in Biblical and Cuneiform Literature*. Edited by Hayim Tadmor and Moshe Weinfeld. Jerusalem: Magnes, 1983.

________. *Canaanite Myth and Hebrew Epic: Essays in the History of the Religion of Israel*. Cambridge, Mass.: Harvard University Press, 1973.

________. "Epigraphic Notes on the ᶜAmmān Citadel Inscription." *BASOR* 193 (1969): 1–13. Repr., pages 95–99 in *Leaves from an Epigrapher's Notebook: Collected Papers in Hebrew and West Semitic Paleography and Epigraphy* (HSS 51; Winona Lake, Ind.: Eisenbrauns, 2003.

________. *From Epic to Canaan: History and Literature in Ancient Israel*. Baltimore: The Johns Hopkins University Press, 1998. Pages 53–70 revised and expanded from his essay "Reuben, First-Born of Jacob." *ZAW* 100 suppl. (1988): 46–65.

________. "The Themes of the Book of Kings and the Structure of the Deuteronomistic History." Pages 274–89 in *Canaanite Myth and Hebrew Epic: Essays in the History of the Religion of Israel*. Cambridge: Harvard University Press, 1973. Repr., pages 79–94 in *Reconsidering Israel and Judah: Recent Studies on the Deuteronomistic History*. Edited by G. N. Knoppers and J. G. McConville. SBTS 8. Winona Lake, Ind.: Eisenbrauns, 2000. Originally published as "The Structure of the Deuteronomistic History." Pages 9–24 in *Perspectives in Jewish Learning*. Annual of the College of Jewish Studies 3. Chicago: College of Jewish Studies, 1968.

________, et al. *1–2 Samuel*. Vol. 12 of *Qumran Cave 4*. DJD 17. Oxford: Clarendon, 2005.

Crumley, Carole L. "Sacred Landscapes: Constructed and Conceptualized." Pages 269–76 in *Archaeologies of Landscape: Contemporary Perspectives*. Edited by Wendy Ashmore and A. Bernard Knapp. Malden, Mass.: Blackwell, 1999.

Curtis, John Briggs. "A Folk Etymology of *nābîᵓ*." *VT* 29 (1979): 491–93.

Crüsemann, Frank. *Der Widerstand gegen das Königtum: Die antiköniglichen Texte des Alten Testaments und der Kampf um den frühen israelitischen Staat*. WMANT 49. Neukirchen-Vluyn: Neukirchener Verlag, 1978.

Cryer, F. H. "David's Rise to Power and the Death of Abner: An Analysis of 1 Samuel xxvi 14–16 and Its Redaction-Critical Implications." *VT* 35 (1985): 385–94.

Dahood, Mitchell J. *Psalms I: 1–50*. AB 17. Garden City, N.Y.: Doubleday, 1966.

________. "New Readings in Lamentations." *Bib* 59 (1978) 174–97.

Dalman, Gustaf. "Jahresbericht des Deutschen Evangelischen Instituts für Altertumswissenschaft des Heiligen Landes für das Arbeitsjahr 1912/13." *PJ* 9 (1913): 1–75.

________. *Sacred Sites and Ways: Studies in the Topography of the Gospels*. Translated by Paul Philip Levertoff. New York: Macmillan, 1935.

Davies, G. Henton. "Judges viii 22–23." *VT* 13 (1963): 151–57.

Davies, Philip R. *In Search of "Ancient Israel."* JSOTSup 148. Sheffield: Sheffield Academic Press, 1992. Repr., 1999.

________. *Scribes and Schools: The Canonization of the Hebrew Scriptures*. LibAncIsr. Louisville, Ky.: WJKP, 1998.

Dawson, Andrew, and Mark Johnson. "Migration, Exile and Landscapes of the Imagination." Pages 319–32 in *Contested Landscapes: Movement, Exile and Place*. Edited by Barbara Bender and Margot Winer. Oxford: Berg, 2001.

Day, John. "Bedan, Abdon or Barak in 1 Samuel xii 11?" *VT* 43 (1993): 261–64.

De Vries, Simon J. *1 Kings*. WBC 12. Waco: Word Books, 1985.

________. "David's Victory over the Philistines as Saga and as Legend." *JBL* 92 (1973): 23–36.

Dearman, J. Andrew. "Baal in Israel: The Contribution of Some Place Names and Personal Names to an Understanding of Early Israelite Religion." Pages 173–91 in *History and Interpretation: Essays in Honour of John H. Hayes*. JSOTSup 173. Sheffield: Sheffield Academic Press, 1993.

________. *Studies in the Mesha Inscription and Moab*. Atlanta: Scholars Press, 1989.

Deflem, Mathieu. "Ritual, Anti-Structure, and Religion: A Discussion of Victor Turner's Processual Symbolic Analysis." *JSSR* 30 (1991): 1–25.

Deist, Ferdinand. "Coincidence as a Motif of Divine Intervention in 1 Samuel 9." *OTE* n.s. 6 (1993): 7–18.

Delekat, Lienhard. "Tendenz und Theologie der David-Salomo-Erzählung." Pages 26–36 in *Das ferne und nahe Wort: Festschrift Leonard Rost zur Vollendung seines 70. Lebensjahres am 30. November gewidmet*. Edited by Fritz Maass. BZAW 105. Berlin: Töpelmann, 1967.

Demsky, Aaron. "Geba, Gibeah, and Gibeon: An Historico-Geographic Riddle." *BASOR* 212 (1973): 26–31.

Dever, William G. "ʾAbel-Beth-Maʿacah: 'Northern Gateway of Ancient Israel." Pages 207–22 in *The Archaeology of Jordan and Other Studies: Presented to Siegfried H. Horn*. Edited by Lawrence T. Geraty and Larry G. Herr. Berrien Springs, Mich.: Andrews University Press, 1986.

Dhorme, Paul. *Les livres de Samuel*. Paris: Gabalda, 1910.

Dick, Michael B. "The 'History of David's Rise to Power' and the Neo-Babylonian Succession Apologies." Pages 3–19 in *David and Zion: Biblical Studies in Honor of J. J. M. Roberts*. Edited by Bernard F. Batto and Kathryn L. Roberts. Winona Lake, Ind.: Eisenbrauns, 2004.

Dietrich, Walter. "David in Überlieferung und Geschichte." *VF* 22 (1977): 44–64.

________. *David, Saul und die Propheten: Das Verhältnis von Religion und Politik nach den prophetischen Überlieferungen vom frühesten Königtum in Israel*. BWANT 122. Stuttgart: Kohlhammer, 1987.

________. *The Early Monarchy in Israel: The Tenth Century B.C.E.* Translated by Joachim Vette. SBLBibEnc 3. Atlanta: SBL, 2007. Translation of *Die frühe Königszeit in Israel: 10. Jahrhundert v. Chr*. Biblische Enzyklopädie 3. Stuttgart: Kohlhammer, 1997.

________. "Das Ende der Thronfolgegeschichte." Pages 38–69 in *Die sogenannte Thronfolgegeschichte Davids: Neue Einsichten und Anfragen*. Edited by Albert de Pury and Thomas Römer. OBO 176. Fribourg: University Press; Göttingen: Vandenhoeck & Ruprecht, 2000. Repr., pages 32–57 in *Von David zu den Deuteronomisten: Studien zu den Geschichtsüberlieferungen des Alten Testaments*. BWANT 156. Stuttgart: Kohlhammer, 2002.

________. "Die Erzählungen von David und Goliat in 1Sam 17." *ZAW* 108 (1996): 172–91. Repr., pages 58–73 in *Von David zu den Deuteronomisten: Studien zu den Geschichtsüberlieferungen des Alten Testaments*. BWANT 156. Stuttgart: Kohlhammer, 2002.

________. "Prophetie im deuteronomistischen Geschichtswerk." Pages 47–65 in *The Future of the Deuteronomistic History*. Edited by T. Römer. BETL 147. Leuven: University Press, 2000. Repr., pages 236–51 in *Von David zu den Deuteronomisten: Studien zu den Geschichtsüberlieferungen des Alten Testaments*. BWANT 156. Stuttgart: Kohlhammer, 2002.

________. *Prophetie und Geschichte: Eine redaktionsgeschichtliche Untersuchung zum deuteronomistischen Geschichtswerk*. FRLANT 108. Göttingen: Vandenhoeck & Ruprecht, 1972.

Dietrich, Walter, and Thomas Naumann. *Die Samuelbücher*. EdF 287. Darmstadt: Wissenschaftliche Buchgesellschaft, 1995.

Domar, Evsey D. "The Causes of Slavery or Serfdom: A Hypothesis." *JEconHist* 30 (1970): 18–32. Cited by Lawrence E. Stager, "Response," in *Biblical Archaeology Today: Proceedings of the International Congress on Biblical Archaeology, Jerusalem, April 1984* (Jerusalem: Israel Exploration Society, 1985), 85.

Dornemann, Rudolph H. "The Beginning of the Iron Age in Transjordan." Pages 35–40 in *Studies in the History and Archeology of Jordan* 1. Edited by Adnan Hadidi. Amman: Jordanian Department of Antiquities, 1982.

Dorsey, David A. *The Roads and Highways of Ancient Israel*. Baltimore: The Johns Hopkins University Press, 1991.

Dozeman, Thomas B. "The Way of the Man of God from Judah: True and False Prophecy in the Pre-Deuteronomic Legend of 1 Kings 13." *CBQ* 44 (1982): 379–93.

Driver, S. R. *An Introduction to the Literature of the Old Testament*. 1897. Repr., Cleveland: Meridian, 1967.

________. *Notes on the Hebrew Text of the Books of Samuel*. Oxford: Clarendon, 1890.

Edelman, Diana. "The Asherite Genealogy in 1 Chr 7:30–40." *BR* 33 (1988): 13–23.

________. "The 'Ashurites' of Eshbaal's State (2 Sam 2:9)." *PEQ* 117 (1985): 85–91.

________. "The Deuteronomistic Story of King Saul: Narrative Art or Editorial Product." Pages 207–20 in *Pentateuchal and Deuteronomistic Studies*. Edited by C. Brekelmans and J. Lust. BETL 94. Leuven: Leuven University Press, 1990.

________. "Hezekiah's Alleged Cultic Centralization." *JSOT* 32.4 (2008): 395–434.

________. *King Saul in the Historiography of Judah*. JSOTSup 121. Sheffield: JSOT Press,1991.

________. "Mahanaim." *ABD* 4:472–73.

________. "Saul's Journey through Mt. Ephraim and Samuel's Ramah (1 Sam. 9:4–5; 10:2–5)." *ZDPV* 104 (1988): 44–58.

________. "Saul's Rescue of Jabesh-Gilead (I Sam 11 1–11): Sorting Story from History." *ZAW* 96 (1984): 195–209.

Eissfeldt, Otto. "Amos und Jona in volkstümlicher Überlieferung." Pages 4:137–42 in *Kleine Schriften*. Edited by Rudolf Sellheim and Fritz Maass. 6 vols. Tübingen: Mohr Siebeck, 1962–1979.

________. "Deuteronomium und Hexateuch." *Mitteilungen des Instituts für Orientforschung* 12 (1966): 17–39. Repr., pages 4:238–58 in *Kleine Schriften*. Edited by Rudolf Sellheim and Fritz Maass. 6 vols. Tübingen: Mohr Siebeck, 1962–1979.

________. *Geschichtsschreibung im Alten Testament: Ein kritischer Bericht über die neueste Literatur dazu*. Berlin: Evangelische Verlagsanstalt, 1948.

________. "Die Geschichtswerke im Alten Testament." *TLZ* 72 (1947): 71–76.

________. *Die Komposition der Samuelisbücher*. Leipzig: Hinrichs, 1931.

________. *The Old Testament: An Introduction*. Translated by Peter R. Ackroyd. New York: Harper & Row, 1965. Translation of *Einleitung in das Alte Testament*. 3d ed. NTG. Tübingen: Mohr Siebeck, 1934.

Elitzur, Yoel. *Ancient Place Names in the Holy Land: Preservation and History*. Jerusalem: Magnes; Winona Lake, Ind.: Eisenbrauns, 2004.

Engnell, Ivan. *Gamla testamentet: En traditionshistorisk inledning*. Stockholm: Svenska Kyrkans Diakonistyrelses Bokförlag, 1945.

________. "The Pentateuch." Pages 50–67 in *A Rigid Scrutiny: Critical Essays on the Old Testament*. Edited by Ivan Engnell. Translated by John T. Willis with Helmer Ringgren. Nashville: Vanderbilt University Press, 1969. Published in Great Britain as *Critical Essays on the Old Testament*. London: SPCK, 1970.

Eppstein, Victor. "Was Saul also among the Prophets?" *ZAW* 81 (1969): 287–303.

Eslinger, Lyle. "Viewpoints and Point of View in 1 Samuel 8–12." *JSOT* 26 (1983): 61–76.

Evans, William E. "An Historical Reconstruction of the Emergence of the Israelite Kingship and the Reign of Saul." Pages 61–77 in *Scripture and Context II: More Essays in the Comparative Method*. Edited by William W. Hallo, James C. Moyer, and Leo G. Perdue. Winona Lake, Ind.: Eisenbrauns, 1983.

Eves, Terry L. "One Ammonite Invasion or Two? 1 Sam 10:27–11:2 in the Light of 4QSam[a]." *WTJ* 44 (1982): 308–26.

Eynikel, Erik. *The Reform of King Josiah and the Composition of the Deuteronomistic History*. OTS 33. Leiden: Brill, 1996.

________. "The Relation between the Eli Narratives (1 Sam. 1–4) and the Ark Narrative (1 Sam. 1–6; 2 Sam. 6:1–19)." Pages 88–106 in *Past, Present, Future: The Deuteronomistic History and the Prophets*. Edited by Johannes C. de Moor and Harry F. van Rooy. *OtSt* 44. Leiden: Brill, 2000.

Faber, Alice. "Second Harvest: *šibbōlεθ* Revisted (Yet Again)." *JSS* 37 (1992): 1–10.

Faust, Avraham. "Settlement Patterns and State Formation in Southern Samaria and the Archaeology of [a] Saul." Pages 14–38 in *Saul in Story and Tradition*. Edited by Carl S. Ehrlich with Marsha C. White. FAT I/47. Tübingen: Mohr Siebeck, 2006.

Feld, Steven, and Keith H. Basso. "Introduction." Pages 3–11 in *Senses of Place*. Edited by Steven Feld and Keith H. Basso. Santa Fe, N.M.: School of American Research, 1996.

Fenton, Terry L. "Deuteronomistic Advocacy of the *nābîʾ*: 1 Samuel ix 9 and Questions of Israelite Prophecy." *VT* 47 (1997): 23–42.

Fichtner, Johannes. *Das erste Buch von den Königen*. BAT 12/1. Stuttgart: Calwer Verlag, 1964.

Field, Frederick. *Origenis Hexaplorum*. 1867–1875. Repr., Hildesheim: Olms, 1964.

Finkelstein, Israel. *The Archaeology of the Israelite Settlement*. Jerusalem: Israel Exploration Society, 1988.

Firth, David G. "The Accession Narrative (1 Samuel 27–2 Samuel 1)." *TynBul* 58 (2007): 61–81.

Fischer, Alexander A. "Flucht und Heimkehr Davids als integraler Rahmen der Abschalomerzählung." Pages 43–69 in *Ideales Königtum: Studien zu David und Salomo*. Edited by Rüdiger Lux. ABG 16. Leipzig: Evangelische Verlagsanstalt, 2005.

________. "Die Saul-Überlieferung im deuteronomistischen Samuelbuch (am Beispiel von I Samuel 9–10)." Pages 163–81 in *Die deuteronomistischen Geschichtswerke: Redaktions- und religionsgeschichtliche Perspektiven zur "Deuteronomismus"-Diskussion in Tora und Vorderen Propheten*. Edited by Markus Witte et al. BZAW 365. Berlin: de Gruyter, 2006.

________. *Von Hebron nach Jerusalem: Eine redaktionsgeschichtliche Studie zur Erzählung von König David in II Sam 1–5*. BZAW 335. Berlin: de Gruyter, 2004.

Flanagan, James W. "Chiefs in Israel." *JSOT* 20 (1981): 47–73. Repr., pages 136–61 in *Social-Scientific Old Testament Criticism*. Edited by David J. Chalcraft. Biblical Seminar 47. Sheffield: Sheffield Academic Press, 1997.

________. "Court History or Succession Document? A Study of 2 Samuel 9–20 and 1 Kings 1–2." *JBL* 91 (1972): 172–81.

________. "Judah in All Israel." Pages 101–16 in *No Famine in the Land: Studies in Honor of John L. McKenzie*. Edited by James W. Flanagan and Anita Weisbrod Robinson. Missoula, Mont.: Scholars, 1975.

Fohrer, Georg. *Introduction to the Old Testament*. Translated by David E. Green. Nashville: Abingdon, 1968. Translation of *Einleitung in das Alte Testament*. 10th ed. Heidelberg: Quelle & Meyer, 1965.

Fokkelman, Jan P. *King David (II Sam. 9–20 & 1 Kings 1–2)*. Vol. 1 of *Narrative Art and Poetry in the Books of Samuel*. Assen: Van Gorcum, 1981.

Foresti, Fabrizio. *The Rejection of Saul in the Perspective of the Deuteronomistic School: A Study of 1 Sm 15 and Related Texts*. Studia Theologica (Teresianum) 5. Rome: Edizioni del Teresianum, 1984.

Foucault, Michel. *Discipline and Punish*. New York: Vintage, 1977.

Franken, H. J. "Deir ᶜAllâ." *EAEHL* 1:322. Cited by Jean-Baptiste Humbert, "L'occupation de l'espace à l'âge du Fer en Jordanie," in *Studies in the History and Archaeology of Jordan* 4 (ed. Muna Zaghloul et al.; Amman: Jordanian Department of Antiquities, 1992), 200.

Franken, H. J. "Deir ᶜAllā and Its Religion." Pages 25–52 in *Sacred and Sweet: Studies on the Material Culture of Tell Deir ᶜAlla and Tell Abu Sarbut*. Edited by Margreet L. Steiner and Eveline J. van der Steen. ANESSup 24. Leuven: Peeters, 2008.

Freedman, David N. "Early Israelite History in the Light of Early Israelite Poetry." Pages 3–35 in *Unity and Diversity: Essays in the History, Literature, and Religion of the Ancient Near East*. Edited by Hans Goedicke and J. J. M. Roberts. Baltimore: The Johns Hopkins University Press, 1975.

________, and Francis I. Anderson. *Hosea: A New Translation with Introduction and Commentary*. AB 24. New York: Doubleday, 1980.

Fretheim, Terence E. *Deuteronomic History*. IntBT. Nashville: Abingdon, 1983.

Friedman, Richard Elliot. *The Exile and Biblical Narrative: The Formation of the Deuteronomic and Priestly Works*. HSM 22. Chico, Calif.: Scholars Press, 1981.

________. "From Egypt to Egypt: Dtr^1 and Dtr^2." Pages 167–92 in *Traditions in Transformation: Turning Points in Biblical Faith*. Edited by J. D. Levenson and B. Halpern. Winona Lake, Ind.: Eisenbrauns, 1981.

Fritz, Volkmar. "Die Deutungen des Königtums Sauls in den Überlieferungen von seiner Entstehung I Sam 9–11." *ZAW* 88 (1976): 346–62.

Frolov, Serge. "Bedan: A Riddle in Context." *JBL* 126 (2007): 164–67.

________. "Evil-Merodach and the Deuteronomist: The Sociohistorical Setting of Dtr in the Light of 2 Kgs 25, 27–30." *Bib* 88 (2007): 174–90.

________. "The Semiotics of Covert Action in 1 Samuel 9–10." *JSOT* 31 (2007): 429–50.

________. "Succession Narrative: A 'Document' or a 'Phantom'?" *JBL* 121 (2002): 81–104.

________, and Vladimir Orel. "A Nameless City." *JBQ* 23 (1995): 252–56.

Garbini, Giovanni. "'Narrativa della Successione' o 'Storia dei Rei'?" *Hen* 1 (1979): 19–41.

Garr, W. Randall. *Dialect-Geography of Syria-Palestine, 1000–586 B.C.E.* Philadelphia: University of Pennsylvania Press, 1985.

Gennep, Arnold van. *The Rites of Passage*. Translated by Monika B. Vizedom and Gabrielle L. Caffee. 1909. Repr., Chicago: University of Chicago Press, 1960.

Gellner, Ernest. "Introduction: Approaches to Nomadism." Pages 1–9 in *The Desert and the Sown: Nomads in the Wider Society*. Edited by Cynthia Nelson. Berkeley: Institute of International Studies, University of California at Berkeley, 1973.

________. *The Saints of the Atlas*. London: Weidenfeld & Nicholson, 1969.

Geoghegan, Jeffrey C. "'Until This Day' and the Preexilic Redaction of the Deuteronomistic History." *JBL* 122 (2003): 201–27.

________. *The Time, Place, and Purpose of the Deuteronomistic History: The Evidence of "Until This Day"*. BJS 347. Providence: Brown University, 2005.

George, Mark K. "Constructing Identity in 1 Samuel 17." *BibInt* 7 (1999): 389–412.

Gerbrandt, Gerald Eddie. *Kingship According to the Deuteronomistic History*. SBLDS 87. Atlanta: Scholars Press, 1986.

Gluckman, Max. "*Les Rites de Passage*." Pages 1–52 in *Essays on the Ritual of Social Relations*. Edited by Max Gluckman. Manchester: Manchester University Press, 1962.

Gluckman, Mary, and Max Gluckman. "On Drama, and Games and Athletic Contests." Pages 227–43 in *Secular Ritual*. Edited by Sally F. Moore and Barbara G. Meyerhoff. Assen: Van Gorcum, 1977.

Glueck, Nelson. *Explorations in Eastern Palestine, II*. AASOR 15. New Haven: ASOR, 1935.

Gonçalves, Francolino J. *L'expédition de Sennachérib en Palestine dans la littérature hébraïque ancienne*. Ebib n.s. 7. Paris: Gabalda, 1986.

Gooding, David W. "An Approach to the Literary and Textual Problems in the David-Goliath Story: 1 Sam 16–18." Pages 55–86 in *The Story of David and Goliath: Textual and Literary Criticism*. Edited by Dominique Barthélemy et al. OBO 73. Fribourg: University Press; Göttingen: Vandenhoeck & Ruprecht, 1986.

________. "Response." Pages 99–106 in *The Story of David and Goliath: Textual and Literary Criticism*. Edited by Dominique Barthélemy et al. OBO 73. Fribourg: University Press; Göttingen: Vandenhoeck & Ruprecht, 1986.

Goody, Jack. "Against 'Ritual': Loosely Structured Thoughts on a Loosely Defined Topic." Pages 25–35 in *Secular Ritual*. Edited by Sally F. Moore and Barbara G. Meyerhoff. Assen: Van Gorcum, 1977.

Gordon, Robert L. "Notes on Some Sites in the Lower Wādī ez-Zerqa and Wādī Rāġib." *ZDPV* 103 (1987): 67–77.

________, and Linda E. Villiers. "Tulul edh Dhahab and Its Environs Surveys of 1980 and 1982: A Preliminary Report." *ADAJ* 27 (1983): 275–89.

Gottwald, Norman K. *The Tribes of Yahweh: A Sociology of the Religion of Liberated Israel, 1250–1050 BCE*. Maryknoll, N.Y.: Orbis, 1979. Repr., Biblical Seminar 66. Sheffield: Sheffield Academic Press, 1999.

Gray, John. *I & II Kings*. 2d ed. OTL. Philadelphia: Westminster, 1970.

________. *Joshua, Judges and Ruth*. NCB. London: Nelson, 1967.

Green, Barbara. *How Are the Mighty Fallen? A Dialogical Study of King Saul in 1 Samuel*. JSOTSup 365. Sheffield: Sheffield Academic Press, 2003.

________. *Mikhail Bakhtin and Biblical Scholarship: An Introduction*. SemeiaSt 38. Atlanta: Society of Biblical Literature, 2000.

Gressmann, Hugo. *Die Schriften des Alten Testaments*. 1910. 2d. ed. Göttingen: Vanderhoeck & Ruprecht, 1921.

Grimes, Ronald L. *Deeply into the Bone: Re-Inventing the Rites of Passage*. Berkeley and Los Angeles: University of California Press, 2000.

Grønbaek, Jakob H. *Die Geschichte vom Aufstieg Davids (1. Sam. 15–2. Sam. 5): Tradition und Komposition*. ATDan 10. Copenhagen: Munksgaard, 1971.

Gunn, David M. *The Story of King David: Genre and Interpretation*. JSOTSup 6. Sheffield: JSOT Press, 1978.

Habel, Norman. "The Form and Significance of the Call Narratives." *ZAW* 77 (1965): 297–323.

Hackett, Jo Ann. "1 and 2 Samuel." Pages 85–95 in *The Women's Bible Commentary*. Edited by Carol A. Newsom and Susan H. Ringe. London: SPCK, 1992.

________. *The Balaam Text from Deir ʿAllā*. HSM 31. Chico, Calif.: Scholars Press, 1984.

________. "Religious Traditions in Israelite Transjordan." Pages 125–36 in *Ancient Israelite Religion: Essays in Honor of Frank Moore Cross*. Edited by Patrick D. Miller, Paul D. Hanson, and S. Dean McBride. Philadelphia: Fortress, 1987.

________. "Response to Baruch Levine and André Lemaire." Pages 73–84 in *The Balaam Text from Deir ʿAlla Re-Evaluated: Proceedings of the International Symposium Held at Leiden 21–24 August 1989*. Edited by J. Hoftijzer and G. van der Kooij. Leiden: Brill, 1991.

________. "Some Observations on the Balaam Tradition at Deir ʿAllā." *BA* 49 (1986): 216–22.

________. "'There Was No King in Israel': The Era of the Judges." Pages 177–218 in *The Oxford History of the Biblical World*. Edited by Michael D. Coogan. New York: Oxford University Press, 1998.

Haelewyck, Jean-Claude. "L'assassinat d'Ishbaal (2 Samuel iv 1–12)." *VT* 47 (1997): 145–53.

Hagan, Harry. "Deception as Motif and Theme in 2 Sm 9–20; 1 Kgs 1–2." *Bib* 60 (1979): 301–26.

Hall, Thomas N. "The Reversal of the Jordan in Vercelli Homily 16 and in Old English Literature." *Traditio* 45 (1990): 53–86.

Halpern, Baruch. "Biblical or Israelite History?" Pages 103–39 in *The Future of Biblical Studies: The Hebrew Scriptures*. Edited by Richard Elliot Friedman and H. G. M. Williamson. Atlanta: Scholars Press, 1987.

________. *The Constitution of the Monarchy in Israel*. HSM 25. Chico, Calif.: Scholars Press, 1981.

________. *David's Secret Demons: Messiah, Murderer, Traitor, King*. Grand Rapids, Mich.: Eerdmans, 2001.

________. "Erasing History—The Minimalist Assault on Ancient Israel." *BRev* 11.6 (1995): 26–35, 47.

________. *The First Historians: The Hebrew Bible and History*. University Park: Pennsylvania State University Press, 1988.

________. "Levitic Participation in the Reform Cult of Jeroboam I." *JBL* 95 (1976): 31–42.

________. "Sacred History and Ideology: Chronicles' Thematic Structure—Indications of an Earlier Source." Pages 35–54 in *The Creation of Sacred Literature: Composition and Redaction of the Biblical Text*. Edited by Richard Elliott Friedman. UCNES 22. Berkeley and Los Angeles: University of California Press, 1981.

________. "Sectionalism and the Schism." *JBL* 93 (1974): 519–32.

________. "The State of Israelite History." Pages 540–65 in *Reconsidering Israel and Judah: Recent Studies on the Deuteronomistic History*. Edited by G. N. Knoppers and J. G. McConville. SBTS 8. Winona Lake, Ind.: Eisenbrauns, 2000.

________, and David S. Vanderhooft. "The Editions of Kings in the 7th–6th Centuries B.C.E." *HUCA* 62 (1991): 179–244.

Hamilton, Gordon J. "New Evidence for the Authenticity of *bšt* in Hebrew Personal Names and for Its Use as a Divine Epithet in Biblical Texts." *CBQ* 60 (1998): 228–50.

Hamilton, Mark W. "The Creation of Saul's Royal Body: Reflections on 1 Samuel 8–10." Pages 139–55 in *Saul in Story and Tradition*. Edited by Carl S. Ehrlich with Marsha C. White. FAT I/47. Tübingen: Mohr Siebeck, 2006.

Hanson, Paul D. *The Dawn of Apocalyptic: The Historical and Sociological Roots of Jewish Apocalyptic Eschatology*. Rev. ed. Philadelphia: Fortress, 1979.

Hartmann, Richard. "Zum Ortsnamen aṭ-Ṭajjiba." *ZDMG* 65 (1911): 536–38.

Hauer, Christian A. "Does I Samuel 9 1–11 15 Reflect the Extension of Saul's Dominions?" *JBL* 86 (1967): 306–10.

Havrelock, Rachel S. "The Jordan River: Crossing a Biblical Boundary." Ph.D. diss., University of California, Berkeley, 2004.

________. "The Two Maps of Israel's Land." *JBL* 126 (2007): 649–67.

Hawks, Tony. *Playing the Moldovans at Tennis*. New York: Thomas Dunne, 2000.

Hayes, John H., and J. Maxwell Miller, eds. *Israelite and Judaean History*. OTL. Philadelphia: Westminster, 1977.

Heider, George C. *The Cult of Molek: A Reassessment*. JSOTSup 43. Sheffield: JSOT Press, 1985.

Hentschel, Georg. *1 Könige*. NEchtB 10. Würzburg: Echter Verlag, 1984.

________. *2 Könige*. NEchtB 11. Würzburg: Echter Verlag, 1984.

Herbert, Edward D. "4QSam[a] and Its Relationship to the LXX: An Exploration in Stemmatological Analysis." Pages 37–55 in *IX Congress of the International Organization for Septuagint and Cognate Studies, Cambridge, 1995*. Edited by Bernard A. Taylor. SBLSCS 45. Atlanta: Scholars Press, 1997.

Herr, Larry G. "Social Systems in Central Jordan: Moving toward the First Millennium BC and the Earliest Iron Age Politics." Pages 275–83 in *Studies in the History and Archaeology of Jordan* 7. Edited by Ghazi Bisheh. Amman: Jordanian Department of Antiquities, 2001.

Herrmann, Siegfried. "Operationen Pharao Schoschenks I. im östlichen Ephraim." *ZDPV* 80 (1964): 55–79.

Hertzberg, Hans Wilhelm. *I & II Samuel: A Commentary*. Translated by John S. Bowden. OTL. London: SCM, 1964. Repr. Philadelphia: Westminster, n.d. Translation of *Die Samuelbücher*. 2d ed. DATD 10. Göttingen: Vandenhoeck & Ruprecht, 1960.

________. "Mizpa." *ZAW* 47 (1929): 161–96.

Hess, Richard S. *Israelite Religions: An Archaeological and Biblical Survey*. Grand Rapids, Mich.: Baker, 2007.

Heyd, Michael. "The Reaction to Enthusiasm in the 17th Century: From Structure to Anti-Structure." *Religion* 15 (1985): 279–89.

Hillers, Delbert R. "A Note on Some Treaty Terminology in the Old Testament." *BASOR* 176 (1964): 46–47.

Hodder, Ian. "Converging Traditions: The Search for Symbolic Meanings in Archaeology and Geography." Pages 134–45 in *Landscape and Culture: Geographical and Archaeological Perspectives*. Edited by J. M. Wagstaff; Oxford: Basil Blackwell, 1987.

Hoffmann, Hans-Detlef. *Reform und Reformen: Untersuchungen zu einem Grundthema der deuteronomistischen Geschichtsschreibung*. ATANT 66. Zurich: Theologischer Verlag, 1980.

Hoffner, Harry A. "Propaganda and Political Justification in Hittite Historiography." Pages 49–62 in *Unity and Diversity: Essays in the History, Literature, and Religion of the Ancient Near East*. Edited by Hans Goedicke and J. J. M. Roberts. JNHES. Baltimore: The Johns Hopkins University Press, 1975.

Hoftijzer, J., and G. van der Kooij, eds. *Aramaic Texts from Deir ʿAlla*. Leiden: Brill, 1976.

Hölscher, Gustav. "Bemerkungen zur Topographie Palästinas, 1: Die Feldzüge des Makkabäers Judas (1. Makk. 5)." *ZDPV* 29 (1906): 133–51.

________. "Das Buch der Könige, seine Quellen und seine Redaktion." 1:158–213 in *ΕΥΧΑΡΙΣΤΗΡΙΟΝ: Studien zur Religion und Literatur des Alten und Neuen Testaments*. Edited by Hans Schmidt. FRLANT 36. Göttingen: Vandenhoeck & Ruprecht, 1923.

________. *Geschichtsschreibung in Israel: Untersuchungen zum Jahvisten und Elohisten*. SHVL 50. Lund: Gleerup, 1952.

Hoppe, Leslie J. "The Meaning of Deuteronomy." *BTB* 10 (1980): 111–17.

Horowitz, Wayne, Takayoshi Oshima, and Seth Sanders. "A Bibliographical List of Cuneiform Inscriptions from Canaan, Palestine/Philistia, and the Land of Israel." *JAOS* 122 (2002): 753–66.

Howard, David M. "The Transfer of Power from Saul to David in 1 Sam 16:13–14." *JETS* 32 (1989): 473–83.

Huehnergard, John. "Remarks on the Classification of the Northwest Semitic Languages." Pages 282–93 in *The Balaam Text from Deir ʿAlla Re-Evaluated: Proceedings of the International Symposium Held at Leiden 21–24 August 1989*. Edited by J. Hoftijzer and G. van der Kooij. Leiden: Brill, 1991.

Humphreys, W. Lee. "From Tragic Hero to Villain: A Study of the Figure of Saul and the Development of 1 Samuel." *JSOT* 22 (1982): 95–117.

________. "The Rise and Fall of King Saul: A Study of an Ancient Narrative Stratum in 1 Samuel." *JSOT* 18 (1980): 74–90.

________. "The Tragedy of King Saul: A Study of the Structure of 1 Samuel 9–31." *JSOT* 6 (1978): 18–27.

Hurvitz, Avi. *A Linguistic Study of the Relationship between the Priestly Source and the Book of Ezekiel: A New Approach to an Old Problem*. CahRB 20. Paris: Gabalda, 1982.

________. "Hebrew and Aramaic in the Biblical Period: The Problem of 'Aramaisms' in Linguistic Research of the Hebrew Bible." Pages 24–37 in *Biblical Hebrew: Studies in Chronology and Typology*. Edited by Ian Young. JSOTSup 369. London: T&T Clark, 2003.

Hutton, Jeremy M. "'Bethany Beyond the Jordan' in Text, Tradition, and Historical Geography." *Bib* 89 (2008): 305–28.

________. "Isaiah 51:9–11 and the Rhetorical Appropriation and Subversion of Hostile Theologies." *JBL* 126 (2007): 271–303.

________. "Jordan River." *NIDB* 3:385–92.

________. "The Left Bank of the Jordan and the Rites of Passage: An Anthropological Interpretation of 2 Samuel xix." *VT* 56 (2006): 470–84.

________. "The Levitical Diaspora (I): A Sociological Comparison with Morocco's Ahansal." Pages 223–34 in *Exploring the* Longue Durée*: Essays in Honor of Lawrence E. Stager*. Edited by David Schloen. Winona Lake, Ind.: Eisenbrauns, 2009.

________. "'Long Live the King!' 1 Sam 10:17–27 in Light of Ahansali Intra-Tribal Mediation." Paper presented at the annual meeting of the SBL, Boston, Mass., Nov. 23, 2008.

________. "Mahanaim, Penuel and Transhumance Routes: Observations on Genesis 32–33 and Judges 8." *JNES* 65 (2006): 161–78.

________. Review of Y. Elitzur, *Ancient Place Names in the Holy Land*. *Maarav* 14 (2007): 77–97.

________. "Southern, Northern, and Transjordanian Perspectives." In *Religious Diversity*. Edited by John Barton and Francesca Stavrakopoulou. London: T&T Clark, forthcoming.

________. "Topography, Biblical Traditions, and Reflections on John's Baptism of Jesus." In *Proceedings of the Princeton-Prague Symposium on the Historical Jesus*. Edited by J. H. Charlesworth. Grand Rapids, Mich.: Eerdmans, forthcoming.

Hutton, Rodney R. *Charisma and Authority in Israelite Society*. Minneapolis: Fortress, 1994.

________. "What Happened From Shittim to Gilgal? Law and Gospel in Micah 6:5." *Currents in Theology and Mission* 26 (1999): 94–103.

Hutzli, Jürg. "Mögliche Retuschen am Davidbild in der masoretischen Fassung der Samuelbücher." Pages 102–15 in *David und Saul im Widerstreit–Diachronie und Synchronie im Wettstreit: Beiträge zur Auslegung des ersten Samuelbuches*. Edited by Walter Dietrich. OBO 206. Fribourg: University Press; Göttingen: Vandenhoeck & Ruprecht, 2005.

Hylander, Ivar. *Der literarische Samuel-Saul-Komplex (1. Sam. 1–15) traditionsgeschichtlich untersucht*. Uppsala: Almqvist & Wiksell; Leipzig: Otto Harrassowitz, 1932.

Ignatius, Peter. "1 Sam 9,1–10,16: Have the Davidic Propagandists Capitalized on the Folktales about Saul to Enhance the Image of David?" *BiBh* 28 (2002): 632–55.

Ingold, Tim. "The Temporality of the Landscape." *WorldArch* 25 (1993): 152–74.

________. "The Picture Is Not the Terrain: Maps, Paintings and the Dwellt-In World." *ArchDial* 4 (1997): 29–31.

Irwin, W. A. "Samuel and the Rise of the Monarchy." *AJSL* 58 (1941): 113–34.

Ishida, Tomoo. "Adonijah the Son of Haggith and His Supporters: An Inquiry into Problems about History and Historiography." Pages 165–87 in *The Future of Biblical Studies—The Hebrew Scriptures*. Edited by Richard Elliot Friedman and H. G. M. Williamson. Atlanta: Scholars Press, 1987. Revised and repr. as part of "Solomon's Succession to the Throne of David." Pages 102–36 in *History and Historical Writing in Ancient Israel: Studies in Biblical Historiography*. SHCANE 16. Leiden: Brill, 1999.

________. *The Royal Dynasties in Ancient Israel: A Study on the Formation and Development of Royal-Dynastic Ideology*. BZAW 142. Berlin: de Gruyter, 1977.

________. "'Solomon Who is Greater than David': Solomon's Succession in 1 Kings i–ii in the Light of the Inscription of Kilamuwa, King of Yʾ DY-Śamʾal." Pages 145–53 in *Congress Volume: Salamanca, 1983*. Edited by J. A. Emerton. VTSup 36. Leiden: Brill, 1985. Repr., pages 166–74 in *History and Historical Writing in Ancient Israel: Studies in Biblical Historiography*. SHCANE 16. Leiden: Brill, 1999.

________. "Solomon's Succession to the Throne of David—A Political Analysis." Pages 175–87 in *Studies in the Period of David and Solomon and Other Essays*. Edited by Tomoo Ishida. Winona Lake, Ind.: Eisenbrauns, 1982. Revised and repr. as part of "Solomon's Succession to the Throne of David." Pages 102–36 in *History and Historical Writing in Ancient Israel: Studies in Biblical Historiography*. SHCANE 16. Leiden: Brill, 1999.

________. "The Story of Abner's Murder: A Problem Posed by the Solomonic Apologist." Pages 109*–13* in *ErIsr* 24. Edited by S. Aḥituv and B. A. Levine. Jerusalem: Israel Exploration Society, 1993. Repr., pages 158–65 in *History and Historical Writing in Ancient Israel: Studies in Biblical Historiography*. SHCANE 16. Leiden: Brill, 1999.

________. "The Succession Narrative and Esarhaddon's Apology: A Comparison." Pages 166–73 in *Ah, Assyria...: Studies in Assyrian History and Ancient Near Eastern Historiography Presented to Hayim Tadmor*. Edited by M. Cogan and I. Ephʿal. Jersalem: Magnes, 1991. Repr., pages 175–85 in *History and Historical Writing in Ancient Israel: Studies in Biblical Historiography*. SHCANE 16. Leiden: Brill, 1999.

Jackson, Kent P. *The Ammonite Language of the Iron Age*. HSM 27. Chico, Calif.: Scholars Press, 1983.

________. "The Language of the Mesha Inscription." Pages 96–130 in *Studies in the Mesha Inscription and Moab*. Edited by Andrew Dearman. Atlanta: Scholars Press, 1991.

Jacobs, Jonathan. "The Role of the Secondary Characters in the Story of the Anointing of Saul (1 Samuel ix–x)." *VT* 58 (2008): 495–509.

Jacobson, Howard. "Bedan and Barak Reconsidered." *VT* 44 (1994): 108–9.

________. "The Judge Bedan (1 Samuel xii 11)." *VT* 42 (1992): 123–24.

Jagt, K. A. van der. "What Did Saul Eat When He First Met Samuel? Light from Anthropology on Biblical Texts." *BT* 47 (1996): 226–30.

Jamieson-Drake, David W. *Scribes and Schools in Monarchic Judah: A Socio-Archaeological Approach*. JSOTSup 109. SWBA 9. Sheffield: Almond, 1991.

Janssen, Enno. *Juda in der Exilszeit: Ein Beitrag zur Frage nach der Entstehung des Judentums*. FRLANT 69. Göttingen: Vandenhoeck & Ruprecht, 1956.

Jason, Heda. "The Story of David and Goliath: A Folk Epic?" *Bib* 60 (1979): 36–70.

Jenni, Ernst. "Zwei Jahrzehnte Forschung an den Büchern Josua bis Könige." *TRu* 27 (1961): 1–32, 97–146.

Jensen, Hans J. L. "Desire, Rivalry and Collective Violence in the 'Succession Narrative'." *JSOT* 55 (1992): 39–59.

Jepsen, Alfred. *Die Quellen des Königsbuches*. Halle: Niemeyer, 1953.

Ji, Chang-Ho C. "Iron Age I in Central and Northern Transjordan: An Interim Summary of Archaeological Data." *PEQ* 127 (1995): 122–40.

Jobling, David. "Jonathan: A Structural Study in 1 Samuel." Pages 4–25 in *The Sense of Biblical Narrative: Three Structural Analyses in the Old Testament (I Samuel 13–31, Numbers 11–12, I Kings 17–18)*. JSOTSup 7. Sheffield: JSOT Press, 1978.

________. "'The Jordan a Boundary:' Transjordan in Israel's Ideological Geography." Pages 88–133, 142–47 in *The Sense of Biblical Narrative II: Structural Analyses in the Hebrew Bible*. JSOTSup 39. Sheffield: JSOT Press, 1986.

Kaiser, Otto. "Beobachtungen zur sogenannten Thronnachfolgeerzählung Davids." *ETL* 44 (1988): 5–20.

________. "David und Jonathan. Tradition, Redaktion und Geschichte in I Sam 16–20: Ein Versuch." *ETL* 66 (1990): 281–96.

________. *Grundriß der Einleitung in die kanonischen und deuterokanonischen Schriften des Alten Testaments*. 3 vols. Gütersloh: Gerd Mohn, 1992.

Kallai, Zecharia. "Conquest and Settlement of Trans-Jordan: A Historiographical Study." *ZDPV* 99 (1983): 110–18.

________. "Samuel in Qumrān: Expansion of a Historiographical Pattern (4QSam[a])." *RB* 103 (1996): 581–91.

Kamp, Kathryn A., and Norman Yoffee. "Ethnicity in Western Asia During the Early Second Millennium B.C.: Archaeological Assessments and Ethnoarchaeological Perspectives." *BASOR* 237 (1980): 85–104.

Kapelrud, Arvid S. "König David und die Söhne des Saul." *ZAW* 67 (1956): 198–205.

Keys, Gillian. *The Wages of Sin: A Reappraisal of the "Succession Narrative"*. JSOTSup 221. Sheffield: Sheffield Academic Press, 1996.

Kim, Uriah Y. *Decolonizing Josiah: Toward a Postcolonial Reading of the Deuteronomistic History*. The Bible in the Modern World 5. Sheffield: Sheffield Phoenix, 2005.

King, Philip J., and Lawrence E. Stager. *Life in Biblical Israel*. LibAncIsr. Louisville, Ky.: WJKP, 2001.

Kitchen, K. A. *The Third Intermediate Period in Egypt (100–650 B.C.)*. Warminster: Aris & Phillips, 1986.

Klein, Ralph W. *1 Samuel*. WBC 10. Waco: Word Books, 1983.

Knapp, A. Bernard, and Wendy Ashmore. "Archaeological Landscapes: Constructed, Conceptualized, Ideational." Pages 1–30 in *Archaeologies of Landscape: Contemporary Perspectives*. Edited by Wendy Ashmore and A. Bernard Knapp. Malden, Mass.: Blackwell, 1999.

Knauf, Ernst Axel. "The Mists of Ramthalon, or: How Ramoth-Gilead Disappeared from the Archaeological Record." *BN* 110 (2001): 33–36.

Knierem, Rolf P. "The Messianic Concept in The First Book of Samuel." Pages 20–51 in *Jesus and the Historian: Written in Honor of Ernest Cadman Colwell*. Edited by F. Thomas Trotter. Philadelphia: Westminster, 1968.

Knight, Douglas A. "Deuteronomy and the Deuteronomists." Pages 61–79 in *Old Testament Interpretation: Past, Present, and Future: Essays in Honor of Gene M. Tucker*. Edited by James Luther Mays, David L. Petersen, and Kent Harold Richards. Nashville: Abingdon, 1995.

Knoppers, Gary N. "Introduction." Pages 1–18 in *Reconsidering Israel and Judah: Recent Studies on the Deuteronomistic History*. Edited by G. N. Knoppers and J. G. McConville. SBTS 8. Winona Lake, Ind.: Eisenbrauns, 2000.

Köhler-Rollefson, Ilse. "A Model for the Development of Nomadic Pastoralism on the Transjordanian Plateau." Pages 11–18 in *Pastoralism in the Levant: Archaeological Materials in Anthropological Perspectives*. Edited by Ofer Bar-Yosef and Anatoly Khazanov. Madison, Wis.: Prehistory Press, 1992.

Kooij, Arie van der. "The Story of David and Goliath: The Early History of Its Texts." *ETL* 68 (1992): 118–31.

Kratz, Reinhard G. *The Composition of the Narrative Books of the Old Testament*. Translated by John Bowden. London: T&T Clark, 2005. Translation of *Die Komposition der erzählenden Bücher des Alten Testaments*. Göttingen: Vandenhoeck & Ruprecht, 2000.

Krause, Hans Joachim. "Gesetz und Geschichte: Zum Geschichtsbild des Deuteronomisten." *EvT* 11 (1951–52): 415–28.

Kreuzer, Siegfried. "Saul—Not Always—at War: A New Perspective on the Rise of the Kingship in Israel." Pages 39–58 in *Saul in Story and Tradition*. Edited by Carl S. Ehrlich with Marsha C. White. FAT I/47. Tübingen: Mohr Siebeck, 2006.

Kuenen, Avraham. *Historische-kritische Einleitung in die Bücher des Alten Testaments*. Translated by Th. Weber. Leipzig: Reisland, 1890. Translation of *Historisch-kritisch onderzoek naar het ontstaan en de verzameling van de boeken des Ouden Verbonds*. Leiden: Engels, 1861.

________. *Het onstaan van de Historische Boeken des Ouden Verbonds*. Vol. 1 of *Historisch-kritisch onderzoek naar het ontstaan en de verzameling van de boeken des Ouden Verbonds*. 3 vols. Leiden: Engels, 1861.

Kuhrt, Amélie. *The Ancient Near East: c. 3000–330 BC*. 2 vols. London: Routledge, 1995.

Kutsch, Ernest. "Gideons Berufung und Alterbau Jdc 6,11–24." *TLZ* 81 (1956): 75–84.

Laberge, Léo. "Le deutéronomiste." Pages 47–77 in *"De bien des maniéres": La recherche biblique aux abords du XXIe siècle*. Edited by Michel Gourgues and Léo Laberge. LD 163. Paris: Cerf; Montreal: Fides, 1995.

LaBianca, Øystein S., and Randall W. Younker. "The Kingdoms of Ammon, Moab and Edom: The Archaeology of Society in Late Bronze/Iron Age Transjordan (ca. 1400–500 B.C.E.)." Pages 399–411 in *The Archaeology of Society in the Holy Land*. Edited by Thomas E. Levy. London: Leicester University Press, 1998.

Lane, Edward William. *An Arabic-English Lexicon*. 8 vols. London: Williams & Norgate, 1865).

Langlamet, François. "Absalom et les concubines de son père: Recherches sur II Sam., xvi, 21–22." *RB* 84 (1977): 161–209.

________. "Ahitofel et Houshaï: Rédaction prosalomonienne en 2 S 15–17?" Pages 57–90 in *Studies in Bible and the Ancient Near East: Presented to Samuel E.*

Loewenstamm on His Seventieth Birthday. Edited by Yitschak Avishur and Joshua Blau. Jerusalem: Rubinstein, 1978.

________. “David et Barzillaï. 2 Samuel 19:32–41a: le récit primitif et sa ‘forme’.” Pages 149–69 in *Isac Leo Seeligman Volume: Essays on the Bible and the Ancient World*. Edited by Alexander Rofé and Yair Zakovitch. 3 vols. Jerusalem: Magnes, 1983.

________. “David et la Maison de Saül: Les épisodes ‘benjaminites’ de II Sam. ix; xvi, 1–14; xix, 17–31; 1 Rois ii, 36–46.” Parts 1–5. *RB* 86 (1979): 194–213, 385–436, 481–513; 87 (1980): 161–210; 88 (1981): 321–22.

________. “De ‘David, fils de Jessé’ au ‘Livre de Jonathan’: Deux editions divergentes de l’‘Ascension de David’ en 1 Sam 16–2 Sam 1?” *RB* 100 (1993): 321–57.

________. “‘David—Jonathan—Saül’ ou le ‘Livre de Jonathan’: 1 Sam 16,14–2 Sam 1,27*.” *RB* 101 (1994): 326–54.

________. “David, fils de Jessé: Une edition prédeutéronomiste de l’‘Histoire de la Succession’.” *RB* 89 (1982): 5–47.

________. “Pour ou contre Salomon? La rédaction prosalomonienne de 1 Rois i–ii.” Parts 1–2. *RB* 83 (1976): 321–79, 481–528.

________. Review of E. Würthwein, *Die Erzählung von der Thronfolge Davids—theologische oder politische Geschichtsschreibung?* and T. Veijola, *Die ewige Dynasty*. *RB* 83 (1976): 114–137.

Lapp, Nancy L. “Rumeith, Tell er-.” *NEAEHL* 4:1291–93.

Lapsley, Jacqueline E. “Feeling Our Way: Love for God in Deuteronomy.” *CBQ* 65 (2003): 350–69.

Lattimore, Owen. *Inner Asian Frontiers of China*. 1940. Irvington-on-Hudson, N.Y.: Capitol, 1951.

Lawton, Robert B. “David, Merob, and Michal.” *CBQ* 51 (1989): 423–25.

Layton, Robert. *An Introduction to Theory in Anthropology*. Cambridge: Cambridge University Press, 1997.

Lemaire, André. “Les benê Jacob: Essai d’interprétation historique d’une tradition patriarcale.” *RB* 85 (1978): 321–37.

________. “Galaad et Makîr.” *VT* 31 (1981): 39–61.

________. “Les inscriptions sur plâtre de Deir ᶜAlla et leur signification historique et culturelle.” Pages 33–57 in *The Balaam Text from Deir ᶜAlla Re-Evaluated: Proceedings of the International Symposium Held at Leiden 21–24 August 1989*. Edited by J. Hoftijzer and G. van der Kooij. Leiden: Brill, 1991.

________. “Toward a Redactional History of the Book of Kings.” Pages 446–61 in *Reconsidering Israel and Judah: Recent Studies on the Deuteronomistic History*. Edited by G. N. Knoppers and J. G. McConville. Translated by Samuel W. Heldenbrand. SBTS 8. Winona Lake, Ind.: Eisenbrauns, 2000. Translated from “Vers l’Histoire de la Rédaction des Livres des Rois.” *ZAW* 98 (1986): 221–36.

Lemaire, Ton. “Archaeology between the Invention and the Destruction of the Landscape.” *ArchDial* 4 (1997): 5–21.

________. “Ambiguous Landscape(s).” *ArchDial* 4 (1997): 32–38.

Lemardelé, Christophe. “Saül le *nazir* ou la Légende d’un roi.” *SJOT* 22 (2008): 47–62.

Lemche, Nils P. “David’s Rise.” *JSOT* 10 (1978): 2–25.

Lemke, Werner E. “The Way of Obedience: I Kings 13 and the Structure of the Deuteronomistic History.” Pages 301–26 in *Magnalia Dei: The Mighty Acts of God*. Edited by Frank Moore Cross, Werner E. Lemke, and Patrick D. Miller. Garden City, N.Y.: Doubleday, 1976.

Lestienne, Michel. *Premier Livre des Règnes*. Vol. 9.1 of *Le Bible d'Alexandrie*. Paris: Cerf, 1997.

Leuchter, Mark. "The Literary Strata and Narrative Sources of Psalm xcix." *VT* 55 (2005): 20–38.

________. "'The Levite in Your Gates': The Deuteronomic Redefinition of Levitical Authority." *JBL* 126 (2007): 417–36.

________. "'Now There Was a [Certain] Man': Compositional Chronology in Judges–1 Samuel." *CBQ* 69 (2007): 429–39.

________. "Samuel, Saul, and the Deuteronomistic Categories of History." Pages 101–110 in *From Babel to Babylon: Essays on Biblical History and Literature in Honour of Brian Peckham*. Edited by Joyce Rilett Wood, John E. Harvey, and Mark Leuchter. Library of Hebrew Bible/Old Testament Studies 455. London: T&T Clark, 2006.

________. "Something Old, Something Older: Reconsidering 1 Sam. 2:27–36." *Journal of Hebrew Scriptures* 4 (2003): art. 6. www.jhsonline.org.

________. "Why Is the Song of Moses in the Book of Deuteronomy?" *VT* 57 (2007): 295–317.

Levenson, Jon D. "1 Samuel 25 as Literature and as History." *CBQ* 40 (1978): 11–28.

________. "From Temple to Synagogue: 1 Kings 8." Pages 143–66 in *Traditions in Transformation: Turning Points in Biblical Faith*. Edited by J. D. Levenson and B. Halpern. Winona Lake, Ind.: Eisenbrauns, 1981.

________. "The Last Four Verses in Kings." *JBL* 103 (1984): 353–61.

________. *Sinai and Zion: An Entry into the Jewish Bible*. San Francisco: HarperCollins, 1985.

________. "Who Inserted the Book of the Torah?" *HTR* 68 (1975): 203–33.

________, and Baruch Halpern. "The Political Import of David's Marriages." *JBL* 99 (1980): 507–18.

Levin, Christoph. *Der Sturz der Königin Atalja: Ein Kapitel zur Geschichte Judas im 9. Jahrhundert v. Chr*. SBS 105. Stuttgart: Verlag Katholisches Bibelwerk, 1982.

Levine, Baruch A. "The Balaam Inscription from Deir ᶜAlla: Historical Aspects." Pages 326–39 in *Biblical Archaeology Today: Proceedings of the International Congress on Biblical Archaeology, Jerusalem, April 1984*. Jerusalem: Israel Exploration Society, 1985.

Levine, Nachman. "Twice as Much of Your Spirit: Pattern, Parallel and Paranomasia in the Miracles of Elijah and Elisha." *JSOT* 85 (1999): 25–46.

Lévi-Strauss, Claude. *The Savage Mind*. Chicago: The University of Chicago Press, 1966.

Lincoln, Bruce. *Emerging from the Chrysalis: Rituals of Women's Initiation*. New York: Oxford University Press, 1981.

Lindars, Barnabas. "Gideon and Kingship." *JTS* n.s.16 (1965): 315–26.

Lingen, Anton van der. *David en Saul in I Samuel 16–II Samuel 5: verhalen in politiek en religie*. 's-Gravenhage: Boekencentrum, 1983.

Lods, Adolphe. *Israel from Its Beginnings to the Middle of the Eighth Century*. Translated by S. H. Hooke. London: Routledge, 1932, page 11. Cited by Edward L. Greenstein, "The Formation of the Biblical Narrative Corpus," *AJSR* 15 (1990): 154.

Lohfink, Norbert. "Kerygmata des Deuteronomistischen Geschichtswerks." Pages 87–100 in *Die Botschaft und die Boten: Festschrift für Hans Walter Wolff*. Edited by Jörg Jeremias and Lothar Perlitt. Neukirchen-Vluyn: Neukirchener Verlag, 1981.

________. "Zur neueren Diskussion über 2 Kön 22–23." Pages 24–48 in *Das Deuteronomium: Entstehung, Gestalt und Botschaft*. Edited by Norbert Lohfink. BETL 68. Leuven: University Press and Peeters, 1985.

Long, Burke O. *1 Kings: With an Introduction to Historical Literature*. FOTL 9. Grand Rapids, Mich.: Eerdmans, 1984.

________. *2 Kings*. FOTL 10. Grand Rapids, Mich.: Eerdmans, 1991.

Lundbom, Jack R. "Psalm 23: Song of Passage." *Int* 40 (1986): 5–16.

Lust, J. "David dans la Septante." Pages 243–63 in *Figures de David à travers la Bible: XVIIe congrès de l'ACFEB (Lille, 1er–5 septembre 1997)*. Edited by Louis Desrousseaux and Jacques Vermeylen. Paris: Cerf, 1999.

________. "The Story of David and Goliath in Hebrew and in Greek." Pages 5–18 in *The Story of David and Goliath: Textual and Literary Criticism*. Edited by Dominique Barthélemy et al. OBO 73. Fribourg: University Press; Göttingen: Vandenhoeck & Ruprecht, 1986.

________. "Second Thoughts on David and Goliath." Pages 87–91 in *The Story of David and Goliath: Textual and Literary Criticism*. Edited by Dominique Barthélemy et al. OBO 73. Fribourg: University Press; Göttingen: Vandenhoeck & Ruprecht, 1986.

Mabry, Jonathan, and Gaetano Palumbo. "Environmental, Economic and Political Constraints on Ancient Settlement Patterns in the Wadi al-Yabis Region." Pages 67–72 in *Studies in the History and Archaeology of Jordan* 4. Edited by Muna Zaghloul et al. Amman: Jordanian Department of Antiquities, 1992.

Machinist, Peter B. "Biblical Traditions: The Philistines and Israelite History." Pages 53–83 in *The Sea Peoples and Their World: A Reassessment*. Edited by E. D. Oren. Philadelphia: University Museum, University of Pennsylvania, 2000.

________. "Hosea and the Ambiguity of Kingship in Ancient Israel." Pages 153–81 in *Constituting the Community: Studies on the Polity of Ancient Israel in Honor of S. Dean McBride Jr*. Edited by J. T. Strong and S. S. Tuell. Winona Lake, Ind.: Eisenbrauns, 2005.

________. "Outsiders or Insiders: The Biblical View of Emergent Israel and Its Context." Pages 35–60 in *The Other in Jewish Thought and History: Constructions of Jewish Culture and Identity*. Edited by Laurence J. Silberstein and Robert L. Cohn. New York: NYU Press, 1994.

Macholz, Georg Christian. "Untersuchungen zur Geschichte der Samuel Überlieferungen." Th.D. diss., Heidelberg, 1966.

Macy, H. R. "The Sources of the Book of Chronicles." Ph.D. diss., Harvard University, 1975.

Maeir, Aren M., et al. "A Late Iron Age I/Early Iron Age II Old Canaanite Inscription from Tell eṣ-Ṣâfī/Gath, Israel: Palaeography, Dating, and Historical-Cultural Significance." *BASOR* 351 (2008): 39–71.

Mahdi, Louise Carus, Nancy G. Christopher, and Michael Meade, eds. *Crossroads: The Quest for Contemporary Rites of Passage*. Chicago: Carus, 1996.

Malamat, A. "The Punishment of Succoth and Penuel by Gideon in Light of Ancient Near Eastern Treaties." Pages 69–71 in *Sefer Moshe: Studies in the Bible and the Ancient Near East, Qumran, and Post-Biblical Judaism*. Edited by Chaim Cohen, Avi Hurvitz, and Shalom M. Paul. Winona Lake, Ind.: Eisenbrauns, 2004.

Marcus, David. "Ridiculing the Ephraimites: The Shibboleth Incident (Judg 12:6)." *Maarav* 8 (1992): 95–105.

Marfoe, Leon. "The Integrative Transformation: Patterns of Sociopolitical Organization in Southern Syria." *BASOR* 234 (1979): 1–42.

Marx, Emanuel. "Are There Pastoral Nomads in the Middle East?" Pages 255–60 in *Pastoralism in the Levant: Archaeological Materials in Anthropological Perspectives*. Edited by Ofer Bar-Yosef and Anatoly Khazanov. Madison, Wis.: Prehistory Press, 1992.

________. "The Tribe as a Unit of Subsistence: Nomadic Pastoralism in the Middle East." *AmAnthropol* n.s. 79 (1977): 343–63.

Mayes, A. D. H. "The Rise of the Israelite Monarchy." *ZAW* 90 (1978): 1–19.

________. *The Story of Israel between Settlement and Exile: A Redactional Study of the Deuteronomistic History*. London: SCM, 1983.

Mays, James L. *Hosea: A Commentary*. OTL. Philadelphia: Westminster, 1969.

Mazar, Benjamin. "The Campaign of Pharaoh Shishak to Palestine." Pages 57–66 in *Volume du Congrès: Strasbourg, 1956*. Edited by G. W. Anderson et al. VTSup 4. Leiden: Brill, 1957.

________. "Geshur and Maacah." *JBL* 80 (1961): 16–28.

________. "David's Reign in Hebron and the Conquest of Jerusalem." Pages 235–44 in *In the Time of Harvest: Essays in Honor of Abba Hillel Silver on the Occasion of His 70th Birthday*. Edited by Daniel Jeremy Silver. New York: Macmillan, 1963.

McCarter, P. Kyle. *I Samuel: A New Translation with Introduction and Commentary*. AB 8. Garden City, N.Y.: Doubleday, 1980.

________. *II Samuel: A New Translation with Introduction and Commentary*. AB 9. New York: Doubleday, 1984.

________. "The Apology of David." *JBL* 99 (1980): 489–504. Repr., pages 260–75 in *Reconsidering Israel and Judah: Recent Studies on the Deuteronomistic History*. Edited by G. N. Knoppers and J. G. McConville. SBTS 8. Winona Lake, Ind.: Eisenbrauns, 2000.

________. "The Balaam Texts from Deir ᶜAllā: The First Combination." *BASOR* 222 (1980): 49–60.

________. "The Dialect of the Deir ᶜAlla Texts." Pages 87–99 in *The Balaam Text from Deir ᶜAlla Re-Evaluated: Proceedings of the International Symposium Held at Leiden 21–24 August 1989*. Edited by J. Hoftijzer and G. van der Kooij. Leiden: Brill, 1991.

________. "The Historical David." *Int* 40 (1986): 117–29.

________. "'Plots, True or False': The Succession Narrative as Court Apologetic." *Int* 35 (1981): 355–67.

McCarthy, Dennis J. "The Inauguration of Monarchy in Israel: A Form-Critical Study of I Samuel 8–12." *Int* 27 (1973): 401–12.

________. "The Uses of *wᵉhinnēh* in Biblical Hebrew." *Bib* 61 (1980): 330–42.

McGovern, Patrick E. "Central Transjordan in the Late Bronze and Early Iron Ages: An Alternative Hypothesis of Socio-Economic Transformation and Collapse." Pages 267–73 in *Studies in the History and Archaeology of Jordan* 3. Edited by Adnan Hadidi. Amman: Jordanian Department of Antiquities, 1987.

________. *The Late Bronze and Early Iron Ages of Central Transjordan: The Baqᶜah Valley Project, 1977–1981*. University Museum Monograph 65. Philadelphia: University of Pennsylvania Museum of Archaeology, 1986.

________. "Settlement Patterns of the Late Bronze and Iron Ages in the Greater Amman Area." Pages 179–83 in *Studies in the History and Archaeology of Jordan*

4. Edited by Muna Zaghloul et al. Amman: Jordanian Department of Antiquities, 1992.

McKenzie, John L. "The Four Samuels." *BR* 7 (1962): 3–18.

McKenzie, Steven L. *The Chronicler's Use of the Deuteronomistic History*. HSM 33. Atlanta: Scholars Press, 1984.

________. *King David: A Biography*. Oxford: Oxford University Press, 2000.

________. "Mizpah of Benjamin and the Date of the Deuteronomistic History." Pages 149–55 in *"Lasset uns Brücken bauen...": Collected Communications to the XVth Congress of the International Organization for the Study of the Old Testament, Cambridge 1995*. Edited by Klaus-Dietrich Schunk and Matthias Augustin. BEATAJ 42. Frankfurt a.M.: Lang, 1998.

________. "Saul in the Deuteronomistic History." Pages 59–70 in *Saul in Story and Tradition*. Edited by Carl S. Ehrlich with Marsha C. White. FAT I/47. Tübingen: Mohr Siebeck, 2006.

________. "The So-Called Succession Narrative in the Deuteronomistic History." Pages 123–35 in *Die sogenannte Thronfolgegeschichte Davids: Neue Einsichten und Anfragen*. Edited by Albert de Pury and Thomas Römer. OBO 176. Fribourg: University Press; Göttingen: Vandenhoeck & Ruprecht, 2000.

________. *The Trouble with Kings: The Composition of the Book of Kings in the Deuteronomistic History*. VTSup 42. Leiden: Brill, 1991.

Mendelsohn, I. "Samuel's Denunciation of Kingship in Light of the Akkadian Documents from Ugarit." *BASOR* 143 (1956): 17–22.

Mendenhall, George E. "The Hebrew Conquest of Palestine." *BA* 25 (1962): 66–87.

________. *The Tenth Generation: The Origins of the Biblical Tradition*. Baltimore: The Johns Hopkins University Press, 1973.

Merleau-Ponty, Maurice. *Phenomenology of Perception*. 1945. Translated by Colin Smith, 1962. Repr., London: Routledge, 2002.

Mettinger, Tryggve N. D. *King and Messiah: The Civil and Sacral Legitimation of the Israelite Kings*. ConBOT 8. Lund: Gleerup, 1976.

Meyerhoff, Barbara G. "We Don't Wrap Herring in a Printed Page: Fusion, Fictions and Continuity in Secular Ritual." Pages 199–224 in *Secular Ritual*. Edited by Sally F. Moore and Barbara G. Meyerhoff. Assen: Van Gorcum, 1977.

Meyers, Carol. Review of P. King and L. Stager, *Life in Biblical Israel*. *BASOR* 331 (2003): 84–86.

Mildenberger, Friedrich. "Die vordeuteronomistische Saul-Davidüberlieferung." Ph.D. diss., Tübingen, 1962.

Miller, J. Maxwell. "The Elisha Cycle and the Accounts of the Omride Wars." *JBL* 85 (1966): 441–54.

________. "Geba/Gibeah of Benjamin." *VT* 25 (1975): 145–66.

________. "Saul's Rise to Power: Some Observations Concerning 1 Sam 9:1–10:16; 10:26–11:15 and 13:2–14:46." *CBQ* 36 (1974): 157–74.

________, and John H. Hayes, eds. *Israelite and Judaean History*. OTL. Philadelphia: Westminster, 1977.

Miller, Patrick D., and J. J. M. Roberts. *The Hand of the Lord: A Reassessment of the "Ark Narrative" of 1 Samuel*. JHNES. Baltimore: The Johns Hopkins University Press, 1977. Repr., Atlanta: SBL, 2008.

Miller, Robert D. *Chieftains of the Highland Clans: A History of Israel in the 12th and 11th Centuries B.C.* Grand Rapids, Mich.: Eerdmans, 2005.

Minokami, Yoshikazu. *Die Revolution des Jehu*. Göttinger Theologische Arbeiten 38; Göttingen: Vandenhoeck & Ruprecht, 1989.

Miscall, Peter D. "Michal and Her Sisters." Pages 246–60 in *Telling Queen Michal's Story: An Experiment in Comparative Interpretation*. Edited by D. J. A. Clines and T. C. Eskenazi. JSOTSup 119. Sheffield: Sheffield Academic Press, 1991.

Mittmann, Siegfried. "Amathous, Essa, Ragaba: Drei hellenistische Festungen im östlichen Randbereich des mittleren Jordangrabens." *ZDPV* 103 (1987): 49–66, pls. 1–7.

________. *Beiträge zur Siedlungs- und Territorialgeschichte des nördlichen Ostjordanlandes*. ADPV 2. Wiesbaden: Harrassowitz, 1970.

________. "Die Steige des Sonnengottes (Ri. 8,13)." *ZDPV* 81 (1965): 80–87.

Moberly, Gregory. "Glimpses of the Heroic Saul." Pages 80–87 in *Saul in Story and Tradition*. Edited by Carl S. Ehrlich with Marsha C. White. FAT I/47. Tübingen: Mohr Siebeck, 2006.

Moenikes, Ansgar. "Zur Redaktionsgeschichte des sogenannten Deuteronomistischen Geschichtswerks." *ZAW* 104 (1992): 333–48.

Möhlinbrink, Kurt. "Sauls Ammoniterfeldzug und Samuels Beitrag zum Königtum des Sauls." *ZAW* 58 (1940/1941): 57–70.

Mommer, Peter. "David und Merab—eine historische oder eine literarische Beziehung?" Pages 196–204 in *David und Saul im Widerstreit—Diachronie und Synchronie im Wettstreit: Beiträge zur Auslegung des ersten Samuelbuches*. Edited by Walter Dietrich. OBO 206. Fribourg: University Press; Göttingen: Vandenhoeck & Ruprecht, 2005.

________. "Ist auch Saul unter den Propheten? Ein Beitrag zu 1 Sam 19,18–24." *BN* 38/39 (1987): 53–61.

________. *Samuel: Geschichte und Überlieferung*. WMANT 65. Neukirchen-Vluyn: Neukirchener Verlag, 1991.

Moore, George Foot. *Judges*. ICC. New York: Scribner, 1895.

Moore, Michael S. "Jehu's Coronation and Purge of Israel." *VT* 53 (2003): 97–114.

Moore, Sally F., and Barbara G. Meyerhoff. "Secular Ritual: Forms and Meanings." Pages 3–24 in *Secular Ritual*. Edited by Sally F. Moore and Barbara G. Meyerhoff. Assen: Van Gorcum, 1977.

Moran, William L. "The Ancient Near Eastern Background of the Love of God in Deuteronomy." *CBQ* 25 (1963): 77–87.

Morgenstern, Julian. *Amos Studies*. 2 vols. Cincinnati: Hebrew Union College Press, 1941.

Morris, Brian. *Anthropological Studies of Religion: An Introductory Text*. Cambridge: Cambridge University Press, 1987.

Muilenburg, James. "The Site of Ancient Gilgal." *BASOR* 140 (1955): 11–27.

Müller, Reinhard. *Königtum und Gottesherrschaft: Untersuchungen zur alttestamentlichen Monarchiekritik*. FAT II/3. Tübingen: Mohr Siebeck, 2004.

Na'aman, Nadav. "Hazael of ᶜAmqi and Hadadezer of Beth-rehob." *UF* 27 (1995): 381–94.

________. "The Pre-Deuteronomistic Story of King Saul and Its Historical Significance." *CBQ* 54 (1992): 638–58.

Nelson, Richard D. *The Double Redaction of the Deuteronomistic History*. JSOTSup 18. Sheffield: JSOT Press, 1981.

________. "The Double Redaction of the Deuteronomistic History: The Case is Still Compelling." *JSOT* 29 (2005): 319–37.
________. *First and Second Kings*. Interpretation. Atlanta: John Knox, 1987.
________. "Josiah in the Book of Joshua." *JBL* 100 (1981): 531–40.
Nelson, William Boyd, Jr. "1 Samuel 16–18 and 19:8–10: A Traditio-Historical Study." Ph.D. diss., Harvard University, 1992. Reviewed in *HTR* 85 (1992): 499–500.
Nentel, Jochen. *Trägerschaft und Intentionen des deuteronomistischen Geschichtswerks: Untersuchungen zu den Reflexionsreden Jos 1; 23; 24; 1 Sam 12 und 1 Kön 8*. BZAW 297. Berlin: de Gruyter, 2000.
Nicholson, E. W. *Deuteronomy and Tradition*. Philadelphia: Fortress, 1967.
Nicholson, Sarah. *Three Faces of Saul: An Intertextual Approach to Biblical Tragedy*. JSOTSup 339. Sheffield: Sheffield Academic Press, 2002.
Niditch, Susan. *Oral World and Written Word: Ancient Israelite Literature*. LibAncIsr. Louisville, Ky.: WJKP, 1996.
Niemann, Hermann Michael. *Herrschaft, Königtum und Staat: Skizzen zur soziokulturellen Entwicklung im monarchischen Israel*. FAT I/6. Tübingen: Mohr Siebeck, 1993.
Nihan, Christophe. "Du voyant au prophète: Royauté et divination en Israël selon 1 Samuel 9,1–10,16." *Foi & Vie* 38 (1999): 7–25.
________. "Saul among the Prophets." Pages 88–118 in *Saul in Story and Tradition*. Edited by Carl S. Ehrlich with Marsha C. White. FAT I/47. Tübingen: Mohr Siebeck, 2006.
Noll, K. L. "Deuteronomistic History or Deuteronomistic Debate? (A Thought Experiment)." *JSOT* 31 (2007): 311–45.
North, Robert. "David's Rise: Sacral, Military, or Psychiatric?" *Bib* 63 (1982): 524–44.
________. "Quirks of Jordan River Cartography." Pages 205–15 in *Studies in the History and Archaeology of Jordan* 2. Edited by Adnan Hadidi. Amman: Jordanian Department of Antiquities, 1985.
Noth, Martin. *The Deuteronomistic History*. Sheffield: Sheffield Academic Press, 2001. Repr. of *The Deuteronomistic History*. Translated by J. A. Clines et al. JSOTSup 15. Sheffield: JSOT Press, 1981. Translation of *Überlieferungsgeschichtliche Studien*. 2d ed. Tübingen: Niemeyer, 1957.
________. "Gilead und Gad." *ZDPV* 75 (1959): 14–73. Repr., pages 1:489–543 in *Aufsätze zur biblischen Landes- und Altertumskunde*. 2 vols. Neukirchen-Vluyn: Neukirchener Verlag, 1971.
________. *The History of Israel*. 2d ed. Translated by P. R. Ackroyd. London: Adam & Charles Black, 1960. Translation of *Geschichte Israels*. 2d ed. Göttingen: Vandenhoeck & Ruprecht, 1958.
________. "Das Land Gilead als Siedlungsgebiet israelitischer Sippen." *PJ* 37 (1941): 50–101. Repr., pages 1:347–90 in *Aufsätze zur biblischen Landes- und Altertumskunde*. 2 vols. Neukirchen-Vluyn: Neukirchener Verlag, 1971.
________. "Die Wege der Pharaonenheere in Palästina und Syrien, IV: Die Schoschenkenliste." *ZDPV* 61 (1938): 277–304.
Nübel, Hans-Ulrich. "Davids Aufstieg in der frühe israelitischer Geschichtsschreibung." Ph.D. diss., Bonn, 1959.

O'Brien, Mark A. *The Deuteronomistic History Hypothesis: A Reassessment*. OBO 92. Fribourg: University Press; Göttingen: Vandenhoeck & Ruprecht, 1989.
________. "The Protrayal of Prophets in 2 Kings 2." *ABR* 46 (1998): 1–16.

Oded, B. "Observations on Methods of Assyrian Rule in Transjordania after the Palestinian Campaign of Tiglath-Pileser III." *JNES* 29 (1970): 177–86.

Olivier, Hannes. "Remarks on Landscape Resources and Human Occupation in Jordan According to Some Nineteenth Century Travelogues." Pages 393–98 in *Studies in the History and Archaeology of Jordan* 6. Ed. Ghazi Bisheh, Muna Zaghloul, and Ina Kehrberg. Amman: Jordanian Department of Antiquities, 1997.

Palmer, Carol. "Traditional Agriculture." Pages 621–29 in *The Archaeology of Jordan*. Edited by Burton MacDonald, Russell Adams, and Piotr Bienkowski. Sheffield: Sheffield Academic Press, 2001.

Pardee, Dennis. "The Linguistic Classification of the Deir ᶜAlla Text Written on Plaster." Pages 100–105 in *The Balaam Text from Deir ᶜAlla Re-Evaluated: Proceedings of the International Symposium Held at Leiden 21–24 August 1989*. Edited by J. Hoftijzer and G. van der Kooij. Leiden: Brill, 1991.

Peckham, Brian J. *The Compostion of the Deuteronomistic History*. HSM 35. Atlanta: Scholars Press, 1985.

________. "The Composition of Deuteronomy 5–11." Pages 241–61 in *The Word of the Lord Shall Go Forth: Essays in Honor of David Noel Freedman in Celebration of His Sixtieth Birthday*. Edited by Carol L. Meyers and M. O'Connor. ASORSVS 1. Winona Lake, Ind.: Eisenbrauns, 1983.

________. "The Composition of Joshua 3–4." *CBQ* 46 (1984): 413–31.

Peleg, Yaron. "Love at First Sight? David, Jonathan, and the Biblical Politics of Gender." *JSOT* 30 (2005): 171–89.

Perdue, Leo G. "'Is There Anyone Left of the House of Saul...?' Ambiguity and the Characterization of David in the Succession Narrative." *JSOT* 30 (1984): 67–84.

________. "Liminality as a Social Setting for Wisdom Instructions." *ZAW* 93 (1981): 114–26.

Person, Raymond F. *The Deuteronomic School: History, Social Setting, and Literature*. SBLStBL 2. Atlanta: SBL, 2002.

Piccirillo, Michele. "The Jerusalem-Esbus Road and Its Sanctuaries in Transjordan." Pages 165–72 in *Studies in the History and Archaeology of Jordan* 3. Edited by Adnan Hadidi. Amman: Jordanian Department of Antiquities, 1987.

Pickering, W. S. F. "The Persistence of Rites of Passage: Towards an Explanation." *BritJSociol* 25 (1974): 63–78.

Pigott, V. C., P. E. McGovern, and M. R. Notis. "The Earliest Steel from Transjordan." *MASCA Journal* 2 (1982): 35–39.

Pisano, Stephen. *Additions or Omissions in the Books of Samuel*. OBO 57. Fribourg: University Press; Göttingen: Vandenhoeck & Ruprecht, 1984.

Polzin, Robert. *Late Biblical Hebrew: Toward an Historical Typology of Biblical Hebrew Prose*. HSM 12. Missoula, Mont.: Scholars Press, 1976.

________. *Samuel and the Deuteronomist*. San Francisco: Harper & Row, 1989.

Porter, R. "Old Testament Historiography." Pages 125–62 in *Tradition and Interpretation: Essays by Members of the Society for Old Testament Study*. Edited by G. W. Anderson. Oxford: Clarendon, 1979.

Preuß, Horst Dietrich. "Zum deuteronomistischen Geschichtswerk." *TRu* 58 (1993): 229–64, 341–95.

Provan, Iain. *1 and 2 Kings*. NIBCom. Peabody, Mass.: Hendrikson, 1995.

________. *Hezekiah and the Books of Kings: A Contribution to the Debate about the Composition of the Deuteronomistic History*. BZAW 172. Berlin: de Gruyter, 1988.

________. "Why Barzillai of Gilead (1 Kings 2:7)? Narrative Art and the Hermeneutics of Suspicion in 1 Kings 1–2." *TynBul* 46 (1995): 103–16.

________, V. Philips Long, and Tremper Longman III. *A Biblical History of Israel*. Louisville, Ky.: WJKP, 2003.

Pury, Albert de, and Thomas Römer, eds. *Die sogenannte Thronfolgegeschichte Davids: Neue Einsichten und Anfragen*. OBO 176. Fribourg: University Press; Göttingen: Vandenhoeck & Ruprecht, 2000.

Pury, Albert de, and Thomas Römer. "Einleitung: Zu den wichtigsten Problemen der sogenannten Thronnachfolgegeschichte." Pages 1–3 in *Die sogenannte Thronfolgegeschichte Davids: Neue Einsichten und Anfragen*. Edited by Albert de Pury and Thomas Römer. OBO 176. Fribourg: University Press; Göttingen: Vandenhoeck & Ruprecht, 2000).

Rad, Gerhard von. *Das formgeschichtliche Problem des Hexateuchs*. BWANT 78. Stuttgart: Kohlhammer, 1938.

________. *Studies in Deuteronomy*. Translated by D. Stalker. SBT 9. London: SCM, 1953. Repr., 1961. Translation of *Deuteronomium-Studien*. 2d ed. Göttingen: Vandenhoeck & Ruprecht, 1948. Pages 74–91 repr. as "The Deuteronomic Theology of History in *I* and *II Kings*." Pages 205–21 in *The Problem of the Hexateuch and Other Essays*. Translated by E. W. T. Dicken. Edinburgh: Oliver & Boyd, 1966.

________. *Old Testament Theology*. Translated by D. M. G. Stalker, with an introduction by W. Brueggemann. 2 vols. OTL. Edinburgh: Oliver & Boyd, 1962. Repr., Louisville, Ky.: WJKP, 2001. Translation of *Theologie des alten Testaments*. 2 vols. 2d ed. Munich: Kaiser, 1957.

Radjawane, Arnold Nicolaas. "Das deuteronomistische Geschichtswerk: Ein Forschungsbericht." *TRu* 38 (1974): 177–216.

Rainer, Albertz. "Die Intentionen und Träger des deuteronomistischen Geschichtswerks." Pages 37–53 in *Schöpfung und Befreiung: Für Claus Westermann zum 80. Geburtstag*. Edited by Rainer Albertz, Friedemann W. Golka, and Jürgen Kegler. Stuttgart: Calwer Verlag, 1989.

Rainey, Anson F. "Whence Came the Israelites and Their Language?" *IEJ* 57 (2007): 41–64.

________. "Redefining Hebrew—A Transjordanian Language." *Maarav* 14 (2007): 67–81.

Regev, Eyal. "Josephus on Gibeah: Versions of a Toponym." *JQR* 89 (1999): 351–59.

Rendsburg, Gary A. "Hurvitz Redux: On the Continued Scholarly Inattention to a Simple Principle of Hebrew Philology." Pages 104–28 in *Biblical Hebrew: Studies in Chronology and Typology*. Edited by Ian Young. JSOTSup 369. London: T&T Clark, 2003.

________. *Israelian Hebrew in the Book of Kings*. Bethesda, Md.: CDL, 2002.

________. "Some False Leads in the Identification of Late Biblical Hebrew Texts: The Cases of Genesis 24 and 1 Samuel 2:27–36." *JBL* 121 (2002): 23–46.

Rendtorff, Rolf. "Beobachtungen zur altisraelitischen Geschichtsschreibung anhand der Geschichte vom Aufstieg Davids." Pages 428–39 in *Probleme biblischer*

Theologie: Gerhard von Rad zum 70. Geburtstag. Edited by H. W. Wolff. Munich: Kaiser, 1971.

________. *The Old Testament: An Introduction*. Translated by John Bowden. Philadelphia: Fortress, 1986. Translation of *Das Alte Testament: Eine Einführung*. Neukirchen-Vluyn: Neukirchener Verlag, 1983.

Rezetko, Robert. *Source and Revision in the Narratives of David's Transfer of the Ark: Text, Language, and Story in 2 Samuel 6 and 1 Chronicles 13, 15–16*. Library of Hebrew Bible/Old Testament Studies 470. New York: T&T Clark, 2007.

Richter, Wolfgang. *Die Bearbeitungen des "Retterbuches" in der deuteronomistischen Epoche*. BBB 21. Bonn: Hanstein, 1964.

________. *Die sogenannten vorprophetischen Berufungsberichte: Eine literaturwissenschaftliche Studie zu 1 Sam 9,1–10,16, Ex 3f. und Ri 6,11b–17*. FRLANT 101. Göttingen: Vandenhoeck & Ruprecht, 1970.

________. *Traditionsgeschichtliche Untersuchungen zum Richterbuch*. BBB 18. Bonn: Heinstein, 1963.

________. "Die Überlieferungen um Jephtah: Ri 10,17–12,6." *Bib* 47 (1966): 485–556.

Robinson, Theodore H. *The Old Testament: A Conspectus*. London: Duckworth, 1953.

Rofé, Alexander. "The Acts of Nahash According to 4QSam[a]." *IEJ* 32 (1982): 129–33.

________. "The Battle of David and Goliath: Folklore, Theology, Eschatology." Pages 117–51 in *Judaic Perspectives on Ancient Israel*. Edited by Jacob Neusner, Baruch A. Levine, and Ernest S. Frerichs. Fortress: Philadelphia, 1987.

________. "Classes in the Prophetical Stories: Didactic Legenda and Parable." Pages 143–64 in *Studies on Prophecy: A Collection of Twelve Papers*. Edited by G. W. Anderson et al. VTSup 26. Leiden: Brill, 1974.

________. *The Prophetical Stories: The Stories about the Prophets in the Hebrew Bible—Their Literary Types and History*. Jerusalem: Magnes Press, 1988.

Rollston, Christopher A. "Scribal Education in Ancient Israel: The Old Hebrew Epigraphic Evidence." *BASOR* 344 (2006): 47–74.

Römer, Thomas. "Entstehungsphasen des 'deuteronomistischen Geschichtswerkes." Pages 45–70 in *Die deuteronomistischen Geschichtswerke: Redaktions- und religionsgeschichtliche Perspektiven zur "Deuteronomismus"-Diskussion in Tora und Vorderen Propheten*. Edited by Markus Witte et al. BZAW 365. Berlin: de Gruyter, 2006.

________, ed. *The Future of the Deuteronomistic History*. BETL 147. Leuven: University Press; Leuven; Peeters, 2000.

________. *Israels Väter: Untersuchungen zur Väterthematik im Deuteronomium und in der deuteronomistischen Tradition*. OBO 99. Fribourg: University Press; Göttingen: Vandenhoeck & Ruprecht, 1990.

________. *The So-Called Deuteronomistic History: A Sociological, Historical, and Literary Introduction*. London: T&T Clark, 2005.

________, and Albert de Pury. "Deuteronomistic Historiography (DH): History of Research and Debated Issues." Pages 24–141 in *Israel Constructs Its Identity: Deuteronomistic Historiography in Recent Research*. Edited by A. de Pury, T. Römer, and J.-D. Macchi. JSOTSup 306. Sheffield: Sheffield Academic Press, 2000. Translation of "L'histriographie deutéronomiste: Histoire de la recherche et enjeux du débat." Pages 9–120 in *Israël construit son histoire: L'historiographie deutéronomiste à la lumière des recherches récentes*. Edited by A. de Pury, T. Römer, and J.-D. Macchi. *MdB* 34. Geneva: Labor et Fides, 1996.

Rooker, Mark F. *Biblical Hebrew in Transition: The Language of the Book of Ezekiel.* JSOTSup 90. Sheffield: JSOT Press, 1990.

________. "Diachronic Analysis and the Features of Late Biblical Hebrew." *BBR* 4 (1994): 135–44.

Rösel, Hartmut N. *Von Josua bis Jojachin: Untersuchungen zu den deuteronomistischen Geschichtsbüchern des Alten Testaments*. VTSup 75. Leiden: Brill, 1999.

Rosenbaum, Jonathan. "Hezekiah's Reform and the Deuteronomistic Tradition." *HTR* 72 (1979): 23–43.

Rost, Leonhard. *The Succession to the Throne of David*. Translated by Michael D. Rutter and David M. Gunn, with an introduction by Edward Ball. HTIBS 1. Sheffield: Almond, 1982. Translation of *Die Überlieferungen von der Thronnachfolge Davids*. BWANT 42. Stuttgart: Kohlhammer, 1926. Repr., pages 119–253 in *Das kleine Credo und andere Studien zum Alten Testament*. Heidelberg: Quelle & Meyer, 1965.

Roth, Wolfgang. "The Deuteronomic Rest Theology: A Redaction-Critical Study." *BR* 21 (1976): 5–14.

________. "Deuteronomistisches Geschichtswerk/Deuteronomistische Schule." *TRE* 8 (1981): 543–52.

Rowlett, Lori. "Inclusion, Exclusion, and Marginality in the Book of Joshua." *JSOT* 55 (1992): 15–23.

Rowton, Michael B. "Urban Autonomy in a Nomadic Environment." *JNES* 32 (1973): 201–15.

________. "Dimorphic Structure and Topology." *OrAnt* 15 (1976): 17–31.

________. "Dimorphic Structure and the Problem of the ᶜApirû-ᶜIbrîm." *JNES* 35 (1976): 13–20.

________. "Dimorphic Structure and the Parasocial Element." *JNES* 36 (1977): 181–98.

Rudman, D. "The Commissioning Stories of Saul and David as Theological Allegory." *VT* 50 (2000): 519–30.

Rudnig, Thilo Alexander. *Davids Thron: Redaktionskritische Studien zur Geschichte von der Thronnachfolge Davids*. BZAW 358. Berlin: de Gruyter, 2006.

Sacon, K. K. "A Study of the Literary Structure of the 'Succession Narrative'." Pages 27–54 in *Studies in the Period of David and Solomon and Other Essays*. Edited by Tomoo Ishida. Winona Lake, Ind.: Eisenbrauns, 1982.

Said, Edward W. "Reflections on Exile." *Granta* 13 (1984): 159. Cited in Beverley Butler, "Egypt: Constructed Exiles of the Imagination," in *Contested Landscapes: Movement, Exile and Place* (ed. Barbara Bender and Margot Winer; Oxford: Berg, 2001), 315.

St. John, Robert. *Roll Jordan Roll: The Life Story of a River and Its People*. Garden City, N.Y.: Doubleday, 1965.

Sakenfeld, Katharine Doob. *Just Wives? Stories of Power and Survival in the Old Testament and Today*. Louisville, Ky.: WJKP, 2003.

________. "Loyalty and Love: The Language of Human Interconnections in the Hebrew Bible." *Michigan Quarterly Review* 22 (1983): 190–204. Repr., pages 215–29 in *Backgrounds for the Bible*. Edited by Michael Patrick O'Connor and David Noel Freedman. Winona Lake: Eisenbrauns, 1987.

Sanders, Seth L. "Writing and Early Iron Age Israel: Before National Scripts, Beyond Nations and States." Pages 97–112 in *Literate Culture and Tenth-Century Canaan:*

The Tel Zayit Abecedry in Context. Edited by Ron E. Tappy and P. Kyle McCarter Jr. Winona Lake, Ind.: Eisenbrauns, 2008.

________. "What Was the Alphabet For? The Rise of Written Vernaculars and the Making of Israelite National Literature." *Maarav* 11 (2004): 25–56.

Satterthwaite, Philip E. "The Elisha Narratives and Coherence of 2 Kings 2–8." *TynBul* 49 (1998): 1–28.

Schicklberger, Franz. *Die Ladeerzählungen des ersten Samuel-Buches: Eine literaturwissenschaftliche und theologiegeschichtliche Untersuchung*. FB 7. Würzburg: Echter Verlag, 1973.

Schipper, Jeremy. "Did David Overinterpret Nathan's Parable in 2 Samuel 12:1–6?" *JBL* 126 (2007): 383–407.

________. "Disabling Israelite Leadership: 2 Samuel 6:23 and Other Images of Disability in the Deuteronomistic History." Pages 103–13 in *This Abled Body: Rethinking Disabilities in Biblical Studies*. Edited by Hector Avalos, Sarah J. Melcor, and Jeremy Schipper. SemeiaSt 55. Atlanta: SBL, 2007.

________. "'Why Do You Still Speak of Your Affairs?' Polyphony in Mephibosheth's Exchanges with David in 2 Samuel." *VT* 54 (2004): 344–51.

Schloen, J. David. *The House of the Father as Fact and Symbol: Patrimonialism in Ugarit and the Ancient Near East*. SAHL 2. Winona Lake, Ind.: Eisenbrauns, 2001.

Schmid, Konrad. "Hatte Wellhausen Recht? Das Problem der literarhistorischen Anfänge des Deuteronomismus in den Königebüchern." Pages 19–43 in *Die deuteronomistischen Geschichtswerke: Redaktions- und religionsgeschichtliche Perspektiven zur "Deuteronomismus"-Diskussion in Tora und Vorderen Propheten*. Edited by Markus Witte et al. BZAW 365. Berlin: de Gruyter, 2006.

Schmitt, Hans-Christoph. "Das sogenannte vorprophetische Berufungsschema: Zur 'geistigen Heimat' des Berufungsformulars von Ex 3,9–12; Jdc 6,11–24 und I Sam 9,1–10,16." *ZAW* 104 (1992): 202–16.

Schmidt, Ludwig. *Menschlicher Erfolg und Jahwes Initiative: Studien zu Tradition, Interpretation und Historie in Überlieferungen von Gideon, Saul und David*. WMANT 38. Neukirchen-Vluyn: Neukirchener Verlag, 1970.

Schniedewind, William M. *How the Bible Became a Book: The Textualization of Ancient Israel*. Cambridge: Cambridge University Press, 2004.

Schulte, Hannelis. *Die Entstehung der Geschichtsschreibung im Alten Israel*. BZAW 128. Berlin: de Gruyter, 1972.

Schumacher, G. *Across the Jordan*. New York: Scribner & Welford, 1886.

________. "Das südliche Basan." *ZDPV* 20 (1897): 65–227.

Schunk, Klaus-Dietrich. *Benjamin: Untersuchungen zur Entstehung und Geschichte eines israelitischen Stammes*. BZAW 86. Berlin: Töppelman, 1963.

________. "Erwägungen zur Geschichte und Bedeutung von Maḥanaim." *ZDMG* 113 (1963): 34–40.

Schüpphaus, Joachim. "Richter- und Prophetengeschichten als Glieder der Geschichtsdarstellung der Richter- und Königzeit." Th.D. diss., Bonn, 1967.

Schwartz, Theodore. Review of V. Turner, *The Ritual Process*. *AmAnthropol* n.s. 74 (1972): 904–8.

Seebass, Horst. "Die Vorgeschichte der Königserhebung Sauls." *ZAW* 79 (1967): 155–71.

Seeligmann, Isac Leo. "Hebräische Erzählung und biblische Geschichtsschreibung," *TZ* 19 (1963): 305–25. Repr., pages 119–36 in *Gesammelte Studien zur Hebräischen Bibel* (FAT I/41; Tübingen: Mohr Siebeck, 2004.

Seeman, Don. "The Watcher at the Window: Cultural Poetics of a Biblical Motif." *Proof* 24 (2004): 1–50.

Segal, M. H. "The Composition of the Books of Samuel." *JQR* 55 (1964–1965): 318–39.

Segal, Robert A. "Victor Turner's Theory of Ritual." *Zygon* 18 (1983): 327–35.

Seidl, Theodor. "David statt Saul: Göttliche Legitimation und menschliche Kompetenz des Königs als Motive der Redaktion von I Sam 16–18." *ZAW* 98 (1986): 39–55.

Seiler, Stefan. *Die Geschichte von der Thronfolge Davids (2 Sam 9–20; 1 Kön 1–2): Untersuchungen zur Literaturkritik und Tendenz*. BZAW 267. Berlin: de Gruyter, 1998.

Sellin, Ernst. *Introduction to the Old Testament*. Translated by W. Montgomery. London: Hodder & Stoughton, 1923. Translation of *Einleitung in das Alte Testament*. ETB 2. Leipzig: Quelle & Meyer, 1910.

Seow, Choon-Leong. *Ecclesiastes: A New Translation with Introduction and Commentary*. AB 18C. New York: Doubleday, 1997.

________. *Myth, Drama, and the Politics of David's Dance*. HSM 44. Atlanta: Scholars Press, 1989.

Shaviv, Shemuel. "*nābîʾ* and *nāgîd* in 1 Samuel ix 1–x 16." *VT* 34 (1984): 108–113.

Shehadeh, Numan. "The Climate of Jordan in the Past and Present." Pages 25–37 in *Studies in the History and Archaeology of Jordan* 2. Edited by Adnan Hadidi. Amman: Jordanian Department of Antiquities, 1985.

Shenkel, James Donald. *Chronology and Recensional Development in the Greek Text of Kings*. HSM 1. Cambridge, Mass.: Harvard University Press, 1968.

Simons, Jan Jozef. *Geographical and Topographical Texts of the Old Testament: a Concise Commentary in XXXII Chapters*. Nederlands instituut voor het Nabije Oosten. Studia Francisci Scholten memoriae dicata 2. Leiden: Brill, 1959.

Smith, Henry Preserved. *A Critical and Exegetical Commentary on the Books of Samuel*. ICC. New York: Scribner, 1899.

Smend, R., Sr. "J E in den geschichtlichen Büchern des AT." *ZAW* 39 (1921): 181–217.

Smend, Rudolf. *Die Entstehung des alten Testaments*. 1978. 4th ed. Stuttgart: Kohlhammer, 1989.

________. "The Law and the Nations: A Contribution to Deuteronomistic Tradition History." Pages 95–110 in *Reconsidering Israel and Judah: Recent Studies on the Deuteronomistic History*. Edited by G. N. Knoppers and J. G. McConville. Translated by P. T. Daniels. SBTS 8. Winona Lake, Ind.: Eisenbrauns, 2000. Translation of "Das Gesetz und die Völker: Ein Beitrag zur deuteronomistischen Redaktionsgeschichte." Pages 494–509 in *Probleme biblischer Theologie: Gerhard von Rad zum 70. Geburtstag*. Edited by H. W. Wolff. Munich: Kaiser, 1971.

Snaith, Norman H. "The Historical Books." Pages 84–114 in *The Old Testament and Modern Study: A Generation of Discovery and Research*. Edited by H. H. Rowley. Oxford: Clarendon, 1951.

Soggin, J. Alberto. "The Davidic-Solomonic Kingdom." Pages 332–80 in *Israelite and Judaean History*. Edited by John H. Hayes and J. Maxwell Miller. London: SCM, 1977.

________. "Deuteronomistische Geschichtsauslegung während des babylonischen Exils." Pages 11–17 in *Oikonomia: Heilsgeschichte als Thema der Theologie*. Edited by Felix Christ. Hamburg-Bergstedt: Herbert Reich Evangelische Verlag, 1967.

________. "Der Entstehungsort des Deuteronomistischen Geschichtswerkes: Ein Beitrag zur Geschichte desselben." *TLZ* 100 (1975): 3–8.

________. *Joshua: A Commentary*. OTL. London: SCM, 1972.

________. *Judges: A Commentary*. Translated by J. S. Bowden. OTL. Philadelphia: Westminster, 1981.

________. *Das Königtum in Israel: Ursprünge, Spannungen, Entwicklung*. BZAW 104. Berlin: Töpelmann, 1967.

________. "Problemi di storia e di storiografia nell'antico Israele." *Hen* 4 (1982): 1–16.

________. "The Reign of ᵓEšbaᶜal, Son of Saul." Pages 31–49 in *Old Testament and Oriental Studies*. BibOr 29. Rome: Biblical Institute Press, 1975.

Soriano, Matthew J. "The Apology of Hazael: A Literary and Historical Analysis of the Tel Dan Inscription." *JNES* 66 (2007): 163–76.

Spencer, John R. "Priestly Families (or Factions) in Samuel and Kings." Pages 387–400 in *The Pitcher is Broken: Memorial Essays for Gösta W. Ahlström*. Edited by Steven W. Holloway and Lowell K. Handy. JSOTSup 190. Sheffield: Sheffield Academic Press, 1995.

Spieckermann, Hermann. *Judah unter Assur in der Sargonidenzeit*. FRLANT 129. Göttingen: Vandenhoeck & Ruprecht, 1982.

Staalduine-Sulman, Eveline van. *The Targum of Samuel*. Studies in Aramaic Interpretation of Scripture 1. Leiden: Brill, 2000.

Stager, Lawrence E. "Archaeology, Ecology, and Social History: Background Themes to the Song of Deborah." Pages 221–34 in *Congress Volume: Jerusalem, 1986*. Edited by J. A. Emerton. Leiden: Brill, 1988.

________. "The Archaeology of the Family in Ancient Israel." *BASOR* 260 (1985): 1–35.

________. "Forging an Identity: The Emergence of Ancient Israel." Pages 123–75 in *The Oxford History of the Biblical World*. Edited by Michael D. Coogan. New York: Oxford University Press, 1998.

________. "Jerusalem and the Garden of Eden." Pages 183*–94* in *ErIsr* 26. Edited by Baruch A. Levine et al. Jerusalem: Israel Exploration Society, 1999.

________. "The Patrimonial Kingdom of Solomon." Pages 63–74 in *Symbiosis, Symbolism, and the Power of the Past: Canaan, Ancient Israel, and Their Neighbors, from the Late Bronze Age through Roman Palaestina*. Edited by W. G. Dever and S. Gitin. Winona Lake, Ind.: Eisenbrauns, 2003.

________. "Response." Pages 83–87 in *Biblical Archaeology Today: Proceedings of the International Congress on Biblical Archaeology, Jerusalem, April 1984*. Jerusalem: Israel Exploration Society, 1985.

Stahl, Rainer. "Aspekte der Geschichte deuteronomistischer Theologie: Zur Traditionsgeschichte der Terminologie und zur Redaktionsgeschichte der Redekompositionen." Ph.D. diss., Jena, 1982.

Steck, Odil Hannes. *Israel und das gewaltsame Geschick der Propheten: Untersuchungen zur Überlieferung des deuteronomistischen Geschichtsbildes im Alten Testament, Spätjudentum und Urchristentum*. WMANT 23. Neukirchen-Vluyn: Neukirchener Verlag, 1967.

Steen, Eveline J. van der. "Aspects of Nomadism and Settlement in the Central Jordan Valley." *PEQ* 127 (1995): 141–58.

________. *Tribes and Territories in Transition: The Central East Jordan Valley in the Late Bronze Age and Early Iron Ages. A Study of the Sources*. OLA 130. Leuven: Peeters, 2004.

________. "A Walk through the Wadi Zerqa." Pages 109–133 in *Sacred and Sweet: Studies on the Material Culture of Tell Deir ᶜAlla and Tell Abu Sarbut*. Edited by Margreet L. Steiner and Eveline J. van der Steen. ANESSup 24. Leuven: Peeters, 2008.

Steuernagel, Carl. "Der ᶜAdschlūn (Bogen 1–3)" *ZDPV* 48 (1925): 191–240.

________. *Der ᶜAdschlūn*. Leipzig: Hinrichs, 1927.

________. "Wo lag Pnuel?" *JPOS* 8 (1928): 203–13.

Stipp, Hermann-Josef. *Elischa—Propheten—Gottesmänner*. Arbeiten zu Text und Sprache im Alten Testament 24. St. Ottilien: EOS Verlag, 1987.

Stoebe, Hans Joachim. *Das erste Buch Samuelis*. KAT 8/1. Gütersloh: Mohn, 1973.

________. *Das zweite Buch Samuelis*. KAT 8/2: Gütersloh: Gütersloher Verlagshaus, 1994.

________. "David und Mikal: Überlegungen zur Jugendgeschichte Davids." Pages 224–43 in *Von Ugarit nach Qumran: Beiträge zur alttestamentlichen und altorientalischen Forschung*. Edited by J. Hempel et al. BZAW 77. Berlin: Töpelmann, 1958. Repr., pages 91–110 in *Geschichte, Schiksal, Schuld und Glaube*. BBB 72. Frankfurt a.M.: Athenäum, 1989.

________. "Die Goliathperikope 1 Sam. xvii 1–xviii 5 und die Textform der Septuaginta." *VT* 6 (1956): 397–413.

________. "Noch einmal die Eselinnen des *Kîš* [1 Sam IX]." *VT* 7 (1957): 362–70.

________. "Zur Topographie und Überlieferung der Schlacht von Mikmas, 1. Sam. 13 und 14." *TZ* 21 (1965): 269–80.

Stone, Ken. "Sexual Power and Political Prestige." *BRev* 10.4 (1994): 28–31, 52–53.

Sturdy, John. "The Original Meaning of 'Is Saul Also among the Prophets (1 Samuel x 11, 12; xix 24)?'" *VT* 20 (1970): 206–13.

Sweeney, Marvin A. *I & II Kings: A Commentary*. OTL; Louisville, Ky.: WJKP, 2007.

Tadmor, Hayim. "Autobiographical Apology in the Royal Assyrian Literature." Pages 36–57 in *History, Historiography and Interpretation*. Edited by H. Tadmor and M. Weinfeld; Jerusalem: Magnes, 1983.

________. "The Southern Border of Aram." *IEJ* 12 (1962): 114–22.

Tanret, Michel. "The Works and the Days…On Scribal Activity in Old Babylonian Sippar-Amnānum." *RA* 98 (2004): 33–62.

Tappy, Ron E., et al. "An Abecedary of the Mid-Tenth Century B.C.E. from the Judaean Shephelah." *BASOR* 344 (2006): 5–46.

________, and P. Kyle McCarter Jr., eds. *Literate Culture and Tenth-Century Canaan: The Tel Zayit Abecedry in Context*. Winona Lake, Ind.: Eisenbrauns, 2008.

Thackeray, H. St. John. *The Septuagint and Jewish Worship: A Study in Origins*. London: Oxford University Press, 1921.

Thenius, Otto. *Die Bücher Samuels*. 3d ed. EHAT. Leipzig: Hirzel, 1898, page 165. Cited in Alexander A. Fischer, "Flucht und Heimkehr Davids als integraler Rahmen der Abschalomerzählung," in *Ideales Königtum: Studien zu David und Salomo* (ed. Rüdiger Lux; ABG 16; Leipzig: Evangelische Verlagsanstalt, 2005), 50 n. 27.

Thompson, J. A. "The Significance of the Verb *Love* in the David-Jonathan Narratives in 1 Samuel." *VT* 24 (1974): 334–38.

Thompson, Thomas L. *The Mythic Past: Biblical Archaeology and the Myth of Israel*. New York: Basic Books, 1994.

Thornton, T. C. G. "Charismatic Kingship in Israel and Judah." *JTS* 14 (1963): 1–11.

________. "Solomonic Apologetic in Samuel and Kings." *CQR* 169 (1968): 159–66.

Tilley, Christopher. *A Phenomenology of Landscape: Places, Paths and Monuments*. Oxford: Berg, 1994.

________. "Rocks as Resources: Landscapes and Power." *CornArch* 34 (1995): 5–57.

________. "The Powers of Rocks: Topography and Monument Construction on Bodmin Moor." *WorldArch* 28 (1996): 161–76.

Timm, Stefan. *Die Dynastie Omri: Quellen und Untersuchungen zur Geschichte Israels im 9. Jahrhundert vor Christus*. FRLANT 124. Göttingen: Vandenhoeck & Ruprecht, 1982.

Todd, Judith A. "The Pre-Deuteronomistic Elijah Cycle." Pages 1–35 in *Elijah and Elisha in Socioliterary Perspective*. Edited by Robert B. Coote. Atlanta: Scholars Press, 1992.

Toorn, Karel van der. "Saul and the Rise of Israelite State Religion." *VT* 43 (1993): 519–42.

________. *Scribal Culture and the Making of the Hebrew Bible*. Cambridge, Mass.: Harvard University Press, 2007.

Tosato, A. "La colpa di Saul (1 Sam 15,22–23)." *Bib* 59 (1978): 251–59.

Tov, Emanuel. "The Nature of the Differences between MT and the LXX in 1 Sam. 17–18." Pages 19–46 in *The Story of David and Goliath: Textual and Literary Criticism*. Edited by Dominique Barthélemy et al. OBO 73. Fribourg: University Press; Göttingen: Vandenhoeck & Ruprecht, 1986.

________. "The Composition of 1 Samuel 16–18 in the Light of the Septuagint Version." Pages 97–130 in *Emperical Models for Biblical Criticism*. Edited by Jeffrey H. Tigay. Philadelphia: University of Pennsylvania Press, 1985.

Trebolle Barrera, Julio C. *Salomón y Jeroboán: Historia de la recensión y redacción de I Reyes 2–12, 14*. Bibliotheca Salmanticensis, Dissertationes 3. Salamanca: Universidad Pontificia, Inst. Español Bibl. y Arqueologico, 1980.

________. "The Story of David and Goliath (1 Sam 17–18): Textual Variants and Literary Composition." *BIOSCS* 23 (1990): 16–30.

Tsevat, Matitiahu. "Ishbosheth and Congeners: The Names and Their Study." *HUCA* 46 (1975): 71–87.

Tsumura, D. T. "Bedan, a Copyist's Error? [1 Samuel xii 11]." *VT* 45 (1995): 122–23.

Tuan, Yi-Fu. "Geography, Phenomenology and the Study of Human Nature." *CanGeogr* 15 (1971): 181–92.

________. "Strangers and Strangeness." *GeogrRev* 76 (1986): 10–19.

________. *Topophilia: A Study of Environmental Perception, Attitudes, and Values*. New York: Columbia University Press, 1974.

Turner, Terence S. "Transformation, Hierarchy and Transcendence: A Reformulation of van Gennep's Model of the Structure of Rites of Passage." Pages 53–70 in *Secular Ritual*. Edited by Sally F. Moore and Barbara G. Meyerhoff. Assen: Van Gorcum, 1977.

Turner, Victor. *The Ritual Process: Structure and Anti-Structure*. Ithaca, N.Y.: Cornell University Press, 1969.

________. "Variations on a Theme of Liminality." Pages 36–52 in *Secular Ritual*. Edited by Sally F. Moore and Barbara G. Meyerhoff. Assen: Van Gorcum, 1977.

Ulrich, Eugene Charles. *The Qumran Text of Samuel and Josephus*. HSM 19. Missoula, Mont.: Scholars Press, 1978.

Van Seters, John. "Histories and Historians of the Ancient Near East: The Israelites." *Or* 50 (1981): 137–85.

________. *In Search of History: Historiography in the Ancient World and the Origins of Biblical History*. New Haven: Yale University Press, 1983. Repr., Winona Lake, Ind.: Eisenbrauns, 1997.

Van Zeist, W. "Past and Present Environments of the Jordan Valley." Pages 199–204 in *Studies in the History and Archaeology of Jordan* 2. Edited by Adnan Hadidi. Amman: Jordanian Department of Antiquities, 1985.

Vanderkam, James C. "Davidic Complicity in the Deaths of Abner and Eshbaal: A Historical and Redactional Study." *JBL* 99 (1980): 521–39.

Vanoni, Gottfried. "Beobachtungen zur deuteronomistischen Terminologie in 2 Kön 23,25–25,30." Pages 357–62 in *Das Deuteronomium: Entstehung, Gestalt und Botschaft*. BETL 68. Edited by Norbert Lohfink; Leuven: University Press and Peeters, 1985.

Vaux, Roland de. "Notes d'histoire et de topographie transjordaniennes." Pages 16–47 in *Vivre et Penser I: Recherches d'exégèse et d'histoire I* (=*RB* 50 [1941]).

Vehse, Charles Ted. "Long Live the King: Historical Fact and Narrative Fiction in 1 Samuel 9–10." Pages 435–44 in *The Pitcher is Broken: Memorial Essays for Gösta W. Ahlström*. Edited by Steven W. Holloway and Lowell K. Handy. JSOTSup 190. Sheffield: Sheffield Academic Press, 1995.

Veijola, Timo. "David und Meribaal." *RB* 85 (1978): 338–61.

________. "Deuteronomismusforschung zwischen Tradition und Innovation." Parts 1–3. *TRu* 67 (2002): 273–327, 391–424; 68 (2003): 1–44.

________. *Die ewige Dynastie: David und die Entstehung seiner Dynastie nach der deuteronomistischen Darstellung*. AASF B 193. Helsinki: Suomalainen Tiedeakatemia, 1975.

________. *Das Königtum in der Beurteilung der deuteronomistischen Historiographie: Eine redaktionsgeschichtliche Untersuchung*. AASF B 198. Helsinki: Suomalainen Tiedeakatemia, 1977.

________. "Solomon: Bathsheba's Firstborn." Pages 340–57 in *Reconsidering Israel and Judah: Recent Studies on the Deuteronomistic History*. Edited by G. N. Knoppers and J. G. McConville. Translated by Peter T. Daniels. SBTS 8. Winona Lake, Ind.: Eisenbrauns, 2000. Translation of "Salomo: Der Erstgeborene Bathsebas." Pages 230–50 in *Studies in the Historical Books of the Old Testament*. Edited by J. A. Emerton. VTSup 30. Leiden: Brill, 1979.

Veldhuijzen, Xander, and Eveline van der Steen. "Iron Production Center Found in the Jordan Valley." *NEA* 62.3 (1999): 195–99.

Vermeylen, Jacques. "L'affaire du veau d'or (Ex 32–34): Une clé pour la 'question deutéronomiste'?" *ZAW* 97 (1985): 1–23.

________. *La loi du plus fort: Histoire de la rédaction des récits davidiques de 1 Samuel à 1 Rois 2*. BETL 154. Leuven: University Press, 2000.

Vette, Joachim. *Samuel und Saul: Ein Beitrag zur narrativen Poetik des Samuelbuches*. BVB 13. Münster: LIT Verlag, 2005.

Wagner, David. *Geist und Tora: Studien zur göttlichen Legitimation und Delegitimation von Herrschaft im Alten Testament anhand der Erzählungen über König Saul*. ABG 15. Leipzig: Evangelische Verlagsanstalt, 2005.

Walker Bynum, Carol. "Women's Stories, Women's Symbols: A Critique of Victor Turner's Theory of Liminality." Pages 105–25 in *Anthropology and the Study of Religion*. Edited by Robert L. Moore and Frank E. Reynolds. Chicago: Center for the Scientific Study of Religion, 1984.

Wallace, H. N. "The Oracles Against the Israelite Dynasties in 1 and 2 Kings." *Bib* 67 (1986): 21–40.

Wallis, Gerhard. *Geschichte und Überlieferung: Gedanken über alttestamentliche Darstellungen der Frühgeschichte Israels und der Anfänge seines Königtums*. AzTh 2/13. Stuttgart: Kohlhammer, 1968.

Walters, Stanley D. "Saul of Gibeon." *JSOT* 52 (1991): 61–76.

Weber, Max. *Economy and Society: An Outline of Interpretive Sociology*. Edited by Guenther Roth and Claus Wittich. 2 vols. Berkeley and Los Angeles: University of California Press, 1968.

Weinfeld, Moshe. *Deuteronomy and the Deuteronomic School*. Oxford: Clarendon Press, 1972.

________. "The Emergence of the Deuteronomic Movement: The Historical Antecedents." Pages 76–98 in *Das Deuteronomium: Entstehung, Gestalt und Botschaft*. Edited by Norbert Lohfink. BETL 68. Leuven: University Press and Peeters, 1985.

________. "The Extent of the Promised Land—The Status of Transjordan." Pages 59–75 in *Das Land Israel in biblischer Zeit*. Edited by Georg Strecker. Göttingen: Vandenhoeck & Ruprecht, 1983.

Weippert, Helga. "Die Ätiologie des Nordreiches und seines Königshauses (1 Reg 11:29–40)." *ZAW* 95 (1983): 344–375.

________. "Die 'deuteronomistischen' Beurteilungen der Könige von Israel und Juda und das Problem der Redaktion der Königsbücher." *Bib* 53 (1972): 301–39.

________. "Das deuteronomistische Geschichtswerk: Sein Ziel und Ende in der neueren Forschung." *TRu* 50 (1985): 213–49.

________. "Der Ort, den Jahwe erwählen wird, um dort seinen Namen wohnen zu lassen: Die Geschichte einer alttestamentlichen Formel." *BZ* 24 (1980): 76–94.

Weippert, Manfred. "Fragen des israelitischen Geschichtsbewusstseins." *VT* 23 (1973): 415–42.

________. "Israélites, Araméens et Assyriens dans la Transjordanie septentrionale." *ZDPV* 113 (1997): 19–38.

Weiser, Artur. "Die Legitimation des Königs David: Zur Eigenart und Entstehung der sogen. Geschichte von Davids Aufstieg." *VT* 16 (1966): 325–54.

________. *The Old Testament: Its Formation and Development*. Translated by Dorothea M. Barton. New York: Association, 1961. Published in Great Britain as *Introduction to the Old Testament: The Canon, the Apocrypha and Pseudopigrapha*. London: Darton, Longman & Todd, 1961. Translation of *Einleitung in das Alte Testament*. 1939. 4th ed. Repr. Göttingen: Vandenhoeck & Ruprecht, 1957.

________. "Samuel und die Vorgeschichte des israelitischen Königtums: 1. Samuel 8." *ZTK* 57 (1960): 141–61.

________. *Samuel: Seine geschichtliche Aufgabe und religiöse Bedeutung*. FRLANT 81. Göttingen: Vandenhoeck & Ruprecht, 1962.

Weitzman, Steven. "The Samson Story as Border Fiction." *BibInt* 10 (2002): 158–74.

Wellhausen, J. *Die Composition des Hexateuchs und der historischen Bücher des Alten Testaments*. 4th ed. Berlin: de Gruyter, 1963. Repr. of 3d ed., 1895. Originally published as vol. 2 of *Skizzen und Vorarbeiten*. 6 vols. Berlin: Reimer, 1885.

________. *Prolegomena to the History of Israel*. Translated by J. S. Black and Allan Menzies, with a preface by W. Robertson Smith. 1885. Repr., with a foreword by Douglas A. Knight, Atlanta: Scholars, 1994. Translation of *Prolegomena zur Geschichte Israels*. Berlin: Reimer, 1883.

Wesselius, Jan Wim. "The First Royal Inscription from Ancient Israel: The Tel Dan Inscription Reconsidered." *SJOT* 13 (1999): 163–86.

________. "Joab's Death and the Central Theme of the Succession Narrative (2 Samuel ix–1 Kings ii)." *VT* 40 (1990): 336–51.

Westermann, Claus. *Basic Forms of Prophetic Speech*. Translated by H. C. White, with a forward by G. M. Tucker. Louisville, Ky.: Westminster, 1967. Repr., 1991. Translation of *Grundformen prophetischer Rede*. Munich: Kaiser, 1960.

Wharton, J. A. "A Plausible Tale: Story and Theology in II Samuel 9–20, I Kings 1–2." *Int* 35 (1981): 341–54.

White, Ellen. "Michal the Misinterpreted." *JSOT* 31 (2007): 451–64.

White, Hayden. *Tropics of Discourse: Essays in Cultural Criticism*. Baltimore: The Johns Hopkins University Press, 1978.

White, Marsha C. *The Elijah Legends and Jehu's Coup*. BJS. Atlanta: Scholars, 1997.

________. "'The History of Saul's Rise': Saulide State Propaganda in 1 Samuel 1–14." Pages 271–92 in *"A Wise and Discerning Mind": Essays in Honor of Burke O. Long*. Edited by Saul M. Olyan and Robert C. Culley. BJS 325. Providence: Brown Judaic Studies, 2000.

________. "Saul and Jonathan in 1 Samuel 1 and 14." Pages 119–38 in *Saul in Story and Tradition*. Edited by Carl S. Ehrlich with Marsha C. White. FAT I/47. Tübingen: Mohr Siebeck, 2006.

________. "Searching for Saul: What We Really Know about Israel's First King." *BRev* 17.2 (2001): 22–29, 52–53.

Whitelam, Keith W. "The Defence of David." *JSOT* 29 (1984): 61–87.

Whybray, R. N. *The Succession Narrative: A Study of II Samuel 9–20; I Kings 1 and 2*. SBT II/9. Naperville, Ill.: Allenson, 1968.

Wiesemann, Gerd. "Remarks on the Geomorphogeny of the Yarmuk Valley, Jordan." Page 79 in *Studies in the History and Archaeology of Jordan* 2. Edited by Adnan Hadidi. Amman: Jordanian Department of Antiquities, 1985.

Wildberger, Hans. "Samuel und die Entstehung des israelitischen Königtums." *TZ* 13 (1957): 442–69.

Wilkinson, T. J. *Archaeological Landscapes of the Near East*. Tucson, Ariz.: The University of Arizona Press, 2003.

Williams, Reginald. *Hebrew Syntax: An Outline*. 2d ed. Toronto: University of Toronto Press, 1976.

Williams, William. "Guide Me Ever, Great Redeemer." Hymn #343 in *Lutheran Book of Worship*. Translation composite. Minneapolis: Augsburg, 1978.

Willi-Plein, Ina. "ISam 18–19 und die Davidshausgeschichte." Pages 138–71 in *David und Saul im Widerstreit—Diachronie und Synchronie im Wettstreit: Beiträge zur Auslegung des ersten Samuelbuches*. Edited by Walter Dietrich. OBO 206. Fribourg: University Press; Göttingen: Vandenhoeck & Ruprecht, 2005.

_______. "Michal und die Anfänge des Königtums in Israel." Pages 401–19 in *Congress Volume, Cambridge, 1995*. Edited by J. A. Emerton. VTSup 66. Leiden: Brill, 1997. Repr., pages 79–96 in *Sprache als Schlüssel: Gesammelte Aufsätze zum Alten Testament*. Edited by Michael Pietsch and Tilmann Präckel. Neukirchen-Vluyn: Neukirchener Verlag, 2002.

_______. "Frauen um David: Beobachtungen zur Davidshausgeschichte." Pages 349–61 in *Meilenstein: Festgabe für Herbert Donner*. Edited by S. Timm and M. Weippert. Wiesbaden: Harrassowitz, 1995. Repr., pages 97–115 in *Sprache als Schlüssel: Gesammelte Aufsätze zum Alten Testament*. Edited by Michael Pietsch and Tilmann Präckel. Neukirchen-Vluyn: Neukirchener Verlag, 2002.

Willis, J. T. "The Function of Comprehensive Anticipatory Redactional Joints in 1 Samuel 16–18." *ZAW* 85 (1973): 294–314.

Wilson, Kevin A. *The Campaign of Pharaoh Shoshenq I into Palestine*. FAT II/9. Tübingen: Mohr Siebeck, 2005.

Wilson, Robert R. *Prophecy and Society in Ancient Israel*. Philadelphia: Fortress Press, 1980.

Winckler, Hugo. *Geschichte Israels in Einzeldarstellung*. 2 vols. Leipzig: Pfeiffer, 1895–1900, pages 2:233–35. Cited in Alexander A. Fischer, "Flucht und Heimkehr Davids als integraler Rahmen der Abschalomerzählung," in *Ideales Königtum: Studien zu David und Salomo* (ed. Rüdiger Lux; ABG 16; Leipzig: Evangelische Verlagsanstalt, 2005), 49.

Witte, Markus, et al., eds. *Die deuteronomistischen Geschichtswerke: Redaktions- und religionsgeschichtliche Perspektiven zur "Deuteronomismus"-Diskussion in Tora und Vorderen Propheten*. BZAW 365. Berlin: de Gruyter, 2006.

Wolf, Herbert M. "The Apology of Ḫattušiliš Compared with Other Political Self-Justifications of the Ancient Near East." Ph.D. diss, Brandeis, 1967. Cited in Michael B. Dick, "The 'History of David's Rise to Power' and the Neo-Babylonian Succession Apologies," in *David and Zion: Biblical Studies in Honor of J. J. M. Roberts* (ed. Bernard F. Batto and Kathryn L. Roberts; Winona Lake, Ind.: Eisenbrauns, 2004), 4–5.

Wolff, Hans Walter. "The Kerygma of the Deuteronomic Historical Work." Pages 62–78. in *The Vitality of Old Testament Traditions*. Edited by W. Brueggemann and H. W. Wolff. Translated by F. C. Prussner. 2d ed. Atlanta: John Knox, 1982. Repr. pages 62–78 in *Reconsidering Israel and Judah: Recent Studies on the Deuteronomistic History*. Edited by G. N. Knoppers and J. G. McConville. SBTS 8. Winona Lake, Ind.: Eisenbrauns, 2000. Translation of "Das Kerygma des deuteronomistischen Geschichtswerks." *ZAW* 73 (1961): 171–86. Repr. pages 308–24 in Hans Walter Wolff, *Gesammelte Studien zum alten Testament*. Munich: Kaiser, 1964).

Wolters, Al. "The Balaamites of Deir ᶜAllā as Aramean Deportees." *HUCA* 59 (1988): 101–113.

Woźniak, Jerzy. "Drei verschiedene literarische Beschreibungen des Bundes zwischen Jonathan und David." *BZ* n.s. 27 (1983): 213–18.

Wright, David P. *Ritual in Narrative: The Dynamics of Feasting, Mourning, and Retaliation Rites in the Ugaritic Tale of Aqhat*. Winona Lake, Ind.: Eisenbrauns, 2001.

Wright, G. Ernest. "Deuteronomy: Introduction." *IB* 2:311–30.

_______. Introduction to *Joshua: A New Translation with Notes and Commentary*, by Robert G. Boling. AB 6a. Garden City, N.Y.: Doubleday, 1982.

Würthwein, Ernst. *Die Bücher der Könige: 1. Könige 1–16*. ATD 11/1. Göttingen: Vandenhoeck & Ruprecht, 1985.

________. *Die Bücher der Könige: 1. Kön. 17–2. Kön. 25*. ATD 11/2. Göttingen: Vandenhoeck & Ruprecht, 1984.

________. *Die Erzählung von der Thronfolge Davids—theologische oder politische Geschichtsschreibung?* ThSt B 115. Zurich: Theologischer Verlag, 1974. Repr., pages 27–79 in *Studien zum deuteronomistischen Geschichtswerk*. BZAW 227. Berlin: de Gruyter, 1994.

Wyatt, N. "Jonathan's Adventure and a Philological Conundrum." *PEQ* 127 (1995): 62–69.

Yeivin, S. "The Benjaminite Settlement in the Western Part of Their Territory." *IEJ* 21 (1971): 141–54.

Zakovitch, Y. "יפתח = בדן." *VT* 22 (1972): 123–25.

Zehnder, Marcus. "Exegetische Beobachtungen zu den David-Jonathan Geschichten." *Bib* 79 (1998): 153–79.

Zevit, Ziony. "Deuteronomistic Historiography in 1 Kings 12–2 Kings 17 and the Reinvestiture of the Israelian Cult." *JSOT* 32 (1985): 57–73.

________. *The Religions of Ancient Israel: A Synthesis of Parallactic Approaches*. London: Continuum 2001.

Zohary, Michael. *Vegetation of Israel and Adjacent Areas*. BTAVO A/7. Wiesbaden: Reichert, 1982.

Zwickel, Wolfgang. *Eisenzeitliche Ortslagen im Ostjordanland*. BTAVO B81. Wiesbaden: Reichert, 1990.

Index

Scriptural Citations

Extra-Biblical Citations

Greco-Roman Sources

Talmud

Northwest Semitic Epigraphic Sources

Hittite and Akkadian Sources